KENNETH McLEISH

THE PENGUIN COMPANION TO

THE ARTS
IN THE
TWENTIETH
CENTURY

VIKING

VIKING

Penguin Books Ltd, Harmondsworth, Middlesex, England
Viking Penguin Inc., 40 West 23rd Street, New York, New York 10010, U.S.A.
Penguin Books Australia Ltd, Ringwood, Victoria, Australia
Penguin Books Canada Ltd, 2801 John Street, Markham, Ontario, Canada L3R 1B4
Penguin Books (N.Z.) Ltd, 182–190 Wairau Road, Auckland 10, New Zealand

First published 1985

Typeset in VIP Times
Typeset, printed and bound in Great Britain by
Hazell Watson & Viney Limited,
Member of the BPCC Group,
Aylesbury, Bucks

BRITISH LIBRARY CATALOGUING IN PUBLICATION DATA

McLeish, Kenneth
    The Penguin companion to the arts in the
    twentieth century.
    1. Arts, Modern – 20th century –
    Dictionaries
    I. Title
    700'.9'04   NX456

ISBN 0-670-80127-5

For
Simon McLeish

CONTENTS

PREFACE

As we live our day-to-day lives, humanity's achievement often seems less apparent than its struggle, and our dominant forces and preoccupations are (in the wide view) economics, politics and strategy, and (in the narrow) child-rearing, making a living and relaxing. By hindsight, however, these activities tend to be paralleled or eclipsed by the creations of human imagination: we remember 5th-century Athens as much for Sophocles as for the Peloponnesian War, Augustan Rome as much for Virgil as for a stable economy, Medicean Florence for art and architecture as much as for mercantile or military expertise. I believe that the same will prove true of our own century: however ragged and bestial human life seems as we struggle to continue it, future ages will look back not on famines, cold wars and totalitarian oppression but on one of the greatest flowerings of cultural activity since the Renaissance. From inside the century, it is easy to mistake the arts for escapism or irrelevance; by hindsight, they channel and express the finest endeavours of humanity, they offer models for excellence and propose roads to decency no politicians, generals or financial pundits can. They are a reminder and guarantee of human potential, our life-raft and our reward.

The problem, for would-be consumers of 20th-century arts, is not so much the complexity as the variety of work on offer. Choosing what to read, hear or see can be a daunting and enervating job – and it is made no easier by the welter of technical and analytical advice available, manuals often larger and more complex than what they seek to clarify. When one visits a new country, the most useful guides are straightforward statements of what is available, how and where – and this book sets out to provide the same thing for the arts. I have tried, throughout, to write from the point of view of someone experiencing the books, plays, films, paintings, buildings or pieces of music for the first time – indeed, in many cases that was exactly the position I was in. So far as possible I have avoided critical ideologies in favour of the endorsement of eclecticism, and while I agree with Matthew Arnold's lofty view that criticism is 'a disinterested endeavour to learn and propagate the best that is known and thought in the world', I have been equally bound by John Osborne's remark that 'asking a working writer what he thinks about critics is like asking a lamp-post what it thinks about dogs'.

In a book of this size, it was impossible to include everyone. I have (with varying degrees of regret) left out performers, pundits, entrepreneurs (such as publishers or producers), and those many genre-creators (such as Harold Robbins, David Thompson or Jerome Kern) whose work is everywhere enjoyed but hardly needs explanation or introduction. I have excluded such culturally programmatic but artistically contentious subjects as photography, fashion and television. Accessibility to the English-speaking reader was an important but not an over-riding factor. And just as I omitted several marginal figures (Margaret Drabble, Luigi Nono and Douglas Sirk, for example) whose claims on art leave me cold, so I put in several others because I like them: in the end this is a personal book reflecting personal delight.

Standing back and taking stock of a century's artistic achievement is an activity as daunting as it is presumptuous. At the start of the project, suffering from the opposite problem to Proust's parish-priest of Combray (who 'cared nothing for the arts, but knew a great many genealogies'), I was greatly encouraged by the enthusiasm of Will Sulkin and Hilary Rubinstein; Frederic Raphael and Valerie McLeish have read and advised on every word, and kept me going; Pamela Heath and Anne Nash typed and typed. I am warmly grateful to them all.

Kenneth McLeish

An asterisk before a name (e.g. *Picasso) means that that person is discussed in his or her alphabetical place in the same section of the book. The date given for each art-work is the year when it first appeared before the public, or (in the case of some literature) the date of its first English edition or most important revision. The cut-off date for inclusion in this edition of the Companion was 31 October 1984. The idea of adding selected (additional) information in smaller type at the end of the entries was Justin Wintle's (in his 'Makers of Culture' series); I found it invaluable, and thank him for it.

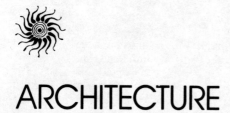

ARCHITECTURE

INTRODUCTION

KEY DATES

1871　Great Chicago fire prepared ground for new architectural style

1900　Wright's 'prairie house' designs given wide publicity in *Ladies' Home Journal*

1900　Vienna Secession exhibition (including Mackintosh designs): vital impetus to arts-and-crafts movement in Austria and Germany

1919　Bauhaus established under Gropius

1923　Le Corbusier published *Towards a New Architecture*, containing theory of buildings as 'machines for living'

1939　Outbreak of Second World War, which, with the first systematic bombing of European cities, opened the door for more widespread and radical rebuilding than ever before

1960　Inauguration of Brasilia (latest, greatest and most emblematic architectural folly of the century)

1970　Arcosanti begun in Arizona: archetypal new town of the future?

FUNCTION AND FORM

The 20th century has seen the debate between function and form (begun in the tavernas of ancient Athens) carried to its concrete conclusion, with advocates of either side taking up extreme positions while ordinary people – who actually have to use the buildings which result – stand respectfully and helplessly out of range. The argument is between art and applied art, between aesthetics and practicality, between the claims of individual creativity and those of social politics.

In the 19th century the division was clear enough. Anyone requiring new buildings (whether he was Napoleon II commissioning a redesigned French capital or a small-town industrialist in search of a new mill or a row of workers' houses) went to a civil engineer for the basic structure, and to an architect only if grand façades, unavailable from pattern-books, were the order of the day. Artisans, builders, saw to function; the artist, the architect, provided ornament (which Ruskin dubbed in 1853 the 'principal part' of architecture). Thus, the thrusting new cities of the industrial revolution grew in much the same haphazard way as their pre-industrial forerunners; function dictated the placing and type of most new buildings, and the exceptions were as likely to be triumphant monuments to engineering innovation (the Crystal Palace, Brooklyn Bridge, the Eiffel Tower) as works of primarily aesthetic enterprise. The nearest the 19th century came to a Palladio was Baron Haussmann (who laid out the new Paris) and he was a politician, a bureaucrat working to a strategic rather than an artistic brief. As for 19th-century Christopher Wrens, they built glass-and-steel railway termini, utilitarian cathedrals to the god of speed. The exceptions, the great builder-architects, perhaps in reaction to such vulgar and streamlined novelty, abandoned the attempt to match a new age with new materials and designs, and fled instead to the archaizing certainties of the glorious past. Neo-classicism and neo-baroque produced results which had grandeur and confidence (the Bank of England, the Altes Museum in Berlin, the Paris Opéra), but lacked contemporary relevance, artistic dynamism and originality – a lack which was, in the eyes of the bourgeoisie, precisely their reassuring charm.

THE CHICAGO PLAN

The moment of change, the birthdate of 20th-century architecture, can be precisely identified: the Chicago fire of 1871. (Architecture has benefited ever since from the space cleared by colossal disasters, from the San Francisco earthquake to the pattern-bombing of modern wars; the Chicago fire set a scorching precedent.) Until 1871 Chicago was a shanty-town of wooden-frame buildings, constructed to no overall plan and without thoughts of lasting merit or beauty. The fire left a whole city population in need of buildings of every conceivable kind, from factories to finishing schools, kiosks to cathedrals. Architects were drawn to the ruins like flies to a carcase – not merely neo-Palladians (though there were some of those) but also engineers trained in new building techniques and city planners inspired by the assertive success of Haussmann's Paris plan. Chicago was redesigned from scratch, the city blocks parcelled out along a symmetrical grid of streets. The rebuilders were consciously working to construct a city of the future, the first fully integrated, custom-built metropolis of the modern age. To this end – and spurred on by a ready-made population waiting at their elbows – they largely abandoned the time-consuming and cumbersome building methods of the past in favour of steel-and-glass techniques developed in Europe in the preceding twenty years. Virtually overnight, what had once been no more than engineers' showing-off, examples not built to last – the Crystal Palace, the Galerie des Machines and the Eiffel Tower were all built for exhibitions, intended for demolition after a few gleaming months – became the maquettes for solid city architecture, built for permanence. The skyscraper-prototypes of Richardson, Jenney, Holabird and Roche, Burnham and Root, Adler and Sullivan changed not only the Chicago cityscape, but also the whole relationship between function and form in architecture. They were manifestly practical (indeed, a skyscraper is one of the most practical buildings ever invented, so long as the elevators work and the arsonists don't), and they were strikingly beautiful as well, with a novel beauty unrelated to any buildings of the past. The penthouse betokened a literally new view of life.

The success of the Chicago plan was celebrated by the holding of the World's Fair there in 1893. Although this pandered to 19th-century European tastes by being laid out like a superannuated barracks from ancient Rome, it drew universal attention to the innovative architecture of the city itself. So began the dissemination of the Chicago style around the world. The style was particularly influential on young designers in northern Europe. Its unaffected methods and angular grace – the result of the use of modern materials – appealed especially to believers in the arts-and-crafts movement. (This had begun, in the workshops of people like Morris, as a revolt against the prevailing ugliness of mass-produced goods, and was now setting out to reverse that trend by applying the highest standards of art and craftsmanship to the design of machine-made goods.) Behrens' work for the Berlin Electrical Company in the 1900s – he designed everything from factories to pension certificates – was typical of a widespread belief that functional articles could and even necessarily would be beautiful; its marriage of technology and artistry was exactly analogous to that of engineering and architecture in Chicago. After Behrens came the Bauhaus (a depressing and significant move, viewed with hindsight: from an individual craftsman to a team), and from the Bauhaus eventually came the International Style.

THE INTERNATIONAL STYLE

The International Style sounds impeccably, even self-evidently 'right' in principle. Mass-produced sections, designed to the highest technical and artistic standards, could be quickly and cheaply assembled into buildings anywhere. Although the designs could be sophisticated, the building processes (welding, pouring concrete, fitting glass) remained simple; the basic patterns left plenty of scope for local variation and individual ingenuity. It was an adult's box of bricks: a few basic shapes allowed infinite variety of assembly.

There were two serious problems – and it took a generation and world-wide acceptance of the style to reveal them. The first is that jerry-building has catastrophic results on such an all-or-nothing style: all over the world, badly made tower-blocks (high-rise housing and offices are the most widespread application of the International Style) crumple and collapse like card-houses. The second is that soulless buildings oppress the humanity of those who live in them. Designed to be functional, many of these buildings leave no room for human individuality or self-expression – nowhere to play or to exercise the dog, nowhere to hang washing, nowhere to dawdle or to gossip. And the higher the floor, the higher the crime-rate: it has been calculated that above the sixth floor, the incidence of rape, mugging and murder increases, floor by floor, at an exponential rate. Sullivan famously said that 'form follows function'; the work of Gropius, Le Corbusier and thousands of untalented, cheapskate imitators across the globe has proved that this is not at all the same as claiming that 'function *leads* to form'. Ours has been a century of disastrous dogmas; doctrinaire adherence to the precepts of International architecture and its dismal progeny Brutalism and Megabuilding has led to a universal distress far from the uptown utopian dreams of those who evolved them. The machine-architects, the levellers, have destroyed more than they ever built. (Significantly, both Gropius and Le Corbusier, in their own work, soon left dogmatic Internationalism to others, and began designing buildings of ever-increasing eclecticism and individuality.)

It would be unfair, even so, to blame the miseries of modern inner-city or clearance-area slums on the International Style itself. Unthinking or untalented application of a theory does not invalidate the theory. The concept of terraced housing, for example, led in the 19th century to the appalling back-to-backs of the industrial north of England – but it also lent style to Bath, Cheltenham and Edinburgh. In the same way, when the International Style has been used by people of genius to build for people of wealth, the results have been some of the most beautiful (and practical) buildings made this century. (Mies van der Rohe's and Johnson's Seagram Building in New York, for example, is an Alhambra.) Form has followed function, but individual inventiveness and fidelity to materials have also played crucial parts. The balance is elusive, but with care (and cash) it can certainly be achieved.

If the branch-line of the International Style was mistaken for a main track of architecture (especially in the 1930s–50s), the principal reason was a tendency to regard it less as one style among many than as the road to utopia, the expression in building-materials of a philosophical programme for rescuing humanity. Other people in this century have shared the architects' conviction that there was a rational answer to the question 'What is the nature of humankind?', that solutions to practical and social problems could be found as naturally elegant as the equations of science, and that if these solutions were stated with sufficient force and clarity the scales would at once fall from every eye. The failure of modern architecture is not inherent in the architects' intentions; it is humanity's own failure, the result of a general departure from the light of humane reason in which that architecture was conceived. The problem for architectural consumers, however, is the obstinate permanence of what the builder makes for them. Buildings, by and large, must be endured long after the assumptions which led to them have been abandoned or discredited. It is no comfort to the inhabitants of Brasilia or Peterlee to know that their prizewinning environments represent the very best liberal thinking of a generation ago, if actually living there today is a life-sentence without remission. People do adapt – as they have, for example, to Le Corbusier's Unité d'Habitation in Marseilles – but the question remains: should we adapt to concrete or should it adapt to us?

Thus the charge against the International Style is not that it was the fruit of criminal arrogance, but that it was quite simply not the panacea it seemed to be; and the problem for architects is that unlike most failed philosophers they have to live – and see other people live – amid the wretched wreckage of their own ideals. The fact that architecture has been failed by human beings, not human beings by architecture, is small comfort when the failure is on so grand a scale.

INDIVIDUALISM

Fortunately, human individuality (that of both creator and consumer) has been the guiding force of a robust alternative tradition in 20th-century architecture: regarded in the heyday of Internationalism as eccentric or wilfully dissident, it emerged in the 1970s as a warming and tempering force, a reminder that buildings can reflect human beings' disorderly romanticism as well as our penchant for the cerebral. In the 19th century a tradition had developed of comfortable, unpretentious villas architect-designed for the affluent middle class. Architects such as Shaw and Lutyens built to suit their patrons, in a 'vernacular' style closer to farmhouses and gentlemen's hunting lodges than to the grandiose mock palaces or temples of big-city buildings. In the USA Wright made his reputation – and most of his income – from designing private houses; he transformed the genre from conservative to radical, using the force of his personality to persuade his clients that what each of them wanted was a striking, brand-new and unique design. (His combination of mass-producible basic structures and custom-built detail is similar to the way in which such talents as Mies van der Rohe made the International Style their own.) The best buildings of many of America's finest architects (e.g. Wright, Breuer, Johnson) are private houses or unusual, even fantastical, large buildings made for institutions or industrialists prepared to break away from the International Style. (The idea of celebrating your social standing or wealth by commissioning a lavish and eye-catching building is exactly analogous to the rich aristocrat's patronage of fine art – and a building offers the added attraction of usefulness. Certainly the claims of 20th-century architecture to be an art-form have been justified more often by privately commissioned buildings than by monuments to civic enterprise or need.)

In Europe, where the cities into which new buildings must fit are older and offer a more dominating variety of past styles, the vernacular tradition has had even more success. The buildings of Hoffmann, Mackintosh and Gaudí at the beginning of the century and those of Asplund, Aalto and Nervi later on are effective and functional without straitjacketing their users; they are also striking and original to look at without the four-square stridency of Behrens or Gropius, the Smithsons' implacable symmetry or Rudolph's bulge and bulk. As the century proceeds, more and more public buildings are being erected to what would once have seemed arbitrary and exotic designs: Japanese architects (e.g. Kurokawa, Tange, Mayakawa) have evolved a particularly successful mixture of geometric and organic forms. The idea of a 'garden city' (pioneered over a century ago in Bedford Park and Port Sunlight, and later in Bournville, Hampstead Garden Suburb and Letchworth) is once more prevalent: the pressure of ecology (that is, the desire to harmonize with, and neither to deplete nor to pollute, the environment) and the feeling that, despite the continuing and overwhelming need for cheap mass housing, 'small is beautiful' are leading to many innovative and promising designs, from Kiesler's pumpkin-shaped 'endless houses' and Fuller's geodesic domes to visionary communities like Soleri's Noah's-ark Arcosanti, Arizona. These 21st-century designs often have a philosophical rationale just as rigorous as any of the city-programmes of the Internationalists, but because they start from a respect for the human owner rather than for building-methods or geometry, their radicalism is pragmatic, and so far from being ruthlessly iconoclastic, takes its place in the tradition of 'real' housing for 'real' people which has been the main preoccupation of builders since the first stone-age architect designed extensions for his or her client's cave. This kind of contract, between individual patron and individual architect, has always made the best architecture; when, as so often nowadays, both parties are replaced by committees, the results suffer. In this respect, at least, the creation of high-quality architecture is analogous to that of any of the other arts.

◙

The list of architects is short, confined to those who made crucial or influential innovations, to those who made buildings which combine practicality with aesthetic appeal, or (wherever possible) to those who did both at once.

AALTO, Alvar (1898–1976)
Finnish architect

Aalto's first buildings were in the white-shoebox International Modern Style: cubes of reinforced concrete with narrow horizontal strips of window and no mouldings or decoration to interrupt the functional plainness. The Sanatorium at Paimio (1933) is typical: handsome from a distance, when its contours are softened by pine and spruce, but close-to the epitome of chilly efficiency. In his later buildings he still used a basis of steel and concrete, but clad the walls in warm wood or brick, restricted the height (two storeys are common, more than five are rare), and above all broke up the cubes with S-shaped edges, wedges and diamonds. This style (perhaps influenced by work on bentwood furniture, which he was developing in the 1930s) was thrillingly announced by the Finnish Pavilion at the New York World's Fair of 1939, chiefly a sinuous outward-leaning wall of panelled wood, its three upper galleries (each proportionately higher than the one below) inset with huge photographs of Finnish woodland and industrial scenes, its ground floor an eye-pleasing tumble of mirrored, pillared walls and Aalto furniture. Curves and broken outlines (jutting balconies, zig-zag walls) are the main feature of his buildings – the best include the dormitory he made for MIT in 1947 and the oast-house-shaped House of Culture in Helsinki (1958) – and he is also notable for the care he devoted to the interiors, incorporating decoration and furniture to the harmony of overall design.

Good, if dry, study: M. Quantrill: *Alvar Aalto* (1982). Good study of early work: P. D. Pearson: *Alvar Aalto and the International Style* (1978).

ARUP, Ove (born 1895)
Danish/British civil engineer and architect

A joyful problem-solver, Arup helped to realize a handful of delightful and fanciful buildings, in each of which a dominant feeling is of sheer ingenuity, of impossible engineering feats made possible. In the Penguin Pool at London Zoo interlocking concrete boomerangs make walkways over blue water; in the converted oast-house concert-hall at The Maltings, Snape (home of the Aldeburgh Festival), open-work wooden girders not only seem to float the roof high overhead, but also provide superb acoustics; the thrusting, unfolding-petal roofs of the Sydney Opera House, like jet-engine cowlings or the wing-cases of Martian insects, challenge both their stiff medium (concrete) and our imagination – *why*, never mind *how*, do they work so well?

BEHRENS, Peter (1868–1940)
German architect and designer

Influenced by William Morris, Behrens was a firm believer in the applied arts as a normative, dynamic force. He designed furniture, glassware and cutlery, was interested in book-illustration and type-design, and wanted to apply fine-art principles to the design of all mass-produced goods from wallpaper to kitchen utensils. (In his view that overall artistic integration of the environment was possible, he was a precursor of the Bauhaus; in his view that art and architecture can symbolize – not to say programme – national energy and self-esteem, he foreshadowed the architects of National Socialism.) In 1907 he was a founder-member of the applied-arts ginger group Deutscher Werkbund, and was also appointed architectural and design consultant for the General Electricity Company of Berlin. The turbine factory he built for this company in 1909 – the first steel-and-glass building in Germany – is typical both of his intellectual approach to architecture (it is conceived to *look* like the casing of a turbine) and of his lumpishness of execution (it is a squat, glowering building too tall for its width, planted four-square like a railway terminus). His German Embassy, St Petersburg (1912), suffers from the same over-emphasis: it is neo-classical (complete with massive sculptured men and horses rearing from the roof) in everything but grace; it is long, fat and forbidding. In the 1920s he abandoned crushing grandiosity for the International Modern Style – he has the doubtful distinction of building the first-ever flat-roofed white cube seen in Britain, in Northampton in 1925 – but he remains more an interesting bridge between two earnest orthodoxies (19th-century work-ethic and Nazi social engineering) than an architect of any strong personal style or vision. He was an influential teacher (notably as director of the Vienna Academy School of Architecture from 1920): among those he taught were *Gropius, *Le Corbusier and *Mies van der Rohe.

BREUER, Marcel (1902–81)
Hungarian/American architect

In the 1920s Breuer worked in the furniture section of the Bauhaus, producing a series of suave-lined, none-too-comfortable, tubular-steel chairs. He went to America in 1937, and worked for a time in partnership with *Gropius. In the 1950s and 1960s, beginning with the Unesco Building in Paris (1956, on which he collaborated with Zehrfuss and *Nervi), he designed some of the most impressive and individual large public buildings put up this century. The IBM Research Centre, La Grande Var, France (1962), for example, consists of two huge Y-shaped buildings joined at the stems; at one side they rest on the ground, at the other on broad concrete pylons (shaped like abstract Atlases with upraised arms). The façades of the buildings are a grid of tall rectangular windows, deep-set like the cells of a cubist honeycomb. The buildings' curves satisfyingly echo those of the surrounding wolds – in fact landscaping is one of their most attractive features. In the USA, as well as the Whitney Museum of American Art, New York (1966), Breuer made many particularly imaginative and striking university buildings. His Lecture Hall for New York University (1961), for example, is a plain concrete box perched on a pair of inverted Vs, one at each side; the entrance hangs from the centre like a waiting elevator; the whole graceful structure is like an upside-down Monopoly house or a Spielberg space vehicle parked in a wide paved square – a conception as successful as it is startling. His masterpiece is St John's Abbey Church, Collegeville, Minnesota (1953), made in collaboration with Hamilton Smith. This shows all Breuer's flair for combining functionality with cheekiness. The (separate) bell-tower is a huge, flat stone slab set in A-shaped stone supports; one of the walls of the main building is covered with row on row of interlocking hexagons, another has huge brick buttresses, deep-set and shadowed as if in a Chirico painting; the church's interior roof is a perspective of square stone arches, like the supports of a box-girder bridge, at once simple and mysterious. Breuer's ideas must look stunning on paper – their intellectual logic, based each time on a handful of brashly juxtaposed shapes, is compelling – but they differ from those of some architects in that they also look stunning on the ground, and work excellently as buildings for human daily use.

Breuer's publications include Sun and Shadow: The Philosophy of an Architect (1956); Marcel Breuer: Buildings and Projects 1921–1961 (1962).

COSTA, Lúcio (1902–63)
Brazilian architect

After satisfactory but not overly original work (e.g. the apartment blocks in Guinle Park, Rio de Janeiro, 1954, discards from *Le Corbusier), Costa won the competition for the design of Brasilia, Brazil's new capital and one of the greatest architectural triumphs and sociological disasters of the modern age. Its shape, on paper or seen from the air, is breathtakingly beautiful. It is a rounded cross, or a swallow with outspread wings. At one end are grouped all administrative buildings, at the other is the railway station. In between, separated by parkland and joined by multi-lane arterial highways (in the manner of Le Corbusier's *ville radieuse*) are sectors for industry, tourism and commerce. Houses for the inhabitants are placed in the arms of the cross or the swallow's wings: tall apartment blocks standing on guard round grassy 'supersquares'. If this city-design (and the designs for the individual buildings, many of them by *Niemeyer) existed merely on paper, in the abstract, it would remain one of the most civilized and attractive plans-for-living-space in the history of humanity. But the claims of real people, alas, conflict with Costa's aesthetics. The city dwarfs its inhabitants; it has no cheap housing, no pedestrian communication between one area and another, no common land, no opportunities for anyone not rich or upper-middle-class. These problems may one day be sorted out (for who but a Mogul emperor can treat a whole city as disposable?); but in the meantime Brasilia remains two cities, an upmarket environment for the wealthy on the one hand and appalling shanty-suburbs on the other. It is a broken toy, a bronzed but fast-corroding monument to the folly of those architects who put art first and human beings nowhere at all.

FOSTER, Norman (born 1935)
British architect

Starting from a distaste for the social pretensions of so many contemporary architects (and the 'ill-conceived, ill-mannered, uncomfortable, anti-social environments' they tend to create), Foster has evolved a stunning style for large public buildings. Like *Wright's Johnson Wax Factory, it is based partly on simple pragmatism (careful analysis of future patterns of use for the building), and partly on confident, dogmatic general principles (extensive use of glass, access wherever possible to natural light, open-plan interiors). Foster's finest building, the Willis, Faber and Dumas office-block in Ipswich (1976), for example, has an exterior curved to fit the flow of an existing street, and its three storeys conform with the height of the surrounding, older buildings. It is entirely clad in black mirror-glass, an unbroken, smooth surface which by day reflects its surroundings and by night becomes transparent, allowing clear views of the lit interior of the building, and of the ground-floor swimming-pool (not a common feature of insurance offices). Its roof is turfed and gardened; its interior flourishes with trees and growing plants. In 1978 Foster Associates completed another astonishing building, the Sainsbury Centre for the Visual Arts at the University of East Anglia. This is a vast steel hangar, large enough for a squadron of Concordes and clad in glass. It is a crystal palace set in a grassy park, and its shape (five times as wide as it is high) integrates it snugly with the landscape and the existing campus in a way remarkable for such an uncompromising design.

These buildings are typical of Foster's work: not only of his style but of the sort of commissions he undertakes. He has so far not turned his talents in the direction of a well-conceived, well-mannered, comfortable and social *living* environment: his nearest approach, a development plan for Hammersmith, London, was scrapped by the authorities (to the anger and regret of the people of Hammersmith, whose views and needs had otherwise been consulted at every stage). Foster Associates have worked on shipping terminals, computer headquarters, shops and banks (notably the headquarters of the Hong Kong and Shanghai Bank in Hong Kong). It would be good to think that they will one day use their superb skills to enhance ordinary living environments as well. Why should civic housing always be designed by doctrinaire Brutalists or the also-ran?

FULLER, Richard Buckminster (1895–1983)
American designer

What are the great inventions of architecture? The brick? The arch? The geodesic dome? A hundred years from now, Fuller (who invented the dome) may well be to housing what the inventor of the wheel was to transport. His elegant domes – the culmination of years of work on the design of cheap, prefabricated buildings – are like puffballs or silvery jelly-fish settling on the landscape. At present their use is small-scale and piffling (e.g. as greenhouses or in place of army tents); but they can be built to any size – the largest so far housed the entire American Pavilion at Expo 67, Montreal (1967), and Fuller's feasibility studies include one for a single dome covering the whole mid-area of Manhattan Island, stretching from river to river in one direction and for forty-two city blocks in the other. Such science-fiction wonders – if they can successfully be applied to the scale of everyday housing – may one day make *Le Corbusier's Unité d'Habitation look as obsolete as the Lascaux Cave.

Fuller's prolific, polemical writings, offering a pound of outrageousness for every grain of sense, include *Inventory of World Resources, Human Trends and Needs* (1963), *Explorations* (ed. McLuhan, 1967), *Operating Manual for Spaceship Earth* (1968), *Utopia or Oblivion* (1969) and *Synergetics* (1975); a useful anthology is *The Buckminster Fuller Reader* (ed. Mellor, 1970). Good study of the man and his creations (though not of his extraordinary world-view, visionary or muddled according to taste): J. McHale: *R. Buckminster Fuller* (1962).

GAUDÍ, Antonio (1852–1926)
Spanish architect and sculptor

Architecture-pundits are discomforted by Gaudí. His buildings, with their curved vegetable shapes, sloping pillars and avoidance of straight lines or right angles, flout every masonic rule – and work. His decoration (fish-scale patterns carved in or plastered on the stone, mosaics of broken tiles and pottery) raises sandcastle-ornament to the solemn Alhambra perfection of Moorish art. He was no dilettante (like the eccentric Rodia who built Disney towers of junk in Watts, San Francisco): he made a cathedral, several apartment buildings, a dozen private houses and a public park, all in his native Barcelona. Worst of all, he conformed to no tradition – diligent comparisons with such things as 'the Catalan tradition' are wishful thinking – and he had no artistic heirs. He was successfully and irritatingly unique.

Fortunately architecture is not built for pundits, and to everyone else the joys and merits of Gaudí's buildings are self-evident. People sit happily and talk in the worm-shaped benches in Güell Park, and children ride bicycles and play tag down the mole-tunnel corridors and walkways underneath. The slender openwork spires of the Sagrada Familia Church (his unfinished masterpiece, on which he worked for forty years), and the extraordinary decoration of its Portal of the Nativity – vine-tendrils, worm-casts and leaf-clusters, seemingly organic rather than carved – these make stone romantic, full of secrets, comfortable. Other Gaudí buildings are merely witty (merely! How witty is a *Niemeyer tower-block?): the house he built for his patron Güell, for example, has wrought-iron gates made like outspread pterodactyl wings; his luxury apartments, the Milà House, are built without a single straight line and their six storeys overlap and flop like fungi or cream oozing from a well-filled sponge sandwich-cake. But the Sagrada Familia and Güell Park add warmth and are built to human scale; squashy, warty and unkempt, they replace the dignity of 'proper' buildings (the Parthenon; Notre Dame; the Law Courts at Chandigarh) with sensuality, irrepressibility and beguiling fantasy.

Good studies: Le Corbusier: *Gaudí* (1958); G. R. Collins: *Antonio Gaudí* (1960). Particularly well illustrated: G. R. Collins and J. B. Nonell: *The Designs and Drawings of Antonio Gaudí* (1982).

GROPIUS, Walter (1883–1969)
German designer and architect

At the Bauhaus (which he founded in 1919 and ran until 1928) Gropius was a Diaghilev of the applied arts, binding talented creators of all kinds to a single purpose, that of designing an artificial environment which would combine utilitarian methods with artistic excellence. Its actual products (furniture, cutlery, kitchenware, lighting) and its apartment designs now seem stiff and clumsy – but Bauhaus designs still form the basis for many of the things in everyday home use. Others have refined the recipe, but the Bauhaus staff invented it.

The same aims of practicality and elegance mark Gropius's own buildings. In the best of them unfussy design (intended for mass-production and prefabrication) leads to remarkable symmetry and refinement. The Fagus Shoelace Factory, for example (1916, in collaboration with Meyer), is a cube of glass and steel on a brick base, as severely functional as a pair of wire-rimmed spectacles. What gives it grace are careful proportions between length and height and between density and void: the glass curtain-walls, which could easily loom and threaten (as do the walls of *Behrens' Turbine Factory, an important influence), are controlled by strips of brick trim at top and bottom – a structural necessity put to aesthetic use. Gropius built a larger sibling of this building in the Workshop Wing of the Bauhaus (1926), and a comparison between the two (the Fagus Factory nowadays seems cautious and slightly self-conscious, the Bauhaus Workshop as confident as if built yesterday) shows not only how in ten years the style reached its perfect form, but also how nearly right the original conception was – in view of its novelty, a triumph of designing skill.

In the 1930s Gropius left Germany and settled first in Britain (where, among other things, he designed the Village College at Impington, 1936, the first of those low-slung, windowy school buildings we now see everywhere), and then moved to the USA, where he became Professor of Architecture at Harvard. His later buildings (most, e.g. the Harvard Graduate Center, 1949, or the US Embassy, Athens, 1961, designed with the Architects' Collaborative, which he founded), though graceful and elegant enough, look perfectly anonymous – and the reason is not that he lost his flair, but simply that the language he pioneered became, during his own lifetime, an efficient and attractive worldwide common speech.

Gropius's writings include *The New Architecture and the Bauhaus* (English edn 1936) and *Scope of Total Architecture* (English edn 1956). Good on Gropius: J. M. Fitch: *Walter Gropius* (1960); good on the Bauhaus: H. M. Wingler, *Bauhaus, Weimar, Dessau, Berlin* (1969).

HOFFMANN, Josef (1870–1956)
Austrian architect

If architecture is art, then Hoffmann's buildings are art for art's sake, designed to give aesthetic pleasure far more than for practicality. He was an admirer of William Morris and of *art nouveau*, but the main influence on his style was the work of *Mackintosh exhibited at the Vienna Secession in 1900. There is an uncontrolled, ivy-tendril sprawl about *art nouveau*; Mackintosh's style is one of prim rectangles and ladder-shapes; Hoffmann's work distinctively combines the two. Even in intentionally functional buildings (e.g. the Convalescent Home at Puckersdorf, Austria, 1904) he broke up flat white walls with multi-paned windows and edged them (in true Mackintosh style) with lines of black bricks. His masterpiece is the Palais Stoclet in Brussels (1911), a gorgeous rectangular Christmas cake in white marble with black-edged corners, gutters and windows, *art-nouveau* interior mosaics by Klimt and furniture and lighting designed by Hoffmann. It is a building not for living in (though the Stoclet family did) but for walking round open-mouthed, not part of an architectural mainstreet but a glorious parking lot. Hoffmann's importance in his own day (i.e. the 1900s; he made many rich private villas later, but nothing better or stylistically new) was as founder of the Vienna Werkstätte (1903), a craft-guild forerunner of the Bauhaus. He is now celebrated, in this book at least, less for this than as the creator of just one masterpiece, a decadent, superb and superfluous *jeu d'esprit*.

HORTA, Victor (1861–1947)
Belgian architect

There are very few successful *art-nouveau* buildings (as opposed to ordinary buildings enriched with *art-nouveau* windows, railings and architraves). Those that work well include Guimard's 1900s stations for the Paris Métro, Jourdain's 1905 La Samaritaine Department Store, Paris – and the buildings of Horta. These include civic buildings (e.g. Maison du Peuple, Brussels, 1899), stores (e.g. À l'Innovation, Brussels, 1901, now alas demolished) and – most thorough-going of all in style – private houses and hotels (e.g. Hôtel Tassel, Brussels, 1892). Why was this exuberant, attractive style so short-lived? Even Horta himself, in the 1920s, turned away from it towards neo-classicism (e.g. Palais des Beaux Arts, Brussels, 1929). Is it the cost of all those coloured glass panels and wrought-iron curlicues – or has 20th-century humanity simply no time for beauty which is fantastical and frivolous?

JOHNSON, Philip (born 1906)
American architect

Johnson did not become prominent as an architect until he built the Glass House, New Canaan, Connecticut (1949). This is a one-storey rectangular house of steel girders filled in with glass and sparsely furnished with beautiful objects (each sofa, carpet or rubber plant a work of art). The style has since been endlessly copied and varied in rich people's villas throughout the world: it is even a Hollywood cliché, now, that media success involves living in a Johnson house by a Californian beach or on an alsatian-guarded private estate. Johnson went on to collaborate with *Mies van der Rohe on such glass-and-steel towers as the Seagram Building, New York (1958) – and carried the style to its born-again apotheosis in the (literally) dazzling Crystal Cathedral, Los Angeles (1980), built (of 10,000 mirror-glass panels) for the television evangelist Robert Schuller. But his main legacy to the US landscape is a series of less pretentious buildings, each tailor-made to harmonize with its surroundings (a rarer architectural ambition than it ought to be). Thus, some of his buildings are forbidding stone boxes in bleak countryside (e.g. the Munson-Williams-Proctor Institute, Utica, New York, like an enlarged wartime pillbox); others take inspiration from ethnic styles (e.g. the shrine at New Harmony, Indiana, 1960, incorporating Red Indian themes). His masterpiece is the New York State Theater (1964), which combines modern steel-and-concrete building-techniques (allowing a huge unpillared auditorium with a vast domed roof) with the rococo splendour of traditional theatre design (a spectacular horseshoe sweep of stalls, circle, upper circle and balcony facing a cavernous proscenium arch). This building shows a recurring Johnson characteristic: the exterior is dull, not to say uninspired; all his inventive genius is reserved for the interior. His buildings may look unprepossessing from the air – so much modern architecture seems to have been designed to look marvellous as you jet overhead – but as environments for human activity they work just fine.

Useful anthology: *Writings* (1979).

KAHN, Louis (1901–74)
American architect

Like *Johnson, Kahn was a leader in the movement to combine mass-production techniques with stylistic individuality, to take monotony out of the great conformity that characterized American architecture in the late 1940s. His buildings are as grand in scale as those of *Mies van der Rohe, his main influence; but he broke up Mies's monumental, monolithic shapes, thus allowing intimacy, and was not afraid of wit. (For example, the Richards Medical Research Building, University of Pennsylvania, Philadelphia, 1961, a set of perfectly respectable Miesian glass-and-steel towers, looks like nothing so much as neat stacks of plastic culture-boxes from a medical research laboratory; the Kimbell Art Museum, Fort Worth, Texas, 1972, is a phalanx of stone dutch barns set round a paved piazza – storing art like hay against the winter?) His theory that the functional guts of a building (pipes, ducts, stairways, elevator shafts) are essential to its 'meaning' and should be made a visible and integral part of its design led him to plan buildings as unconventional and extraordinary as those of the 1920s Russian Constructivists: his model for Philadelphia City Hall (1957), for example, is first cousin to Tatlin's famous twisted-Eiffel-Tower model for the Third International (1920). Few of Kahn's experimental buildings have, alas, so far been built – though if Piano and Rogers' Centre Pompidou in Paris (1977) is any indication, the notion of Industrial Baroque is gaining ground.

LASDUN, Denys (born 1914)
British architect

The suitability of the International Style in architecture for an ancient city like London has been endlessly debated, not least by those old enough to remember London before the Second World War Blitz which gave high-rise Le Corbusians their chance. Even in 1935, Highpoint I, an eight-storey block of flats designed by Tecton (an architectural partnership including Lasdun), was as highly controversial as it was high; the same partnership's buildings for London Zoo have never pleased the public, though the animals seem content enough; Lasdun's own National Theatre and the grey-concrete South Bank Complex of which it is part still provoke apoplexy in the nostalgic. The buildings may be soullessly ugly, but they *work* extremely well – visiting the cavernous National Theatre is a unique, exciting and above all *theatrical* experience, even if you do keep glancing over your shoulder to see the Minotaur – and should we really ask anything more of architecture? Of course we should. Just because your buildings are utilitarian and huge doesn't mean you need abandon style. Wren and Nash in London – and *Aalto, *Breuer and *Saarinen elsewhere, Lasdun's contemporaries – could have taught him that.

LE CORBUSIER (Charles-Édouard Jeanneret) (1887–1966)
Swiss/French architect

The Moses of the International Style, Le Corbusier gave its followers their tablets in his book *Towards a New Architecture* (1923). This contains the dogma – and the fanatical, uncompromising tone – which has made the idea of 'modern architecture' stink all over the inhabited world. The fault is hardly Le Corbusier's: his philosophy of a totally planned environment, of the house as a 'machine for living', one part of a streamlined and efficient city at the service of those who live in it, is no more inhumane or megalomaniac than any other radical programme for the human race. But wherever miserable people live in vandalized, graffiti-scrawled tower-blocks of box-like flats, 20th-century tenements, the cause of their misery is the Le Corbusier plan put into practice by lesser talents.

Le Corbusier's basic building unit, as designed for the Domino Housing Project (1914 – prophetic name), is a rectangular framework of steel girders supporting concrete floors. The walls, exterior and interior, are lightweight prefabricated panels hung from this frame. The frame can be one storey high or many; Le Corbusier liked to place multi-storey buildings on stilts or piers, so that the street level is open-air and open-plan. For expensive private versions of this basic structure (e.g. the Villa Savoye, Poissy, France, 1930) he provided specially designed extra effects (in this case a cylindrical tower – the stairwell – rising high above the flat roof); on larger buildings (e.g. the Swiss Dormitory, Cité Universitaire, Paris, 1932) he left the plain rectangles of the structure and the repeated pattern of window- and wall-sections to do powerful aesthetic work. His masterpiece in the transcendental-Lego style is the UN Secretariat, New York (1951), an abstract-sculpture slab of glass and concrete as stunning as one of Brancusi's 'endless columns'.

The point about Le Corbusier's prefabricatable buildings – the point ignored by almost every purse-bound town-planner since – was not that they should be erected haphazardly in every slum area throughout the world, regardless of their environment or the people's social needs, but that they should form the basis for clean, new suburbs or entire new cities. An important part of his theorizing involved the making of city plans: *Ville contemporaine* (1922), *Plan voisin* (1925), *Plan for Algiers* (1930) and above all *Ville radieuse* (1935), a pattern-book city based on parks and freeways, with each centre (commercial, industrial, residential) placed separately but interconnected like the organs of a human body. Once again, others have put this attractive theory into disastrous practice: Brasilia is the most notorious example, a whole city designed for Brazilians without the needs of a single Brazilian borne in mind. Le Corbusier himself supervised one such 'total city', Chandigarh in the Punjab, India (begun 1951). Here the inhabitants live in neat blocks on a flat plain, and look upwards to a line of hills to the north, at whose feet are built three sumptuous and dominating bureaucratic palaces, the

Assembly, the Secretariat and the High Court. The Orwellian aspects of this arrangement are more apparent than real: by all accounts the city is a harmonious, effective machine for living, Le Corbusier's greatest work and the vindication of a lifetime's theories.

It is impossible to be objective about Le Corbusier. His own buildings are successful human environments, and often sensational to look at too. (Even the notorious Unité d'Habitation, Marseilles, 1952, after thirty years of teething troubles caused by people who hated being rehoused there, is now not merely another soulless block of flats but a bustling, and increasingly happy, village community complete with shops, schools, play-areas, 'internal piazzas' and apartments all under a single gardened-and-swimming-pooled flat roof.) At the same time, his influence on the world at large can only be deplored. Like Marx, like Freud, like Keynes, he put forward unignorable theories which have since been catastrophically misapplied.

Le Corbusier's other writings include *Almanac of Modern Architecture* (1926), *When the Cathedrals Were White* (1937) and the technical, mathematical – and seminal – *The Modulor* (1949). Good critical study: C. Jencks: *Le Corbusier and the Tragic View of Architecture* (1973). T. Benton: *Villas of Le Corbusier 1920–1930* (1984) is magnificently illustrated with sketches, plans and photographs, showing the progress of each work from conception to completion.

LOOS, Adolf (1870–1933)
Austrian architect and designer

Loos's own buildings are chiefly forgettable villas for the rich, cubic palaces with Mackintoshy interior designs. His main importance is his influence on such radical International Stylists as *Gropius and *Le Corbusier, who in 1920 reprinted Loos's article 'Ornament and Crime'. In this, drawing on lessons learned from *Sullivan during three years in Chicago in the 1890s, Loos attacked the self-indulgent, decadent and non-functional ornamentation of the *art-nouveau* Vienna Secession style (see van de Velde), and proposed instead a lucid, 'bespoke' style based on geometric forms and fidelity to natural materials. The nearest he himself came to conforming with these principles was in his two years as chief architect of the Vienna Housing Department (1920–22), during which he designed an estate (the Heuberg Estate) of cubic terrace-houses, each with its own greenhouse and allotment, which have been a model for inexpensive urban terraces ever since. In the 1920s tower-block apartments swept such notions away; but nowadays, when the tower-block itself is in disgrace, Loos-like terraces are increasingly being built, in particular as replacements or updatings of the successful 19th-century terrace-housing in many European cities.

Good study: L. Münz and G. Künstler: *Adolf Loos, Pioneer of Modern Architecture* (1966).

LUTYENS, Edwin (1869-1944)
British architect

Lutyens belongs in a long tradition of British architectural individualists: in eclecticism and creative arrogance he is the heir of such men as Hawksmoor, Vanbrugh or Norman Shaw. His finest buildings are a series of fanciful country houses, each designed to suit both the surrounding countryside and the character of whoever commissioned it. Tigbourne Court (1899), for example, is a miniature red-brick mansion, with gables and chimneys in a delirious combination of Tudor and *art-nouveau* styles, mock-Georgian windows and front porch and pompous oast-house roofs – not style but a bourgeois dream of style. The apotheosis of this amiable, eccentric art is Lindisfarne Castle (1903), in which a gaunt military ruin is turned into a faery palace for Rossetti's Blessed Damozel or a Burne-Jones medieval princess. The borderline between fancy and whimsy, folly and foolishness, has never been so nimbly pranced. Lutyens's public buildings (churches, banks, insurance buildings and liberal clubs) are in a neo-classical style which is both more grandiose and more anonymous. Its apogee is his buildings for New Delhi, India (1913–30), the consummation of Edwardian self-importance, Greek temples and colonnades dumped – with superb disregard for a whole continent's artistic heritage and practical needs – on subject soil. He was extraordinarily prolific – among his other creations are the Cenotaph in Whitehall (1920), the British Embassy in Washington (1926) and the lumpish Britannic House in London (1928) – but his individualism and eclecticism make him the last of the great dilettantes rather than a significant member of any school or trend.

Authoritative three-volume study: A. S. G. Butler (ed.): *The Architecture of Edwin Lutyens* (1950). Good life: C. Hussey: *The Life of Edwin Lutyens* (1950). A beautifully illustrated, charming book on Lutyens's country houses and the gardens Gertrude Jeckyll designed for them is J. Brown: *Gardens of a Golden Afternoon* (1982). Sympathetic study: R. G. Irving: *Indian Summer: Lutyens, Baker and Imperial Delhi* (1981).

MACKINTOSH, Charles Rennie (1868-1928)
British architect and designer

As an interior designer, Mackintosh made full use of the tendrils and lily-pads of *art nouveau*: his pillars and banisters in particular writhe and coil like creepers in a jungle, and his window-seats and stair-treads are often curved and moulded to suggest that they grew naturally rather than were shaped by human hand. But in his buildings he replaced vegetable exuberance with geometric austerity of line and plainness of surface. He favoured bare whitewashed walls (often edged in black like mourning-cards), elongated or tapering windows and tall, sloping and high-chimneyed roofs. Inside his high-ceilinged, narrow rooms he placed spindly furniture (tall ladder-chairs are his hallmark) against plain-panelled or white-distempered walls. Thus, controlled *art-nouveau* riot (in window-panes, light-fittings, ceilings) is set against a background as dour as a Calvinist chapel. (The buildings are carefully planned for the effect of light: the tall windows funnel incoming daylight as if spotlighting a stage-set.) His best buildings are in and around Glasgow; the finest is the Glasgow School of Art (1909). He was the first British architect since the 18th century to have both international fame and influence: his designs, exhibited at the Vienna Secession in 1900, gave vital impulse to the Vienna Werkstätte (see Hoffmann) and to *Behrens, and so made their mark on the style of the Bauhaus, both in buildings and in furniture.

Good study: R. Macleod: *Charles Rennie Mackintosh* (1968).

MIES VAN DER ROHE, Ludwig (1886–1969)
German/American architect

A pupil of *Behrens and a member of the Bauhaus (indeed, its director from 1930 to 1933), Mies fully imbibed the cocktail of beauty-through-function which characterized German architecture in the 1910s and 1920s. His plans included fantastic schemes (fantastic for 1920) for huge skyscrapers; but his actual buildings, in accordance with his favoured motto 'Less is more', were orderly solutions to the problems of providing mass housing that was both cheap and dignified. In 1929 he built the German Pavilion at the World Exhibition, Barcelona: a single-storey open-plan building with walls of green glass framed with polished green marble and onyx, the whole building a mass of mirrors mirrored in a courtyard pool. The blend in this pavilion of Bauhaus modular building-techniques and luxury finish became the chief characteristic of Mies's work throughout his life: he was less an architect than a sculptor of genius, his materials being metal girders, pillars and poles of marble and sheets of coloured glass. This makes his work – before 1933 mainly private villas, e.g. the Tugendhat House, Brno, 1930; after his 1938 arrival in the USA mainly large public buildings – some of the most expensive and beautiful of all modern architecture: he is at once the Mondrian and the Rolls-Royce of the International Style. His first important US structure was the Minerals and Metals Research Building, IIT, Chicago (1943), part of an outstandingly attractive campus devel-opment scheme – his buildings are always set in large open areas, given room to breathe and to be admired, and the IIT plazas and piazzas are some of its most striking features. His masterpieces are Lake Shore Drive Apartments, Chicago (1951), and the Seagram Building, New York (1958) – gorgeous slabs of steel and coloured glass, skyscrapers as stunning as cathedrals – and the long, low glass-and-stone Crown Hall built for IIT, Chicago, in 1956. Mies's combination of simple modular construction and super-extravagant, fastidious finish has been widely imitated, but no other architect has yet surpassed him for care or flair.

He is one of the few creators of modern buildings who could with justice echo Wren's self-composed epitaph: 'If you seek my monument, look around'.

Good study: P. Blake: *Mies van der Rohe* (1966).

NERVI, Pier Luigi (1891-1979)
Italian engineer and architect

Nervi was the maestro of reinforced concrete. His buildings are beautiful, but more than that, they are amazing: you think not only 'How wonderful!' but also 'How ingenious! However does that stay up?' He devised many of his techniques as a builder of hangars for the Italian Air Force from 1935 to 1941; their huge size, and the need for vast uninterrupted roof spans, pushed concrete technology into the realms of artifice. His post-war buildings are notable, most of all, for fantasy: they may be built from cheap, prefabricatable modules, but Nervi's profusion of pattern and ornament makes them look rich and extravagant – the Crystal Palace in London and the Eiffel Tower in Paris once worked the same magic in glass and iron. In particular, Nervi's ceilings – sprays of symmetrical rayons and arches quilted with windows – are as dazzling as the carved cathedral ceilings of the Middle Ages. He was consultant engineer for the Unesco Building in Paris (1956) and the Pirelli Building in Milan (1958); his masterpieces are the Sports Palace, Rome (1960), a fluted concrete dome supported on rows of Y-shaped pillars – they look like firemen trying to hold down a billowing rescue-sheet – and the Audience Hall, Vatican City (1971), with its roof like an outspread fan, a peacock's tail gaudy with windows.

Useful publications: P. L. Nervi: *The Works of Pier Luigi Nervi* (1957); *Aesthetics and Technology in Building* (1965). Good interim study: A. L. Huxtable: *Pier Luigi Nervi* (1960).

NIEMEYER, Oscar (born 1907)
Brazilian architect

Niemeyer built his quota of rational Le Corbusian tower-blocks – an apartment building for the collaborative housing estate Interbau Hansa-Viertel, Berlin (1957), office blocks and plain administrative buildings in Brasilia (from 1951) – but his most distinctive work is in a different style altogether. He uses standard components (steel frames, prefabricated window panels, ceramic tiles and poured concrete) but controls them with vegetable shapes as original and fantastical as those of *Gaudí. His Church of St Francis, Pampulha, Brazil (1943), for example, has a domed concrete roof the shape of an italic letter 'm'; its flat front wall is an abstract mosaic of ceramic tiles. His Arts Centre, Le Havre (1982), constructed in the area of the old port, cheekily (and superbly) combines ultra-modern building-techniques with a shape reminiscent of a berthed liner; a feature of the interior is the lighting, subdued and at times, in misty greens, mauves, violets and pinks, suggesting reflected underwater light. In Brasilia, whose chief architect he became in 1957, he interspersed office blocks so banal they could have been designed by an apprentice with individual luxury buildings of dazzling originality and beauty. The cathedral, for example, is a series of inbending curved stone ribs locked together by windows; from a distance it is reminiscent both of a crown of thorns and of a crown of lamb. The best Brasilia building of all, the Palace of the Dawn (1959), is a straightforward window-fronted rectangle with a flat roof – which Niemeyer makes unique by a screen of soaring concrete pillars (this time shaped like italic 'w's): the contrast between the curves of the pillars and the straight-edged windows behind lifts an ordinary building to the spectacular. There is a creative arrogance about Niemeyer's best work – the same self-importance which governed *Costa's, and made Brasilia an ice palace – and his buildings often seemed designed as showcases rather than as environments for human life. But for all his wilfulness and lack of compromise, he certainly knew the meaning of the word 'superb'.

RUDOLPH, Paul (born 1918)
American architect

Rudolph is an exponent of the style brutally dubbed Brutalism. Its main characteristics are the use of rough-cast concrete (exterior) or untreated brickwork (interior), and the chunkiness of its appearance – many of Rudolph's buildings look as if they were originally designed from children's building blocks. His municipal buildings have a lumpish expressionist solidity not seen since *Behrens: a good example is the Mental Health Building, Boston Government Center (1971), thick, straight stone bands supported on pillars as bulbous and out of proportion (too fat for their height) as those which carry the upper tiers of a wedding cake. His university buildings are better: the new campus for Southeastern Massachusetts University (1963), for example, though full of aggressively jutting shapes and the usual massive pillars, looks as if it belongs to its landscape (a grassy campus) instead of – like the Boston Health Building – challenging it like a punch-drunk pugilist. Inside, his exposed-concrete stairwells, rough-cast walls and cold balconies – exactly like *Lasdun's at the London National Theatre – dwarf the humans. This style was regarded as radical and functional in the 1960s; in the (more humane?) 1980s, 'dated' and indeed 'brutal' seem better words.

SAARINEN, Eero (1910–61)
Finnish/American architect

The son of a distinguished architect (Eliel Saarinen, 1873–1950, whose works range from the expressionist Helsinki Railway Terminal of 1914 to the Scandinavian-severe Tabernacle Church of Christ, Columbus, Ohio, 1942) Saarinen designed a large number of workmanlike and 'conventional' – i.e. *Miesian, *Le Corbusian, *Kahnian – modern buildings, for example the decorously rectangular Vivian Beaumont Theater, Lincoln Center, New York (1965), or the forbidding skyscraper of the CBS Building, New York (1964), a mass of lowering vertical stone pillars fit to deter any latter-day Harold Lloyd. But his best work escapes from doctrinaire rigidity into a version of 1930s futurism – many of his buildings have the same appealing absurdity as the stage-sets of a Busby Berkeley musical. He was particularly good at airports: the main building of Dulles Airport, Chantilly, Virginia (1962), is roofed like a flat-dish radio-telescope receptor; the TWA Terminal, Kennedy Airport, New York (1962), is a swirl of horizontal curves held up by thin vertical uprights, looking from a distance like a concrete eagle poised for flight. Other important buildings include a General Motors factory (1950), the US Embassies in Oslo (1959) and London (1961), the Yale University Hockey Rink (1959) and the Watson Research Center, Yorktown, New York (1961). More a man-for-all-buildings than a great architect, Saarinen nevertheless shows how effective the marriage of talent and fantasy can be, how modern buildings which are perfectly functional can still be *jeux d'esprit*.

Saarinen's publications include *The City* (1943), *Search for Form* (1948), and an autobiography, *Eero Saarinen* (1968); useful anthology: *Eero Saarinen at His Work* (1962). Good study: A. Temko: *Eero Saarinen* (1962).

SMITHSON, Alison (born 1928) and **Peter** (born 1923)
British architects

The Smithsons are the most thorough-going and influential British disciples of *Mies van der Rohe. Their first major building, a secondary school at Hunstanton (1954), even refers back to the Bauhaus roots of the Miesian style: it is functional shoebox architecture, one large rectangular block (the administration centre and main classrooms) flanked by several smaller boxes (classrooms), the runt of the litter being the bicycle shed. This type of school building has now swept Britain, and become a useful if unlovely (and unloved) feature of post-war suburbs in almost every town. In the late 1950s the Smithsons, with *Lasdun, became the leading British exponents of Brutalism: architecture designed solely for use, not ornament. They specialize in long chains of tower-blocks, whose similarity to chains of molecules seen under a microscope is their only concession to vitality. The best (i.e. worst) example is their dour Robin Hood Gardens Estate, London (1972) – and again, others have eagerly parroted this charmless style, notably Wilson in Cumbernauld New Town. Just as poorly designed tower-blocks have engulfed many older British city centres – Bradford and Birmingham, for example, are concrete wildernesses dead, except to vandals, after nine p.m. – so these soulless Smithsonian living-factories are eating up new towns everywhere. Human beings are not battery chickens – but how are we to squawk this fact loud enough to convince the planners and the architects, those cocks of every walk? That the Smithsons themselves are not slaves to their own glum conventions is shown by one dazzlingly successful work, the Economist Building in London (1964), a Miesian tower of glass and polished stone. This was commissioned for St James's, one of London's most stylish 19th-century streets, and its success is due to the Smithsons' willingness to harmonize with, rather than to dominate, such a suave environment.

SPEER, Albert (1905–81)
German architect and politician

The architecture of 20th-century totalitarianism is treated by many authorities as if it was tainted by the plague it so often served: Speer, for example, Hitler's architect, is little more than a grudgingly admitted figure in most histories of modern architecture. True, his buildings are none too original, being chiefly derived from the grandiose monuments of the more megalomaniac Roman emperors (Domitian, Caracalla, Constantine). His work – notably the Chancellery in Berlin and the Stadium at Nuremberg – totally dwarfed the people who made use of it: it was architecture for giants, for uniform masses, for the state conceived as a living force. It was overwhelming, vulgar – and magnificent.

Like the buildings of Domitian or Caracalla, Speer's work looks best now that it lies in ruins. He thought he was building for eternity, but his marble suppliers (a Jewish firm, it would be satisfying to think) sent shoddy stone which in fifty years has crumbled and collapsed – aided, perhaps, by Speer's unshakable belief that there was no need to bind the huge blocks with metal cramps. The ruins are grand and inspiring, and – as in the case of the Nazi film-maker Riefenstahl (page 277), whose *Triumph of the Will* shows Speer's Nuremberg Stadium in its most lamentable and finest hour – raise embarrassing questions (for liberals) about the potential of extreme political systems for creating works of art. Speer's enduring legacy is the German *autobahn* system, the result of fascist ruthlessness applied to a practical problem rather than to the promulgation of political ideas in stone.

Speer published several wide-eyed, innocent books about his time with Hitler, of which the best (and most disingenuous, perhaps) is *Inside the Third Reich* (1970).

STIRLING, James (born 1926)
British architect

There was a time when the phrase 'the groves of Academe' suggested bosky campuses beside ivy-clad, warm-stoned buildings of mellow dignity and age, a humane environment for a university education largely consisting of the humanities. The architects of Brutalism have changed all that. In our universities now, harsh rectangles rule; all lines are straight, all corners square; every tender tendril is pruned away. A social environment for the children of Sociology – or ideal buildings for a brutal age? In the UK, the leading exponent of this style is Stirling, working either on his own or with his partner James Gowan. The Department of Engineering, Leicester University (1964), is typical: a foreshortened glass-and-stone tower like an upended plastic slide-rule case, enlivened (or engloomed) by box-shaped offices and balconies angled, it seems, so as never to catch the sun. It is a building wholly in keeping with the popular image of a midlands university as a cheerless depressant to the soul. His History Faculty building for Cambridge University (1968) is better imagined – a glass-and-steel *ziggurat* thrusting out from a V-shaped Miesian office-block – but whatever has it to do with the architecture of the rest of academic Cambridge? There is a new building by Stirling at Queen's College, Oxford (1970), again spectacular and just as spectacularly out of style. This is brilliant work, brilliantly chasing its own tail, oblivious of the people it is supposed to serve – desecration of genius. Or will our descendants, three hundred years from now, experience the same satisfaction and uplift from Stirling's monuments as we feel now from his forebears' dreaming spires?

In the 1970s, Stirling found it hard to get work – perhaps not surprisingly, when so many people complained so vociferously about the buildings he did complete. At the end of the decade he widened his scope, turned from university buildings and had greater success: the Stuttgart Art Gallery (1984), like an enormous wartime pillbox, is one of the first fruits, and work in progress includes a government building in Berlin, laboratories in New York, and the new building to house the Turner Collection at the Tate Gallery, London. His buildings are going to be around, love 'em or loathe 'em, for years to come.

SULLIVAN, Louis Henry (1856–1924)
American architect

Grandfather of the modern skyscraper cityscape, Sullivan was one of many architects attracted to Chicago after the great fire of 1871. His intention was to create a new, forward-looking building style for the city of the future; his imagination was liberated by such recent technological innovations as the passenger elevator and the fireproof steel frame (both perfected in the 1880s). The first Sullivan building inspired by these inventions was the Auditorium (1890); it was designed to fit one half-block of the Chicago grid and consisted of a large concert-hall (seating over 4,000) flanked by an eleven-storey hotel and office building. Skyscrapers were imminent, and soon followed in the massive form of Burnham and Root's block-filling Monadnock Building (1891) and their smaller Reliance Building (1894) with its fifteen-storey corner tower. Sullivan himself built graceful multi-storey buildings (e.g. the Wainwright

Building, St Louis, 1891, and the Guaranty Trust Building, Buffalo, 1894); but their use of stone cladding and carved decoration, added to shapes which are four-square rather than tall, makes them seem stacks of horizontal storeys rather than single buildings vertically designed.

In 1899 Sullivan began his masterpiece, the Carson, Pirie, Scott Department Store (completed 1904). This, despite its rounded corners and interior decoration of rococo ironwork, is the first genuinely 'modern' multi-storey building, a clear forerunner of *Behrens' work and of the International Style. The building is conceived as a single unit, a steel frame with large rectangular windows hung on it in regular rows separated by bands of stone; inside, it offers the essential features of steel-frame buildings, unbroken floor-space (no interior retaining walls) and plentiful natural light. Earlier multi-storey buildings had seemed experimental or awkward, gawky children of the mills and factory towers of the industrial revolution; Sullivan's store has self-confidence and stylistic coherence, and makes references to nothing but itself.

Sullivan's inventive genius is overpraised. His fame, fanned by his polemical writings such as *Kindergarten Chats* (1902), in which the catch-phrase 'form follows function' first appeared, and enthusiastically endorsed by his disciple *Wright, rapidly eclipsed that even of his partner Adler. Indeed, the impression from some accounts is that he built Chicago and gave birth to modern architecture single-handed, after which, unappreciated, he drank himself to death. In fact, from 1880 onwards the trend was there, and many people followed it – it took only a decade for the new building style to become widespread. Sullivan's importance, then as for later generations, was inspirational: he was the most vociferous, the most individual, and the greatest architect around.

The history of skyscrapers and their 'social ethics' is entertainingly discussed in *The Skyscraper* (1982) by Paul Goldberger, who has also published a detailed study of the buildings of one major city: *The City Observed: New York* (1982). Good study of Sullivan: J. Szarowski: *The Idea of Louis Sullivan* (1956).

TANGE, Kenzo (born 1913)
Japanese architect

Tange's work – he became internationally known after his Hiroshima Peace Memorial (1955) – is as eclectic and sensational (in every sense) as *Saarinen's, practicality deliriously enlivened by fantasy. His Yamanishi Press Centre, Kofu (1967), is a child's-construction-set palace of sixteen slender service tubes linked by horizontal office buildings in the shape of industrial containers – as ruthless a piece of Industrial Baroque as the Paris Pompidou Centre itself. His city plans for Skopje and Tokyo also look like child's-toy designs, slot-together motorways and sinuous plastic office blocks balanced by aseptic, tower-block housing estates. His buildings range from town halls to hotels, from churches to golf clubs; the best known (and most striking) of all are his sports arenas originally made for the 1964 Tokyo

Olympics. These are based on parabolic curves, the interiors like seashells, the roofs like feathers or water-lily pads. Like much modern architecture, they yield their full beauty only to an observer in an aeroplane – surely one of the most bizarre aesthetic results of humanity's taking to the air. From inside, their high, domed and arched ceilings (like suspended canopies) and their vast airiness unexpectedly cosset and cocoon the visitor: if any modern architecture can provide a 'womb-like experience', Tange's does.

VAN DE VELDE, Henri (1863–1957)
Belgian designer and architect

Originally a painter, van de Velde moved into house and furniture design in the 1890s. His own house, Bloemenwerf in Brussels (1895), was a manifesto, an assertion of the building as 'total artwork', with every brick, pane of glass, dado, dish or chair playing its part in an overall harmonious effect. In 1896 he designed interiors for the shop L'Art Nouveau in Paris: so a whole movement (and van de Velde's own style) acquired its name. The art-nouveau designers and architects, although they shared aesthetic principles, were individualists: there is far less homogeneity of style in the movement than there is, for example, in the International Modern Style. Van de Velde's interior decoration is like extravagant Morris, his furniture like miniature *Mackintosh, his architecture an eclectic mixture of *Gaudí's ooze and the black-bordered rectangles of *Horta. He made only a few buildings – he was predominantly a designer, indeed from 1907 director of the Weimar School of Arts and Crafts which later, under *Gropius, became the Bauhaus – but all his buildings are comfortable, unassuming and eclectic, conforming to no movements but those of his own fantasy. The Werkbund Exhibition Theatre, Cologne (1914, now alas destroyed), for example, was a series of round-cornered rectangular blocks of varying heights, like a squashed ziggurat; its striking main entrance was a large, mouth-like doorway set between two eye-shaped windows, making it a building with a welcoming smile. His masterpiece, the Kröller-Müller Museum at Otterlo, Holland (1937–54), is relaxed and unfussy in just the same way, contoured to harmonize with the gentle undulations of the surrounding countryside. Van de Velde's quiet style (like Mackintosh's) raises interesting speculations about how different (how much better?) our 1980s architecture might have been if the organic symmetries of art nouveau had not been swept away by Bauhausian angularity. Certainly his leadership of the arts-and-crafts movement in Germany – he was a (notably tetchy) colleague of *Behrens in the Deutscher Werkbund of the 1910s – and his theoretical writings (e.g. the jaw-breakingly titled Formulations of Modern Architectonic Beauty, 1917) were a crucial bridge between the art-for-art's sake style of late-19th-century design and the form-through-function of the 20th.

Good autobiography: Story of My Life (1962). Good study: H. Tierlinck: Henry van de Velde (1959).

WRIGHT, Frank Lloyd (1869–1959)
American architect

Wright's active career spanned seventy years, from the Oak Park house he built for himself in 1890 to the completion of the Guggenheim Museum in 1959. He was an energetic and heterodox theoretician: in both his work and his writings he implacably opposed two vital 20th-century architectural orthodoxies, that machine-shapes, production-line methods and 'group design' were the best way ahead, and that form follows function. His contrary assertions, that successful buildings result from individuality not consensus, and that function and form are equally important but need not be consequentially linked, both led to his own exciting architecture and had crucial influence on those architects who began to move away, in the 1960s and 1970s, from International Geometry towards more humane and individual styles. (In this respect, Wright's influence is most clearly visible in Japan, in the buildings of Kurokawa, Otani and *Tange; but the work of Seidler in Australia, Erskine and Gracie in Britain, and in the USA the private houses of even such giants as *Breuer and *Johnson owe him clear debts.) Wright also established two important 'schools', Oak Park Studio, Chicago (1895–1909), and the community at Taliesin, near Phoenix, Arizona (1920s onwards): these attracted groups of students and others sympathetic to Wright's ideals, much in the manner of an art-studio (say Rubens's) in the 17th century. (There is a paradox in the notion of a school dedicated to individualism; it is a sign of the forcefulness of Wright's personality, and also of his certainty of his own stature and rightness, that he was quite happy to inspire disciples.)

The first phase of Wright's creative work began in the early 1890s, when (astonishingly young) he designed many of the private houses undertaken by the firm headed by *Sullivan. These were the first examples of what became a standard luxury style for 20th-century American homes (Wright christened them 'prairie houses'). They were single-storey, long houses surrounded by terraces and patios, with gardens and house-floors at the same level instead of separated by steps and hedges; the rooms, low-ceilinged and interconnecting, often had floor-to-ceiling windows and smaller raised or sunken 'living-areas'. The low-pitched roofs often had wide projecting gables: like the rest of the design, this idea was adapted by Wright from Japanese houses he saw first at the Chicago Exposition of 1893 and then in several visits to Tokyo (where he worked particularly in the 1910s). The basic designs were published in the *Ladies' Home Journal* in 1900–1901, and were widely admired and imitated; the best of Wright's own prairie houses were built in Oak Park, Chicago, and Riverside, Chicago; the finest of them all (like a Japanese pagoda rife with flowering plants) is the Robie House (1909). As his fame increased, he also built a number of outstanding public buildings: Unity Church, Oak Park (1906), the Larkin Building (1904, a five-storey office building in the form of a vast centre well surrounded by galleries), and the now-demolished Midway Gardens, Chicago (1914), a restaurant-and-beer-garden complex capable of seating several thousands.

In the 1920s and 1930s Wright continued to build private houses (Falling Water, Bear Run, Pennsylvania, 1936, cantilevered out over a waterfall, is one of the most spectacular), and published ever more exotic and radical plans (e.g. the Broadacre City Project, first conceived in 1938, a 'dispersed city' of the future, the antithesis of *une ville radieuse* in that it restored the contours of the natural landscape and there was neither a street-grid nor a tower-block anywhere in sight). He designed a superb administration building for the Johnson company at Racine, Wisconsin (1939): its main feature is a gigantic hangar-like hall filled with thin, mushroom-shaped concrete pillars supporting a wide glass roof. He began to experiment with ideas for 'organic' office-buildings, the working-areas growing from a central trunk like tree-branches or cactus-pads, the whole structure surrounded by a sheath of glass. (These designs were finally realized in the Johnson Wax Tower added to the Racine administration building in 1950, and in the Price Tower, Bartlesville, Ohio, 1956. He also used spiral designs, as in the Morris store, San Francisco, 1948, and in his last and one of his most impressive buildings, the Guggenheim Museum, New York, 1959.)

Because his style (both personal and architectural) was so out of keeping with the predominant aesthetic of Western architecture in the 1920s–70s, Wright still has the reputation of a maverick of genius. It may well be, however, that future generations will regard the trend towards towering uniformity as a characteristic 20th-century aberration (to do with our fascination with the production line and our deferential view of the machine). In that case, Wright will be seen for what he is, a true heir to the great individual architects of the Renaissance and beyond, a master-builder whose concern for the relationship of building to user and environment rivals not so much Palladio (that 16th-century *Le Corbusier) as the anonymous, pragmatic creators of medieval castles, cathedrals and mansions: men who used stone, wood and glass certainly to glorify human beings, but also and chiefly to serve their needs.

Wright's writings include *An Autobiography* (1943), *A Testament* (1957) and *The Work of Frank Lloyd Wright* (1965). Good study: V. Scully: *Frank Lloyd Wright* (1960).

FICTION AND
POETRY

INTRODUCTION

KEY DATES

1909   Apollinaire's *The Putrid Enchanter* and Stein's *Three Lives*: stylistic precursors of many 20th-century trends including fragmented narrative, inconsequential dialogue, destructured form and the use of irony and parody as creative modes

1914   *Blast* magazine published by Pound and Lewis: gauntlet of modernism flung in face of bourgeoisie, who were none the less far more preoccupied by (and eventually to be far more shattered by) the First World War

1922–4   *The Waste Land, The Magic Mountain* and first publication of complete *Ulysses*: three of the major masterpieces of 20th-century literature, impossible without modernist techniques. (The literary equivalent of, say, Picasso's *Les Demoiselles d'Avignon* or Stravinsky's *The Rite of Spring*: unequivocal, seminal and unquestionably 'modern')

1936   Many writers join the International Brigade to fight fascists in Spain; Stalin's purges of former Bolsheviks begin to come to light. Beginning of collapse of left-wing idealism, the parallel driving-force (with social satire) of much 1920s and 1930s writing. The dilemmas of the European left-wing intellectual (as documented in, say, Sartre's *The Roads to Freedom*, 1945–9, and producing such anguished and bitter fruit as Orwell's *Animal Farm*, 1945, and *1984*, 1949) start here

1942   Camus's *The Outsider*: programmatic account of philosophical and intellectual alienation

1951   *The Catcher in the Rye*: birth of American 'Me-generation', the quintessence of flip, self-obsessed alienation (wise-cracking US counterpart to *The Outsider*, and just as influential both on writers and on the social attitudes of a whole generation)

1960   Trial for obscenity in Britain of *Lady Chatterley's Lover* leads to virtual abandonment of literary censorship. (Same function served in USA by trial of *Last Exit to Brooklyn*, 1964, an otherwise vile and unmemorable book.) In English literature now the censoring forces are the 'good taste' of writer or publisher, or commercial forces, less obviously the wishes of the Establishment

1961   *Catch-22*: inauguration or vindication of anti-Establishment mood

in USA, in wake of Beat literature and the poetry of the Flower
people, but (because better written) far more influential

1974 Exile to West of Solzhenitsyn, whose denunciations (of both the
culture he left and the culture he found) may seem to future
generations to have begun, or given impetus to, a new era of
puritanism and born-again repressiveness

WRITERS AND READERS

In the time of Alcuin (the 8th-century scholar at Charlemagne's court
who first put forward the idea of 'seven liberal arts', and thus laid the
foundation for half the education of half the world), a thinking person's
library might contain fewer than fifty books. Their purpose was not,
primarily, to entertain: they were a repository of knowledge, a platform
for new speculation and analysis. Books liberated the mind and inspired
the imagination; literature led to thought and thought to action. Is it
surprising that to the unlettered masses books appeared magic, and those
capable of reading them figures equipped with almost superhuman
powers?

The idea that reading is merely the start, that books are the armature
of thought and that what matters is what you build on them, persisted
until the end of the 19th century (and still lingers in the minds of those
who write advertising copy for 'serious' book clubs). The Hundred Best
Books, or (more exhaustingly) the thousand volumes of Everyman's
Library, were once furniture for every educated English-reading mind.
There was sometimes argument about the choice of titles (though there
was never much doubt about Homer, the Bible, Rabelais), but few
seriously questioned the fact of choice itself.

In our century of Babel, we have changed all that. Mass education and
mass publishing have made every form of reading accessible to everyone.
There is a glut of books, far too many for any one person to read. They
are a commodity to be shifted, merchandise to be sold by the cubic yard.
The parcelling of 'education' itself, the encapsulating in a few hundred
volumes of all the knowledge and experience of the human race, has
become impossible. Knowledge is like Proteus: the more you grasp at it,
the more it changes shape and wriggles free. No single mind could
encompass all the 20th century knows; Renaissance Man is dead;
selection is an essential modern skill.

GENRE WRITING

For literature, the uses of literacy have been both good and bad. The
most striking effect of mass appetite has been on the development and
exploitation of genre. Genre writing is by no means new: there have
always been essays, biographies, short stories and novels. But in this

century each genre has become a distinct literary form, with its own rules, its own conventions and very often its own exclusive audience. The stories of 19th-century writers like Dumas or Wilkie Collins may have had generic themes (adventure or detection, for example), but in general they followed the stylistic ground-rules of fiction at large: there was realistic narrative, character was depicted through both incident and reflective description, and above all (a characteristic of the 19th century), the events of each story were treated as specific examples of general moral points, specific instances of and reactions to the general human condition. From the very beginning of the 20th century, by contrast, genre writers began to follow discrete rules. Already in the detective, historical and adventure stories of Conan Doyle, the nature stories of London, the science fiction of Verne and Wells, the historical romances of Orczy, Hope and Farnol, there was a narrowing of focus, a selection, a concentration on one or more of the specific features which characterize a type. Detective fiction, for example, began to concentrate on the puzzle (often at the expense of character or credible setting); romance treated incident (including 'real' historical events) in terms of character alone; nature stories reversed anthropomorphism, so that instead of animals taking on human characteristics, the human reader was invited to look at events through animal eyes; science fiction concentrated on technology, sociology, or both. Genres of non-fiction appeared – gardening-books, autobiography, travel-writing – each with its own accepted rules.

For reader and writer alike, the fixed parameters of genre provide security. The existence of conventions almost guarantees the standard as well as the nature of the experience; genre writing is above all reassuring. Many highly inventive or capable writers (Agatha Christie, Georgette Heyer, P. G. Wodehouse) remain within their chosen boundaries – their strength and appeal lie in the variations they work on their own well-established conventions. Other writers (Wells, Simenon, Greene) sometimes use the conventions of genre as springboards towards the discussion of broader issues and wider themes. In the period since 1960, in particular, the ground-rules of genre have been expanded and exploded in what at first sight seems a radical manner: writers like John le Carré, Margaret Drabble or Arthur C. Clarke are regularly praised (not to say overpraised) for writing 'serious' novels within a generic style. The rules of genre have become traditional, and creative writers use them as they have always used tradition: they follow, adapt, revise or overturn. But whatever their approach, it is tradition and its ground-rules which validate their art.

The cushioning effect of genre (where even the unpredictable comes in the official envelope of predictability) is one of the main reasons for its popularity (and perhaps for its critical relegation). The genre writers are, however, paradoxically set free by their rules. Because they and their readers are walking in familiar territory, they can introduce startling ideas, radical or lateral changes of style, without alienating more than the most timid members of their audience. (The stylistic innovations of Haydn and Mozart were no less startling, in themselves, than those of

Beethoven; but because they were contained in a less radical frame, they seemed less shocking. Of course, Haydn and Mozart made creative use of this dichotomy – as did Beaumarchais or Swift in literature. They were as keenly self-aware, as vigilant for the effects of their art, as any romantic radical or 20th-century parodist.) At its most creative (in, say, Highsmith's thrillers, Graves's historical novels, Theroux's travel books) today's genre writing treats its own conventions with a respectful irony verging at times on that kind of parody which is such a characteristic and creative force in 20th-century art, and so allows meaning to transcend form. There are many writers of 'serious' fiction of different kinds (e.g. Bennett, Maugham, West, Cheever, Dürrenmatt) whose style derives impetus and formal tension precisely from the use of selected generic conventions, though they are by no means genre writers. Eclecticism is a feature of 20th-century writing, and genre offers the writer an inexhaustible source of conventions to draw upon.

But the use of genre can restrict as well as liberate. Of its essence, genre writing is conservative: it relies on the variation and repetition of traditional elements rather than on innovation. True radicalism and experiment are rare; the genre writer and reader are to a large extent isolated from convulsive change in the world at large. Even when such change *is* reflected – for example in the choice of Nazis or Russians as villains in Western thrillers, or in the use of sexual explicitness in romance – its effect is often at odds with the generic surroundings. (Sex in romances works against the general atmosphere of anticipation and speculation; villains of an explicit political stance over-particularize a thriller's moral conflict and so distance it from the reader, who is concerned more with sensation and empathy than with their specific causes.) Formal innovation, too (for example stream-of-consciousness or poetically descriptive writing), works against the narrative drive and cohesive realism which characterize genre writing at its best.

The fact that popular literature (like popular art in general) has turned away from experiment may be a reflection of our century's recurring uneasiness in the face of change. For previous generations, change (political, moral, scientific), although not always welcome, was part of the general forward and upward movement of humanity. It was disturbing, but also a dynamic and generative force. In the 20th century, by contrast, every advance, every discovery (from totalitarianism to birth control, from relativity to plastic) has its dark side. We are as often bewildered as we are reassured by change; each new direction seems to lead to the disintegration of life, not to its cohesion; the more of the pattern we perceive, the more we see that there is no pattern. In such a situation – and given the resistance to radicalism characteristic of all mass audiences – it is not surprising that the limited certainties of genre writing sell, and that 'high literature', with its limitless interest in experiment and innovation, is often more talked about than read.

REALITY AND THE OBSERVER

Two crucial factors, in imaginative literature of any kind, are the nature and presentation of reality. In the 19th century the favoured modes were Realism and its handmaid Naturalism. 'Realistic' writers such as George Eliot and Dickens (or Tolstoy, Balzac and Flaubert) presented minutely accurate images of the here-and-now. Everything, from the texture of cloth to the passing of 'real' time (as opposed to the selective, 'dramatic' time in, say, *Tom Jones* or *Gulliver's Travels*) was described in Dutch-interior detail. The reader was drawn into the narrative as an observant visitor is drawn into the business of a bustling street. Mimesis (or imitation of reality) extended to emotion and motive: we were shown the symptoms and effects of feeling in such a way that their assumed causes were also declared. This surface appearance of reality (like the conventions of genre today) allowed writers great freedom of allusion, and of illusion: the Realism in George Eliot, in Dickens, in Tolstoy, is selected, presented and carefully shaped, is a vehicle for other things. (An assertive political view, not the detail of everyday events, is the main burden of *Middlemarch*; a (somewhat saccharine) humanism underlies *David Copperfield*; moral pessimism flavours *War and Peace*.) Adherents of Naturalism, such as Zola, went further still, arranging the events and behaviour in their books to demonstrate specific theories of determinism or causality.

Increasing emphasis on selection and presentation led gradually to a new view of what Realism in literature actually was. Observed, 'photographic' reality is an illusion; the things that give it depth and guarantee life are the observers' viewpoint and empathy. And as we know from day-to-day experience, reality for the observer is not precisely ordered, a trim narrative sequence; it is a bubbling stew of observations, memories and interpretations, discontinuous and chaotic. The observers' reality is not defined by what they see; the reality of what they see is defined by them. For each one of us, the world exists only as we perceive or 'read' it, as we link each moment of perception to our memory or to the accounts we receive from others. Reality is a subjective, not an objective phenomenon. The romantics' claim for subjectivity was that it individualized character through emotion; in 20th-century writing, by extension, the whole exterior world is seen and validated as a facet, a projection, of interior individuality.

The idea that the movement of life is a continuum, not a progression, is by no means new. ('Everything flows,' Heraclitus observed in the 6th century BC.) It can be argued that a governing feature of the 20th century has been the replacement of a Christian metaphysic (life as an optimistic upward progression, animated by aspiration and rewarded by redemption) with a new form of the old pagan view that things are what they are, that the only movement, the only change, is in our perception of a static (though swirling) universe. This process was galvanized in the late 19th century by the new disciplines of psychology and anthropology (both of them liberated by Darwinism, which for the first time allowed the human race to be studied dispassionately, as a case instead of the junior partner in a transcendental relationship). Freud and Frazer (in *The Golden Bough*) declared both the universality of human feelings, motives and beliefs, and also that they were what they were regardless of any objective correlative. In addition, these writers opened speculation wide about human behaviour, prised it free from the constrictions of particular dogmatic theories. The science of the external world underwent similar convulsions. Quantum mechanics, and Einstein's theories of time and space, replaced former notions of fixity and permanence with the infinite (and to some, infinitely disorienting) possibilities of relativity and flux. Suddenly, nothing at all was reliably permanent; random humanity inhabited a random universe; the only certainty was the need for choice.

Emphasis on the observer, on the one who makes the choice, has been a major feature of 20th-century literature. Whether Proust's Marcel (who picks over facets of remembered experience like jewels on a tray), Kafka's Josef K. or Camus's Meursault (who choose as rats choose in a maze, endlessly, painfully testing principle against experience), the assertive hero of Hemingway or Mishima (who flings his choices in the face of circumstance), or the abstracted, 'anonymous' protagonist of much French new fiction, the central characters of modern imaginative writing define themselves: they are not defined. When we see the island through Robinson Crusoe's eyes, or London through those of Oliver Twist, the place, the circumstance does not change: the observer grows and changes as he or she learns about it, comes to terms with it – the process is a literary parallel to the Christian soul's reconciliation with an undeviating God. But Stephen Dedalus, J. Alfred Prufrock, Holden Caulfield, Herzog, or Márquez' Colonel (in *No One Writes to the Colonel*) do not change: their world changes, comes into focus for the reader as it is revealed through them.

The inchoate nature of human observation and memory has crucially influenced the form and style of 20th-century poetry and fiction. The form of *À la recherche du temps perdu* is like a guided but random tour through the mansion of one man's mind. *Ulysses* takes the events of a single day, shuffles them with a whole pack of memories and allusions, and deals them in a new order. A favourite 20th-century form (of which Eliot's *The Waste Land*, Dos Passos's *Manhattan Transfer*, Berryman's *Dream Songs* and Woolf's *The Waves* are widely different examples) is that of the mosaic or jigsaw, a tumble of separate impressions collated to make a coherent whole. The observer is a camera, and what he or she takes is a series of self-contained slides whose order and presentation are his or hers to choose. The style of film-cutting has had great influence on literary form (just as it has in fine art and in music). Where narration-by-sequence was the governing structure of 19th-century writing (so that even in short lyric poems, such as those of Keats, there was usually a strong sequential armature), modern writing prefers narrative-by-juxtaposition, what the critic Kenneth Burke called 'perspective by incongruity'. And as in films, the cut itself, the moment of juxtaposition, is the articulating factor, the contributor of pace and climax. Even in poetry as understandable as Frost's, in novels as formally straightforward as Powell's or Roth's, the principle of the cut is regularly and sometimes thrillingly employed.

MORAL COMMITMENT

A major problem of centring imaginative writing on the figure of the observer is that of moral neutrality. The Christian correlative gave earlier writers a clear, and widely understood, moral system to use as framework or rubbing-post. (It still does, in the case of 20th-century writers otherwise as disparate as Eliot, Mauriac and Greene: the duality between personal choice in an incoherent universe and the authoritarian certainties of received religion provide them with endless thematic and philosophical material.) But in its unreplaced absence – for a time it seemed as if a socialist social conscience was the new morality, but that feeling ebbed with the collapse of communist fellow-travelling in the late 1930s – is the moral risk not one of mindless nihilism? The answer, at one extreme, is yes. Not only such *angst*-ridden poets as Lowell, Jones or Berryman, but practitioners of French new fiction and German novelists such as Böll and Lenz have regularly worked in a framework of bleak, post-apocalyptic doom. For them, humanity is 'absurd', out of step with itself and the surrounding world. The same vision – generally more genially articulated – underlies the work of many more conventional writers, such as the later Lawrence, Mann, Auden, even Faulkner and Hemingway. For still other writers, nihilism is a joyous and positive force. Humanity's case may be hopeless, but it is also hopelessly funny. In Hašek, Heller, Márquez, Grass and Frisch, for example, the need for human beings to re-create themselves, to build on their own ashes, unlocks all the zestfulness and creativity which dogmatism (religious or otherwise) has long suppressed. Work of this kind is in line with that of past writers who once seemed eccentric and unique: Aristophanes, Petronius, the Wandering Scholars, Rabelais. It is a pagan vision, humane and strong.

Commitment to such a personal vision (whether pagan or otherwise) is one of the hallmarks of the 'serious' 20th-century writer. It is no longer enough (as it was for Balzac, say, or Dostoievski) to be generally concerned about humanity. In our age of uncertainty we expect specific commitment, specific views. At the same time, we are convinced that the truth of life lies in the flight from the enchanter, in statistics and objective facts; we feel that if events are somehow accurately and fully reported, everything will be revealed without need of comment. 20th-century warfare, in particular, has a bloody immediacy which over-rides philosophy and makes a series of demands which deny individuality. No one is a mere observer: we may be powerless, but we are all involved. The truly moral, truly didactic writing about (say) the trenches or Hiroshima is factual, not imaginative; Belsen has its own moral reality, and needs no gloss. Where modern war *has* produced work of quality (whether Owen's poems, Graves's memoirs, or the novels of Malraux and Ford), its tone is markedly anti-war. Today's general revulsion against mass slaughter (documented in detail, as never before, by modern news media) provides writers with precisely the moral correlative they need to universalize their art. Novels like Hašek's *The Good Soldier Švejk*, Remarque's *All Quiet on the Western Front*, Heller's *Catch-22*, even Mailer's *The Naked and the Dead*, are badged with a notable creative paradox: the more their authors personalize and particularize their rage, the more obsessively they detail actual armies and actual wars, the more objective and dispassionate are the points they make. The catalyst is irony: its presence articulates alienation in a precise and morally engaging way.

Moral engagement of a different but no less galvanic kind has been with politics, the relationship of individual with individual, individual with group, group with group. The advances of technology and science (in such areas as travel, food production and preservation, medicine and birth control) have been matched by social upheavals (arising both from circumstance and from wilfully applied theory) on a previously unparalleled scale. Politics, sociology and less obviously programmatic studies like anthropology and demography have become ever more polyvalent, dogmatic and dominant. Many of those who in earlier ages might have expressed a personal philosophy by writing imaginative literature are now analysts, essayists or pamphleteers. Non-fiction (for so it is called, though it is often wilder and more fantasy-oriented than any fiction) is a major growth-industry in contemporary letters, and it is here, not in novels (*pace* such authors as Koestler or Sinclair Lewis), that radical social thought is normally expressed.

The result, for writers of 'committed' fiction, is that their work tends to reflect rather than to programme change. They are, so to speak, guardians of the human dimension. Their concern for the individual leads them to consider effects before causes, means before ends. This can be clearly seen in the novels of D. H. Lawrence. His essays and letters show that he had an aggressive interest in social change, and several times in his life he expressed this polemicism in action, political or artistic. But in his novels, although social change is a major theme (for example the evolution of industrial society or the emancipation of women), there is no feeling of a politically propagandist stance, such as shaped his presentation of religion or sex. What the characters do in *Sons and Lovers*, *The Rainbow* or *Women in Love* arises, in part, from specific social or political circumstances and illustrates specific views of change, but Lawrence is concerned more with the effects of change on his characters than with the movements of change itself. For once (and it is rare for him) acceptance, not anger, is the prevailing tone. And Lawrence is by no means an isolated case. In 'political' writers as covert as Mann and Hesse, or as overt as Sartre or Orwell, there is the same feeling that fiction is about reaction not action, people not politics. A favourite 20th-century form is the *bildungsroman* or biographical novel, in which the growing of a passive hero is the vehicle for a description of all kinds of political, social and philosophical developments and influences. The writers of such books (and others, like Solzhenitsyn or Upton Sinclair, whose political assertion sits less happily with the novel form) are neither quietists nor pamphleteers. Their concern, like that of any essayist, preacher or activist, is with society and humanity; but their role is to paint pictures not blueprints, to remind not tell. Thus, the readers' response is only partly coloured by their own political or social views. They can accept the fiction on its own terms, suspend disbelief even in a repugnant moral ambience for the sake of the general humanity it articulates. (Can one do this entirely in Orwell, in Solzhenitsyn? If not, if the balance is distorted, the fault is not politics but craft. Theme oppresses form, and we are irritated by the imbalance even as we are convinced by the story-line.)

PRIVATE OBSESSIONS

Many of the greatest 20th-century writers turn in a different direction altogether. Their commitment is not to externals, to the common red meat of life; it is to the detail and significance of obsessive, private, even eccentric themes. They do not enter the reader's world, they invite him or her into theirs. In the fiction of Joyce, Proust or Singer, or in the poetry of Rilke or Cavafy, for example, the social minutiae through which the characters articulate their lives are described with exhaustive care. Their people live in engrossing and credible worlds – but those worlds have few references outside themselves, they are meticulous fantasies whose reality defines and delimits itself.

Even when the philosophical armature of such writing is strong, keeping it in balance can be tricky. The danger is obscurity. Who will deny that Mann, Joyce or Eliot have plenty to say, or that the worlds which flesh their themes are fully imagined, persuasive and thrilling? None the less, their works can sometimes seem wilfully obscure. The reader hardly likes to skip, but feels that the same impression could have been given in simpler sentences and in far less time. In Mann's *Joseph and His Brethren* or *Doctor Faustus*, in Joyce's *Finnegans Wake*, in Eliot's *Four Quartets*, writing is elevated from an accessible art-form to a sort of shrine, a repository of meaning fully accessible only to devotees. Once again (as in Alcuin's time) books are invested with magic properties. Authors (and not only 'philosophers' like Mann or Hesse, but simple fantasists like Tolkien) become *gurus*, the subject of fads and cults.

Perhaps solemnity is one reason: for a true 20th-century prophet must rarely be seen to smile. Certainly wit, light-heartedness and entertainment have often seemed disturbing qualities, inimical to true greatness, in modern art. Stravinsky and Picasso were regularly chided for their lack of seriousness; Nabokov is still regarded (as they once were) as a dilettante, a prancer, a pasticheur. It has taken us fifty years (and two generations of 'Absurd' humorists) to see that Kafka is often wildly funny; we still undervalue Singer's wit.

In all of this, the duality is the familiar one between content and style. For readers, content matters most of all. They want to know what writers have to say. For writers, style is often far more important. They *know* what they want to say; their problem is finding a suitable form of words. (Crane committed suicide when the words he found failed to convey what he wanted them to say.) In much 19th-century writing, the underlying themes were precise, well-understood ideas from the common stock. The language could therefore be prolix, allusive and even impressionistic without disturbing the basic flow of thought. In the 20th century it is the themes which have become prolix, personal and impressionistic, and the language has been stripped down, made precise and clean. Pound and Eliot prised the language of English poetry clear of rhetoric and imprecision; London and Hemingway did the same for prose. In the world outside literature, communication has become an industry, with detailed (not to say sinister) research into the effects of the choice of words. The result is that we tend to be highly conscious of literary style, and suspicious of writers whose language seems over-colourful; gaudy content, on the other hand (whether it be the bizarre social behaviour in McCullers or Márquez, the sexual exoticism of Gide, or the obsession with cooks, nuns and left-wing politics of Grass) is exactly what the consumer of literature requires.

THE HEALING VISION

It could be argued that obsessive particularity is a characteristic of all great literature. Do we not always expect a writer to show us the universal relevance of specific circumstance? Rabelais, Cervantes, Defoe; Fielding, Stendhal, Gogol – it is as easy to scribble a list of pre-20th-century writers whose themes are selective, particular and even eccentric as it is to isolate 20th-century writers like Lowry, Crane or Wolfe. Who reads Aristophanes for the detail of 5th-century Athenian politics, Petronius for the social history of Imperial Rome, or Boccaccio for insight into the pastimes of Renaissance Florentines? The circumstance of each author's work is unique to him or her, and its uniqueness is a major part of its attraction – but the points the writer makes reach beyond particularity and tell us about total experience, about life at large.

The vast majority of 20th-century fiction – and a good deal of its poetry – is genre writing, intended to provide entertainment and little else. But the greatest writers of the century, whether their style is flamboyant or serious, offer in addition a consistent vision of humanity. It is precisely in our obsessions, our devoted concentration on esoteric pursuits and arcane rituals, that we define ourselves. Each of us is a unique reality, the lone focus of a private world; to see it clearly we bring ourselves, and no one else, to bear on it. This can be a salutary vision. In a world shorn of confidence and mortified by allegiance to brutal creeds and very strange gods, what more should we ask of writers than to provide us with models for moral integrity and the prospect of decency?

◻

Although critics (including such able writers as Wilson, the Leavises, the Trillings, Burke and Steiner) have played a dogmatic and dominating part in 20th-century literary activity – a notable case of the taster fattening on the dishes he or she guarantees – they are excluded from this section, along with other writers of non-fiction (e.g. biographers or travel-writers) for lack of space. For the same reason, many talented 'real' writers are excluded. I have confined myself to 'essential' or 'outstanding' authors, or when in doubt to those I particularly admire.

AIKEN, Conrad (1889–1973)
American poet and novelist

Like the British First-World-War poets *Owen and *Brooke, Aiken spent his first creativity in fine but unfocused imitation of the writers he admired (in his case, Whitman and Dickinson); like them, he found a personal voice only when he came to terms at last with what was to be the great theme of his work. Here the comparison ends. Owen and Brooke were forced by the horrors of war into an outward-looking, compassionate utterance, expressed in strict metrical forms (e.g. sonnets); they wrote their best work in a single creative span, with neither stylistic repetition nor decline. Aiken's creativity was unlocked by his reaction to his parents' suicide-pact when he was ten; but the unlocking process took another thirty years – although he wrote plenty of verse, he produced nothing of stature until with *Preludes for Memnon* (1931) he began a protracted series of psychological ruminations on death and the corruption of innocence. His style was introverted (close, indeed, to the later 'confessional' style of *Lowell); he wrote for preference not in tight forms, but in a controlled free verse reminiscent of both Browning and *Eliot; he outlived his own greatness, producing in the 1940s and 1950s more work in his 1930s style, without development. His best poems are in *Preludes for Memnon* and *Time in the Rock* (1936); these outshine both the folksy, early 'symphonies', ballads like *The Jig of Forslin* (1916) or *The House of Dust* (1920), and later, self-consciously 'great man's' collections like *Brownstone Eclogues* (1942) or *A Letter from Li Po and Other Poems* (1955). As well as poems, Aiken also published criticism, short stories, and five novels, of which *Blue Voyage* (1927), a 'voyage of psychological discovery' influenced by *Ulysses*, and the comparatively straightforward tale *A Heart for the Gods of Mexico* (1939) are the most accessible.

Collections: *Collected Short Stories* (1960); *Collected Novels* (1964); *Collected Criticism* (1963, also known as *A Reviewer's ABC*, 1958). Autobiographical sketch, excellent on both the period of his parents' suicide and his 1930s literary life (he knew Eliot, *Cummings and *Lowry, among others): *Ushant* (1952). Good introduction: F. J. Hoffman: *Aiken* (1962).

AKHMATOVA, Anna (1889–1966)
Russian poet

Akhmatova's early poems (in *Rosary*, 1914, *White Flock*, 1917, and *Anno Domini*, 1921) are sad, precise lyrics about the dismays of love: she writes with the same precise clarity as the young *Nabokov, though the world of her feeling is nearer to Chekhov or Pushkin than to Nabokov's lustily nostalgic émigrés. Her family consistently suffered political oppression: her first husband (the poet Gumilyov) was executed in 1917; her son and second husband spent years in labour camps; she herself was prohibited from publishing between 1925 and 1940 and between 1946 and 1956. During this enforced silence she continued to write, and two further collections eventually appeared: *Poem Without a Hero* (1942) and *Requiem* (1963). These are badged with a bitter and at times impenetrable private grief: like the artist Kollwitz (page 409) she makes art out of suffering so painful that the spectator feels inhibited from approaching it.

Akhmatova's crisp style makes translation more effective than is usual with Russian verse; a good collection (both characteristic and accessible), translated by Richard McKane and introduced by Andrei Siniavski, is *Selected Poems* (1969). A fascinating book linking key Akhmatova poems to her historical view of her native city is S. Leiter: *Akhmatova's Petersburg* (1983).

ALLINGHAM, Margery (1905–66)
English novelist

Allingham's Albert Campion books are among the most satisfying detective novels of the century. The basic genre requirements are all there: swift plots, crisp style, engaging characters and bizarre settings. But her novels offer more. Minor characters proliferate, of sub-Dickensian richness – she has an eye for the significant detail which makes every paperboy, postman or shopkeeper leap to life; her feeling for place (especially for teeming London) is sensitive and unsentimental; the incidents in her plots are often splendidly surrealist, though hilarity is used to salt, not swamp the dish. Her best books are *Traitor's Purse* (1941, a Buchanesque tale, world-as-we-know-it saved against all odds), *The Tiger in the Smoke* (1952) and *Hide My Eyes* (1958) – in both of which London is as vividly, as lovingly characterized as Los Angeles is in *Chandler; and *The Beckoning Lady* (1955), an absurdist story set in a timeless English countryside filled with *Wodehouse characters.

Allingham's other books include the black comedies *Sweet Danger* (1933) and *More Work for the Undertaker* (1949), and the more serious, *Highsmithian *Black Plumes* (1940) and *The Mind Readers* (1965). After her death her husband Youngman Carter continued the Campion series for three further books, of which the (excellent) best is the high-jinks spy-novel *Mr Campion's Farthing* (1969). His memoir *All I Did Was This* (1983) is also recommended, both for his own life and for what it reveals of Allingham.

AMIS, Kingsley (born 1922)
British novelist

Amis's first novel, *Lucky Jim* (1954), caught a prevalent British mood: scathingly smug self-satire, sunnily certain that however absurd we are (and my goodness, aren't we *silly?*) we're really the salt of the earth. It's a smart, but never literary, send-up of intellectual one-upmanship (madrigal-singing, wine-savouring, reading the right newspapers), very funny but lacking the genuine satirical snap of Amis's predecessor *Waugh and his successors Bradbury, Lodge and Sharpe. A string of similarly undemanding novels followed; the best are *That Uncertain Feeling* (1955), about small-town ambition and lust, *Take a Girl Like You* (1960), a sexual comedy, like *Murdoch in a woolly cardigan, *Ending Up* (1974), about senile malice in a macabre old people's home, and *Jake's Thing* (1978), whose hero (a menopausal, nympholeptic Oxford don) frets and fumes like Lucky Jim arthritically made over for the seventies. As well as this pleasant output (and some urbanely tart light verse, gathered in *Collected Poems*, 1979), Amis has also tried his hand at pastiche (e.g. *The Green Man*, 1969, a poor science-fiction fantasy, and *The Riverside Villas Murder*, 1973, a 'sociological' murder novel), and at books with more serious satirical pretensions. The best of these is *The Alteration* (1976), about a golden-voiced choirboy marked for preferment – if he consents to castration – in a Catholic 1990s Britain (the Reformation has never happened); the worst is *Russian Hide and Seek* (1980), set in a future Britain ruled by the Russians. This is a neat, if unoriginal theme (it is a rerun, for example, of Saki's *When William Came*, where the conquering enemy is Kaiser Bill), but shallow political tetchiness and lazy writing enfeeble it. In truly Swiftian hands the all-swallowing, bland and bureaucratic Russians would have turned out to be us ourselves; in Amis's they remain the horrid 'them', and the satire is as deep as that of a boy pulling faces behind teacher's back.

Amis's other books include *One Fat Englishman* (1963), *I Want It Now* (1968), *Girl, 20* (1971), the serious *The Anti-Death League* (1966), *What Became of Jane Austen?* (1970, a collection of amiable articles from the period of *Lucky Jim*), and the politically bilious, anti-everything farce (would it ever have been published if he were not famous and formidable?) *Stanley and the Women* (1984).

ANDERSON, Sherwood (1876–1941)
American writer

At the age of thirty-six Anderson abandoned his job as manager of a paint-factory (literally and dramatically: he was halfway through dictating a letter) and became a writer. Four books later he produced his masterpiece, *Winesburg, Ohio* (1919), a group of twenty-three stories of small-town life, drawing their themes from Anderson's own observations and their easy, anecdotal style (the narrator's personality very much colouring the tales he tells) from *Huckleberry Finn*. The book became an instant classic, in the manner of Masters' *Spoon River Anthology* or Agee's and Walker's *Let Us Now Praise Famous Men* – and like Masters and Agee, Anderson never quite managed a worthy sequel. He published thirty books in all, and became both a respected journalist (his 1920s leaders, archetypal small-town-paper vignettes and cracker-barrel wisdom, are collected in *Return to Winesburg*, 1967) and the acknowledged literary master of such geniuses of the short story as *Hemingway (who satirized him mercilessly in *The Torrents of Spring*) and *Faulkner. There are seven novels (the best is *Poor White*, 1920), a dozen non-fiction books (with contents as folksy or down-to-earth as their titles, e.g. *Hello Towns!*, 1929, or *Puzzled America*, 1935), and four books of stories, of which *The Triumph of the Egg* (1921) is the best. Despite this prolificity (and despite the critical admiration heaped on him in the 1930s), *Winesburg, Ohio* is his only real achievement, and his own estimate of himself is exact: 'the minor author of a minor classic'.

Collections: *The Portable Sherwood Anderson* (1949); *Short Stories* (1962). Good books of autobiography: *A Story-Teller's Story* (1924, rev. 1968); *Tar: A Mid-West Childhood* (1926, rev. 1969); *Memoirs* (1942, rev. 1969).

APOLLINAIRE, Guillaume (1880–1918)
French poet, novelist and critic

When Apollinaire settled in Paris in 1902, modernism in the arts was still largely a backward-looking, end-of-epoch trend: *art nouveau*, the writings of Jarry, Huysmans and Wilde (e.g. *Salome*), the music of Delius and Richard Strauss. When he died in 1918, modernism was a thriving, bawling child of the 20th century: the avant-garde, whether Stravinsky's music, Picasso's paintings or Cocteau's drama, was all the rage. Apollinaire himself helped to bring about the change. He was a man-about-the-arts, active (and polemical for novelty) in every field at once: he was friendly with men like Satie, Diaghilev and Braque, and zealously promoted the careers of new poets (in critical works like *The New Spirit and the Poets*, first published in the 1910s) and painters (e.g. in his influential, and still informative, book *The Cubist Painters*, 1913). He wrote several plays; in the best known, the surrealist farce *The Breasts of Tiresias* (first published 1918, set as an opera by Poulenc in 1944), the balloon-breasts of the heroine Thérèse float away on the breeze, revealing her as the ancient Greek prophet Tiresias, while her husband, by the power of thought alone, brings into being no less than 40,049 children. (The play's première provoked a scandal, rivalling the juicy first night of Jarry's *Ubu roi*.) Apollinaire's prose (e.g. the short-story collections *The Heresiarch and Co./The Wandering Jew*, 1910, and *The Assassinated Poet*, 1913; the novel *The Seated Woman*, 1920) is sometimes sinisterly atmospheric (reflecting the contemporary French taste for Poe, or like Chagall's paintings transmuted into words) and sometimes in an incoherent, experimental style, as if pages of *Firbank were cut up and reassembled as a collage. His most lasting work is his poetry (in two major collections, *Alcohols*, 1913, and *Calligrammes*, 1918). At times – e.g. when he compares a woman's body to that of a violin, or writes a lion-shaped poem about a lion – the chief impression it gives is of experimental silliness; but at its best (poems of *accidie* and loss like 'Hôtel' or 'Sanglots'; the war-poems in *Calligrammes*) it is in a line from Baudelaire and Verlaine, and as good as that pedigree suggests.

Collections (in French): *Poetic Works* (1956); *Complete Works* (1966); (in English): *Selected Writings* (1950). Good introduction: D. Oster: *Guillaume Apollinaire* (1978).

AUDEN, Wystan Hugh (1907–73)
British poet

To approach Auden first through the 700 pages of his *Collected Poems* (1976) is to risk starving amid abundance: he is as garrulous as Browning, as coy as Byron, as unstoppable as Wordsworth. Seen in large, his *forte* is footloose, effortless verse, poetic table-talk which only just tempers tedium. The world would surely turn untroubled by the loss of squibs like 'Uncle Henry' (1931), waffly, arcane ramblings like *New Year Letter* (1941), or the piffling 'shorts' which fly across his work like lead balloons. (*Academic Graffiti*, 1952/1970, is the cleverest collection of these. Each must in its time have set High Table on a roar, but they keep about as well as grapes.)

Scythe this undergrowth away, and roots of genuine poetry appear. Auden's collections of the 1930s (*Poems*, 1930/1933; *Look, Stranger!*, 1936) contain his purest work. The rhythms are spare and fresh and the language nicely blends a heightened, slangy 'everyday speech' with extravagant and often brilliant images – Auden's aptitude for the cunning adjective was at its sharpest then. Above all, the poems look outward, the poet discovering the world, and himself in the world, not (as in the post-war poems) buzzing in ever-decreasing circles round his own navel. It is from this period that Auden's most often anthologized and quoted poems come: 'Our Hunting Fathers', 'Who's Who' ('A shilling life will give you all the facts . . .'), 'On This Island', 'As I Walked Out' and the magnificent 'Twelve Songs'. There are fine things, too, in three long works of the 1940s, the meditation on Shakespeare's *Tempest The Sea and the Mirror*, the Christmas sequence *For the Time Being* (both in the collection *For the Time Being*, 1945) and the 'baroque eclogue' *The Age of Anxiety* (1948), a despairing pastoral for our jazz-and-aspirin culture.

One of the reasons for the discipline (leading to success) in these longer poems, compared to the endless *Letters*, is their use of dramatic form. Auden is at his best when he writes with performance in mind – the amputation of the poet's self is surgery always beneficial to his muse. In the 1930s, with *Isherwood, he wrote three Brechtian moralities, *The Dog Beneath the Skin* (1935), *The Ascent of F6* (1936) and *On the Frontier* (1938); in the 1950s and 1960s, with Chester Kallman, he wrote some of the finest 20th-century opera librettos since Hofmannsthal's for Strauss: they include *The Rake's Progress* for Stravinsky and *The Bassarids* (based on Euripides' *Bacchae*) for Henze. He also wrote lucid and pointed critical essays: *The Dyer's Hand* (1963) collects the best.

All this is a large and significant output of quality work. The short post-war poems (eight collections from *Nones*, 1952, to *Thank You, Fog*, 1974) add little to his reputation. They are mainly versified maunderings about ageing, city life, the countryside and friendships – snippets from the commonplace mind of a celebrated, bored man of letters, alternately Olympian (e.g. 'Unpredictable but Providential' from *Thank You, Fog*) and puppyishly confiding, as in the banal collection *About the House* (1966), which offers a poem and a neat philosophical reflection for every room from cellar to attic. There are intermittent gleams of the sharp-witted word-magic of the 1930s, but on the whole the undergrowth is rife again. If Auden is the great poet many critics claim, it is because of the opera librettos, the short poems in *Look, Stranger!* and the two long sequences in *For the Time Being*.

Recommended introduction: J. Fuller: *A Reader's Guide to W. H. Auden* (1970). Good biography: C. Osborne: *Auden: The Life of a Poet* (1980). Good critical anthology: J. H. Haffenden (ed.): *W. H. Auden, The Critical Heritage* (1983).

BALDWIN, James (born 1924)
American novelist and pamphleteer

If, as Gore *Vidal once said, the three great literary themes are money, death and sex, their most assiduous interpreters for 1960s–70s America were *Weidman, *Mailer and Baldwin. Weidman's novels are equally about money and the death of principle; Mailer's work deals with killing and its corrupting effect on the killer; a main strand of Baldwin's writing is ambivalence, usually in sex or in that other great American preoccupation of the 1970s, race. The hero of *Giovanni's Room* (1956) has agonizingly to choose between heterosexual and homosexual love; *Another Country* (1962) – for some, Baldwin's most typical book – is about racial and sexual imbroglios in Europe and New York; *If Beale Street Could Talk* (1974), his least sensational novel, deals with Harlem ghetto-life and racial pressure; *Just Above My Head* (1979), about a travelling preacher, contains sexual wrestling-bouts as interminably explicit as any in contemporary fiction – it is Tennessee Williams's *The Night of the Iguana* made over for *Hustler* magazine.

In general, Baldwin's non-fiction is less feverish and more effective. The best of it is on race, and unanswerably passionate: *Notes of a Native Son* (1955); *Nobody Knows My Name* (1961); the vitriolic *The Fire Next Time* (1963), and *No Name in the Street* (1971), his best-argued and finest book. As he became more and more famous, the same thing happened to his work as overcame Mailer's: it ballooned into posturing (e.g. *A Rap on Race*, 1971, with Margaret Mead). Notable throughout his writing is another theme shared by Weidman and Mailer: the disillusion and despair at the heart of modern American life. Is this, too, merely a mirror held up to fashionable attitudes? Of all three writers, Weidman is the only one who talks warmly and with enthusiasm of humanity's better side; the absence of such optimism in Baldwin's work is a reader-alienating defect, leading to propaganda instead of fact and to rant instead of argument – and to explain, as he would, that the situation has 'gone beyond nice' is a small, indeed self-defeating, excuse.

Baldwin's other novels include *Go Tell It on the Mountain* (1953), an (autobiographical) account of a boy-preacher growing up in Harlem; and *Tell Me How Long the Train's Been Gone* (1968), an experimental tale of a disintegrating personality. Short stories: *Going to Meet the Man* (1965). Plays include *The Amen Corner* (1955) and *Blues for Mr Charlie* (1964). Good, if partisan, introduction: S. Macebuh: *Baldwin: A Critical Study* (1973).

BEAUVOIR, Simone de (born 1908)
French novelist and philosopher

For more than forty years Beauvoir lived and worked with Sartre, and some of her non-fiction (e.g. *The Ethics of Ambiguity*, 1947, her major philosophical work, and the essays collected in *Must Sade Burn?/The Marquis de Sade*, 1955) are expositions of existentialism as demanding, though not as lengthy, as Sartre's *Being and Nothingness* itself. (She was co-editor with Sartre of the journal *Modern Times*; their symbiotic professional relationship may remind British readers of the Leavises, Americans of the Trillings.) The quest for existentialist self-determination is a main theme of her six novels. At their simplest (e.g. *Les Belles Images/Pretty Pictures*, 1966; *The Woman Destroyed*, 1968), these deal compassionately with suffering heroines, rather like upmarket versions of the novels of Penelope Mortimer or Alison *Lurie (and no less readable). In others, by minutely describing the daily life of past decades, she adds to sympathetic characterization a remarkable feeling for the ebb and flow of intellectual attitudes of the recent past. *The Blood of Others* (1945) takes its (left-wing) characters through the difficult idealistic years of the late 1930s; *She Came to Stay* (1943) is set in the early years of the Second World War; *The Mandarins* (1954), her fictional masterpiece, is a story of 1940s and 1950s radical intellectuals equal in interest to, and as digestible as, *Gide's *The Counterfeiters*, to which it owes stylistic debts.

Overlapping with Beauvoir's fiction, and dealing in a different way with the subjects of intellectual and moral self-determination, integrity and the overcoming of spiritual panic in the absence of any kind of divinity, are her volumes of autobiography (*Memoirs of a Dutiful Daughter*, 1958; *The Prime of Life*, 1960; *The Force of Circumstance*, 1963). These tread the same intellectual territory, and discuss the same kind of dilemmas, as Lillian Hellman's autobiographies (see page 488), though the ambience is European rather than American and the writing is very much better; their pendant is a painful memoir of her mother's suffering and death from cancer, *A Very Easy Death* (1964). Her chief non-fiction work is *The Second Sex* (1949), a philosophical examination of the status and nature of women, which has been a feminist primer for three decades.

Beauvoir is, in some ways, a derivative and scolding pundit, immune to humour and resentful of criticism. But much also derives from her, and the world may end up the better for her reproaches.

Beauvoir's other writings include a parallel study to *The Second Sex*, *Old Age* (1970), a play, *Useless Mouths* (1945), and a quantity of classy but ephemeral journalism. Her other novel (the least impressive of the six) is *All Men Are Mortal* (1946). *When Things of the Spirit Came First: Five Early Tales* (published in English 1982) is an excellent early story-collection, reminiscent of *Camus or *Gide at their best. Good study: C. Ascher: *Simone de Beauvoir: A Life of Freedom* (1981). Interesting interviews: A. Schwarzer: *Simone de Beauvoir Today* (1984).

BECKETT, Samuel: see page 463.

BEERBOHM, Max (1872–1956)
British essayist and cartoonist

An urbane satirist, Edwardian *Punch* personified, Beerbohm published meticulously waspish cartoons of eminent contemporaries, and a large number of ironical essays (of which the most lasting are those in *Seven Men*, 1919, a set of imaginary portraits including that of the unknown novelist Enoch Soames who sells his soul to Satan for a glimpse of the literary reviews of the next century, only to find that he is still there unknown except as an unknown novelist who sold his soul, etc.). Beerbohm's own slim immortality is guaranteed by his one novel, *Zuleika Dobson* (1911). This tells of the devastating effects of Beauty (Zuleika) on the beastly aesthetes of Edwardian Oxford and in particular on the Peacockian, Scythropian Duke of Dorset, a young aristocrat deeply absorbed in his own doom-laden destiny. The book is as fresh, as sly and as affectionate a send-up of 1910s campus affectations as *Jarrell's *Pictures from an Institution* is of those of the 1950s.

Good biography: D. Cecil: *Max: A Biography* (1964). Good selection: D. Cecil (ed.): *The Bodley Head Beerbohm* (1970). Good evaluation of Beerbohm's satirical drawings: J. Felstiner: *The Lies of Art* (1973).

BELLOW, Saul (born 1915)
American novelist

The philosopher Husserl (developer of phenomenology) said that in the examination of 'essence' or 'meaning', all considerations of cause, effect and circumstance are irrelevant or a hindrance. The philosopher Heidegger (developer of existentialism) proposed that each individual human being is initially bland and characterless, and that he or she chooses character and destiny by a series of imaginative decisions much as a Christian achieves

Christianity by making the leap of faith. Bellow's unhappy heroes are caught in the no-man's-land between these philosophies. They are colourless – it is a triumph of artistry to make people so flabby sustain long books; they search desperately for their own essence, trying to eliminate inessentials (such as anger, remorse, other people or their own past lives); they are tripped by circumstances every time they attempt the self-defining leap. This is a dry theme for novels, and Bellow softens it by making his secondary characters bizarre (a B-movie tumble of inept crooks, drunken poets, no-good relatives and predatory lawyers), and by inventing settings and incidents which are often hilarious and always extraordinary (a car is beaten up with a baseball bat; a man hunts lizards with an eagle; a US businessman becomes a rain king in darkest Africa). The mixture is unique and rich; but in some of the books (notably *Henderson the Rain King*, 1959, and *Mr Sammler's Planet*, 1970) the ingredients refuse to blend, and the combination of cerebral philosophy and steamy incident seems both pretentious and wished-for, and fails to satisfy.

Bellow's three short novels are fine. *Dangling Man* (1944) is about a young man trying to make up his mind to join the army (the authorities refuse to draft him and so pre-empt his making the decision that will define him to himself); *The Victim* (1947) is a Nabokovian story about a man falsely accused of ruining a stranger's life who (in true Bellow style) comes to wish the charge were true, as it would give him an identity; *Seize the Day* (1956), a masterpiece, is about a middle-aged man trying to bring his own disintegrating personality to terms with that of his outrageous, aggressive father. The vein of these stories is continued in *Mr Sammler's Planet*, a dyspeptic study of life in decaying New York as seen by an elderly middle-European exile, Sammler. (But Sammler's concentration-camp credentials, which should authenticate his personality and the book's seriousness, fail to do so. He irritates everyone around him by his finicky aloofness, and this also makes it hard – alas, for the theme is strong – for the reader to feel engaged.)

Bellow's long novels begin with *The Adventures of Augie March* (1953), 600 pages of picaresque fun set in the Depression. The first half is as plump with detail and observation as *Weidman's books on the theme of pushy Jewish adolescence in the big city; the second half includes a riotous *Hemingway parody, as Augie and his mistress go lizard-hunting in Mexico. It is only after this – as the book romps to a close – that Augie is seen to have grown, to have been changed by his experiences, though this is not so much a leap into character on his part as merely the next adventure along the line. His personality-growth lifts the book from being no more than a hugely enjoyable comic strip – but perhaps it comes too late. *Henderson the Rain King* is Bellow's only real failure. The African adventure (Henderson sets out on an Odyssey, but is captured and forced to become part of someone else's reality, one which he only dimly understands) is packed with Hemingway (again) incident: lion-hunts, rain-ceremonies, initiations and mud-palace intrigues. But the action is interspersed with boring talk between Henderson and the interminably philosophical prince he is trying to understand (his *doppel-gänger* – what a novel *Nabokov would have made of this!). Henderson gets nowhere – he escapes and returns home, just like that – and neither, alas, do we. *Herzog* (1964) is an exploration of the mind of a man driven half-crazy by his own lack of character and the pressure of events. He circles his old haunts and friends like a moth round a candle-flame, always returning and always burnt; he writes endless, unsent letters to famous people ('Dear Professor Einstein, about the universe . . .'); he is racked by causeless agony of soul. The novel's experimental form, cutting backwards and forwards from reality to Herzog's imaginings, from first person to third, from past to present, is brilliant; it is a thorny but compulsive read. (The court-scene is one of the finest passages in modern fiction, with a bleak brilliance and a sense of pain unrivalled since Dostoievski.) *The Dean's December* (1982), in form guilt-ridden musings about Chicago by an elderly journalist-academic on a visit to chilly Romania (a land, for Bellow, whose heart has been chipped by a splinter from the ice-queen's mirror), is Bellow's most political book since *Dangling Man*, fully setting out the view of laid-waste American cities only sketched, by comparison, in *Mr Sammler's Planet*. Dean Corde, another of Bellow's liberal, ineffective and intellectual heroes, feels personally tormented by America's urban and moral decay (if any one person could feel responsible for Chicago, *he* does: he shares no ground at all with Augie March). Instead of the Sartrean philosophy of most Bellow heroes, 'What you make of your life is what you are,' he exemplifies, without ever evolving as a character – the book's main flaw – an even bleaker viewpoint, Hegel's (and, in part, Sammler's and Herzog's) 'This world, as you experience it, is your personal fate'.

Bellow's masterpiece is *Humboldt's Gift* (1975), not least because he allows its narrator-hero Charlie Citrine a neat line in self-deprecation – if the book were a movie, this would be Jack Lemmon's part. Citrine is baffled by his easy riches (and by the easy way they are stripped from him as the book proceeds), by the loss of his talent, by the human predators who dog him, and above all by his dead friend, *his doppelgänger* Humboldt Fleischer, a boozy, bawdy poet (some say based on Delmore Schwartz, but the book transcends à *clef* ingredients). *Humboldt's Gift* is to Bellow as *The Flounder* to *Grass: the work which pulls together and crowns a disparate but dazzling output.

Bellow's other publications include several plays (*The Bellow Plays*, 1966), short stories (e.g. *Mosby's Memoirs and Other Stories*, 1968, and *Him with the Foot in His Mouth*, 1984), the fascinating *Like You're Nobody: The Letters of Louis Gallo to Saul Bellow, 1961–2*, plus '*Oedipus-Schmoedipus*', the Story That Began It All (1966), and a highly political memoir of his visit to Israel, *To Jerusalem and Back: A Personal Account* (1976). Good introduction: S. B. Cohen: *Bellow's Enigmatic Laughter* (1974), which devotees may care to update with the hefty academic study by D. Fuchs: *Saul Bellow, Vision and Revision* (1983).

BENNETT, Arnold (1867–1931)
British novelist

An admirer of Flaubert and Zola, Bennett determined to become, as they had, an *homme de plume*, and devoted himself to a daily stint of words, and to an annual account of earnings from writing which reads more like a factory balance-sheet than the output of a single individual. (His million-word *Journals*, published in selection in 1932–3, are a fascinating record of achievement through endeavour – appropriate for a man who wrote articles on such thrifty subjects as 'How to make do on twenty-four hours a day'; they also record his cosmopolitanism and his love of good food, the theatre, and all things French.) Bennett's journalism (he worked for the magazine *Woman* for some years, and became editor in 1896) largely patronizes the reader and is forgettable, though one of the books he wrote for magazine serialization, the light comedy *The Grand Babylon Hotel* (1902), is still enjoyable. His great achievement is his series of books about the Five Towns, the industrial area of northern England where he grew up. The stories generally tell of young people trying to escape from an environment dominated by rigorous Protestantism and the work ethic, and coming to terms with its effects on their own characters. (The subject is similar to, and the books' quality as high as, the 'town' episodes in *Lawrence's *The Rainbow*; but Bennett's characters forsake Lawrentian dourness for a go-getting bounce reminiscent of *Wells's George Ponderevo (in *Tono-Bungay*) or Mr Kipps: bright optimism rescues his stories, each time, from the relentless pieties of the trooble-at-t'mill school.) The best of the Five Towns books are *Anna of the Five Towns* (1902), *The Old Wives' Tale* (1908) – 'Arnold has written a masterpiece', declared *Maugham – and the trilogy *Clayhanger* (1910), *Hilda Lessways* (1911) and *These Twain* (1916).

Among Bennett's other novels (most of which deserve their present neglect) are *Buried Alive* (1908), *Imperial Palace* (1930), the splendidly Wellsian *The Card* (1911) and *Riceyman Steps* (1923). Good short stories: *Tales of the Five Towns* (1905). *Letters* (1966–70). Good study: M. Drabble: *Arnold Bennett* (1974).

BERNANOS, Georges (1888–1948)
French novelist

A writer on Roman Catholic themes (particularly the search for grace and redemption through repentance), Bernanos has been as neglected outside France as those other great Catholic writers *Claudel and *Mauriac. (His work has tended to reach the international audience in versions made by others, for example Bresson's 1951 film of *The Diary of a Country Priest* and Poulenc's 1956 opera based on *Dialogues of the Carmelites*.) His books tackle big Christian themes in an unfashionable

but engrossing way: *Star of Satan* (1926) is about Satanic possession and
its exorcism, *Monsieur Ouine/The Open Mind* (1943) about a tormented
priest trying to work for his own and his indifferent parishioners'
salvation (it is a steelier version of the plot of *Diary of a Country Priest*,
1936). If serious novels on Christian moral themes ever return, those of
Bernanos will stand high on the list, for despite his old-fashioned, late-
19th-century ambience (at times he can seem as carpet-slippered as
Pagnol), he gives the everyday dilemmas of ordinary characters universal
poignancy.

Bernanos's other novels include *The Deception* (1927), *Joy* (1929), *Mouchette*
(1937) and *A Bad Dream/Night is Darkest* (1935, first published 1950). His non-
fiction includes *Diary of My Times* (1938), not the cheery autobiography the title
might suggest but a passionate denunciation of the support of the Spanish Catholic
Church for fascism.

BERRYMAN, John (1914–72)
American poet

After interesting if derivative early work (derived, however, only from
the best, e.g. from Villon, Donne, *Hopkins or *Auden), Berryman
found his theme and his style in *Homage to Mistress Bradstreet* (1956).
This long sequence draws on the life, philosophy and work of the 17th-
century Massachusetts poet Anne Bradstreet, and on what Malcolm
Bradbury has called the 'domestic metaphysical' tradition in American
letters. Berryman subsumes Bradstreet's persona in his own, thus
announcing the autobiographical drive of his mature work; the poem's
allegorical, allusive style similarly blends Puritan images and messages
with a slangy amorality characteristic of the 1950s. The result is rich,
personal and difficult; but for the engaged reader, Berryman's linguistic
grandeur (seen in lines like 'Headstones stagger under great draughts of
time/after heads pass out, and their world must reel/speechless, blind in
the end/about its chilling star . . .') makes it one of the most thrilling
poetic meditations of the century. *Berryman's Sonnets* (1967) apply the
same aggressive mixture of rhetoric and philosophizing to the more
extrovert (and more accessible) theme of love. Berryman's finest work is
the vast collection of 'Dream Songs' (*77 Dream Songs*, 1964; *His Toy,
His Dream, His Rest: 308 Dream Songs*, 1968; *The Dream Songs*, 1969):
these are works as varied, as personal and as fine as *Pound's *Cantos*.
They are the shambling, tormented thoughts and utterances of an
alcoholic poet-teacher (Henry; Pussycat; Mr Bones) floundering through
middle age and struggling to perceive or produce order in his own over-
educated, reeling mind. Henry is kin to *Salinger's Seymour Glass or to
*Bellow's Moses Herzog: a man formed by his time but out of it, battling
(alternately with wit and in despair) against insanity and suicide. The
Dream Songs' grim brilliance is continued in Berryman's last works,
Love and Fame (1970) and *Delusions etc.* (1972), and in the novel

Recovery (1973), published after his suicide. The opening stanza of *Beethoven Triumphant*, from *Delusions etc.*, sums up not only Beethoven, but also Berryman's Henry and, save that he was an unchary womanizer, the unhappy poet himself:

> Dooms menace from tumults. Who's immune
> among our mightier of headed men?
> Chary with his loins
> womanward, he begot us an enigma.

Other publications: *The Freedom of the Poet* (1976); *Henry's Fate and Other Poems* (1977). Good introduction: J. Conarroe: *Berryman: An Introduction to the Poetry* (1977). Good biography: J. Haffenden: *The Life of John Berryman* (1982), usefully complemented by E. Simpson: *Poets in Their Youth: A Memoir* (1982), a personal account of Berryman, *Lowell, Schwartz, *Jarrell and their friends, by Berryman's psychiatrist wife.

BETJEMAN, John (1906–84)
English poet

In his fifties, Betjeman became a television personality: his apple-cheeked nostalgia for a vanished suburban Britain of tennis-clubs, steam-trains and Meccano was expressed in sharply imaged, rhythmic language, with a nimble blend of facetiousness and genuine wit. These are also the qualities of his verse. Its rhythms and rhymes are as functional as those of *Masefield or *De la Mare, but he adds an element of self-mockery, of bitterness, which gives an edge to both nostalgia and style. His verse autobiography *Summoned by Bells* (1960) lacks this, and is full of cuddly sentimentality; but his short poems (*Collected Poems*, 1958 and 1970; *Uncollected Poems*, 1982) are often precise and fine. He was a minor figure, but he knew where his target was, and regularly hit the mark.

Other writings: *Ghastly Good Taste* (2nd edn 1970), on architecture, *An Oxford University Chest* (1938), on Oxford, and *First and Last Loves* (1952), general essays. Biography (in cliché-spattered prose, but good on Betjeman's work and excellent on his life): P. Taylor-Martin: *John Betjeman: His Life and Work* (1983). F. Delaney: *Betjeman Country* (1983) is a lovely book of interviews, reflections and tracings of the territory of Betjeman's verse, and contains evocative photographs.

BLOK, Alexander (1880–1921)
Russian poet

One of the side-effects of the Russian revolution was to polarize artists, for some time afterwards, into Those who Stayed and Those who Left. For many of those who left (particularly composers and writers of fiction) the nostalgic element in their work, the yearning for a vanished, dream Mother Russia – as in the works of *Nabokov or Stravinsky – lifted individuality to sublime levels. In those who stayed (particularly poets and visual artists) the galvanizing force was revolutionary zeal, the arts of Mother Russia for a time – as in the work of Mayakovsky or Tatlin – being swept away in a flood of peremptory and untried isms, designed to remodel rather than to reflect society. Western critics have tended to fawn on artists of the first kind, Soviet critics on those of the second; insufficient attention has been paid to those caught in the middle, whose artistic maturity coincided with the revolutionary years themselves. Of these, the greatest is Blok – and the effect of revolution was simultaneously to redirect his inspiration and to hobble his muse. His pre-revolutionary poems (*Verses about the Lady Beautiful*, 1904) are love-lyrics like those of a Russian Rossetti, misty visions of the unattainable expressed in language of delicate exactness, innocent of any purpose except to be what they are, 'beautiful' poems. His next published work, the result of a decade of revolutionary enthusiasm, was *The Twelve* (1918), an allegory entwining the Bolshevik Red Guards with Christ and his disciples at the Last Supper: the effect is as if an Orthodox ikon had been repainted by a futurist. His final volume, *The Scythians* (1918), brings together poems from throughout his creative life; there is little in it to match the concentrated impulse of his earlier work. He remains an extraordinarily enigmatic writer, a Russian Rimbaud. While the unconvinced may feel that his artistic dilemma is more interesting than his poetry, his admirers find in his work (especially *The Twelve*, regularly hailed as the greatest Russian poem of the century) an invigorating, tantalizing combination of authority and unfulfilled potential.

The best introduction to Blok's work is *Selected Poems* (1972), translated by Avril Pyman, who has also written a definitive, 800-page biography, *The Life of Alexander Blok* (1980). Blok's poetry itself is analogous to that of another anguished hanger-on, Osip Mandelstam, a survivor of Bolshevik idealism systematically oppressed by later Soviet Russian masters. His work (*Selected Poems*, in English translation, 1973; *Poems*, tr. Green 1977; *Prose*, tr. Brown 1966) is generally not as good as Blok's, but his memory will live forever thanks to the magnificent memoir by his wife Nadezhda Mandelstam, *Hope Against Hope* (1961), *Hope Abandoned* (1974): a classic account of 20th-century inhumanity to stand with *The Diary of Anne Frank* or Bakunin's *Confession*.

BÖLL, Heinrich (born 1917)
German novelist

The subject of Böll's prolific, sombre fiction is post-war Germany, which he depicts as a psychological and philosophical desert, a land bathed in the radiance of an economic miracle but lacking any myth of itself, any fabulous identity against which to measure present prosperity. Böll's books (like those of Lenz, e.g. *The Heritage*, 1978, their clones) describe a people barred (by a race-memory of Nazism) from their cultural past and (by the absence of any horizon but that of enough-to-eat) from future cultural possibility. If future generations want to know what life under the threat of nuclear extinction was like, these will be the books to read. Characteristic novels, with characteristic themes, are *Adam, Where Art Thou?* (1951), on the moral collapse of Nazism; *Acquainted With the Night* (1953), about an ex-prisoner-of-war trying to come to terms with the new Germany, with his wife and with himself; *Billiards at Half Past Nine* (1959), the ironic case-study of a present-day family and the previous generations who made it the way it is; and *The Safety Net* (1979), which brings the gloom into the second post-war generation, and takes in urban terrorism, religious mania and the whole despairing ethos of what the guilt-ridden hero (the target of terrorists, and therefore at the core of a ludicrous but sinister security barrage) calls this 'era of nice monsters'.

The most accessible of Böll's books, for English-speaking readers, are *The Clown* (1963), on another favourite theme, the Catholic's quest for God in a secular wasteland, and *Group Portrait with Lady* (1971), perhaps his best novel, a study, through the reports of those who knew her, of a 'typical' German woman from her birth before the war to the present day. *Group Portrait with Lady* is fast and fascinating, told in a panorama of short scenes like a Godard film; eschewing ambitions to grandeur or breadth of statement, it achieves both.

Böll's other books include *The Unguarded House* (1954), savage about miracles, economic or otherwise; *The Lost Honour of Katherine Blum* (1974), scathing about gutter journalism; *The Train Was on Time* (1949); *The Unguarded House* (1954); short stories (e.g. *Absent Without Leave and Other Stories*, 1964; *Traveller, If You Come to Spa*, 1950; *Children are Civilians Too*, 1964); and *Irish Journal* (1967), on his time spent in Ireland and his enthusiasm for the Celtic culture of such men as O'Casey, Synge and Behan.

BORGES, Jorge Luis (born 1899)
Argentinian writer

Borges is a mesmeric miniaturist. His favoured form is the first-person short story of some half-dozen pages or less. (There are poems – a good, late collection is *The Gold of the Tigers*, 1972 – but they seem limp and inconsequential in translation; there are essays – a representative selection is in the anthology *Labyrinths*, 1962 – but they are often on subjects peripheral to the English reader, for example the gaucho tradition in Argentinian letters, or deal with matters more fully covered in the stories.) His favourite subject is the illusory nature of reality – he will write a story in which a man exactly, and convincingly, rewrites *Don Quixote*, and another about a man by a river meeting a mysterious stranger who turns out to be himself – and his pieces often lay silken traps for the reader, not sprung until the very last sentence. (*Borges and I*, for example, proposes that there are two simultaneous but increasingly divergent Borgeses, the man who experiences life and the man who writes about it, ending with the sentence 'I do not know which of us has written this page'.) In this respect at least, his stories owe debts to *Kafka (e.g. 'There Are More Things', from the collection *The Book of Sand*, 1975, or 'The Gospel According to Mark', from *Doctor Brodie's Report*, 1970); there are also reminiscences (sometimes disconcerting in their banality) of *Conrad ('The Intruder', from *Doctor Brodie's Report*) and even of *Hemingway ('Avelino Arredondo', from *The Book of Sand*). In short, Borges is multi-faceted, and his work ranges from the fascinating to the slight. By far the best introduction to it is the anthology *Labyrinths*, which includes a complete volume of stories (*Fictions*, among his best), and a representative selection of his essays and teasing 'parables'. This book is notably well translated, too: later volumes, rendered into English by Borges himself in collaboration with Norman Thomas di Giovanni, are full of odd grammatical solecisms and outworn American slang – or do these features, perhaps, seem to Borges truly to represent his Spanish style? He is a riddling writer, and a bit of a riddle; not the giant of 20th-century letters some admirers imagine, but intriguing and satisfying just the same.

Other publications include *The Aleph* (1949), *Dreamtigers* (1960), *Other Inquisitions* (1964), *The Book of Imaginary Beings* (1969) and *A Universal History of Infamy* (1972). Best introduction: M. S. Stabb: *Jorge Luis Borges* (1970). Good heavyweight study: G. H. Bell-Villada: *Borges and Fiction: A Guide to His Mind and Art* (1981).

BROOKE, Rupert (1887–1915)
British poet

Although he was twenty-eight when he died, Brooke's poetry (*Collected Poems*, ed. Keynes, 1946) has the qualities of adolescence, not maturity. The shallowness of its perceptions is balanced by all-or-nothing passion of utterance; its verse-style is alternately clumsy and skilful (he is over-fond of feminine endings, which sap the vitality particularly of his blank verse; he is best at more extrovert and complex verse-forms, especially the sonnet); he is appealingly self-absorbed. All these qualities, good and bad, are seen at their peak in poems such as 'Song' ('Oh! that apple-bloom, and the pale spring sun . . .') or the school-magazine-titled 'Lines Written in the Belief that the Ancient Roman Festival of the Dead was Called Ambarvalia' ('Swings the way still by hollow and hill,/And all the world's a song . . .'). The appeal of his verse, for many, is enhanced by the biographical knowledge that this bud of youthful exuberance was doomed never to flower. Brooke is the archetype of the glowing upper-middle-class subaltern blotted out by the First World War – and by now, it is easy to think that he is famous merely for being famous. But in a score of poems, at least (e.g. 'The Hill', 'Sometimes even now . . .' or 'The Great Lover'), he stands with Shelley (for lyricism) and *Housman (for gravity): not a great poet, but a good one. The war sonnets, and the self-conscious 'The Old Vicarage, Grantchester', give a false idea of his themes and his quality; far more characteristic are poems of passion (so Edwardian in their delicate, hot-blooded gush) like 'Beauty and Beauty' or 'Lust'. Clearly, for the right bee, there *is* honey still for tea.

Critical biography: T. Rogers: *Rupert Brooke* (1971).

BURGESS, Anthony (born 1917)
British novelist

As his writing career progressed – fifty books since 1956 – it became apparent that if Burgess ever found a theme to match his talent, or to engage his whole mind, he might well turn out to be a great romantic European novelist, the Victor Hugo of the age. Each of his books was individually interesting, and he often reworked well-worn material in an unusual or technically intriguing way: *A Clockwork Orange* (1962), for example, is an ordinary tale of urban violence given pretensions above pulp by the extraordinary street-argot which Burgess invents to tell it in; *Napoleon Symphony* (1974), a novel about Napoleon, borrows the form of Beethoven's *Eroica* symphony and the swashbuckling vigour of Raphael Sabatini. Readers picking over the magpie's-hoard of his books in search of more of the same will find jewels of almost every other kind, from (say) *The Malayan Trilogy* (1956–9, republished in 1981 as *The Long Day Wanes*), stories of colonial despair as sober as those of P. H. Newby, to *MF* (1971) and *Abba Abba* (1977), written in a word-juggling experimental style imitated from *Joyce (to whose work Burgess also wrote an excellent and readable critical guide, *Here Comes Everybody/Re Joyce*, 1965).

Throughout and despite this diversity (other worthwhile books include *Inside Mr Enderby*, 1963, an Amissy satire on the literary business (equipped with two splendid sequels, *The Clockwork Testament*, 1974, and *Enderby's Dark Lady*, 1984); *Nothing Like the Sun*, 1964, a funny-serious novel about Shakespeare; and *Tremor of Intent*, 1966, an ironic spy-thriller) there was a feeling of gathering momentum, and each new Burgess novel was wider-ranging than the last. But greatness – the uniting of theme and talent to make a unique statement – seemed elusive. In 1980 Burgess published *Earthly Powers*. This is a 650-page blockbuster, a tumble of real people and real historical incidents thrust into a bubbling fictional stew. (It is, in form, the leathery 'memoirs' of an aged homosexual author, in reflective content a survey of ambition and honour in the 20th-century wilderness.) It could be that the book is just superior collage – the idea of 'evil', for example, suggests to Burgess the incorporation not only of the Holocaust, but also of the mass suicide at Jonestown, Guyana, and (no less portentously treated) the bitchy betrayals of the narrator's catamites. But equally, Burgess magnificently relates malignity and decadence; in particular, his view of a satanic Church (one of his characters tortures and betrays his way to Popehood and sainthood), a Church which is also the one sure repository of goodness and of hope, is central to the book, and is a matter which no one this century has handled with such lubricious authority (he makes *Greene, for example, seem pursed and mean). This theme and its treatment are what align Burgess with Hugo, and what make *Earthly Powers*, at the very least, a 1980s *Les Misérables*.

Burgess's many other works include the novels *Beard's Roman Women* (1977), *Man of Nazareth* (1979) and the apocalyptic satire *The End of the World News* (1982); *Urgent Copy* (1968), a collection of sharp journalism; the radio musical *The Blooms of Dublin* (1982), based on Joyce's *Ulysses*, and a contribution to the extraordinary, savage film *Quest for Fire* (1982), which reconstructs the life and – Burgess's main contribution – language of prehistoric humanity. *This Man and Music* (1982) is his own account of his prolific musical composition, a readable but self-serving exercise in autobiography.

CAMUS, Albert (1913–60)
Algerian-French writer

With Sartre, Camus is one of the greatest existentialist writers. He has the same ability to turn ethical and philosophical dilemmas, and the intellectual processes by which they are confronted, into art. But whereas Sartre's plays and novels are chiefly concerned with the 'leap into being' itself, the sequence of thoughts and events which leads to it and the consequences which follow it, Camus is more interested in the 'nothing-ness' which is there before the leap or, more tragically, which continues to envelop those of his characters who make the self-defining choice and find that it fails. Their failure is shown in different ways. Meursault, the 'hero' of *The Outsider* (1942), commits murder, and instead of being liberated by it into being turns in on himself in the docile, pragmatic manner of *Kafka's K. Caligula, in the 1938 play of that name (published 1944), turns to debauch and excess more as a despairing gesture against the world than in an attempt to 'define' himself. The garrulous 'I' character of *The Fall* (1956), who has failed to make even a literal leap into the Seine to save a drowning girl, never mind any existential leaps, circles round his own failure like a fish in a whirlpool, never able to recapture the moment of choice and hopelessly aware not only that he has missed his one chance, but that if circumstances *did* repeat themselves he would fail again.

Camus's philosophy was set out in two pithy essays. *The Myth of Sisyphus* (1942) says that human beings, so far from trying to combat the irrational world they find themselves in, should conquer it by accepting it in all its absurdity, as Sisyphus in the legend begins to roll his rock uphill again however many times it slips back just as it reaches the top. ('We have to think of Sisyphus as happy' is a key phrase.) The blend of insolence and resolution required to adopt such an attitude was called by Camus 'revolt', and its disintegration when outside events simply become too much (as they did for Camus himself both during the German occupation of France and later, as the Cold War began to develop) is reflected in *The Rebel* (*L'Homme révolté*) (1951), a bitter and thorough refutation of communism as an ethical or moral intellectual stance. (Camus had been a party member, and a communist journalist; but the excesses of Stalinism, as gradually revealed, turned him from that personal choice to the 'outsider' position in life which he explored so tormentedly in literature.)

The philosophical essays are not the best of Camus's work. In his notebook for 1936 he wrote 'People think only in images. If you want to be a philosopher, write novels' – and his three novels exactly follow this advice, each offering a different, equally telling metaphor for a philosophical state of mind and the actions that arise from it. In *The Outsider* the conflict in Meursault's nature between hedonism (he is direct kin to the sun-and-pain-worshipping young men in *Gide) and intellectual despair leads to an 'absurd' action (murder) and to psychological disintegration as he begins to collaborate with his accusers. In *The Plague* (1947) a doctor who refuses to believe in death is caught up in the progress of a remorseless, irrational plague (the book was seen as an allegory of the German occupation of France; but its horrifically detailed account of a community collapsing under the pressure of illogical disaster now needs no such props). *The Fall* is the ironic confession of a man nagged to distraction by his own moral failure: it is Camus's most nihilistic work and also his funniest, close in tone to the monologues of Ionesco's heroes as they battle the absurdity of life.

As well as *Caligula*, Camus wrote three other original plays and several adaptations. His own plays are *Cross Purpose* (1944), *State of Siege* (1948, a stage version of *The Plague*) and *The Just Assassins* (1950). *Exile and the Kingdom* (1957) contains six excellent short stories. *Notebooks (Carnets)* (2 vols., 1962 and 1964) are a transcription of his working notes, full of themes and ideas later absorbed into his work. Good introductions: P. Thody: *Albert Camus 1913–1960* (1961) (plain); P. McCarthy: *Camus: A Critical Study of His Life and Work* (1982) (fancy: some splendid debunking as well as lucid fact).

ČAPEK, Karel: see page 470.

CAPOTE, Truman (1924–84)
American writer

Like *Mailer, Capote began his career with fiction – in his case (e.g. *The Grass Harp*, 1951) dandyish, scented novellas, *McCullers made over for the *New Yorker* crowd – and moved from there first into journalism and then into 'faction', that is, real events treated in a fictional style. (There was litigation, no less, about whether he or Mailer developed this hybrid; they are certainly its most outstanding practitioners.) He also worked in films and television, notably on the screenplays of Huston's joky *Beat the Devil* (1953) and the bizarre *Trilogy: An Experiment in Multimedia*

(1969). His best books are his hallucinatory, Kafka-dream first novel *Other Voices, Other Rooms* (1948), *Breakfast at Tiffany's: A Short Novel and Three Stories* (1958), in which fastidious technique expresses real feeling about alienation and loneliness, and the chilling *In Cold Blood* (1966), a 'faction' account of gruesome mass murders notable not only for its cold-eyed bloodiness but also for its meticulous evocation of both small-town America and the mind of the criminally insane. This last matter subsequently became a preoccupation. Capote's later work (e.g. 'Handcarved Coffins', in the collection *Music for Chameleons*, 1980) was much concerned with death, and though his prose-style was as dazzling as ever, his conceits – not least his vision of himself as the Redeemer of American Letters – tended to get seriously in the way.

Other publications include *A Tree of Night and Other Stories* (1949); *The Dogs Bark: Public People and Private Places* (1973); *Then It All Came Down: Criminal Justice Today Discussed by Police, Criminals and Correction Officers, with Comments by Capote* (1976). Good introduction: W. L. Nance: *The World of Capote* (1970).

CAVAFY, Constantine (1863–1933)
Greek poet

Though his work is precisely located in place and time – he was a civil servant in Alexandria, and many of his poems describe the furtive, fascinating city familiar from the novels of *Durrell – Cavafy was also an exile, with the exile's passionate disdain for the life he led. He kept his work aloof from modern politics, filling it instead with echoes of the whole Greek past, talking of Alexander or Porphyrogenitus as if he'd seen them plain, loading his lines with the memory of Sappho, Callimachus and the poets of the Greek Anthology. The result is the same kind of local cosmopolitanism and momentous timelessness as many travellers find in Greece or Alexandria themselves, a feeling that past and present are alternative views of the same reality, that today and yesterday haunt one another. Poems like 'In a Town of Osroene' (Rhemon, wounded in a tavern brawl, reminds the poet of Plato's Charmides), 'Kleitos' Illness' (with its faith-healer straight from Theocritus) or 'Darius' (in which the poet Phernazis, composing his masterwork on the subject of Darius, is tediously interrupted by news of an irrelevant modern war) blend scholarly, aristocratic sipping of the past with a demotic urgency and bluntness which collapses time: Cavafy is anything but 'difficult'. The many beautiful boys who pass through his pages – he was homosexual, with an unapologetic taste for one-night stands (another factor in the feeling of life as impermanent, of happiness as venal or borrowed, which permeates his work) – owe as much to the bland-smiling *kouroi* of antiquity as to the Alexandrian gutter, and his ability to see and enjoy both aspects together is typical. (There are similarities of mood here with California-exiled *Isherwood and with the drawings of Hockney, page

401; but Cavafy's appropriation of the past makes him a deeper, greater figure than either.) No other 20th-century poet – *Pound comes nearest – has written with such delicate and personal precision about the balance between life (observed by Cavafy from his café-table as a daily self-renewing, 'political' and ironical game) and the duplicitous pull of art: each bedroom encounter leads to and is 'betrayed' by poetry. His best poems – 'Aristoboulos', 'In the Evening', 'The Horses of Achilles', 'I Went' – take the small events of small lives (tears, kisses, ceremonial) and make them resonant with the sadness and hope of a world without boundaries.

A definitive Greek edition of the *Complete Poems* was published in 1963; there are excellent translations in French by Georges Papoutsakis (1958) and by Marguerite Yourcenar and Constantine Dimaras (1958), and in English by Sherrard and Keeley (1975 – a bilingual text) and by Rae Dalven (1961). Good introductions: R. Liddell: *Cavafy: A Critical Biography* (1974); E. Keeley: *Cavafy's Alexandria* (1976).

CHANDLER, Raymond (1888–1959)
American novelist

In his preface to the essays in *The Simple Art of Murder* (1950), Chandler dissociated himself from the hemlock-at-the-vicarage British school of detective fiction (a genteel derivative of the melodramas of coincidence and the clodhopping rural comedies of the Victorian stage), and advocated instead tales of believable crime committed for believable psychological motives and investigated by believable, professional sleuths. None the less, his own writing was as fanciful and artificial as any he deplored. His novels are near to those of *Hemingway (for laconic sadism), *Faulkner (for acidly brilliant descriptions of sleazy backstreets) and *Salinger (for wilful style) – and he is more at home in such literary company than in the pulp-fiction world in which he is regularly placed: he is nothing at all like Hammett, for example, save for his use of a lone, wisecracking and sentimental hero and of abrupt and heartless mayhem. There are seven Marlowe novels, trash-culture of genius: *The Big Sleep* (1939); *Farewell, My Lovely* (1940), his masterpiece; *The High Window* (1942); *The Lady in the Lake* (1943); *The Little Sister* (1949); *The Long Goodbye* (1954); and the tired *Playback* (1958).

Chandler's short stories (thin stuff compared to his novels) are in *Five Murderers* (1944), *Five Sinister Characters* (1945), *Finger Man* (1946) and *Killer in the Rain* (1964). He also wrote five film-scripts, of which *Double Indemnity* (1943, with Billy Wilder, on a story by Cain) is head and shoulders above the rest. *Selected Letters* (ed. MacShane, 1981). Good introductions: P. Durham: *Down These Mean Streets a Man Must Go* (1963); F. MacShane: *The Life of Raymond Chandler* (1976). See also A. Clarke: *Raymond Chandler in Hollywood* (1982).

CHEEVER, John (1912–82)
American writer

Cheever is the author of four novels. *The Wapshot Chronicle* (1957) and *The Wapshot Scandal* (1964) are satirical threnodies for the 'old American decencies', as practised by sturdy village eccentrics with windswept, whitewashed clapboard houses and manners and lives to match. (A stylistic, and stylish, pendant to these Wapshot books is the posthumous novella *Oh What a Paradise It Seems*, 1982.) *Bullet Park* (1969) is a bitter black comedy of suburban despair and the descent to insanity, his grimmest book. In *Falconer* (1977) he changes his subject and details the life of a prison community ('Falconer' is not a character but the 'correctional facility' itself) whose moral compromises and sudden despairs or joys are made a smooth, perhaps overly wished-for, analogue for the human condition at large.

Cheever's novels, however, are minor work compared to his magnificent short stories (collected in *The Stories of John Cheever*, 1978). These are frequently bleak and sad; their subject is happiness snatched away, their milieu either the standard commuter America of fiction or the world of expatriates in Italy. Cheever is outstanding on the flow and particularly the ebb of humdrum relationships; he has a Dostoievskian ability to make drab lives interesting (see, e.g., 'The Pot of Gold', 'The Superintendent' or 'The Brigadier and the Golf Widow') and (especially in such Italian stories as 'The Bella Lingua' or 'The Duchess') shows an unusual and vivid sense of the importance of restlessness as a focus for some people's lives and characters. To some readers his writing seems sleek but shallow, *New Yorker* Gothic at its most elegantly bland; but his best work (*The Wapshot Scandal* and such stories as 'The Trouble of Marcie Flint', 'Marito in Città' and 'The Swimmer') has eloquence and passion as well as artifice.

Good introduction: S. Coale: *Cheever* (1977). Of a similar kind to Cheever's, though not consistently of the same stature, is the work of John Gardner (1933–82). His best novels are set in the past, and finely blend reconstructions of ancient daily life (especially medieval) with psychological tension and wit which are wholly 20th-century: *Grendel* (1971), *Freddy's Book* (1980) and *Mickelsson's Ghosts* (1982) are particularly good at this. His short stories are either extremely Cheeverish, set in modern American suburbia, or are bizarre medieval fables: one of the latter, the novella 'Vlemk the Box-Painter' in *The Art of Living and Other Stories* (1983), is his finest work in any form.

CLAUDEL, Paul (1868–1955)
French poet and playwright

Once regarded as a leading writer, Claudel has suffered almost total eclipse since his death; his work is also unsatisfactory in translation. Nevertheless, though by no means of the stature once claimed for him –

he has been favourably compared with St John himself – he is an important, individual figure, of a status akin to that of *Jones in the UK or *Macleish in the USA. His most accessible poems are the *Five Great Odes* (1910). These seek to marry pagan (especially Greek) and Christian themes: it is as if Walt Whitman had taken up Catholic apologetics, expressing in long, loose lines and sensuous imagery themes of the lust for and love of God. The combination of wistful hedonism and Catholic rigour is also the dominant feature of Claudel's 'plays' (really poetic meditations organized in dialogue), many of which are on religious themes. Out of an enormous and repetitive output, the best are *The Tidings Brought to Mary* (1912), a straightforward Biblical drama influenced by *Everyman*, and *The Book of Christopher Columbus* (1935), originally an opera-libretto for Darius Milhaud. *Partage de midi* (1906), on sublimating fleshly lust, and *The Satin Slipper* (1929), on the nature of love, have grander ambitions and fail grandly (largely because ponderous moralizing replaces dramatic interest). Those who are neither committed Christians nor sympathetic to ecstatic cerebration may find Claudel's work long-winded, narcissistic and elliptical; those who are moved by it may find that it can dominate their poetic experience. Either way, he hardly merits his present neglect.

Good introductions: J. Chiari: *The Poetic Drama of Claudel* (1954); W. Fowlie: *Claudel* (1958).

COLETTE (Sidonie Gabrielle) (1873–1954)
French novelist

Colette's first novels, about a young girl growing up (the *Claudine* series, beginning with *Claudine at School*, 1900), were originally published in the name of her overbearing Svengali of a husband, whom she finally divorced in 1906. Apart from a lacing of – then – heady sex-scenes to make them sell, these books are characteristic of her refined talent. Her descriptions of country life and her sensitivity to the (often bisexual) feelings of adolescence raise them into the class of the first volume of *Proust's *À la recherche du temps perdu*, though they lack the conse-quential themes which make Proust's book a masterpiece. She continued this kind of home-cooked but aromatic autobiographical fiction – British readers may be reminded of Laurie Lee's *Cider with Rosie* or the 'village' books of 'Miss Read' – in *La Retraite sentimentale* (1907), *Les Vrilles de la vigne* (1908), *La Maison de Claudine* (1922) and *My Apprenticeship* (1936). These, together with *Le Blé en herbe/The Ripening Seed* (1923), her best novel, and *Sido* (1929), a memoir of her mother, are outstanding books and justify her reputation.

Other worthwhile novels, though less good than those above, are *Chéri* (1920) and *The Last of Chéri* (1926); *La Naissance du jour/A Lesson in Love* (1928), about a middle-aged woman's seduction of a very young man, the arch (and archly filmed) *Gigi* (1945), and two books based on her life as a pre-First-World-War music-hall artiste, *La Vagabonde* (1910) and *L'Entrave/Recaptured* (1913). *Letters from Colette* (ed. Phelps, 1982) is a selection and translation of delightfully malicious, tender and homely correspondence from the whole of Colette's adult life. *The Collected Stories* (ed. Phelps) (1984). Good biography: Y. Mitchell: *Colette, A Taste for Life* (1975).

COMPTON-BURNETT, Ivy (1884–1969)
British novelist

Something of a highbrow cult in her lifetime – it was said, for example (in the blurb to one of her books), that she wrote 'Freudian case-histories to Aristotelian rules in the style of Jane Austen' – Compton-Burnett is now out of favour. After one immature (and disowned) book (*Dolores*, 1911), she produced eighteen novels in a consistent style and on much the same themes. The setting is a large (usually Edwardian) household; the cast is the family and servants who live in it; the game is letting skeletons out of cupboards – incest, murder, illegitimacy, financial chicanery: the whole Criminal Register is represented, never mind a simple Aristotelian crime like *hubris*. The narrative is largely in dialogue, ornate, stiff and spectacularly unspeakable (e.g. 'We are right not to be afraid of it.' 'But just afraid enough,' murmured Salomon. 'I am terrified,' murmured Reuben. 'I am untouched,' said their brother. 'If it is the truth to you, you are right to say it, Father . . .'). The plots, if not Freudian, are certainly 'family romances'. Indeed, the whole performance is a poker-faced nightmare, Ibsen rewritten by Fellini; if it is to your taste, it is compulsive, stylish, and resonant with lacerating wit. The easiest novels to get into are *Pastors and Masters* (1925), *Parents and Children* (1941), *Elders and Betters* (1944) and *A God and His Gifts* (1963).

A notable follower of Compton-Burnett, whose novels blend poignancy and acid wit in the same way, but interlace the dialogue with stylish narrative, is Edward Candy: his/her (the name is a pseudonym) best books are *Parents' Day* (1967) and *Scene Changing* (1977). The definitive biography of Compton-Burnett is H. Spurling: *Ivy When Young* (1974) and *Secrets of a Woman's Heart: The Later Life of Ivy Compton-Burnett* (1984).

CONRAD, Joseph (1857–1924)
Polish/British novelist

Conrad combines 19th-century melodramatic realism (learned from Hugo and from Zola) with an examination of psychological tension as a motivating force in human behaviour which is close to *Kafka or to *Joyce. He was one of the first novelists to make inner pressures of personality the dominating factor in his plots (as opposed to the external pressures of society or relationships which govern behaviour in most 19th-century fiction); in his books alienation, that crucial element in 20th-century art, is a central and obsessive theme. This icy heart is not immediately apparent, thanks to exotic locations (Indonesia, South America, the Persian Gulf) observed during his thirty years as a merchant seaman, and to the energy of his plots: *The Secret Agent* (1907) and *Under Western Eyes* (1911) concern anarchist intrigues in London and Geneva; *Nostromo* (1904) is about revolutionary politics in a banana republic; *Heart of Darkness* (his masterpiece, a novella published with two others in *Youth*, 1902) centres on an upriver journey into the African jungle in search of a demented, satanic and all but deified crook of a colonist. But under the bustling surface, each of his books is a slow-moving, thoughtful account of individual human lives stretched to snapping point: the intensity of *The Nigger of the 'Narcissus'* (1898), for example, comes from Conrad's detailed picture of the increasing psychological domination of an entire ship's crew by a bedridden, awesome negro haunted by the fear of death; the action of *The Secret Agent* is as much concerned with the hero's desperation as with his comic-opera activities; brooding Kurtz in *Heart of Darkness* stands for darkness in the human soul, and Marlow's search for him leads to a discovery of that darkness; the search for identity by Razumov, the student caught up in the revolutionary politics of *Under Western Eyes*, is far more intriguing than the story's physical location or its events. Among the dozens of later writers who have walked in Conrad's footsteps, Graham *Greene and Tennessee Williams, in their different ways, have come closest to his world of despair and decadence, 'the barren darkness of the heart'. He was also a notably accurate prophet of 20th-century psychological decline. But neither his followers nor his prescience make him a great novelist: he earns that status by the narrative power of his books, by their depth of characterization and above all by the single-mindedness and compassion of his view of the human race.

Conrad's other books include the novels *Almayer's Folly* (1895), *An Outcast of the Islands* (1896), *Lord Jim* (1900), *Chance* (1913) and *Victory* (1915), short stories – chiefly about the sea – collected in *Typhoon and Other Stories* (1912) and *Twixt Land and Sea* (1912), and a volume of memoirs *The Mirror of the Sea* (1906). Good introduction: J. Baines: *Joseph Conrad: A Critical Biography* (1960). See also J. A. MacClure: *Kipling and Conrad: The Colonial Fiction* (1982) and D. R. Schwarz: *Conrad: Almayer's Folly to Under Western Eyes* (1983). Interesting letters and documents from Conrad's early life: Z. Najder (ed.): *Under Familial Eyes* (1983). Conrad's complete letters are being published in an edition by Karl and Davis; Volume 1 appeared in 1983.

COOK, David (born 1940)
British novelist

Cook's early novels *Albert's Memorial* (1972) and *Happy Endings* (1974) placed him in the dour fictional company of Debbie Moggach or Ian MacEwan: that is, he wrote with mandarin fastidiousness (and in prose as sharp as a scalpel, a pleasure to read) about sexual deviation, mental illness, deprivation and cruelty, squalid subjects seemingly out of range of humanity's brighter side. *Albert's Memorial* charts the relationship between two emotional derelicts, a confused widow and a catamite whose protector has died; *Happy Endings* begins with the reception at an assessment centre of a twelve-year-old boy who has molested a five-year-old girl, and ends with a thirty-five-year-old sexual deviant (a luster after teenage girls) becoming house-father at another assessment centre twenty-three years later.

After these promising but unsunny books, however, Cook parted company fast with the video-nasty school in British fiction, and began to reveal his true quality. His third novel, *Walter* (1978, subsequently filmed), was a tender story of a mentally subnormal adult and his love of pigeons; its themes of dereliction and inadequacy were as stony as ever, and its descriptions as unflinchingly clinical, but Cook now added a moral standpoint and a compassion for his characters which lifted the experience. His next two books were masterpieces. *Winter Doves* (1979) is an account of Walter's love for an articulate would-be suicide; *Sunrising* (1984) is about three children coping with rural poverty and with the criminality and destitution of London slums in the 1830s. Outlining their themes does these books as little service as epitomizing *Oliver Twist* or *David Copperfield*. Cook may write about the dispossessed (*Winter Doves* owes debts to *Orwell's *Down and Out in London and Paris*, *Sunrising* to Borrow's *Rural Rides* and Chesney's *The Victorian Underworld*), but he consistently irradiates his material by the tenderness of the relationships he describes, and by the way each new twist of suffering unlocks humanity in both the central characters and the people they encounter. Of present-day British novelists, only Susan *Hill can match his ability to find hope in the blackest despair – and the comparison with Dickens is also just, for although Dickens could never have achieved their concision or elegance of style, both *Winter Doves* and *Sunrising* are books he would have been proud to write.

As well as novels, Cook has written several TV plays including *Willy, Jenny Can't Work Any Faster* and the splendid black comedy *Singles Weekend* (1984). His admirers may well also enjoy the novels of Paul Bailey (born 1937). He has the same Dickensian eye for macabre detail, the same coldly laconic style, and the same vision of human existence as a struggle to find purpose in what to the outsider might seem deprived, shabby or expedient lives. *At the Jerusalem* (1967) and *Old Soldiers* (1980) are both about old age; *A Distant Likeness* (1973) charts the neurotic collapse of a tough policeman (it is a mirror-image *Crime and Punishment*, obsession with a single crime triggering long-suppressed guilt and self-disgust); *Peter Smart's Confession* (1977) is a first-person narrative by a despairing actor.

CRANE, Hart (1899–1932)
American poet

After a volume of pleasant but unspecial short poems (*White Buildings*, 1926), chiefly love-lyrics or nature-poems in the manner of Verlaine and Tennyson (with occasional syntactical or linguistic invigoration derived from the recently published poetry of *Hopkins), Crane set about his major work, a poem which would 'encompass and re-imagine' America. The grand phraseology suggests Whitman; the idea suggests *Wolfe; the poem, when it finally appeared, derived energy from *Eliot, and especially from *The Waste Land*. It was called *The Bridge* (1930), and took Brooklyn Bridge as a symbol both of America's dynamic ambition and of her combination of technological wizardry and aesthetic grace. Where *The Waste Land* details the sterility of 20th-century life, *The Bridge* proclaims its fecundity. Its subject-matter ranges from the Red Indian heritage to the Wright brothers on the one hand and on the other to the hoboes (or, as Crane regarded them, 'free souls') found in the subway (where Crane also, and – as he tells it – magnificently, encountered the ghost of Edgar Allan Poe).

It sounds pretentious and incoherent, and Crane himself felt that it was a failure: he committed suicide in 1932. But it fails only as Wolfe's fiction fails, on a scale so tremendous that it seems to set new bounds for poetry (as Eliot's verse, by contrast, seems to define and delimit it). Many of the individual subjects alluded to in *The Bridge* disappeared in the Depression, and the allusions now seem dated; but Crane's vision of a single, richly dynamic nation, welded from a thousand diverse elements, still has echoes in American mythology, and no one else has found such a compact and enthralling way of expressing it.

Crane's only other verse is *Ten Unpublished Poems* (1972); there are *Letters of Crane and His Family* (ed. Lewis, 1974), and *Crane and Yvor Williams: Their Literary Correspondence* (ed. Parkinson, 1978). Good introductions: S. J. Hazo: *Crane: An Introduction and Interpretation* (1963) and *Smithereened Apart: A Critique of Hart Crane* (1977); R. P. Sugg: *Crane's 'The Bridge': A Description of Its Life* (1977).

CUMMINGS, Edward Estlin (1894–1962)
American poet

Anyone who has seen a film involving an intellectual party in Greenwich Village (such as that held by Audrey Hepburn's friends in *Breakfast at Tiffany's*), or heard Woody Allen or Tony Hancock sending up contemporary poetry, will have some idea of Cummings's style. For fifty years he was at the forefront of the avant-garde, pushing self-expression up to and beyond the border of narcissism. (A typical poem, on middle-aged passion, might read 'i. you. leaffall.'; typical volume-titles include &; (*No title*) and *1 × 1*. This kind of thing either dazzles you with its brilliance, or leaves you stony-faced.) All poets make art by redefining the potentialities of language; Cummings redefined several of them right off the page. He famously dispensed with capital letters; the list of his exclusions also includes punctuation, rhythm, word-sequence, even at times nouns and adjectives. Like *Apollinaire, he wrote animal-poems in the shape of animals; like Lewis Carroll, he wrote poems whose words slipped askew and tumbled off the page. All of this would be merely silly, if he hadn't gone on for so long, and been accepted by so many serious critics as a serious poet. A suitable (lower) case for treatment?

Cummings's major work is collected in *Tulips and Chimneys* (rev. edn 1976); *Poems 1923–1954* (1954); *73 Poems* (1963); *Complete Poems* (2 vols. 1968; 1972). A good introductory selection is G. Firmage (ed.): *Cummings: A Miscellany* (rev. edn 1965). His prose includes a striking war-novel (*The Enormous Room*, 1922, rev. edn 1978), an account of a visit to Russia (*eimi*, 1933), and the appropriately named *i: six nonlectures* (1953). Good introduction (taking as the title suggests, a more positive view than mine): C. Norman: *The Magic-Maker: e.e. cummings* (1958).

DAY LEWIS, Cecil (1904–72)
British poet

In his heyday, Day Lewis was everyone's favourite highbrow poet: he wrote 'quality' verse in an easy idiom, and avoided both the alienating wit of *Auden and the intellectual convolutions of *Eliot. Read now, his poetry still has an attractive manner, but lacks substance – it is, precisely, like winsome Auden or straightened-out Eliot. His main subject is himself, either lost in contemplation of the world's silliness and beauty (e.g. 'Behold the swan/Riding at her image, anchored there/Complacent, a water-lily upon/The ornamental water . . .' from *Overtures to Death*, 1938), or teasing out his own character (e.g. 'Transitional Poem', 1929 – 'Now I have come to reason . . .' – or 'Going My Way', from the early 1970s: 'Now, when there is less time than ever . . .'). His style draws clarity and strength not from Auden's heightened common speech or from Georgian vacuities, but from the great 19th-century hymn-writers (e.g. 'Consider. These are they/Who have a stake in earth/But with no wing on air/Walk not a planet path . . .' from *The Magnetic Mountain*, 1933). If his verse is slighter than it seemed, it is never less than agreeable, of minor excellence: his best collections are *A Time to Dance* (1935) and *The Room and Other Poems* (1965). His translations are variable, his Valéry and Baudelaire good, his Virgil accurate but flat. His detective stories (written under the pseudonym Nicholas Blake) may well outlive his poetry: good examples are *The Beast Must Die* (1938) and *The Tangled Web* (1956).

Good biography (despite family argument about suppression or distortion of specific relationships): S. Day Lewis: *C. Day Lewis: An English Literary Life* (1980).

DE LA MARE, Walter (1873–1956)
British poet

The prolific De la Mare (his *Complete Poems*, 1969, fill nearly 1,000 pages) is usually classified, conveniently but unhelpfully, as 'unclassifiable': a craggy individualist, a verse Vaughan Williams. In fact he belongs in a minor tradition also honoured by Kenneth Grahame, C. S. Lewis, Arthur Ransome and *Tolkien. Its roots are planted in firm English soil – and that means both Edwardian certainty that the British were the gleam in God's eye when he or she separated light from dark and also the moody blend of whimsy and terror in British folk tales, the Celtic twitch beneath the tweed. De la Mare's expressed intention was to 'enshrine the inexpressible' in verse, and perhaps his present elusiveness is a measure of his success. His collections of his own verse for children (e.g. *Peacock Pie*, 1913) and of other people's (e.g. *Come Hither*, 1923) are often quoted as his finest work. They are certainly fine, and have had an immense effect for generations, but they hardly scale his heights. These are to be found in adult collections such as *The Listeners and Other Poems* (1912), *Memory and Other Poems* (1938, Hardyish in tone and quality) and particularly in *Winged Chariot* (1951), his most sustained and most enigmatic work. If he is like Vaughan Williams, it is not only because of his apartness from tradition, but also because he uses easily understood language to express far from easy thoughts (in De la Mare's case, about the yearning and the happiness of the human soul).

A good selection of De la Mare's work, with an outstanding introduction by *Auden, is *A Choice of De la Mare's Verse* (1963).

De VRIES, Peter (born 1910)
American novelist

In his shorter pieces, many of them written for the *New Yorker* (collection, *No, But I Saw the Movie*, 1952), De Vries reveals himself a humorist in the mode of Leacock or Thurber and, like them, finds endless material in the spectacle of metropolitan humanity blundering through the undignified minefield of the everyday. His novels (over two dozen, a sequence of comic excellence sustained for over three decades) inhabit the same world, and their heroes' Long Island or Connecticut commuter lives are a desperate balance between wild inner urges and the risk of irrecoverable social gaffes. His style is sometimes urbane, sometimes frantic: the books are propelled by puns, parodies and ironic wit, a kind of *Nabokovian journalese. He is at his best when dealing with suburban sex (*Comfort Me With Apples*, 1956; *I Hear America Swinging*, 1976), and with self-educators and crackerbarrel wits (*Reuben, Reuben*, 1964; *Through the Fields of Clover*, 1961). His funniest book is also his sharpest: *The Mackerel Plaza* (1958), a deadpan satire on the effects of swinging religion on small-town society.

De Vries's many other books include *The Tunnel of Love* (1954), *Let Me Count the Ways* (1965), *Mrs Wallop* (1970), *Into Your Tent I'll Creep* (1971), *Madder Music* (1977) and *Sauce for the Goose* (1981). *The Blood of the Lamb* (1962) is comparatively serious, about the death of a child.

Dos PASSOS, John (1896-1970)
American writer

A large part of Dos Passos's output was high-quality hardback journalism: he was the *Wells or *Mailer of his age. His best books in this genre include *Facing the Chair* (1927), on Sacco and Vanzetti, *The Villages Are the Heart of Spain* (1937), and a number of sympathetic accounts of American history: *The Ground We Stand On* (1941), *The Men Who Made the Nation* (1957), *Prospects of a Golden Age* (1959), and the outstanding *The Shackles of Power* (1966), the fruit of a lifetime's enthusiasm for Jefferson and his times. Documentary thoroughness and political acuteness also badge his novels. The best are *Three Soldiers* (1921), about young Americans at war, and a striking contrast with Mailer's *The Naked and the Dead*; *Manhattan Transfer* (1925), an enormous panorama of big-city life, discontinuous and impressionistic, a prose equivalent – save that it is streets better – of Elmer Rice's play *Main Street*; and the trilogy *USA* (*The 42nd Parallel*, 1930; *1919*, 1932; *The Big Money*, 1936), which is a left-oriented study of American life between the end of the First World War and the 1929 Wall Street Crash. Dos Passos's commitment (starry-eyed left-wing in the earlier books, disillusioned right-wing in the later) is regularly cited as his most notable quality, but his chief excellence, as one of the finest of all political novelists, is rather the acuity and thoroughness of his political analysis. It is rare, for example, for an American novelist to be so persistently convinced of the need for political engagement. Although he became an almost McCarthyite rightist (to the embarrassment of his friend and admirer Edmund Wilson), Dos Passos had a craving for maturity not to be found in flashier contemporaries. Thus he is a vital source for anyone wanting to know what made 20th-century America the way it was (at least until Vietnam), and in particular how revolutionary zeal, that vitalizing 19th-century force, was modified and adapted there in the stress of 20th-century events.

Dos Passos's other novels include the political trilogy *District of Columbia* (*Adventures of a Young Man*, 1939; *Number One*, 1943; *The Grand Design*, 1949), and the dyspeptic *Century's Ebb* (1975). *Occasions and Protests* (1964) collects essays; *The Fourteenth Chronicle* (ed. Ludington, 1973) letters and diaries. Good introduction: I. Colley: *Dos Passos and the Fiction of Despair* (1978).

DREISER, Theodore (1871-1945)
American writer

If a list of the great unread (unreadable?) books of the 20th century were to be compiled – it would include Broch's *The Death of Virgil* and Musil's *The Man Without Qualities*, as well as more contentious entries like Myers' *The Near and the Far* – Dreiser's *An American Tragedy* (1925) would be a popular choice. It is Zola's *Thérèse Raquin* in transatlantic dress, the story of a bell-hop who impregnates one girl, falls in love with another, then takes the first on a boating-trip during which she drowns. Is he a murderer? (He is certainly tried and executed.) The characters are not 1920s socialites, but the Dull Young Things of real life; the detail is realistic; the style is static and monumental. But *An American Tragedy* is Zolaesque in another way too: piling small details of character and incident into a convincing edifice is the realistic method by which trial evidence is converted into 'truth' – and that is exactly how Dreiser works. His novel, if you allow yourself time to get into it, is both ponderous and magnificent.

Dreiser's eight other novels include *Sister Carrie* (1900, rev. 1970), *Jenny Gerhardt* (1911) and the autobiographical *The 'Genius'* (1915). He also wrote plays (*The Old Ragpicker*, 1918, was a staple of melodramatic 'circuits' storming barns in the 1920s), poems and forgettable journalistic works with titles like *The Carnegie Works at Pittsburgh* (1929) or *America Is Worth Saving* (1941). *Twelve Men* (1919) is a collection of biographical sketches; *A Book about Myself* (1922) is interesting autobiography. Fascinating journals: T. P. Riggio (ed.): *Theodore Dreiser: American Diaries 1902–1926* (1981). Good introduction: D. Pizer: *Dreiser: A Critical Study* (1976).

DURAS, Marguerite: see page 476.

DURRELL, Lawrence (born 1912)
British writer

Durrell has lived most of his life out of England (chiefly in Greece, Egypt and France), and much of both the strength and the weakness of his writing comes from the mixture of an old-fashioned, Foreign-Service British parochialism with an exuberant delight in the extraversion of the Mediterranean world and its culture. Often this duality is reflected in a conflict of theme and style. He writes of love, for example (one of his major themes), with obsessive, meta-Puritan haughtiness (it is, for his characters, no more than a species of higher sex, a duel) – but in engorged, convulsive language, whose surface jauntiness, poetic stream-of-consciousness aspiring to philosophy, often disguises the fact that he has nothing very much to say. (What, for example, does this passage tell us, except that Durrell is a clever writer? 'The Errols are both econo-mists . . . They make love to two places of decimals only. Their children have all the air of vulgar fractions.') The novels proceed in a series of confrontations and set-pieces, each with its own (often experimental) form: for Durrell, the frame outweighs the picture, the external skeleton guarantees life to the bag of nerves and guts. *Tunc* (1968) and *Nunquam* (1970), for example, form a diptych: the two parts of the story fold together into completeness like the pages of a book, and neither makes sense without the other (if they finally do make sense at all). In the first three volumes of *The Alexandria Quartet* (1957–60), Durrell's fictional masterpiece, the same events are viewed from three points of view by successive narrators; the fourth volume moves on in time to complete the story. Each book is thus a kind of commentary on itself and the others, interleaving reactions and events in a particularly dynamic way. Durrell's best work is, first, his poetry (*Collected Poems*, 1980), which has an elegance and a restrained sensuality not unlike that of *Graves; and second, his travel writing – *Prospero's Cell* (1945, about Corfu), *Reflections on a Marine Venus* (1953, about Rhodes) and *Bitter Lemons* (1958, about Cyprus) set standards for evocation of place and for allusive, poetic prose which his fiction can rarely match. *The Alexandria Quartet*, despite passages of impacted brilliance, comes closest: *Balthazar* in particular (the second book) shows the same restraint, the same sharpness of style and of observation, and (a quality largely lacking in his other novels) the same power to move as well as to charm.

Among Durrell's other books are *The Black Book* (1938), the excellent, light *Cefalû/The Dark Labyrinth* (1947), and a sequence of particularly rich (in the sense that clotted cream is rich) novels, an Avignon 'quincunx' of which *Monsieur* (1974), *Livia* (1978), *Constance* (1982) and *Sebastian* (1983) are so far published. *Lawrence Durrell and Henry Miller: A Private Correspondence* (1963) is a fascinating, narcissistic read. Lawrence's brother Gerald Durrell, in *My Family and Other Animals* (1956), one of the best light autobiographical books of the century, definitively proves of 'Larry' that no hero can conceal his feet of clay from irreverent siblings; this is the 'other side' of Durrell's own *Prospero's Cell* – and perhaps explains why he left the family home.

DÜRRENMATT, Friedrich: see page 476.

ELIOT, Thomas Stearns (1888–1965)
American/English poet, critic and playwright

Eliot was an influential critic: *The Sacred Wood* (1920), *The Use of Poetry and the Use of Criticism* (1933) and *Notes Towards the Definition of Culture* (1948) – a useful anthology is *Selected Prose* (1975) – contain important writings, a key not only to the habits of his own thought, but also to that clear-eyed retrospection which was such a programmatic force in 1920s and 1930s 'highbrow' culture. Eliot's essays are the fruit of self-conscious, polyglot eclecticism; his strengths as a critic are in explaining the techniques of literary creation, and in ruthless excommunication of flab and sham; his chosen authors work hard to earn their place.

Eclecticism, intellectuality and moral earnestness are also the driving forces of Eliot's poetry. Sometimes, perhaps, they come a little pat: *Poems, 1920* (especially 'Sweeney Erect', 'Whispers of Immortality' and

'Mr Eliot's Sunday Morning Service') tend to push cleverness beyond parody towards tiresome display; the quotations and allusions in *The Waste Land* (1922) – ranging from the Chaucer parody in the opening lines to the Upanishad references at the end – should work unaided in their places, without need of nudging notes. *The Waste Land*, full of tags and reminiscences, is a true picture of the junkyard of the intellectual mind, a jumble of half-remembered images and instances. But Eliot's jumble is meticulous and organized, fleshing the theme of emptiness with bare, bleak images. It is the world made familiar by later Absurd writers: Eliot is close in spirit to the Beckett of *Endgame* and to the galvanic nihilism of*Lewis's *Childermass*; passages like that beginning 'My nerves are bad tonight. Yes, bad. Stay with me . . .', from the second part of *The Waste Land*, notably anticipate Ionesco's passionate barrenness (e.g. in *The Chairs*).

In Eliot's later poetry, particularly in *Ash-Wednesday* (1930), the play *Murder in the Cathedral* (1935) and *The Four Quartets* (1944), nihilism and negativism were replaced by the warmth of Christian certainty: formerly a Jacobean of the skull-beneath-the-skin variety, Eliot now, by turning his philosophy towards the positive, reached the metaphysical intensity of Donne or Herbert, and borrowed from them too a sensuousness and geniality generally lacking in his earlier work. *The Four Quartets* (his finest achievement) still concerns human striving; but instead of the anguish of *The Waste Land* the search is here conducted in affirmative tranquillity. (Landscape, no longer a symbol of alienation, now stands for home: exploring its contours confirms familiarity. It is a parable of the soul's exploration of its familiar, God.) The closing lines of *Little Gidding* (beginning 'We shall not cease from exploration . . .') are typical – and also show Eliot's true 'metaphysical' genius for expressing impressionistic, indefinite thoughts in language of crystal directness.

After *The Four Quartets*, except for a few minor poems, Eliot's verse was written for the stage. He had already written *Murder in the Cathedral* (1935) and *The Family Reunion* (1939); now followed *The Cocktail Party* (1949), *The Confidential Clerk* (1954) and *The Elder Statesman* (1959). Paradoxically, the plays (collected in *Complete Poems and Plays*, 1969) are for the most part in some of the loosest and least 'dramatic' of all his verse. The personal style of his poetry had been drawn from sources as diverse as Jacobean drama, the lyrics of Donne and Milton and the driving soliloquies of Browning. Its pointing, its cadences and pauses, were built into the texture of the lines. In the plays (with the exception of *Murder in the Cathedral*, whose language is Sophoclean: tight and sharp), crisp articulation is replaced by an urbane metrical flow derived from late Euripides (whose influence also underlies plot and characterization). Eliot's plays are in no tradition, either of verse or of plays; they create their own tradition, an entertainment as civilized and thoughtful as the dialogues of Plato.

Eliot is a complex poet. He is as dry as his detractors claim, and he lacks emotional sympathy. There are occasional signs of intellectual hollowness: *angst*, for example, is too glibly surrendered to the leap of faith (that is, he makes us believe the suffering, but does not quite convince us, as Donne and Herbert do, that God is real). But he had, more than any other poet, his finger on the nerve-ends of this century; he balances sensuality and intellect in a uniquely personal way; above all, his verse is memorable: his phrases haunt the mind.

Good introductions: B. C. Southam: *A Student's Guide to the Selected Poems of T. S. Eliot* (1968); S. Spender: *T. S. Eliot* (1975); H. Gardner: *The Composition of the Four Quartets* (1978). Bumper critical compendium (two fat volumes): M. Grant (ed.): *T. S. Eliot: The Critical Heritage* (1982). Unfussy biography, good on literary matters: P. Ackroyd: *T. S. Eliot* (1984).

FAULKNER, William (1897–1962)
American novelist

Those seeking models for the 'well-made' novel (that is, one in which themes, plot, language and structure are in harmony, all working to provide entertainment which is both engrossing and challenging) need look no further than Faulkner's best work, a dozen novels set in the American Deep South, in the place he invented and named Yoknapataw-pha County. Many of them concern two white groups, the rich Sartoris family (who pass, as the series proceeds, from pre-civil-war supremacy to mid-20th-century impoverishment and bitterness) and the landless, semi-barbarian Snopeses (who neither progress nor regress, but simply – at their brute level – survive). Around these two clans moves an enormous supporting cast of negroes, poor townsfolk, farmhands, North-erners, sleek salesmen and decent but bewildered local officials. The novels' major themes are the see-saw between hope and decadence, and the imbalance – which the benighted, bigoted South, for Faulkner, ideally emblematizes – between high cultural ideals and a moral impoverishment bordering on bankruptcy.

Faulkner's serious, not to say tragic, themes give depth to fiction which is otherwise as smoothly schematic as *Gone With the Wind*. Even so, it is hard at times for non-Americans (perhaps even for non-Southerners) to believe in the verisimilitude of all those inbred relationships, blinkered and steamy emotions and passionate philistinism, the rotten infilling under the courteous veneer. Even if the South is too consistently described by author after author to be merely writers' invention, it still seems melodramatic and overblown – and even Faulkner, its greatest anatomizer, never drew out the wider human resonances of his material as, say, Balzac or Dickens did with theirs. His books already seem like historical fiction, and theirs do not; we are content merely to read about Yoknapatawpha County, without ever wanting to visit it, to test it by experience, as we might gladly visit *Proust's Balbec, *Joyce's Dublin or (even, some of us) *Mann's Magic Mountain.

Faulkner's Southern theme is revealed at its starkest in his short stories

(*Collected Stories*, 1950; *Uncollected Stories*, 1979; the best single collection, containing 'Barn Burning', 'Wash' and 'There Was a Queen', his masterpiece in the genre, is *Dr Martino and Other Stories*, 1934). Then come the great Yoknapatawpha novels: *Sartoris* (1929), *Absalom, Absalom!* (1936), *The Unvanquished* (1938), and *The Hamlet* (1940), which forms a trilogy with the less good *The Town* (1957) and *The Mansion* (1959). The most compelling of them all, *Intruder in the Dust* (1948), is a moving treatment of one of Faulkner's favourite subjects, the awakening of moral sensibility in an adolescent. All these books are straightforwardly, leanly written, in a combination of pacy narrative and inner monologue. In several others, Faulkner used a more experimental technique derived from Joyce: *The Sound and the Fury* (1929), for some his finest novel, uses four stream-of-consciousness monologues to outline the disintegration of the Compson family; its entrance into the minds of the neurotic, suicidal Quentin and the idiot Benjy is an eerily convincing *tour de force*. *As I Lay Dying* (1930) pushes technical virtuosity even further: it consists of fifty-nine separate interior monologues, a whole society self-revealed. (If *The Sound and the Fury* is Faulkner's *Ulysses*, *As I Lay Dying* is his *Finnegans Wake*, and just as thorny to read.)

Faulkner worked in Hollywood (he wrote the screenplays of two of Bogart's best and most brooding films, *To Have and Have Not*, 1944, and *The Big Sleep*, 1946), and produced a deal of fiction and essays to order, efficiently tailored but inferior to his 'real' work. He stands with writers like Hardy and *Lawrence: very good indeed, but kept out of the highest class by a glossy parochialism which makes tourists of his readers, and gives his work, to outsiders, an unintended exoticism, the unlikeliness perhaps of the American South itself.

Faulkner's other writings include the novels *Sanctuary* (1931), *The Wild Palms* (1939), *A Fable* (1954), and *The Reivers* (1962), poems (*This Earth*, 1932; *A Green Bough*, 1933), and the experimental *Requiem for a Nun* (1951), part play and part prose narrative. A good selection from his vast output is *The Portable Faulkner* (ed. Cowley, 1946), for which he wrote valuable introductions. Good biography: J. Blotner: *Faulkner: A Biography* (2 vols., 1974). Good introduction: C. Brooks: *William Faulkner: First Encounters* (1983).

FIRBANK, Ronald (1886–1926)
British novelist

Firbank's novels belong to the homosexual, decadent tradition of Huysmans, Wilde and Rolfe – life is a series of absurd experiences to be sipped to the full; nothing is momentous but the moment; I chatter, therefore I am. His dowagers, cardinals, and negresses endlessly take tea in out-of-season spas, their conversation as jewelled as their fingers, their attitudes and manners cocky as cockatoos. Sequins are not only in season, but for ever. At its best (e.g. in *Valmouth*, 1919, or *Prancing Nigger*, 1924), his dialogue – the most enjoyable component of his books – is as good as Peacock's or *Compton-Burnett's; his masterpiece,

Concerning the Eccentricities of Cardinal Pirelli (1926), about a silky paedophiliac prelate, adds a satirical sharpness close to early *Powell or to *Waugh. His other work (*Vainglory*, 1915; *Inclinations*, 1916; *Caprice*, 1917; *Santal*, 1921; *The Flower Beneath the Foot*, 1923) is perhaps weakened by the absence of such edge – it's often hard to find flesh beneath the conversational plumage, certainly no plot and little consequence, and if you're not in the mood, he's as wearisome as a needle-clawed kitten. But taken in small doses, his books (none longer than 100 pages) not only serve to while time away, but also stick, for no discernible reason, in the memory.

As well as his seven novellas, Firbank also published a play, *The Princess Zoubaroff* (1920). Lively biography: B. Brophy: *Prancing Novelist* (1973).

FITZGERALD, Francis Scott (1896–1940)
American writer

It is easy to pigeon-hole Fitzgerald as the epitome of the vulnerable, cynical Roaring Twenties, the arch-priest of spats, speakeasies, sassy flappers and all that jazz. Certainly if any one book 'catches' the twenties (as *Catcher in the Rye* stands for the fifties, *Catch-22* for the sixties) it is *The Great Gatsby* (1925), which tells of Gatsby's rise to fortune by a succession of *coups* each of which involves single-minded endeavour and the acceptance of yet another moral compromise: he becomes the archetypal self-made Hollow Man. For the reader, *The Great Gatsby* offers the rueful pleasure of cynicism confirmed, and its hardness is matched by the flawless glitter of the prose, as sharp as ice.

But *The Great Gatsby* (with its satellite short stories, published in *Tales of the Jazz Age*, 1922), though excellent, is not Fitzgerald's best or most characteristic work. He is actually a romantic, a frontier novelist whose theme is less the failure of the American dream than its phoenix vitality. But the steely simplicity of his style and his view of innocence and endeavour as the sap of life derive from such writers as *London and Twain; so far from striking brilliant attitudes in a cul-de-sac, he is in the main highway of American fiction, and his followers are *Salinger, *Roth and especially *Updike. His best short stories are autobiographical and deal with the painful acquisition of self-knowledge in adolescence: the Basil and Josephine short stories (published in part in *Taps at Reveille*, 1935, and complete in *The Basil and Josephine Stories*, 1973) tell of this timeless theme in a timeless way – not a charleston in sight – and it is continued into adulthood in the novels *This Side of Paradise* (1920), about a young man discovering his identity at Princeton, and *The Beautiful and the Damned* (1922), which concerns artistic ambition and disillusion. *Tender Is the Night* (1934) is the most overtly anguished of all his books: it describes the collapse of a sensitive idealist, whose *acte gratuit* (marrying an unstable mental patient) triggers his own decline into dissipation, alcoholism and despair. (Those who wish to trace the autobiographical strands in this book – Fitzgerald was always his own best character – should read Nancy Milford's *Zelda Fitzgerald: A Biography*, 1970, and Aaron Latham's *Crazy Sundays: F. Scott Fitzgerald in Hollywood*, 1971). Reading Fitzgerald, although his books invariably end in tears, is by no means a totally downcasting activity: however thin his characters stretch the line of hope, it never snaps, and this makes his work far more than the flawlessly costumed tango to the tomb it seems at first.

Fitzgerald's other writings include the excellent (unfinished) novel *The Last Tycoon* (1941), a group of anguished but revealing autobiographical pieces (collected in *The Crack-Up*, ed. Wilson, 1945), and two volumes of correspondence offering fascinating insights into his creative life: *Dear Scott/Dear Max: The Fitzgerald-Perkins Correspondence*, ed. Kuehl and Bryer, 1971, and *As Ever, Scott Fitz-: Letters between Fitzgerald and His Literary Agent Howard Ober 1919–1940*, ed. Bruccoli, 1972. Good introductions: A. Mizener: *The Far Side of Paradise* (1951); A. Turnbull: *Fitzgerald* (1975).

FORD, Ford Madox (1873–1939)
British writer

In the welter of new publications, good second-rate writers of the past often slip into a limbo of respected obscurity which they hardly deserve. Ford is one of these. He was a friend of *Conrad and *Wells; he founded and edited the *English Review* and the *Transatlantic Review*; under his real name (Hueffer) he published biographical studies (notably *Ford Madox Brown*, 1896, on his grandfather, and *Rossetti*, 1902), memoirs (*Ancient Lights and Certain New Reflections*, 1911), and several novels including *The Good Soldier* (1915). As 'Ford', he concentrated on travel-books, on an enormous literary compendium entitled *The March of Literature from Confucius to Our Own Time* (1939), and above all on the quartet of novels later republished under the joint title *Parade's End* (1951). (The individual titles are *Some Do Not*, 1924; *No More Parades*, 1925; *A Man Could Stand Up*, 1926; *Last Post*, 1928.) These books are about the collapse of upper-middle-class mores and morality under the stress of the First World War. Though the idea suggests *Proust, the effect is rather more of a composite novel, at enormous length, by *Galsworthy and Simon Raven. That said (and especially for those who like Galsworthy or Raven) *Parade's End* is a thoughtful, and by no means unenjoyable, read.

Ford's other writings include *The Fifth Queen* (1906), a trilogy of historical novels; *Joseph Conrad: A Personal Reminiscence* (1924); and *Letters* (ed. Ludwig, 1965). Good biography: A. Mizener: *The Saddest Story* (1965); good, serious-minded literary study: R. Green: *Ford Madox Ford: Prose and Politics* (1981). An intimate account, in letters, of an extraordinary relationship is given in B. Lindberg-Seyerstad (ed.): *Pound/Ford: The Story of a Literary Friendship* (1983).

FORSTER, Edward Morgan (1879–1970)
British novelist

Forster's novels were all written in a single five-year period, 1905–10 (though *A Passage to India* was not completed and published until fourteen years later); thereafter he concentrated on short stories, essays (notably the clear-headed and influential *Aspects of the Novel*, 1927) and occasional biography (e.g. *Goldsworthy Lowes Dickinson*, 1934). His silence in fiction has been variously explained. Some see it as the result of a failure to 'come to terms with' his own homosexuality (an early autobiographical novel on this subject, *Maurice*, appeared posthumously in 1971 and proved, by its literary awfulness, that he had been right to suppress it). Others said that the reasons for his silence were dismay at the way the 20th century was developing (a feeling he surely did not hold alone), or alienation from 1920s 'experimental' or 'confessional' styles in fiction. The most plausible reason of all is that he had said what he had to say: the statement made by his five novels is powerful, persuasive and complete.

Forster's theme is the process of emotional growth, whether achieved by obedience to the famous injunction 'Only connect . . .' (used as the epigraph to *Howards End*, 1910) or by rejection of the connections offered by other individuals or by society. The theme is at its clearest in (the partly autobiographical) *The Longest Journey* (1907), whose hero is an introverted young writer tragically destroyed at the very moment when he 'connects' with his wastrel brother; it is at its most complex in *Howards End*, in which the friendships and moves towards love of a large group of characters are manipulated with schematic, *Murdoch-like dexterity (except that in a Murdoch novel there are fewer unhappy people and fewer deaths). In his three other novels, foreign settings sharply focus themes of exile and separation – Forster is second only to Henry James in his symbolic use of the jar between cultures. *Where Angels Fear to Tread* (1905) and *A Room with a View* (1908) are set in Italy, and concern the development of self-understanding in pliable and boring people (Philip in *Where Angels Fear to Tread*, Lucy in *A Room with a View*): they achieve growth by severing emotional ties, and are then trapped and destroyed by the new ties they choose to make. *A Passage to India* (1924) uses as its symbol of alienation racial hostility in genteel colonial India, and shows the progression in its heroine Adela from boredom to flirtation to hysteria (she falsely accuses an Indian friend, Dr Aziz, of molesting her while on a visit to some caves) and finally to self-awareness and resignation (she recants at Aziz's trial). Like all Forster's characters, she finds that emotional evolution leads only to self-disgust and loneliness; this progress towards dissolution is a paradigm, in Forster's view, of the tendency of human affairs at large.

Forster's elegant tragedies have had a switchback reputation (they are currently down): at his zenith he was called a second Jane Austen, at his nadir a spinster of a less exalted kind. His books are certainly limited in scope, and lack the grand sweep of his master, James. But within their range, it is hard to imagine how *A Room with a View* and *A Passage to India*, in particular, could be differently or more convincingly and movingly done.

Forster's other writings include short stories (*The Celestial Omnibus*, 1911; *The Eternal Moment*, 1928), essays (*Abinger Harvest*, 1936; *Two Cheers for Democracy*, 1951, whose political views now seem old-fashioned), and a splendid travelogue of his own passages to India, *The Hill of Devi* (1953). Good studies: L. Trilling: *Forster* (1964; 1967); M. Colmer: *E. M. Forster: The Personal Voice* (1975). Interesting letters: M. Lago and P. N. Furbank: *E. M. Forster: Selected Letters Vol. 1 1879–1920* (1983).

FOWLES, John (born 1926)
British novelist

A middlebrow novelist of dazzling gifts, Fowles has rashly been compared with Dickens, *Lawrence and even Tolstoy; *Bennett or Priestley would be nearer the mark. His books are long, sumptuously plotted, richly written and absorbing – Victorian three-volume novels renovated for a more liberated and more anguished age. His subject is obsession. In *The Collector* (1963) a young man's obsession for 'owning' a girl leads him to collect her as one might collect a butterfly; the hero of *The Magus* (1966, rev. 1977) is obsessed by his search for reality on a mesmeric, Circean Greek island; *The French Lieutenant's Woman* (1969), his best book, is about a tormented sexual affair in Victorian England; *Daniel Martin* (1977) describes the self-obsession of a successful middle-aged man discovering – in Fowles's least original plot – that as the old snake-skin of his past is sloughed, the new skin underneath is tender and vulnerable. These themes are fascinating, but also melodramatic and trivial: they have the compulsive call of soap-opera, not art. What elevates them is Fowles's prose-style, which is seductive and self-conscious, rich in allusion, metaphor and teasing intellectual games – he writes as well as *Durrell, but avoids Durrell's saucy pretentiousness. Richard Strauss once described himself as 'a supremely gifted genius of the second rank'; Fowles is the Strauss of novelists.

In *Mantissa* (1982) Fowles supplied his heavyweight novels with a short, lightweight and avowedly humorous sibling: the title itself is Latin for a minor work. In it, his standard themes are all present, laced with hallucinatory, explicit sex. Useful introduction to his major work: P. Conradi: *John Fowles* (1982).

FRISCH, Max: see page 480

FROST, Robert (1874–1963)
American poet

In the 19th century there was a vigorous tradition of homespun, Grandma-Moses poetry in the USA. Its pretensions were those of small-town journalism; it reflected with emotional sureness and shallowness the preoccupations of 'ordinary, decent folk', the supporting cast in a Mark Twain story; it survives today principally in hymns, high-school songs and the lyrics of country-and-western music. Its freshness and directness – and its regular rhythms and clean rhymes – are also hallmarks of Frost's style. Throughout his life he promoted himself as a no-fuss, no-frills philosopher of nature, the Gary Cooper of poetry – and the image is by no means entirely false. Poems such as 'Stars' ('How countlessly they congregate/O'er our tumultuous snow . . .') or 'Pan With Us' ('Pan came out of the woods one day . . .'), both from *A Boy's Will* (1913), seem designed to be embroidered on samplers or copied in primary-school handwriting classes; 'The Death of the Hired Man' or 'The Housekeeper', both from the 'book of people' *North of Boston* (1914), have the same clear imagery and emotional simplicity as in Edward *Thomas or *De la Mare, a natural style which goes back through Wordsworth to the (very Frost-like) lyrics in some Shakespeare plays (e.g. 'When icicles hang by the wall', or 'When that I was but a little tiny boy'). In his later collections – he was still publishing at the age of eighty-seven – he also spoke of America itself as a species of philosophical entity, a self-defining being: a good example is 'The Gift Outright' (from *A Witness Tree*, 1942): 'The land was ours before we were the land's . . .'), a piece of laureate verse later used at the 1961 Kennedy inauguration.

All of this is fine and strong. But to discuss Frost simply as a mystic from the New Hampshire backwoods is to explain his popular appeal, not his poetic stature. He is a great poet because he uses uncluttered observation and common speech to confront the world's darkness and the soul's desolation. The beauty of nature (as expressed in, say, 'Stopping by Woods', from *New Hampshire*, 1923: 'Whose woods these are I think I know . . .') is a proof to humanity of the existence and concern of God; but it is the only proof offered, and it merely demonstrates, it explains nothing and makes no demands. We are surrounded by unhappiness and death (see, e.g., the magnificent 'Home Burial', from *North of Boston*, or 'Come In', from *A Witness Tree*), and our comfort, what Frost himself called our 'stay against confusion', lies simply in our aesthetic sense and in the aspiring, philosophical questioning to which it leads. (His view of art is precisely the opposite of the 'comfortable armchair' theory of Matisse.) The integrity of nature is a model for integrity in humankind; love, courage and need are the crucial forces in human life.

This uncompromising material – reminiscent at times of the grave epicureanism of Horace's *Odes* – is best handled in Frost's earlier collections, especially *A Boy's Will*, *North of Boston* and *Mountain Interval* (1916). From the poems of his fifties onwards (that is, those written after the publication of *Collected Poems*, 1930 – which should not be confused with the definitive edition by Lathem of *The Poetry of Robert Frost*, 1971) he tended towards self-repetition on the one hand and boisterous satire on the other. ('Version', or 'Accidentally on Purpose', both from *In the Clearing*, 1962, illustrate these qualities: they are reach-me-down versions of the old Frost themes, in jolly jog-trot lines and full of bobbly rhymes – jungle/bungle; minute/in it; Omnibus/got to us – which direct attention only to themselves and hinder thought.) The two dramatic poems *A Masque of Reason* (1945, about Job) and *A Masque of Mercy* (1947, about Jonah) combine absolute verbal certainty with coyness of content, like a clever college student's parody of Thornton Wilder. And yet in the next breath, at the same period, Frost produced marvellous work: 'There Are Roughly Zones' (from *A Further Range*, 1936), 'The Rabbit Hunter' (from *A Witness Tree*, generally a superb collection) and 'One More Brevity' (from *In the Clearing*) stand high in any pantheon of 20th-century American verse.

Useful collections: *The Poems* (ed. Lathem, 1969); *Selected Letters* (ed. Thompson, 1964); *Selected Prose* (ed. Cox and Lathem, 1966). Good biography: L. Thompson and R. H. Winnick: *Frost: The Early Years* (1966), *The Years of Triumph* (1970), *The Later Years* (1977). Good introduction: E. Isaacs: *An Introduction to Frost* (1962). Good letters: W. R. Evans (ed.): *Robert Frost and Sidney Cox: Forty Years of Friendship* (1981).

GALSWORTHY, John (1867–1933)
English novelist and playwright

Galsworthy's plots (like those of *Snow, which are similar in both outlook and style) are often set in the boardrooms, clubs and Commons committee-rooms of the governing class, and seek to counteract the potential aridity of affairs by precise (sometimes too precise) injections of private emotion, usually suffering. He strove for fairness and docu-mentary balance in his writing – his work followed in the naturalistic footsteps of Zola and Dostoievski, whom he much admired. Like them, he wrote well about social justice and injustice; but he lacked their humane concern for or understanding of character, and his work tends to be stifled both by its limited subject-matter and by its over-earnest, risk-nothing style. He saw human behaviour as a chase, with the hunters motivated by fear and greed, and all pity reserved for the hunted. (The mill-owner and workers in his play *Strife*, 1909, and Soames and Irene in *The Man of Property*, 1906 – the first novel of *The Forsyte Saga*, the first three parts of which, *The Man of Property*, *In Chancery*, 1920, and *To Let*, 1921, are his finest work – exemplify both the types and his approach to them.) With *Kipling, whose genius, wildness and humour he signally lacked, he is a touchstone for his period; his work, not otherwise noted for depth or sensitivity, is at its best when treating of the young. He is a good, bad writer whose books give pleasure and will live for that.

Good introduction: C. Dupré: *John Galsworthy* (1976).

GARCÍA MÁRQUEZ, Gabriel: see page 147.

GASCOYNE, David (born 1916)
British poet

Early precocity (first published book of poems at sixteen; first novel at seventeen) was followed by submersion in surrealism, which swamps such 1930s poems as 'The Cubical Domes' or 'The Very Image', dedicated to Magritte ('An image of my grandmother/her head appearing upside down upon a cloud . . .'). From the publication of *Poems 1937–42* (1943), however – a later volume is *A Vagrant and Other Poems*, 1950; *Collected Poems* appeared in 1970 – it was apparent that so far from being a chic poseur, Gascoyne is a religious or philosophical poet of considerable distinction. His mature work often has the exotic gravity of *Cavafy (e.g. 'Rex mundi', 'Spring MCMXL' – 'London Bridge is falling down, Rome's burnt, and Babylon/The Great is now but dust . . .' – or the fine 'Fragments Towards a Religio Poetae'); *Hopkins is the (by no means traduced) mentor of poems like 'After Twenty Springs' or 'Innocence and Experience'.

Gascoyne's major work is *Night Thoughts* (1956), originally written for radio. Its subjects are (in the poet) a psychological darkness just this side of breakdown, and (in society) the cliché-gabble of what Gascoyne calls the Megalometropolitan Carnival. Like all his work, *Night Thoughts* is absorbed in its own somewhat simplistic view of the sick-parade of human life. Wyndham *Lewis is the only other writer who could have risked – and justified – such banal, bleak statements as *Night Thoughts'* penultimate speech: 'The primary division of the human family at night is that which sets those who are alone apart from those who are together.'

Among Gascoyne's other work is *Collected Verse Translations* (1970), especially good of Hölderlin.

GENET, Jean: see page 483.

GIDE, André (1861–1951)
French writer

Outrage in Gide's youth at his overt bisexuality, and in his old age at his support for the Vichy regime, tended to swamp his critical reputation.

He was at heart a journalist (he founded and edited the influential *La Nouvelle Revue Française*), and stoked controversy sometimes to the detriment of his true talent. He wrote voluminously and gracefully in every conceivable form: plays (e.g. *Oedipus*, 1931; the libretto for Stravinsky's *Perséphone*, 1934), translations (of Shakespeare, Blake and *Conrad), social and political polemic (*Recollections of the Assizes*, 1913; *Corydon, Four Socratic Dialogues on Homosexuality*, 1923; *Return from the USSR*, 1937), and above all autobiography and prose fiction.

Gide documented his own life with a mixture of compulsion and reticence: not since Cicero's *Letters* has a man so garrulously told his readers so little about himself. The *Journals* (4 vols., 1947–9) come nearest to revealing his complex privacy (and are essential and lively reading, the best of Gide's non-fiction); but even they, once he took the decision to publish, began to replace conviction with persuasiveness. In addition there are two volumes of suave autobiography (*Si le grain ne meurt/If It Die*, 1926, on his childhood, and *Journey to the Congo*, 1927, on travels in colonial Africa). There are half a dozen short 'intimate memoirs', of which the most accessible is *Et nunc manet in te/Madeleine* (1951), about his marriage. And there are fat volumes of letters, notably a correspondence (on ethical and moral questions) with *Claudel.

Gide's most lasting work is his novels. They are short, spare and beautifully 'worked': no garrulity here. They are also his most self-revealing writing: if he glossed his autobiographies with fiction, he put true autobiography (the illumination of states of feeling) into his fiction. He was fascinated by two themes above all: the conflict between pagan hedonism and Christian asceticism and the progress of each individual towards an *acte gratuit*. (See Sartre, p. 513.) The soul's liberation from Christian dogma is the subject of *Strait is the Gate* (1909), a *bildungsroman* close in theme and spirit to *Joyce's *A Portrait of the Artist as a Young Man*. *The Immoralist* (1902) charts the withering of intellectual sensibility in a young man coming to terms, in schematic sequence, with marriage, Algeria, bisexuality, corrupt servants (his country estate decays in parallel with his mental state) and Parisian society. The *acte gratuit* is the subject of *The Vatican Cellars* (1914), a lumpishly constructed, ironical book which starts with an account of a man's abrupt discovery of faith (and loss of self), proceeds to update *The Man in the Iron Mask* into a story of confidence tricksters and an imprisoned and impersonated pope, and ends with a chillingly Dostoievskian account of the deterioration of the personality of a murderer (the man who commits the *acte gratuit*). More successful – and on a literary level to equal, say, *Mann's *Death in Venice* – are the novellas *Isabelle* (1911) and *The Pastoral Symphony* (1919), often published together in English as *Two Symphonies*. *Isabelle* is about a young scholar working in an eccentric country household who becomes obsessed with the image of a girl he sees in an old miniature; in *The Pastoral Symphony* a clergyman rehabilitates a waif at the cost of his own soul and self. *The Counterfeiters* (1926), Gide's longest and best novel, describes the lives of a group of turn-of-the-century Parisian adolescents and their elders who guide or prey on them. It is particularly strong on the sexual ambivalence of boyhood friendship, on the blossoming of literary talent, and on the shuttering effect of first experience on the soul. One of its central characters is a novelist, writing the book we are reading, and who buttonholes the reader with alienating effect: e.g. 'I think I'm bored with this explanation of Olivier's . . .'. This apart, *The Counterfeiters* is one of the best French novels of the last 100 years, as characterful as Zola's *Thérèse Raquin* (which influenced it), as philosophically packed as Sartre's *The Roads to Freedom* (which it influenced), and more readable than either.

Gide's many other writings include the Nietzschean, not to say Huysmanic, exhortation to self-fulfilment *Fruits of the Earth* (1897; sequel, *New Fruits of the Earth*, 1945); letters to *Rilke and *Valéry, critical works on Dostoievski and on the novel; and a number of works on classical themes and in neo-classical style (e.g. *Theseus*, 1946). Good introduction: C. Bettinson: *Gide: A Study Guide* (1977). R. Tedeschi (ed.): *Selected Letters of André Gide and Dorothy Bussy* (1983) reveals a sexually involuted 'love-in-the-head' affair, as bizarre as any of his novellas, with his passionate translator (a Bloomsberry, the sister of Lytton Strachey).

GINSBERG, Allen (born 1926)
American poet

In the happy, hippy 1960s it seemed as if Ginsberg, Kerouac and the other artists of beat culture or flower-power were above – or at least out of sight of – criticism. They seemed in touch with a force – it involved taking pot, reciting 'Om' and letting your sexual deviance, if any, out of the closet – which might genuinely redeem our world; to show incomprehension or scorn seemed as impertinent as offering to copy-edit the Sermon on the Mount. In the dismal decades since (though the message they preached has lost none of its urgency) the flower-petals have dropped away one by one, revealing only Bob Dylan and Ginsberg as poets of any durable stature. (Both, by coincidence, were regarded by their fans as pop performers as much as poets.)

Ginsberg's masterpiece (actually produced in the 1950s when flower-power was no more than a seed waiting to germinate) was *Howl* (1956), one of those threnodies for lost innocence so dear to some American hearts. Its firm roots (the 'frontier tradition' in American literature; the verse-style of *Williams) guaranteed vigour, just as in *Kaddish and Other Poems* (1961) the keening tradition of Jewish lament for the dead acts as a binding-force for otherwise trite observation and incoherent philosophy. With fame, increasing age, and the jetlag produced by thousands of miles of recital-tours, Ginsberg's work sagged – and as with Warhol's daubs, the wispier the master's productions became, the more they attracted applause and cash. Typical volume-titles are *Planet News* (1968) or *Bixby Canyon Ocean Path Word Breeze* (1972), the title a Ginsberg poem in its own right. Only in *Ankor-Wat* (1969) is there work of substance, rising above acidic fantasy. Ginsberg is important – but only as a symbol of his times; the simplest Beatles lyrics (*Yesterday*; *Lucy in the Sky with Diamonds*; *All You Need Is Love*) said more with less.

Ginsberg's other books include *Iron Horse* (1972), *The Fall of America* (1972), *Mind Breaths* (1977) and *Plutonium Ode* (1980) – all poetry volumes; *Indian Journals* (1970); *Allen Verbatim: Lectures on Poetry, Politics, Consciousness* (ed. Ball, 1974), and *The Visions of the Great Remembrancer* (1974), on Kerouac; and *Journals: Early Fifties–Early Sixties* (ed. Ball, 1977). The best books on the whole beat/flower-power phenomenon are Ann Charters' *Kerouac: A Biography* (1973), Kerouac's novel *On the Road* (1957), and J. Kramer: *Paterfamilias: Allen Ginsberg in America* (1969). No more harrowing account of the America they were all living in (and off) exists than A. Tuttle (ed.): *The Journal of Andrew Bihaly* (1973), a book to make all liberals (and certainly all politicians) blush with shame.

GOLDING, William (born 1911)
British novelist

Dissatisfaction with the cosy decencies of such children's classics as Ballantyne's *Coral Island* impelled Golding, then a schoolmaster, to write his first novel, *Lord of the Flies* (1954), an attempt to imagine what 'real' children might do if marooned on a desert island. The result was a grim fantasy about the degeneration of humanity, a parable as powerful (and as popular) as *Brave New World* or *Animal Farm*. (It has been especially attractive to schoolteachers, a staple of examination syllabuses for a generation. Why? What kind of experience is it supposed to give the young?) He followed it with *The Inheritors* (1955), which sees the arrival of *homo sapiens* through the eyes of the last, doomed group of neanderthal people, and with *Pincher Martin* (1956), the account of a dying sailor's last moments, when his past life (as Ballantyne might have put it) 'flashes through his mind'.

Apart from their moral subtexts (as blunt as in Balzac or *Conrad, Golding's nearest analogues) all three of these novels are immensely powerful narratives. Golding's plots are streamlined and compulsive (he knows the pull of the bizarre) and his writing is juicy with description and metaphor. His ability to describe sensual impressions (the taste of water, the smell of blood, the feel of lichen at the finger-ends) is unequalled in modern fiction save by *Nabokov, and his descriptions have a primitiveness and earthiness Nabokov shuns. His re-creation of the thought-processes of humanity stripped of sophistication (child; neanderthal; fighting for life) is engrossing and plausible in its quirky and poetic way. (No one probably ever *did* behave or think like Golding's people; his skill is to make his parables appear more lifelike than our knowledge of life itself.)

In *Free Fall* (1959) and *The Pyramid* (1967), Golding abandoned 'primitive' for 'modern' people: both novels concern growing up, the learning of sophistication; both are based on the premise that 'the child is father to the man'. The parable-element is less secure in these books, which are chiefly interesting for their detailed descriptions of childhood – he is good, for example, on bullying and on the fragile cockiness of adolescent sex. *The Pyramid* also essays humour (notably in a wildly slapstick account of a village operetta production). This was unwise: Golding's wit (also seen in the play *The Brass Butterfly*, 1958, about the coming of steam power to an urbanely decadent ancient Rome, and his dull, late novel *The Paper Men*, 1984, about a successful elderly writer dodging a would-be academic biographer) is lumpish and self-indulgent, successful only at the level of an end-of-term revue. The other main subject of these books, love (parent–child, between friends, homosexual and heterosexual), is the principal theme of *Darkness Visible* (1979), a knotty allegory about innocence and corruption, Golding's most personal and most difficult (or least convincing?) book.

The Spire (1964) and *Rites of Passage* (1980) return to what Golding does best of all: reconstructing the imaginative life of people whose experience is remote from ours. *The Spire* is about the building of a too-heavy spire for a medieval cathedral; *Rites of Passage* re-creates life on a ship-of-the-line travelling to Australia during the Napoleonic Wars. In each case the raw detail is brilliant: stones, scaffolding, ropes and tar are evoked with Golding's usual sensual power. The allegories (the spire is a symbol for the earthly *hubris* of the dean who commissions it; the ship's journey is a symbol of the journey of the soul) are unaffected and strong – Balzac again, and Bunyan, come to mind. These books, with *The Inheritors*, are Golding's best, 'content' and 'message' fleshed out in engrossing narrative and compulsive images.

The runaway success of *Amis's *Lucky Jim* in the mid-1950s, and his intimidating critical record (in the *Spectator*, as a don), made unpretentiousness in fiction a governing aesthetic principle of the 1960s and early 1970s, thus depressing the whole level of intent of the English novel (though Amis himself cannot be personally blamed for this). Golding, like *Durrell, *Raphael and to a lesser extent *Burgess, stood out against the trend. As a result, he seemed for a time an impressive, lonely flamboyant. Now that the critical fog has cleared, he can be more easily seen for the landmark he really is.

A Moving Target (1982) is a collection of Golding's speeches, reviews and articles, intermittently fascinating. Good study: M. Kinkead-Weekes and I. Gregor: *William Golding: A Critical Study* (rev. edn 1984).

GORKI, Maxim (1868–1936)
Russian writer

Gorki (the word is a pseudonym meaning 'bitter') was brought up from the ages of five to eight by his brutal bargee grandfather, and from eight onwards spent his childhood in a variety of lowly trades: domestic servant, dish-washer on a cargo-boat, cobbler's apprentice, thief. The insights this appalling childhood – paralleled in great writers only by that of Genet – gave him into the underside of Tsarist Russia were expressed in several books of short stories (the best English selection is *Twenty-Six Men and a Girl*, 1902) and some grim plays about derelicts, of which *The Lower Depths* (1902) – an O'Neill-like piece about human flotsam waiting in vain for a redeemer – is by far the best. Subject-matter of this kind, and its unsparing treatment, made Gorki a rich man in pre-revolutionary Russia (he was able to buy land on Capri, and to retreat there, in 1906), and also made him a favourite writer with the Bolsheviks: a chronicler, so they thought, of all the ills their revolution was setting out to cure.

Unfortunately Gorki himself was never a popular revolutionary figure. After the revolution he went back to Russia, but soon quarrelled with Lenin – ostensibly about religion (which Gorki wanted to incorporate in the brave new Russia, and Lenin didn't); but neither man had a particularly outgoing personality – and returned to Capri. His enthusiasm for the cause remained, however, and he set out to produce a Soviet Russian equivalent of the great Tsarist fiction of Tolstoy. The nearest he came to this, even so, was less in his avowedly 'revolutionary' works (of which the best are the novel *The Artamonov Affair*, 1925, and the play *Dostigaev and Others*, 1933) than in the earlier *Mother* (1906), about a woman elevated by suffering to revolutionary heroism, his one piece of fiction unquestionably in Tolstoy's class. Much of his non-fiction is forgettable propaganda (its titles combine such terms as 'culture', 'revolution' and 'the working class'); but it includes his masterpiece, the autobiographical trilogy *My Childhood* (1913), *My Apprenticeship* (1916) and *My Universities* (1922), in which he exorcised the memory of his fearful past and also – thanks to his savage irony about Tsarist times – produced one of the works still most frequently read in Russian schools. (But the trilogy is more than propaganda, if it is propaganda at all: read with *Nabokov's *Speak, Memory*, about a privileged childhood a generation later, it gives an account of growing up in 19th-century Russia as exotic and bizarrely personal as, say, Chaplin's autobiography and Gosse's *Father and Son* do of Victorian British public and private life.)

Gorki died (some think by no accident, and on Stalin's instructions) in 1936, and is dismally memorialized in the name of the closed city Gorki, once Nijhni Novgorod, now the unwilling home of many a scientific dissident – an irony whose bitterness would certainly have made him smile.

Gorki's other works include the excellent short novels *Foma Gordeyev* (1899) and *A Confession* (1908), the plays *Smug Citizens* (1903), a Gogolish satire, and *Enemies* (1906). His enormous later epics (e.g. the 1920s–1930s tetralogy *Bystander*, *The Magnet*, *Other Fires* and *The Spectre*, or the unfinished *The Life of Klim Samgin*, 1936) are of interest largely to devotees: slabs of interesting description (foreshadowing *Solzhenitsyn) alternate with half-baked and inter-minable political philosophy. Good introductions: A. Kaun: *Maxim Gorki and His Russia* (1932); D. Levin: *Stormy Petrel* (1967).

GRASS, Günter (born 1927)
German novelist and playwright

For a time it seemed as if Grass was strangled by his own versatility: throughout his twenties he produced visual art, poetry and drama, all of it striking (and well received), but none of it outstandingly original. His plays, for example (*Flood*; *Onkel, Onkel*; *Only Ten Minutes to Buffalo* and *The Wicked Cooks*, published together in English in *Four Plays*, 1967), though competent and entertaining, are in a reach-me-down European Absurd style derived ultimately from Ionesco: they have their own likeable personality, but show no hint of Grass's own. (His later play *The Plebeians Rehearse the Uprising*, 1966, a Brechtian critique of Brecht, is better because the influences are absorbed and put to the service of personal – in this case political – ends.) His poetry, too (best collection is *In the Egg and Other Poems*, 1977), is interesting without ever being memorable; also, replacing density of images and tight verse-structure with rather bland moralizing, it loses alertness in translation.

It was in his novels that Grass finally grew to artistic maturity, blending parody, political polemic and eclectic obsessions into a convincingly personal view of humanity's affairs. The catalyst was politics, and at times in *The Tin Drum* (1959), *Dog Years* (1963) and *Local Anaesthetic* (1969) – each of them tracing the effects of Nazi and post-Nazi history on selected individual lives – the detail of post-war German socialism can baffle the general reader; in *From the Diary of a Snail* (1972) this is a disabling flaw. In *The Flounder* (1977) the political themes are generalized (the socialist view is now of humanity at large), and the Absurd style (involving the trial, before a deliciously ridiculous feminist tribunal, of a talking fish) works towards the general theme (human beings defining themselves through relationships, and particularly through differing male and female views of the irrational world). The esoteric detail in the book (of cooking, of medieval history) enhances rather than impedes an intriguing narrative; the style blends limpidity and liveliness, even though the prose is more poetic than the poems which punctuate the book. In short, *The Flounder* is Grass's masterpiece, and earns him a secure place among the best novelists of the age.

Grass's other writings include the short novels *Cat and Mouse* (1961), *The Meeting at Telgte* (1979) and *Headbirths* (1980). Good study of the political novels: J. Reddick: *The Danzig Trilogy of Günter Grass* (1974).

GRAVES, Robert (born 1895)
British writer

Graves was one of the most prolific and protean British men of letters of the century, and produced work of distinction and popular appeal in every field he touched. His experiences in the First World War led to the outstanding autobiography *Goodbye to All That* (1929, rev. 1957), which also deals with 1920s Oxford and Bloomsbury and with his first marriage. He made robust translations of Homer's *Iliad* (*The Anger of Achilles*, 1959), of Apuleius's *The Golden Ass* and of other works, and was a tireless essayist – good collections are *The Long Weekend* (1940), on between-wars Britain, *The Common Asphodel* (1949), on poetry, *The White Goddess* (1948, rev. 1961), an important book on the nature of poetic inspiration, and *The Nazarene Gospel Restored* (1953), on the historical basis of Christianity. His *The Greek Myths* (1955, rev. 1960) is one of his most characteristic books. Its basis is a straightforward telling of the entire corpus of Greek myths, and this is interlarded with notes and a commentary filled with extraordinary lore on all matters to do with folk culture, and with Graves's own hobby-horses and obsessions (e.g. the worship of the moon-goddess, or the sacred intoxication cults he sees mushrooming everywhere). Though heterodox and needing to be taken with a pound or two of academic salt, *The Greek Myths* is an essential book for anyone interested in Greek mythology or folk culture – and, like all Graves's books, is crisply readable as well.

In addition to his non-fiction, Graves produced outstanding historical novels. These cover the whole range of his interests: mythology (*The Golden Fleece/Hercules My Shipmate*, 1944, a 'rationalization' of the myth of the Argonauts; *Homer's Daughter*, 1955, delightfully embroidering Samuel Butler's theory that *The Odyssey* was written by a woman), historical and social (*I, Claudius*, 1934, and *Claudius the God*, 1934, on Imperial Rome; *Count Belisarius*, 1938, on Byzantium and Rome; *Wife to Mr Milton*, 1943, on Puritan England; *Sergeant Lamb of the Ninth*, 1940, and *Proceed, Sergeant Lamb*, 1941, on the American war of independence), and utopian (*Seven Days in New Crete*, 1949, a Shavian future-fantasy). His most extraordinary novel is *King Jesus* (1946), which treats the founder of Christianity in the same manner as the mythological or historical characters who are the subjects of his other books: that is, it makes him simultaneously a figure emblematic of his own age and a repository of wholly modern sensitivity and sensibility – a cultural duality which allows Graves to make (and to get away with) a deliciously, outrageously partial interpretation of the past. Like *The Greek Myths*, this novel simultaneously fascinates and irritates; it is typical of Graves's method and central to his work.

Graves's third – and some say most distinguished – field of activity was poetry. This, like much of his work, was subject to constant and restless revision, so that the latest edition (*Collected Poems*, 1975) is essential for seeing his final thoughts. Anthologies favour witty, modish verses like 'Welsh Incident' (which begins 'But that was nothing to what things came out/From the sea-caves of Criccieth yonder . . .' and ends 'What did the mayor do?' – 'I was coming to that.'); but his truest poetry is all on the theme of love. He writes short lyrics, in simple language and plain syntax; the effect depends on strong rhythms, precise situations and passionate clarity of utterance. He is with *Durrell and *Seferis rather than with *Eliot or *Berryman: a descendant of the poets of Alexandria, of Propertius and of Catullus – and in some pieces (such as 'Dialogue on the Headland', 'Fact of the Act' or 'Three Times in Love') one of the best love-poets of this or any other age.

Interesting correspondence, especially on the background to the poems: P. Prey (ed.): *In Broken Images: Selected Letters of Robert Graves 1914–1946* (1982); *Between Moon and Moon: Selected Letters 1946–1972* (1984). Good biography: M. Seymour-Smith: *Robert Graves, His Life and Works* (1982).

GREEN, Henry (1905–73)
British novelist

Green's first two books, though excellent, are his least characteristic. *Blindness* (1926) is about a young man whose creative ability is unlocked by sudden blindness; *Living* (1929) is set in a British Midlands factory and reflects ordinary working people's attitudes and (especially) speech in a way as detailed as *Anderson's *Winesburg, Ohio*. After he became director of the family business, Green produced seven more novels, in a markedly different style. They are comedies of manners, a blend of gentle satire (in the manner of *Powell) and claustrophobic, malicious dialogue (like that of the families in *Compton-Burnett). The best are *Party Going* (1939), about smart socialites, *Caught* (1943), set in the London Blitz, *Loving* (1945), exploring the balance in Green's characters between love (vulnerable and menaced) and lust (menacing and ridiculous), and *Back* (1946), about a man's agonizing self-rehabilitation after prison. Green's last three novels, *Concluding* (1948), *Nothing* (1950) and *Doting* (1952), are largely for devotees, the characteristic aloofness and abrupt punctuation of his prose taken to alienating extremes, rather as *Salinger in his later work over-polished an already gleaming style. (The last two books, in particular, read like *Woolf's *The Waves* written with tongue in cheek.) Green is now something of a writer's writer, unduly neglected; but anyone who enjoys the authors mentioned above (or *Updike, who once said that no other novelist had influenced him more) will find plenty to like in his understated, sardonic work.

Green's early autobiography, *Pack My Bag* (1940), largely about his business experiences and acquaintances, is as lively and as malicious as any of his novels.

GREENE, Graham (born 1904)
British writer

The influences on Greene are easy to see: Buchan (intriguing plots; laconic style), *Mauriac (concern for the torments of the lapsed Roman Catholic soul) and above all *Conrad (bleakness; obsession with alienation and despair; fast action in exotic locations contrasted with slow exploration of the characters' inner emptiness). After *The Power and the Glory* (1940, about a failed priest caught up in a Mexican revolution), his course was set: in subsequent novels he repeated and extended the same formula – some say to the point of self-parody – varying only the locations and the events which began his characters' journey into hell. The quest for redemption can take place in the African jungle (*The Heart of the Matter*, 1948; *A Burnt-Out Case*, 1961), Vietnam (*The Quiet American*, 1955), Haiti (*The Comedians*, 1966), Latin America (*The Honorary Consul*, 1973) or even quiet Berkhamstead, England (*The Human Factor*, 1978) – but it is always the same quest and it is always doomed because of the same flaw in the seeker, *accidie* or inertia of the soul.

In addition to his major novels, Greene published a large number of what he called 'entertainments': shorter, lighter books usually more concerned with incident than with character (though Pinkie in *Brighton Rock*, 1938, and the vacuum-cleaner salesman Wormold in *Our Man in Havana*, 1958, are characters as solid and as racked as any in the 'serious' books). Several of these books are straightforward (and excellent) thrillers: *Stamboul Train* (1932), *A Gun for Sale* (1936), *The Ministry of Fear* (1943), *The Third Man* (1950). Others (notably *Our Man in Havana* and *Travels with My Aunt*, 1969, a picaresque story not unlike *Mann's *The Confessions of Felix Krull* in tone) are humorous or whimsical. All, however, deal with Greene's major themes, the nature of loyalty (to family, class, religion, political creed or self), and the forces which corrupt and diminish it. Greene also wrote a number of successful plays (notably two tragicomedies about suburban marriage, *The Potting Shed*, 1958, and *The Complaisant Lover*, 1959), essays and travel books (e.g. *Journey Without Maps*, 1936, about a journey through Liberia) and a deprecatory autobiography (*A Sort of Life*, 1971; *Ways of Escape*, 1982). Since the 1960s, when many other writers (e.g., in their different ways, *Highsmith, *Le Carré and *Updike) began exploring his desolate landscapes, the soul's no-man's-land nicknamed 'Greeneland', he has begun to lose stature: in a crowded field, he stands out less well than once seemed possible. But his novels are consistent, thoughtful and highly entertaining – and one at least, *The Power and the Glory*, outclasses all imitations, whether by other writers or by Greene himself.

Greene's other writings include the novels *The Man Within* (1929), *The Confidential Agent* (1939), *The End of the Affair* (1951), *Dr Fischer of Geneva* (1980), and *Monsignor Quixote* (1982); short stories (*Collected Stories*, 1972); biography (*Lord*

Rochester's Monkey, 1974); essays, chiefly on writers (*Collected Essays*, 1969); lively criticism of 1930s films (*The Pleasure Dome*, 2nd edn 1972). He also produced a notable piece of 'faction', *J'accuse* (1982), a hatcheting, Mailer-with-teeth exposé of the *milieu* (gangsterdom) of the Côte d'Azur. Useful, if evasive, interviews: M. F. Allain: *The Other Man* (1983). Brisk, clear survey: J. Spurling: *Graham Greene* (1983).

GUNN, Thom (born 1929)
British/American poet

On present showing, Gunn is living proof of that sad cliché that first thoughts are always best. In his twenties he belonged in the class of Logue or *Hughes: he was regularly anthologized with them, and shared their quality. His collection *Fighting Terms* (1954, rev. – and rhythmically weakened – in 1962) was one of the best poetry-books of its time: a combination of urgent style and that sparky, intellectual involvement with 'issues' (there were a lot of issues in 1953) characteristic of the Oxbridge generation of the day – the seeds were already being sown that not much later produced *Beyond the Fringe*. Gunn and his contemporaries contrasted both with austere *Eliot and elegant *Auden, but still seemed set to claim their crowns. But Auden and Eliot are still admired; Logue and Hughes moved on (among other things, to *War Music* and to *Crow*); Gunn became a professor at Berkeley, California. He continued to publish, and has been an authoritative teacher and enthusiastic editor. But the great 1960s American poets are *Jarrell (Gunn's nearest stylistic analogue) and *Lowell; of Gunn's own work only *My Sad Captains* (1961) contains anything to match with theirs, or remotely to rival his own spectacular early work.

The best of Gunn's other collections are *The Sense of Movement* (1957) and *Jack Straw's Castle* (1976). *The Passages of Joy* (1982) is soft-centred, easy, *Auden without tears. 'Collected' and 'revised' editions are generally to be avoided, as slacker than the originals. Good essays: *The Occasions of Poetry* (1982). Good on Gunn and the other poets of his generation, especially Larkin: B. Morrison: *The Movement: English Poetry and Fiction of the 1950s* (1980).

HARTLEY, Leslie Poles (1895–1972)
British novelist

Hartley's main themes (sexual repression, and the guilt and selfishness involved in making relationships) and his spare style (which can equal *Forster's) are best seen in his *Eustace and Hilda* trilogy (*The Shrimp and the Anemone*, 1944; *The Sixth Heaven*, 1946; *Eustace and Hilda*, 1947) and in the novel *The Go-Between* (1953, exquisitely filmed in 1971). *Eustace and Hilda* is about a brother and sister growing up in Britain between the wars; its evocation of comfortable middle-class life is balanced by an exploration of the siblings' tight relationship: they are claustrophobic kin to the tormented children in James's *The Turn of the*

Screw, haunted not by real ghosts but by the implications of their own relationship (symbolized by that between anemone and shrimp). Hartley's vision of childhood corrupted is equally well expressed in *The Go-Between*, which is about a thirteen-year-old boy used as a message-carrier by two Edwardian lovers. As their doomed affair flowers (he is a tenant farmer, she the daughter of 'the big house') the boy's own sexuality is blighted: the book is movingly told by the go-between himself as a crabbed, unsatisfied old man. Hartley's other work (eight more novels; five volumes of short stories) is slight and sometimes cranky; but in *The Go-Between* and in *The Shrimp and the Anemone* (which deals with Eustace and Hilda as children) he wrote minor classics.

Of Hartley's other novels, the best is *The Hireling* (1957), an exploration of sexual jealousy and introversion. The best collection of stories is *The Killing Bottle* (1932). *The Novelist's Responsibility* (1967) contains lively essays on literature and on the British novelists he admired.

HAŠEK, Jaroslav (1883–1923)
Czech author

From the age of seventeen, Hašek lived as a kind of anti-hero in the ironical fiction of his own life. He was phenomenally productive: he wrote more than 1,200 short stories and articles, an average of one a week throughout his working life, if he had kept regular hours. But he spent weeks and months at a time as a kind of beatnik *avant la lettre*, tramping the countryside, boozing, begging, a member of the alternative society of gipsies, army deserters, vagabonds and thieves which had thrived in Eastern and Middle Europe for centuries, and was given a new 19th-century impulse by the Napoleonic and Franco-Prussian wars. His regular employments are typified by his post as editor of the Prague journal *The Animal World*, from which he was sacked for writing articles about fictitious animals. In 1906 he joined the anarchist movement; in 1915 he volunteered; he was captured at the Russian front, imprisoned and subsequently employed by the Bolsheviks.

All of this is transformed and transmuted into the tumbling detail of Hašek's masterpiece *The Good Soldier Švejk* (1923). He began the novel to support his wife and young son, but left it incomplete at his death. (It was finished, unsatisfactorily, by Karel Vanek; but the picaresque, circular form of the book in fact makes completion unimportant – the 700 extant pages work very well as they stand.) *The Good Soldier Švejk* relates the day-to-day military life (much of it spent on an interminable train journey) of the Falstaffian Švejk himself, an amiable, self-pro-claimed simpleton who uses wide-eyed innocence as a devastating mirror for the venal, arrogant and deadly fools he finds on every side. He is a medieval rogue strayed into the modern world, a *Simplex Simplicissimus* of the War that was to End War. *The Good Soldier Švejk* is one of the world's finest pieces of fiction: it ranks with the work of Rabelais (in particular with *Gargantua*, whose structure and form it resembles), and it may remind modern readers strongly of *Heller's *Catch-22* (a novel similar in theme, tone and method), or of such other masterworks of humour as Gogol's *Dead Souls*, Goncharov's *Oblomov* or *Mann's *The Confessions of Felix Krull*.

Earlier, much-cut translations of *The Good Soldier Švejk* were superseded by Cecil Parrott's magnificent version (1973). Parrott has also translated a selection of Hašek's shorter works in *Jaroslav Hašek: The Red Commissar* (1981), and written a useful critical study, *Jaroslav Hašek* (1982), particularly revealing on *The Good Soldier Švejk*.

HEANEY, Seamus (born 1939)
Irish poet

An appealing strand of British 20th-century literature – perhaps of that of most countries – is a series of delicately evocative memoirs of childhood (often rural): minor writing of high quality. (Good prose examples are Raverat's *A Cambridge Childhood*, Beer's *Mrs Beer's House*, Durrell's *My Family and Other Animals* and Lee's *Cider with Rosie*.) Heaney belongs to this tradition – and evades the problem of poeticizing by writing in dense, image-rich verse, full of mind-catching and original metaphor. (The bubbles from rotting canal weeds 'gargle delicately', while bluebottles 'weave a strange gauze of sound around the smell'.) Since Heaney is from Ireland, he has not been able to avoid writing about 'the troubles', and one of his most heart-felt books, *Station Island* (1984), is a threnody for the rape of a culture, raw with the sense of personal loss and the furious helplessness of the sensitive individual caught up in insane mass politics. But his finest poems are not political but autobiographical – or rather 'biographical', since he has the rare gift, in writers of childhood, of making his evocations seem our own memory, of making us nostalgic for his nostalgia. The opening lines of 'A Drink of Water' (from *Field Work*, 1979) show both his method and his quality:

> She came every morning to draw water
> Like an old bat staggering up the field:
> The pump's whooping cough, the bucket's clatter
> And slow diminuendo as it filled,
> Announced her.

Apart from *Field Work* and *Station Island*, Heaney's books are *Death of a Naturalist* (1966), *Door into the Dark* (1969), *Wintering Out* (1972) and *North* (1975), the most concerned with politics. Good anthology: *Selected Poems 1965–1975* (1980). *Preoccupations: Selected Prose 1968–1978* (1980) is especially good on the writing of poetry, and on *Yeats. Good, brief study: B. Morrison: *Seamus Heaney* (1982). Critical compendium: T. Curtis (ed.): *The Art of Seamus Heaney* (1983).

HELLER, Joseph (born 1923)
American novelist

Heller is a New Yorker, an academic though not a scholar (he taught creative writing) and a wit. His first novel, *Catch-22* (1961), was one of the most brilliant books of its generation. In particular, it seemed to sum up (and partly to create) a sharply cynical public view of war as the subject of a choking, existentialist joke, the world dying not with a whimper but with a wisecrack. This feeling is by no means new (Aristophanes, for one, was there before), but became of devastating emblematic relevance to the Vietnam-haunted America of the 1960s – 'We had to destroy it in order to save it' is history imitating art. In *Catch-22* the US Air Force is depicted as a lunatic, engulfing machine: if you're sane enough to want to get out, you're sane enough to fight. The humour is black and bleak, relying chiefly on hyperbole and deadpan wit. The vein has been over-exploited since (outstanding examples are Altman's film *M*A*S*H* and the fine TV series to which it gave birth); but *Catch-22* will outlive its imitators, a satirical masterpiece in the class of *Don Quixote* or *The Good Soldier Švejk*.

Heller's later novels are less successful. *Something Happened* (1974) explores one man's private agony, in a bureaucratic hell (business as a family; family relationships as a business) which lacks the deadly universal relevance of the military and which *Kafka and others have more chillingly appropriated. Slocum is too shallow, too bland a hero; lacking the wit of *Catch-22*, the tone of *Something Happened* is too flat for its theme – it is a scream of anguish uttered in a monotone. *Good as Gold* (1979) is better, and its picture of (Jewish) family life is occasionally as acerbic as anything in *Catch-22*. It is, however, flawed by its attention to particular (and evanescent) real events and people (mid-1970s American politics, and the character of Henry Kissinger). *God Knows* (1984) is a presentation of King David of Israel (in first-person monologue) as the Jewish father-figure to end them all, a rueful, all-knowing patriarch doomed to eternal disappointment in his progeny and a one-sided, wise-cracking conversation with an unhelpful deity. It is Heller's funniest book since *Catch-22*, salted with quotations from everyone from Moses to Marx, *Hamlet* to Fanny Brice, but its unremitting melancholy, for all the jokes, makes it a less life-enhancing read. Like *Something Happened* and *Good as Gold*, it is an also-ran – but how could things be otherwise, when *Catch-22* is such a front-runner even among masterworks?

Admirers of *Catch-22*, in particular, will find plenty of similar pleasures in the novels of John Irving (born 1942). His subjects are apparently less bizarre than Heller's – small-town US life of the 1950s and 1960s, the pangs and pains of adolescent sex – but he grafts on to them obsessions (Vienna; bears; baseball; incest; freaks) as weird as anything in *Grass and as matter-of-fact as anything in Vonnegut. The mixture of farce, fantasy and pain is not fully controlled in his early novels, but by his fourth, *The World According to Garp* (1976), it is brilliantly, mesmerically right, and he managed the feat of topping that performance in *The Hotel New Hampshire* (1981).

HEMINGWAY, Ernest (1899–1961)
American writer

It is easy to dispraise Hemingway – and to do so has seemed to many recent critics a salutary antidote to two generations of preposterous adulation which carried the man, his legend and his work beyond the reach of sensible assessment. He did not invent redneck literature (*London and *Lardner were there before, and their stories are scandalously undervalued in comparison with his); but he gave it an impetus and a stylishness which planted its gruff certainties deep in American letters (and, some would say, in American life) long after its time was past. Women, in Hemingway's world, are ciphers: decorative or slatternly, they have no existence beyond the need to support their men. The reason for this is that Hemingway men are almost without exception effeminate, achieving masculinity only by *macho* activities like hunting, boozing and the ruthless elimination of sentiment for anything but a noble piece of game or a game old buddy. The natural kingdom exists to be hooked, impaled or shot – and the orgasmic satisfaction such slaughter produces in the hunter extends to warfare: one of the most serious charges against Hemingway is not that he glorified war but that he reduced the killing of other men (especially lower-caste aliens such as spics, wops, dagoes and krauts) to a callously schematic ritual about as moving (to the killer) as blowing his nose. In this, it could be argued, Hemingway merely reflected in his work a prevalent morality; but his books (and their countless imitations in both pulp fiction and B movies) promoted uncivilized brutalism in western humanity to an extent unrivalled by any other single creative artist. Nick Adams (the hero of many of his short stories, a surrogate for Hemingway himself) is a bloodthirsty, callous boor, despite Hemingway's attempts to suggest a sensitive soul inside by constant throwaway references to Adams's (otherwise unsubstantiated) ability as a writer. The quintessential Hemingway hero is Harry Morgan in *To Have and Have Not* (1937). Despite the irony in this story – which sees, among other things, every *macho* Morgan act deprive him of limbs, livelihood and finally life – the many fights and killings are described with a lipsmacking relish totally absent from the more 'moral' parts of the book. The description of Morgan machine-gunning the Cubans who have commandeered his boat is a piece of pornography-of-violence unsurpassed even in the goriest sub-Hemingway pulp magazine.

Hemingway's preoccupation with death is often adduced by critics as somehow an extenuation of his art as well as an explanation of it. In the same way, the laconicism of his style – no one has used short, adjectiveless sentences better – has blinded many readers to the facts that his themes are limited and threadbare and his character-drawing is non-existent. (His characters are, exactly, the cast-list of Punch and Judy; even the hangman, the string of sausages and the crocodile play featured roles.) He has no range, no depth and no humanity; his work is slick and sick, a gutter journalism of the arts.

All that is easily said, and undeniable. But for all his faults, the awkward fact is that Hemingway is also a superb writer, one of the finest and most individual novelists of the century. The reasons are to do with the complexities of his own character, and the presence of the man himself in every line of his work. First of all, his fastidious (homosexual?) withdrawal from messy human emotion, coupled with an ability to see beauty in the most unlikely activities, leads to descriptive passages unequalled by any writer until *Nabokov. His account of the bull-running and festival at Pamplona in *Fiesta/The Sun Also Rises* (1926) and his descriptions of bull-fighting in *Death in the Afternoon* (1932) combine the verve and punch of a journalist hot with a scoop – no one had 'done' these subjects in English before – with a sense of individual involvement rare in his work. Although many of his short stories (e.g. 'On the Quai at Smyrna', 'The Snows of Kilimanjaro' and most of those in *In Our Time*, 1925) are trivial and narcissistic, others (e.g. 'Fifty Grand' and 'Now I Lay Me', from *Men Without Women*, 1927, and 'The Gambler, the Nun and the Radio' and 'Fathers and Sons', from *Winner Take Nothing*, 1933, his finest collection) propose a view of decent, doomed humanity which is powerful, moving and persuasive. In the same way, although his later novels (e.g. *For Whom the Bell Tolls*, 1940, set in the Spanish civil war, and the doomily symbolic – duck-shoots an emblem for the fate of humankind – *Across the River and into the Trees*, 1950) are overblown, his early books (*Fiesta*, and the First-World-War novel *A Farewell to Arms*, 1929, memorable as the only piece of Hemingway writing to depict a warm man–woman relationship, both partners of equal interest and on equal terms) show us, with compassion, grace and often wit, a human condition it is possible to recognize, even to admire. *A Farewell to Arms* is his masterpiece: the dying-fall ending, in particular, reaches heights he never otherwise achieved. His Nobel-Prize-winning book *The Old Man and the Sea* (1952) is of debated status. Some see it as slack self-repetition, reworking in particular many of the themes of *To Have and Have Not*; for others it is the pinnacle of his art, a description in clear, clean prose of the elemental conflict between human beings and the unreasoning and overwhelming force of nature, the power within matched against the power without. Either way, potboiler or masterpiece, the book is essential Hemingway; together with *Winner Takes Nothing* and *A Farewell to Arms*, it is one piece of 20th-century fiction sure to last.

Good, if hefty (611 pages), critical compendium: *Hemingway: The Critical Heritage* (ed. Meyers, 1982). Good biography: C. Baker: *Ernest Hemingway: A Life Story* (1969).

HESSE, Hermann (1877–1962)
German/Swiss novelist

Hesse was immensely prolific, producing poems (*Collected Poems*, in English, 1970), thousands of reviews and articles, important autobiographical works (*Autobiographical Writings*, ed. Ziolkowski, 1972; *My Belief: Essays on Life and Art*, ed. Ziolkowski, 1974), and no less than 35,000 letters (*The Hesse/Mann Letters*, 1968, for example, contains a fascinating, reserved correspondence between two wary giants). His first novels, *Peter Camenzind* (1904), *Under the Wheel/The Prodigy* (1905) and *Gertrud* (1910), though written in a straightforwardly realistic style he later abandoned, set out some of his characteristic themes. *Gertrud*, for example (the most elegant and moving of his early books), examines the pull between the intellectual and carnal sides of humankind, and the place of love in self-fulfilment: it is a formally perfect account of the developing relationship between a young composer, his close friend and the girl they love.

The crucial period in Hesse's artistic development was the early 1910s. Suffering both from a creative block and from marriage problems, he travelled to India in 1911, seeking spiritual regeneration; he underwent psychoanalysis; at the beginning of the First World War, unable to accept German militarism, he settled in Switzerland. The fruits of this turmoil are among his finest books: *Rosshalde* (1914), a beautiful, limpid novel about an estranged couple bound together by their obsessive love for their house and child; *Demian* (1919), an opaque, mystical book about violence and the healing power of culture, and *Siddhartha* (1922), a short novel describing Buddha's growth to spiritual maturity, in which the balance between the internal human world, symbolized by intellectuality and spirituality, and our coming-to-terms with the external world, symbolized by sexual and business prowess, is once again a major theme. In *Steppenwolf* (1927) – the most 'German' of his books, with vital echoes of German folklore and of the stories of Hoffmann and Keller – Hesse dealt at length, for the first time, with the theme of redemption. Haller, the reclusive 'Steppes-wolf' of the title, is saved from self-destructive hate by two forces: his love for Hermine (and his acceptance of hers for him) and a realization that fantasy and imagination are forces in human consciousness as dynamic as logic or causality. Hermine is the finest female character in Hesse's work: usually his women are there merely to project the feelings of his male characters, but Hermine is vividly imagined and characterized in her own right, a lively and sunny counterpart to sombre Haller.

Hesse's next major novel, *Narciss and Goldmund* (1930), is a panoramic story set in the Middle Ages. Its philosophy is perhaps over-schematic (the two halves of human nature, in the persons of Narciss the intellectual recluse and his friend Goldmund the feckless, bohemian artist, go their separate ways in youth, live their lives to the full, and are finally reunited), but the colour and thrust of the narrative are irresistible. In particular, the descriptions of Goldmund's vagabond life, and of his apprenticeship to the craft of wood-carving, reveal in Hesse an understanding of the meaning of medieval society that was to reach its full expression in his last novel, *The Glass Bead Game* (1943). This is his masterpiece: the story of Jacob Knecht, the *magister ludi*, unites and brings to fruition all his major themes. Knecht, who devotes his being to the mystic perfections of the Game, and then comes to see that the outside world has charms, and claims, as well, is in the long line of Hesse heroes: in him are united the peasant creativity of Peter Camenzind, the artistic sensitivity of Veraguth (in *Rosshalde*), the suffering of Haller (in *Steppenwolf*) and the spiritual resignation of Siddhartha. The 'balance that makes a human being' is the book's subject, the interplay of inner and outer selves, reason and feeling, weaknesses and strengths. *The Glass Bead Game* combines poetry, reflection and narrative drive; it seems to speak directly to our need; with *Rosshalde*, *Siddhartha* and *Steppenwolf*, it is one of the great German novels of the century.

Other short novels: *Knulp* (1915); *Klingsor's Last Summer* (1920). Dreamlike short stories: *Pictor's Metamorphosis and Other Fantasies* (ed. Ziolkowski, 1982). Good critical introduction: T. J. Ziolkowski: *The Novels of Hermann Hesse* (1965). Brief life: B. Zeller: *Hermann Hesse: The First Biography* (1963).

HIGHSMITH, Patricia (born 1921)
American novelist

Highsmith's first crime novel, *Strangers on a Train* (1951), was filmed by Hitchcock, and it is easy to see why: the book has exactly the combination of continuous surprise and the closing in of inexorable circumstance (two strangers agree on a train to commit 'perfect' murders for each other – and everything goes wrong) which characterizes Hitchcock's best work. It is a Highsmith characteristic too: in *The Two Faces of January* (1964) or *The Story Teller/A Suspension of Mercy* (1965) she explores further the workings of circumstance on the amoral mind. Her heroes are hollow people; it takes only the slightest chance to trigger a remorseless, meticulously reported descent into splintered emptiness. Even Ripley, the successful criminal hero of a sequence of books (beginning with *The Talented Mr Ripley*, 1957, in which he practises his skills at forgery, impersonation and murder), has husk for heart. Like *Le Carré, Highsmith is often described as a 'real novelist' working within the frame of genre, and her aim, like Le Carré's, is chiefly entertainment – it is the bleakness of her moral vision which gives her fiction relevance, and seems to give it depth.

Highsmith's other Ripley books are *Ripley under Ground* (1970), *Ripley's Game* (1974) and *The Boy who Followed Ripley* (1980). Her other crime books include *The Tremor of Forgery* (1969), *The Snail-Watcher and Other Stories/Eleven*

(1970), short stories, *Edith's Diary* (1977) and *The Black House* (1981). *The People Who Knock on the Door* (1982) is an interesting departure: a moving story of the tensions in a Middle Western family when the father becomes a 'born-again' Christian. Her *Plotting and Writing Suspense Fiction* (1983) is nothing like the dry primer proposed by the title, but is lively and full of engrossing sidelights on how several of her most bizarre books came to be written.

HILL, Susan (born 1942)
British novelist and playwright

Apart from two early books (*The Enclosure*, 1961; *Do Me a Favour*, 1963), the bulk of Hill's distinguished fiction – she is one of the most gifted English-language novelists of her generation, and it is a classy generation – was written in a concentrated burst of activity from 1969 to 1974. Shortly afterwards, she announced her temporary (and so far unbroken) retirement from writing fiction, married, and devoted her creative energies to literary journalism and to radio drama (including a stint as scriptwriter for the soap-opera *The Archers*). The six novels she produced between 1969 and 1974 are tragedies about relationships, normally involving one emotional predator and one victim: husband and wife, and mother and daughter, in *A Change for the Better* (1969); two small boys in the magnificent and sombre *I'm the King of the Castle* (1970); a manic-depressive artist and his loyal friend in *The Bird of Night* (1972), notable for its painful delineation of mental illness. The theme of emotional depredation is common in English writing, from the books of the Brontë sisters to Rattigan's *Separate Tables*; but no writer in the post-war period has tackled it as well as Hill – at her best, she equals her two great models, de Maupassant and *Mansfield. Her finest novel is her last to date: *In the Springtime of the Year* (1974). This is about a young woman's sudden bereavement, and the solace she finds from observing and accepting the daily round of life in the countryside. The same kind of heart's ease, one feels – the result of marriage and the upbringing of her small daughter, about which she has movingly written in the memoir *The Magic Apple-Tree* (1982) – has left Hill herself no time for the emotional tension and dismay about which she wrote so well. It is to be hoped, none the less, that she will soon return to fiction.

Hill's other novels are *Gentleman and Ladies* (1969) and *Strange Meeting* (1971). Her short stories are collected in *The Albatross and Other Stories* (1971) and *A Bit of Singing and Dancing* (1973). Her radio plays include the outstanding *The End of Summer* (1970), *The Cold Country* (1972) and *Consider the Lilies* (1973). *The Woman in Black* (1983) is a Poe-ish ghost story.

HOPKINS, Gerard Manley (1844–89)
British poet

Although Hopkins's poetry was written in the Victorian age (and its patterns of thought and some of its turns of style are second cousins of

Morris or the Pre-Raphaelites as well as of Cardinal Newman) it was not published until 1918, and its thorny syntax and impacted imagery were important factors in freeing English poetry from the Georgian treacle of such men as Bridges (Hopkins's friend who published his verse, in a generous and surely conscious act of artistic suicide). Even so, and although Hopkins belongs with *Pound and *Joyce rather than with Tennyson, the pull in his work is between a 'modern' intellectual style and scented Victorian subject-matter, a sentimental mysticism nearer to Pusey than to Blake. He was a classical scholar, and his poems are reminiscent of those of Pindar: abrupt, dense syntax, treating uninflected English as if it had cases and moods like Greek. All these qualities, from grittiness to gush, can be seen in *The Wreck of the Deutschland*, a 1,000-line meditation occasioned by the death of five nuns in a shipwreck. It begins, typically,

> Thou mastering me
> God! Giver of breath and bread;
> World's strand, sway of the sea;
> Lord of living and dead;
> Thou has found bones and veins in me, fastened me flesh,
> And after it almost unmade, what with dread,
> Thy doing: and dost thou touch me afresh?
> Over again I feel thy finger and find thee.

There is strength in these lines, but also a surrender to self missing in both earlier and later metaphysical poets. Undisciplined imagery, word-play for its own sake, weakens much of Hopkins's non-religious verse (e.g. the travel-brochure 'Duns Scotus's Oxford' – 'Cuckoo-echoing, bell-swarmed, lark-charmed, rook-racked, river-rounded . . .' – or 'Inversnaid' – 'This darksome burn . . .'). His religious poems, especially those using his favourite sonnet form, are his finest work, and a handful of them (e.g. 'The Windhover', 'Hurrahing in Harvest', 'God's Grandeur') combine mysticism and warm observation, and use imagistic language as a firm vehicle for thought, in a way matched only by such masters of religious poetry as Donne or *Eliot. We are used, in the 20th century, to making a chiefly intellectual response to poetry – and 20th-century poets organize their work with this in mind. Hopkins's fastidious language admirably suits this approach, but his all-or-nothing content also demands something present-day poets like *Hughes or *Heaney are just rediscovering, total sensual immersion and intellectual submission, the leap of faith which, in verse as in religion, is one of the 19th century's most characteristic legacies.

Collected editions: *The Letters of Gerard Manley Hopkins* (ed. Abbott, 3 vols., 1955–6); *The Journals and Papers of Gerard Manley Hopkins* (ed. House and Storey, 1959).

HOUSMAN, Alfred Edward (1859–1936)
British poet

A classical scholar, a don and a precise recluse (he was a closet homosexual, devastated by the trial of Oscar Wilde), Housman published two slim volumes of verse, *A Shropshire Lad* (1896) and *Last Poems* (1922); *More Poems* appeared posthumously in 1936. He is like those minor German lyricists set to music by Schubert and Wolf (and indeed he is one of the most frequently set of all British poets). He writes in uncomplicated metres with honest rhymes; his work has the lilt and sway of English ballad. His prevailing subject, doomed youth, acquired poignant point after the First World War. His art is minor, but fine-drawn and neat, a blend of cool pastoral (he is good on ploughed fields, rooks and sunlit views from hills) and a pursed-lipped, look-but-don't-touch hedonism drawn from Horace and the Silver Latin poets he admired.

Complete Poems (1959, rev. 1971); *Selected Prose* (1961). Good biography: N. Page: *A. E. Housman: A Critical Biography* (1984).

HUGHES, Richard (1900–1976)
British writer

After early, undistinguished attempts at plays and poetry Hughes found his form with the novel *A High Wind in Jamaica* (1929). This is an ironical story about a group of children captured by pirates: at first a jolly, Stevensonian escapade, it becomes ever more sinister as the children's isolation and terror unlock in them more and more of 'the beast in us'. The end is murder, lies, and a hysterical recantation in court distinctly recalling the climax of *Forster's *Passage to India*. The book is bizarre and many-layered, Hughes's one masterpiece. His later novels are *In Hazard* (1938), fashionably making a storm at sea an allegory for other, emotional storms, and the unfinished trilogy *The Human Predicament* (whose first volume, *The Fox in the Attic*, 1961, about a middle-class British life in the 1920s, is clearly plotted and good, and whose second volume, *The Wooden Shepherdess*, 1973, is *Woolfish and over-fanciful).

Hughes's other work includes short stories (*A Moment of Time*, 1926), and three unduly neglected children's books, *The Spider's Palace* (1931); *Don't Blame Me* (1940); *Gertrude's Child* (1966). *Collected Poems* (1926); *Plays* (1966).

HUGHES, Ted (born 1930)
British poet

Hughes is a nature poet – but instead of celebrating soaring larks, lovable otters and rippling streams he shows us icy mud, hawks' talons and pikes' teeth, savagery, dark and death. His images are as raw as his themes: parrots shriek 'as if they were on fire', faces 'sweat like hams', kisses 'suck life'. His predatory, expressionist world was first revealed in *The Hawk in the Rain* (1957) and further explored in *Lupercal* (1960) and the less satisfactory *Wodwo* (1967), which contains Dylan-*Thomasy short stories and a gloomy radio play as well as poems. His harsh philosophy (that clawing nature is a paradigm for humanity, and each human being is, like Lear, no more than a cruel forked radish in a thunderstorm) is most powerfully articulated in *Crow* (1972), in which raucous, prancing Crow embodies all the world's dark imaginings, and in the 'alchemical cave drama' *Cavebirds* (1978).

The bleakness of Hughes's thought and the energy of his language are usually enough to offset poor rhythm: he slips into a jogging, free-verse pit-a-pat, occasionally too flimsy to bind his images. Over-confident jitteriness hampers many of the poems in *The Remains of Elmet* (1979) and *Moortown* (1979), his most mannered and least convincing collections. As well as in poetry, he has worked in other media (for example he scripted the harsh theatre-piece *Orghast*, with its weird invented language of clicks and shrieks, for Peter Brook) and he has written several books for children. These include the superb *The Iron Man* (1968), a fable of good and evil (about a starving iron man fed on scrap metal by humans who in gratitude destroys, in an epic single-handed contest, a marauding being from the void of space) entirely original and in the same imaginative class as *Alice in Wonderland* or *Charlotte's Web*.

Hughes's other publications include *Season Songs* (1975) and *Moon-Bells* (1978), both for children; *Poetry in the Making* (1967), and an excellent collection of *Selected Poems* (1982). Vast (400 pp.) but helpful critical tome: K. Sagar (ed.): *The Achievement of Ted Hughes* (1983).

HUXLEY, Aldous (1894–1963)
British writer

Bitter glitter is the chief quality of Huxley's early novels, *Crome Yellow* (1921), *Antic Hay* (1923), *Those Barren Leaves* (1925) and *Point Counter Point* (1928): Juvenalian disgust at the hopeless, self-inflicted plight of 20th-century humanity (especially Society and Intellectual Humanity) is expressed in terms of *Firbankian sprightliness – death-prattle, the prance of death. Huxley's characters (it would be more correct to call them 'attitudes', except that they are often, and libellously, based on real people, cold dazzlers like Noël Coward or the Bloomsberries) tread the wheel of country-house parties, smart balls and ironic love-affairs as if their lives, and the future of the human race, depended on it. Their tragedy (and Huxley's, too, as a novelist) is that it does not: his books are gorgeous anatomies of desolation but the barrenness is his, not ours. Only in *Point Counter Point*, in the character Rampion (based on his friend *Lawrence), does he depict a human being with potential for warmth and hope. The climax of this dystopianism is *Brave New World* (1932), his fantasy of a dreadful, antiseptic future, and one of the most stylish examples of satirical rage since Swift.

It would have been hard for anyone to have progressed further into despair without contemplating suicide, and particularly hard for so intelligent a person as Huxley not to begin using his brains to search for cures as well as to diagnose sickness – the more terminal the ills, the greater the challenge to the doctor's art. From the mid-1930s onwards, Huxley poured out articles and essays, alternating between solutions based on radical humanism (e.g. in *Ends and Means*, 1937, and *Science, Liberty and Peace*, 1946) and a quirky mysticism enhanced by hallucinogenic drugs (*The Doors of Perception*, 1954). His personal tragedy now became that the more he preached and the louder we clapped, the less we listened: like *Orwell, he was overwhelmed by a combination in his readers of high regard and inattention. His novels became less racked and more utopian: the best are *Eyeless in Gaza* (1936) and *Ape and Essence* (1948), after *Brave New World* his tautest book, because their disgust at the human predicament belongs to the characters and not to the author, and so makes their frivolous lives poignant as well as pointless. Even so, Huxley is hardly a novelist to place on a shelf with *Mann or *Proust (or even with *Powell or *Waugh): he is a pamphleteer who squats in rather than inhabits the novel form – and this, unless you find his obsessions interesting, makes him a tediously over-assertive read. After *Brave New World*, his short stories (especially those in *Mortal Coils*, 1922, and *Brief Candles*, 1930) are the best introduction to his fascinating, cold-hearted work.

Collected Short Stories (1957); *Letters* (1969); *Collected Poems* (1971). Huxley's other writings include the novels *Time Must Have a Stop* (1944) and *The Genius and the Goddess* (1955), and self-declaring non-fiction such as *Vulgarity in Literature* (1930), *The Art of Seeing* (1942), *The Devils of Loudun* (1952) and *Brave New World Revisited* (1969). Good introductions: S. Bedford: *Aldous Huxley: A Biography* (1974); C. S. Ferns: *Aldous Huxley, Novelist* (1980).

ISHERWOOD, Christopher (born 1904)
British/American writer

Few British writers of the 1930s showed more dazzling promise than Isherwood – and like the 1950s of *Amis, Larkin and Wain, the 1930s were a time when new talents were sky-rocketing. He collaborated with *Auden on three verse plays (*The Dog Beneath the Skin*, 1935; *The*

Ascent of F6, 1936; *On the Frontier*, 1938) and on a travel book (*Journey to a War*, 1939); above all, he produced the fiction about pre-Nazi Berlin which made his reputation, the episodic novel *Mr Norris Changes Trains* (1935) and the linked-story collection *Goodbye to Berlin* (1939, later filmed, made into the stage-play *I Am a Camera* and the musical *Cabaret*). These works are set in a world of sleazy decadence where innocent students tremble to the sound of jackboots in the night, the most innocuous relationships (e.g. that of landlady and tenant) are riven with duplicity, and the singer in every nightclub is a Marlene Dietrich world-wearily performing Brecht to entertain audiences straight from a Grosz cartoon. In 1939 Isherwood went to California to teach literature and to write films; in 1944 he became an American citizen, discovered Indian mysticism (he wrote a notable translation of the *Bhagavad-Gita* in 1944), and lost his creative identity. Of his (several dozen) later books, the best are the novels *Prater Violet* (1945), the autobiographical *A Single Man* (1964), and *A Meeting by the River* (1967, about two brothers, and on one of the things Isherwood describes best, a developing relationship), and the autobiography *Christopher and His Kind* (1977), distinctly unreticent about his and others' homosexuality.

Among Isherwood's 'Indian' books are *Vedanta for Modern Man* (1951) and a translation of *How to Know God: The Yoga Aphorisms of Patanjali* (1953). *The Condor and the Cows, a South American Travel Diary* (1949), and *Exhumations: Stories, Articles, Verse* (1966) are worthwhile non-fiction. Good study: B. Finney: *Christopher Isherwood: A Critical Biography* (1979).

JARRELL, Randall (1914–65)
American poet

Jarrell taught poetry and creative writing, and his critical writings (*Poetry and the Age*, 1953; *A Sad Heart at the Supermarket*, 1962; *The Third Book of Criticism*, 1969; *Kipling, Auden and Co.*, 1979) are perceptive, dogmatic and fascinating. His satirical novel *Pictures from an Institution* (1954) is a warmly funny account of a small American college: Dr Rosenbaum the advanced composer, President Robbins and his wife, and Gertrude the tortured novelist are rounded comic characters, their humanity thrusting from the page. This novel achieves what Jarrell's poetry sometimes misses: an unselfconscious balance between feeling and form. Many of his 1930s poems, for example, are too schematic to make their full effect: the structure is rather obviously that of specific observation followed by generalized reflection, and Jarrell the narrator can seem too detached from the reality of his subjects, too aware that he is 'making poetry' out of what he sees. In the poems of the Second World War ('Pilots, Man Your Planes' is magnificent) he was able to put himself into the experience, to see the experience in himself, and this true involvement warms all his later work. The collections *Losses* (1948) and *The Woman at the Washington Zoo* (1960) show him at his most consistent: supple lines, uncluttered imagery, poise and resonance of thought – at his best, he is the equal of *Rilke. This untitled poem (1965, first published in *The Complete Poems*, 1969) distils his essence:

The old orchard in the middle of the forest
Through which, six years ago, I walked in misery,
My beggar's-lice-streaked trousers wet with the dew of dawn,
Is a road now, and some houses, and two apple trees,
And I am no longer miserable.

Jarrell's other publications include translations of Chekhov's *Three Sisters* (1969) and Goethe's *Faust* (1974; 1978), and several children's books including the outstanding *The Animal Family* (1965). Good critical assessment: S. Ferguson: *The Poetry of Jarrell* (1971).

JARRY, Alfred: see page 491.

JONES, David (1895–1974)
British poet and artist

Discovered by *Eliot ('I was deeply moved . . . work of genius . . .'), admired by *Auden (as the author of 'very probably the finest long poem written in English this century'), Jones remains for many readers a bafflingly difficult poet. *In Parenthesis* (1937) is a book-length meditation on the experience and spiritual meaning of the First World War; *Anathemata* (1952) is an equally long examination of spirituality in the condition of 20th-century humanity, what Jones calls 'one's own thing . . . part and parcel of the Western Christian *res*'. Each line comes garlanded with footnotes, on matters as diverse (and central to Jones's meaning) as Platonism, Gnosticism, Welsh oral poetry and the anthropological byways of Frazer's *The Golden Bough*. The language itself is a mixture of bardic rhetoric, *Kiplingesque 'common speech' (Jones's Tommies stand next in line to Kipling's Indian volunteers) and *Joycean polysyllables and neologisms, the Dead Sea fruit of *Finnegans Wake*. For the ordinary reader, the problem is that when you've spent the necessary minutes disentangling the meanings and pondering the implications of such lines as 'The lord Cunedda/*conditor noster*/*filius Aeterni*, son of Padarn Red Pexa, son of Tacitus,/came south over the same terrain . . .' you're very often left wondering if it was worth the effort: after the notes, the text often seems pure bathos. And yet clever poets like Eliot and Auden thought Jones a clever poet. He was also an artist (of fine-lined, explicit work blending Chagall-like mysticism with the etiolated draughtsmanship of Nicholson) and a calligrapher; this graphic work may, in the end, outlive his poetry.

Jones's other published poems are *The Wall* (1955); *The Sleeping Lord* (1974); *The Dying Gaul* (1978). Helpful guide: R. Hague: *Commentary on the Anathemata* (1977). Fascinating conversations and letters: W. L. Blisset: *The Long Conversation: A Memoir of David Jones* (1981).

JOYCE, James (1882–1941)
Irish novelist

Few other 20th-century authors have proved such a don's delight. Joyce's books offer professional explainers almost unlimited opportunities for work: hardly a sentence (indeed, in *Finnegans Wake*, 1939, hardly a word) fails to benefit from a learned note, and the books grow in stature and intellectual fascination the more you read about them. A typical passage, the discussion in *Ulysses* (1922) which takes place in Barney Kiernan's Bar between Bloom (the novel's Jewish protagonist), a nationalist, anti-Semitic Citizen and assorted other speakers, requires knowledge of, among other things, Irish history and the politics of the 1900s, Roman Catholic liturgy, Darwinism, the Polyphemus episode from Homer's *Odyssey*, alchemy, numerous medieval heresies about the Holy Family (and their Jesuitical refutations), and a smattering of at least seven languages. (This section is comparatively straightforward, in terms of narrative: others require syntactical and linguistic explanation as well.) The question is whether such scholarly treasures are also riches for the ordinary reader – does the conversation in Kiernan's Bar make coherent sense (or pointful lack of sense) as you read it, or is it merely an impressive gallimaufry, the pickings of one man's brilliant but overheated brain?

From the layperson's point of view (and leaving aside Joyce's collection of straightforward short stories, *Dubliners*, 1914, elegant vignettes of Dublin life), the most accessible book is *A Portrait of the Artist as a Young Man* (1916). This is an autobiographical novel (based, in part, on the earlier, unfinished *Stephen Hero*), an account of the education and spiritual growth of a sensitive, intellectual boy in the last twenty years of the 19th century. It has its complexities – an acquaintance with the Greek myth of Daedalus and the intricacies of Jesuitical religious teaching will enhance enjoyment – but by and large it is perfectly clear at each moment what Joyce is telling us and what sort of people his characters are. The unfolding of Stephen's character, his growth to maturity as he examines and sheds one by one the influences of both environment and education (influences which, for all his rejection, are none the less forming him: the book is strong on anguished irony) is as engrossing and convincing as that of the boy Marcel in the first part of *À la recherche du temps perdu* – and, like Proust's account, it makes its effect by the observation and meticulous description of those tiny events (the sound of a plopping gas-jet, the feel of mud on a playing-field, the smart of being unjustly smacked, the ecstasy of confession and absolution) which both form Stephen himself and link his humanity to ours. Joyce's other books impress; *A Portrait of the Artist as a Young Man* has the power to move as well. (It also contains, as they do not – save for Molly Bloom – sensitively imagined and sympathetic female characters. Stephen's world is not yet circumscribed by Guinness, political and religious hair-splitting and, oddly, literature

– all areas reserved in Joyce's later work for men, leaving women chiefly to wait on their backs with their legs apart.)

Ulysses is about the mundane events of a single day in 1904: the characters progress somewhat aimlessly from bed to privy to work to pub to brothel and back to bed. But its Odyssey, its epic journey, is through those characters' minds and memories: every moment of the day is enriched by associations and conjectures. In structure, *Ulysses* parodies twenty-three sections from Homer's *Odyssey* (Joyce however ends with the Penelope section, making no use of the final battle with the suitors or the reconciliation between the world Odysseus left and what he has become: unlike Odysseus, Bloom does not grow, but is displayed, piece by piece, for our attention). The opening depicts Stephen Dedalus as Telemachus; Molly's operatic audition in the Ormond Hotel is based on the story of the Sirens; the Nighttown sequence draws on Homer's Circe episode, and so on. As the book proceeds, and we become more and more familiar with Bloom's habits of mind, the language becomes ever richer and more fragmented: half-sentences, words which collapse and coalesce as we take them in, puns and distortions of every kind. The over-riding influence is Urquhart's 'translation' (re-creation) of Rabelais, but every other kind of literature is used as well, from trashy romantic magazines (in the Nausicaa sequence, the seaside scene involving Gerty MacDowell and her teenage friends) to the stream-of-consciousness case-histories of Freud (most notably in Molly Bloom's soliloquy which ends the book).

Not all of *Ulysses'* richness is apparent at first glance. If it is – as many claim – the greatest novel of the century, that is because it grows in depth and fascination with each re-reading: it is a book of infinitely self-renewing promise, consistently fulfilled. Whether this is also true of *Finnegans Wake* is dubious. In essence, the book is an extension of the method of Molly Bloom's soliloquy: in 600 pages it shows us the dreams and nightmares of one man, H. C. Earwicker, in a single night. Its language is an Alhambra of puns, sound-play, rhythmic virtuosity and syntactical dislocation. A typical sentence reads 'When every Klitty of a scolderymeid shall hold every yard-scullion's right to stimm her uprecht for whimsoever, whether on privates, whether in publics.' This is clever and has meaning (once you tease it out) – but what in the end are we really experiencing more than a dazzling, heartless show whose only point is its technique? Joyce was nearly blind for most of the book's composition, and had to carry large portions of it in his head until his amanuenses could catch up with his inspiration, a method of composition from which sound gains but unity suffers. Just as avant-garde critics sometimes claim that if you study and understand every permutation of every note-row in 12-note music, the whole musical fabric becomes clear, so with *Finnegans Wake* total dedication can mean total comprehension. But for readers who simply want to absorb themselves in the experience (as one can with *Proust or *Mann, say, even at their most difficult), the book remains an unfulfilling read. (For determined postulants, *Burgess's *A Shorter Finnegans Wake*, 1966, which cuts the book by half and also supplies paragraphs of guidance and explanation, is a useful introduction.)

Letters (1957–66). Good on the man: R. Ellmann: *James Joyce* (rev. edn 1982); B. Bradley: *James Joyce's Schooldays* (1982); good introductions to the work: A. Burgess: *Here Comes Everybody/Re Joyce* (1965); M. J. C. Hodgart: *James Joyce: A Student's Guide* (1978).

KAFKA, Franz (1883–1924)
Czech writer

After Kafka's death his manuscripts were not burnt (as he had requested), but were put in order and published by Max Brod, as an act of self-conscious piety to his dead friend's genius. Next, so far as the English-speaking reader is concerned, they were given a dry and witless translation by Edwin and Willa Muir, who also treated Kafka from the start as an object of reverence rather than familiarity. The result is that we still have a false impression of him as an unsmiling, surrealist neurotic, the haunted, thin-faced invalid shown in the usual jacket-photograph rather than the man who reputedly fell about with laughter as he read his stories to his friends. If Leacock or Thurber were translated without humour into German, similar results would be achieved.

In fact Kafka belongs in a robust tradition of surrealist humour in Russia and Europe (one seldom accorded its proper due). His nearest equivalents are Gogol (especially in such stories as *The Nose*, in which a nose takes on an independent, opinionated life of its own), Goncharov (whose hero Oblomov is alienated from the pressure of the mundane world in exactly the way of Kafka's K., except that he causes his own alienation by simply refusing to get out of bed) and *Hašek, whose absurd functionaries and terrifying bureaucracies come from the very world of Kafka's Castle and Kafka's Court. Kafka's hero tilts at windmills with the same doomed doggedness as Don Quixote; his bureaucrats split exactly the same hairs as those in Rabelais' *Pantagruel*; the absurd logic of his hero's harassment is precisely that of *Heller's US Air Force, *Grass's Women's Tribunal, or the whole ambience in Ionesco and the other Absurd dramatists. Kafka the author is not a lonely outsider: he is a central figure in a vigorous and attractively subversive tradition.

His humour is most apparent in his three long works, *The Trial* (1925), *The Castle* (1926) and *America* (1927). In *The Trial* Joseph K. is arrested one morning 'although he had done nothing wrong' but is then allowed to return to the boring routine of his normal life until, with equal abruptness, he is taken from his bed on a later morning and executed. (He is by now convinced of his own guilt, since the Court is not known for making mistakes – though he is ignorant of any crime save possibly that of being alive itself.) The arrest, and his attempts to bring his case to trial and so pin it down, colour and define his life, hitherto as bland as that of the Belgian clerks in Magritte's surrealist paintings. It is like a negative image of religious faith, proposing as many questions as it answers; it is horrible and horrifying, a nightmare fleshed. But it is also absurd. We are made to feel always that if K. had had a shred of humour, if he had only once said, like Alice, 'Why, you're nothing but a pack of cards', the whole edifice would have blown away like mist. (In*Nabokov's *Invitation to a Beheading* the hero finally does just this: he throws up his hands in exasperation and embraces death.) In the same way, K.'s attempts to win official recognition for his post as Land Surveyor in *The Castle* have been described as a parable of the 'search for grace'; but again, his dogged battering on official doors which turn out to have been open all the time and to lead nowhere, and his absurd sexual and domestic adventures – e.g. the brilliant scene in which he sets up house in a school gymnasium, trying to brew coffee and dress while the children mill about waiting for a lesson – are hilarious just as much as they are hopeless. Karl's picaresque adventures in a fantasy America (a pilgrimage of the soul?) are the embodiment of every adolescent's dream of a country paved with gold, dreams to which the hero clings despite being patronized, bullied and cheated at every turn. Karl is a farce hero in all but name, cousin to the desperate innocents in Feydeau or Travers, though insulated from their panic by total unawareness of what is being done to him. (His life as a lift-boy is one of the most satisfyingly funny episodes in 20th-century literature.)

Even so, it must be said that Kafka is far more than just a humorist, and that the three long books (none finished at his death) are not his sharpest or most typical work. His short stories are bleaker, sparer and far more barbed. In the novels, the heroes' simple innocence is a guarantee of humanity and of the phoenix nature of human hope; in the stories, where characterization is deliberately reduced, there is little humanity and far less hope. Gregor Samsa (the man in 'Metamorphosis', 1915, who wakes up one morning to find he has turned into a giant beetle) is treated by his family with terror and hatred: even his sister, who seems still to love him, rejoices harshly at his death. The creature in 'The Burrow' (1931, one of Kafka's most haunting works) builds a system of runways and tunnels so perfect and so impregnable that he finds himself being subsumed into it, taken over and engulfed by the magnificence of his own creation. The commandant in 'In the Penal Colony' (1919) chooses ecstatic death at the hands of his own punishment machine (a harrow whose needles write each criminal's crime in his flesh, deeper and deeper until he dies) rather than see it broken up – and the machine's malfunction gives him death but denies him ecstasy. 'The Great Wall of China' (1931) and 'The Giant Mole' (1931) are about humanity's erection of useless and illusory edifices (actual walls, or walls of rumour) which, if they are ever allowed to crumble, crush all reason for hope from human life.

If Kafka's themes are baffling and appalling, events inexorably circling round themselves with the logic of dreams not life, his style is notably

clear and smooth: his work draws you on, is by no means hard to read.
Many of his stories (e.g. 'The Vulture', 'The Married Couple', 'The
Knock at the Manor Gate' and 'The Proclamation', all published in an
exemplary new translation by Malcolm Pasley in *Kafka's Shorter Works*,
1971) have the same clarity of exposition and wide-eyed inconsequentiality as the dreams reported to Freud and recorded in his case histories.
Kafka's *Diaries* (1948), essential for the understanding of his fiction,
exhibit the same bland lunacy, the lunatics' (or humorists') conviction
that theirs is the only true logic in the world. The paradox – as delicious
as it is terrifying – is that as 'modern life' proceeds, many people have
come to regard his writings less as fantasies than as accurate predictions.
But if life is absurd, can we not do what Kafka's heroes never do, and
what *he* did as he read his work, that is, exert free-will and laugh?

Good introduction: A. Thorlby: *Kafka: A Study* (1972). Extraordinary letters, to
the woman who was Kafka's friend and Muse during the writing of *The Trial* and
'Metamorphosis': *Letters to Felice* (ed. Heller and Born, 1973).

KAZANTZAKIS, Nikos (1883–1957)
Greek writer

Outside Greece, Kazantzakis is best known for two novels of peasant
life. *The Life and Politics of Zorba the Greek* (1946) is a fictionalization
of the ethical conflict in humanity between Apollonian asceticism and
Dionysian earthiness – and the Dionysian principle, exemplified by the
thigh-slapping, ouzo-swilling leading character, wins every bout.
(Another, less touted, episode, the stoning to death by the villagers of a
prostitute, shows a darker aspect of the same dilemma: humanity's fear
of the irrational pleasure-principle.) Schematic demonstrations of
morality also appear in *Christ Recrucified/The Greek Passion* (1954), in
which rehearsals for a village passion-play arouse in the participants the
same kind of impulses and actions as those of the characters they portray;
the central character, the priest-producer who tries to keep the elements
in check, is at once (and memorably) a version of the objective narrator-
figure (the gospel-writer; Kazantzakis), and, as he gets drawn into events,
of Pontius Pilate.

Readers encouraged by these full-blooded novels to explore Kazantzakis's work further will find it resistant to translation. He used an
uncouth form of demotic Greek (to say nothing, on occasion, of Cretan
dialect), and his plots and characters are far from the easy Greece of the
tourist circuit. (It is as if a French writer confined himself to Provence
and Provençal: Daudet's *Tartarin de Tarascon* is a near analogue.) The
exceptions are a group of powerful verse plays on Biblical or allegorical
themes, of which the best are *Melissa* (1939), *Julian the Apostate* (1945),
Kapodistrias (1946) and *Sodom And Gomorrha/Burn Me to Ashes* (first
produced 1963), and a vast epic poem, *The Odyssey* (1938), a 33,333-line
sequel to Homer exploring Odysseus's memory of his adventures, and his

reflections on their effects on his beliefs and character. This work is not only a 20th-century masterpiece (as grand as, say, *The Magic Mountain* or *Ulysses*); it is one of only half a dozen or so world epics (Virgil's *Aeneid* is another) to use Homer's form for their own purposes with distinction and to descant effectively on Homer's original.

KIPLING, Rudyard (1865–1936)
British story-writer and poet

Just as Elgar's music often seems to show the private sensibility behind bluff Edwardian certainties, so Kipling's best work lays bare the framework of everyday lives behind the British Imperial façade. His own classlessness (he was a lower-middle-class boy elevated by talent to the cultural bourgeoisie), his knowledge of Hindustani and his extensive travels as a journalist (he visited India, China, Japan, Africa, Australia and America) reinforced his already warm feeling for the underdog: he always writes better of common soldiers, coolies, servants and children than of their employers/elders/betters. At times (e.g. in the ballad-and-music-hall-influenced verse of *Barrack-Room Ballads*, 1892) this sympathy trapped him into a blend of naïvety and bitterness – the sense of class betrayal is strong, and prescient of later First-World-War writers – which patronizes his subjects. But his 'low life' short stories are excellent, filled with a journalist's brevity and eye for telling detail: the best collections are *Plain Tales from the Hills* (1888), *Actions and Reactions* (1909) and *Debits and Credits* (1926). He wrote well for children (*The Jungle Book*, 1894; *Puck of Pook's Hill*, 1906), less well for adolescents (*Stalky and Co.*, 1899, is one of the bloodiest-minded school yarns ever penned), and for infants with a breath-taking blend of imagination and archness (*Just-So Stories*, 1902). He wrote three novels. *The Light that Failed* (1891) and *Captains Courageous* (1897) are run-of-the-mill, but *Kim* (1901) – about a white boy brought up as a native in India, torn (as Mowgli was, as Kipling was) between his two cultures, and working as a spy for the Raj in a superbly depicted rural India – is outstanding, his masterpiece in any form.

Other good story collections: *The Day's Work* (1898); *Traffics and Discoveries* (1904); *Thy Servant a Dog* (1930); *Limits and Renewals* (1932). Complete *Verse* (1940). His autobiography *Something of Myself* (1937) tells even less than its title promises, and may usefully be supplemented by A. *Wilson: The Strange Ride of Rudyard Kipling* (1977), which is good on his sexual and political ambivalence, and on his increasingly fervent racism. Also of interest: J. A. MacClure: *Kipling and Conrad: The Colonial Fiction* (1982).

KOESTLER, Arthur (1905–83)
Hungarian/British writer

*Orwell and *Sartre not excepted, Koestler was the finest radical writer of the century. His perception was that western civilization is tottering to its end, hastened by barbarian oppressors and by the spineless liberalism of its intellectual defenders. This theme led his writing in two distinct directions. His journalism and fiction deals obsessively with the causes of revolutionary failure; his non-fiction, an examination of humanistic science, both surveys the achievements of past science (notably astronomy, physics, psychology and the natural sciences) and also proposes the re-establishment of a pagan, synthetic and cross-cultural scientific system for human thought, a return to the highroad to progress blocked by organized religion (for Koestler, one of the great oppressive forces) and largely abandoned in Europe since the death of Newton.

Koestler's scientific books (e.g. *The Sleepwalkers*, 1959–60, about ancient and medieval astronomy, *The Ghost in the Machine*, 1967, an attack on scientific and para-scientific reductionism, and *The Case of the Midwife Toad*, 1971, on Kammerer's attempts to duplicate Lamarck's experiments and so to prove his anti-Darwin evolutionary theory), though fascinating to laypeople, have regularly been attacked by specialists as journalism, slick but superficial. No such charge has been levelled at his political writing (save by doctrinaire Marxists), perhaps because his views and perceptions here seem closer to general experience. The heart of this work, a trilogy of novels about failed revolutionaries, was prescriptive reading during the cold-war 1950s. *The Gladiators* (1939), about Spartacus and the Roman slave-revolts of the first century BC, tackles the theme of the rise to power and inevitable relapse into dictatorship of a charismatic revolutionary leader. *Darkness at Noon* (1940), Koestler's masterpiece, about the arrest, moral collapse and show-trial of one of the original Bolshevik revolutionaries, is a savage indictment of all that Soviet communism became under Stalin. In *Arrival and Departure* (1943) a one-time revolutionary gradually comes to realize that his whole life's struggle has been the result of self-deception, of delusion masquerading as idealism.

Koestler's collected work is plentiful (more than thirty books); his influence on European radical thought was greater, for half a century, than that of almost any other individual; for many politicians and scientists now in their prime, he is (to use *Eliot's phrase) 'what we know', the originator of patterns of thought now taken for granted. Indeed, he is in danger of becoming dated. Like *Solzhenitsyn, he prophesied the collapse of hope into decadence, and was not heeded; like *Wells, he moved in the course of a fifty-year writing career from idealism to despair, from prescriptions for humankind to threnodies. His non-fiction is fascinating, his fiction moving and thought-provoking; he is an essential writer.

The most useful of Koestler's other books is a 900-page digest of his lifetime's writings, *Bricks to Babel* (1980): equipped with a running commentary on his view now of what he said then, this eclipses his volumes of actual autobiography. Of his two other novels, the best is *Thieves in the Night* (1946), about the struggle for a Jewish homeland. Good interim biography: I. Hamilton: *Koestler: A Biography* (1982).

LAGERKVIST, Pär (1891–1974)
Swedish writer

Lagerkvist's reputation outside Scandinavia was boosted by the Nobel Prize in 1951 – and the highbrow distinction such an award suggests was almost immediately undercut by the pasteboard epic film made of his novel *Barabbas* (1950), in which Anthony Quinn as Barabbas roared round the Roman world in search of spiritual salvation. The dichotomy (ascetism or barnstorming?) is present in most of Lagerkvist's work. His earliest success was with drama: he wrote an influential treatise on non-realism (*Modern Theatre*, 1918), and a dozen plays in an expressionist, symbolist idiom like that of Strindberg's *Dream Play*. (The best are *The Difficult Hour*, 1918, and *Heaven's Secret*, 1919; *Modern Theatre: Seven Plays*, 1966, also contains an essay summing up his later view of this art.)

In the 1930s, Lagerkvist began experimenting with philosophical allegory, the presentation of ethical argument in a particularly austere, spare style. He first did this in plays (e.g. *The Man Without a Soul*, 1936, and *Victory in the Dark*, 1939), but then used it in novels – and found exactly the form he needed. His fiction is far from the mainstream of Scandinavian writing (of which the lengthy Martinsson and Undset are examples); its tone and style are more like Bergman's films, both his medieval allegories and his anguished dissections of modern marriage. Lagerkvist's masterpieces in this style are *The Dwarf* (1944), the pitiless study of a stunted soul in a heartless medieval court, and *The Sibyl* (1956), the memoirs of a peasant girl chosen to be the Sibyl in ancient Delphi, to experience (and agonizingly to seek to understand) the torment and ecstasy of union with God. It is in these two books, no more than 400 pages altogether, that Lagerkvist's world stature becomes plain: more than all his other work, they justify his Nobel Prize.

The best of Lagerkvist's other novels are the autobiographical *Guest of Reality* (1925), about growing up in Calvinist 19th-century Sweden, and *The Death of Ahasuerus* (1960). Other plays include *Midsummer Night's Dream in the Work-house* (1941), *The Philosopher's Stone* (1947) and *Let Man Live* (1949). There is also poetry (*Anguish*, 1916), and there are short stories (*The Eternal Smile and Other Stories*, ed. Vowles, 1954). Readers who enjoy his bony style may find echoes of it in the novels of the American Imagist H.D. (i.e. Hilda Doolittle), especially *Hedylus* (1928); those drawn to the Scandinavian clarity of *Guest of Reality* will appreciate Tove Jansson's *The Summer Book* (1972), about a little girl and her grandmother spending summer on a lonely Finnish island.

LARDNER, Ring (1885–1933)
American story-writer

Magisterial praise from Edmund Wilson – among other things, he said that Lardner's use of language was 'unexcelled, perhaps masterly', and asked 'what bell would he not ring, if he set out to give us the works?' –

has done very little to help Lardner's reputation. Could any newspaper-man, any short-story writer, any humorist, live up to such hyperbole? Lardner's speciality, fictional letters revealing the slobbishness or ignorance of the writer (e.g. *You Know Me, Al: A Busher's Letters*, 1916), can hardly have been what Wilson meant, though they have since been much imitated: with the effortless ease of most humorous journalism, they pass out of the mind as soon as read.

However, Lardner also wrote humorous short stories, pinning his America as firmly on the page as Twain did his or Leacock did his Canada. His style, laconic, full of dialogue and the prose equivalent of the cinema's 'jump-cut' (i.e. points made by rapid and startling juxtaposition, omitting reams of exposition), was an inspiration both to literary heavyweights like *Hemingway and to masters of the stage monologue like Fanny Brice or Woody Allen. His collection-titles give the contents away: *Gullible's Travels* (1917); *Own Your Own Home* (1919); *The Real Dope* (1919); *The Big Town* (1921). This is the world of Buster Keaton's dogged, go-getting comedy, with the physical slapstick replaced by wordplay. In the early 1920s, thanks to his failing health (he was tubercular and alcoholic), Lardner's writing faltered. He wrote two stage shows (*Elmer the Great*, 1928; *June Moon*, with Kaufman of Kaufman and Hart, 1930), and polished and republished his earlier work. To say, as Wilson did, that *How to Write Short Stories: With Samples* (1924), one of his best collections, is 'a series of studies of ordinary American types almost equal to those of Sherwood Anderson and Sinclair Lewis' is preposterous. Lardner is a funny, perceptive writer, great to read – and that's enough.

Good collections: *Round Up: The Stories/Collected Short Stories* (1941); *The Ring Lardner Reader* (1963). Autobiography: *The Story of a Wonder Man* (1927). Biography: J. Yardley: *Ring: A Biography of Lardner* (1977).

LAWRENCE, David Herbert (1885–1930)
English author

Lawrence was a compulsive communicator, always urgent with news, opinion and comment. His letters (*Collected Letters*, 1962) and critical writings (*Selected Essays*, 1950; *Selected Literary Criticism*, 1956) reveal the fascinating rashness of his character: he always had something to say, considered or not; he wore his heart (and soul, and mind) on his sleeve, with the result that the reader can sometimes mistake raucousness for shallowness. The propaganda aspect of his art is, perhaps, least apparent in his poetry (*Collected Poems*, 2 vols., 1964): here, concision of thought and language combine with his outstanding ability to invent images to produce dense, deeply felt verse packed with moral metaphor. (The poems in *Birds, Beasts and Flowers*, 1923, are outstanding.) Concision works well for him in his short stories, too (*Complete Short Stories*, 1955): because their length allows readers time to catch their breath, they are

perhaps the best introduction to his work. (The finest single volume is
England, My England, 1922.) His plays (*Complete Plays*, 1965) have been
occasionally revived. They have a 'poetic' view of ordinary people's lives
which is reminiscent of O'Casey's, but they lack tension – his gift is for
reflective narrative, not for action or dialogue.

Lawrence's thirteen novels crown his work. They are uneven, and often
flawed by strident authorial intervention. He can never let the characters
alone, to express a moral or philosophical point of view in what they are
and what they do; he has to take the reader on one side and preach,
whether the sermon fits its narrative context or not. In a way, this is a
dynamic fault. Our irritation arises not because Lawrence himself or his
characters are bores: we want to know what *he* has to say as much as
what *they* will do, and when conflict arises between creator and creation
we are torn, and do not know which way to look. The novels of the 1920s
(especially *The Plumed Serpent*, 1926, and *Lady Chatterley's Lover*, 1928)
are particularly prone to this failing, simultaneous over-writing of
incident and message and underwriting of character. His best novels are
The White Peacock (1911, his first) and the three so-called 'Nottingham'
books: *Sons and Lovers* (1913), *The Rainbow* (1915) and *Women in Love*
(1920). They have consistency; the autobiographical element is integral
to the characters, not irrelevant; the events articulate the themes; the
characters, and especially the landscapes, are carefully and finely drawn.
Lawrence takes strength from earlier novelists like George Eliot and
Thomas Hardy; his female characters (much more credible than any of
his men) have a depth and sensitivity reminiscent of those of James. In
two of the Brangwen girls in particular (Anna in *The Rainbow*, Ursula in
Women in Love), he pulled off the clinching novelist's trick: they become
'real', draw the reader into their wholeness and tell us things about
ourselves. There are few passages in 20th-century literature better than
the scene in *The Rainbow* (Chapter 6) where pregnant Anna dances
naked before a full-length mirror: Lawrence's views of the mother as
nature and of nature as a mother are embodied in a scene as touching as
it is startling, and given conviction by detachment and restraint in the
writing.

Mr Moon (1984) is a recently discovered comic fictionalization of the first months
of Lawrence's marriage, chiefly for devotees. Good biography: H. T. Moore: *The
Priest of Love* (1974). Good introductions: F. Kermode: *Lawrence* (1973); P.
Hobsbawm: *A Reader's Guide to D. H. Lawrence* (1981). A new, complete edition
of the letters is in progress, edited by G. J. Zyfaruk and J. T. Boulton: two volumes
are so far published.

Le CARRÉ, John (born 1931)
English novelist

Le Carré began his career with two elegant, straightforward murder
mysteries, *Call for the Dead* (1961) and *A Murder of Quality* (1962). His

third book, *The Spy Who Came In from the Cold* (1963), was an international best-seller. The times were propitious (the Philby spy-affair, the 'hot line' and the first test-ban treaty were headline news); the book's vision of spies as the weary functionaries of a stumbling bureaucracy seemed more in tune with our distracted times (President Kennedy was assassinated in November 1963) than did the glamorous cavortings of the James Bond school. The chief reason for the book's success, however, was excellence: it was an absorbing story crisply told. Le Carré's next novel, *The Looking-Glass War* (1965), maintained this excellence. But in his later books he has become increasingly the victim of critical overpraise, writing up to other people's expectations. He is not a major novelist who just happens to use the genre form, but a good genre novelist whose wider aspirations fight the boundaries of his chosen genre and tend, more and more, to lose. In particular, *A Small Town in Germany* (1968) and *Tinker, Tailor, Soldier, Spy* (1974), with their endlessly convoluted puzzles, mazes which lead nowhere, are not (as Le Carré's admirers claim) a devastating reflection of sterile reality; they lack depth of philosophy and of character; they are pretentious, deceptive and boring. In *The Naive and Sentimental Lover* (1971) Le Carré dropped the framework of espionage and achieved some depth: the book is a chilling anatomy of a successful man at loggerheads with inner emptiness. This book and *The Spy Who Came In from the Cold* are Le Carré's best – and while they are not 'great', they are very good indeed.

Le Carré's other books include *The Honourable Schoolboy* (1977), *The Little Drummer Girl* (1983), on urban terrorism rather than spying, and *Smiley's People* (1980), which, together with *Tinker, Tailor, Soldier, Spy*, was republished in a bumper 1,000-page omnibus edition, a true addict's delight, *The Quest for Karla* (1982).

LESSING, Doris (born 1919)
Zimbabwean / British novelist

Use of a natural, 'as-told-to' narrative style gives Lessing's novels a feeling of immediacy: they read more like autobiography than art. In many of her books, this feeling is increased by the subject-matter: her output is, in the broad view, the *bildungsroman* of an outspoken Marxist, feminist creative artist growing up in colonial Africa and then in seedy 1960s Britain. *The Grass is Singing* (1950) and the novellas in *Five* (1953) are concerned largely with Africa, and dismal Rhodesian politics are the subject of her acid non-fiction memoir *Going Home* (1957). Her most ambitious exploration of these themes is the five-novel sequence *Children of Violence* (*Martha Quest*, 1952; *A Proper Marriage*, 1954; *A Ripple from the Storm*, 1958; *Landlocked*, 1965; *The Four-Gated City*, 1969), an examination of the life and circumstances of her heroine/alter ego Martha Quest, similar in scope and style (and, her detractors say, in unsmiling length) to Sartre's novel-sequence about racked left-wing intellectuals,

The Roads to Freedom. This sequence, together with *The Golden Notebook* (1962), a *Woolfish novel (its style a sequence of interlocking narrations) on feminism and the torments of the liberal conscience, is her finest work. Since 1979 she has written an ambitious science fiction allegory, *Canopus in Argos: Archives*. Though set in the far future, it is primarily concerned with the Sartrean themes of the nature of evil and individual freedom of conscience; its five volumes are *Shikasta* (1979); *The Marriage Between Zones Three, Four and Five* (1980); *The Sirian Experiments* (1981); *The Making of the Representative for Planet 8* (1982); and *The Sentimental Agents in the Volyen Empire* (1983).

Lessing's other publications include pithy short stories (assembled in two volumes of *Collected Stories*, 1979), the novels *Briefing for a Descent into Hell* (1971) and *The Summer Before Dark* (1973), and the non-fiction *In Pursuit of the English* (1960) and *Memoirs of a Survivor* (1974). Her *The Diaries of Jane Somers* (1984) is the fruit of an odd literary hoax: she published two novels under a pseudonym and was then somewhat disingenuously surprised at their poor reception. Good, brief guide: L. Sage: *Doris Lessing* (1983).

LEWIS, Percy Wyndham (1884–1957)
British writer and artist

Lewis thought of himself as a wayward genius, a 20th-century amalgam of Gillray and Swift, a major irritant; his enemies thought of him as a fascist pest. He trained as an artist, espoused every anti-bourgeoisism of the 1910s, and with his friend *Pound started a polemical magazine, *Blast (A Review of the Great English Vortex)*, whose launch coincided with the beginning of the First World War and which survived for only two issues. Its erratic typography – it looked like the messages lunatics assemble from snipped-up magazines to taunt the police – startled those of the bourgeoisie who bought it at least as much as its contents, which were chiefly endorsements of Poundian poetry and of a new art-style Lewis called Vorticism. This was the child of a (none too harmonious) marriage between cubism and futurism: angular, violent pictures laid out in a harsh geometry of triangles, cubes and (above all) cones, coloured in flat, matt blocks. It was a short-lived, if strident, style, and produced no master-pieces (though several ugly non-masterpieces by Lewis, such as the Stanley Spencerish *Workshop*, now hang in the Tate Gallery, London); unlike cubism or futurism, it said nothing except how cleverly nihilistic it was, and it now looks as dated as old subway posters. Lewis himself abandoned it after the war, and his art thereafter was in a straightforward Modigliani-like neo-classical style (for example the portraits of Pound, *Eliot and Edith *Sitwell also in the Tate Gallery). By denying himself originality, he discovered his talent.

Lewis had greater success with fiction. Indeed, though few would now claim him as a great painter, some critics regard him as one of the best satirical novelists of the century. His simplest book is one of his earliest (and exorcises, perhaps, his own artistic frustration): *Tarr* (1918), about a blocked painter, is as good on artistic creativity as Michael Ayrton's *The Maze-Maker* or Stuart Evans's more recent *The Caves of Alienation*. (In their different ways, Ayrton – once Lewis's amanuensis – and Evans are the only subsequent British creators to show any marked Lewis influence.) *The Apes of God* (1930) is Lewis's funniest book, a satirical demolition of English literary life, and particularly of the Bloomsbury cult. Other lively novels include *The Snooty Baronet* (1932), *Rotting Hill* (1951) and the outstanding *The Revenge for Love* (1937, rev. 1982), a knockabout political farce about the events leading up to the Spanish civil war. Huxleyan wit also infuses Lewis's unfinished tetralogy *The Human Age*. Its first volume, *Childermass* (1928, rev. 1956), depicts the souls of the dead massing for judgement, like troops milling across an empty plain, in the after-life, and finding that their judge is a deformed, malignant Punch-and-Judy-man, for whom the Apocalypse is a private Mardi Gras. The work was continued, nearly thirty years later, with *Malign Fiesta* (1955) and *Monstre gai* (1955), which again depict the after-life as a Becketty, Fellinian distortion of our present, unpleasant and pointless reality. (Lewis died before writing the fourth novel, which was to draw together the threads of his denunciation; the three surviving books are a huge and philosophically cumbersome torso.)

In addition to this and other fiction, Lewis produced dozens of letters, essays, pamphlets and book-length diatribes, all putting forward his awkward, hopeless view of 20th-century life. The tone is furious and denunciatory, as if he were sitting on a goad; the books were – and are – as hard to like as his Vorticist art. He said what he had to say much better in his satires, and particularly in *The Human Age*.

Lewis's other works include the satirical novel *The Red Priest* (1956) and the short stories *Unlucky for Pringle* (1973). He wrote lively autobiography (e.g. *Blasting and Bombardiering*, 1937; *Rude Assignment*, 1950), and two autobiographical novels, *The Vulgar Streak* (1941, rev. 1974) and *Self-Condemned* (1954). A good selection of his non-fiction is *Wyndham Lewis: An Anthology of His Prose* (1969). *Collected Poems and Plays* (1978). Good on the art: W. Michel: *Wyndham Lewis: Paintings and Drawings* (1971). Good on the man: J. Meyers: *The Enemy: A Biography of Wyndham Lewis* (1980). Sharp critical essays: J. Meyers (ed.): *Wyndham Lewis: A Revaluation* (1980).

LEWIS, Sinclair (1885–1951)
American novelist

For a time, in the 1920s, it seemed as if no aspect of contemporary American life had any validity until it was made the subject of one of Lewis's exhaustive documentary satires. His freshness, and his eagerness to attack every species of sacred cow from religion and the 'negro question' to the American home, caused outrage and procured success; he was taken to be the most honest (and some said greatest) American writer since Twain; like his friend Mencken, he acquired a reputation for plain-speaking thanks to a combination of trenchant cleverness and downright rudeness. *Main Street* (1920) is about hypocritical, cultureless Mid-Western life, and shows the apple-cheeked home-town folks of American legend as bigoted fools. *Babbitt* (1922) depicts twenty-four hours in the life of a smug, empty-headed city businessman who has been on every Dale Carnegie course, remembered everything and learned nothing. *Arrowsmith* (1925, Lewis's best book) is set among doctors; *Elmer Gantry* (1927) attacks evangelical religion; *Dodsworth* (1929) is about an honest American seeking happiness (that is, culture and a second wife) abroad. After *Dodsworth* the standard of Lewis's work began a decline accelerated by alcoholism. Of his following dozen novels, only *It Can't Happen Here* (1935), on creeping fascism, has anything like the quality of his earlier books; the rest are trash. The reason is that he was utterly dependent on his 'ear' (especially for dialogue); when this failed him, the weakness of his plotting and characterization was clearly shown. Even his 1920s novels now live less because of their literary quality (debatable) or humour (dated) than because of their fly-in-amber description of their chosen worlds: reading them is like watching the flickering newsreels of a vanished and unlikely age.

Selected Short Stories (1935). Good anthologies: *The Man from Main Street: Selected Essays and Other Writings* (ed. Maule and Kane, 1953); *From Main Street to Stockholm: Letters of Lewis 1919–1930* (ed. Smith, 1952).

LONDON, Jack (1876–1916)
American writer

A busy adolescence (he was, successively and for short periods, a tramp, a convict and a seal-hunter; he took part in the Klondike gold rush and came home $4.50 better off) gave London the background and material for his fiction; avid reading of Twain (especially *Huckleberry Finn*) and of *Kipling (especially *Plain Tales from the Hills*) gave him his style. In 1899 he settled down to write 1,000 words a day, and by 1902 he was earning upwards of $2,000 a week. Much of his output was hackwork, magazine stories and serials in which he professedly sought to do for North America what Kipling had done for India; but at his best he had a vision of human beings proving themselves by courage, and a laconic style, which set standards in American fiction for three generations. His most famous books, *The Call of the Wild* (1903), about a tame dog stolen and brutalized in the Klondike, and *White Fang* (1906), about the love-hate relationship of a dog and his several owners, show human beings as the dismal end of a brutal, bloody evolutionary chain; they also deal more sensitively and convincingly with the feelings of animals than the works of any other writer except Henry Williamson. (The sensitivity remains, even so, sleight of hand – for who is to say that animals have 'feelings' at all, let alone those London attributes to them?) His restless view of human nature led him to a Wellsian form of early socialism (tempered by an equally strong belief in the artist-superman, the creative free spirit), best expressed in his horrific account of British slums (*The People of the Abyss*, 1903) and in a savage political novel of the future, *The Iron Heel* (1907), showing Chicago oppressed by a totalitarian dictatorship. These four books are his best – much of the rest is as trashy as Sax Rohmer's *Fu Manchu* series or Edgar Wallace's low-life potboilers – and at his best he is both a fine writer on his own account and a clear forerunner of *Orwell and *Camus (for themes) as well as of *Hemingway (for style).

London published forty-eight books and three plays. Typical of his he-man short stories are those in *Moonface and Other Stories* (1906). Worthwhile novels include *Sea Wolf* (1904), *Martin Eden* (1909) and *John Barleycorn* (1913). *The Kempton-Wace Letters* (1903) is an extraordinary and revealing sequence of letters between London and Anna Strumsky, who decided (so characteristically of their time and artistic class) to experiment with 'making love intellectually, by mail', and soon replaced epistolary passion with physical. Good biographies: Irving Stone: *Sailor on Horseback* (1938); A. Sinclair: *Jack: A Biography of Jack London* (1977).

LORCA, Federico García (1898–1936)
Spanish playwright and poet

Multi-talented – he was musician, actor and painter as well as author – Lorca was at the height of his career when he died in unmysterious circumstances (he was shot by Spanish fascists) but for mysterious reasons (sympathy with the peasants? homosexuality?) at the age of thirty-eight. Since then a legend worthy of a Hollywood biopic has grown up around him: that of the vagabond genius who squanders his talent and snaps his fingers at both life and death. This reputation has inflated the status of his work, which is intensely Spanish and parochial, exploiting folk themes in a bardic, incantatory manner – Synge is a near English-language equivalent. (The crucial importance for his work of folk-poetry is shown by the poems in *Poet in New York*, written in 1930, published in 1940. These are fine enough – surrealist, urban splinters of the jazz age – but uncharacteristic, as unlike his 'natural' (and great) style as, say, Mondrian's *Boogie-Woogie* pictures differed from 'real' Mondrian after he first went to the United States.)

Lorca's early plays include two charming fantasies, *The Butterfly's Evil Spell* (1920) and *The Love of Don Perlimplin and Belisa in the Garden* (1933), and a historical drama about a 19th-century revolutionary martyr, *Mariana Pineda* (1928); there are also interludes, sketches and full-length plays in his 'folk' style. His stage masterpiece is the trilogy *Blood Wedding* (1933), *Yerma* (1934) and *The House of Bernarda Alba* (1936). These plays are tragedies of peasant life in rural surroundings; their evocation of lives bounded by superstition, family ritual and relentless work is matched only by Rossellini's Italian realist films; their rich, poetic prose recalls O'Casey's. Their importance on later theatre (particularly before the mid-1950s, when realistic styles fell out of fashion) cannot be exaggerated: among the authors Lorca influenced were giants like Miller, O'Neill and Tennessee Williams; even Albee's *Who's Afraid of Virginia Woolf?*, from the mid-1960s, owes its theatrical impact as much to Lorcan passion and rhetoric – actors of the time were well used to playing the style, in Lorca's plays themselves – as to its careful use of the conventions of the Absurd.

Lorca's poetry ranges from short lyrics, many in folk-style (*Book of Poems*, 1921; *Songs*, 1927; *Gipsy Ballads*, 1928), to dark, impassioned incantations like *Lament for Ignacio Sanchez Mejias* (1935), apart from the dramatic trilogy his best-known work. He preferred performance to publication, and his poems, like those of Dylan *Thomas, were written primarily for himself to read aloud. The result, as with Thomas's poems, is that unless you respond to their incantatory power, they die. A line like Thomas's 'Do not go gentle into that good night' looks flat on the page, deprived of Thomas's voice; it would look (and sound) flatter still in Spanish. Similarly, the refrain-line of Lorca's *Lament* (which is for a dead bull-fighter), 'A las cinque de las tardes', sounds at once menacing, threnodic and grand in Spanish, with tolling 'a's' and harshly repeated 's's' – whereas its English translation, 'At five in the afternoon', is no more than an invitation to vicarage tea. For reasons such as this, and because of the knowledge of Spanish culture (both literary and folk) needed fully to understand his work, Lorca remains – at least for *estranjeros* – a special taste.

Lorca's other plays include *When Five Years Pass* (1931), *The Frame of Don Cristobal* (1935) and *Dona Rosita the Spinster, or The Language of Flowers* (1935). His other published collection of poems is *The Divan at the Tamarit* (1936). *Sonnets of Dark Love*, a projected collection which, with its echoes of *Rilke, sounds potentially magnificent, was never completed, as was his play *The Public*, begun in 1933. Good collections in English: *Lorca* (1960), a poetry anthology; *Three Tragedies* (1961); *Five Plays* (1963). Good introduction: M. Adams: *García Lorca, Playwright and Poet* (1977).

LOWELL, Robert (1917–77)
American poet

If literature has in the last thirty years been going through a second Alexandrian age, neo-classical rather than neo-romantic, then Lowell is its greatest poet, its Callimachus. His output was not large – a few hundred pages – and the majority of his poems are short. But his images (and these include remembrances of and references to past literature) are complex, intellectual and personal; he wrote them down in language of great concentration – and the result is poetry which grows and branches in the mind. A good, typical example is the opening of 'Terminal Days at Beverley Farm', from a sequence about his dying father in *Life Studies* (1959):

At Beverley Farm, a portly, uncomfortable boulder
bulked in the garden's centre –
an irregular Japanese touch.
After his Bourbon 'old-fashioned', Father,
Bronzed, breezy, a shade too ruddy,
swayed as if on deck-duty
under his six-pointed star-lantern . . .

Verse of that quality calls on the reader not merely for a response, but for intelligence: like Alexandrian poetry (or the poems of those past-haunted Romans Catullus and Horace, Lowell's great masters), its appeal is at once sensual and intellectual – or rather it is, precisely, sensual intellectuality.

Some of Lowell's verse is slight: the poems in *Life Studies* dedicated to Ford, Santayana, Schwartz and Crane, for example, are Audenish *vers d'occasion* ('When the Pulitzers showered on some dope/or screw who flushed our dry mouths out with soap,/few people would consider why I took/to stalking sailors . . .'). But in general his work adds to that technical adroitness a strengthening self-obsession: the neurosis which plagued his life was in his work a liberating and defining force. No one since Keats has equalled the romantic intensity of (say) 'Waking Early Sunday Morning', from *Near the Ocean* (1967): 'O to break loose, like the chinook/salmon jumping and falling back . . .'; no one at all has bettered his raising of autobiography into art in *For the Union Dead* (1964) – 'Returning', 'July in Washington' and 'The Flaw' are three of the steeliest American poems of the century. Many writers have made a career out of rhetorical confession; Lowell's strength is his fastidiousness, which leads him to show us the *context* of each self-portrait, to make himself the emblem or messenger of wider human experience. This is particularly so in *The Dolphin* (1973), where Lowell's own travels, his reading and his marriage are turned (in a sequence of sonnets) into an impressive commentary on those alienated, sensitive figures so prevalent in modern artistic life (and in life at large?), those whom Lowell sees as drunkenly eloquent actors who 'totter off a strewn stage'. (The combined obsession and attraction of this one-sided view of art and life today are typical of his work.)

As well as his original work, Lowell's translations have been much admired – some people even place them above his own poetry, on the grounds that they allow his verbal gifts to flourish without the inhibition of neurosis. He is best at 'imitations' (i.e. free translations) of short lyrics, whether by Horace, Villon, Baudelaire or Montale: the collection *Imitations* (1962), one of his most attractive books of verse of any kind, shows this ability at its peak. In longer works, the quality varies. His translations of Aeschylus (*Prometheus Bound*, 1969; *The Oresteia*, 1979) are full of eye-catching phrases, but seriously misrepresent Aeschylus and are also, literally, unspeakable (the lines die on an actor's lips). His version of Racine's *Phaedra* (1960), on the other hand, and his three verse plays based on stories by Melville and Hawthorne (*The Old Glory*, 1965) show exactly how the difficult task of diffidently but definitively inhabiting someone else's work can best be done.

Selected Poems (1976). Good introduction: J. Crick: *Lowell* (1974). Good account of his life, especially acute on the links between his madness and his creativity: I. Hamilton: *Robert Lowell, a Biography* (1983).

LOWRY, Malcolm (1909–57)
British novelist

Lowry's nearest analogue is the scabrously brilliant Genet of *The Thief's Journal:* that is, he lived an unspeakable life, and turned it into art so stylish that many critics regard him as a genius. Lowry was an alcoholic and a drug-addict. He had a private income (and was classily educated at Cambridge); he spent his life bumming across the world, or holed up in remote parts (fifteen years, for example, in the Canadian wilderness), writing up his experiences, thoughts and hallucinations. Like *Wolfe, he poured out reams of intoxicated, rambling prose, out of which novels were later assembled by Lowry himself or by patient editors. All his work is autobiographical. *Ultramarine* (1933, re-issued 1963) describes his time as a boy-sailor, and at Cambridge; *Lunar Caustic* (1968) is set in the 'drying-out' unit of a New York hospital; *Dark as the Grave Wherein My Friend is Laid* (1968) concerns a boozy tour of Mexico just after the Second World War. None of these books is wholly satisfactory: there are too many editorial fingers in the pie. Lowry's masterpiece, the work which occupied most of his dismal lucid hours (it took him thirty years to get it into shape), is *Under the Volcano* (1947; filmed by Huston in 1984), a novel about two days in the life of a drunken, self-pitying British consul in 1930s Mexico. Lowry's admirers compare the book with *Ulysses*; for others, the lachrymose, shattered brilliance of the writing and unsavouriness of the contents make Lowry no more than an upmarket Henry Miller.

Lowry's other fiction is the novel *October Ferry to Gabriola* (1970) and the short-story collection *Hear Us O Lord from Heaven Thy Dwelling-Place* (1961). *Selected Letters* (1967); *Malcolm Lowry: Psalms and Songs* (1975). Good introductions: R. Binns: *Malcolm Lowry* (1984); R. K. Cross: *Malcolm Lowry: A Preface to His Fiction* (1980).

LURIE, Alison (born 1926)
American novelist

Lurie's first two novels, *Love and Friendship* (1962) and *A Nowhere City* (1966), were competent but derivative: *Love and Friendship* (about a gossipy campus love-affair) owes its wit to *McCarthy and its creaky plotting to Grace Metalious; *A Nowhere City*, in a darker, more fragmented style, owes debts to *Bellow and to early *Roth. It was with *Imaginary Friends* (1967) that she found her own voice. This is a short, elegant study of an unhappy woman, in a stripped prose that makes Lurie one of the most enjoyable stylists in modern fiction. *Real People* (1969) is an ironical tale about artists in a beautiful creative colony; its central character (a confused 'lady writer') is drawn with cheerfully malicious sympathy – Lurie's ordinary people, living out the quiet tensions of daily life, are always superbly imagined. *The War Between the Tates* (1974), her finest book, is the story of a fastidious liberal marriage falling apart; *Only Children* (1979) shows us knockabout adult sex-comedy through the sharp eyes of a pair of little girls, one of whom (Mary Ann) is going to grow up, if she doesn't watch herself, to be an ironist.

Lurie's other books include *The Language of Clothes* (1981), a serious-minded study on the lines of (but not half so good as) Reay Tannahill's *Food in History* and *Sex in History*. So far as social history is concerned, fiction is Lurie's forte.

McCARTHY, Mary (born 1912)
American author

McCarthy is the author of an excellent autobiography (*Memoirs of a Catholic Girlhood*, 1957) and of widely praised books on travel and culture (*Venice Observed*, 1956; *The Writing on the Wall*, 1970). Her novels, in a clean, incisive style, take a satirical view of ivy-league, liberal America, the urbane agonies of the upper middle class. They include *The Groves of Academe* (1952), a funny campus novel, *A Charmed Life* (1955) and *The Group* (1963). *The Group* was acclaimed on publication as a readable feminist novel, because it showed a group of women coming to terms with their own nature and their life. Adventitious topicality apart, it remains an enjoyable but by no means outstanding book. *Birds of America* (1971) is an elegant *bildungsroman*, in style and flavour not unlike the early novels of *Hesse. Like *Murdoch, McCarthy always seems to be hovering on the threshold of greatness. Her books are perceptive and stylish; it is perhaps unfair (though true) to say that they promise more than they deliver.

McCarthy's other books include the novel *Cannibals and Missionaries* (1979), and the stingingly political *The Mask of State: Watergate Portraits* (1974). Good studies: B. McKenzie: *Mary McCarthy* (1966); D. Grumbach: *The Company She Kept* (1967).

McCULLERS, Carson (1917–67)
American novelist

Human beings as corrupt angels are the theme of McCullers' fine, slight work. Set in the American Deep South, her stories tell of lonely, oppressed individuals struggling for decency against the impacted weight of lassitude and bigotry inherited from the past. These are people for whom the lost world of *Gone With the Wind* is a mirage of culture and excellence, for whom military and racial hierarchies are the code of life itself. Her two full-length novels, *The Heart is a Lonely Hunter* (1940, about a deaf mute) and *Clock Without Hands* (1961, about two adolescent half-brothers, black and white, coming to terms with the casual bigotry which is the dead heart of the adult life around them), have magnificent set-pieces – usually sad conversations at table or in the kitchen – but lack the tightness of her best work. This is in her three novellas, *Reflections in a Golden Eye* (1941, a study of boredom and yearning set in an army camp), *The Member of the Wedding* (1946, a static and sensitive account of an emerging adolescent) and her masterpiece, *The Ballad of the Sad Café* (1951), a grand-guignol tale of freakishness and emotional deprivation among poor whites in a swamp village, told with a warmth of human engagement which gives its tawdry characters depth and dignity. McCullers' output is small, and her themes are restricted. But she is stylish and a compassionate observer, and her best writing has a poise and sad gravity reminiscent of the shorter works of *Gide or *Mann, no less.

Good studies: O. Evans: *McCullers: Her Life and Work* (1965); V. S. Carr: *The Lonely Hunter: A Biography of Carson McCullers* (1975).

MACLEISH, Archibald (born 1892)
American poet

Macleish had a distinguished public career (editor of *Fortune* magazine; librarian of Congress; assistant Secretary of State; Harvard professor), and knew famous and important people (e.g. *Cummings, *Hemingway and Muir). He published several good critical works, notably *Poetry and Opinion* (1950), on *Pound's *Pisan Cantos* and the role of poetry in society, and *Poetry and Experience* (1961). All in all, his role in American letters, for most of his life, was analogous to that of vice-president in politics: essential but unimportant. Until his fifties, for example, he was a prolific but unoriginal poet: his work read like early drafts by *Eliot or Pound. It was not until the death or retirement of most of his great contemporaries that his muse was liberated, in the writing of verse radio-plays, a form to which he was one of this century's most outstanding contributors. (His work in this field, later published, includes *The American Story*, 1944, ten linked plays on historical themes; *The Trojan Horse*, 1952, and *This Music Crept by Me on the Waters*, 1953). He also wrote well for the stage: *J.B.*, 1958, an updating of the book of Job; *Herakles*, 1967; *The Great American Fourth of July Parade*, 1975.) Once Macleish found his own voice, his poetry leapt into the class to which it had once only aspired. His finest poems are the short lyrics (usually on love, as experienced, or reflected upon, in old age) published after 1952 (when a useful set of his earlier verse, *Collected Poems 1917–1952*, also appeared); they yield in quality to no one, not even to the work of *Jarrell or *MacNeice, which they superficially resemble. The books are *Songs for Eve* (1954), *The Wild Old Wicked Man and Other Poems* (1968), and *New and Collected Poems* (1976). In them, the vice-president steps into the president's shoes, and finds them seven-league boots.

Macleish's own selection of his verse, *The Human Season: Selected Poems 1926–1972* (1972), is the best anthology. Also of interest: W. V. Busch (ed.): *The Dialogues of Macleish and Mark van Doren* (1964); *Riders of the Earth: Essays and Reminiscences* (1978). Recommended autobiography: *A Continuing Journey* (1968); recommended interim study: E. C. Smith: *Macleish* (1971).

MacNEICE, Louis (1907–63)
British poet

Being lumped with *Auden, *Isherwood, *Day Lewis and Spender as a quintessential 'poet of the thirties' (all left-wing dogmatism and tripping up-to-dateness) did MacNeice's reputation neither good nor justice. He is an individual and a great poet, writing at his best with a gravity and precision worthy of *Eliot or *Lowell. His work moves between the poles of Augustan restraint (he was a classical scholar) and clubbable Irishness. He has engaging things to say (notably about the trivialities of daily life – and their importance); but he also affects a dryness which can get in the words' way. (A persistent bad habit, for example, is over-clever enjambement, which gives a pointlessly self-mocking tinge to poems as far separated as 'Glass Falling', 1926, 'The North Sea', 1948, and the otherwise fine 'Charon' of 1962.) His anthology pieces tend either to Audenish skittishness (e.g. *Bagpipe Music* – 'It's no go the merrygoround, it's no go the rickshaw . . .') or to an equally enjoyable cod-intellectual smartness (e.g. 'The British Museum Reading Room' – 'Under the hive-like dome the stooping haunted readers/Go up and down . . .'). In the two book-length sequences *Autumn Journal* (1939) and *Autumn Sequel* (1954), the rambling diary-format allows him to explore every side-alley of allusion on the one hand and of semantic exuberance on the other; similarly, in his best work, the grave late poems in *Solstices* (1961) and *The Burning Perch* (1963), he draws together every thread of meaning and style, and sets in order the gathering and jottings of a lifetime's magpie intellectual curiosity. ('Apple Blossom', 'Soap Suds' and 'Birthright', *Jarrell-like, find resonant general meaning in apparently banal phenomena; 'Tree Party', 'Notes for a Biography' and 'Homage to Wren' make his characteristic cleverness work for meaning as well as effect.)

In any final assessment – and MacNeice still lacks proper critical attention – his translations will also stand high, particularly those of Goethe's *Faust* (1951) and of *Agamemnon* (1936, one of the truest English versions of Aeschylus ever made). *Collected Poems* (ed. Dodds), 1966. MacNeice's other books include *The Poetry of W. B. Yeats* (1941), and an unfinished autobiography, *The Strings are False* (1965). Good study: R. Marsack: *Louis MacNeice and His Poetry* (1983).

MAILER, Norman (born 1923)
American author

If the 'Me-generation' heroes of *Salinger manage not to commit suicide,
they probably grow up into people like Mailer: loud, larger than life (five
divorces; prize-fights; auto-didact film-directing; mayoral candidature),
full of crinkly-eyed, life-tousled charm – and enormously talented. In
fact the way in which his talent has been simultaneously trumpeted and
squandered – the advance royalties paid for his books are as hyped, and
sometimes as interesting, as the books themselves – *is* a kind of suicide:
how can people be as good as Mailer is consistently claimed to be and
still rubbish themselves like that? In *The Naked and the Dead* (1948) he
wrote one of the great *macho* novels of the century. It is about bewildered
young soldiers in the Second World War, an orgiastic predecessor of
Coppola's Vietnam film *Apocalypse Now*; Kate Millett (in *Sexual Politics*)
rightly tore into its orgasmic descriptions of sex-as-violence and violence-
as-sex, without making clear whether Mailer was in her view inventing or
(God forbid) merely documenting the sick fantasies of real American
men. (With *Hemingway, you know it's just a story; with Mailer, fiction
via faction equals fact.)

Mailer's later novels (e.g. *The Deer Park*, 1955; *An American Dream*,
1965) are full of the same shambling, loud-mouthed excellence; but their
surface energy conceals lack of substance – they are packed with ideas
(e.g. How We Need Great Americans or How Release of Orgone Energy
is a Liberating Force), but empty of persuasive logic or conclusions, and
their characters are cut from plangent cardboard. *Ancient Evenings*
(1983) is a unique departure: a 700-page novel about ancient Egypt,
whose hero undergoes three reincarnations in 150 years. It is as dense
with detail as *Graves's *I, Claudius* (its chief stylistic progenitor), but
neither as good on Egypt as Joan Grant's *The Winged Pharaoh* nor as
exciting a story as Mika Waltari's *Sinuhe the Egyptian*. Like *Vidal's
Creation it is a massive, impressive and singularly arid re-creation of the
past. His non-fiction is either superb (e.g. *The Armies of the Night*, 1968,
about the Peace March on the Pentagon, or *The Executioner's Song*, 1979,
a meditation on the murders, mind and execution of Gary Gilmore), or
else it is over-wrought and nasty. (Good, bad examples are *Marilyn*,
1973, a purple-prose panegyric to Marilyn Monroe and the meaning of
her death, garnished with ravishing photographs, and its ghoulish and
masturbatory sequel *Of Women and Their Elegance*, 1980, a collection of
imaginary interviews with Monroe whose overblown, banal title tells
everything.) His best book, *Advertisements for Myself* (1959), is a collage
of journalism and fiction: it takes the form of a collection of (often
superb) early writings, linked by a rambling and riotous autobiographical
commentary.

Mailer's many other publications include the novels *Why Are We in Vietnam?*

(1967) and *Tough Guys Don't Dance* (1984), a tumescent thriller, and the non-fiction anthology *The Long Patrol: 25 Years of Writing from the Works of Mailer* (ed. Lucid, 1971). Good, battling assessment: R. Solotaroff: *Down Mailer's Way* (1974), which could usefully be supplemented by the more recent H. Mills: *Mailer: A Biography* (1983). *The Essential Norman Mailer* (1982) contains much self-regarding garbage, but also some pacy fiction from his good early period, hitherto uncollected.

MALAMUD, Bernard (born 1914)
American novelist

After an admired but lacklustre first novel, *The Natural* (1952), a B-movieish story reworking Arthurian legend in a 20th-century baseball setting, Malamud found his form in *The Assistant* (1957). In this novel, a hoodlum who robs a Jewish shop expiates his guilt first by being taken on as an assistant, then by entering into the condition of his employers to the extent of circumcision and conversion. In *A New Life* (1961), a failing writer joins a college community and is destroyed by his inability to make or keep relationships; the tragi-comic tone of *Roth's *Letting Go* (published a year later) owes this book debts. In *The Tenants* (1971), two writers, one white, one black, form a relationship in which each tries to swamp and then to 'become' the other; the resemblance here is to *Bellow, and to the early menace-plays of Pinter. *Dubin's Lives* (1979) is again about a failing writer, this time a middle-aged biographer coming to terms with the fact that he is loved for what he is, even though he himself despises that self. *God's Grace* (1982) is a curious novel about the sole human survivor of a nuclear holocaust, who makes a relationship with quizzical, intelligent apes. In addition to these tragi-comedies of relationships, Malamud wrote a historical novel about early 20th-century Russian Jews (*The Fixer*, 1966), and several volumes of stories, some of which were worked into an episodic novel (*Pictures of Fidelman: An Exhibition*, 1969, about an artist trying to 'find' himself by travelling abroad).

Short-story collections: *The Magic Barrel* (1958); *Idiots First* (1963); *Rembrandt's Hat* (1973); *The Stories of Bernard Malamud* (1983). Good anthology: P. Rahv (ed.): *A Malamud Reader* (1967). Good study: S. Cohen: *Malamud and the Trial by Love* (1974).

MALRAUX, André (1901–76)
French novelist

Malraux's life was spent at the heart of affairs. He was an archaeologist in Indo-China at the time of Chiang Kai-shek's revolution; he fought against the fascists in Spain and was in the French Resistance; after the Second World War he was an active Gaullist politician, and ended his career as the Fifth Republic's minister of culture. (It was, in fact, he who proposed the idea of the *musée imaginaire*, the sitting-room collection of all the world's great art, the anthology of human achievement to whose modern shelf this present book is, in part, a guide.) In his novels, Malraux had the knack of taking events he knew from personal experience, and remounting and relighting them as art. His work is as detailed and *parti-pris* as an Eisenstein film, and is written in a baroque, artificial style – an unusual and appealing combination, which produces the feeling, rare in fiction, that there is a 'humane' continuum between behaviour and its description, between life and art.

Malraux's first novel, *Paper Moons* (1921), is surrealist, inconsequential and immature; his fifth and last, *The Walnut Trees of Altenburg* (1943), is blandly philosophical about the artist-superman, and contains an appropriate and memorable account of Nietzsche. His three other novels are at once the core of his work and uniquely approachable 'documents' about key moments in 20th-century history, analogous to *All Quiet on the Western Front* or *Battleship Potemkin*. La Condition humaine (1933 – the 1948 translation *Man's Fate* is the best of several) is about the 1923 Kuomintang triumph and Chiang Kai-shek's bloody and treacherous purge of his communist allies which followed. *Days of Contempt* (1935) is on the rise of Nazism in Germany; *Days of Hope* (1937) – from which he directed his own film, *L'Espoir* – concerns the Spanish civil war. These novels, ranking with Sartre's or *Koestler's fiction for their effect on later left-wing thinking, are balanced by some notable non-fiction, including a book strikingly prescient of the hippy 1960s – except that it is sensibly, logically argued, not impulsive and addle-pated – *The Temptation of the West* (1926), which proposes a philosophical accommodation between east and west, and *The Voices of Silence* (1951), setting out Malraux's views on the cultural importance of art.

The conventional critical view of Malraux is that he was an interesting thinker and agitprop novelist who 'went soft' at the end of his life as he lost his faith in action. The glum progression of human affairs since his death has proved him, rather, right: now, more than ever, humankind needs art, needs culture, not as a sticking-plaster or an ornament but to guarantee identity.

Malraux's *Antimemoirs* (2 vols., 1967, 1971) are smooth as syrup, the work of a man who has turned aside from the affairs he takes part in, an epicurean looking with detached amusement at the crazy funfair of Kissinger, Vietnam and all that fuss. It is witty or infuriating, depending on your own political involvement. Good survey of both man and work: A. Madsen: *Malraux* (1977).

MANN, Thomas (1875–1955)
German novelist

Mann was a prolific essayist, propagandist and pamphleteer. Much of his political writing (he was a tireless anti-fascist) is now largely of historical or biographical interest: a useful collection is *Order of the Day* (1930).

His essays on philosophy and the arts are likely to prove more durable; many are collected in *Essays of Three Decades* (1947). His views on Goethe, Tolstoy, Nietzsche, Wagner and Dostoievski are particularly valuable, both as criticism and as clues to Mann's own creative mind. Often, his literary essays are concerned with the major theme of all his writing, the place and task of the artist in a troubled world. In this, he is often a glum poet of decadence: his creative spirits more often end up as victims than redeemers of society. In *Buddenbrooks* the enterprise and thrust of a great mercantile family gradually flickers and dies, as bourgeois energy seemed to Mann to have died in Germany; in *The Magic Mountain* Castorp – symbolizing the old bourgeoisie – learns flexibility of thought, only to be swept away by the First World War; *Dr Faustus* is a parable of how the individual soul (Leverkühn) maintains dignity in the face of totalitarian evil (for Mann, Nazism; for Leverkühn, the devil). Only Felix Krull survives, and his survival is ironical: he wins not so much because of his own amorality as through the unblinkingly rigid morality of those he preys upon. Politically – and perhaps creatively – Mann is a pessimist; his writing is at its most pretentiously awful when intellectuality (always pessimistic) rules, at its lightest and best when human character (always optimistic) is his theme.

His fiction falls into three categories, identifiable by bulk. There is, first, a group of fine short stories, including his masterpiece, 'Death in Venice': they are available in separate volumes, and are also collected in *Stories of a Lifetime* (1961). 'Death in Venice' (1913), a parable about the internal and external pressures which destroy creativity, is written with a studied terseness Mann never surpassed; it is as elegant as Henry James, as eloquent as Dostoievski; the humanity of Aschenbach is both a symbol and of engrossing interest in its own right; above all, the book's brevity prevents that endless philosophical rhetoric which sometimes, in the long novels, becomes mannerism unmaking Mann. Absence of rhetoric also benefits the second group of his works, a series of medium-length novels, sometimes anticipating themes of the major books – *Mario and the Magician* (1929), for example, about demonic possession, foreshadows *Dr Faustus* – and sometimes dealing with lighter themes in a self-contained manner that sets them apart from the mainstream of Mann's work. Thus *Royal Highness* (1909) is an unserious romance, Mann's equivalent of *The Prisoner of Zenda* or *Arms and the Man*; *Lotte in Weimar* (1939), partly – since its hero is Goethe – about creativity, is chiefly a love story; *The Holy Sinner* (1951) is an ironic parody of medieval heroic legend, a ridiculous tale of incest and magical transformation told in a mixture of Old High German pomposity and Hollywoodish one-liners, as if Groucho Marx were to retell Wagner's *Ring*; *The Black Swan* (1953), about a 'free spirit' in the 1910s who has an unhappy love-affair, suffers cancer of the womb and dies, is strongly reminiscent in style and theme, though not in its clinical doominess, of the early novels of *Hesse.

The third group, of long novels, stands head and shoulders above Mann's other work and puts him, as a writer, in the heady class of Balzac, Tolstoy or Dickens. He begins, in *Buddenbrooks* (1901), with a *tour de force*. The book appears to be – and is – an old-fashioned 'generation novel', tracing the fortunes of a family as it grows and adapts to changing circumstances (a *bildungsroman*, in fact, with a dynasty at its centre instead of an individual). But this family *fails* to grow, fails to adapt, and finally chokes itself to death. Thus a sappy, energetic novel form is turned inside-out and made a vehicle for political parable. The strength of the book lies partly in its traditional roots (Tony Buddenbrook, for example, Mann's finest character until Felix Krull, is straight out of Stendhal, even has links with the wittily disenchanted secondary characters in Jane Austen), but more especially in the way it subverts the tradition even as it uses it. The same is true of *The Magic Mountain* (1924): apparently a straightforward *bildungsroman*, this uses its charming central character as a symbol of Germany grappling with progress. As in *Buddenbrooks*, the devastating inner point of the book is not apparent till the end. Castorp learns his lessons, but leaves to fight in the War to End Wars; the ironical contrast between his ideals and our hind-knowledge of what that war actually led to is punched home in a series of ever more dislocated and surrealist closing chapters – it is as if Castorp's disease has finally eaten him away, as if he is in the delirious last rallying-time before death.

The Magic Mountain is stylistically and thematically the finest of Mann's long novels. After it, he seems to have lost control of both material and style. Who has read, for pleasure, every word of *Joseph and His Brothers* (1933–43)? The Biblical myth gives Mann a solid foundation – but instead of a single edifice, he builds *Kafka's Castle, a tower of philosophical and stylistic Babel. What does it all mean? And could it not all be said at half the length? *Dr Faustus* (1947) is just as pretentious, but convincingly shorter. Its theme (like that of *Joseph*) is the plight of the visionary individual struggling to maintain his or her creative identity against hostile forces. (Again, it is an inverted *bildungsroman*, with the influences tending to corrupt instead of teach.) Joseph wins the battle because of his clinching faith, an absolute force; Leverkühn (who makes a Faustian pact with the devil, bartering his soul for creative inspiration) loses because he abandons faith even in himself. The philosophical platform of *Dr Faustus* is sound and clear, and the book also offers the persevering reader a well-argued and convincing exposition in words of what 'modern music' is all about.

Mann's last book, the unfinished *Confessions of Felix Krull* (1954), is one of his finest works. In it, he abandons themes and concentrates on people, always his greatest strength. The characters are no longer symbols: like those in *Buddenbrooks*, they are human individuals who engage us not by what they mean but by who they are – their idiosyncrasies (charming, extraordinary or both) make the book. The women in *Felix*

Krull are Mann's best since *Buddenbrooks*; the places (especially Paris and Lisbon) are presented with a sensuality of description unmatched in his other work; above all, the comedy is relaxed and warm, and we are invited to smile at, not recoil from, the foibles of humanity.

Good introductions: E. Heller: *The Ironic German* (1958); T. E. Apter: *Thomas Mann: The Devil's Advocate* (1978). Good biography of the young Mann: R. Winston: *Thomas Mann* (1981). A good English-language selection from Mann's diaries is *Diaries 1918–1939* (ed. Kesten, 1983).

MANSFIELD, Katherine (1888–1923)
New Zealand writer

Mansfield's private life contained three events particularly crucial to her work. In 1908 she settled in Britain, and this led to the discovery of European, and particularly French, life and culture: many of her stories are set in hotels and *pensions*, and concern middle-class women in slightly bewildered exile (they are akin to such Black Sea visitors in Chekhov as 'The Lady with the Little Dog'). The death of her brother in the First World War drove her into a protracted and nostalgic reverie of their New Zealand childhood, which she evoked in three fine stories, 'Prelude' (from *Bliss and Other Stories*, 1920), 'At the Bay' (from *The Garden Party and Other Stories*, 1922) and 'The Doll's House' (from *The Dove's Nest and Other Stories*, 1923). Thirdly, her entry in 1911 into the Bloomsbury circle not only encouraged her blunt freedom of spirit (she has been claimed, despite the absurdity of such labels, as one of the first feminist writers), but also led, in her literary style, to a self-absorbed refinement and impressionistic elegance – character-through-dialogue; 'musical' construction – sometimes tending to the fey. She produced three volumes of stories (the first was *In a German Pension*, 1911, which she later rejected as immature); after her death her husband brought out *The Dove's Nest* and *Something Childish and Other Stories* (1924); there are seventy-six complete stories altogether.

Mansfield was particularly sensitive to the joys and terrors of very small children. Not only the New Zealand stories show this, but also the best stories in *Something Childish*: 'Sixpence', about a small boy's outburst of hysterical 'naughtiness' and his father's remorse after he beats him, 'How Pearl Button Was Kidnapped', or 'The Little Girl', about a child's feelings of fear and love for her father. But her main characters are the vain, empty-headed bourgeoisie, the strutting men, bored women and bullied children of the suburbs. It is here that she most nearly approaches Chekhov (to whom she is regularly compared), and stories such as 'A Cup of Tea' (from *The Dove's Nest*), 'The Man Without a Temperament' (from *Bliss*) and the superb 'The Garden Party' and 'The Daughters of the Late Colonel' (both from *The Garden Party*) share Chekhov's ability to reveal humanity and tragedy in vapid lives. Other stories suggest de

Maupassant, notably those with New Zealand outback settings such as 'Ole Underwood' or 'The Woman at the Store' (both from *Something Childish*). In short, her work is wide-ranging and subtle, and she ranks with the greatest exponents of her craft.

As well as stories, Mansfield wrote one of the best of all the Bloomsbury journals (*The Journal of Katherine Mansfield*, 1927) and conducted a fascinating correspondence (*Letters*, 2nd edn 1951), not least with *Lawrence, with whom she had a friendship which kept both of them trembling with fury. ('Why don't you *die?*' he asked her once.) Good biography: A. Alpers: *The Life of Katherine Mansfield* (1980). Interesting literary criticism: A. Gurr and C. Hanson: *Katherine Mansfield* (1981). Her *Letters* are currently appearing in an edition by V. O'Sullivan and M. Scott: the first volume was published in 1984.

MÁRQUEZ, Gabriel García (born 1928)
Colombian novelist

Like *Faulkner's Yoknapatawpha, Márquez' mythical community Macondo was invented to stand for every aspect of a decadent, collapsing society – in his case, a typical banana-republic township of fatcat landowners, jack-booted police, dull-witted peons and duller-witted revolutionaries. The satire is as viciously affectionate as Voinovich's or Zinoviev's of the Soviet Union; but Márquez is a greater writer than either, because he uses scabrous satire as the cloak for a serious and compassionate examination of the godforsaken plight of modern humanity. Macondo first appeared in *Leaf-Storm and Other Stories* (1955) – and it is typical of Márquez that though the idea of a storm of leaves sounds ludicrous, it is actually an image taken from the guard's speech in Sophocles' *Antigone*, a description of nature's alarm at the horror and irrevocability of what human beings are about to do. The town and its various inhabitants appear again in *No One Writes to the Colonel* (1961), the brief, Borgesian fantasy *In Evil Hour* (1962), and in Márquez' satirical masterpieces *One Hundred Years of Solitude* (1967) and *The Autumn of the Patriarch* (1975). *One Hundred Years of Solitude* is at once an example and a parody of such 'disintegrating great family' sagas as *Mann's *Buddenbrooks*, the Buendia family exemplifying the whole crumbling society in which they live; *The Autumn of the Patriarch* is a Swiftian portrait of a military dictator, written in page-long sentences which twist and grip like vines. Márquez' biographer Lhosa grandly calls him a 'deicide'; other admirers invoke Cervantes or Rabelais. He is really more like the Emperor Nero's 'arbiter of elegance' Petronius (author of the *Satyricon*). He luxuriates in the corruption he excoriates; he is a deadpan farceur, a man with appalling news to tell, if only he can keep his face straight long enough to announce it.

Márquez' other books include *Big Mama's Funeral* (1962), *Innocent Erendira and Other Stories* (1972), and *Chronicle of a Death Foretold* (1982), a pendant to *One*

Hundred Years of Solitude and one of his best short books, about two Macondan brothers driven to murder the man they think has seduced their sister. (It is as macabre and witty as a Buñuel film.) The only contemporary writer to match Márquez' baroque imagination, event for event, phrase for phrase, bizarrerie for bizarrerie, is Salman Rushdie (born 1947). His two novels in this style (there is an earlier, uncharacteristic one) are both 'histories of families', in the sense that the fantastic events which befall Márquez' Buendia family are 'history': *Midnight's Children* (1981) is set in India and *Shame* (1983), a masterpiece on the scale of *One Hundred Years of Solitude*, in Pakistan, but both lie really in the unfettered, logically illogical world of the imagination, the boundary of consciousness which seemed, before Rushdie, to be Márquez' own private domain.

MASEFIELD, John (1878–1967)
British poet

In one of his two moods, Masefield was a no-nonsense boy's-own-paper balladeer, one of the most rollicking in the language. Such poems as 'Sea Fever' ('I must go down to the sea again . . .'), 'Cargoes' ('Quinquereme of Nineveh . . .') or the long, narrative *Reynard the Fox* (1919, his masterpiece) show his unpretentious muse at her trimmest: short, end-stopped lines, trotting rhythms, honest rhymes and above all a feeling that every emotional or pictorial target is hit dead centre. In his other mood, he tends to mawkishness and faery whimsy; this became a persistent fault after 1930, when he was appointed Poet Laureate and overnight became the Mabel Lucie Attwell of English letters. His early verse (especially *Salt Water Ballads*, 1902, *Ballads and Poems*, 1910, and *The Everlasting Mercy*, 1911), and his adventure novels (*Jim Davis*, 1911, and *Sard Harker*, 1924, are magnificent) are his most durable work, as fine as any of the Victorians (Stevenson, Newbolt, Clough) whose heir he was.

Masefield's manifold other writings include an autobiography, *So Long to Learn* (1952). His *Letters to Reyna* (ed. Buchan, 1984) movingly chart how his sad declining years were warmed by friendship for a young concert-violinist.

MAUGHAM, William Somerset (1874–1965)
British novelist and playwright

Few writers (*Hemingway is one) have so baffled the critics. Is Maugham a first-rate artist prone to regular and alarming lapses, or a hack with pretensions to genius? The problem has never worried Maugham's reading public, which has always been large and appreciative. His excellences – and defects – have been deployed in three distinct fields. In the 1910s and 1920s he wrote light comedies for the stage, out-styling Lonsdale and anticipating, if never quite matching, Coward (who once said 'Everyone but Willy said I was the new Somerset Maugham'): the best are *Home and Beauty* (1919), *The Circle* (1921), *Our Betters* (1923) and *The Constant Wife* (1927). (His more serious plays, of which the best is *Sheppey*, 1932, are now less well regarded.) His short stories, as well as being staple fodder of 1930s and 1940s film melodrama – 'Rain' alone, thanks to its superb central character, Sadie Thompson, was filmed in half a dozen versions – are spare and exact, often recounting incidents from the love-life of expatriate westerners in the Far East. ('Ashenden, or the British Agent', 1928, is the exception, initiating a genre to which Buchan and *Greene later made notable contributions.)

The heart of Maugham's work is his eighteen novels. Like his short stories, many are based on real incidents from his own past life or on anecdotes heard on his travels in exotic parts. Some (e.g. *Catalina*, 1948) are historical trash; but a handful raise popular story-telling (Maugham's real métier) to the realms of art. These include the Zolaesque *Liza of Lambeth* (1897), his first book, bruisingly set in the London slums, the partly autobiographical *Of Human Bondage* (1915), a masterly 'outsider' novel, *The Moon and Sixpence* (1919), about a Gauguinesque painter's escape to artistic freedom in the South Seas, and *Cakes and Ale* (1930), a beautifully carpentered, waspish satire on the London literary scene.

Among Maugham's other plays (he wrote more than thirty) are the splendidly melodramatic *East of Suez* (1922), a love-triangle set in Hollywood-Chinese locations, and the serious *For Services Rendered* (1932). His non-fiction includes the autobiographical *The Summing Up* (1938) and *A Writer's Notebook* (1949). *Complete Short Stories* (1951); *Collected Plays* (1952); *Selected Novels* (1953). Good biography: Ted Morgan: *Somerset Maugham* (1980), which should be complemented, for a well-illustrated overview of both man and work, by F. Raphael: *Somerset Maugham and His World* (1978).

MAURIAC, François (1885–1970)
French novelist

The background to Mauriac's score of novels is the wine-country around Bordeaux; the period is generally pre-First-World-War; the characters almost without exception come from rich land owning families or are the priests, lawyers, bankers and prostitutes who serve their needs. The motivating forces are love (or its sour alternatives lust and loyalty to family or caste), money and religion. No Mauriac character enjoys all three; most of his characters possess two of them, and their lives are blighted by a despairing search for the third. In *Genitrix* (1923) the blighting force is love: the plot is a triangle between a young woman, the husband she dotes on and his possessive, monstrous mother. In *The Desert of Love* (1925), an adolescent and his estranged father both love the same woman, who cares for neither of them; the characters are trapped by longing, like the damned in Dante's Hell forever yearning for a paradise they glimpse but can never reach; hope for them is cancerous, not a healing force. In *The Knot of Vipers* (1932) greed for money destroys three generations of a rich family: the book is the 'confession' (save that he is an atheist) of a miserly grandfather surrounded on his deathbed by vulturine relatives, and tormented by the thought that whenever in his life he faced the choice between making money and showing love, he chose cash. His agony of soul, for Catholic Mauriac, is a paradigm of the human being who has no knowledge of God and is therefore trapped in himself or herself, denied freewill. (Sartre famously attacked Mauriac, and Catholicism, for denying his characters precisely that.) In *Gide, the same torment often leads to a liberating *acte gratuit*; in Mauriac, if it fails to lead to a conversion – which is about as convincing in literary terms as the *deus ex machina* is in classical drama – it leads to misery and self-disgust. Mauriac's two finest novels are *Thérèse Desqueyroux* (1927), which shows a woman on a train journey reliving in her mind the emotions which led her to poison her husband, and her feelings when he recovered and refused to testify against her, and *The Woman of the Pharisees* (1941), a marvellous fusion of two of his most frequent themes, adolescent love and the sterile energy of religious bigotry in the unlovely middle-aged. Mauriac's world is narrowly circumscribed (he makes Henry James seem profligate) and bleak; but his novels (none longer than 200 pages; all packed) offer the satisfactions of an unfamiliar milieu brought completely to life, and of crucial questions about humanity painstakingly, painfully discussed.

Mauriac's other writings include several volumes of journals (*Journal of Adolescence*, 1934, important on his fictional aims and means; *Journal 1932–39*, 1947; *Journal*, 1950; and *The Black Notebook*, 1944, published under the pseudonym Forez and about his wartime resistance work), a number of gloomy plays (of which the best is *Fire on the Earth*, 1951), and collections of essays – he was a vociferous Gaullist and a prolific right-wing political journalist, notably in *Le Figaro*. Good biography (in French): J. Lacouture: *François Mauriac* (1980).

MAYAKOVSKY, Vladimir: see page 496.

MISHIMA, Yukio (1925–70)
Japanese novelist

His sensational suicide (by *hara-kiri*) brought Mishima's name before a worldwide public at a time when his books' nihilism and view of violence as a wholesome cathartic force were likeliest to make ripples among the alienated western young of the early 1970s. This led to exaggeration of his stature and to the confusion of posturing (e.g. in the lumbering allegory *The Sailor Who Fell from Grace with the Sea*, 1963) with meaningful philosophy. He was a prolific writer, in a rapid, gestural style akin to that of Vonnegut: if you stuff a book with references, reminiscences, parodies, views and statements on anything and everything, the chances are that some of them will strike fire with someone. His best and least prolix books treat a single obsessive theme (often the nature of pure evil) with unremitting narrative tension – there is no doubt about his hypnotic story-telling skill. *Confessions of a Mask* (1949), about a man trying to burrow down to the heart of himself, and *The Temple of the Golden Pavilion* (1956), about a young man torn between meditation and psychopathic violence, are immediately accessible books – Japanese equivalents of *Greene's *Brighton Rock* or *Gide's *Les Caves du Vatican*. Mishima's masterpiece is the tetralogy *The Sea of Fertility* (1965–70), studies of 20th-century Japanese life as bitter and as eloquent as the novels of *Böll or *Grass, to which they are similar in tone.

Mishima's other books include the novels *The Sound of Waves* (1954) and *After the Banquet* (1960); *Five Modern Noh Plays* (1956), and the play *Madame de Sade* (1965). Good study: H. S. Stokes: *The Life and Death of Yukio Mishima* (1975). P. Schwenger: *Phallic Critiques: Masculinity and 20th-Century Literature* (1984) interestingly sets his *macho* philosophy against those of *Hemingway, *Mailer and others.

MONTHERLANT, Henri de: see page 499.

MOORE, George (1852–1933)
Irish writer

Unfashionable today, Moore was one of the leading English-language novelists of the turn of the century, and as good as the *Wharton of *Ethan Frome* or the Hardy of *Tess of the d'Urbervilles*. His earlier books, in a realistic style derived from Balzac (no jigsaw-piece of the human comedy left out of place), include the superb *Esther Waters* (1894), about a servant-girl who has a bastard child, and *Evelyn Innes* (1898) and *Sister Teresa* (1901), exploring the effects of divine and profane love. At this time he also travelled in Europe (notably to Paris), was a London art-critic, and published several books of pacy, scurrilous memoirs and reviews, of which *Confessions of a Young Man* (1888), *Impressions and Opinions* (1891) and *Modern Painting* (1893) are in the class of Shaw.

In the 1910s Moore began a study of the ancient world which resulted both in a fine translation of Longus's *Daphnis and Chloe* (1924) and in three of his own most eloquent novels, *The Brook Kerith* (1916), his masterpiece, about Joseph of Arimathea, *Heloise and Abelard* (1921) and *Aphrodite in Aulis* (1930), one of the most engrossing novels about ancient Greece until Renault's *The King Must Die*. Moore continued to publish memoirs – the most important are *Reminiscences of the Impressionist Painters* (1906) and *Hail and Farewell* (*Ave*, 1911; *Salve*, 1912; *Vale*, 1914) – and collections of outstanding short stories, of which *Celibate Lives* (1927) is the best. Of all the 'unknown' writers of the century, he is one of those most deserving rediscovery. He was hardly a quiet genius – he was far too opinionated and pugnacious for that – but it is lamentable that his books, now, should languish in libraries while his name is regularly shouted aloud in guides like this.

Among Moore's many other novels (often with finely drawn women as central characters) are *A Mummer's Wife* (1885), *A Drama in Muslin* (1886), *The Untilled Field* (1903), *The Lake* (1905) and *Perronik the Fool* (1924). Story-collections include *Celibates* (1895), and among his books of reminiscence are the once-notorious *Conversations in Ebury Street* (1924), a spectacular graveyard for reputations of the time. Good selection: *George Moore's Mind and Art* (1968). There is no good biographical or literary study; it's time there was.

MOORE, Marianne (1887–1972)
American poet

Moore is regularly compared with Emily Dickinson, but she is much closer in quirkiness of style as well as reticence of temperament to Stevie Smith. She began adult life as a teacher of shorthand (a discipline the cynical might wish on several modern poets), and was a friend and publisher (she edited, for a time in the 1920s, the literary journal *Dial*) of such people as *Pound and Hilda Doolittle. None the less, she avoided their occasional preciousness: like Smith (and Dickinson) she prefers to play the part of the objective observer – one of her early collections is actually called *Observations* (1924) – who first describes and then draws conclusions. (Later, *Jarrell too was good at this.) She deliberately set out to abandon rum-ti-tum, to combine prose rhythms with the sharp imagery and compressed symmetry of verse. Her best poems are about animals (typical collections are *The Pangolin and Other Verse*, 1936, and *The Arctic Ox*, 1964), and not only draw out human comparisons with the jerboas, unicorns and sea-beasts she describes, but also make the point that animals have a secret dignity of their own, unthreatened by humanity. She once, characteristically, thus addressed a snail:

> If 'compression is the first grace of style',
> you have it. Contractility is a virtue
> as modesty is a virtue.

Selected Poems (1935); *Collected Poems* (1951); *The Complete Poems* (1967). Literary criticism: *Predilections* (1955); *Poetry and Criticism* (1965). Translation: *The Fables of La Fontaine* (1951): fine; less translations (or even 'imitations' in Lowell's word) than 'reinhabitation' of the original thought. Good introductions: P. W. Hadas: *Moore: Poet of Affection* (1977); B. Costello: *Marianne Moore: Imaginary Possessions* (1981).

MURDOCH, Iris (born 1919)
British novelist

Murdoch is the thinking person's Ethel M. Dell. Her work is plentiful and comfortable – if you like one of her books, you'll like them all. She has invented an implausible but convincing world; her functional prose hooks the reader from the first mouthful, like fast food; her characters are a tumbling, exotic crew. The intellect is tweaked by the throwaway use of cultural brand-names (Plato, *Hamlet*, Wittgenstein, Laforgue), though it it is more often intrigued by bizarrerie than satisfied with depth of perception or human analysis. Her subject is sexual politics, and her tone is that of a detached observer, half-smiling at the moral contortions she describes. In short, her books offer self-confident, chic fun. Their anguished heroes (the 'mid-life crisis' is a favourite theme), taloned women and fluffy adolescents perform intricate charades of love and life in a never-never-land of bosky country estates and mid-fifties big-town lodgings, back-streets and coffee-bars. Some of her early books, it's true, do shoulder their way out of this pleasant rut. Her first two novels, *Under the Net* (1954) and *The Flight from the Enchanter* (1956), appealingly mix the blurry fantasy of Cocteau's films (*Orphée* and *Les Enfants terribles* are important influences) with a slapstick wit like that of *Queneau. *The Sandcastle* (1957) deals believably (it may be her best book) with a middle-aged man's passion for a young girl and its effects on his family; *The Bell* (1958) is a sombre study of religious and erotic possession; *A Severed Head* (1961) is an amiably satirical account of musical beds among the tart, smart set (Georgie loves Antonia loves Palmer loves Martin loves Georgie – and where does Honor Klein come into it?). Of her later books, *The Black Prince* (1973) and *The Sea, the Sea* (1978) stand out. To her critics, the unvarying, prolix mixture of gaminess and adolescent intellectual bravura makes her easily resistible; to her addicts, she is unputdownable.

Murdoch's other books include *Sartre: Romantic Rationalist* (1953), clear-headed, *The Fire and the Sun: Why Plato Banned the Artists* (1977), polemical and philosophical, and the novels *Bruno's Dream* (1969), *A Fairly Honourable Defeat* (1970) and *A Word Child* (1975). Good study: E. Dipple: *Iris Murdoch: Work for the Spirit* (1981). Encouraging, brief introduction: R. Todd: *Iris Murdoch* (1984).

NABOKOV, Vladimir (1899–1977)
Russian novelist

Exile gave Nabokov both a theme and an attitude. His key characters are all aliens, whether literally (Godunov-Cherdyntsev in *The Gift*; Pnin; the egregious Kinbote in *Pale Fire*) or metaphorically (Krug in *Bend Sinister*, a 'dissident' against totalitarianism; the psychological exile who narrates *Despair*; Humbert Humbert in *Lolita*, exiled from conventional morality). He writes about their lives with a dandyish aloofness which is also a trademark of exile. (His security, like that of most exiles, seems to lie in himself and in his fly-in-amber view of what he had to leave; he observed events around him wryly, self-consciously, as if reality and not he himself were alien and transient.) Nabokov's characters are chess-pieces. They delight their creator, but seldom move him; they have intriguing and delicate mechanisms, but seldom hearts. (His female characters, in particular, have very little verisimilitude. Even Lolita and Ada, the best of them, are described – and behave – more like living dolls than living flesh.) In his 'autobiography revisited' *Speak, Memory* (1967) he turns the spotlight of garrulous reticence on himself, and the same thing happens: the more he tells us about his actions and memories, the more shadowy a figure he becomes.

Until the late 1940s Nabokov's novels and stories were written in Russian: the majority were Englished (brilliantly, by Nabokov himself, or under him) during the 1960s, after the success of *Lolita*. They are the work of a less self-conscious and less dazzling stylist than the later novels; the feeling that Nabokov is a leading character in his own books (one of his most enjoyable later attributes) is less pervasive. His Russian short stories are some of his finest work – those collected in *Tyrants Destroyed* (1975) and *Details of a Sunset* (1976) combine a wry view of human absurdity and suffering with a notably crisp, dry style. The novels include several 'psychological thrillers'. (Nabokov might have deplored the vulgar term, but it aptly describes their concern for the intricacies of motivation and feeling in the characters rather than for the often melodramatic action.) The best are *King, Queen, Knave* (1928), *Laughter in the Dark* (1933) and *Despair* (1934), about a man haunted by his own double, his *doppelgänger*, whom he finally kills, only to find that he has destroyed himself. (Fassbinder later made a haunting film of this story, scripted by Tom Stoppard.) There are two Kafkaesque novels of political oppression, *Invitation to a Beheading* (1935) and *Bend Sinister* (1947). *Bend Sinister*, about the pressure placed on an individual to serve the repugnant state, is Nabokov's most savage book, the 20th-century nightmare described with anger and an anguish rare in his work. Of the other earlier novels, several are 'biographies', usually of men of heterodox, distressed genius: an emotionally stunted chess champion (*The Defence*, 1929), an elusive and arrogant author (*The Real Life of Sebastian Knight*, 1941), and in *The Gift* (1937–8) – Nabokov's major Russian novel, so rich in allusions to Russian life and literature that the English reader feels at times like an uninvited guest – the aristocratic émigré man-of-letters Godunov-Cherdyntsev. *The Gift* is the most 'Nabokovian' of the earlier books. It is full of parody, word-play and teasing conceits of every kind; it even anticipates *Pale Fire*, by including both the hero's critical biography of Chernyshevski *and* a critique of that critique. And for the first time in Nabokov's work, systematic use is made of parenthesis: a series of self-indulgently baroque passages in which author communes with reader about nothing particularly relevant to the action, but crucial to the book. The accounts of the hero's father's expeditions (to Tibet, the Gobi Desert and China) stand out, evocations of scientific field trips as memorable as any of the lepidopterical passages in *Speak, Memory*.

Nabokov's English novels dazzle. *Lolita* (1955) is the worst of them, his *Lady Chatterley's Lover*. The reader must believe in Lolita's bitten-nail, scratched-shin charm not only with the fervour of Humbert's self-disgust but because the prose convinces; if not, the story remains grubby and wished-for, more successful as a hymn to the motel way of life and the American school system than to the reality of its characters. *Pnin*

(1957) is a campus novel given depth by our sympathy for desperate Pnin himself, and with a stunning final set-piece. *Look at the Harlequins!* (1974), an urbane reversion to Nabokov's earlier style, is the 'biography' of an émigré writer. There remain his two most coruscating books, *Pale Fire* (1962) and *Ada* (1969). He never contrived more artificial plots, never wrote prose so rich or arch. If those are the qualities that make him a great writer as well as an enjoyable one, these are his finest books. The form of *Pale Fire*, perhaps the most self-consciously original of any modern novel, is that of a long poem and an even longer critical commentary incorporating parodies of Ruritanian royal-escape stories, American college novels of the *McCarthy school and pulp murder stories. (The killer, Gradus, hampered by inadequacy and diarrhoea, is one of Nabokov's funniest creations.) *Ada* is about a passionate love-affair between half-brother and half-sister, begun in childhood and continued into extreme old age. Its prose is as heady and exotic as the emotions it describes (the prose *is* the emotions); its setting is the ultimate example of Nabokov's lifelong fascination with 'doubles' (it takes place on a planet exactly like Earth, except that White Russia and America are a single country, and the 19th and 20th centuries a single time); authorial tongue-in-cheek is its galvanizing force. Whether it shows us a great writer at full gallop, or a sumptuous literary circus act, *Ada* is 'the Nabokov experience' in apogee.

Good critical essays, appealingly blending the impish and the acute: *Lectures on Literature* (1980); *Lectures on Russian Literature* (1982). Good introduction: G. M. Hyde: *Vladimir Nabokov: America's Russian Novelist* (1977). Good on *Lolita* and *Pale Fire*, outstanding on *Ada*: D. Packman: *Nabokov: The Structure of Literary Desire* (1983).

NARAYAN, Rasipuran Krishnaswami (born 1907)
Indian novelist

Like *Márquez' Macondo or *Faulkner's Yoknapatawpha County, Narayan's invented place Malgudi seems more real than reality itself. It is a small Indian town and the surrounding villages and countryside, and Narayan's characters are its shopkeepers, civil servants, craftsmen and intellectuals. He writes in a vein of gentle social comedy (analogous, for westerners at least, to that in such Satyajit Ray films as *The Chess Players*), but what his people think, the centre of their being, is rooted in Hindu orthodoxy, and this gives the novels a poetic depth and intangibility equalled, in the west, only in the work of *Hesse (the well-springs of whose work also lie in Indian mysticism). We recognize the Malgudians' feelings and actions – which are always direct and unequivocal – as like our own, and yet the otherworldliness of their motivation, of their inner selves, simultaneously makes them mysterious and seems to tell us more about ourselves.

There are more than a dozen Malgudi novels, all of the same high quality. Among the more rollicking (verging at times on social farce rather than comedy) are *The Maneater of Malgudi* (1962), about a demented taxidermist bent on showing his skill with animals of every size and kind, until he rashly proposes to shoot and stuff the town's sacred elephant, and *A Tiger for Malgudi* (1983), told in the first person by a circus tiger which escapes only to become first a film star and then the companion of an absurd wandering guru. Of Narayan's more mystical works, the finest are *The English Teacher/Grateful to Life and Death* (1945), about a selfish, simple-hearted man who grows into spiritual self-knowledge after the death of his beloved wife, and *The Guide* (1958), which begins farcically as the roguish tourist-guide Raju makes himself the manager of a pin-headed dancer, and ends with his own inner transformation, slowly and beautifully described, until he becomes in reality the holy man everyone takes him for.

Narayan's finest novel, combining social observation, mysticism and comedy as if there were no other mode for life, is *The Vendor of Sweets* (1976). Its hero, Jagan, is a self-made businessman, bustling, well-meaning and simple-hearted, but with a wastrel son. When the son brings home a non-Indian wife and sets up a ludicrous business enterprise based on a machine for writing novels, Jagan begins to feel that he is being driven not only out of his home but out of the belief which has sustained his entire existence. He turns increasingly to memories of his happy past, and to the rituals and patterns of Hinduism – but the novel's resolution, in a splendid final twist, comes from none of this but from outside, as the inevitable end of what seemed like a random and unfocused sequence of events.

Narayan's other Malgudi novels include *Swami and Friends* (1935), *The Bachelor of Arts* (1937), *Mr Sampath* (1949), *The Financial Expert* (1952) and the outstandingly comic *The Painter of Signs* (1977). Short story collections: *An Astrologer's Day* (1947); *Dodu* (1950); *Lawley Road* (1956); *A Horse and Two Goats* (1970). Essays: *Next Saturday* (1973); *Reluctant Guru* (1974). Memoirs: *My Days* (1974).

NERUDA, Pablo (1904–73)
Chilean poet

A professional diplomat, Neruda spent twenty years abroad, chiefly in the Far East and in Spain (where the civil war confirmed his left-wing sympathies: he was later one of Allende's chief ministers, and was murdered after Allende was overthrown). Absence from home evoked nostalgia for his native landscape and people: he writes mainly descriptive, panoramic poetry, rather in the manner of *Masefield's nature verse or of *Heaney. His verse is prolific, easy on the ear (he frequently went on tours, reading to appreciative audiences) and translates well into English. His principal works – all topographical or autobiographical – are *Residence on Earth* (Vols. 1–2, 1931–5, strong on the feeling of the expatriate; Vol. 3, 1947, an excitable, bardic celebration of Chile and its people); *Canto general* (1950), a poetical history of South America, written in exile and full of the overwhelming impact of an earlier visit to Macchu Picchu, and the predominantly nature-poems of *Elemental Odes* (1954). Neruda is seldom a great poet, and never an intellectual one; but he is a splendid sensualist, and couples this with a vivid feeling of the outsider, the visitor preoccupied with himself as much as with the magnificent sites he describes.

Among Neruda's other volumes of verse are *Twenty Love Poems and a Song of Despair* (1924); *Spain in My Heart* (1937), his most politically committed work; *Estravagario* (1958); *Memorial de Isla Negra* (1964). Good collections in English: *Selected Poems* (ed. Tarn, 1970); R. Pring Mill: *Pablo Neruda: A Basic Anthology* (1975). Also recommended: *Memoirs* (1974) and *Passions and Impressions* (1983), both of them bonhomous but interesting: he went to exotic places and took part in fascinating events.

O'CONNOR, Flannery (1925–64)
American writer

Those who like the blacker young novelists of today (Martin Amis, say, or Ian McEwan), or who 'enjoy' the books of O'Connor's close American analogue *McCullers, will find this author much to their taste. O'Connor wrote two novels (*Wise Blood*, 1952; *The Violent Bear It Away*, 1960) and two books of short stories (*A Good Man Is Hard to Find/The Artificial Nigger*, 1957; *Everything That Rises Must Converge*, 1965). They are set in the American South, and deal with souls in the grip of Satan, who seek salvation and instead find crime, ugliness and death. (*Wise Blood*, for example, is the story of a soulless preacher whose discovery of the true God brings him to madness, self-blinding and death: it is a version in modern terms of *Oedipus the King*. *The Violent Bear It Away*, as tense as, say, *Hill's *I'm the King of the Castle*, is about the struggle for a small boy's soul between the forces of evil, i.e. false religion, and good.) The stories also deal in religious fanaticism, sadism and despair. Their contents sound as lurid as those of exploitation-shocker films like *Damien* or *The Exorcist* – and are. But O'Connor writes always with delicacy, precision and restraint. (She was a sickly, retiring woman, and famously recoiled from reading *Lolita* because of its 'shocking contents'.) There is critical argument about whether she is a minor writer of genius or merely a repressed religious maniac with literary style.

Collections: *The Complete Stories* (1971); *The Habit of Being: Letters* (1978). Good study: J. R. May: *The Pruning Word: The Parables of O'Connor* (1976).

O'HARA, John (1905–70)
American writer

O'Hara once said that he saw it as his duty to 'record the way [Americans] talked and thought and felt, and do it with complete honesty and variety'.

This is analogous to Balzac's intention, in *The Human Comedy*, to take 2,000 characters, from every layer of society, and to describe them with such sympathy and in such detail that the reader would be left in no doubt either about France in the 1850s or about the nature of humankind. Does this make O'Hara Balzac? No. His plots are more sensationalist, his characterization is shallower and his overview makes far fewer demands on his material. He is nearer to the best of the old picture-newspapers, the *Illustrated News* or *Picture Post*: his people and themes are recognizably everyday and they are reported honestly rather than 'written up'.

O'Hara's subject is materialistically pushy and philosophically self-doubting America between 1910 and 1970, and he is particularly good on the 1930s, when his work has both the literary quality of (his friend) *Fitzgerald and the authenticity of a good Hollywood melodrama of the time. He wrote eighteen novels. The best are *BUtterfield 8* (1935), the story of the fame and mysterious death of a beautiful 'jazz-age queen', and *From the Terrace* (1958), O'Hara's own favourite, a *Weidmany story about a small-town boy who rises to fame, prosperity and public service, and finds them lonely eminences. The novel-length sometimes overburdened O'Hara's muse: at his worst (e.g. in *Pal Joey*, 1940, cobbled together from a dozen short stories) he can be as slick, if never as quick, as Harold Robbins. His best work, his true 'American comedy', is in his 374 short stories. Often witty, self-declaring first-person narratives (in a style imitated from *Lardner), these tell single incidents or capture single moods with skill. There are fourteen story-collections altogether; the best are *Files on Parade* (1939), *Hellbox* (1947), *The Hat on the Bed* (1963) and *The O'Hara Generation* (1969).

The best of O'Hara's other novels include *A Rage to Live* (1949), a fine account of small-town life, *The Big Laugh* (1962), a funny Hollywood novel, *Elizabeth Appleton* (1963) and the family saga *The Lockwood Concern* (1965). Collections: *Here's O'Hara* (1946); *The Great Short Stories of John O'Hara* (1956); *49 Stories* (1963). Good non-fiction: *An Artist Is His Own Fault: O'Hara on Writers and Writing* (ed. Bruccoli, 1977). *Selected Letters* (1978). Good biographical study: M. J. Bruccoli: *The O'Hara Concern: A Biography* (1975).

ORWELL, George (1903–50)
British novelist and essayist

Orwell, an Etonian, belongs to a small but fascinating group in 20th-century British life: that of the passionate upper-middle-class radical. Heirs to centuries of eccentricity in the remoter Shires, its members often gave the state distinguished service, as maverick insiders (e.g. Roman Catholic rather than Anglican, navy rather than the Guards, leftish liberals rather than High Tory). They tended particularly to distinguish themselves in the Far-Eastern Civil Service and in the 1930s and 1940s Secret Service; some were led by zealous if purblind patriotism (and by membership of a homosexual group which was itself a secret society within society) to become double agents or spies for the 'other side'. No less individual, and no less passionate about the need for change, were those members of the group (like Orwell) who chose to criticize society not from the corridors of power but from outside – though, unlike their less alienated peers, they were often hampered by the very wealth of targets on display. Orwell's own early – and highly autobiographical – books, for example (*Burmese Days*, 1934; *A Clergyman's Daughter*, 1935; *Keep the Aspidistra Flying*, 1936), are somewhat unfocused novels of revolt (about depressed heroes in the colonial service or the provincial bourgeoisie); their chief appeal is in the precision of Orwell's social observation and the sharpness of his style. The best of his early books are *Down and Out in London and Paris* (1933), a succinct, unsentimental evocation of exactly what its title says, and *The Road to Wigan Pier* (1937), in which left-wing social reformers are given the sociological equivalent of a public-school cold bath, that is, their proposals are bitingly contrasted with the conditions of provincial poverty they came down from their ivory towers to amend. (Like Engels' *The Condition of the Working Class*, this book offers no comfort to anyone at all.)

Orwell's genius was clearly more as an essayist and journalist than as a novelist, and the Spanish civil war and Second World War gave his work the focus it required. His account of his civil war experiences, *Homage to Catalonia* (1938), and his wartime writings (a useful anthology is *Collected Essays, Journalism and Letters*, 1968) reveal him as one of the most clear-headed of all 20th-century analysts of discontent, merciless to cant and with a particularly sharp eye for that bland humbug which was (and still is) the cancer of British life. He wrote three more novels, *Coming Up for Air* (1939), the anti-Stalinist fable *Animal Farm* (1945) and *1984* (1949). *1984* takes its place in a long line of prescient dystopian fiction including *Wells's *The War of the Worlds*, *Huxley's *Brave New World* and *Burgess's *A Clockwork Orange*. All share the same faults and excellences: melodramatic plots and thin characterization on the one hand and jagged-toothed sociological and political prediction on the other. *Animal Farm* is his masterpiece: the artificial framework of fable allowed him (as it did Swift with Gulliver) to distance and therefore to shape his rage. By pretending that it's just a story about animals, he uses innocent blandness (the establishment's own most powerful weapon) to rend and tear.

Although at first sight much of Orwell's matter may seem dated, the clarity of his ideas and the incisiveness of his style remain compelling, and sad present-day reality makes him still a prophet whose message is both discomforting and quite unanswerable.

Good introduction: Meyers (ed.): *George Orwell: The Critical Heritage* (1975). Good biography: B. Crick: *George Orwell, A Life* (1980). Outstanding on Orwell's early life: P. Stansky and W. Abraham: *The Unknown Orwell* (1972). Useful, stimulating compendium: J. R. Hammond: *A George Orwell Companion* (1983).

OWEN, Wilfred (1893–1918)
British poet

The early poems (e.g. 'To the Bitter Sweetheart: A Dream', which begins 'One evening Eros took me by the hand . . .') give no indication of Owen's greatness: they are competent school-magazine lyrics, the work of a clever magpie. His experiences in the First World War and his acknowledgement of his homosexuality carried Owen's talent to the edge of genius. His verse still has a heroic impulsiveness derived from Keats and Tennyson, but his terrible theme (war's mutilation of body and spirit) provides tension and anger, and these qualities elevate him far above such other elegists of doomed youth as *Brooke, *Housman or Sassoon. It is, in the end, the *austerity* of (say) 'Smile, Smile, Smile', 'Futility' or 'Strange Meeting' which stays in the mind: Owen's images (e.g. 'Be slowly lifted up, thou long black arm,/Great gun towering towards Heaven, about to curse . . .' from 'Sonnet') are stylistically and emotionally precise, their power derived from understatement rather than from rhetoric. His work is political, his view of human humbug as uncompromising as *Orwell's; though he writes of trench warfare, this icy rage gives his poetry a general relevance which both keeps it from dating and guarantees its quality. Britten's choral work *War Requiem* introduced Owen's poetry to millions in the early 1960s.

Good critical edition: J. Stallworthy (ed.): *The Complete Poems of Wilfred Owen* (2 vols., 1984). *Collected Poems* (ed. *Day Lewis, 1963) has the added interest of a critical introduction by one poet (Day Lewis) and a memoir by another (Blunden). Good biography: J. Stallworthy: *Wilfred Owen: A Biography* (1974).

PASTERNAK, Boris (1890–1960)
Russian poet

Pasternak's reputation in Russia was as translator (among others, of Goethe, Schiller and Shakespeare), and as lyric poet. His style is simple and mystical (akin to the best of *De la Mare), and his subjects are generally autobiographical. His most famous collection is his earliest: *My Sister Life* (1922). This was written during – and reflects – the 1917 revolution, but uses historical events to frame a private love-affair: the interaction of people's public and private selves is a recurring theme in Pasternak's work. More lyric poems followed (*Themes and Variations*, 1923; *Second Birth*, 1932, about another, adulterous, love-affair), and two prose memoirs, *Childhood* (written 1918, rev. and published 1925) and *Safe Conduct* (1931). At the same time, he tried his hand at the 'official' poetry demanded of good 1920s Soviet artists: *Lofty Malady* (1924), *1905* (1926) and *Lieutenant Schmidt* (1927) go through the epic motions, but sound neither convinced nor convincing. In the 1930s and 1940s he continued writing lyric verse (a late-published collection is

When the Weather Clears, 1959), but his main effort went into the novel *Doctor Zhivago* (1958), essentially a reworking of the themes of *My Sister Life*, the counterpointing – as in *War and Peace* – of private and public affairs, love-story and politics. This book earned him the disapproval of the Soviet authorities, the Nobel Prize (which he was forbidden to accept) and the wide fame brought by a slushy 'epic' film version. Pasternak is a noble writer (if not so significant as anti-Soviet journalists once proclaimed); his best work (*My Sister Life*; *Childhood*) is intensely Russian and intensely personal, factors which simultaneously enhance and restrict his appeal.

Translations include: *The Poetry of Boris Pasternak* (1959); *50 Poems* (1963, translated by Pasternak's sister); *Collected Prose* (ed. Barnes, 1977); *Selected Poems* (ed. and trans. Stallworthy and France, 1983); *Letters to Georgian Friends* (1967); *Zhenia's Childhood* (1924), four evocative short stories intended as the beginning of a long novel, were published in English in 1982. Good study: G. de Mallac: *Boris Pasternak, His Life and Works* (1983).

PAVESE, Cesare (1908–50)
Italian novelist and poet

The themes of Pavese's work are emptiness of soul and the despairing human search for a still centre to life, whether it be love, religion or political engagement. His settings, Turin and the surrounding Piedmont region, are realistically described, and each detail of his subjects' lives is meticulously supplied. The effect is as if *Mauriac had collaborated with *Dos Passos; Pavese has less in common with directors of the Italian realist cinema (i.e. Rossellini or de Sica, with whom he is often compared) than with the fanciful symbolists who followed them, notably Antonioni (who filmed his novella *Tra donne sole*) and Pasolini and Bertolucci, whom he influenced. (They found particularly stimulating his combination of rich subject-matter and a sparse, not to say arid, narrative style.) He was interested in the formative effect of childhood experience, and his books are rich with descriptive 'flashbacks' – an action in the present is juxtaposed with the past events (mother's whoredom, father's brutality, grandmother's death) which 'caused' it. This technique is most effective in his last novel, *The Moon and the Bonfires* (1950), about a man restlessly revisiting the scenes of his former life, only to realize that 'happiness' lies not in explanations of the past but inside himself. Other novels available in English include *The Harvesters* (1941), *The Comrade* (1947) and *The House on the Hill* (1949); Pavese also published short stories (*The Political Prisoner*, 1947; *Nice Summer*, 1949), and two books of poetry, of which the second, *Death Will Come and Have Your Eyes* (1951), a collection of love-lyrics, is fine.

Selected works in English: *A Mania for Solitude* (1969), a poetry anthology; *Selected Letters* (1969); Journal: *This Business of Living: A Diary 1934–1950* (1961). Important non-fiction, on his theories and literary methods: *Dialogues with Leukothea* (1947). Good study: D. Thompson: *Cesare Pavese: A Study of the Major Novels and Poems* (1982).

PIRANDELLO, Luigi: see page 510.

POUND, Ezra (1885–1972)
American poet

As a midwife of 20th-century modernism, Pound had no equal but Diaghilev. He had the knack of cutting through others' artistic flab and sham, and showing them exactly what they were trying to do. The list of authors he 'helped' includes *Joyce (the publication of whose *Portrait of the Artist as a Young Man* Pound organized), *Yeats (whose style he completely changed), *Moore and *Williams (whose styles he helped to form) and *Eliot (whose *The Waste Land* he licked into shape from hesitant draft to self-confident publication). Pound freed English poetry from the windy syntax and ponderous sentimentality of the 19th century (and part of his poem *Hugh Selwyn Mauberley*, 1920, wittily describes what the problems were); he called for a verse-style consisting of clear images expressed with terse beauty, as in Anglo-Saxon, Japanese or Greek. (The call was famously answered by the 'Imagists', a group of poets who reduced their art, phrase by phrase, to little more than striking, random images, exquisite cobwebs of sound. But the effect of Pound's preaching on greater writers, from Eliot to *Berryman, was far-reaching and prescriptive. As with Schoenberg in music or Picasso in painting, it was impossible, after Pound, for his art ever to be done again in the way it had been before.)

Once the birth-pangs of 20th-century poetry were over, Pound proceeded to midwife poets of earlier cultures by 'translating' or adapting them into sharp modern English, as if they were real people, our contemporaries, instead of corpses mummified in scholarly notes. His greatest work in this vein was *Homage to Sextus Propertius* (1917), a recycling of the introverted love-poetry of a minor Roman poet of the first century BC, who in Pound's hands become rough-edged, unpredictable and strikingly, even if inaccurately (cf. *Graves's denunciations), up to date. Other writers as diverse as Confucius (*The Digest*, 1937; *The Unwobbling Pivot and the Great Digest*, 1947) and Sophocles (*The Women of Trachis*, 1956) also benefited from his attentions.

Unfortunately for Pound, to be an efficient midwife is not necessarily to be a good mother: one can inspire without being inspired. His own poetry – particularly set against that of followers and friends such as Eliot – is confused, wobbly in inspiration, rhythmically uncertain and distinctly difficult: he had too much to say and too little technique to say it with. (His mental state throughout his life – not only for the years he spent in a Washington asylum, atoning for his anti-Semitic, pro-fascist activities before and during the Second World War – was unstable. He walked always the dividing-line between genius and madness, and was temperamentally incapable of the artistic self-discipline he recommended to others.) The great work of his life was a series of *Cantos* begun in the 1910s, published in parts throughout his life, and finally issued 'complete' (117 in all) in 1972. They seek to offer the reader a 'guided tour' of 20th-century life, philosophy and letters similar to Dante's tour of Inferno; in fact they lead nowhere but into the labyrinth of Pound's own mind. Because that mind was brilliant, parts of the *Cantos* – notably the *Pisan Cantos* (1948), on his imprisonment by the allies after the fall of Italy – are inspired and exciting; but there is also dross in plenty. Of his other verse, the short poems of his youth (especially those in *A lume spento*, 1908, and *Lustra*, 1916) are good minor work; *Hugh Selwyn Mauberley*, an Eliotish piece in which a writer with problems of his own (shades of both *Prufrock* and *Sweeney Agonistes*) is set against a survey of the previous fifty years of English letters, is a precise and 'finished' work whose images really are clear and really do haunt the mind:

> 'Daphne with her thighs in bark
> Stretches towards me her leafy hands' –
> Subjectively –

is typically brief and fine.

Pound is, in short, a puzzle. He carried pretension to absurd and arrogant heights, inventing for himself a *persona* as bizarre as any of the characters in his verse, 'Old Ez', a sort of 'Papa Pound' for versifiers, and a role it took immense concentration and effort to sustain. A third of his work is among the best poetry of the century; no one has bettered some of his translations; he was a crucial figure in the forming of 20th-century verse. Why, though, is it so hard to *like* his verse? Alienation of audience is, in view of all his protestations about 'Kulchur', just about the last quality he would have chosen for himself.

Selected Prose 1909–1965 (1973); *Selected Poems 1908–1959* (1975); *Collected Early Poems* (1976). Translations (other than those mentioned) include *Certain Noble Plays of Japan* (1916) and *Love Poems of Ancient Egypt* (1962). He published over forty critical and polemical works (several in Italian), on subjects ranging from *ABC of Reading* (1934, a guide which famously excludes Shakespeare) and *Guide to Kulchur/Culture* (1938) to *If This Be Treason* (1948). *Literary Essays* (ed. Eliot 1954); *Pound/Joyce: The Letters of Ezra Pound and James Joyce* (ed. Read 1967); *Pound and Music: The Complete Criticism* (ed. Shafer 1977); *Selected Letters* (1907–41) (1982): excellent choice. Good biography: N. Stock: *The Life of Pound* (1970). Good critical studies: H. Kenner: *The Poetry of Ezra Pound* (1971); E. Homberger (ed.): *Pound: The Critical Heritage* (1972). Brief, well-illustrated life: P. Ackroyd: *Ezra Pound and His World* (1981).

POWELL, Anthony (born 1905)
British novelist

It was inevitable that Powell's major work, the twelve-novel sequence *A Dance to the Music of Time* (1951–75), would on completion be labelled 'Proustian' – and in one way at least the description is fair enough. Powell's work is structured in four blocks of three novels each, and each block relates a particular period in his characters' lives to the ongoing progress of the century. Thus, a main factor in the book is memory: our corporate historical memory colours and is coloured by the specific incidents recalled from his characters' past. The idea is Proustian, but the technique is not: Powell belongs to an altogether gentler tradition. His novels are comedies of manners, recalling Thackeray and even – in the urbanity of their dialogue – the plays of Sheridan. The first three books (*A Question of Upbringing, A Buyer's Market, The Acceptance World*), dealing with his characters' interlocking lives at Eton and Oxford in the gilded teens and twenties, and the three about their Second-World-War experiences (*The Valley of Bones, The Soldier's Art* and *The Military Philosophers*) are the most sharply satirical in the set; their light-hearted farce gives way to darker comedy – Powell has depth as well as edge – in the trio set in the deb-and-dance set during the Depression (*At Lady Molly's, Casanova's Chinese Restaurant, The Kindly Ones*) and to (somewhat lack-lustre) melancholy in the last three novels of all (*Books Do Furnish a Room, Temporary Kings, Hearing Secret Harmonies*), where looking back, remembering the steps of the dance, has become an engulfing obsession, and the past has overtaken and blurred the present.

Powell has a comedian's ability to create instantly striking vignettes of incident or character, and the flowing, developing nature of his work allows his characters not only frozen moments of eccentricity or tragedy (a mirror-version of *Joyce's 'epiphanies'), but also growth: events and memory play leapfrog at every stage. In fact it is Powell's eye for character which makes his art: his four-volume autobiography *To Keep the Ball Rolling* (1976–82; 1-volume reduction 1983) covers the same period, social milieu and historical events as *A Dance to the Music of Time*, but, lacking the novels' delirious invention, seems by comparison both conceited and dull.

The claim that *A Dance to the Music of Time* is Proustian exaggerates its stature; but as dry entertainment it is excellent. Its fame has unjustly eclipsed that of Powell's earlier novels, which are self-contained, prancing farces-of-manners. *Afternoon Men* (1931), about London's upper-middle-class party set between the wars, and *What's Become of Waring* (1939), about a seedy firm of publishers whose best-selling travel-writer, the obnoxious and enigmatic Waring, disappears, are English social comedy at its funniest.

A good chart to the pools and rapids of Powell's *roman fleuve* is H. Spurling: *A Reader's Guide to Anthony Powell's The Music of Time* (1977).

POWYS, John Cowper (1872–1963)
British writer

Until his 60s, Powys was a lecturer and teacher of literature, particularly in the United States. (He later distilled this work into a number of books, including studies of *Dostoievski*, 1946, *Rabelais*, 1948, and Homer, in *Atlantis*, 1954, and *Homer and the Aether*, 1959. Disrespected, on the whole, by today's specialists in these authors, the books remain revealing accounts of Powys's general view of literature and of the authors he admired.) In his later life he began publishing enormously long novels, in a philosophical, mythological and fantastic style: the effect is as if Homer had written epics on the Holy Grail, the kings of Wales or the iron-age inhabitants of Dorset, and those had then been translated into ponderous English prose by *Tolkien. The most accessible are *Wolf Solent* (1929, rev. 1961) and *A Glastonbury Romance* (1932, rev. 1965), on the Grail legend; other worthwhile titles are *Weymouth Sands/Jobber Skald* (1934), *Maiden Castle* (1936), *Owen Glendower* (1940) and *The Brazen Head* (1956). Powys's half dozen other novels, his verse (*Lucifer*, 1956) and his *Autobiography* (1934) are material chiefly for his addicts, those for example who share the critic George Steiner's view that Powys, not *Lawrence, is the greatest English novelist of his day.

Powys's brothers Llewelyn (1884–1939) and Theodore Francis (1875–1953) were also writers. T. F. Powys's books, dark with Christian symbolism, include *The Left Leg* (1923), *Mr Tasker's Gods* (1925), *Mr Weston's Good Wine* (1927) and the short-story collections *The White Paternoster* (1930), *Fables/No Painted Plumage* (1934) and *God's Eyes A-Twinkle* (1947). Llewelyn Powys, by far the jolliest of the three, published a handful of light novels and some entertaining books of autobiography and travel, including *Black Laughter* (1924), *The Verdict of Bridle-Goose* (1927), *A Pagan's Pilgrimage* (1937) and *Dorset Essays* (1935). He and J. C. Powys collaborated on the autobiographical *Confession of Two Brothers* (1916), which should be complemented by R. P. Graves's outstandingly evocative biography *The Brothers Powys* (1983).

PRIESTLEY, John Boynton: see page 511.

PROUST, Marcel (1871–1922)
French novelist

Apart from a collection of short magazine articles (*Les Plaisirs et les jours*, 1896), translations of two works by Ruskin (*The Bible of Amiens* and *Sesame and Lilies*) and one unfinished novel (*Jean Santeuil*, published 1952), Proust's lifework consists of a single book, *À la recherche du temps perdu/Remembrance of Things Past* (1912–27). Its 3,000 pages tell a continuous story, but it is divided into seven sections, each treating a different principal theme. (In *Swann's Way* the theme is childhood; in

166 · **Fiction and Poetry**

Within a Budding Grove the awakening of first love, for people and the arts; in *The Guermantes Way* high society; in *Cities of the Plain* natural and unnatural love; in *The Captive* how we are possessed by other people; in *The Sweet Cheat Gone* loss; in *Time Regained* the cycle of human life and regeneration through memory.)

The book is told in the first person: it is partly the *bildungsroman* of its narrator Marcel, and partly his account of the disintegration of French aristocratic society over a period of some fifty years (from the reign of Napoleon III to the end of the First World War). As the society crumbles in its beliefs and purposes, Marcel grows in self-knowledge and self-confidence, until at the end of the book he is ready 'to begin work', that is to write the novel we have just read. The investigation and presentation of Marcel's character is one of Proust's main objectives. Every event and every character is seen through Marcel's eyes and glossed by his comments and memories: even his heartbreaking love-affair with Albertine begins with him saying to her 'I feel that my friendship would be of value to you, that I am just the person who could give you what you lack', and ends (1,500 pages later) with a book-long reflection on his misery and remorse after she is gone. (We are told nothing of *her* feelings: the relationship is emotionally as predatory as that of the homosexual Baron de Charlus and his catamite Morel.)

Telling the story through Marcel's eyes allows Proust (as nothing else would have done) to observe with a marvellous combination of admiration, compassion and bitchy satire the obsessively self-centred world in which his characters move. Very few of them need to work – those who do are high-ranking civil servants, diplomats or creative artists – and their days are devoted to improving or enjoying their own situation in life. Connections are everything: either family connections (your place in the hierarchy of birth) or sexual connections (your personal power to dominate others). The most interesting characters are invincibly in one camp or another (the members of the Guermantes family, so well connected that they look down even on themselves; Jupien the sexual pander, and Mme Verdurin who panders to the artistic snobbery of her 'little clan'); the finest comic character of all, the Baron de Charlus, has a foot in both camps (he uses his Guermantes ancestry to dominate his low-life sexual partners, and his sexual raffishness to dominate his high-life acquaintanceship).

Because the society is enclosed and inward-looking, it is particularly susceptible to outside threats. One of Proust's themes is the series of stresses which weakened and finally destroyed the power of the French upper class in the period he is describing. There was libertarianism (symbolized in the novel by the gradual erosion of ritual 'manners' in social life, and by sexual frankness and freedom). There was the growth in importance of the middle class (symbolized by Marcel himself, acceptable everywhere; by creative artists such as Bergotte, Vinteuil, Elstir and above all Bloch, who sheds the aura of his Jewishness as his work makes him increasingly 'respectable'; and by the social-climbing

Mme Verdurin, who ends up, through sheer persistence and honesty to herself and her purposes, Princesse de Guermantes). And above all there were politics: the Dreyfus affair, and the shift it caused in the motivating ethics of the ruling class from caste loyalty to abstract justice, reverberate through the novel (and incidentally give it a prescience about the rise of fascism, and its malign manifestation McCarthyism, of which Proust can hardly have been aware).

At times, the incessant detail of Proust's writing, and its leisurely pace, cause *longueurs*: the social pirouettes in *The Guermantes Way* in particular – to say nothing of such passages as the 100-page meditation in *The Prisoner* about whether Marcel is going to get up or stay in bed – require perseverance in the reader. But this same concentration also produces the glories of the book. It is the meticulous detailing of tiny events, each with associations and evocations, which makes the life of Marcel's great-aunt at Combray, of Elstir at Balbec, of the Verdurins at La Raspalière, touching, funny and above all evocative of life. (The more particular and specific Proust's creations are, the more he reveals in them of the generality of humankind.) The finest passage in the whole novel, the evening party in *Time Remembered* (when Marcel, returning to society after years in a sanatorium, finds his friends like aged caricatures of his memory of them, realizes that he, too, is a walking ghost – and then, in Proust's greatest *coup* of all, discovers in the person of Mlle de Saint-Loup, the daughter of his greatest friend and his first love, both the key to his own past and the regenerative force both he and exhausted society need) gains its power not only from its gathering together of all the threads and themes of the preceding 2,600 pages, but also from a determined and precisely organized examination of every wrinkle, faded fold of flesh and attitude of old to young and young to old. Just as the Nighttown sequence in *Joyce's Ulysses* is at once the climax and the vindication of the novel's whole style, so this passage is what every word in *Remembrance of Things Past* was organized and set in place to make. The *craft* in Proust's art is clearly visible and is meant to be seen; it is one of its main attractions, just as it is in (say) Bach's music; but as with Bach, Proust combines intellectual density and febrility of method with a totally relaxed content: he is entirely at ease with what he wants to tell us and with every aspect of the technique and style required.

Few other writers (Rabelais is one) have been so well translated into English as Proust. The version by C. K. Scott-Moncrieff and Andreas Mayor was once even claimed to be superior to the original. It is hardly that, but in Terence Kilmartin's revision (1981) is an excellent substitute for anyone daunted by the prospect of more than a million words of French. Several fascinating satellite works also exist, each shedding light on the original novel or its author: George Painter's *Marcel Proust, a Biography* (1959–65), George Pickering's *Creative Malady* (1974), a study of – among others – Proust's neuroses as a creative force, André Maurois' *À la recherche de Marcel Proust/Quest for Proust* (1949) and Harold Pinter's amazing (and successful) distillation *The Proust Screenplay* (1978). *Monsieur Proust* (1970), by his housekeeper Céleste Albaret, is a wonderfully, unconsciously funny memoir by the unwitting original of Françoise. P. Kobb (ed.): *Selected Letters of Marcel Proust, 1880–1903* (1983).

QUENEAU, Raymond (1903–76)
French novelist

Queneau was a polymath (editorial director of Gallimard's Pléïade encyclopaedia) and an experimental novelist of stylish originality and wit. His usual subject is childhood (often in a Paris suburb), and he tells his stories in a combination of childlike observation – recapturing the phrases, distorted impressions of life and anarchic humour of children (a talkative aunt can seem ten feet tall and has a megaphone-mouth) – and a virtuoso display of puns and ironic hyperbole. His French is difficult: the best 'translation' is Malle's slapstick film of *Zazie dans le métro* (from Queneau's 1959 novel about a wisecracking little girl who wreaks havoc in a surrealist Montmartre); but sensitive English versions have been made of *The Bark-Tree* (1933), his masterpiece and the first and best of a set of autobiographical novels, of *Pierrot* (1942), *The Sunday of Life* (1952) – a hilarious send-up of, among others, Beckett – and of *Les Fleurs bleus/Between Blue and Blue* (1965). Queneau published poetry (*The Fatal Moment*, 1948; *Dog with Mandolin*, 1965), and a collection of articles and essays, *The Journey to Greece* (1973). He is also known for two elaborate, brilliant literary jokes: *Exercises in Style* (1947), ninety-nine different ways of telling the same simple tale, and *One Hundred Thousand Billion Poems* (1961), a sample-book for would-be poets in which verse and verse-forms are systematically demolished. Those who enjoy Ionesco's wilder plays will warm to Queneau; the best first approach, perhaps, is Barbara Wright's splendid 1960 translation of *Zazie*.

A good counterpart to *Zazie* – one which cries out for a film – is *We Always Treat Women Too Well* (English edn 1982), a rip-roaring Mickey Spillane spoof set in Ireland.

RAPHAEL, Frederic (born 1931)
American/British novelist and screenwriter

In 1965 Raphael's second screenplay *Darling* (sourly witty about 'swinging London') was garlanded with awards, including an Oscar. From then on, his career has oscillated between dazzling media success and the more private concerns of fiction, until in 1976 his six-part television series *The Glittering Prizes* (later published as a novel) fixed him firmly (and unfairly) in the public mind as the man who wrote, with shallow, Byronic brilliance, about the unhappy private lives of successful middle-class people, usually Oxbridge graduates and usually in the public eye. (Many of Raphael's Cambridge contemporaries, now stage producers, television anchor-persons and dons, searched anxiously for portraits of themselves in *The Glittering Prizes*; only the most narcissistic found them.) As Raphael's public reputation grew, his reception from the critics became ever frostier: an unjust state of affairs, since he is one of the most talented novelists of his generation, a man – like *Burgess, whom in every other way he outclasses – never content to write the same book twice. His best novels are *Lindmann* (1963), the study of one man's twenty-year guilt feelings at being a (Jewish?) survivor of the Holocaust, *April, June and November* (1972), the study of a 'hollow man' (witty, successful and tiresome) trying, Don-Juan-like, to discover himself through his relationships with women, and *Heaven and Earth* (1985), Raphael's most impressive work in any form. Set in the English Midlands and in Suffolk, this is about varieties of love, and particularly about close friendship and the tie between parents and children. More than any other of his books, *Heaven and Earth* establishes Raphael as a major novelist, a worthy companion (however unfashionable it may seem in British critical circles) to *Nabokov (for stylistic dazzle) and to *Roth (for emotional perception).

Of Raphael's other novels, the best are *The Limits of Love* (1960), *Orchestra and Beginners* (1967), and *Like Men Betrayed* (1970), a *Camusian story of the making of a reluctant revolutionary leader in a fascist (Greek?) dictatorship. His other films include *Two for the Road* (1967), and he has written several stage-plays, notably the Millerish tragedy *From the Greek* (1980). His short stories are published in *Sleeps Six* (1979) and *Oxbridge Blues* (1980); a selection was filmed for television in 1984.

RICHLER, Mordecai (born 1931)
Canadian novelist

To be a poor, ambitious and wisecracking Jewish boy or girl living by your wits in the big city is to be one of the Great Themes of 20th-century American fiction. The character seems as emblematic and as protean as the handsome rogue was to 18th-century novelists or the racked paterfamilias to the Edwardians. The theme is rich – and Richler, by setting his novels not in New York but in his native Canada, adds another fertile strand, provincialism. His heroes, though by no means hicks from the sticks (Montreal and Toronto are, after all, quite large), have to work just a little harder for sophistication and world-weariness. He is as sharp about Jewishness as *Roth – in a Gentile writer, such asperity would seem anti-Semitic – and as funny about endeavour (sexual, family and business) as *Heller. His best books add fascinating detail about growing up in the slums and suburbs, of first- and second-generation immigrants thrusting their way from poverty to (often rueful) affluence. The broth is rich, and needs to be stirred with a steady spoon. Sometimes Richler's writing spills into slapstick: *Cocksure* (1968), for example, a silly Mafia fantasy, is an unsatisfying cross between Terry Southern and Donald Westlake. But when he's on form, he's an entertainer as sharp and as smooth as glass. His best books are *The Apprenticeship of Duddy Kravitz* (1957), a Canadian equivalent of *What Makes Sammy Run?*, and *Joshua Then and Now* (1980), about a successful middle-class failure rerunning his past to see why a lifetime's energy, ambition and achievement produces such a bitter aftertaste. Joshua Shapiro is a *Weidman hero, just as Duddy Kravitz's stepfather is Sammy Glick. But if Richler's themes come from common stock, his exuberance and slapstick are his own, and his eye for the hollowness of fulfilled ambition makes these two novels, at least, rather more than sprawling Jewish jokes.

Richler's other books include *Shovelling Trouble* (1973), the stories in *Notes on an Endangered Species and Others* (1974), and *The Street* (1975), a book of memoirs. *Home Sweet Home* (1984) is a collection of witty, no-holds-barred essays on contemporary Canadian 'life' and 'culture' – the quotation marks sum up Richler's wry approach.

RILKE, Rainer Maria (1875–1926)
Austrian/Czech poet

If Rilke had lived in the 1960s, he might well have been a hippy; as it was, he was one of those restless 1890s, 1900s artists for whom life was an uncomfortable quest for spiritual identity. (No one quite knew what that was, but the ways to achieve it included freedom from political, social, moral and intellectual restraint and an uninhibited, not to say mystical, surrender to impulse.) Though enervating to lesser intellects, this soulful anarchy, the aleatory impulse, inspired some of the most substantial and innovative figures of the time: the list includes Rimbaud, Gauguin, Wilde and Strindberg at the beginning of the period, and *Proust, Munch, Debussy, Kandinsky and Kaiser at the end of it. For many of these artists, the door leading from unsettled busyness (what the critic Seymour Smith has called 'the existential sickness') into directed creativity was a single moment of shock and revelation (ranging from Proust's dipped *madeleine* to Strindberg's vision of Christ in the Tuileries Gardens); for Rilke, it was the result of a year (1905–6) working as Rodin's secretary – Rodin's character and working-method (notably the way in which excess stone is gradually chipped away to unclothe the immanent sculpture), though practical enough, affected him profoundly.

The 'existential quest', as applied to love, to God and above all to art, is the subject of Rilke's work. His novel *The Notebook of Malte Laurids Brigge* (1910), about a Scandinavian poet's self-tormenting life in Paris – it is a lacerating analogue of Strindberg's non-fiction *Journal of a Descent into Hell* – describes the anguish of the search; his immature poetry (e.g. *The Book of Hours*, written in the 1890s, published 1905; *New Poems*, 1907–8) shows the chaotic brilliance of genius shooting off ideas and phrases like a machine-gun. Rilke's solution to the soul's quest was (as in Rodin's sculpture) a search for latent 'truth', a paring down and simplification of experience until the desired goal became at least clear, if not attainable. It may sound pretentious and pointless; but in *The Duino Elegies* (published in 1923, after ten years' work) and in *Sonnets to Orpheus* (1922) Rilke pointfully drew out the analogies between the poet's artistic quest (symbolized by Orpheus's 'harrowing of hell'), the lover's search for the contentment only the ideal beloved can bring, and the soul's yearning for mystical possession. Rilke's poetry requires from the reader both sympathy for his predicament and patience with his style (which, for English readers, lies somewhere between *Hopkins and *Eliot); but few writers in the first half of the century so clearly lived the torment of creative genius, or produced from that torment work of such impassioned power.

Selected Letters of Rainer Maria Rilke 1902–1926 (trans. Hull, 1946) and *Letters to a Young Poet* (trans. Norton, 1954) are essential to the understanding of Rilke's work, as revealing of their author as *Kafka's *Diaries* are of theirs. Useful collection (including *The Life of Mary*, set to music by Hindemith): F. Wright (trans.): *The Unknown Rilke* (1984). The best English translations of Rilke's poetry are by Leishman and Spender; the best introductory studies are F. Wood: *Rainer Maria Rilke: The Ring of Forms* (1958) and E. C. Mason: *Rilke* (1963). The best biography is J. F. Hendry: *The Sacred Threshold: A Life of Rainer Maria Rilke* (1983).

ROBBE-GRILLET, Alain (born 1922)
French novelist

After several years as an agronomist, Robbe-Grillet took up full-time writing in his forties. He is the most readable of the French authors of 'new fiction', a genre analysed by 'new critics' (structuralists, to name only the most notorious) until the average novel-reader fears that he or she will never 'unpack' the new novelists' secret. In Robbe-Grillet's case, the secret is simple: there *is* none. He writes perfectly ordinary stories (often about searches, often with detective-heroes), and replaces psychological tension (such as animates the work of *Chandler or *Simenon) with unemotional, detailed description of every paving-stone, bread-roll or bullet-scar his characters encounter on their way. It might be argued that absence of psychological subtlety is a crippling fault, the major flaw in (say) the pulp thrillers of Mickey Spillane; but in Robbe-Grillet's hands its absence produces a dream-like atmosphere, in which lack of subtlety, even of ordinariness itself, is made to seem both improbable and intriguing. (This is a form of that dandyism which often accompanies the programmatic writer: Robbe-Grillet substitutes externals – the dandy's domain – for the 'sincerity' which can never produce genuine smartness. The 'programme' in his work is thus a dare of the reader, not a serious insight: he asks us to abandon the old tools, as he does, and still make reliable furniture. Chic replaces authenticity, and becomes the only hallmark of an Art from which genuine commitment has been purged.) Anyone who saw Resnais' 1961 film *Last Year at Marienbad*, scripted by Robbe-Grillet, will know exactly what to expect: elegant bafflement, teasing and gorgeous approximations of reality, the stuff of dreams. (Robbe-Grillet started making films himself in the 1970s: they are slow and plotless, influenced less by Resnais than by the 'constant presents' of Andy Warhol's films.)

Admirers of *Last Year at Marienbad*, or those who enjoy the stories of *Borges, should find Robbe-Grillet's novels decidedly to their taste. The best to begin with, the quintessence of his method and also a highly entertaining book, is *Jealousy* (1957), a study of exactly what it says; other novels are *The Erasers* (1953), *The Voyeur* (1955) and *In the Labyrinth* (1959). *The House of Assignation* (1965), *Project for a Revolution in New York* (1970), *Topology of a Phantom City* (1976) and *Souvenirs of the Golden Triangle* (1978), dealing as they do with drug-pushing, urban decay and teenage hooliganism, are dispassionately violent, echoing the unemotional style of exploitation movies like *Death Wish* or *The Warriors*.

Among Robbe-Grillet's published filmscripts are *Trans-Europe Express* (1967), *The Liar* (1968) and *Eden and After* (1970). Other practitioners of the 'new novel' include Sarraute (*Tropisms*, 1939, rev. 1957; *The Golden Fruits*, 1963), Simon (*The Wind*, 1957; *The Flanders Road*, 1960), and – after Robbe-Grillet the most accessible – Butor (*Second Thoughts/A Change of Heart*, 1957; *Degrees*, 1960; *Mobile*, 1963). The best critical introduction is Robbe-Grillet's own essay 'Towards a New Fiction', in *Snapshots* (1963); S. Heath: *The Nouveau Roman* (1972) makes helpful points without lapsing into the jargon of new criticism. Excellent brief study: J. Fletcher: *Alain Robbe-Grillet* (1983).

ROTH, Philip (born 1933)
American author

Like *Heller, though more aggressively, Roth draws inspiration from New-York-Jewish roots. His headline-catching books are among his weakest. *Portnoy's Complaint* (1969) is a cocky, stand-up comic book about Jewish family life, and sex, whose wise-guy brilliance has an enervating effect: the style is masturbatory, never mind the theme. *Our Gang* (1971) is a prescient satire about the Nixon presidency, rendered obsolete by events. *The Breast* (1972) is a fantasy in which a man becomes a gigantic tumescent breast – and nothing much else happens. Roth's quieter novels will wear better. They are generally about relationships, with a fineness of style and sharpness of perception characteristic of post-war American writing in this area (*McCarthy, *Updike, *Lurie). The best are *Letting Go* (1962), *When She Was Good* (1967) and *The Professor of Desire* (1977). His most impressive books are *Goodbye, Columbus* (1959), a collection of six beautifully crafted stories about the loss of innocence, and *The Ghost Writer* (1979), a short novel on one of Roth's favourite themes, the writer's urge to write and its effect on his ordinary human relationships. (Its sequels, *Zuckerman Unbound*, 1981, on being the very successful author of a very dirty book, and *The Anatomy Lesson*, 1984, are less convincing.)

Roth's other publications include a revealing anthology of his articles and interviews, *Reading Myself and Others* (1975).

SALINGER, Jerome David (born 1919)
American writer

The Catcher in the Rye (1951), Salinger's only full-length novel, brilliantly launched the 'Me-generation' of sophisticated, alienated young people on the post-Second-World-War world. It tells of Holden Caulfield's gloomy three-day spree in New York between running away from school and going home. Holden is never clear what exactly he's searching for, but he's very clear what he's rejecting: the entire sum of western consumer civilization – though, like all Salinger characters, he smokes cigarettes till the reader's lungs wheeze and ache in sympathy. The feeling of Frankenstein Humankind betrayed by its own monstrous civilization is continued in *Nine Stories/For Esmé, with Love and Squalor* (1953), which contain some of Salinger's finest writing about children. Like all his work, these stories are technically magnificent: few writers, even in the *New Yorker*, have produced more satisfyingly Rolls-Royce prose, whose style no less than its content makes it a joy to read. The stories introduce the Glass family, intellectuals ruefully, defiantly out of step with the modern world. The rest of Salinger's work to date – he publishes sparingly, and has even declared publication a 'terrible invasion of privacy' – presents further episodes in the life of this family. *Franny and Zooey* (1961) movingly charts Franny's nervous breakdown and the way in which her actor-brother Zooey, in his most dazzling 'performance', talks her out of it. *Raise High the Roof Beam, Carpenters* (published in 1963 with *Seymour, an Introduction*) is a wry account of Seymour Glass's wedding day, a painful, comic *tour de force* like the script for a Mike Nichols film. By contrast, *Seymour, an Introduction*, about intellectual genius and how we come to terms with it, is obsessed and difficult, comprehensible only in terms of Salinger's other writings about the Glass family. Salinger was the most important US writer of the 1950s, as prescient and as disdainful of coming social change as *Amis (a far smaller talent) was in Britain. A generation later, his themes have shrunk in scope, but the precision of his social and emotional observation, his humour, and above all the economy and elegance of his prose, make him a rewarding writer still.

Good, if wide-eyed, critical anthology: Belcher and Lee (eds.): *J. D. Salinger and the Critics* (1962). Good study: H. A. Grunwald (ed.): *Salinger: A Critical and Personal Portrait* (1962).

SAROYAN, William (1908–81)
American story-writer and playwright

Saroyan was to the United States what Priestley was to Britain: a purveyor (in enormous quantities: three dozen fiction books, two dozen non-fiction, nearly fifty plays) of warm-hearted, reliable and wry literary entertainment, the observing author very much written into what he wrote. There is argument about his quality (caused, perhaps, by puritan critics' dismay that anyone so prolific and so easy to read should be so 'good'), but, though his plays and novels are routine, his short stories are superb, the equal of any by *Faulkner or *Cheever (who learned much from him). The best approach to his work (which describes the fears, fantasies and foibles of 'ordinary' America) is through such collections as *48 Saroyan Stories* (1942) or *Best Stories of Saroyan* (1964); collections of individual excellence include *The Daring Young Man on the Flying Trapeze and Other Stories* (1934), *The Insurance Salesman and Other Stories* (1941) and *Love and Other Stories* (1959). His best novel is *The Human Comedy* (1943), and his best plays are *My Heart's in the Highlands* and *The Time of Your Life* (published with *Love's Old Sweet Song* in *Three Plays*, 1940).

Among Saroyan's non-fiction are five volumes of autobiography, of which the best are *The Bicycle-Rider in Beverly Hills* (1953), *Here Comes, There Goes, You Know Who* (1961) and *Sons Come and Go, but Mothers Hang in Forever* (1976), and several other books of urbane reflections such as *Famous Faces and Other Friends: A Personal Memoir* (1976). Good interim introduction: H. R. Floan: *Saroyan* (1966). *Last Rites* (1982), by his son Aram Saroyan, is a scabrous memoir about as sensationalist as Joan Crawford's daughter's *Mommie Dearest*, proving – to the author's satisfaction, at least – that Saroyan *père* had feet of clay extending right to the top of his head.

SARTRE, Jean-Paul: see page 513.

SAYERS, Dorothy Leigh (1893–1957)
British novelist

Sayers was a leading exponent of that extraordinary genre of between-the-wars detective fiction claimed to be the bedside reading of every bishop in Britain and later categorized (by Colin Watson) as 'snobbery with violence'. Her suave sleuth Wimsey, with an apt quotation ever on his lips and with patronizing ease, solves bizarre crimes committed by low-class thugs or degenerate bounders in exotic locations like East Anglian belfries, London advertising agencies or Oxford on Gaudy Night. Whether or not Sayers intended Wimsey to be insufferable, he is: the books' chief delight, apart from the recondite detail of their backgrounds, is his brisk charm, the 'nerve' of the old landed upper class. Sayers' best books are her earlier ones, especially *Strong Poison* (1930), *The Five Red Herrings* (1931) and *Murder Must Advertise* (1933). Her later novels (e.g. *Gaudy Night*, 1935) tend to pretentiousness: they are overlong, over-written and overly self-involved. She also wrote a twelve-part sequence of radio plays on the life of Christ (*The Man Born to be King*, 1941), influential and much admired in its day, and one of the flattest and most arch translations of Dante ever committed to paper (*Inferno*, 1949; *Purgatorio*, 1955). If she had stopped writing in 1933, after *Hangman's Holiday*, her reputation today would stand much higher than it does, for her first five books are excellent.

Good, no-holds-barred biography: J. Hitchman: *Such a Strange Lady: An Introduction to Dorothy L. Sayers, 1893–1957* (1975).

SEFERIS, George (1900–1971)
Greek poet

Refinement of language and distillation of experience should make Seferis accessible; but the very act of refinement makes many of his poems seem elusive and private, far less universal than those of *Cavafy, which they superficially resemble. He is a 20th-century equivalent of the poets of ancient Greece, expressing single moments of intense feeling (love, despair, sensual rapture) in restrained language which puts the reader at a 'classical' distance. The beloved is enfolded by sleep as a tree is by its leaves ('Quid platanon opacissimus', from *Mythistorema*, 1935); the poet, gazing at a wrecked ship in shallow water, hears the whispered confidences of its past ('The Wreck of the Thrush', from the splendid collection *The Thrush*, 1947); ancient Greek experience simultaneously thrusts aside and validates the present – as Seferis himself put it (in a line which could be the epigraph for his entire output): 'Wherever I travel, Greece keeps wounding me' ('In the Manner of GS', from *Logbook 1*, 1940).

All of this is as close to the age of Sappho as to our own, and yields nothing in quality to the ancient lyricists: the content may be slender, but the style is superb. None the less, Seferis is robuster than his Greek forerunners. He wrote about *Eliot, translated *The Waste Land* and was influenced by it; he was a diplomat (ambassador to Britain in the late 1950s); he spoke out gravely against the fascist Colonels in the 1960s; he was awarded the Nobel Prize in 1963. There are (well-dissembled) signs of this cosmopolitanism and toughness in the collections *Logbook I* and *The Thrush*, and they elevate Seferis's otherwise decorative art to greatness. Poems such as 'Mathios Paschalis Among the Roses', from *Logbook I* (in which love, a garden and the passing of happiness are perfectly combined – Eliot's *Little Gidding* is a near equivalent) or the unusually and overtly political 'The House near the Sea', from *The Thrush* ('They took away my houses . . .') justify his reputation – and there is nothing in the Greek Anthology so fine as 'Helen', from *Logbook III* (1955), which delineates the whole experience of Greece. Perhaps in the end Seferis's work yields its secrets only to those willing to immerse themselves in Greece and Greek culture: this is another marked difference from Cavafy, whose use of the Greek heritage is eclectic and exotic by comparison.

Seferis's work has been well translated in selection by Rex Warner (1960), and published in a bilingual edition (*Collected Poems*, 1969). His *A Poet's Journal: Days of 1945–1951* was published in English in 1974.

SIMENON, Georges (born 1903)
Belgian novelist

The excellent Simenon has an equivocal reputation with English-speaking readers. The nuances of his style resist translation – and he has been scandalously badly served, in this respect, by his British publishers; the huge success of the Maigret books has tended to eclipse his other, less formulaic output. This is not to say that the Maigret books are bad (many are excellent; *Le Chien jaune*, 1931, *Signé Picpus*, 1944, *Le Port des Brumes*, 1963, and *La Patience de Maigret*, 1966, are outstanding), merely that the non-Maigret novels are even better. Simenon's desperate characters inhabit the same desert of the soul as those of *Highsmith: their only proof to themselves that they are alive is action, and action inevitably leads to destruction. The psychological intensity (a major part of the Maigret books as well) is as unremitting as it is persuasive. Simenon's output is vast (over eighty Maigret novels, over 200 others), but at its best (for example *L'Assassin*, 1936, *En cas de malheur*, 1956, or *Le Président*, 1958), his work ranks with that of *Conrad or *Greene.

Revealing, haunting autobiography: *When I Was Old* (1970). Good study: F. Boesler: *The Mystery of Georges Simenon* (1982).

SINCLAIR, Upton (1878–1968)
American novelist

*Nabokov once mischievously invented a composite 'great American novelist' named Upton Lewis, devoted to the production of realistic 'documentary' fiction and utterly unable to produce a specific artistic signature. If this is unfair to *Lewis, it seems to describe Sinclair to a T. He was inordinately prolific: in a sixty-year writing life he produced ten plays, a volume of poetry, forty-two novels and no less than sixty-seven non-fiction works. The non-fiction is the least interesting. Its hectoring political tone and reach-me-down philosophizing can be deduced from its titles (e.g. *War: A Manifesto Against It*, 1909; *I, Governor of California, and How I Ended Poverty*, 1933; *Expect No Peace!*, 1939); much of it was dictated and remained untouched (even, one imagines, for editing) by Sinclair's own pen; by and large it has died unmourned. His plays (except for the jolly *Wally for Queen!*, 1936, and *A Giant's Strength*, 1948) are negligible; his verse (*Songs of our Nation*, 1941) is piffling. If, therefore, he still has claims on our attention, it must be as a novelist. For the average reader, the problem here is sorting out worthwhile books from two or three shelves of dross. Clearly books with titles like *100%: The Story of a Patriot* (1920) or *The Gnomobile: A Gnice Gnew Gnarrative with*

Gnonsense but Gnothing Gnaughty (1936), with their evocation of the *Reader's Digest* on the one hand and Disney Studios on the other, seem to rule themselves out (and are, in fact, appalling). But there is a string of excellent books, impressive enough to place Sinclair in the class of artist as well as word-monger, and (saving Nabokov's sneer) to link him with Lewis for quality as well as for industry. (This may not be a high artistic claim, but it is a claim.) Almost all of his novels are long, polemical studies of political or social evils of their time. *The Jungle* (1906), for example – his best-known book, and perhaps his best – is about union politics in the Chicago stockyards; *King Coal* (1917) deals with the struggle of organized labour in the Colorado coalfields (and has a 1977 sequel, *The Coal War*); *Boston* (1928) attacks both the socially privileged and the police they buy. There seem to have been no bounds to Sinclair's wrath: he took aim, among other targets, at false religion (*The Profits of Religion*, 1918), the school system (*The Goose-Step*, 1923) and the car industry (*The Flivver King*, 1937). His political stance, apparently leftish, was in fact liberal and woolly: his books are vehement with social indignation, but propose few solutions. In 1940, in *World's End*, he invented a hero who was a surrogate for the author himself: an observer, making notes and plans for the improvement of humankind. (The character was used in several more books, often now together called the *World's End* series.) If he had had the talent, Sinclair could have been the American *Wells. As it is, as hardback-journalist supreme, he remains an extraordinary, and extraordinarily American, phenomenon.

The best study of Sinclair is not in his own autobiographies (e.g. *My Lifetime in Letters*, 1960; *The Autobiography of Sinclair*, 1962), but in the more dispassionate account (particularly good on the link between art and propaganda) in L. Harris: *Sinclair: American Rebel* (1975).

SINGER, Isaac Bashevis (born 1904)
Polish/American writer

Singer writes in Yiddish, and maintains that his work is seriously weakened in translation. The same is true of *Borges in Spanish and *Mann in German – but as with them, Singer even in translation is magnificent, one of the finest writers of the century. At first sight his subject seems hermetic and obscure: the world of middle-European Jews (especially Polish) in the last three centuries, and in particular the conflict between orthodoxy and 'advanced' thinking. If that were all, if Singer were merely the chronicler of a lost way of life, his books would be the literary equivalent of dated tourist postcards. But exotic colour, though fascinating, is only the surface. His greatness lies in his warm humanity, his articulate vision of the place of change in human lives. He writes of yeshiva boys, bewigged matrons, rag-pickers and dybbuks, and makes us see our own reality. His characters are haunted – by the past, by longing for change, by the conflict between flesh and spirit, by the turmoils and urgencies of daily life. This conflict in the soul is often expressed as a direct confrontation between natural and supernatural worlds, as in the fine novels *The Magician of Lublin* (1960) and *The Slave* (1960); in other books (e.g. *Shosha*, 1975) the demonic forces are partly those within (lust, religious fervour, despair) and partly devastating political pressure from outside (particularly nazism). Other novels (e.g. *The Estate*, 1969, and *Enemies, a Love Story*, 1966) deal with the warm continuum of human relationships: *The Family Moskat* (1950), for example, his first and longest novel, charts the decline of a close-knit family in much the same way – and it is as fine a book – as Mann's *Buddenbrooks*. *The Penitent* (1974) interestingly (and movingly) sends a Polish-American Jew back to his native land and faith, and charts his journey of self-discovery: a marvellous synthesis of all Singer's major themes.

The qualities of the novels are even more apparent in Singer's superb short stories. Many of these (e.g. 'The Blasphemer', from *A Friend of Kafka*, 1971; 'Yochna and Shmelke' and the brilliant 'Elka and Meir', from *Old Love*, 1979) have Singer's familiar Polish-Jewish setting; others (e.g. 'The Cafeteria', perhaps his masterpiece in the short-story form, from *A Friend of Kafka*) are set among Yiddish-Jewish exiles in New York, haunted by the holocaust; others (e.g. 'The Briefcase', from *A Crown of Feathers*, 1973: 'The Bus', from *Old Love*) agreeably send up the idea of an elderly Jewish writer-celebrity touring America, visiting Europe and Israel, trying to cope with fans, fame and the lusts of the failing flesh. (Genuine autobiography appears in the 1966 volume of memoirs, *In My Father's Court*.) Apart from the story-collections mentioned, others include *Gimpel the Fool* (1957), *The Spinoza of Market Street* (1961), *The Séance* (1968) and *Passions* (1975); his *Collected Stories* were published in 1981.

Recognition of Isaac Singer's greatness (he won – belatedly – the Nobel Prize for Literature in 1978) has eclipsed the work of his once better-known brother Israel Joshua Singer (1893–1944). One book of Israel's, at least, is a neglected masterpiece, a novel similar in theme and quality to Isaac's best: *The Ashkenazy Brothers* (1936). Good studies of Isaac Singer: I. Malin (ed.): *Critical Views of Singer* (1969); I. Malin: *Singer* (1972). Good study, of I. B. Singer especially: C. Sinclair: *The Brothers Singer* (1983).

SITWELL, Edith (1887–1964), **Osbert** (1892–1969) and **Sacheverell** (born 1897)
British writers-about-town

In the 1920s and 1930s the rich, aristocratic Sitwell siblings were as famous in London as the Algonquin Set later became in New York; but while the Algonquins were celebrated for something serious (wit), the Sitwells' reputation at first seems to have been for nothing more than outrageousness, a poker-faced high camp topped only by Noël Coward's cruel skit on them in his 1925 revue *On With the Dance*. Behind group narcissism, however, lay genuine talent. The Sitwells knew everybody – and that included *Huxley and Walton as well as nonentities; the first performance of *Façade* (1922), with nonsense-verse by Edith and music by Walton, was a society scandal – but it also introduced 'modernism' to stuffy British society and so made possible more substantial achievements (such as Walton's own 1929 *Viola Concerto*); the Sitwells' poetry-anthologies were plump with their own verse – but they also introduced undiscovered writers like *Owen and Dylan *Thomas.

Of their own work, the best is Osbert's five-volume autobiography, a witty account of the whole bizarre bazaar. (The titles are *Left Hand, Right Hand*, 1945; *The Scarlet Tree*, 1946; *Great Morning*, 1948; *Laughter in the Next Room*, 1949, and *Noble Essence*, 1950). Sacheverell's books (mainly on travel, art and architecture) are well anthologized in *For Want of a Golden City* (1973); his *Poltergeists* (1940) deals delightfully with a preoccupation of the Sitwells' father, an eccentric turn-of-the-century spiritualist. Edith's poetry begins with modish nonsense, but progresses to work of minor excellence in the books *Gold Coast Customs* (1929), *Street Songs* (1942) and *The Canticle of the Rose* (1949); her *Collected Poems* appeared in 1954 (rev. 1957), and she was a tireless and excellent anthologist. Her non-fiction includes *Aspects of Modern Poetry* (1934), *English Eccentrics* (1933), and an autobiography, *Taken Care Of* (1965). Her *Selected Letters* were published in 1970.

Good study of the family and its entourage: J. Pearson: *Façades* (1978). Good study of Edith, making out an impassioned case for her poetry: V. L. Glendinning: *Edith Sitwell: A Unicorn Among Lions* (rev. edn 1983).

SNOW, Charles Percy (1905–80)
English novelist

Snow's 1959 lecture *The Two Cultures and the Scientific Revolution* dealt with the failure of our traditionally 'arts'-based culture to come to terms with the transformation of our lives by science and technology. In his novels, he tried to bridge this gap, and in particular to propose a new 'scientific' morality, a kind of rational humanism which would be a valid alternative to the more arbitrary moral systems of the past. This, and his dogged evocation of the hustle and importance of affairs, is the main attraction of his novels: politics (both public and personal) are their liveliest ingredient. The eleven-novel sequence *Strangers and Brothers* (1940–70) has been both overpraised and (more recently) unfairly dismissed. At its best (*The Light and the Dark*, 1947, on friendship; *The New Men*, 1954, on the morality of working on the development of atomic weapons; *The Conscience of the Rich*, 1958, on inherited influence and the 'new man') his work has something to say, and says it well. He ranks with *Galsworthy: a solid craftsman, dour but interesting.

Snow's other books include a study of a not dissimilar (though wittier) novelist,

Anthony Trollope (1975), two readable crime novels, *Death under Sail* (1932), his first book, and *A Coat of Varnish* (1979), his last, and the fine *The Search* (1934, rev. 1958) which puts across with passion and clarity the appeal a truly abstruse science (in this case, X-ray crystallography) has for its practitioners. Fascinating letters from the 1930s and 1940s: P. Snow: *Stranger and Brother: A Portrait of C. P. Snow* (1982), which can be intriguingly supplemented by J. Halpern: *C. P. Snow, an Oral Biography* (1983), taped interviews, largely filling in the gaps in his brother's account and particularly good on the originals of some of Snow's characters.

SOLZHENITSYN, Alexander (born 1918)
Russian writer

For some years after his Nobel Prize in 1970, Solzhenitsyn was the world's most famous Russian author. His labour-camp novels *One Day in the Life of Ivan Denisovich* (1962) and *First Circle* (1968), and his enormous and minutely documented exposé of the Soviet prison system *The GULAG Archipelago* (3 vols., 1974–8), were published everywhere in the western world, and acclaimed; when he was expelled from the USSR in 1974, he was welcomed in Switzerland like a prodigal son. (His popularity waned thereafter, as he began uttering and publishing denunciations of ideal-less western materialism just as blistering as his attacks on the USSR: titles like *Warning to the West*, 1976, are typical.) In the midst of all the enthusiasm – he was regularly compared to Tolstoy, though never to *Gorki, whose propaganda mirrors and whose style equals his – the actual literary quality of his work was ignored. The terrible subject-matter of *One Day*, *First Circle* and *The GULAG Archipelago* is so demanding and so compulsive that we read on regardless of the prose which treats of it. But Solzhenitsyn's work lacks depth and human understanding (as opposed to sympathy or pity): it is journalism or jeremiad, nothing else. Its essential shallowness is shown by the fact that when he writes about less sensational subjects - hospital life in *Cancer Ward* (1968, a work which admirably shows up the greatness of *Mann's *The Magic Mountain*), or the First World War and the stirrings of the Russian revolution in *August 1914* (1971, which performs the same function for *Pasternak's *Doctor Zhivago*, and is said, ominously and significantly, to be the first of a projected ten-book saga) – his intricate historical detail, pacy plotting and swift narrative are reminiscent less of Dostoievski or Tolstoy than of the Lew Wallace of *Ben Hur*: there is length without depth, verve without engagement, moralizing without morality. It is less for his quality than for the sheer fury of his invective that Solzhenitsyn commands attention.

Solzhenitsyn's other works include a short novel, *Matryona's Place* (1963), short stories (*For the Good of the Cause*, 1964; *Stories and Prose Poems*, 1971), plays (*The Love-Girl and the Innocent*, 1969; *The Victor's Feast*, 1971; *Candle in the Wind*, 1973), and several collections of speeches, essays and notebooks, of which *The Oak and the Calf* (1979), on his life from 1967 to his deportation from the

USSR, is the longest and most revealing (especially in conjunction with L. Labedz's collection of biographical primary sources, *Solzhenitsyn: A Documentary Record*, 1970).

SPARK, Muriel (born 1918)
British novelist

Memento mori (1959), her third book, a blackly funny novel about eccentric elderly people phoned up and reminded that one day they must die, announced Spark as a talented literary confectioner, a combination of *Firbank and *Compton-Burnett. Since then she has produced a string of novels set in the same shabby-genteel *milieux* and flaying their characters with the same ironic malice. It is a world where the characters are pegs for the author's wit, not people: dewy-eyed young heroines (whose sensible shoes and Scottish ancestry are none the less signs of sturdier qualities), shaky professional men (often publishers, lawyers or churchmen), high Anglicanism or low Catholicism, seaside resorts and fashionable foreign towns out of season, the Lyons Corner House, the *trattoria* and the coffee bar. It is genre fiction, comforting and changeless – but it is a genre Spark herself created and in which she alone works. (She is like *McCarthy or *Murdoch in this, and like them seems always on the edge of distinction without ever achieving it.) Her best books are not those where she 'makes statements' (e.g. *Robinson*, 1958, or *The Mandelbaum Gate*, 1965), but her slighter novels, written for the glittering, shallow fun of it: *The Prime of Miss Jean Brodie* (1961, later staged and filmed), *The Girls of Slender Means* (1963) and the particularly self-absorbed (autobiographical?) *Loitering with Intent* (1981).

Spark's other books include *Child of Light: A Reassessment of Mary Shelley* (1951) – she also edited *Mary Shelley's Letters* in 1953; *Collected Stories I* (1967), and the novels *The Takeover* (1976), *Territorial Rights* (1979), *The Only Problem* (1984), about a writer working on (and reliving) the Book of Job, and *The Abbess of Crewe* (1974), which wittily rewrites the Watergate affair in terms of convent politics. Good interim study: P. Kemp: *Muriel Spark* (1974).

STEIN, Gertrude (1874–1946)
American writer

Stein was rich and bright, and spent her life indulging herself like a little girl in a sweetshop. She lived for many years in Paris, and knew everybody: she patronized (among others) Braque, Matisse and Picasso, and was as essential a 'sight' for visiting writers (*Pound, *Hemingway, *Anderson, *Fitzgerald) as the Crazy Horse saloon or the Eiffel Tower. Driven by no artistic necessity but her own whim – and an opinion of her own literary quality that ranked her with Homer and Shakespeare – she published regular literary experiments, trying to do in words what cubist artists had done in paint (for example, to write a three-dimensional description of a box). She never actually said or wrote 'a rose is a rose is a rose'; her experimental style is better exemplified by her libretto for Virgil Thompson's 1928 opera *Four Saints in Three Acts*, which consists entirely of squeaks, grunts, whistles and nonsense syllables (and which many listeners profess to find a moving experience), or by her syntaxless 'prose poems' in *Tender Buttons: Objects, Food, Rooms* (1914), in which, she said later, 'I struggled with the ridding myself of nouns . . .' on the grounds that 'if you feel what is inside (a) thing you do not call it by the name by which it is known'.

Though these experiments represent Stein at her most typical, the best approach to her work is through a number of simpler works in more straightforward English. In *Three Lives* (1909) she tells plain tales of ordinary folk: 'Melanchtha', the second story, is a brilliantly successful stream-of-consciousness monologue depicting the 'movement' of the character's mind, interspersed with hilarious, 'tape-recorder-ear' dialogue. (Like Hemingway and many other, lesser writers, Stein learned much from the no-cant pointedness of American popular journalism.) *The Autobiography of Alice B. Toklas* (1933) is nothing of the kind: written by Stein and not by Toklas (her life's companion), it gives an account of Stein herself as a kind of artistic queen bee, and details the movement of *her* artistic mind. Other perfectly comprehensible writings include *The Making of Americans* (1925), a fictional 'history' of the USA, *Ida: A Novel* (1941), and *Matisse, Picasso and Gertrude Stein, with Two Shorter Stories* (1933). Anyone drawn to her experimental writings should begin with *Tender Buttons* and *Have They Attacked Mary. He Giggled.* (1917), and then seek elucidation in *Composition as Explanation* (1926), which piles Pelion on an Ossa of confusion: seemingly tongue-in-cheek, it is actually, disarmingly and deadly serious.

Among Stein's other recommendable non-fiction (there are over fifty titles to choose from) are *How to Write* (1931), fancy, and *Wars I Have Seen* (1945), plain. Selections include *Selected Writings* (ed. van Vechten, 1946), *Writings and Lectures 1911–1945/Look at Me Now and Here I Am* (ed. Meyerowitz, 1971) and the compendious *A Primer for the Gradual Understanding of Stein* (ed. Haas, 1973). Also recommended: *Dear Sammy: Letters from Stein and Alice B. Toklas* (ed. Steward, 1977); *The Flowers of Friendship* (letters to Stein, ed. Gallup, 1953); A. B. Toklas: *What Is Remembered* (a genuine autobiography, 1963). Good studies: E. Sprigge: *Gertrude Stein: Her Life and Works* (1957); J. Hobhouse: *Everybody Who Was Anybody* (1975).

STEINBECK, John (1902–68)
American novelist

Steinbeck's first novel was a swashbuckling yarn entitled *Cup of Gold: A Life of Henry Morgan, Buccaneer, with Occasional References to History* (1929); his last, *The Winter of Our Discontent* (1961), was an ironic comedy of modern life, in which the only way an ordinary American citizen can make his way in the world is to become (as successfully as he can) a buccaneer of crime. The progression from romp to parable mirrors the change of Steinbeck's view of his own status, from story-teller to Great American Novelist. The bulk of his books (eighteen fiction titles; thirteen non-fiction) is agreeable and forgettable; the half-dozen exceptions rank with the best American writing of the age, their style as polished as *Hemingway's, their combination of parochialism and universality as striking as *Faulkner's. Steinbeck was at his best writing about the deprived: the childlike giant Lennie in *Of Mice and Men* (1937), who accidentally kills everything he loves, the poor sharecroppers in *The Grapes of Wrath* (1939), struggling west to a better life in California, or the O'Neill-like urban derelicts and hopefuls of *Cannery Row* (1945). His literary models were often high – *Tortilla Flat* (1935), for example, reworks Malory's *Morte d'Arthur* in terms of Mexican wetbacks in California; *East of Eden* (1952) reworks the Genesis story of Adam, Eve and their quarrelling sons, with side-glances at the Greek myth of Atreus and Thyestes – and his story-telling was clear and compelling. His critics find him over-prone to whimsy and to irony, and complain that when he excludes those qualities from a book (as from *East of Eden*), the result is hysterical melodrama; but these cavils scarcely impede a reader looking simply for interesting allegorical stories, interestingly told.

Apart from *The Grapes of Wrath* (one of the best American novels of the century), Steinbeck's finest work is in short forms: the spare *Of Mice and Men*; the four linked stories of *The Red Pony* (1937), about a boy's growth to maturity; the short story 'The Pearl' (1947), about a 'base Indian, who threw away a pearl greater than all his tribe'. He was, above all, concerned with the acquisition and loss of decency, and the lack of direction in his 1950s and 1960s work was due less to artistic weakness than to the changing times: *Salinger's 1951 *The Catcher in the Rye*, and the wise-cracking Me-generation it introduced, drove out gentler fictional ruminations on the meaning and morality of life. This was tough on Steinbeck, but his best books are toughly made, and will remain.

Steinbeck's other works include the novels *To a God Unknown* (1933) and *In Dubious Battle* (1936), the study of a strike; the fine short-story collection *The Long Valley* (1938); several travel books (notably *A Russian Journal*, 1948, and *Travels with Charley in Search of America*, 1962). *The Journal of a Novel* (1969) is a moving account of how he overcame 'writer's block' and produced *East of Eden*; *The Acts of King Arthur and His Noble Knights* (1977) is a translation of Malory, a life-long passion. Collections: *The Portable Steinbeck* (1971 edn); *Steinbeck: A Life in Letters* (ed. E. Steinbeck and Wallsten, 1975). Good introduction: N. Valjean: *Steinbeck, the Errant Knight* (1975).

STEVENS, Wallace (1897–1955)
American poet

An insurance lawyer, Stevens published no poetry until he was forty-two. From then onwards he produced a dozen slim volumes, but was forever revising and polishing, so that only the last book of all, *Collected*

Poems (1954), contains the work he thought worthy to survive. (Other poems, and two short plays, were published in *Opus Posthumous*, 1957.) Few of his business associates ever knew he was a poet; few of his readers ever knew he was in business. The quality of secrecy this suggests in Stevens's character is mirrored in his verse. He was concerned – in a way much followed since by the avant-garde, who however learned it not from him but from Japanese poetry and art – with the sudden, unexpected moments of sensual or intellectual perception which *Joyce called 'epiphanies': moments when the veils of memory and tradition are briefly lifted and we see things exactly as they are. (Many of Stevens's titles, e.g. 'Thirteen Ways of Looking at a Blackbird', or 'Transport to Summer', also suggest Far-Eastern art.)

Often, the objects perceived in this epiphanic way are simple (sunsets, geese on a pond, the effect of wind in trees); but in his most complex poems (e.g. 'Invective Against Swans', or 'Sunday Morning', his master-piece), the perception Stevens seeks is metaphysical, a search for some guiding principle behind a random if beautiful world. It is this philosophical probing that makes his poetry difficult – it has been compared to the work of both *Eliot and *Pound, a singular feat in view of their disparity. But however complex the underlying thought, the language of his poems is simple and direct, in cadences as straightforward as those of *Masefield (whose nature-poetry is nearer to Stevens than any later verse). Above all, his view that there is in everyone a 'still centre', obscured by the world's turmoil but still fathomable through contemplation and the acceptance of ordinary events, still speaks (more loudly than action) to the condition of 1980s humankind.

As well as poetry, Stevens published three books of philosophical and literary essays, all in 1951: *Two or Three Ideas*; *The Relations Between Poetry and Painting*; *The Necessary Angel: Essays on Reality and Imagination*. *Letters* (ed. H. Stevens, 1967). Good, clear study: H. Bloom: *Stevens: The Poems of Our Climate* (1977).

STOREY, David: see page 522.

THEROUX, Paul (born 1941)
American writer

Long residence abroad (in Africa, Singapore and Britain, where he has made his home) has sharpened and perfected Theroux's preferred stance in his work: that of wry observer. He is the author, for example, of two quizzical, captious travel books (*The Great Railway Bazaar*, 1975; *The Old Patagonian Express*, 1979), in which the enormous discomforts of railway travel in remote places take second place to the traveller's bland astonishment at the people he meets at every stop – this is anthropology for the *New Yorker*, never for the *National Geographical Magazine*. (A third book, *The Kingdom by the Sea*, 1983, on Britain, equally beady-eyed, pleased nobody at all.) Theroux's novels usually centre on cultural misfits, amused or harassed, coping as best they can with the society in which they live. His lighter novels are reminiscent of *Greene's 'entertainments', tales of doleful inadequates feeding on the leftovers of imperialism: *Jungle Lovers* (1971), for example, is set in Africa, *Saint Jack* (1973) in Singapore. His best novels use the same deadpan style to probe deeper into 'outsider' characters: *The Black House* (1974) is about anthropologists, home from Africa, dismayed in rural Dorset; *Picture Palace* (1978), an outstanding book, is the memoirs of a veteran photographer, the observer-figure herself observed. *Mosquito Coast* (1981) is a marvellously *Conrady story of a maniac back-to-nature father and his bewildered, loving son.

Other novels: *Waldo* (1967), *Fong and the Indians* (1968), *Girls at Play* (1969), *The Family Arsenal* (1976) and *Doctor Slaughter* (1984), a sexual-comic novella, a high-camp equivalent of *Fowles's *Mantissa*. Theroux has also published short stories (*World's End*, 1980; *Sinning with Annie*, 1972; *The Consul's File*, 1977, and its sequel *The London Embassy*, 1982) and the critical study of an author with whom he has much in common, *V. S. Naipaul* (1972).

THOMAS, Dylan (1914–53)
British poet

By the end of his life, Thomas was one of the great cult figures of 20th-century letters. He stomped and growled his way round the lecture circuits boozing, chain-smoking, whoring and roaring, a magician exhaling intoxicating spells of words. If you wanted a bard, Thomas was your man. His voice and his presence (as his many recordings still attest) had mesmeric power.

It is less easy to see why Thomas was such a favourite of intellectual critics in the late 1950s. His poetry is hollow bombast. It belongs in a rhetorical tradition going back to *Beowulf* (sound-effects replacing sense), and owes allegiance both to non-conformist sermons and to the delicious, solipsistic 1920s word-games (imaginative Scrabble) of such Dada, gaga figures as Edith *Sitwell and Gertrude *Stein. Like all bad rhetoric, it does not survive the amputation of the voice: stripped of the sound of Thomas himself, nothing remains on the page but weedy words. In a few poems ('In My Craft or Sullen Art', 'Over St John's Hill', 'A Winter's Tale', 'Fern Hill') his vision does match his effects, and he produces great work, like that of a secular, despairing *Hopkins; others ('On No Work of Words', 'Holy Spring', 'Poem on His Birthday' are typical) are no more than sound and fury, hot air attempting to balloon out flabby or non-existent thoughts.

Thomas's best work is not in his *Poems* (1971, rev. 1974, ed. Jones), but in his far less pretentious prose writings. Here, although there is still occasional imagistic excess, a strong narrative drive harnesses the words and sends them cantering. In the short pieces in *Quite Early One Morning*

(1954), originally written for broadcasting, the lively and charming 'fictional autobiography' *Portrait of the Artist as a Young Dog* (1940), and the disciplined *Under Milk Wood* (1954) he has interesting things to say and says them well.

Good biographies: A. Sinclair: *Dylan Thomas: Poet of His People* (1975); P. Ferris: *Dylan Thomas* (1977).

THOMAS, Edward (1878–1917)
British poet

A summary of Thomas's life reads like the synopsis of an Edwardian novelette. He married at twenty-one, supported his family by literary hackwork, showing few signs of his genius, until he went to fight in the Great War and was killed. After his death his *Poems* (1917) were published, and found to be masterworks. Although he wrote a few war-poems (e.g. 'As the Team's Head-Brass Flashed' or the gentle 'In Memoriam, Easter 1915'), he was chiefly a nature-poet, writing about the English countryside with unsentimental, unrhetorical precision, and in particular describing the poet's own emotions as they are stirred by what he sees. He was first encouraged to write verse by his friend *Frost; but the modern American poet he most closely resembles is *Jarrell – he has the same sense of the frailty of human happiness and the inexorable entropy of both material and spiritual things. Even in poems of apparent optimism (such as the four-line 'Thaw'), this underlying sense of loss is what gives Thomas's work its quality:

> Over the land freckled with snow half-thawed
> The speculating rooks at their nests cawed
> And saw from elm-tops, delicate as flower of grass,
> What we below could not see, Winter pass.

Collected Poems (latest edn 1978). Of Thomas's prose, the best is in his later books about the countryside: *The Heart of England* (1906); *The South Country* (1909); *In Pursuit of Spring* (1915). He also wrote an autobiographical novel, *The Happy-Go-Lucky Morgans* (1913). The best biography is his wife's, a minor classic: H. Thomas: *As It Was* (1926) and *World Without End* (1931), which can usefully be supplemented by their daughter Myfanwy Thomas's memoir *One of These Fine Days* (1982). Good critical study: A. Motion: *The Poetry of Edward Thomas* (1980).

TOLKIEN, John Ronald Reuel (1892–1973)
English author

20th-century feelings of disillusion and alienation have made us particularly receptive to *gurus*: anyone who speaks with conviction and personal authority, on almost anything, is likely to attract a following. These are the outstanding qualities in Tolkien's fiction (*The Hobbit*, 1937, the simplest and best of his books; *The Lord of the Rings*, 1954–5; and the less satisfactory *The Silmarillion*, 1977). It is basically escapist fantasy, weak on character but strong on narrative, and with an appealing (or to some, stifling) overlay of pseudo-scholarship: he details the languages, manners and history of his invented world with dotty academic precision. To make a cult of this is harmless – dressing up as hobbits or talking elvish is no stranger than centring your imaginative life on Pooh, Anne Shirley or Mr Toad. For the devotee, Tolkien offers more: his books are founded on rock-solid moral certainty, a conviction that people are essentially honourable, that openness and decency will triumph in the end. This moral optimism, added to the bubbling detail of the stories, gives them vitality and zest: Tolkien's world is magnificently imagined, complete and satisfying. It is hardly his fault if some of his followers mistake it for reality, mistake a game for life.

Other writings include *Farmer Giles of Ham* (1949); *Adventures of Tom Bombadil* (1962); *Unfinished Tales* (1980). Good biography: H. Carpenter: *J. R. R. Tolkien* (1977).

UPDIKE, John (born 1932)
American writer

Updike's verse, essays and reviews have had wide magazine and journal currency; good representative collections are *Midpoint* (1969, poems) and *Picked-Up Pieces* (1975, prose). He has written many short stories, collected in *The Music School* (1966), *Museums and Women* (1972) and *Problems* (1979). Intended for single magazine publication, these are variable and enervating in the mass; even taken singly, they tend towards sleekness rather than depth – dinner-table anecdotes (witty or serious) written up in oyster-smooth prose. (Characteristic are the 'Maple' stories from the *New Yorker*, a series of vignettes from a commuter marriage. The reader feels – and is perhaps made to feel – that Chekhov is Updike's master, but the stories parrot the terse triviality of Chekhov's style without ever capturing its universal resonances. The best stories are in *Museums and Women*, which also contains such typically Updike squibs as 'During the Jurassic' and 'Under the Microscope', in which, respectively, dinosaurs and microscopic creatures are treated as if they were guests at a New England cocktail party.)

Updike's true and lasting work is in his novels. Just occasionally these are flawed by the same narcissistic glossiness as the shorter prose. For example in *Couples* (1968), about ten Connecticut couples indulging in snail-slow upper-middle-class musical chairs in the imaginary village of Tarbox, in its deadpan, black-magic, black-comedy companion-piece *The Witches of Eastwick* (1984), and in *A Month of Sundays* (1975), about a comically distraught and randy clergyman, the characters' verisimilitude and the precision of the situations are constantly undercut by the predatory brilliance of Updike's style: his creations are coat-hangers on which he hangs gaudy wraps of words. Better controlled – style at the service of theme – are *Rabbit, Run* (1960) and its sequels *Rabbit Redux* (1971) and *Rabbit Is Rich* (1981), about an 'ordinary' and decent man ambushed by his own inadequacies, and *Marry Me* (1976), the finest of Updike's books about the anguish of sexual love. His best books are those (influenced by the British novelist Henry *Green) which treat of other subjects than unhappy marriage: *The Poorhouse Fair* (1958), a dystopian fable set in an old people's home, *The Centaur* (1963), his masterpiece, about a failing schoolmaster and his adolescent son, and *Bech: A Book* (1970), and its sequel *Bech Is Back* (1983), groups of linked stories about a self-tormenting writer. Updike writes better than any living novelist about the teetering relationship between fathers and their children: this is superbly done in *The Centaur*, and is the galvanizing strength of *Of the Farm* (1965) and *Rabbit Redux*. *The Coup* (1978) is an interesting departure for another continent: a novel about revolution in Africa, applying Updike's acute perception of the balance of benefit and loss, not only to the politics of personal relationships but also to those of state and state.

Other publications include the suave story collections *The Same Door* (1959) and *Pigeon Feathers* (1962); *Seventy Poems* (1972) and several other poetry collections including *Tossing and Turning* (1977), and a handful of children's books including the Shakespeare adaptation *Bottom's Dream* (1969). Interesting non-fiction (chiefly on literary topics): *Hugging the Shore* (1984). Good introductions (less trivial than their titles suggest): J. B. Markle: *Fighters and Lovers: Theme in the Novels of John Updike* (1973); E. P. Vargo: *Rainstorms and Fire: Ritual in the Novels of John Updike* (1974).

VALÉRY, Paul (1871–1945)
French philosopher and poet

Valéry's chief contribution to the intellectual life of the century was as a philosopher, a latter-day Pascal. His interest was in the potentiality of humankind (expressed in the phrase *Que peut un homme*, 'What can a man do?'), and his search for an answer involved investigations of both art (e.g. *The Soul and Dance*, 1921) and science (e.g. *L'Idée fixe*, 1932), as well as into exemplars of what seemed to Valéry humanity at its intellectual peak (*Introduction to the Method of Leonardo da Vinci*, 1895; *Eupalinos*, 1923, about the architect as an artist-scientist wrestling with brute material). He invented a character to stand as thinking, quizzical Everyman, Monsieur Teste ('Mr Head/Tester/Testicle'), and used him in several books in Socratic-dialogue form (e.g. *An Evening with Mr Teste*, 1896; *Eupalinos*), even equipping him with a wife as down-to-earth and shrewish as Socrates' Xanthippe or Mrs Noah in the medieval mystery play. (*Letter from Mrs Émilie Teste*, 1924, is her ironical, sceptical contribution to Valéry's/Teste's Great Debate.) Throughout his life,

Valéry also jotted down observations and aphorisms, in the manner of Pascal's *Pensées*: these were collected after his death and published in two volumes of *Notebooks* (1957; 1961).

The search for a synthesis of the arts, science and philosophy, and particularly for one which omits the supernatural, has been in many 20th-century writers' minds, and the work of *Gide, *Joyce, *Koestler, *Mann and *Rilke, among others, reflects Valéry's influence. His three volumes of poetry, though no less admired than his philosophical and critical works, have been less influential. (His verse also loses much in translation.) The first two books, *Le Jeune Parque* (1917) and *Album de vers anciens* (1920) collect the work of three decades, much of it in a lusciously decadent style close to that of Mallarmé or even of Maeterlinck. The third volume, *Charmes* (1922), is stylistically harder-edged, and blends sensual description of such things as sea, sky, trees and plants with a sustained philosophical commentary on humanity's eternally aspiring, eternally failing nature. *Charmes* influenced *Eliot (notably in *The Waste Land*) and *Pound; but Valéry's nearest stylistic equivalent is neither of these writers, but a poet with the same refinement of style and the same sense of the world's decadent, fragile beauty: *Cavafy. (*Le Cimetière marin*, 'The sea-side cemetery', for example, Valéry's best-known single poem, though much longer, expresses the same mood as Cavafy's 'Exiles', from *Passions and Ancient Days*.)

Collected essays: *Variétés* (1924–44); *Autres rhumbs* (1927); *Tel quel* (1941–3). Collected works in English (15 vols., 1956–75). *Letters to and from Gide*, (in English, 1966). Good introduction: C. G. Whiting: *Paul Valéry* (1978). C. Crow: *Paul Valéry and the Poetry of Voice* (1982) is a worthy, if finally defeated, attempt to explain Valéry's poetical and 'scientific' ideas (doomed partly because of the author's – and Valéry's – confusion of mind and over-solemnity of style).

VIDAL, Gore (born 1925)
American novelist and essayist

Vidal's combination of relaxed good manners and acid tongue has made him the ideal chat-show guest, and he has devoted much time to pointing out the puerilities and pretensions of those in power. This is also the main theme of his fiction. He delights in taking great figures from history and wittily, lengthily, anatomizing their feet of clay. Since paradox is the essence of this approach, he must also take those the world regards as scoundrels, fools or failures and elevate them. Thus, in *Julian* (1962), the apostate emperor who tried to stem the rush of early Christianity is presented as a kind of earthy saint; in *Burr* (1973) the 'dark shadow over the emerging American nation' Aaron Burr is shown as a Cincinnatus, the only truly honest man; in *Creation* (1981) the Greek victory over the Persians in 490 BC is claimed as either a bad thing or as an utter irrelevance for civilization – true greatness in human culture lay thousands of miles to the east of Marathon. The research in all Vidal's historical novels is wide-ranging and impeccable; the conclusions he draws from it are bizarre and compelling, the fruit of his own conviction that if only the cynics could inherit the earth, all would be well. None the less, his books are fascinating for their detail and compulsive to read: the best are *Julian*, the trilogy on corruption and idealism in American politics *Washington DC* (1967), *Burr* and *1876* (1976), the urbane end-of-civilization-as-we-know-it thrillers (as full of twists as a paper-chain), *Kalki* (1978) and *Duluth* (1983), and his very first book, a sensitive war-novel, *Williwaw* (1946). (His worst books, *Myra Breckinridge*, 1968, and *Myron*, 1974, try to send up and at the same time excoriate sex and Hollywood, and find them squashy targets.) He also wrote film-scripts, television plays (notably *Visit to a Small Planet*, 1955) and the excellent political stage-play *The Best Man* (1960). His essays – distilling his fastidious disdain for human society – are gathered in *Collected Essays* (1974), *Matters of Fact and Fiction* (1977) and *Pink Triangle and Yellow Star and Other Essays 1976–1982* (1982). Like most of his work, they conform to our present fashions in style and 'literary excellence'; it is none the less debatable whether Vidal's smooth-running limousines of books, compared to the buggies of such men as *Bellow, *Golding or *Márquez, are genuinely built to last.

Vidal's other writings include the novels *In a Yellow Wood* (1947), *The Judgement of Paris* (1952), *The City and the Pillar* (rev. edn 1965), *Messiah* (rev. edn 1965) and *Lincoln* (1984). Good introduction: B. F. Dick: *The Apostate Angel: A Critical Study of Vidal* (1974).

WALPOLE, Hugh (1884–1941)
New Zealand/British novelist

In his tart 1930 satire on the London literary world *Cakes and Ale*, *Maugham caricatured, among others, a prolific, famous and humourless novelist who never over-reached himself, never betrayed his readers' expectations and never fulfilled his talent. Walpole recognized the description as of himself, virtually word-for-word – and Maugham's reply was a predictably silky denial, coupled with the clear message 'If the cap fits . . .'. Like most caricatures, this one was as true as it was unfair. Walpole inherited the mantle (if not the wit) of Trollope, and produced a score of estimable, crafty novels, none likely to set the Thames on fire, but never (in their day) left lying long on library shelves. (He tried, now and then, to darken his style, and produced 'shockers' in an idiom by Edgar Wallace out of Wilkie Collins: *The Man with Red Hair*, 1925, is the best.) His finest single book is *Mr Perrin and Mr Traill* (1911), about a couple of schoolmasters; but his most characteristic, most enjoyable work comes in three fat novel-cycles. *Jeremy* (1919), *Jeremy and Hamlet* (1923), and *Jeremy at Crale* (1927) are a (partly autobiographical) account of a middle-class Edwardian youth growing up; the Polchester novels (beginning with *The Cathedral*, 1922) are set in a gossip-riven cathedral city, and are reminiscent not so much of Trollope as of Mrs Gaskell (or her 20th-century equivalent Angela Thirkell); *The Herries Chronicle* (1942, originally in four separate volumes) is the saga of a northern British family from the mid 18th to the mid 20th century. *The Herries Chronicle* has been influential on later middlebrow literature, affecting the style of authors otherwise as disparate as Du Maurier, Delderfield and *Fowles, and inspiring such family sagas as Winston Graham's *Poldark* books. None the less, Walpole was a classier writer than any of these successors; saving Maugham's sarcasm, he was very nearly as able a writer as Maugham himself.

Walpole's other writings include the novels *Maradick at Forty* (1910) and *Fortitude* (1913); an able study of *Joseph Conrad* (1916); and *Four Reminiscences* (1933) of people and scenes he knew. Good biography: R. Hart-Davis: *Hugh Walpole* (1952).

WAUGH, Evelyn (1903–66)
British novelist

One of the most agreeable minor strands of 20th-century English literature has been genteel black satire, treating outrageous or slapstick subject-matter with deadpan elegance. The line stretches from *Beerbohm's *Zuleika Dobson* (1911) to Bradbury's *The History Man* (1975); it takes in stylists as different as *Firbank and *Wodehouse, and its leading talents were *Powell (in his earlier novels) and Waugh. Waugh's 1930s novels, his best books (*Decline and Fall*, 1928; *Vile Bodies*, 1930; *Black Mischief*, 1932; *A Handful of Dust*, 1934; *Scoop*, 1938), send up such subjects as preparatory schools, journalism and above all the pleasure-hungry upper class; studied prose gives the books a sharpness which belies their soft centres (Waugh has warm affection for his characters, however ridiculous the things they do); the plots continually – and enjoyably – teeter on the brink of the preposterous; the technique is visible, and fine. In most of the books, Waugh's intention is simply to entertain, and this means that when he does deepen his approach (e.g. in *A Handful of Dust*), creating a chain of events which carries his characters from folly to farcical tragedy, the result is both moving and reflective in a way outside most farce's range.

A more conscious, almost smug striving for this excellence, never entirely successful, mars Waugh's later books, especially the toadying and snobbish *Brideshead Revisited* (1945) and the trilogy of wartime novels later united under the title *Sword of Honour* (1965). In each of them Catholic manipulation replaces observation, to fatal effect. Increasingly Waugh became the victim of the real-life character he invented for himself, that of a belligerent 18th-century Tory squire, and his work became polemical (e.g. his numerous Catholic books, such as his biography of Ronald Knox, 1959) or desultory (e.g. the limp satire *The Loved One*, 1948). Only in the autobiographical *The Ordeal of Gilbert*

Pinfold (1957), the study of a schizophrenic and paranoid author on a detestable ocean voyage, did he recapture the dazzle of his finest work. His personal decline and fall were sad; but his *Decline and Fall*, and the half-dozen novels that followed it, are an ornament to letters and a lasting memorial.

Waugh's other writings include mordant travelogues, collected in *When the Going was Good* (1946), the novels *Put Out More Flags* (1942), *Helena* (1950) and *Love Among Ruins* (1953), the autobiography *A Little Learning* (1964), and the alternately wicked and maudlin *Diaries* (ed. Davie, 1975), both a picture of their tormented author and a gleeful debagging of everyone else in sight. Good biography: C. Sykes: *Evelyn Waugh: A Biography* (1980). See also M. Stannard (ed.): *Evelyn Waugh: The Critical Heritage* (1984).

WEIDMAN, Jerome (born 1913)
American novelist

Weidman's usual subject is the life of Jewish immigrants to New York in the first three decades of this century, often viewed through the eyes of the prosperous, successful and compromising Americans those immigrants or their children become in later life. His style is warm, sentimental and vivid; he is particularly good at evoking the child's-eye view of harsh material reality (as in *Fourth Street East*, 1971, a witty, beady-eyed book about Lower East Side life in the 1920s). Another favourite theme is that of the pushy adolescent making his way (as in the early *I Can Get It for You Wholesale*, 1937, his toughest book, with a bitter sting in the tail). His later novels are more relaxed, and tackle broader themes without relinquishing the documentary vividness that animates his style. *Other People's Money* (1957, about friendship and duty) and *The Temple* (1975, about Jewishness in contemporary America) are among his most successful works.

Weidman's other books include the sharp short stories in *The Horse That Could Whistle 'Dixie'* (1939), several plays (including *Ivory Tower*, 1968, and *Asterisk! A Comedy of Terrors*, 1969), and the novels *The Center of the Action* (1969) and *Last Respects* (1972) – these form a trilogy with *Fourth Street East* – and *A Family Fortune* (1978).

WELLS, Herbert George (1866–1946)
British writer

Wells's vision was of a united, balanced and peaceful universe in which the barriers of class, sex, religion and politics would be swept away, humanism based on scientific reason would enlighten all people's minds, and the globe would become a single, busy nation-state devoted to the welfare of its inhabitants. His work charts the disintegration of this vision: his insistent theme is the victory of experience over hope. In his first (and for some, finest) books, a series of allegorical science-fiction stories including *The Time Machine* (1895), *The Invisible Man* (1897), *The War of the Worlds* (1898) and *The First Men in the Moon* (1901), his heroes stumble, often thanks to some scientific accident, on one or other form of the ideal state – and find it disastrously wanting; in *The Island of Dr Moreau* (1896) and the savagely pacifist *The War in the Air* (1908) human bestiality, the satanic side of *homo sapiens*, is depicted as an all-conquering force.

Just as these books, in both their view of shattered idealism and their unblinking descriptions of horrific pain, are closer to Poe or Stevenson than to 20th-century science-fiction, so Wells's social 'comedies' (his description) are derived from Dickens. In each of these novels (the best are *Kipps*, 1905, *Tono-Bungay*, 1909, *Ann Veronica*, 1909, and *The History of Mr Polly*, 1910) engaging but socially disadvantaged heroes try to better themselves and fail; the tension is between bright-eyed optimism and grinding fate. As he grew older, Wells's ambitions for society led him away from fiction into pamphleteering: his 1920s and 1930s novels are generally dispraised in favour of such pointed predictions as *The Shape of Things to Come* (1933) and *The Fate of Homo Sapiens* (1939). His best-known non-fiction work is the bulky *Outline of History* (1920), an attempt to show the unity of human endeavour and achievement through the ages, from the stone age to the enlightened harnessing of science in the 20th century. (The notion of human progress as ever upwards as well as onwards is another 19th-century legacy in Wells's thinking. It took the 1930s, and the horrors of the subsequent world war, finally to turn him from hope to panicky despair: books like *Mind at the End of Its Tether*, 1945, chart his own descent – and are still, alas, uncomfortably relevant.)

Wells was a characteristic man of his time, straddling the chasm between Victorian radiance and post-League-of-Nations gloom. His view of science and sociology as the great healing forces for humankind was as widely held among intellectuals (and ultimately as useless and short-lived) as utopian republicanism in 17th-century Britain. Wells's sour sermons have badly dated; but (as in the case of *Owen, with whom he would have agreed that the artist's duty was to warn, or of those other writers for whom the interface between utopia and political reality was an unfailing theme, *Lewis and *Grass), the sombre partiality of his subject-matter should not distract attention from the excellence of his actual work.

The best of Wells's many other writings (over 100 publications) include the novels *Mr Britling Sees It Through* (1916) and *Mr Blettsworthy on Rampole Island* (1928), the tract *The Work, Wealth and Happiness of Mankind* (1932), the short stories in *The Country of the Blind and Other Stories* (1911) and the lively *Experiment in Autobiography* (1934). Good, readable critical summary – managing, with astonishing success, to survey all of Wells's vast output: J. R. Reed: *The Natural History of H. G. Wells* (1982). Good, knockabout criticism of Wells's intellectual and philosophical pretensions, an antidote to reverence: P. Kemp: *H. G. Wells and the Culminating Ape* (1983). A. West: *H. G. Wells* (1984): controversial because of its attacks on the author's mother Rebecca West, but a sympathetic account of his father's (Wells's) complex personality, and good on his literary and philosophical stature.

WELTY, Eudora (born 1909)
American writer

The Southern states of the USA have generally been depicted in 20th-century literature as places of glum despair: the plays of O'Neill and Williams, the novels and stories of *Faulkner, *McCullers, *O'Connor and others hardly encourage the reader to pack a carpet-bag and head south. It is a pleasure, therefore, to read an author who views the Mississippi heartlands and their inhabitants with stylish glee, writing comedies of manners as rumbustious as *Huckleberry Finn* and as full of bejewelled irony as *Mansfield Park*. Welty uses the same cast of characters as any other 'Southern' writer (poor whites, redneck landowners, negroes of every kind from corporation lawyers to Uncle Toms); the events of her plots are slapstick and bizarre (ranging from incest to a car-smash which results in a judge having to spend the night in the farm of one of the prisoners he has condemned); her dialogue, and her characters' iron codes of behaviour, are depicted with sly social observation and a lipsmacking relish for revealing cliché. Apart from the early (and uncharacteristic – except where it sends up *Gone With the Wind* or *Forever Amber*) historical romance *The Robber Bridegroom* (1942), there are two short novels (*The Ponder Heart*, 1954; *The Optimist's Daughter*, 1972) and two longer ones (*Delta Wedding*, 1946, her masterpiece; *Losing Battles*, 1970). She has also published four books of short stories (*A Curtain of Green*, 1941; *The Wide Net*, 1943; *The Golden Apples*, 1949; *The Bride of Innisfallen*, 1955), which – saving the mockery of *Jarrell, who satirized her in *Pictures from an Institution* as the jejune 'Miss Batterson' – read like *Updike, *Cheever or other Massachusetts smoothies wintering in the South.

Collections: *Selected Stories* (1954); *The Eye of the Story: Selected Essays and Reviews* (1979). Literary essays: *Short Stories* (1949); *Place in Fiction* (1957); *Three Papers on Fiction* (1962). Good interim study: J. A. Bryant Jr: *Welty* (1968).

WEST, Nathanael (1906–40)
American novelist

West earned his living as a Hollywood screenwriter, turning out high-gloss rubbish like *Ticket to Paradise* (1936), *Born to Be Wild* (1938) or *Let's Make Music* (1940). He put about as much of himself into this work as a tea-lady does into hers: there is no trace in his filmscripts either of his ornate literary style or of his Swiftian satirical imagination, the chief qualities of his novels. *The Dream Life of Balso Snell* (1931) is a scatological, surrealist and distinctly sub-Joycean fantasy about a dream-journey through the bowels of the Wooden Horse (alias contemporary society). 'O Anus Mirabilis!' gasps the hero upon entry, before conversing with religious maniacs (one writing the biography of a saintly flea which lived in Christ's armpit), murderous children and busty schoolteachers. The book ends, like a wet dream, with pointless orgasm – West's own metaphor for the sticky sterility of contemporary life. His third novel, *A Cool Million* (1934), is a similarly extravagant send-up of those Frank Capra comedies in which the honest boy from out-of-town arrives to set the world straight: West's hero Lemuel Pitkin is raped, cheated and (literally) torn apart while the society he tries to redeem degenerates into a goose-stepping fascist hell.

West's best novels are no less despairing but far less showy. *Miss Lonelyhearts* (1933) concerns an unnamed agony-column writer who is gradually seduced and destroyed by the world of the emotional derelicts he counsels, and sometimes invents. The painter Edward Hopper has exactly equalled West's vision of America in this book: a world where every insurance clerk is an emperor on the brink of discovering that he wears no clothes. The slapstick misery of the human condition is also the theme of *The Day of the Locust* (1939), a satire on Hollywood seen through the eyes of a Goyaesque painter whose *Horrors of War* will one day depict boardroom battles and casting-couch skirmishes – an easy target, but hit dead centre. West's bilious brilliance has something in common with the bitterer books of *Waugh, or even with the dystopian 1930s farces of Thorne Smith; he died (in a car crash) before writing the black masterpiece for which his talents were clearly primed.

Good introduction: I. Malin: *West's Novels* (1972).

WHARTON, Edith (1862–1937)
American novelist

Wharton's friendship with Henry *James (who magisterially commended her novel *The Reef*, 1912, as 'Racinian') has led to the common critical view that she is no more than a clay-footed disciple of the Master. In fact *The Reef* is the only one of her two dozen novels which reads anything at all like James – it is a sparer, tighter doublet of *The Wings of the Dove*, about the spiritual torment of a woman who discovers that her future husband once had an affair with the girl who is about to marry her son. Wharton's other novels are predominantly social satire, in a solid 19th-century style reminiscent of Gaskell or Thackeray. She is particularly good at evoking the snobbish upper-middle-class life of late-19th-century New York, under siege either from charming *parvenus* (e.g. the social adventuress Undine Sprague in *Custom of the Country*, 1913), or from the moral dilemma of characters who can neither endure the empty, stifling luxury of their lives nor live without it (e.g. *The House of Mirth*, 1905). After 1918, unable or unwilling to accommodate to the social changes in American manners, she lapsed into self-repetition or self-parody; the exception is *The Age of Innocence* (1920), at once a novel of moral dilemma (is the hero to marry his stuffy fiancée or the unconventional girl he loves?) and a loving evocation of 1870s New York. In addition to her long novels, Wharton also produced a number of fine shorter books (notably *Ethan Frome*, 1911, and *Summer*, 1917, both set in a New England of Hardyesque, uncompromising gloom, and dealing with intense, doomed love affairs) and some atmospheric ghost stories (e.g. those in *Tales of Men and Ghosts*, 1910, and *Ghosts*, 1937).

Wharton's other worthwhile books include a reticent autobiography (*A Backward Glance*, 1934, good on her friendship with James), the novels *Madame de Treymes* (1907) and *The Buccaneers* (1938, unfinished), the four novellas published together as *Old New York* (1924) and the short stories in *Xingu and Other Stories* (1916). A useful anthology of her work is *A Wharton Reader* (1965), edited by Louis Auchincloss (himself a prolific and recommendable novelist somewhat in the Wharton vein).

WHITE, Patrick (born 1912)
Australian novelist

After a handful of lesser books, White leapt to fame – and to excellence – with *Voss* (1957), the account of a doomed 1880s expedition into Australia's barren heartland which is made, *Conrad-like, to stand for the quest for the soul's identity in humankind at large. Gigantic themes of this sort are typical of White, a weighty (and occasionally ponderous) allegorist whom some have compared with *Lawrence or even *Mann. In two novels, *Riders in the Chariot* (1961) and *The Solid Mandala* (1966), he made the soulless Sydney suburbs a potent metaphor for the soul's waste-land; *Riders in the Chariot* is also a study of the outsider, in this case a persecuted Jewish zealot. White's most sombre treatment of the search for salvation, and his toughest books, are *The Vivisector* (1970) and *The Eye of the Storm* (1973), novels whose 'Scandinavian' darkness of theme and style rouses memories less of Mann than of the racked historical novels of Undset. His later books are less pretentious. *A Fringe of Leaves* (1976), perhaps the most accessible of all – its feeling is close to that of such 1970s Australian films as *The Getting of Wisdom* or *My Brilliant Career* – is about a shipwrecked Edwardian lady captured (and subsequently brought, through suffering, to a crisis of cultural and spiritual identity) by an Aboriginal tribe; *The Twyborn Affair* (1979) is a baroque 'comedy' (with strictly rationed laughs) about sexual identity. These last two books inhabit the same world, respectively, as *Golding's *Darkness Visible* and *The Pyramid*, and like them use irony and lucid style to help the reader with allegories and resonances as dense as any in the author's grander, more unremitting works.

White's other novels include *Happy Valley* (1939), *The Living and the Dead* (1941), *The Aunt's Story* (1948) and the Faulknerish epic of a 1890s settler in bush-country *The Tree of Man* (1956). He has also published short stories (collected in *The Burnt Ones*, 1964, and *The Cockatoos*, 1974), and an autobiography, *Flaws in the Glass* (1981), which contains a particularly moving account of homosexual love. *Four Plays* (1965); *The Ploughman* (1935): poems. Good, brief introduction: J. Colmer: *Patrick White* (1984).

WILDER, Thornton: see page 538.

WILLIAMS, William Carlos (1883–1963)
American poet

A doctor, Williams wrote poetry largely for his own or his friends' pleasure – most of his early books were vanity-pressed – and in an attempt to capture the world around him objectively on paper, with none of the fancy phrase-making of the Imagists or the fancy philosophizing of almost everyone else. He also set out (as he described in *I Wanted to Write a Poem: The Autobiography of the Works of a Poet*, ed. Heal, 1958) to create a verse-style free from the ti-tum-ti-tum iambic rhythms used by most English-language poets from Chaucer onwards. He devised a system (based on speech-rhythm) of three linked lines of varying lengths and stresses, with what he called a single main 'beat' to each line. The tropes of rhetoric (e.g. 'this man is a fool, a cretin, an ignoramus') use this pattern, with three beats spread over regularly increasing phrase-lengths; Williams's lines are subtler and rhythmically more varied:

> Only the imagination is real!
> I have declared it
> time without end

or:

> The smell of the heat is boxwood
> when rousing us
> a movement of the air.

As those examples show, the risk Williams ran in using ordinary speech-patterns to describe ordinary thoughts or events – his subjects include the weather, his patients, his garden and above all his beloved wife – is that your work varies between the flatness of unconsidered prose and a mannered coyness which approximates it to classy gibberish. If there are 'no ideas but in things', as Williams claimed, and you write about dull things, then the dullness of the things must be part of your 'idea'. In his earlier verse (gathered in *The Complete Collected Poems 1906–1938*, 1938) he hardly avoids this trap; it was not until the work of his middle age and retirement (notably the five-volume description of 'ordinary American history' *Paterson*, begun in the 1940s but not published complete until 1963, and the superb *Pictures from Brueghel*, 1962, his finest collection) that he began regularly to say things at all worth saying. The reason for the change, very largely, was that despite his avowed intentions he began increasingly to see things not objectively but *his* way, to put his own personality into his work: the much-anthologized 'Asphodel', for example, from *Pictures from Brueghel*, is an emotion-filled love-poem to his wife. Just as the earlier objectivity had seemed to echo the poise of Far-Eastern verse – not for nothing was Williams a friend of *Pound – so this new way of rendering emotion through objective description repeats, in American speech-rhythms, the method of Chinese and Japanese calligraphy. (There is also a hint, in Williams's later prosody, of the cadences of the King James Bible.)

For all his claims to simplicity and ordinariness, Williams is a difficult poet, an austere 20th-century equivalent to Walt Whitman. It is hard to thrill to his porridgy verse in the way one can respond to *Yeats or to *Lowell: lack of grandeur tends to make his work forgettable. What is interesting about the late poetry is less the lines themselves than the glimpses they give, willy-nilly, of their author, not so much the questing Dr Kildare as the reassuring Dr Gillespie of contemporary verse.

Collections and anthologies: *A Williams Reader* (ed. Rosenthal, 1966); *The Collected Early Poems* (1951); *The Collected Later Poems* (rev. edn 1961); *Selected Letters* (ed. Thirlwall, 1957). Williams also wrote novels (the trilogy *White Mule*, 1937, *In the Money*, 1941, and *The Build-Up*, 1952), short stories (*The Knife of the Times and Other Stories*, 1932; *Life Along the Passaic River*, 1938; *Make Light of It: Collected Stories*, 1950; *The Farmers' Daughters: Collected Stories*, 1961), and some outstanding non-fiction, among his best-regarded work (*In the American Grain*, 1925; *The Autobiography*, 1951). Good biography: R. Whittemore: *Williams: Poet from Jersey* (1975); outstanding literary studies: L. W. Wagner: *The Poems of Williams* (1964); *The Prose of Williams* (1970).

WILSON, Angus (born 1913)
British writer

Wilson's theme – sensibility, and its polar derivatives sensitivity and censoriousness – allies him to such Regency writers as Austen, Words-worth, or even (in his blacker, more apocalyptic flights) Blake. But his prose-style follows later models, notably Wilkie Collins, and his detail is entirely 20th-century: the locations are post-industrial towns, and the characters are as likely to be divorced middle-aged ladies or tormented 'professional men' as any of his models' aspiring or mordant young. He has written particularly well about homosexuality: this is a recurring theme in his short stories (especially those in *The Wrong Set*, 1949, and *Such Darling Dodos*, 1950), and in the novels *Hemlock and After* (1952) and *As If by Magic* (1973). In other books, notably *Anglo-Saxon Attitudes* (1956), *The Old Men at the Zoo* (1961) and the story-collection *A Bit off the Map* (1957), he indulges in sharp black satire, rather in the manner of *Spark or the later *Amis. His best novels blend all these themes and methods to produce 'family' or 'panorama' stories of failing human relationships. *The Middle Age of Mrs Eliot* (1958), one of his best books, is about a widow's Odyssey (literally, across the world; metaphorically, in search of meaning in her own life); *Late Call* (1964) is about a widowed mother forced to come to terms with her son's uncongenial life in a 1960s British New Town; *Setting the World on Fire* (1980) is about the love between two dissimilar brothers in post-war Britain. All of these are interesting stories, and make worthy books. None the less, Wilson remains sturdily in the ranks of 'reliable' rather than 'great' novelists: he belongs in the beta-class of *Murdoch, *Snow or Priestley.

Wilson's other publications include *Death Dance: 25 Stories* (1969), the novel *No Laughing Matter* (1967), *For Whom the Cloche Tolls* (1953), a 'scrapbook of the Twenties' as agreeably waspish as its title, and some excellent biographical/critical writing (*Emile Zola: An Introductory Study of His Novels*, 1952, rev. 1965; *The World of Charles Dickens*, 1970; *The Strange Ride of Rudyard Kipling*, 1977). Collected essays and reviews, especially good on such 'fine second-rate' writers as *Galsworthy: K. McSweeney (ed.): *Diversity and Depth in Fiction: Selected Critical Writings of Angus Wilson* (1983).

WODEHOUSE, Pelham Grenville (1881–1975)
British novelist

A prolific lyricist, Wodehouse in the 1920s and 1930s wrote twenty-two stage musicals (*Oh Boy* is the best known) and worked with composers as eminent as Lehár, Gershwin and Jerome Kern. He also wrote plays with George Grossmith and Ian Hay. But his finest theatrical writing is in his novels – or rather 'novel', for he reworked the same rich material in every book. His novels are farces in the great stage tradition; their gormless heroes, puffed-up colonels, predatory relatives, eccentric millionaires and dewy-eyed *ingénues* go back to Plautus, and his plots, hingeing on withheld inheritances, long-lost relatives, mistaken identity and amiable blackmail ('Do this, or you'll never eat one of Anatole's meals again') are purest *commedia dell'arte*. Clipped staginess also wings his prose – its pace comes from dialogue – though the novel form also allows him such splendid, prosy flights as Bertie Wooster's literary musings ('What sort of cove was Macbeth, and how could he have coped with Aunt Agatha?') and apt, ludicrous similes and hyperboles (butlers are like galleons under sail; happy endings are distributed in 'heaping handfuls'; an inane laugh stuns a passing thrush). There are over 100 books; the Jeeves series (e.g. *The Inimitable Jeeves*, 1924; *The Code of the Woosters*, 1938) and the Blandings series (e.g. *Summer Lightning*, 1929, a masterpiece; *Uncle Fred in the Springtime*, 1939) are the most highly regarded, but there are equally funny books with American characters (e.g. *Quick Service*, 1940) and a shoal of engaging short stories (e.g. those in *The Man Upstairs*, 1914). No other humorists, and few other writers of any kind, have been both so prolific and so consistent: if Wodehouse's mine was shallow, the lode was rich.

Recommended autobiographical letters: *The Performing Flea* (1953). Good study of themes and characters: R. Usborne: *Wodehouse at Work to the End* (1976).

Good biography: F. Donaldson: *P. G. Wodehouse, the Authorised Biography* (1982).

WOLFE, Thomas (1900–1938)
American novelist

Under the combined influences of Whitman, *Joyce and Sinclair *Lewis, and driven by a creativity as heady as any hallucinatory drug, Wolfe poured out several million words of autobiographical fiction. It is rhetorical, grandiose, incantatory, hypnotic and overwhelming, an epic torrent consciously striving to create an American 'mythology' to rival that of Homer's Greece. Out of the swirling waters of Wolfe's verbosity he and the editor Maxwell Perkins drew one reasonably coherent novel, *Look Homeward, Angel* (1929): the story of a boy growing up in North Carolina, it dips a Proustian *madeleine* (and brews a storm) in every available teacup. Perkins and Wolfe also assembled a sequel, *Of Time and the River* (1935), but Wolfe later complained that he was rushed to publish before the work achieved final shape – a criticism amply justified by the novel's intricate, formless sprawl. He published a number of (long) short stories, later collected in *From Death to Morning* (1935) and *The Short Novels* (1961): most were also worked into the fabric of his longer work. After his death, the editor Edward Aswell hewed from his surviving manuscripts another two enormous novels, *The Web and the Rock* (1939) and *You Can't Go Home Again* (1940), as well as another volume of stories, *The Hills Beyond* (1941). They repeat earlier themes in an even more baroque style, to smothering effect – indeed, and although Wolfe was certainly the Great American Novelist he set out to be, his whole output tends to choke his reader with magnificence.

Other writings include *Letters to His Mother* (1968), and two books which shed useful light on the way he worked, both alone (*The Story of a Novel*, 1936) and with Perkins (*The Notebooks*, 2 vols., 1970). In his youth he wrote plays and poetry; there is also a travel journal (*A Western Journal: A Daily Log of the Great Parks Trip, June 20–July 2, 1938*, 1951). An excellent introduction to his work is *The Portable Thomas Wolfe* (1946). Good study: R. S. Kennedy: *The Window of Being: The Literary Career of Wolfe* (1952).

WOOLF, Virginia (1882–1941)
British novelist

One justification for the exhaustive critical attention devoted to the Bloomsbury Group (of which Woolf was a leading 'member') is the light it sheds on both the content and the style of her novels. To extract most from them it is essential to know something of Woolf's own circumstances and habits of mind. (A good guide is Woolf's own *A Writer's Diary*, 1953.) This is because she largely replaced *story* (i.e. plot, consecutive narrative and incident) with *reflection*; her novels are subjective not objective; they have been called 'prose poems', but are more like erratic, digressive monologues whose goal is the exposition of states of *being* rather than (as in plotty Victorian novels) the processes of *becoming*. Woolf herself, in her essay 'Modern Fiction' (in *The Common Reader*, 1925), described the purpose of literature as 'the illumination of life' for the reader, and went on to define 'life' as 'not a series of gig lamps symmetrically arranged . . . [but] . . . a luminous halo, a semi-transparent envelope surrounding us from the beginning of consciousness to the end'.

The method of revealing that halo, of opening that envelope, is Proustian: precise descriptions of a multitude of minute sensual perceptions which combine to give a cumulative picture of a character's state of being. Woolf's strength is her sensitivity to such details: she is excellent at describing textures, tastes, sensations, the play of emotion and the blur of present and memory which is her characters' chief mode of thought. Her weakness is that all her characters are essentially herself: her men are feeble and her attempts to enter into the condition of the working class, though diligent, are condescending and inept. But for describing the genteel turmoil of middle-class, intellectual ladies (Bloomsberries all) she has no equal: it is as if the characters of Henry James opened doors into their own interiors and showed us a Freudian charnel-house behind the frail façade. The most interesting of Woolf's eight novels are *Mrs Dalloway* (1925), *To the Lighthouse* (1927) and *Between the Acts* (1941). *Mrs Dalloway*, *Ulysses*-like, describes the thoughts and memories of a group of characters on a single day, and in particular shows how Mrs Dalloway herself, a society hostess, is 'created' as a person by the way she reworks in her memory the events of her life so far. *To the Lighthouse* is about the inner lives of a philosophy don, his family and their guests in a summer house on the Isle of Skye. It is a thoughtful evocation of the way we are shaped by our relationships and by our struggle to define and understand them, an English counterpart to the books of Hilda Doolittle and Gertrude *Stein. *Between the Acts* readably and stylishly examines the feelings of a group of people involved in a patriotic pageant in an English village on one June day.

If these are the most accessible of Woolf's novels, *Orlando* (1928) and *The Waves* (1931) are the most extraordinary. The action of *Orlando* (which is a spoof, the result of a dinner-table conversation about tracing the literary ancestors of Woolf's friend Vita Sackville-West) takes place over several centuries; its hero Orlando is reincarnated (indifferently as of either sex) in one literary or historical *milieu* after another; the book is by turns vivacious and ponderous, as if Nancy Mitford had written episodes alternately with Sigmund Freud. *The Waves* shows us the thoughts of six characters as they gaze out at changing seascapes; its rhythms are hypnotic, its characters elusive and its movement lateral. For admirers of Woolf's method, it is the consummation of her art; for others, it can be one of the most boring novels of the century – and this dual response is typical: she is a novelist you either like or loathe.

Woolf's other books include *Collected Essays* (1966–7), the novel *The Voyage Out* (1915), *Jacob's Room* (1922) and *The Years* (1937), and *Flush* (1933) a whimsical 'biography' of Elizabeth Barrett's dog at the time of its mistress's elopement with Robert Browning. Good biography: Q. Bell: *Virginia Woolf: A Biography* (1-volume edn 1982). See also R. Poole: *The Unknown Virginia Woolf* (1978), an interesting examination of her 'madness'.

YEATS, William Butler (1865–1939)
Irish playwright and poet

Yeats was a passionate man, and gave himself wholeheartedly to whatever cause he espoused: Irish politics, the Celtic revival, verse drama, modern poetry. His first reputation was as a playwright (he was founder-director of the Irish Literary Theatre in 1899 and the Abbey Theatre, Dublin, in 1904). He wrote talky verse epics (modelled on Victor Hugo rather than Shakespeare) on themes from Irish legend and history: the best-known are *The Countess Cathleen* (1892), *The Land of Heart's Desire* (1894), *Cathleen ni Houlihan* (1902), and the self-revealing *The King's Threshold* (1903), about a poet who sacrifices his life for a political cause. From this fruitful early period there are also several one-act plays on themes from the Irish legend of Cuchulain, in a style modelled on Sophocles': they include the fine *On Baile's Strand* (1904) and *Deirdre* (1907, on the same theme as the unfinished *Deirdre of the Sorrows* by Yeats's friend Synge). Yeats's poems of this time (*Poems*, 1895; *Poems*, 1899) are also part of his efforts for the Celtic revival: many are on Irish themes, and use the rhythms and cadences of traditional ballads. (Such well-anthologized works as 'The Lake Isle of Innisfree', 'Down by the Salley Gardens' and 'The Fiddler of Dooney' date from this time.) In 1908 Yeats published his *Collected Works*, and the first phase of his creativity was done.

The work of his second great period was unlocked by the young *Pound, who acted as his secretary from 1913 to 1916. Just as Robert Craft turned the elderly Stravinsky's creative style in a new and unpredicted direction (serial music), so Pound turned Yeats from romanticism to modernism, and from lavishness to austerity. In drama, he introduced Yeats to Japanese Noh plays; in poetry, he introduced him to Arthur Waley's translations of Chinese verse, with its tight syllabic forms, and to the theories of such experimental groups as the Imagists. (He also encouraged Yeats's interest in spiritualism, but this had less effect on Yeats's work than on his life: his book setting out his mystical philosophy, *A Vision*, 1925, is of interest chiefly to specialists.) As he did with all new experiences, Yeats transmuted these new artistic ideas into the gold of his own style. He wrote a dozen 'plays for dancers', one-act verse plays in Noh style intended not for large theatres but for closet-performance to audiences of not more than fifty (they work well, too, on radio). Their themes are once again from Irish and Christian legend (e.g. the Grail saga), and they are in a particularly non-naturalistic, ritualistic style. The best are *At the Hawk's Well* (1917), *A Full Moon in March*

(1935), and *Purgatory* (1939), Yeats's dramatic masterpiece.

Yeats's late poetry less immediately shows Pound's influence. He still kept rhyme, and remained faithful to the iambic rhythms and regular line-lengths of 19th-century verse. But the thought is denser and more elusive; the poems live by the meaning packed into the lines as much as for their verbal music; there is discipline where once there was headiness or gush. In 'September 1913', from *Responsibilities* (1914), Yeats firmly dismissed his former Irish themes ('Romantic Ireland's dead and gone . . .'), and now regularly chose mystical or transcendental subjects (e.g. 'Easter 1916' or 'The Second Coming', both from *The Tower*, 1928; the superb 'The Collarbone of a Hare', from *The Wild Swans at Coole*, 1919; and 'The Choice', from *The Winding Stairs*, 1933, one of his finest collections).

In 1922 Yeats became a member of the Irish Senate (sitting for a protestant suburb of Dublin); in 1923 he was awarded the Nobel Prize for Literature; in 1928 he retired from public affairs, and spent the rest of his life as a very Grand Old Man of poetry (there are, for example, fascinating recordings of him reading his own verse in a thin, elderly voice, a bardic whisper, as suited to his later style as Dylan *Thomas's windy bass was to his poetry or *Eliot's toneless rasp to his). Yeats's poetic achievement (he ranks with Browning or Tennyson – and like them, wrote some of the most memorable, and remembered, phrases in the English language, ranging from 'When you are old and grey . . .' or 'I will arise and go now . . .' to 'Things fall apart. The centre cannot hold . . .') has tended to eclipse his plays. This is a pity, because although the early dramas now seem lush and overblown, the later 'plays for dancers' are among the sparest dramatic works of the century, ancestors not only of Eliot or Fry but also of the leaner visions of men like Beckett or Pinter.

Collected Poems (1950, variorum edn 1957); *Collected Plays* (1952, variorum edn 1966). *Letters* (1954) – and see *Theatre Business* (ed. Saddlemeyer, 1982), an anthology of letters between Yeats, Synge and Lady Gregory about the trials and triumphs of running the Abbey Theatre, Dublin; *Autobiographies* (1955); *Essays and Introductions* (1961); *Memoirs* (1973). Good biography: R. Ellmann: *Yeats: The Man and the Masks* (1949); *The Identity of Yeats* (1954); good critical introduction: J. Unterecker: *A Reader's Guide to W. B. Yeats* (1959).

YEVTUSHENKO, Yevgeni (born 1933)
Russian poet

In the 1960s Yevtushenko was the darling of the west, holding the place – and speaking to many of the same audiences – as Dylan *Thomas before him and *Solzhenitsyn after him. He presented the human face of the USSR at a time when the Cold War seemed capable of thaw; to the middle-aged he demonstrated that highbrow poetry can be comprehensible and even fun; to the young he seemed living proof of the unity of humankind through art. His (well-timed) hatred of the Stalin era made him an acceptable figure in Khrushchev's Russia, too: even when he supported Solzhenitsyn in 1968 his civil liberties went unimpaired.

Since the 1960s, criticism of Yevtushenko's work (as opposed to his nationality or his politics) has been sniffy: he has been called derivative, a playboy, a populist and a poetaster. All these charges, save the last, are true. He works in the tradition of *Pasternak's autobiographical poetry (and does it no dishonour); he has enjoyed his success (and why should he not?); he has introduced poetry to a wide international audience. But although he works in a comfortable mainstream tradition (nearer, say, to *Heaney or *Jarrell than to *Auden or *Berryman), he is no fake poet. *Babi Yar* (on the extermination of the Jews, harrowingly set by Shostakovich and reworked in D. M. Thomas's fine 1982 novel *The White Hotel*), and his evocations of childhood (in *Zima Junction*, 1956) and of the sterility of modern city life (in *The Bratsk Station*, 1967) are, by any standards, very good indeed.

Yevtushenko's recent work includes *A Dove in Santiago*, excellently translated (1982) by D. M. Thomas. *Selected Poems* (tr. Milner-Gulland and Levi, 1962) is the best English-language anthology of Yevtushenko's earlier work; *The Face behind the Mask* (tr. Boyars and Franklin, 1979), a collection of poems organized to tell a story in the manner of a novel, is his most characteristic recent work. His (prose) *Precocious Autobiography* (tr. 1963) provides an evocative background to the poems in *Zima Junction*, and is an interesting pendant to *Nabokov's *Speak, Memory*, on growing up in the Soviet 1930s and 1940s instead of the Tsarist 1900s.

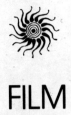

FILM

INTRODUCTION

KEY DATES

1872   Muybridge photographed a horse in motion: the first 'film'
1891   Edison invented Kinetograph (first practicable cine camera)
1895   Lumière gave first public live-action film show
1905   First 'nickelodeon' (cinema) opened (in Pittsburgh, USA)
1912   *Quo Vadis?* (first known epic feature-film)
1915   Griffith's *The Birth of a Nation* (first film masterpiece)
1927   *The Jazz Singer* (first effective commercial sound film)
1933   Disney's *Flowers and Trees*: first animated Technicolor film. (The first Technicolor live-action feature-film was Mamoulian's *Becky Sharp*, 1935)
1937   *Snow White and the Seven Dwarfs* (first animated feature-film)
1947   Appearance of 'Hollywood ten' before Unamerican Activities Committee: resultant convulsions and bannings (coupled with increasing age of moguls and competitive new film-styles from Sweden, France and Japan) accelerated decline of US studio system, with its contract stars, formula films and (often brilliantly and artistically successful) production-line techniques
1959   Truffaut's *Les Quatre Cent Coups* and Resnais' *Hiroshima mon amour*: first masterpieces of French New Wave in films

FILM AND THE 20TH CENTURY

Film, as an art-form, is a true child of the modern age. It was born out of scientific experiments (into the nature of animal locomotion) characteristic of the radical reinvestigations of nature triggered by Darwin's *The Origin of Species*; from their very first showing motion pictures were a prime example of the application to mass entertainment of the principle of the production line; film-makers have always been receptive to the latest ideas in drama, music and the visual arts, and have made them available (in however vulgar a form) to audiences everywhere; the interaction of films and fashion, social development, even military and political events, is so powerful that some people have suggested that cinema is not a passive art-form but a dangerous and distorting mirror, that movies are making the image of the century as much as reflecting it.

A characteristically 20th-century feature of films, shared by no other art-form (since every other art reached our century after hundreds of years, matured and distilled by time), is speed of development. From the 1887 publication of Muybridge's *Animal Locomotion* (sequential photographs of animals, birds and insects in motion, instantly identifiable by modern eyes as the first-ever film strips) to Griffith's *The Birth of a Nation* (1915), the first cinema masterpiece, is a single generation; from *The Birth of a Nation* to the coming of sound is a dozen years; from the coming of sound to the present day is the span of one creative life. There are, still working in films, several pioneers of the early days: 'tradition' in cinema has nothing to do with passing years.

Another phenomenon unique in the arts to cinema is its instant and universal appeal. The images and stereotypes of film transcend nationality, race, class and above all artistic and intellectual sophistication: audiences in Papua New Guinea respond to Chaplin in much the same way as audiences in Chelsea or Manhattan. Film may be a new art-form, but its power is such that it seems, now, always to have been there.

The public hunger for films, coupled with their breakneck evolution, has led to an uneasy alliance between artifice and art, between production methods and product. The movie moguls of the old days – most of whom entered films from other trades, such as glove-making (Goldwyn), scrap-dealing (Mayer) or song-plugging (Cohn) – were in the business to make money. 'If it works, do it – then I'll tell you if it works or not' (Cohn) and 'If I want a message, I'll call Western Union' (Mayer) are possibly apocryphal but certainly fair statements of an attitude of mind. When Warner Brothers screened *The Jazz Singer* in 1927, the other studios' derision at the new, short-lived gimmick (sound) lasted as long as it took *The Jazz Singer* to start making money: within eighteen months every major studio was committed to sound, and (with a few notable exceptions such as Chaplin's *City Lights* and *Modern Times*) silent films were as dead as buggies after the arrival of the Model T Ford. The same thing happened when colour processing became cheap and reliable (with the marketing, in 1949, of Eastmancolor stock). Who nowadays makes black-and-white films, unless they are also making a firm statement about their artistic intentions and/or economic situation? These innovations, not necessarily improvements or deteriorations, were accepted for marketing reasons first; those in the business of art had to follow as best they might or be left behind. (There are people, for example, who still maintain that silent cinema was the true artistic form, and that the coming of sound – replacing simplicity with technical complexity and the poetic representation of action with brute verisimilitude – made films coarser, more strident and far less malleable by the artist's shaping hand.)

At first sight, headlong development and the dominance of the market-place might indeed seem to limit the choices for artistic excellence. If films are made and promoted as a constantly self-renewing novelty (with the built-in obsolescence this implies), what place is left for intellectual integrity or moral depth? The cynic, observing their development over the last seventy years, might well answer 'None'. Is not the gulf between coterie and popular cinema as wide as that between the 'high' and 'low' aspects of any other art? Are not those critics (such as Truffaut) who find artistic excellence in the work of journeymen (in Truffaut's case, Hitchcock) talking self-regarding and inflated nonsense? If films have indeed never been more than fashionable, unpretentious mass entertainment with an arty-crafty fringe (as, to many people, television still seems to be today), then claims to artistic excellence are entirely out of place. But the fact remains that of all 20th-century arts film is not only the most popular, but also the most widely influential and understood. One of the reasons is a phenomenon that no one in Griffith's day could possibly have predicted: the sequences and images of film, so far from being ephemeral, lodge themselves in the mind and can be recalled years later in detail and with ease. How many people, for example, if asked to describe what Chaplin did or how Astaire danced, will describe particular scenes (from films seen perhaps once, years before) with apparently total recall and – even more strikingly – with a clear understanding and appreciation of the artistic techniques involved? Our memory-bank of past film sequences provides the basis for a sophisticated and knowledgeable response to every new film we see.

Audience sophistication, coupled with the need for each film-maker to go on being successful simply to stay in business, has led – whatever the greedy motive – to a rare hunger in the film industry for new ideas. The avant-garde, that characteristic and sometimes wan appendage of every art, is very soon assimilated into the mainstream of cinema: this morning's outrageous experiments become the standard practice of this afternoon. (Good examples are the whip-pans, voice-overs, dislocation of narrative sequence and unsynchronized sound pioneered by the 1950s French New Wave. All these procedures are now so much part of the ordinary processes of film-making that every pop video or television advertisement makes use of them – and the founding work of Godard or Resnais, overtaken by its own discoveries, can seem self-conscious, over-careful and out of date.) Cinema is unique less for its assimilation of the avant-garde than for the short time such assimilation takes.

The flow of ideas is by no means one way. (The two-way flow between experiment and tradition is a sure guarantee that an art-form is full of life.) Avant-garde cinema often draws its strength from an awareness of the processes of popular films, from a common vocabulary, in a far more thorough-going way than any other art. Such figures as Griffith, Disney, Hitchcock, Ford and Groucho Marx have had incalculable influence in areas far beyond their own artistic scope. Their work is not merely parodied (and parody is a fertile method for all avant-garde art); it is used as a platform, a body of material needing no explanation which the avant-garde artist can develop or react against as he or she chooses. (In western literature, classical legend and the Bible have in their time fulfilled a similar function.) In the same way, the international comprehensibility – the *lingua franca* – of cinema has led to a unique cultural cross-fertilization. When eastern music is plundered by western artists (e.g. Stockhausen) or vice versa (e.g. Takemitsu), it tends to be used superficially, for its exotic or traditional appeal; but when Japanese films draw on those of Hollywood, or Russian and Italian cinema-styles interact, exotic differences are soon absorbed. We don't notice the Japanese Noh-style in Eisenstein, or the influence of Eisenstein on Kurosawa: we simply see Eisenstein or Kurosawa films.

The result of all this is to make film a uniquely cohesive and unified art-form. The maker of a block-busting epic uses the same techniques and draws on the same subtleties as the maker of an art-cinema documentary. Whatever the difference in artistic intent, there is no difference in quality between (say) *The Seventh Seal* and *Singin' in the Rain*; the 'trash-culture' of cinema (for example the films of Garbo, Bogart and Wayne) is not the degenerate child of some higher art-form, but is an artistic manifestation in its own right. What *are* the masterpieces of cinema? They are *Battleship Potemkin* and *Wild Strawberries*, but also and equally *The Gold Rush*, *The Seven Samurai* and *Citizen Kane*. In no other contemporary art-form is the marriage between entertainment and excellence so consistently, systematically harmonious.

THE EFFECTS OF FILM

Self-consistent cinema may be – but what of its relationship with the larger world? Has it really any serious claims to 'art'? Are its geniuses (Buñuel, Bergman, Fellini and a handful of others) comparable with Leonardo, Mozart or Shakespeare – and if not, where does the difference lie? The disparity is evident between a masterpiece of 'trash' cinema like *Citizen Kane* and a masterpiece of 'high' art like Mozart's G minor Quintet. The difference is not in basic intention (to entertain) or in technical expertise, but in the degree of creative seriousness. *Citizen Kane* declares Welles a showman, a magician – its brilliance is self-conscious and wilful rather than integral. By contrast, Mozart's personality is subsumed in the notes he writes. Thus *Citizen Kane* is frivolous and Mozart's quintet is not. But are those critics right who find a similar frivolousness, a similar moral and artistic pulling-back, in *all* cinema? Is it an endemic 'fault', the hurdle to greatness which *Twelfth Night* has leapt and *Viridiana* and *The Burmese Harp* have not? For all the 'permanence' of a finished film (and films are more often 'remade' by others than withdrawn and revised by their original creators – Spielberg's reworking of *Close Encounters of the Third Kind* was a piece of artistic commitment, and of self-criticism, almost unique in cinema history), cinema is an art primarily of editing, of choice. (It reflects the liberty of modern humanity, free of religiously imposed or demanded choices; it is supremely secular.) Choice entails that we may have chosen badly; it cannot be good since it could always be better; it is never *finished*.

The question of choice, of editing, raises an issue far more important than these artistic conundrums (which in any case intrigue critics far more than those who choose, merely, to enjoy the arts). That is the moral problem posed by cinema's effect on our century's consciousness of itself. It hardly matters that fashion has always aped the cinema, that people have modelled their bathrooms on Cedric Gibbons's décor or their sweaters and hairstyles on those of their favourite stars. But it does matter that the world tends to think of 1920s Chicago or the American prison system in Warner Brothers terms, or to assume that all Swedes are as glum as Bergman's, all the British as stiff-upper-lipped or eccentric as those of Ealing Studios, all Japanese as inscrutable or hysterical as those of Kurosawa. One of the inescapable effects of cinema is a paradigmatic, insidious corruption of general moral values. Cinema stereotype evolves into real-life norm – for example in the depiction of love, heroism, sincerity or enterprise. All art is deceptive; but the camera, because it appears objectively to photograph reality, tells the most egregious lies of all.

The selection and distortion of real events have latterly been demonstrated in the matter of television news film. In the Vietnam war, for example, reporters and cameramen 'staged' events for the camera, for no more sinister reasons (one hopes) than that they'd arrived too late to film the actual real events, or that unedited reality, in the living room, would not seem real enough. Then Coppola, in *Apocalypse Now*, completed the degeneration from reality by basing his depiction of the Vietnam war – and the moral conclusions he drew from it – not on real conditions or events but on *reports*. Without our knowledge of Vietnam newsfilm, many of his images would baffle – and if we can't trust his images, how can we trust his moral messages? In exactly the same way, fiction films tend to re-invent every aspect of corporate reality in a more processed form. It may even be an essential feature of cinema (the result of editing?) that it *casts* its audience, makes its spectators actors, creates stereotypes and masks. Tragedy, in the ancient theatre, humanized its spectators through formality; the informality and apparent realism of film dehumanize them. The ethical correlative, which gives art moral power, is replaced by an aesthetic correlative, which gives it shallow and dangerous forcefulness. (An example is the 'star system', which allows personal magnetism the force once reserved for moral excellence. We now routinely demand 'star quality' of politicians – with what incalculable results?)

This normative power in film makes questions about its purpose and stature particularly relevant. We can ask of every art-form whether it reflects surrounding culture or programmes it – but because of our susceptibility to cinema images, because of their universal forcefulness, the question is nowhere more pertinent than here. Just as the processes of cinema are artistically unique, so is its relationship with society. For this reason alone it demands – though seldom gets – to be taken more seriously than any other 20th-century art.

NOTE: THE DIRECTOR AS 'AUTEUR'

In most art-forms, ultimate responsibility rests with a single individual –
other hands may be involved in *presenting* the work, but his or hers is the
genius that creates the poem, the symphony, the painting or the play. But
films, because of the technical complexity of their making, are synthetic
creations. Script, lighting, camera-work, music and editing all play vital
parts, and inadequacy in any one of them can destroy the effect of the
others, however fine. So who is the 'author' of a film, the guarantor of its
uniqueness and its quality – writer, star, director, editor or cinematographer?

This is a long-standing and still unresolved controversy. One of the
most convenient answers – the one which governed the choice of film-
makers for this book, less for ideological reasons than because it allows
the widest possible survey of the industry and its achievement – is that the
'author' of a film is the one person in absolute artistic control, the
director. Especially since the decline of the great studios in the 1940s,
but frequently before then, he – there have been very few shes – has been
the commanding source (so long as he is not himself deposed) from whom
all creative decisions flow. So far from merely telling the actors how to
speak and when to move (a producer's definition of the director's job),
he often writes or rewrites the script, commissions the music and chooses
– in the dubbing room – when and how loudly it will be heard, selects
camera angles and lighting – in short, he not only organizes the film's
dramatic ebb and flow but controls its visual appearance too. As the
editor is to a newspaper, so the director is to a film: a figurehead, a
trimmer, a guarantor.

ALLEN, Woody (born 1935)
American writer, actor and director

After a successful early career as solo comedian and writer (among his scripts was that for Donner's 1965 comedy *What's New, Pussycat?*), Allen began directing his own films in 1969. The first three, *Take the Money and Run* (1969), *Bananas* (1971) and *Everything You Always Wanted to Know About Sex* (1972), though fast and full of splendid individual gags, suffer from immature directorial technique: they are as unpretentiously rambling as home movies. In *Play It Again, Sam* (1972, from his own stage play; the film was co-directed by Herbert Ross), *Sleeper* (1973) and *Love and Death* (1975), the technique is surer, and everything works to articulate Allen's own splendid central performance as a little man baffled by contingent circumstance, responding with wry pessimism to the buffets of the world – a comic hero as emblematic of the 1970s as Lloyd was of the go-getting 1920s or *Tati of the bumbling 1950s. The apogee of this style came in *Annie Hall* (1977), in which Allen treated a serious theme (loss and recovery of dignity) with farcical earnestness and made a masterpiece, and in *Broadway Danny Rose* (1984), a welcome return to farce after several more solemn films.

As his films have improved in technique – they are now spectacularly and glossily streamlined – it has become clear that though Allen is an inventive and stylish director, he lacks a style. At first (in *Manhattan*, 1979, notable for its gorgeous black-and-white photography and its big-band sound-track), the results were charming and appealing, though never as good as *Annie Hall*. But *Interiors* (1978) and *A Midsummer Night's Sex Comedy* (1982) are director's, not performer's, films, homage paid to *Bergman by a brilliant devotee. (*Interiors* is as serious as *Six Scenes from a Marriage*; *A Midsummer Night's Sex Comedy*, for all its wisecracking anachronisms, is as autumnally comic as *Smiles of a Summer Night*.) The clue to this development is perhaps in *Stardust Memories* (1980), Allen's *Eight and a Half*, about the agony of a clown prevented by his fans and critics from playing Hamlet. As a clown, and as a writer, Allen is in the front rank; as a serious director, he is overshadowed by the towering company he keeps. He is reported as saying that his 'chief regret is that he is not someone else' – and this is beginning to show in his work. (In *Zelig*, 1983, he played a man so anodyne that he took on the colour of his surroundings, whether those were a Jack Dempsey fight, a Hitler rally at Nuremberg or an audience with Pope Pius XI. The result is technically superb, but short on both laughs and point.)

Allen's characteristic (and very funny) writings for such journals as the *New Yorker* are collected in the books *Getting Even* (1973), *Without Feathers* (1976) and *Side Effects* (1980). A collection of his screenplays from *Annie Hall* to *Stardust Memories* was published in 1982. Good study: D. Jacobs: *The Magic of Woody Allen* (1982).

ALTMAN, Robert (born 1922)
American director, producer and writer

The first film to reveal Altman's mature style was *M*A*S*H* (1970). Everything about it is characteristic of his work: its exploration of a single aspect of contemporary American life (in this case, although the action is set in Korea, the attitudes of young people to the Vietnam war); its blend of caustic wit with a kind of detached sentimentality (although these young doctors send up every aspect of militarism, patriotism, valour and the wholesomeness of conformity, they are at heart as loyal, as honourable and finally as cuddly as Andy Hardy); and most importantly, its creative method. Altman, the autocrat and manipulator, used a large cast of relatively unknown actors, with no stars, and allowed them time to rehearse, to develop depth of performance, to improvise and interact in a democratic way more common in the theatre than in the hasty cinema. That the result made stars of Sally Kellerman, Donald Sutherland and Elliott Gould does not diminish the film's remarkable unity of purpose.

Since *M*A*S*H*, the same three elements have been the dominating features of Altman's work. At times, one or other outweighs the rest and overbalances a film. The sense of egalitarian cast unity, for example, where the actors are free to develop or submerge their scenes and characters as they see fit, produces in *A Wedding* (1978) a feeling of randomness that inhibits enjoyment. As at a real wedding, a large number of relatives mutter or shout their way through a jumble of events, while the camera (and thus the spectator) picks its way among them, trying to find coherence in what is finally and intentionally chaotic. In *California Split* (1974, about a couple of ne'er-do-well gamblers) there are so many lovable rogues, so many cameos of character, that the spectator is choked by richness: the film bustles like a Dickens novel but lacks a Dickens plot. In *Buffalo Bill and the Indians* (1976), a kind of comic-strip history of the American West, the sheer rumbustious Americanness of the whole thing is embarrassing and exhausting (even the nasty guys exude zap and bounce): well before the end you long for a cold compress and a darkened room.

Altman's best films are those where exuberance and anarchy are held in control by a sharp, tight script. *McCabe and Mrs Miller* (1971) is a send-up of the 1900s Northwest, a kind of *M*A*S*H Comes Home* whose humour, parodying the heroics of American fantasy rather than blood-boltered Korean reality, can afford to be relaxed and engaging without losing its cutting edge. *The Long Goodbye* (1973) is a splendid updating of Chandler in the mellow, inconsequential Californian lifestyle of the 1970s. *Nashville* (1975) represents the American dream as a festival of country music; *Health* (1979) is a political satire set, with biliously funny accuracy, at a health convention; they are the films before all others in which Altman's style, a loose progression of random incidents, an imprecise collage of precise observations, triumphantly justifies itself.

Altman's other films include *The James Dean Story* (1957), and its outstanding follow-up *Come Back to the Five and Dime, Jimmy Dean* (1982), a Bogdanovichy film about the reunion of a Dean fan-club in McCarthy Ear, Texas.

ANDERSON, Lindsay (born 1923)
British director

In the 1950s and 1960s Anderson was a respected stage director and a dogmatic film theoretician and critic. He has occasionally (and contro-versially) directed for television, and began his film career with a number of admired short documentaries. His feature-films are stunning with images, the fruit of a documentarist's eye for detail. The rugby-matches in *This Sporting Life* (1963), for example, are convincing both as entertainment (the action is exciting) and as emotional narration (the action tells us what the participants are as well as what they do). But his films also exhibit a damaging creative arrogance: he uses rhetoric instead of argument and can thus, for those not convinced, seem no more than pretentious. Thus, *If . . .* (1968) begins as a promising attack on fascist attitudes in a contemporary Britain symbolized as a public school; but in the end, because the characters are not fully imagined except as puppets of Anderson's dystopian propaganda, the collapse of the society into violence and anarchy seems gratuitous and excessive rather than a persuasively prepared apocalypse. *O Lucky Man!* (1973), *In Celebration* (1974) and *Britannia Hospital* (1982), an over-the-top rerun of Hiller's black farce *Hospital* (scripted by Chayevsky: see page 470), and depicting Britain in terms of a class-ridden, strife-ridden and decaying National Health hospital, widen the scope of Anderson's rage, take on nothing less than the degeneracy of society at large – and once again slide into overassertion expressed in images of heartless brilliance.

Good on Anderson's aims, and on his early career: E. Sussex: *Lindsay Anderson* (1969).

ANTONIONI, Michelangelo (born 1912)
Italian director and writer

After a distinguished early career as scriptwriter and documentarist, Antonioni made his first feature, *Cronaca di un amore* (*Chronicle of an Affair*) in 1950. This film (about a rich woman, her lover, and the mysterious death of her husband) and *La signora senza camelie* (*The Lady Without Camelias*, 1953, the story of a shopgirl who is promoted to film stardom and then relapses into obscurity) follow well-worn Holly-wood conventions both of plot and method. But *Le amiche* (*The Girlfriends*, 1955) and *Il grido* (*The Cry*, 1957) are more individual, and reveal for the first time the dominating themes of Antonioni's mature work. These are, first, the exploration of lack of communication in close relationships, often using incident more to reveal emotion than to carry forward a coherent plot; second, a fascination for landscape, and especially cityscape, photographed with self-conscious and often sensuous beauty; third, a general feeling of alienation from bourgeois society, of disgust with people in the mass, which first drives the central characters together and then separates them. These are the main elements of Antonioni's three finest films: *L'avventura* (*The Adventure*, 1960), *La notte* (*The Night*, 1961) and *L'eclisse* (*The Eclipse*, 1962). *L'avventura*, a masterpiece, chronicles an insubstantial love-affair from the woman's point of view, and contains a performance of outstanding mystery and sensuality from Monica Vitti, as if Garbo had gone to work for the 1950s French New Wave. *La notte* shows twenty-four hours in the life of an ebbing marriage; visits to a nightclub and a party are used to highlight the hollowness of the main relationship, and the characters' inner emptiness is counterpointed with marvellously bleak camera images of the streets and skyscrapers of Milan. *L'eclisse* again centres on a powerful performance by Vitti, this time as a woman who drifts out of one affair and into another. There are strong elements of Absurd drama in all these 'plots'; but Antonioni's nihilist vision is expressed not in a gaunt stage setting but in screen images of swooping, glowing richness – a surface gloss which has deceived some critics into thinking his work corrupted by its own technique. Certainly *Il deserto rosso* (*The Red Desert*, 1964, his first colour film) and *Blow-Up* (1967) are based on the flimsiest of incidents, and rely for effect on the mystery and poetry of their images. But *Zabriskie Point* (1970) binds landscape, human relationships, alienation and the idea of the soul's journey into a single powerful narrative, animated by political disgust. Its central sequence, dozens of lovers coupling in the enormous barrenness of Death Valley, is characteristic of Antonioni's metaphorical art at its most illuminating and most opaque. His films are as individual, and to some as baffling, as those of *Resnais. But they are substantial visions, with power to move the emotions as well as to ensnare the eye.

Antonioni's other films include *The Oberwald Mystery* (1981), loosely based on Cocteau's *The Eagle Has Two Heads* and somewhat fuzzily processed from videotape to film, and the stunningly photographed but unoriginally plotted – it is his version of *Fellini's *La dolce vita*, and also of Fellini's *Eight and a Half* – *Identification of a Woman* (1982).

BALCON, Michael (1896–1978)
British producer and executive

Balcon was the guiding spirit behind two characterful British production companies, Gainsborough Pictures and Ealing Studios. His years with Gainsborough (1924–37) were marked by a series of unpretentious entertainment films using such theatre stars as Ivor Novello, Jack Hulbert, Cicely Courtneidge and the Aldwych farceurs Tom Walls, Ralph Lynn and Robertson Hare. (Ben Travers' farces *Rookery Nook*, filmed in 1930, and *A Cuckoo in the Nest*, filmed in 1933, are among the best films of these years.) After Balcon left, the company specialized in slapstick comedies using popular music-hall comedians (notably George Formby and Will Hay, whose *Oh, Mr Porter*, 1938, and *My Learned Friend*, 1944, are as fine as any Hollywood comedies of the time) and in light-hearted, romantic and sado-masochistic melodramas starring some or all of Margaret Lockwood, Phyllis Calvert, James Mason and Stewart Granger (among the best are *The Man in Grey*, 1943, and *The Wicked Lady*, 1945).

At Ealing, which he joined in 1938, Balcon continued and developed the Gainsborough tradition, and founded a 'house style' as recognizable as those of any of the great American studios. Ealing became known for reliable action films (*The Foreman Went to France*, 1942; *Dead of Night*, 1945; *The Overlanders*, 1946; *Scott of the Antarctic*, 1948; *The Cruel Sea*, 1952), and for idiosyncratic comedies combining whimsy and tangerine irony (*Whisky Galore*, 1949; *Passport to Pimlico*, 1949; *The Lavender Hill Mob*, 1951; *The Man in the White Suit*, 1951; *The Titfield Thunderbolt*, 1952). Part of the Ealing appeal is unassuming insularity, based on British stars, its own stable of writers (notably John Dighton and T. E. B. Clarke), and the use of attractive British locations, filmed with documentary attention to detail. (Ealing films also reflected, and in part fostered, a feeling of national identity and pride during and after the Second World War: their characters' qualities of understatement, individuality and quirky reliability were thought typical of the British nation as a whole.) Two of the best Ealing comedies add blackness to the humour without losing this endearing dottiness: *Kind Hearts and Coronets* (1949, about the successive murders of eight eccentric relatives, all played by Alec Guinness) and *The Ladykillers* (1955, about an old lady and a gang of freakish hoodlums, with macabre touches worthy of *Hitchcock himself).

Balcon's brand of low-budget, workmanlike film-making did not (alas) survive the 1950s. Its essentially local audience and its unflashy creative style were taken over by television, and English-language films (unlike those in many European countries) became ever larger, more international and more grandiose. Balcon wound up Ealing in 1955. He worked for a number of other companies (including Rank and British Lion), but seems never again to have been able to create the team unity and sense of identity which marked the British industry in its finest years.

Interesting autobiography: *Michael Balcon Presents: A Lifetime of Films* (1969). Enjoyable illustrated study, rich in description of films: G. Perry: *Forever Ealing* (1981). Good study of British films in general: R. Durgnat: *A Mirror for England: British Movies from Austerity to Affluence* (1971). Anyone who enjoys Ealing comedies will find them marvellously reincarnated in the work of Bill Forsyth (born 1941): his comedies are less slapstick than Ealing, but as good at the quiet development of incident and exploration of character. *Gregory's Girl* (1981), on first love, and *Local Hero* (1983), about the events in a Shetlands village after an American oil millionaire tries to buy the foreshore, and *Comfort and Joy* (1984), about a mini-Mafia 'ice-cream war' in Glasgow, are the best of them.

BERGMAN, Ingmar (born 1918)
Swedish director and writer

Bergman's films are striking to look at and beautifully photographed. The sensuous black-and-white textures of *Summer with Monika* (1953), the wood-block graininess of *The Seventh Seal* (1957) and the bleached pastel shades of *A Passion* (1969) (to take three films at random) are in each case an exact emotional correlative to the landscapes and characters they show. The acting is intense, personal and convincing: even in the most outlandish sequences, we have no difficulty in accepting the reality of these characters in these situations. In short, Bergman is a fine technician, and uses the medium with unobtrusive skill.

But so do a thousand other directors. Technical excellence is mandatory (and taken for granted) in modern films in a way it is not, for example, in all stage productions, television shows, music and ballet performances. Bergman's genius is not visual, but literary. His scripts make the films his own, raise them from craftsmanship to art. Viewed as a creator of 'literature', he stands with some of the finest dramatists of the century: his vision is as powerful as Beckett's, his articulation of that vision as enriching, idiosyncratic and appropriate as O'Casey's. (We are not used to evaluating cinema in terms of the other arts; because it is a public, popular medium, it is usually judged in terms of itself alone. But the work of a handful of cinema creators – *Chaplin, *Renoir, *Kurosawa, Bergman – transcends particularity and takes its place, objectively, with the productions of the finest, most programmatic 20th-century minds.) In Scandinavian literature, Bergman follows Undset (for narrative power), Lagerkvist (for poetic bareness and precision) and above all Strindberg (for the self-validating and self-destructive energy of his characters).

Bergman's principal subject is human loneliness; he has no time for happy friendships, fulfilled marriages or contented souls, except as mirrors or precursors of alienation. The fullest exposition of this theme is in three films of the early 1960s, *Through a Glass Darkly* (1961), about the cannibalistic force of family relationships; *Winter Light* (1962), about humanity's withdrawal from warmth and friendliness in search of the love of a non-existent God; and *The Silence* (1963), in which the human condition is reduced, Beckett-like, to a dying woman and her sister locked together by hostile surroundings (an oppressive foreign land whose language they do not speak). The danger of alienation as a theme is obviously that of systematic artistic introversion, and some of Bergman's later films (notably *A Passion*, *Cries and Whispers*, 1972, and *Scenes from a Marriage*, 1974) are so nervous with private pain that they

can make the spectator feel an embarrassed voyeur, make us wonder
what the need or value is of eavesdropping on such anguish – in other
words, Bergman's documentary intensity is not balanced by artistic point.
Persona (1966, in part a reworking of the female relationship in *The
Silence*) and the magnificent *Autumn Sonata* (1978) show how it should
be done: because we sympathize with the characters' pain, each film has
something to say outside the story it simply tells.

Bergman's finest films are those of the 1950s. They include two
comedies, *Smiles of a Summer Night* (1955) and *A Lesson in Love* (1956),
not unlike Anouilh in tone. There are three magnificently acted films
exploring the fears and feelings of their female characters, *Waiting
Women* (1952), *Summer with Monika* and *Journey into Autumn* (1954).
Particularly striking is an examination of the artist as outsider, set in (for
Bergman) the uncharacteristically extrovert world of the circus (*Sawdust
and Tinsel*, 1953; the theme of the alienated artist reappears in two of his
emptiest and most pretentious films, *The Face*, 1958 and *Hour of the
Wolf*, 1968). The two finest 1950s films are *The Seventh Seal*, an
apocalyptic journey through a world of Bosch-inspired medieval despair,
and *Wild Strawberries* (1957), a beautifully organized story of old age,
loneliness and, above all, the heartlessness of memory, and with fine
performances from Gunnar Björnstrand and Victor *Sjöström. These
films are the most 'achieved' of all Bergman's works. Their stories,
characters and philosophy are as glacial as ever, but there is a compen-
sating warmth in the story-telling, a persuasive sympathy between creator
and creation which communicates with the spectators, draws us into the
experience, moves us and changes us in the prescriptive way claimed for
all great art.

Bergman's other films include *The Virgin Spring* (1960), *The Rite* (1969) and *From
the Life of the Marionettes* (1981) – all bleak and bare – an ebullient version of
Mozart's opera, *The Magic Flute* (1974), and a sensitive study of Edwardian
childhood (partly autobiographical), *Fanny and Alexander* (1982), claimed at the
time as likely to be his swan-song. Excellent study: P. Cowie: *Ingmar Bergman:
A Critical Biography* (1983). Interesting first-hand information: S. Björkman, T.
Mannis and J. Simon: *Bergman on Bergman: Interviews with Ingmar Bergman*
(English edn 1973). Good on Bergman's non-cinema work: L. L. and F. Marker:
Ingmar Bergman: Four Decades in the Theatre (1981).

BERKELEY, Busby (1895–1976)
American choreographer and director

Berkeley began his career in the Broadway theatre, directing those
musical revues familiar to modern audiences from the films of Fred
Astaire: a chorus of natty gentlemen in tails and dozens of leggy girls
pirouetting or parading on improbable stairways while sumptuously
orchestrated, unmemorable songs are sung. His passion for plastic
geometry was given its head in many 1930s Hollywood musicals: if you

see what look like thousands of identical girls arranged like flower-petals, fountains or fireworks, that's Berkeley's work. The apotheosis of the style came in *Forty-Second Street* (1933), *Gold-Diggers of 1933* (1933), *Dames* (1934) and *Gold-Diggers of 1935* (1935). In the 1940s Berkeley adapted to the new, individual dancing style epitomized by Fred Astaire and Mickey Rooney. His direction of *Babes in Arms* (1939 – which actually contains the line 'Let's do the whole show right here!'), *Strike Up the Band* (1940), *For Me and My Gal* (1942) and *The Gang's All Here* (1943) is expert and likeable, but lacks the absurd grandeur of his earlier style. Later, 'dramatic' style in musicals (pioneered by Gene *Kelly, and brought to a peak in Robbins's *West Side Story*, 1957) eclipsed his style; but in his heyday he set a standard for gargantuan frivolity that is unsurpassed.

BERTOLUCCI, Bernardo (born 1940)
Italian director and writer

Bertolucci's recurring subject is politics, the balance of power or influence in individual relationships and in their mirror, public affairs. His early features *Before the Revolution* (1964) and *Partner* (1968) treat this subject with assertive anger: his screen images assault the audience and leave no room for compromise or alternative opinion. In *The Spider's Stratagem* (1970, a story of political gangsterism adapted from Borges and set in the 1930s Po valley), the technique is more mature and anger no longer swamps narrative. *The Conformist* (1970) is one of Bertolucci's most controlled and finest films to date. Again set in 1930s Italy, it avoids stridency by concentrating on the personal dilemma of its temporizing hero; its handling of the themes of political decadence and guilt is reminiscent of the work of novelists like Camus and Grass (it is in fact based on a story by Moravia), and the performances (especially that of Jean-Louis Trintignant as the 'hero') are excellent. *Last Tango in Paris* (1972) was uneasily received because of its sexual explicitness and savagery. Its central metaphor, relating the politics of personal contact and exploitation to those of state and individual, now seems contrived – or perhaps the wished-for sex obliterates any other message in the spectator's mind. *1900* (1976) deliberately sets a close relationship (between two friends, master and servant) against the events of a social revolution. The 1900 setting is meticulously presented, but the film suffers from length and over-assertion. *La luna* (1979) is better controlled, though its view of the alienated young of modern Rome seems curiously second-hand, *Easy Rider* uneasily riding with *La dolce vita* ten years on. Its main strength is its depiction of an incestuously seesawing relationship between bewildered mother and hippie-adolescent son. Must she lose her identity to help him discover his? (The same theme is the basis of *The Tragedy of a Ridiculous Man*, 1981, a much flatter, more neo-realistic film about the effects on a father's character of his son's abduction by kidnappers.)

Bertolucci's work challenges the spectators, makes us do more than merely watch. His films are as brash and as cunning as those of *Coppola, but he is more single-minded than Coppola and therefore more prone to lose his dramatic balance.

BOGDANOVICH, Peter (born 1939)
American director, writer and critic

Bogdanovich's first feature, *Targets* (1967), was a stunning thriller – shot in eleven days – centred on the balance between delusion and reality in the minds of a young psychopath and an elderly horror star (beautifully underplayed by Boris Karloff). The technical expertise of the film and its nostalgia for the good old days of Hollywood kitsch – its resonances demand a knowledge and love, in its audience, for both the best and worst movies of the great past, for cinema itself – are repeated in *The Last Picture Show* (1971), an evocation of 1950s small-town American life, and in *What's Up, Doc?* (1972), a fast-paced 'screwball' comedy in the tradition of *Capra and *Hawks. After this scintillating start, Bogdanovich seemed momentarily to lose his touch. *Paper Moon* (1973), about an engaging pair of confidence tricksters in the Depression, is kept fresh by the delightful performances of its stars, Ryan and Tatum O'Neal; but *Daisy Miller* (1974), *At Long Last Love* (1975) and *Nickelodeon* (1976) work hard to achieve lacklustre results. Impatient critics were beginning to write Bogdanovich off (some with malicious headmasterly glee, as if having been so talented so young were some kind of impertinent threat), when he returned to form with *Saint Jack* (1979), the story of a grubbily endearing confidence man peddling rest and especially relaxation to the troops during the Vietnam war, and followed it up with *They All Laughed* (1982), a bitter-sweet comedy (starring Audrey Hepburn) which uses the mode of *The Last Picture Show* to tell a story of Neil-Simony wit and charm.

BOULTING, John and Roy (born 1913)
British film-makers

The Boulting twins have taken joint responsibility for producing, directing and occasionally writing some of the best popular entertainment produced by the British film industry in the last forty years; their work is as polished, consistent and individual as that of any of their immediate Hollywood rivals – *Lumet, say, or Preminger. At the start of their career they concentrated on thrillers (*Thunder Rock*, 1942; *Brighton Rock*, 1946) and on films reflecting issues of social or political conscience (*Fame Is the Spur*, 1946, about personal integrity in politics; *The Guinea Pig*, 1948, about a working-class boy sent to a public school). In the 1950s and 1960s they made a string of light comedies spiced by a satirical view of sacred British institutions like the army (*Private's Progress*, 1956), the law (*Brothers in Law*, 1956), the universities (*Lucky Jim*, 1957), the trade unions (*I'm All Right, Jack*, 1959), the church (*Heavens Above*, 1963) and the Northern family (*The Family Way*, 1966). Their comedy has begun to seem dated, but in its time it caught a mood of amiable self-deprecation as exactly as Ealing did post-war breeziness; another generation will probably enjoy their films as nostalgically and respectfully as today's audiences do *The Lavender Hill Mob* or *Passport to Pimlico*.

BRESSON, Robert (born 1907)
French director and writer

Bresson's work has a harsh philosophical basis, in which isolation and pain have almost transcendental power as steps along the road to a mystical state of grace. His film technique follows the style of the more highbrow silent directors (notably *Eisenstein). In particular, he uses cutting to reiterate the 'grammar' of a film's meaning: repetition of images highlights their significance, and momentary insertions of extreme close-up (e.g. of tears, twisted fingers or staring eyes) tell the spectator things about the characters of which the characters themselves are unaware. It is a sophisticated, personal style, and has earned Bresson a fanatical following in esoteric film journals. Unfortunately, his relegation of actor and performance in favour of montage tends to make his films both cerebral and hermetic. His two most accessible films are based on stories by Bernanos: *Diary of a Country Priest* (1951, remarkable for its successful depiction of states of mind – the subtlest thing of all to show on film) and *Mouchette* (1966, about a young girl's spiritual ennoblement through isolation and suffering, a mirror – for Catholic-oriented Bresson – of the human condition). *A Condemned Man Has Escaped* (1956), *Pickpocket* (1959) and *The Trial of Joan of Arc* (1962) are all concerned with the effects of oppressive circumstance (respectively prison, crime and the intransigence of the 'system') on the individual soul.

Bresson's most remarkable films are *Au hasard Balthazar* (1966, a film of Buñuel-like power, in which the brutal suffering and mute acceptance of injustice of a donkey – the dehumanization of the actor taken to its logical conclusion – makes a grey but moving parable for human endurance), and the extraordinary *Lancelot of the Lake* (1974). In this film Bresson makes mud, blood and rain the external correlatives for despair and the brutalizing ritual of chivalric life. His characters are like chessmen in a thunderstorm, puppets of their own heroic code forever grasping for a reality in life which is not really there. (Reverent spectators may be reminded of *Kurosawa, irreverent spectators of *Monty Python and the Holy Grail*.) Like Eisenstein's, Bresson's slow-moving, hypnotic style can repel the less patient spectator. But his films have the enigmatic authority of dreams. He is like *Resnais or *Antonioni: because he tells us things beyond the reach of logic, he has to run the risk that we mistake his visions for shallowness, misread his personal authority as posturing.

Bresson's other films include *Four Nights of a Dreamer* (1971), an updating of

Dostoievski's story 'White Nights', about a girl's despairing, soul-destroying wait for a faithless lover, and *Money* (1983), based on Tolstoy's story about how wealth cocoons the rich and destroys the poor. Good study: I. Cameron (ed.): *The Films of Robert Bresson* (1970).

BROOKS, Mel (born 1927)
American director, actor and writer

After two successful decades as a television scriptwriter (and occasionally as performer: his sketch, with Carl Reiner, *Interview with a 2000-Year-Old Man*, is brilliant), Brooks burst into cinema prominence with a series of lunatic comedies, *Blazing Saddles* (1974), *Young Frankenstein* (1974), *Silent Movie* (1976), *High Anxiety* (1977) and *History of the World, Part One* (1981). He is the nearest modern equivalent of *Sennett, and like Sennett sacrifices everything to hilarity. His films are crude, slapdash and very funny; *Young Frankenstein*, the best organized, underpins the farce with amiable parody of the directorial clichés of such horror gurus as James Whale. (*High Anxiety* tries to do the same for *Hitchcock, but fails – Hitchcock is himself tongue-in-cheek, and parody dissipates itself.) Brooks's best film is *The Producers* (1967), a comparatively restrained and structured farce about the mounting of an appalling Broadway musical entitled *Springtime for Hitler*.

Brooks's other films include the uncharacteristically serious *The Twelve Chairs* (1967); he is also the guiding spirit of a production company whose films include *The Elephant Man* (1979), and a lively remake (starring Brooks and his wife Anne Bancroft) of *Lubitsch's *To Be or Not To Be* (1984), and which is dedicated to realizing the work of young, untried or unfashionable film-makers. Good study: M. Yakowar: *The Comic Art of Mel Brooks* (1982).

BUÑUEL, Luis (1900–1983)
Spanish director and writer

The driving force of Buñuel's art was the exact antithesis of *Bergman's: he believed that liberation of spirit lies in anarchy, that human beings are inherently free but systematically repressed by a doctrinaire bourgeois society oppressed by its own impotence and fear. Affectations of anarchy also permeate his style: he favoured an (apparently) inconsequential narrative, animated by surrealism and black comedy and sharpened by a consistent use of blasphemous images (washing of feet, breaking of bread, even stigmata and crucifixion) and eroticism, often twined together in a uniquely startling way. His vision of humanity was medieval: he would entirely have understood the erotic and spiritual ecstasy of the flagellants, the cheerfully fatalistic corpse-robbing which took place during the Black Death, the arbitrariness of mailed-fist power or the psychic hysteria which periodically and inexplicably attacked individuals or groups and as inexplicably disappeared. In particular, the sappy pragmatism of medieval life, the constant discovery of hope in hopelessness, purpose in purposelessness, is reflected in the swarming modern exuberance of his films. Anarchy is the true condition of humanity, and its rediscovery is a form of fulfilment, almost of happiness. There are many parallels between the medieval world and the 20th century – and this may be one reason why Buñuel seemed such a true prophet, why his initially frightening art now seems prescriptive and comforting. (His films are also entertaining – not the least factor in their importance or appeal.)

After a brilliant debut with *The Andalusian Dog* (1928, a two-reel sequence of surrealist sight-gags devised with Salvador Dali) and *The Golden Age* (1930, a satirical assault on bourgeois values – beggars are thrashed instead of helped, fathers shoot dead their disobedient sons), Buñuel worked for nearly two decades on a formless variety of projects ranging from documentary (*Land Without Bread*, 1932) to genre comedy (*The Great Madcap*, 1949); indeed for ten years he directed no films at all, but worked in America as dubbing editor and studio producer. His first great feature was *Los olvidados* (*The Young and the Damned*, 1950). This film, about three Mexican street urchins and the brutal society which preys on them and on which they try to prey, deals in a characteristic way (loose narrative structure, images of horrifying brutality entwined with sudden moments of iridescent happiness) with the typical Buñuel theme that the dispossessed actually do possess the earth – a theme developed further in the film that is perhaps his masterpiece, *Viridiana* (1961), in which an unworldly novice nun and her cynical, grasping cousin stand for dispossession and possession in society. His assault on bourgeois self-deception continued in *Nazarín* (1958, a scalding attack on the hypocrisies of religion), *The Exterminating Angel* (1962, a kind of psychic 'disaster movie' in which a group of people, trapped together at an interminable dinner party, degenerate from elegance to cannibalistic barbarism – it is an adult's *Lord of the Flies*), and its mirror-image, the deliriously ironical *The Discreet Charm of the Bourgeoisie* (1972), where the rich socialites, for all their efforts, are prevented by a series of alarming and ridiculous events from ever enjoying their promised meal.

All these films concern the annihilating effect of 'civilization' and 'custom' on the natural impulses of humanity, and our violent or ironic efforts to reassert our individuality. The theme appears at its most zestful in Buñuel's many comedies about sex. Sexual liberation was a consistent theme of *The Golden Age*, and of *Depths of Passion* (1953), an under-rated parody of *Wuthering Heights* (of which Buñuel had directed a 'straight' version the previous year). It becomes a subject for splendid black humour – sex rather than love, eroticism and fetishism rather than sublimation – in *The Criminal Life of Archibaldo de la Cruz* (*Ensayo de un crimen*, 1955), *Diary of a Chambermaid* (1964 – at first a frothy comedy, but with a savage and violent conclusion), *Belle de jour* (1966) and *That Obscure Object of Desire* (1977).

Buñuel's work has provoked violent reactions, particularly in Catholic or authoritarian countries (it was regularly banned, for example, in his native Spain). Sadism and blasphemy are the overt reasons, perhaps –

though these became standard ingredients in cheap, non-banned thrillers of the late 1970s. Disturbing at a deeper level is his view of the power of anarchy: it is not surprising that although his films seldom achieved general release, they had a vast campus following, particularly in the 1960s and early 1970s. Method and 'vision' apart – and he is one of the most influential artistic figures of the century, the Picasso or Stravinsky of his art – he has, simply, made a handful of masterpieces (*Los olvidados, Viridiana, The Exterminating Angel, Belle de jour, That Obscure Object of Desire*), and his work demonstrates time and again that art can be serious and of the highest quality without abandoning popular appeal.

Engaging autobiography, as bizarrely inconsequential as his films: *My Last Breath* (1983). Good critical and biographical study: G. Edwards: *The Discreet Charm of Luis Buñuel* (1982).

CAPRA, Frank (born 1897)
American director and writer

Capra's sense of pace, his respect for the craft and placing of jokes, was sharpened by his early days in the *Sennett studios, and is shown to perfection in three silent features starring the enigmatic, slow-paced comedian Harry Langdon (*The Strong Man*, 1926, *Tramp Tramp Tramp*, 1926, and *Long Pants*, 1927). Capra went on to make a string of dazzling comedies, including *Platinum Blonde* (1931, the quintessential Jean Harlow film), *Lady for a Day* (1933), *It Happened One Night* (1934, a screwball comedy starring Clark Gable and Claudette Colbert, a favourite nomination for lists of 'the best comic films of all time'), *You Can't Take It With You* (1938) and *Arsenic and Old Lace* (1944). His reputation rests equally on a pair of 'social comedies', *Mr Deeds Goes to Town* (1936) and *Mr Smith Goes to Washington* (1939). In these, wide-eyed, gentle heroes (played respectively by Gary Cooper and James Stewart) triumph, in a distinctly Mark Twain-like manner, over the seductively corrupt societies (money and politics) into which they make their way. The slow-talking American Candide is a potentially sugary character, but these films avoid sentimentality thanks to Capra's blend of satire with a light, ironical touch.

Showbizzy, fascinating autobiography, the author very much star of every scene: *The Name Above the Title* (1971).

CARNÉ, Marcel (born 1909)
French director

Carné's high reputation is the result of half a dozen atmospheric films made in the 1930s and 1940s in collaboration with the scriptwriter Jacques Prévert. (He made eleven more films after the partnership broke up, but they seldom rise above routine.) Apart from *Drôle de drame* (1937), a farce, the Carné–Prévert films are all marked by intensity of atmosphere, plots which swoop between portentousness and melodrama, and brilliantly written parts for some of the finest French performers of the time. Two of the films, *Quai des brumes* (1938) and *Le Jour se lève* (1939), are stories of Dostoievskian grimness: a man commits murder in a fit of rage, and in his subsequent flight from justice falls in love with a young girl; a man murders his rival, and after barricading himself in his room relives his past life before shooting himself just as the police break in. For all their visual richness (they look at times like *Eisenstein, at others like *Bergman), there is a coldness about these films, a view of the arbitrariness of fate, which can alienate the spectator. It is also present, but softened by character-warmth and a less pervasive feeling of gloom and doom, in *Les Visiteurs du soir* (1942) and *Les Enfants du paradis* (1945). *Les Visiteurs du soir* may remind modern spectators, again, of Bergman. Its plot concerns a seduction in a 15th-century castle, the arrival of the devil, lovers changed into statues whose hearts still beat, minstrels and a wedding-feast; its script is as smooth-running as clockwork; its direction is detached and slow-moving, building tension by remorseless concentration on detail. The film has a hallucinatory, hypnotic effect which finally over-rides the feeling that it has nothing much to say. (The anti-Nazi symbolism read into it by French audiences in 1942 is no longer apparent.) *Les Enfants du paradis* is about a beautiful 19th-century actress and her lovers, including the mime artist Deburau. In this film, Carné's masterpiece and generally acknowledged as one of the finest films in cinema history, portentousness is leavened by the light-hearted wit of the backstage community. The story is slight, and everything rests on the main performances, on Pierre Brasseur's flamboyance as the actor-manager, Pierre Renoir's bumbling charm, the vivacity of Arletty as the heroine, and above all Jean-Louis Barrault's mesmeric dignity and grace as Deburau – the elusive apartness of the great performer has seldom been better shown. Like *Les Visiteurs du soir*, *Les Enfants du paradis* engulfs the spectator. Carné's richness may be more decorative than dynamic, baroque style rather than poetry – but in these two films, at least, he works the clinching performer's magic and makes illusion seem substantial, dream-visions true.

CASSAVETES, John (born 1929)
American director and actor

Like *Welles, Cassavetes has had a double career: as an actor (often on television, or in thrillers such as *A Man Is Ten Feet Tall*, *The Dirty Dozen*, *Rosemary's Baby* and *Capone*), and as an independent-minded and experimental director. He works with a regular team of actors, who discuss and improvise their scenes until a definitive shape is achieved. The camera is often static and detached, as if casually eavesdropping; the dialogue is fragmentary and half-inaudible; the films have a looseness of structure similar to those of *Altman. The danger, when the single shaping hand is removed, is of chaos or lack of involvement – and both *Shadows* (1960) and *Husbands* (1970) are flawed by this: moments of great point and tension are succeeded by slapdash ramble or sloppy camera-work, as if Uncle Arthur had suddenly stepped in to direct a scene. Cassavetes' most successful films are those where he uses a proper script, built up from improvisation, certainly, but then used as a reliable fixed point in the filming. *Faces* (1968), *Minnie and Moskowitz* (1971), *Killing of a Chinese Bookie* (1976) and *Love Streams* (1984) contain magnificent scenes of relationship-through-dialogue (often the most striking feature of improvised drama), and *Opening Night* (1977) is a moving and convincing depiction of the creative tension inside a star performer (Gena Rowlands, as the actress undergoing self-appraisal, is outstanding). This film vindicates Cassavetes' method: could it have been made so poignant or persuasive in any other way? *Gloria* (1981) offers the same depth of observation and characterization in a gangland comedy; once again Rowlands is superb, as a Bogart-like gangster's moll who finds herself landed with a mouthy seven-year-old orphan.

CHABROL, Claude (born 1930)
French director

Chabrol was one of the most influential theorists of the mid-1950s, helping to liberate film criticism from choking intellectuality: his and *Rohmer's *Hitchcock* (1957) was one of the first books to treat an 'entertainment' director as if he had something personal to say. Chabrol's own films are predominantly thrillers, combining Hitchcockian psychological suspense with a critique of bourgeois society: he is a philosophizing Simenon, with radical political overtones. His best films are *The Cousins* (1959), an atmospheric thriller set among Parisian students; *The Beast Must Die* (1969); *The Butcher* (1969), a story of sex-murders in a charming but stifling Dordogne village setting; and *Violette Nozière* (1978), an elegantly creepy study (based on a real-life, controversial murder case) of an alienated 1930s teenager.

Chabrol's most recent films – none matching the intensity of those discussed above – include *Le Cheval d'orgeuil/The Proud Ones* (1982), a semi-documentary of peasant life in 1910s Brittany.

CHAPLIN, Charles (1889–1977)
British/American film-maker

The music-hall roots of Chaplin's art can be clearly seen in his early short films. In several, stage routines are performed unaltered, in front of a static camera. *Work* (1915), for example, is a series of house-decorating gags still familiar (though never as well performed) in modern pantomime; the delivery of the bottle-filled trunk in *The Cure* (1917), and the series of customers with objects to pawn and the running fight between Charlie and the second assistant in *The Pawnbroker* (1917) are variations of standard music-hall ideas. Two films, *Charlie at the Show* (1915) and *One AM* (1916, a balletic compendium of drunk routines), are screen adaptations of Chaplin's legendary stage performances for Fred Karno, whose 1913 American tour first introduced him to Hollywood. Other of the early films place music-hall 'business' and gag-routines in less studio-bound settings, and the camera itself begins to move, to isolate the action by means of pans and close-ups, to select, to frame and comment. This fluidity of movement, and the uncramped settings, liberate Chaplin's athletic style: the fights in *Easy Street* (1917) and *The Idle Class* (1921), the acrobatics in *The Floorwalker* (1916 – for example Charlie's battle with an escalator going the other way) and *The Rink* (1916 – breathtaking roller-skating, repeated and, incredibly, improved in *Modern Times* 1936), the skittering chases of *The Immigrant* (1917) and *A Dog's Life* (1918) – all these would have been impossible on the stage. *Shoulder Arms* (1918) is wholly cinematic in conception and performance.

If that were all, if Chaplin merely performed music-hall routines with outstanding dexterity in a variety of more-or-less interesting locations, he would be no different from a dozen skilful silent clowns (Chester Conklin, Fatty Arbuckle, Larry Semon, Ben Turpin). Their art is funny, and combines grace and excitement to an outstanding degree. But it is essentially heartless: they are mechanistic puppets, never really hurt or out of sorts, and our admiration of them owes nothing to a perception of shared humanity, but depends entirely on their revelation of ever more impressive and unlikely skills. (Because the vital element of this kind of comedy is surprise, the possibilities for surrealism inherent in film make it an ideal vehicle.) Some of Chaplin's earliest films, and certain sequences in his later ones, are purely physical in a similar way: he is like a slapstick robot running out of control. But from the very start he adds a unique ingredient which raises him to genius – and it is not pathos, but poetry. His poetry is based on metaphor: he shows us one physical object or action, and turns it before our eyes into another. His cane momentarily becomes a flower, a violin, a sword; bread-rolls do dance-routines; a boot becomes steak and its laces spaghetti; a broken clock (in *The Pawnbroker*) becomes a patient on the surgeon's table. In *The Cure* he tipsily spills water on the floor, then looks accusingly at a tiny (toy) dog; *City Lights* opens with the unveiling of a grandiose statue, and the tramp is discovered asleep in its arms. He is a magician, making reality his toy and the expression of his moods and whims. He undergoes metamorphosis himself, both fleetingly and throughout a film: the tramp becomes soldier (*Shoulder Arms*), father (*The Kid*), stern guardian of law and order (*Easy Street*), rich idler (*The Idle Class*), conscientious employee (*Pay Day*) and preacher (*The Pilgrim*). The apotheosis of this process comes in *The Great Dictator* (1940), where, apart from smaller metamorphoses, Chaplin enacts both the embodiment of human evil and the epitome of decency and ordinariness.

This ability to make us see the world in whatever terms he chooses is dangerous, and in some of his later films (after 1923 he made only nine more films, all features) the balance between poetry and rhetoric is not always maintained. It is, basically, the *small* metaphors and meta-morphoses which interest the audience: we understand and enjoy Charlie as a circus acrobat (*The Circus*), a robot or a waiter (*Modern Times*) more readily than as the embodiment of suffering humanity or a David battling every Goliath in the world. Over-solemnity (self-consciousness becoming self-pity) is a persistent danger in Chaplin's longer films, and mars works as diverse as *The Kid* (1920), *The Great Dictator* and *A King in New York* (1957). In his best-controlled features, we are kept on a knife-edge of expectation throughout – not only to see what Charlie will show us next, but also to observe the flow between sadness and puncturing glee. Constant expectation and its fulfilment or frustration: the tramp in *The Gold Rush* (1925) and the tired comedian in *Limelight* (1952) manage the transitions perfectly.

The problem with Chaplin (and that there is a problem at all is probably more apparent to critics than to audiences) is that he defies standards. He is to film comedy what Shakespeare is to tragedy or Beethoven to the symphony. Everyone else, however high they climb, remains in his foothills; to call any of his films 'better' or 'best' is to measure him only against himself. His excellence is also, perhaps, too familiar for proper appreciation. He is *sui generis*; he is magnificent; he *is* his art.

Chaplin's *My Autobiography* (1964) is a classic, particularly good on his Dickensian childhood. Good studies: I. Quigley: *Charlie Chaplin: Early Comedies* (1968); J. McCabe: *Charlie Chaplin* (1978). Unusually revealing (magazine articles by men like Stan Laurel, Fred Karno, Graham Greene): P. Haining (ed.): *The Legend of Charlie Chaplin* (1982), which can usefully be supplemented by D. Robinson (ed.): *Chaplin: The Mirror of Opinion* (1983).

CLAIR, René (1898–1981)
French director and writer

Clair's films range from ironical comedies (*An Italian Straw Hat*, 1927, *Le Million*, 1931, *À nous la liberté*, 1931, *The Ghost Goes West*, 1935, *Les Belles de nuit*, 1952) and light-hearted melodrama like that of *Lubitsch (*Sous les toits de Paris*, 1930, *Porte des Lilas*, 1957) to an affectionate send-up of the early film industry itself (*Silence is Golden*, 1947) and a parody of the Faust legend (*La Beauté du diable*, 1950). They are notable for their visual style (often balletic, geometric, following the logic of music rather than drama) and for their brilliant use of sound – sound-effects, music and dialogue (sparse, often mere grunts or murmurs) are 'composed' together in an individual and striking way.

Clair's comedies are the nearest thing in cinema to the plays of Ionesco. Their mode is surrealist farce, in a style learned from *Chaplin and *Keaton, and passed on to *Tati. In particular, he sees the longing for social dignity as the most absurd and most dangerous feature of human life. Whenever people gather for an organized function – a wedding, an opera, a political meeting or to hear a speech – chaos ensues. (The abiding mental image of *An Italian Straw Hat*, for example, is of a long line of wedding-guests in dishevelled formal clothes, clutching presents and shuffling in a despairing conga from one disaster to another.) When human beings join together for unified action, they dehumanize themselves. The neighbours in *Le Million*, for example, at first unite to harass the artist hero (for unorthodox behaviour like painting and not paying his bills); then, when he wins a million-franc lottery ticket, they crowd round him with brass bands, fawning smiles and meaningless congratulation delivered by a bashful child – he is no more accepted into their society, as himself, than he ever was. *À nous la liberté* sees factory life in terms of prison (the factory is actually owned by an ex-convict), and the heroes' escape from its regimented monotony is like a Warner Brothers prison-break.

If Clair shows organized society as composed of heartless idiots, an ants' nest of pointless energy (one sequence of *Le Million* sets police and gangsters backstage in an opera house, in an anarchic trailer for the Marx Brothers), his heroes, the people whose individuality allows them to break free of the absurdity around them, are characterized with ironic sentimentality, a sugary niceness which is never allowed to conceal the fact that they are basically as unreal as everyone else. Sometimes the hero is a single individual, harassed by events like a fox by hounds (Fadinard in *An Italian Straw Hat* is the archetype); but usually the films centre on a pair of friends who band together to win a common prize (often money), but whose friendship, apart from the impetus it derives from this single common purpose, is bonded with emotional treacle.

It could be argued that these criticisms are too unsmiling, that all Clair is doing is entertaining us, that he is a *Sennett farceur and not a moralist. His best films are structured, in Sennett style, on a picaresque and slapstick chase: towards a wedding (*An Italian Straw Hat*), to win a girl back from a gang of crooks (*Sous les toits de Paris*), to track down a lottery ticket (*Le Million*), in pursuit of a castle being shipped to America (*The Ghost Goes West*), and, climactically, as a Keatonesque trip through the history of humanity from the Stone Age to the present, in *Les Belles de nuit*. His view of the folly of human hierarchies (the harder-faced the pyramid, the more certain its collapse) and his harried heroes are learned from Sennett, and his use of slapstick surrealism belongs to the Sennett tradition of 'use anything, providing it's funny' rather than (say) to that of Chaplin, where surrealism is used for poetic point.

None the less, Clair's films do contain more than expertly paced slapstick. There is a consistent message in them, a pessimistic view of human nature expressed in whimsical irony but none the less devastating for that. This is what allies him with Black Comedy, with Ionesco. The ending of *À nous la liberté* is typical. Work is abolished, and all the people in the world become singing, dancing buddies who go fishing in beautiful sunshine. Pigs never actually fly – but at any moment, one is made to feel, they might.

Clair's writings include *Reflections on the Cinema* (English edn 1953) and *Cinema Yesterday, Cinema Today* (1970).

COCTEAU, Jean: see page 471.

COPPOLA, Francis Ford (born 1939)
American film-maker

Coppola was executive producer of the likeable *American Graffiti* (1973), and the author or co-author of several notable screenplays including that of the award-winning *Patton* (1970), whose view of the corrupting effects of killing foreshadows a major theme of his later work. His films as director include two quietly paced studies of young people coping with the first stresses of adult life, *You're a Big Boy Now* (1967) and *The Rain People* (1969), and an impressive thriller, *The Conversation* (1974). This is interesting work, and its low-budget amiability is in marked contrast to his three multi-million-dollar blockbusters *The Godfather* (1972), *The Godfather Part Two* (1975) and *Apocalypse Now* (1979). The two *Godfather* films, about the Mafia, make gangster movies of the 1930s look like a Sunday School picnic (though we know, in Bogart's or Cagney's hands, what could get into *those* sandwiches). *Apocalypse Now* sets Conrad's story *Heart of Darkness* in 1970s Vietnam, and its theme (the seductive power of violence, the transcendental joy of pain) is sharpened by Coppola's blend of realistic and sympathetic characters with a detached, almost anthropological view of the rituals and horrors they perform – it is as if Lorenz or Lévi-Strauss had discussed their theories of hierarchical aspiration and aggression in the form of pulp fiction instead of academic lucubration. Disturbingly, *Apocalypse Now* photographs napalm and bullets with vertiginous brilliance – it is debatable whether to depict the thing you hate in such seductive images (the scene of helicopters making a strafing run, tracer bullets searing the sky to Wagner's *Ride of the Valkyries*, is one of the most unforgettable in modern cinema) is not to succumb to enthralling vulgarity, to drown the message in the medium.

After *Apocalypse Now*, Coppola poured his energy and money into Zoetrope Studios, which he founded and ran as an avowed successor to the great 1940s Hollywood studios. His one substantial film, the musical romance *One from the Heart* (1982) – streets better than his earlier *Finian's Rainbow* (1968), a fey piece about leprechauns – ran him and Zoetrope into financial trouble, thanks to disagreements between Coppola and his co-distributors Paramount. In 1982 and 1983 he also made two effective, low-budget films about teenagers, *The Outsiders* and *Rumble Fish*, referring back to the understated style of his 1960s films, and proving, financially at least, that small is still more beautiful than large.

CURTIZ, Michael (1888–1962)
Hungarian/American director

After a prolific career in Hungary (sixty films in fifteen years), Curtiz moved to Hollywood in 1928 and became a one-man dream-factory in his own right, turning out over 100 films of all kinds – romance, action, gangster, comedy and musical. A large part of his output was instantly forgettable; but consistently over the years about one film in four was excellent. His finest achievement is a series of swashbuckling costume adventures with Errol Flynn (including *Captain Blood*, 1935; *The Charge of the Light Brigade*, 1936; *The Adventures of Robin Hood*, 1938; *The Sea Hawk*, 1940): these have a swagger and pace to rival Fairbanks. With James Cagney he made *Angels with Dirty Faces* (1938) and the outstanding *Yankee Doodle Dandy* (1942); he directed Joan Crawford's best weepie, *Mildred Pierce* (1945); and in *Casablanca* (1942) he made one of the best known, not to say canonized, of all Hollywood romances. No single ingredient in *Casablanca* is excellent: the story is tosh, the script average, the music so-so, the performances (apart from that of Claude Rains) nothing like each actor's best. But the *blend* of ingredients is exactly right, and the film as a whole outclasses each component. It is, in that, characteristic of the best of Curtiz's work.

De MILLE, Cecil B. (1881–1959)
American director and producer

De Mille was one of the great Hollywood pioneers. Between the 1913 version of *The Squaw Man* and its first remake in 1918, he made no less than thirty-four features, chiefly westerns. When he began, the film medium was generally regarded as a fascinating but crude toy, and it was due as much to his work as to that of (say) *Griffith, inventing techniques and processes as he went along, that it developed in five years to a sophisticated art-form with patterns of style and models of excellence all its own. In five years, De Mille and his colleagues created a tradition.

Between 1919 and 1923, De Mille made a series of comedies notable for their pert, vivacious heroines. The fashions and interior decoration in his films were avidly copied – wherever they were shown, real life fell over itself to imitate what passed for art. Bathroom scenes in particular (delirious décor and nudging nudity) led to sanitary extravagance in the houses of the rich only surpassed in later years by the plunge into swimming pools. The best of these comedies, *Male and Female* (1919), *The Affairs of Anatol* (1921) and *Adam's Rib* (1923), still stand up today, though more because of their delightful heroines and shiny-eyed 1920s nostalgia than for inherent excellence in the direction.

Like many of his pioneer colleagues, De Mille reserved sophistication for the technical side of film-making. His films are innovatory, subtle and precisely judged. But in every aesthetic sense, his taste never rises above *Reader's Digest* vulgarity, a cosy common denominator of meaning ('Such is Life') and thought ('The World's Most Unforgettable Character'). This is most clearly seen in the costume spectacles which are, alas, his enduring legacy. In them human wisdom, honour and fortitude (and evil, pride and greed) are depicted with fairground shallowness: his tuppence-coloured morality has no more subtlety than that of a comic strip. In westerns (*The Plainsman*, 1936; *Union Pacific*, 1939) or in 'historical' action films (*The Crusades*, 1935; *Reap the Wild Wind*, 1942) consistent trivialization hardly matters: the torrent of events carries all before it. But when the Bible is reduced to thick slices of spectacular ham, we are witnessing not religious but artistic sacrilege. There is a story that De Mille first turned to the Old Testament as a way of evading the new Hays Code rules about showing scenes of eroticism and debauchery – certainly the orgy before the golden calf in *The Ten Commandments* (1923), his first Biblical venture, is one of his most voluptuous and explicit sequences. Tongue-in-cheek, such an approach would be fine: irony and wit (as in Fairbanks' treatment of the heroic past) can stand for depth. But De Mille's single-minded pursuit of 'authenticity', his poker-faced belief that it is sufficient merely to depict or enact greatness, denies humanity.

That said, for spectators satisfied to reserve their awe for spectacle (often building construction – for example, the Pyramids – or demolition – for example, Babylon), De Mille's epics are just the ticket. Their crowds and sets are huge; their special effects (parting seas, burning bushes, writing on walls) are immaculate; their themes have a universal grandeur that no amount of wooden acting or clay-footed dialogue can totally destroy. Sophisticates may well go to *The Sign of the Cross* (1932) or *The Ten Commandments* (1956) to scoff, and stay to gasp. One can truly say, in short, of all De Mille's work that if this is what you like, then you'll certainly like this.

The Autobiography of Cecil B. De Mille was published in 1959. Good study: G. Ringgold and D. Bodeen: *The Films of Cecil B. De Mille* (1969).

De SICA, Vittorio (1901–74)
Italian actor and director

De Sica's acting performances, in over 100 films, are generally those of an expert light comedian, the Cecil Parker or Edward Everett Horton of Italian cinema. The films he directed combine the same disarming lightness of touch with an unsentimental view of social reality which gives them edge. The blend of the two elements is vital. Without comedy, films like *Shoeshine* (1946, about two children in wartime Rome forced by circumstances into begging, theft and murder) would be strident; without social edge, comedies like *Marriage Italian Style* (1964, a version of Eduardo di Filippo's *Filumena*) and *After the Fox* (1966) would slump into glossiness. De Sica's best films were all based on scripts by Cesare Zavattini. They are *Bicycle Thieves* (1948), about a man and his son searching for a stolen bicycle in the slums of Rome; *Miracle in Milan* (1951), his masterpiece, about a gentle, miracle-working boy, again in the slums; and *Umberto D* (1952), the study of a lonely old man, a film combining whimsicality and pain with outstanding success. Of his later films, the best is *The Garden of the Finzi-Continis* (1971), a well-acted story based on Bassani's novel about a rich Jewish family under fascism.

DISNEY, Walt (1901–66)
American producer and artist

Disney, a commercial artist, began experimenting with animation in the early 1920s, moved to Hollywood in 1923, and invented Mickey Mouse in 1928. Sound was used almost from the start (in *Steamboat Willie*, 1928), and colour followed in 1933. The first full-length cartoon was *Snow White and the Seven Dwarfs* (1937); it is still one of the best. By now, in the mid-1980s, the greatest tribute to Disney is the vast industry he spawned, a shoal of imitators many of whom have surpassed him in sophistication, style and taste.

Disney's short cartoons (produced, like all his studios' products, by a large creative team, but still in the 1930s benefiting from his own original input and turn of mind) are based on anarchic, surrealist violence. Their heroes (especially gormless Pluto and aggressive Donald Duck) are assailed by hostile objects and gadgets of every kind: if all else fails, their own clothes, necks and tails take on a malign will and turn on them. Mickey Mouse himself (and Goofy, who is patterned on John Doe, the ordinary little man at the mercy of conmen, salesmen, sharks and officials of every kind) is softer-edged; in fact the growth of subsequent non-Disney cartoon series, for example the magnificent Tom and Jerry, has meant that he has rather been left behind by more forceful, violent avatars. The pattern of violence usually follows the mutual destruction, tit-for-tat style perfected in live action by Laurel and Hardy. It reaches its apogee in Donald Duck's endless ritual battles with his nephews or with the chipmunks – and as with Laurel and Hardy, our knowledge that no one in the end is hurt allows us to revel in scenes of mayhem that would be appalling in more 'serious' cinema. (The cathartic value of this harmless violence was well understood by children, though it caused Disney occasional problems with humourless censors.)

Witty mayhem, however, was in Disney's view not enough to sustain a full-length cartoon. From *Snow White* onwards, he packed his features with other ingredients, particularly songs and a wholesome whimsy which titters and teeters just this side of archness. Even so, the best full-length cartoons are those which retain a measure of slapstick violence: *Pinocchio* (1939), *Peter Pan* (1953), *One Hundred and One Dalmatians* (1961) and *The Jungle Book* (1967). Self-indulgent 'niceness' and the vulgarity of imagination of which it is a symptom mar others, notably *Lady and the*

Tramp (1956), *The Sword in the Stone* (1963) and several films combining
cartoon sequences with live action, like *Bedknobs and Broomsticks*
(1971) and *Pete's Dragon* (1978); *Mary Poppins* (1964) only avoids it
because of the asperity of the central character. Vulgarity is a crippling
flaw in *Fantasia* (1940) – neither music nor the visual arts are well served
by Disney's appalling, appealing visions of bluebirds nesting (to Beethoven) and hippos dancing (to Ponchielli). (The same is true of the
famous 1950s nature documentaries, *True Life Adventures*. The animals
are stunningly filmed, but the film is then edited to a cute anthropomorphism which destroys the dignity of nature.)

  In the 1950s the Disney studios began a long series of live-action,
'family' films with the splendid *Treasure Island*. There have been dozens
since, as reliable and filling as supermarket bread. Sometimes a particular
star, or a particular theme, strikes gold. *The Absent-Minded Professor*
(1961), a vehicle for Fred MacMurray, the spectacular space adventure
The Black Hole (1979) and the agreeable *Popeye* (1981, directed by
*Altman), for example, offer entertainment not only to children but also
to the adults who accompany them. But if it comes to that, why should
children or anyone else be fobbed off with the undiscriminating blandness
which, more and more since Disney's death, has become his studios'
chief ingredient? In 1977 his old animators were so dismayed at the way
things were going that they resigned *en masse*, and *Tron* (1982), computer
graphics notwithstanding – it is about a man trapped in his own video
game – is a dismal portent of what may take their place.

For those with limitless purses or access to a good library, F. Thomas and O.
Johnston: *Disney Animation: The Illusion of Life* (1981) is a huge, gorgeous
anthology of everything from working drawings to finished frames of many of the
cartoons from the 1930s to the end of the 1970s. Less expensive: L. Maltin: *The
Disney Films* (1972); A. Bailey: *Walt Disney's World of Fantasy* (1983).

DREYER, Carl-Theodor (1889–1968)
Danish director

In an industry which systematically rewards flair above genius, Dreyer
was always at a disadvantage. He spent much of his career echoing, with
dogged brilliance, themes or styles which in hastier hands led to more
integrated and spectacular results. His *Pages from Satan's Book* (1921),
for example, tells four separate stories about the power of evil in the
world in an uneasy mixture of Strindbergian gloom with the camera-
techniques and grandiose directorial style of *Griffith's *Intolerance*, but
without its clinching energy; his *Vampire* (1932) is an over-atmospheric
(and over-rated) psychological horror-film outclassed by *Murnau's
Nosferatu; his *Gertrud* (1964), a study of a woman seeking spiritual
fulfilment through successive love-affairs, is a Joan Crawford 'three-
handkerchief' psychodrama as seen by *Bergman. Dreyer would head
the list of superb failures if it were not for *The Passion of Joan of Arc*

(1928) and *The Word* (1955). These are truly integrated works, and the majesty and authority of his technique for once illuminate his themes instead of getting in their way. *The Passion of Joan of Arc*, oddly (for a silent film) based on trial transcripts and dealing with theological argument rather than action, sets up the theme of the search for spiritual truth and the need to express its power in action – and this is picked up and perfected in *The Word*, about a peasant girl's death and miraculous rebirth through love. In both films, Dreyer's powerful and sympathetic view of women (unequalled, in cinema, till Bergman) blends with naturalistic direction and slow-paced, pensive camera-work, making much use of close-up and so allowing the actors an emotional intensity of performance like that of modern television but without its jitteriness – Dreyer cuts on average once a minute, in contrast with a television director's once every twenty seconds. The result is two cinema master-pieces – and two harmonious and successful works.

Good study: D. Bordwell: *The Films of Carl-Theodor Dreyer* (1981).

DWAN, Allan (1885–1981)
Canadian director

As well as pioneers like *Griffith or *De Mille, early Hollywood was full of competent film-makers whose only pretension was to entertain. Neither innovative nor controversial, they combined reliability with enough of an individual touch to catch and keep the public's eye. Dwan was one of these – and went on turning out unassumingly excellent pictures for over sixty years. His silent films include *Robin Hood* (1922), *The Iron Mask* (1929), both starring Fairbanks, and several of Gloria Swanson's sauciest comedies, including *Manhandled* (1924) and the charming *Stage Struck* (1925). His sound films range from *Heidi* (1937), stickily starring Shirley Temple, through enjoyable comedies like *Brewster's Millions* (1945) and *Getting Gertie's Garter* (1946 – little known, but as stylish as its title) to stirring war-pictures like *Sands of Iwo Jima* (1949). He is hardly Tolstoy; but if films truly have a 'trash culture' of quality (see page 210), he is one of its most consistent guarantors.

EISENSTEIN, Sergei (1898–1948)
Russian director

There were three main influences on Eisenstein's style. First, Japan. He went there in 1918, and studied Japanese visual art (especially calligraphy) and the traditional theatre arts of Noh and Kabuki. From calligraphy he learned simplicity of line, and also the associative power of linked images. (The Japanese ideograms for 'dog' and 'mouth' combine to make not only 'dog's mouth' but also 'bark'; in the same way the superimposition of the shadow of wire-netting over a sailor's face in *Battleship Potemkin* symbolizes his imprisoned soul. This marriage of unrelated images to create metaphorical or philosophical meaning is one aspect of film montage. Eisenstein did not invent the process – *Méliès or *Griffith did that – but he used it with a power and propagandist purpose unmatched before or since.) From Japanese theatre he learned a rhetorical, emphatic performing style, gesture and movement stylized into choreography – action is not depicted, but symbolized. (Eisenstein's debt to Japan was, later, amply repaid: the Japanese cinema's Noh-style acting was heavily influenced by his work.)

The second influence was the artistic movement Futurism (see page 540), born in Italy and thriving in Russia immediately after the revolution. (Its uncluttered, dogmatic organization of material made it a favourite style of emerging totalitarianism: it was later the dominant artistic form of both Italian fascism and German national socialism.) From Futurism Eisenstein took, above all, geometric brutality of line and a dehumanized, machine-vision of people in groups. His strikers, soldiers, prisoners and masses move in waves and lines across the screen, huddled or purposeful; each frame is as studiedly composed as an academic painting, and the actors lose individuality and become, so to speak, an artistic medium, making patterns chosen and disposed for their dialectical force. The logic is external and imagistic, and contrasts in a striking way with Eisenstein's use of close-up, which singles out the individual from the throng, makes him or her a facet of the huge, an interiorization of some larger external theme.

The third influence was Griffith's epic *Intolerance*, which, on Lenin's instructions, was widely shown in the USSR in 1919. (The impact of this huge feature-film on audiences new to the medium must have been as overwhelming as its influence was on Russian film-makers. What *can* they have made of it in Georgia, in Siberia, in Kazakhstan?) From *Intolerance* Eisenstein learned the cinema's vast propaganda power (it can say complex things in a uniquely direct and forceful way) and also the basic grammar of epic. Alternation of long shots and close-ups, in particular, is a Griffith-devised technique central both to *Intolerance* and to Eisenstein's style. (How different would Eisenstein's films have been if Lenin had, God forbid, selected instead of *Intolerance* Griffith's intimate, trashy *Broken Blossoms* or *Way Down East*?)

The effect of these influences was to make Eisenstein's style economical, measured and precise. If ever a director created 'poetry in motion', he did. Nothing is extra: each image both makes a single point and is striking to look at in an objective, almost self-consciously 'artistic' way. Unfortunately, the influences often marry with revolutionary-propagandist elements to produce a grandiose, preconceived and pasteboard view of human motive and emotion. In Eisenstein human beings are never left alone to themselves. They are the victims or component parts of cosmic movements which swallow individuality; they suffer or triumph symbolically, never for themselves; they do plenty but make nothing; they are never quiet. Eisenstein's raucous view of humanity is presented with staggering power, and has seemed to match our savage century. But in reducing individual people to instruments, to vehicles, it trivializes them. There is (as other epic creators – Shakespeare, Goya, Tolstoy – could have told him) far more to life, and to art, than this.

In the darkness of the cinema, it must be said, these doubts seldom arise. With the possible exceptions of *Ichikawa and *Kurosawa, no other film-maker has crammed the screen with shots of such power. Many have followed Eisenstein's methods or parroted his style; no one has ever matched his single-minded eloquence. Astonishingly, he made only about fifteen hours of finished film – his total 'work' is shorter, for example, than Wagner's *Ring*. His first film, *Strike* (1925), shows its subject in a style derived from Futurist theatre (its screenplay was a collective venture by the actors, from the Proletkult Theatre): the oppressed workers rise, surge lemming-like towards the guns of the controlling military, and die; as they are mown down, Eisenstein intercuts scenes from a slaughter-house. *Battleship Potemkin* (1925) reworks much of the same material – the coalescing of individual resentment into an eruption of doomed action; mechanistic, violent repression by the military. But it uses a far more refined technique, notably close-up (e.g. of individual sailors before the strike, or of the soldiers and their victims at the Odessa Steps) and montage (the famous example, the baby's pram careering, infinitely slowly, down through the carnage of the Steps, past a pair of spectacles forlornly crushed, is still the best). The tragic intensity of this film, its economical story-telling and its pictorial impact make it Eisenstein's finest work. Individual parts of later films are greater, but none has such challenging unity or power.

October (1928) lacks thrust. Its best scenes and images (the storming of the Winter Palace, and the workers' amazement or fury at the objects they find inside) are unsurpassed, but the film is glued together by propaganda, not narrative, and falls apart. Not so *Old and New/The General Line* (1929). Here an unpromising story about the coming of collectivization to a rural area is given human warmth and even charm (not a common Eisenstein quality) by its centring on a single peasant whose humanity dignifies and elevates her symbolic role. The unfinished *Que viva México* (part of it shown as *Thunder over Mexico*, 1933) blends the same human sympathy (for individual Mexican peasant lives) with Eisenstein's machine-visions of oppression to impressive effect. *Alexander Nevski* (1938) is a tightly organized costume epic, his nearest approach to 'popular' cinema; the battle on the ice is shot, and mounted, with characteristic force, a sequence visually as amazing as anything in his work and bound up with the controlling themes of the film in an artistically convincing way. His last film, *Ivan the Terrible* (Part I 1944, Part II 1946), is gloomy and protracted, an atmospheric mess. Superb individual elements (e.g. the vision of Ivan himself as a species of vampire spider, haunted eyes and a dark cloak that swells and stains the screen) cannot conceal the fact that, overall, the film is fustian.

Eisenstein's prolific writings include *The Film Sense* (1943); *Film Form* (1949);

Notes of a Film Director (1968). Good general biography: M. Seton: *Sergei M. Eisenstein: A Biography* (1952); good account of Eisenstein's abortive sortie into studio 'discipline': I. Montagu: *With Eisenstein in Hollywood* (English edn 1969). Particularly informative: D. Mayer: *Sergei M. Eisenstein's 'Potemkin': A Shot-by-Shot Presentation* (1972).

FASSBINDER, Rainer Werner (1946–82)
German director and actor

Fassbinder's work was prolific, left-wing (he was an admirer and sometime imitator of *Godard's polemicism) and variable. His characters' morose dullness (they seem always to be mumbling in dark corners or in the rain) reflected a generally pessimistic view of contemporary life; it was relieved by psychological roundness which made us sympathize, if not actually pity them, as they declined towards madness and despair. *Pedlar of the Four Seasons* (1971) is a *Bergmany essay about a man's slide into nervous illness; *Fear Eats the Soul* (1974) deals with the effects of terror (real and self-induced) on the individual. His best films are *The Bitter Tears of Petra von Kant* (1972), a film about a lesbian 'mistress' and her 'slave' reminiscent of Genet's play *The Maids*; *The Wild Game* (1972), a taut thriller about a nymphomaniac girl and the lover she eggs on to despair and murder; *Chinese Roulette* (1976), *Buñuelesque sexual and murderous confrontations in a Norwegian château; *The Marriage of Maria Braun* (1976), a splendid mixture of Lili Marlene-like melodrama with politics as acerbic as those of Grass's *The Tin Drum*; and above all *Despair* (1977), about a man's loss of and desperate search for his own identity. This last film (scripted by Tom Stoppard from a mesmeric Nabokov novel) is Fassbinder's finest achievement, because all his pretensions and obsessions work to serve a single dramatic theme. He died, tragically, just as his career was flowering into greatness.

Fassbinder's many other films – he made thirty-eight features in a dozen years – include *The Third Generation* (1978), on urban terrorism, the expensive and empty *Lili Marleen* (1980), *Veronika Voss* (1982), and a version of Genet's novel *Querelle* (1982), a seedy homosexual Odyssey which is no pleasure cruise. Good study: R. Hayman: *Fassbinder Filmmaker* (1984).

FELLINI, Federico (born 1920)
Italian director

In the history of cinema a score of directors stand out as supreme craftsmen, whose film-making outstrips the common run as a virtuoso's piano-playing eclipses Cousin Harriet's. Fellini's films have dazzling technical accomplishment: viewed simply as workmanship, telling stories through engrossing images, they stun. But unlike some of his colleagues, Fellini offers more. His faultless visual technique serves an equally attractive and engrossing personal vision; his films have bones as well as skin. Once or twice, it is true (e.g. in *Satyricon*, 1969, *The Clowns*, 1970, and *Casanova*, 1976), inspiration falters and technique looks like showing-off; but the bulk of his work satisfies heart and mind as well as the hungry aesthetic sense. His films fall into two groups. In the first, his subject is the ennobling power of innocence. The three films in this group were all written for his wife Giulietta Masina. In *La strada* (1954) she plays a simple-minded girl 'bought' as assistant to a travelling circus (the hinge between illusion and reality is a recurring Fellini theme); in *Cabiria* (1956) she plays a prostitute; in *Juliet of the Spirits* (1965) she plays an 'ordinary' woman who sees 'extraordinary' visions. In each case the heroine's surroundings are irradiated and transfigured by her own pure simplicity; at the same time, Fellini avoids sentimentality by making her not a saint, but a 'holy fool' set in a relentlessly grim or trivial modern world, minutely observed. In the second group of films the central characters are again innocents, but Fellini's theme is darker. For these characters innocence is vulnerability, not strength. Instead of transfiguring their surroundings, they are corrupted and destroyed by them. *I vitelloni* (1953) concerns a group of shiftless, engaging youths in a North Italian town; their aimlessness perhaps symbolizes a cancer presciently diagnosed in Italian society at the time (certainly Fellini was attacked for this). In *Il bidone* (1955) and *La dolce vita* (1960) we see the same shiftless types a dozen years older. The characters in *Il bidone* have 'failed' and turned to crime, those in *La dolce vita* have 'succeeded' and entered high society; but their inner desolation is the same. In *Amarcord* (1974), his finest film on this theme, Fellini sets against the rootlessness of 1930s provincial youth the corrosive energy of fascism – once again 'realistic' observation appears to be used to make an explicit political statement. I say 'appears to be' because no statement about Fellini's film-making can stand unqualified once one has seen his masterpiece, *Eight and a Half* (1963). This is a film about film-making, about truth and illusion, genius and talent, meaning and form. Trite themes (if big ones) – but dressed in Fellini's luminous technique, they have a resonance not often met when movie-makers start picking over their own navel-fluff.

Fellini's other films include *The White Sheikh* (1952) and *And the Ship Sails On* (1984), engaging if uncharacteristic comedies, and *City of Women* (1981), an all-too-characteristic blend of the glossiness of *La dolce vita* and the strenuous vulgarity of *Casanova*, a depiction of middle-aged sexual fantasy which makes Ken *Russell look like Mabel Lucie Attwell. Good interim study: G. Salachas: *Federico Fellini* (English edn 1969). Revealing interviews: A. Keel and C. Strich (eds.): *Fellini on Fellini* (English edn 1977). Well illustrated: T. Perry: *Filmguide to '8½'* (1975).

FLAHERTY, Robert (1884–1951)
American documentarist

Flaherty began his career as an explorer in northern Canada; film-making was initially incidental, or used as a means of raising expedition capital.

His films, conceived as studies of human beings in harmony with their environment, now have un unforeseen value as records of utterly vanished ways of life. They include *Nanook of the North* (1922), about Eskimos, and *Moana* (1926), about the Samoan islanders. In 1931 Flaherty went to Britain, at the invitation of the influential documentary producer John Grierson. For British companies he made *Man of Aran* (1934), about 'primitive' life in the Irish islands, and *Elephant Boy* (1936), set in jungle India. Returning to the USA in 1938, he made *The Land* (1941), the record of a journey through agricultural mid-America, and *Louisiana Story* (1948), about the discovery of oil in the Louisiana swamps. This film, like *Elephant Boy*, partly fictionalizes its material, viewing day-to-day events through the eyes of a young hero. It has zest (and remains a fascinating account of a past way of life), but lacks the documentary drive of his earlier work – you feel that Flaherty is now shaping his material, instead of, as in his finest work, letting the material shape the film.

Good study: R. Griffith: *The World of Robert Flaherty* (1953). Good memoir: F. H. Flaherty: *Odyssey of a Film-Maker* (1960).

FORD, John (1895–1973)
American director

Ford began his Hollywood career at the age of seventeen, and acted (not too well) in a number of films including *The Birth of a Nation*. He began his directing career with a western (*The Tornado*, 1917, in which he also starred) and consolidated it with a series of action films starring Harry Carey. Between *The Prince of Avenue A* (1920) and the appalling *Vietnam Vietnam* (1971) he directed over 150 features; many are excellent, several outstanding. He was adept at showing groups of men under stress (*Men Without Women*, 1930; *The Lost Patrol*, 1934; *Fort Apache*, 1948; and, in a different vein, the splendid Cagney comedy *Mr Roberts*, 1955); he made many excellent films on themes or episodes from American history (e.g. *Young Mr Lincoln*, 1939; *The Grapes of Wrath*, 1940; *Wagonmaster*, 1950). Beyond doubt, however, his finest films are westerns, as his laconic testimony to the Unamerican Activities Committee – 'My name's John Ford. I make westerns' – acknowledges. Many of the best star John Wayne, and several (*Stagecoach*, 1939; *My Darling Clementine*, 1946; *She Wore a Yellow Ribbon*, 1949; *The Searchers*, 1956; *The Man who Shot Liberty Valance*, 1962) transcend the genre. They have a consistent vision of human integrity, of the old-fashioned pioneer virtues, which marks Ford out (for all his frequent disclaimers) as a man with something personal to say, and a uniquely appropriate form to say it in.

Good study: P. Bogdanovich: *John Ford* (1968). Good critical biography: D. Ford: *The Unquiet Man: The Life of John Ford* (1982).

FORMAN, Milos (born 1932)
Czech/American director

Forman's first films, *Talent Competition* (1963) and *If It Weren't for All Those Bands* (1963), are humorous documentaries interwoven with fictional stories. The recipe is reversed in *Peter and Pavla* (1964), *A Blonde in Love* (1965) and *The Fireman's Ball* (1967): these are fictional stories etched with acid social observation, as if Hollywood 'screwball' comedies had been directed by a more than usually dyspeptic *Fellini. In 1968 Forman moved to Hollywood. *Taking Off* (1971), a farce about the would-be-hip middle-aged, is intermittently funny, but shows for the first time in his work a marring tendency towards hysteria, satire becoming cynicism unwarmed by wit. *One Flew Over the Cuckoo's Nest* (1975) is better, and sidesteps the problem of hysteria by being set in a mental hospital. It shows all the best qualities of Forman's work: abrasive observation, black seriousness always underpinned by farce, superbly naturalistic performances. The film – which is somewhat in the mode of *M*A*S*H* or *Catch-22* – was overpraised; it is Forman's best so far (*Hair*, 1979, and the raggedly overblown *Ragtime*, 1981, based on Doctorow's pretentious novel, offer it no challenges), but it leaves him with plenty of potential unexplored.

FRANJU, Georges (born 1912)
French director

Three fine documentaries begin – and in some ways crown – Franju's work. *Le Sang des bêtes* (1949) and *Hôtel des Invalides* (1951), about, respectively, a slaughter-house and a military museum, combine horrific images of pain and blood with a compassionate tone; *The Great Méliès* (1952) is about the inventor of cinema surrealism. Human beings as brutes or angels are the subject of most of Franju's feature-films. *La Tête contre les murs* (1958), about the suffering of the mentally ill, is balanced by his version of Mauriac's novel *Thérèse Desqueyroux* (1962), about the psychological ill-treatment by her stifling family of a woman acquitted of trying to poison her husband. *Eyes Without a Face* (1959) and *The Man Without a Face* (1974) are terrifying horror films, Franju's claustrophobic style and matter-of-fact surgical sequences probing nerves no exploitation shocker knows are there: those who like Wells's *The Island of Doctor Moreau* or the anatomical drawings of Vesalius will find Franju just their man. *Judex* (1963) and *Thomas the Impostor* (1965, to a script by Cocteau) are lesser works.

Good study: R. Durgnat: *Franju* (1968).

GANCE, Abel (1889–1981)
French director

Almost forgotten until the late 1970s (when it was rediscovered and reconstituted by Kevin Brownlow), Gance's *Napoléon* (1927) is one of the finest silent pictures made. In grandeur it rivals *Intolerance*, in atmosphere *Metropolis*, in narrative power *Battleship Potemkin*. Gance's use of experimental techniques – hand-held cameras, colour tinting, superimposition, split-screen, and above all the wide-angle lens and 'polyvision' (the use of three screens at once) – makes the film a breath-taking spectacle. The acting is superb, and the pace of editing and cutting – basically, long continuous takes (which give epic intensity) with brief intercut close-ups (which give intimacy) – at first strikes the spectator as quirky and slow, but soon involves and engrosses us. The film's length (six hours) and expensive screening requirements, added to the arrival of sound, eclipsed both it and Gance in the 1930s. Butchered versions were made and shown (some by Gance himself); but chopped-up and shortened, *Napoléon* seemed a tantalizing failure, a postcard Mona Lisa. (Nevertheless, the 1934 sound score is partly, and successfully, used in the modern reconstruction.) Restored, it has power like that of Wagner's *Ring*.

From Gance's pre-*Napoléon* career, only one film stands out: *J'accuse* (1919, poorly remade in 1937), an anti-war film using sequences shot during the First World War itself. Lack of money and political fatuity (he was ardently pro-fascist, though the fascists were never pro-Gance) made his career after *Napoléon* a symphony of discords. All his cash and energy were poured into tinkering with *Napoléon*, or in further experiments – at the age of ninety he was collecting funds for an epic about Christopher Columbus. He earned his living making routine costume dramas (including the likeable – but anybody's – *Un Grand Amour de Beethoven*, 1936, *Austerlitz*, 1960 and *Cyrano and d'Artagnan*, 1964). His cinema genius ranks with *Eisenstein's – and so would his influence, if lack of financial support had not destroyed his career just as it reached its peak. But what a peak!

Brownlow, who reconstituted *Napoléon*, wrote a fascinating book about it (*Napoléon: Abel Gance's Classic Film*, 1983), and also made a splendid compilation-film of Gance's work (*Abel Gance: The Charm of Dynamite*, 1968).

GODARD, Jean-Luc (born 1930)
French director, writer and critic

Enormously influential in the New Wave 1960s, much of Godard's work now seems obscure, opinionated and out of date. (He would not be dismayed by this. His films are polemical, and it may be that their jumble-sale look today means that they have become part of cinema's common currency, that their point is made. Certainly the techniques of television, both fact and fiction, owe him a tremendous debt.) His critical writings reiterate the value of the personal statement, the film-author's overview: the message is the point, and entertainment-value is a means but not necessarily an end. His directorial procedures swept away the formality of European cinema (he is the antithesis of *Bergman). Establishing shots are non-existent; long takes (often with hand-held cameras) replace composed sequences; locations are preferred to studios; the films are shot in sequence, with few retakes, so that editing is minimal; the sound track and music are not always cued into the action, but follow their own logic; Brechtian alienation-techniques are used, such as superimposing a commentary on the action as it proceeds or making polemical speeches (about the events of the film, or current preoccupations of Godard's, relevant or not) direct to camera. All this, added to left-wing political content, makes his work clamorous with personality – and it solicits (and gets) an equally personal response. In the 1970s he largely abandoned commercial cinema for the intimacy and directness of television, returning to films with characteristic thorniness in *Sauve qui peut (la vie)/Slow Motion* (1980).

Godard's subjects are the literal and metaphorical violence of modern society, and the way people sell themselves to others – again literally (prostitutes or mercenary soldiers) or metaphorically (politicians or the compromising bourgeoisie). Like Camus, he is fascinated by the alienated members of society: criminals, terrorists, strikers, immigrants and revolutionaries. Even when his characters are those of 'ordinary' life, like the housewife in *Une Femme mariée* (1964) or the husband of *Pierrot-le-fou* (1965), two of his best films, their individuality is diminished and depressed by society, and they only reassert their human identity by breaking free.

For the non-partisan spectator, Godard's best films are his earliest. *À bout de souffle* (1960), about a man on the run, *Vivre sa vie* (1962) and *Deux ou trois choses que je sais d'elle* (1966), both about prostitutes, and above all the extraordinary *Weekend* (1967), in which a couple on a weekend drive witness murderous attacks, terrorism, bestiality and cannibalism – Arthur Hiller made a delicious comic parody in *The Out-of-Towners* (1969) – in each of these films Godard shows compassion for his characters, and this human engagement turns polemic into art.

Godard's other films include *Alphaville* (1965), a bleak counterpart to *Tati's *Playtime*, and *Passion* (1982), a mixture of *tableaux vivants* of famous paintings, marxist dialectic, and a story involving a film-maker having an affair with an activist factory-worker trying to organize a strike. *First Name Carmen* (1983) is an appealing change of direction: an absurdist updating of the story behind Bizet's opera, lightweight Godard but lively fun. Good collection of essays from the 1960s: *Godard on Godard* (ed. Milne, 1972). Good study of the 1960s films: P. French (ed.): *The Films of Jean-Luc Godard* (2nd edn 1969).

GRIFFITH, David Wark (1874–1948)
American film-maker

Griffith had the rare ability of a master craftsman to grow by experience, to develop technical skill into an object of excellence in itself. If he had never existed, other directors would have invented film 'grammar' – eventually. As it was, he did it all, much of it in the course of the 500 short films (most of them one reel, or ten minutes, long) he made between joining the industry in 1908 and directing *The Birth of a Nation* in 1915. Before him, film was a sophisticated toy of the illusionist; after *Birth of a Nation* it had pretensions (however red-nosed) to art.

Griffith's technical innovations all arose, in the end, from a single decision: to move his camera nearer to the actors. Previously the camera had taken up a static position, as it were in a seat in the theatre stalls. There was no perspective or depth to film acting, and close-up (for example in Porter's *The Great Train Robbery*) was used as a trick effect, a joke with no motivation or emotional purpose. Griffith put his camera among the actors, thus bringing the spectator into an intimacy with the story; he used close-ups and tracking shots to follow the performers about, to move in and show their feelings and motivation. The result, for actors, meant a scaling-down of barnstorming theatre style and the development of a subtle vocabulary of film gesture and facial expression; for technicians it meant the development of lighting, make-up and above all the choice of camera-angles themselves. These innovations in turn led Griffith to develop 'editorial' techniques in shooting, cutting and film assembly – the camera takes a critical, involved part in the story-telling, and does not merely observe. He developed cross-cutting as a way of showing two simultaneous events and building tension: in *The Birth of a Nation*, for example, as the Ku Klux Klan rides to rescue Elsie from imminent assault, he cross-cuts rapidly from the galloping horsemen to the girl's assailants and her own terrified face, thus making a moral and critical point, focusing the story, by cutting alone. He developed dramatic close-up as a vehicle for registering thought: in the strike sequence of *Intolerance*, for example, he regularly picks out individual strikers and focuses on their snarling or pitiful faces. He developed the long shot and its sister the wide pan as means of achieving epic sweep (for example in the battle vistas of *The Birth of a Nation*). He developed the use of flashback (usually dream-sequences of past happiness), establishing shots (general views of the sites of each scene, before the scene begins), fade-out, irises (opening or closing a circular frame round the action), even split-screen and slow motion. All of these techniques might have remained gimmicks in other hands; Griffith's unique contribution lay in welding them into the vocabulary of story-telling rather than treating them as high spots of story themselves.

That said, it must be admitted that he used this subtle vocabulary and syntax to tell stories of crashing banality. His plots never whisper when they can shriek; his characters never have two thoughts, motives or instincts where one will do. It is a world of grandiose melodrama – and never more so than in the endless tearful, coy or lowering close-ups which mark his style just as much as huge cities or battlefields pullulating with extras. No amount of technical sophistication prevents *The Birth of a Nation* (1915) from being the most offensive piece of racialist propaganda put on the screen until *Riefenstahl's *Triumph of the Will*; *Intolerance* (1916) reduces the human race to pasteboard cutouts enacting scenes of compelling but turgid grandeur (a failing endemic to cinema epic: first-class realization of fourth-class imagination is characteristic of films as diverse as *Ben Hur*, *Gone With the Wind*, *Lawrence of Arabia* and *Apocalypse Now*); the plots and characters of *Broken Blossoms* (1919) and *Way Down East* (1920) are ridiculous. Characteristic titles from some of Griffith's later films show, only too well, the tabloid level of his intellect: *Orphans of the Storm* (1922), *Sally of the Sawdust* (1925), *Drums of Love* (1928), *The Struggle* (1931). Like all trash culture, his films comfort their audience; Griffith only twice (in the war-film *Hearts of the World*, 1918, and in *Isn't Life Wonderful?*, 1924, a harshly realistic story set in war-ruined Germany) used his eloquent language to *say* something, his outstanding artifice to disconcert or shock.

Good studies: I. Bany: *D. W. Griffith, American Film Master* (1965); R. M. Henderson: *D. W. Griffith: His Life and Work* (1972). Wide-eyed, scandalous nonsense, hugely enjoyable: L. Arvidson (Mrs D. W. Griffith): *When the Movies Were Young* (1925), which should be complemented by the splendid autobiography of one of his favourite stars (a far beadier-eyed lady than he ever dreamed): L. Gish: *The Movies, Mr Griffith, and Me* (1969). Well illustrated: F. Silva (ed.): *Focus on 'The Birth of a Nation'* (1971).

HAWKS, Howard (1896–1977)
American director

Hawks made over fifty feature films, all marked by the same relaxed pace and wryness of style. (They are also as enjoyably 'American' in tone as the war-films and comedies of Ealing Studios are 'British'.) He made entertaining films in several genres, for example war-action (*The Dawn Patrol*, 1930; *Only Angels Have Wings*, 1939; *Sergeant York*, 1941), gangster (*Scarface*, 1932) and western (*Red River*, 1948; *Rio Bravo*, 1959). His best films all concern, in one way or another, the battle between the sexes. They include *The Big Sleep* (1946), with *Huston's *The Maltese Falcon* the definitive private-eye film, with a clinching central performance by Humphrey Bogart; an off-beat love story, *To Have and Have Not* (1944), the film in which Bogart and Bacall first fall in love; and a handful of Hollywood's sharpest comedies: *Twentieth Century* (1934 – John Barrymore slicing succulent ham as a megalomaniac theatre director), *Bringing Up Baby* (1938 – Cary Grant as an archaeologist, Katharine Hepburn as a leopard-toting society girl), *His Girl Friday* (1940 – his funniest film, a version of the Hecht–MacArthur play *The Front Page* involving Grant as a ruthless newspaper editor wooing back his ex-wife and ace reporter), and the neglected *Ball of Fire* (1941, about a group of encyclopaedia-compiling professors who shelter a gangster's moll). Hawks is as consistent and as individual a stylist as *Wilder; but his range is wider and his view of humanity more genial.

Good, if solemn, study: R. Wood: *Howard Hawks* (1968). More zestful (particularly good at describing actual sequences): G. Mast: *Howard Hawks, Storyteller* (1983). Splendid interviews: J. McBride (ed.): *Hawks on Hawks* (1982).

HERZOG, Werner (born 1942)
German director

If *Coppola, *Scorsese, *Spielberg and others are the American generation of 'movie brats' (that is, young directors able, it seems, to plan dolly shots and reverses in their cradles and for whom the language of *Bergman, *Hitchcock, *Godard and *Kurosawa was mother's milk), there is a flourishing German equivalent, and its leading light is Herzog. Of all earlier film-makers he perhaps owes most to *Buñuel and to 1920s expressionist directors like *Lang and *Murnau. His fascination is with freaks, or with human beings driven to freakish conduct by etiolating circumstance. *Even Dwarfs Started Small* (1970), for example, is his version of *Lord of the Flies*: dwarfs on a desert island create a ghastly model of human society. *Fata morgana* (1971, set in the Sahara desert) and *The Land of Darkness and Silence* (1971) are in much the same vein; the latter uses a cast of deaf-and-dumb performers. His finest films use the hypnotic talent of the actor Klaus Kinski, who can at one and the same time embody the very consummation of human suffering and the power of the Living Dead. He stars in Herzog's *Aguirre, Wrath of God* (1973), a savage, eerie film about conquistadors in Mexico, reminiscent in tone of *Bresson's *Lancelot*; in *Woyzeck* (1979); in *Nosferatu the Vampire* (1979), a reworking of both of the original Dracula story and of Murnau's masterpiece; and in *Fitzcarraldo* (1982), an extraordinary film about modern Peruvian Indians moving a steamship across a hill by stone-age technology. Herzog is something of a special taste, but in these four films, at least, he is magnificent.

Herzog's other films include *Where the Green Ants Dream* (1984), a fable about Australian aborigines watching one of their sacred places being torn apart by the heavy machines of a mining company. An interesting documentary film, *Burden of Dreams* (1982), charts the making of Herzog's *Fitzcarraldo*, a story almost as bizarre as that of Herzog's film itself.

HITCHCOCK, Alfred (1899–1980)
British director

Hitchcock appeals to highbrow film-critics because of his view of 'total
cinema': each story is told entirely in film terms, with no references
outside the immediate experience. The rhythm and montage of a
Hitchcock film are its dominating features. In *Psycho* (1960), for example,
music, camera positions and cutting set up forebodings about Anthony
Perkins and his motel long before Janet Leigh signs the register; the
film's first climax, the shower scene, is meticulously prepared in the same
way. We know that 'something horrible' (a favourite Hitchcock phrase)
is going to happen to Leigh in the shower simply because its preparation
(turning on taps, undressing, moving the plastic curtain) is dwelt upon
with such deliberation. Then – and this too is characteristic – when the
horrible something actually *does* happen, it is brief, extremely nasty, and
shot with callous technical sophistication – a mosaic of images, some
lasting no more than a couple of seconds. The sheer power of suggestion
creates both tension and horror. Hitchcock never once states what
happens: he simply manipulates the nerve-ends of our imagination.

For most cinema-goers, Hitchcock's appeal is not so much technical
sophistication as his mixture of tension with tongue-in-cheek jauntiness.
There is something irresistibly entertaining, for example, in people fighting for their lives under Jefferson's giant nose on Mount Rushmore, or
clambering for dear life down the torch of the Statue of Liberty; if crooks
threaten the hero, it is not with gun or knife but with a crop-spraying
aircraft; a man keeps a skeleton – literally – not in his cupboard but
sitting in a chair. Hitchcock's best films are those which use stars known
for debonair charm: this is a vital ingredient in establishing from the start
their innocence (or the delicious possibility of their guilt), and in
counterbalancing moments of extreme violence with throwaway, insouciant niceness. In fact niceness is often their only personality-trait.
Hitchcock's characters are anodyne – as in detective fiction, the puzzle
is all-important, the events outweigh the people. (It is also a predominantly masculine world: his films with female leads are among his
weakest.) His style is consistently ironical and cerebral rather than
emotional. We always know more than the characters (we see a drinking
scene *through* the glasses laced with knockout drops; we cut back and
forth from the victim in the crowd to the assassin's gun pointing from a
balcony) – but we never know everything, we learn with the characters,
and when our knowledge fully coincides with theirs, catharsis and the
film are both complete.

This seems a simple recipe (though few other directors have used it
with such consistent excellence), and it stood, largely unvaried, as
Hitchcock's working style for over fifty years. He favoured a 'chase'
structure: the hero (usually innocent but trapped in a situation of
apparent guilt, working against the odds to clear his name) has to travel,

often to a climax in some outlandish spot; he is pursued by both crooks and the law, helped only by the innocent girl he is trying to save, or by the wicked lady who turns out good in the end (a variant of the whore with the heart of gold). In some films, notably the superb, voyeuristic *Rear Window* (1954), the hero is trapped not by events but by physical incapacity: he has to stay in one place, while things happen around or in front of him (a variant of the traditional 'locked-room' mystery).

There are a few stinkers (*Rope*? *Dial M for Murder*? *Marnie*? *Torn Curtain*?) among Hitchcock's films, but the majority are excellent and a handful are among the most enjoyable entertainment the cinema has yet produced. *Notorious* (1946), *Strangers on a Train* (1951), *The Birds* (1963), *Frenzy* (1972) and above all *North by Northwest* (1959 – Cary Grant and a crop-sprayer), together with *Rear Window* and *Psycho*, represent his work at its shallow, splendid best.

Classic studies: C. Chabrol and E. Rohmer, *Hitchcock* (1957); F. Truffaut: *Hitchcock* (1967). Their hagiographical approach is excellently counterbalanced by D. Spoto: *The Life of Alfred Hitchcock: The Dark Side of Genius* (1983), which presents Hitchcock as something of an appalling person, but is also firm about the quality of his work.

HUSTON, John (born 1906)
American director and writer

Huston began as a studio screenwriter, collaborating on such films as *Dr Ehrlich's Magic Bullet*, *High Sierra* and *Sergeant York*. His debut as a director was *The Maltese Falcon* (1941), still perhaps his best film. It shows all the best qualities of his work: fast, wise-cracking action, atmospheric characterization and above all an ability both to control and to pander to star actors (here Bogart, Greenstreet and Lorre). He made several more outstanding films with Bogart (*Across the Pacific*, 1942; *Treasure of the Sierra Madre*, 1948; *Key Largo*, 1948; *The African Queen*, 1952; and the under-rated – by Bogart, among others – gangster comedy *Beat the Devil*, 1953). He did more than anyone else except *Hawks to bring out the acid vulnerability that became Bogart's main screen characteristic. In fact vulnerability has been a consistent theme in all Huston's work – among small-time crooks (*The Asphalt Jungle*, 1950), rookie soldiers (*The Red Badge of Courage*, 1951), creative artists (*Moulin Rouge*, 1952; *Freud*, 1962) and failing boxers (*Fat City*, 1972); the culmination was his version of Lowry's *Under the Volcano* (see page 137) in 1984. He has made some terrible films – especially in the 1960s and 1970s, when he began working with other people's scripts (though *The Night of the Iguana*, 1964, from Tennessee Williams's play, recaptures the tautness of his earlier work). But the films here mentioned are excellent, and those with Bogart are magnificent.

Huston's later films include *The Misfits* (1961), *The Bible* (1966), the expensive but pleasant musical *Annie* (1982), and a gloriously vulgar weepie, *Young Giants* (1983), about how the great footballer Pele (acting here with his kneecaps) gives purpose in life to a bunch of hard-boiled orphanage kids. A fascinating account of Huston at work (on *The Red Badge of Courage*) is given by Lillian Ross in *Picture* (1952). Huston's autobiography, *An Open Book* (1980), is both informative and witty.

ICHIKAWA, Kon (born 1915)
Japanese director

Ichikawa is a prolific and versatile director: his films include documentary (*Tokyo Olympiad*, 1965), melodrama (*An Actor's Revenge*, 1963, based on a famous Kabuki-theatre story of rape, murder and betrayal) and satirical comedy (*Mr Pu*, 1953; *Odd Obsession*, 1959). The finest of his films known in the west – and half his output is still to be seen – are *The Burmese Harp* (1956) and *Alone on the Pacific* (1963). Both deal in a poetic and moving way (and in an underplayed dramatic style nothing like the barking hysteria of *samurai* or kung fu films) with individuals achieving dignity of spirit through heroic endurance or suffering. In *The Burmese Harp* a musician from Japan's defeated army remains in Burma to bury his dead comrades; in *Alone on the Pacific* a man sets out on a single-handed voyage. Both films avoid consecutive plot and incident – past events blur with present; human experience and feeling are shown as individually perceived parts of a continuous whole. The philosophical basis is Buddhist: humanity's ideal state is one of passive receptivity; people define themselves by perception, not action; they are the paper and not the pen. For western spectators, this can be hard going. But in contrast to the often frigid, post-apocalyptic emptiness of *Godard or *Fassbinder or the Bosch-like visions of humanity in such films as *A Clockwork Orange, Death Race 2000* or *The Warriors*, it can also seem humane, hopeful and comfortingly warm.

INGRAM, Rex (1892–1950)
Irish/American director

Ingram's active career ended in the early 1930s: his few sound films are minor works. In the 1920s he was one of the most highly regarded of 'artistic' directors, encouraging performances of notable restraint from his actors and filling the screen with images as well composed and lit as paintings. (When people say that sound films have never matched the visual beauty of the silent cinema, Ingram's are the kind of silent films they mean.) These qualities of control and taste were usually, in his films, applied to lightweight stories (*The Four Horsemen of the Apocalypse*, 1922; *The Prisoner of Zenda*, 1922; *Scaramouche*, 1923), and all but elevated swashbuckle into an art-form. Perhaps Ingram's seriousness (so different from, say, Fairbanks' satirical elegance) was the reason; certainly in his most personal films (*Mare nostrum*, 1926, ostensibly about spies and submarines; *The Magician*, 1926, an Arabian Nights adventure) the events of the stories take second place to the dream-like, poetic style in which they are told. If Ingram had been a European director, making expressionist versions of Frankenstein or the Last Judgement, he would be acclaimed today as a genius. As it is, because he worked in 'trivial' Hollywood, he is hardly known. He remains a genius.

IVORY, James (born 1928)
American director

Working with the producer Ismail Merchant and the Anglo-Indian writer Ruth Prawer Jhabvala, Ivory has made a number of features in a sensitive, low-key style not unlike that of *Ray. (His first four films were set in India, and used some of Ray's actors and also his regular cameraman, Subratha Mitra.) A main theme of Ivory's work is the nature and importance of performance, both public and private. *Shakespeare Wallah* (1965), *Bombay Talkie* (1970) and *Jane Austen in Manhattan* (1980), respectively about a touring Shakespeare company, the pullulating Indian film industry and the production in America of a newly discovered Jane Austen play, concern the effects of performance on an (untutored or sophisticated) audience, and on the performers themselves; the theme of illusion and reality is also at the heart of *The Guru* (1968), about the effects of Indian mysticism on a brash western pop singer. In *Roseland* (1977), *The Europeans* (1979) and *The Bostonians* (1984) Ivory turns to private performance: here are people playing roles to hold together or influence their everyday lives. *Roseland*, about the hollow habitués of an American dance-hall, is like a sad, bad *Tati film; *The Europeans* is based on Henry James's early novel; *The Bostonians* meticulously translates to the screen James's study of a self-confident, attitudinizing and crumbling aristocratic society. *Heat and Dust* (1983) is Ivory's finest film to date, a study (made with *Ray-like intensity and sensitivity) of a mysterious young European coming to terms with herself and the 1920s Raj.

Good study: J. Pym: *The Wandering Company: 25 Years of Merchant–Ivory Films* (1983).

KEATON, Buster (1895–1966)
American actor and director

*Chaplin is extrovert, Keaton introvert; Chaplin understands everything about the world, Keaton nothing; Chaplin is never the waif he seems, Keaton always the waif he never plays. Even their surpassing acrobatic skill articulates these differences. Chaplin always seems relaxed: his acrobatic tricks seem to occur to him as spur-of-the-moment improvisations, self-revealing (and self-delighting) reactions to events, casually begun and as casually abandoned when his mood changes. Keaton by contrast is always wary, alert for the slings and arrows of an implacable universe. His acrobatics look meticulous, the scrupulous products of mind not heart. Chaplin's style looks easy and has had a thousand imitators; Keaton's looks difficult and has had none.

His output was comparatively small (if we exclude a few early performances, for example in Fatty Arbuckle films, and the desolate series of appearances after 1929, when uncongenial working conditions, added to alcoholism, clouded his career). Between 1920 and 1923 he made nineteen two-reel comedies; between 1923 and 1929 he made ten features. In many of the films he plays an earnest, unsmiling Samuel Smiles young man determined to better himself. He builds a do-it-yourself house and boat; he sets out to marry and to win a fortune; he follows the instruction 'Go west, young man'; he dreams of being a famous detective, a boxing champion, a great lover, a hero of the civil war. He is, with Harold Lloyd, the archetype of 1920s get-up-and-go; but unlike Lloyd he rarely succeeds – his films end with tombstones as often as with marriages. The reason is usually the hostility of material things. His home-made house, which he is pushing bodily to its new site on the other side of town, sticks fast on a railway track (and, in typical Keaton style, is wrecked not by the first express, which turns unexpectedly off on a siding, but by the second, which arrives unheralded from behind him); his boat sinks; he finds not one bride but hundreds; realizing that he is inadvertently holding a bomb, he flings it away – into a police march-past. Each film proceeds with unstoppable logic from one disaster to the next – and as the disasters grow in scale and scope, Keaton reacts with ever more galvanic activity, frenzied ingenuity which his unsmiling face lets us know he knows is doomed.

His best films? Of the two-reelers, *One Week* (1920 – the home-made house), *The Boat* (1921 – in which he is a family man, totally at sea, hampered not only by tempest and flood but by a wife and two gravely identical tiny Keatons) and *Cops* (1922 – in which he is pursued by every policeman in town) stand out both for single-minded logic and for lunatic invention. Among the features, *Sherlock Junior* (1924 – where he is a cinema projectionist dreaming himself into the films he shows), *The Navigator* (1924 – Keaton and girl alone on an ocean liner) and *The General* (1926 – Keaton as an engine-driver in the civil war) have unsurpassed individual moments, but suffer from episodic plots. (The decision to end *The General* with triumph – Buster/Johnny saves the day – is weak, for example, and turns satire into whimsy.) The best features – and, with *Cops*, Keaton's finest films – are *Our Hospitality* (1923), *Seven Chances* (1925) and *Steamboat Bill, Jr* (1928). *Our Hospitality* sets him in the feuding South: to win the girl he must not only get away unharmed from a house where everyone is set to murder him, but also canoe down rapids, swim torrents and finally snatch the girl from the brink of a Niagara-sized waterfall (one of his most breathtaking comic stunts). In *Seven Chances* he sets out simply to marry before nightfall, but ends up pursued by hundreds of predatory brides, their relatives, and dozens of huge boulders leaping and plunging down a hill – again, a sequence of outstanding agility and hilarity. In *Steamboat Bill, Jr* he is the wimpish son of a tough riverboat-owner father, and during a cyclone – Keaton's most fantastic stunt-sequence ever – saves his father, saves the girl he loves, saves *her* father, and finally saves a preacher to perform the wedding ceremony.

In the last analysis, Keaton lacks the human resonance of Chaplin. His films have no 'philosophical' overtones, no purpose except to amuse. They represent the apogee of the *Sennett gag-comedy, carried to perfection by Keaton's own unique, balletic skill. He is the greatest acrobat, and the greatest inventive genius, in comic cinema – not so deep as Chaplin, but better controlled and funnier.

Autobiography (so-so, but all there is): *My Wonderful World of Slapstick* (with C. Samuels) (1960). Good biography: T. Dardis: *Keaton: The Man Who Wouldn't Lie Down* (1979).

KELLY, Gene (born 1912)
American dancer, choreographer and director

Before Kelly, musicals were essentially concerned with stage 'numbers', either the backstage squabbles during their creation or the glittering results of such artistic argument. Evening dress was the usual costume, occasionally replaced by 'speciality' dress (for example tennis clothes or exotic costumes for ethnic dances). The dancing was based either on ballroom styles or on tap, soft-shoe and chorus-line routines derived from vaudeville. Kelly himself performed (not often, but well) in all these styles, but his main contribution to the development of the musical was to dispense with them. He used everyday clothes, and whenever possible natural locations (streets, living rooms, the decks of ships – when Astaire dances on a ship, it is as part of a speciality dance group; when Kelly dances on a ship, he is a sailor – even museums, lifts and skyscraper roofs). The dancing, so far as possible, was integrated into the story and developed the plot or the character's emotions. (The exception is a number of pretentious jazz ballets, which interrupt the flow of such films as *An American in Paris*, 1951, and *Invitation to the Dance*, 1956.) Kelly's fluid, narrative style (to say nothing of his actual dancing, which is marvellous – happiness distilled – or of his likeable comic acting) is well seen in *For Me and my Gal* (1942), *Cover Girl* (1943) and *Anchors Aweigh* (1945), and reached its peak in two films he co-directed with Stanley Donen, *On the Town* (1950) and *Singin' in the Rain* (1952). From the mid-1950s onwards (when the style of film musicals again changed, towards Rodgers and Hammerstein on the one hand and *West Side Story* on the other) he turned largely to acting (notably in *Marjorie Morningstar*, 1958, and *Inherit the Wind*, 1960) and to direction (notably in *A Guide for the Married Man*, 1967, and *Hello, Dolly*, 1969).

Enjoyable study: A. Thomas: *The Films of Gene Kelly, Song-and-Dance-Man* (1974).

KORDA, Alexander (1893–1956)
Hungarian /British producer and director

Apart from *Balcon, Korda was the nearest British equivalent to a Hollywood studio boss: a man of extravagant dash and flair, whose personality coloured every film on which he worked. He founded London Films (and built Denham Studios); in the 1930s they produced a string of films to rival anything from Hollywood. Korda specialized in two kinds of film above all. First, historical melodramas, often in a light-hearted satirical style reminiscent of *Lubitsch. The best are *The Private Life of Henry VIII* (1933) and *Rembrandt* (1936), in both of which Korda himself was the director and Charles Laughton the star; but *Catherine the Great* (1934) and *The Scarlet Pimpernel* (1934) are also excellent. Second, 'general interest films', often with exotic plots or locations – for example H. G. Wells's science-prediction film *Things to Come* (1936), the semi-documentary *Elephant Boy* (1936), set in India, and the Arabian Nights story *The Thief of Baghdad* (1940). After the Second World War (during which he worked partly in Hollywood and partly on war-information films in London), Korda took over British Lion Films (based on Shepperton Studios). Although he never here achieved the financial or artistic success of his pre-war film-making, he did supervise a handful of outstanding films, including *Anna Karenina* (1948), *The Fallen Idol* (1948), *The Third Man* (1949) and *Hobson's Choice* (1954). Throughout his career his best work was done in the studios: when he moved to the boardroom (as in his later years at British Lion) his energy and personality had less effect. Perhaps he was at heart a Hollywood flamboyant, out of his element in British mists, but none the less, if British films of the 1930s have a distinctive tang, that tang is his.

Interesting study: M. Korda: *Charmed Lives* (1981).

KRAMER, Stanley (born 1913)
American director and producer

As an independent producer, Kramer worked on several outstanding films, including *The Men* (1950), *Death of a Salesman* (1951), *High Noon* (1952) and *The Caine Mutiny* (1954). As director he has specialized in films with 'concerned' liberal themes: his subjects include the Final Solution, nuclear war, religious bigotry and racism. The topicality such themes lend his films has tended to gild the fact that underneath they are hollow melodrama, whose pretensions to social significance would hardly strain the mental processes of a ten-year-old. But *On the Beach* (1959), *Inherit the Wind* (1960), *Judgement at Nuremberg* (1961), *Ship of Fools* (1965) and *Guess Who's Coming to Dinner* (1967) remain highly entertaining, largely because of such 'thinking' romantic stars as Gregory Peck and Spencer Tracy. *It's a Mad Mad Mad Mad World* (1963), a strident farce, and *The Runner Stumbles* (1980), an old-fashioned 'woman's picture', lacking such reliable performances, fall over themselves. Kramer's best film is *The Defiant Ones* (1958): Sidney Poitier and Tony Curtis as escaped convicts chained together make an effective statement about inter-racial tension and the need for tolerance.

KUBRICK, Stanley (born 1928)
American film-maker

Kubrick works slowly, and his films are technically superb. He uses popular styles (novelettish plots, 'middle-of-the-road' music and fashion-magazine design) and popular actors (Peter Sellers, Kirk Douglas, James Mason) to tell stories of the blackest pessimism and irony. Humanity, in Kubrick's world, is an insane ants' nest: the queen is dead, and individuals twist and writhe while all around them the mindless mass seethes and dies. *The Killing* (1956), a sour caper movie, first established the theme of the doomed individual; this is worked out more fully in *Paths of Glory* (1957), about a warped court-martial in the First World War (the lunacy of military thinking is a recurring Kubrick theme), and reached its climax in the gleefully dystopian *A Clockwork Orange* (1971). His best films are quieter, and cloak his obsessions in a variety of glittering styles. *Spartacus* (1960) is that rare thing, a restrained epic about ancient Rome; *Lolita* (1962) is an unsensational treatment of Nabokov's novel, centring (as the book does) on Humbert's self-torture rather than on tabloid prurience; it was followed by the bleakly funny *Dr Strangelove* (1963), in which humanity rodeo-rides to its death on a phallic nuclear bomb, and by *2001: A Space Odyssey* (1968), whose seductive special effects (space vehicles waltzing in the void to the strains of Strauss) mechanize its vision of the sterility and pointlessness of human existence. The costume drama *Barry Lyndon* (1975), though beautiful to look at, is flatter, and *The Shining* (1980) is a blood-thirsty horror film, ruined by hysterical acting (especially from Jack Nicholson) and a sensational and silly script.

Revealing study of Kubrick at work: J. Agel (ed.): *The Making of Kubrick's '2001'* (1970). Interesting general study: M. Ciment: *Kubrick* (1983).

KUROSAWA, Akira (born 1910)
Japanese director

Western audiences, bemused by the strangeness of some of the conventions used (the actors seem to bark or whine instead of speaking, to leap or flit instead of walking, and there is arcane significance, it seems, in bamboo, slicing rain and mud), have sometimes read more meaning into Kurosawa's *samurai* films than is actually there. They are simple entertainments, as sophisticated and as unassuming as the westerns of *Ford. (Several in fact, have been excellently remade as westerns, and the fact that they lose nothing when one set of conventions replaces another indicates their reliance on the particularity of genre rather than Kurosawa's uniqueness.) The best are *The Seven Samurai* (1954), *The Hidden Fortress* (1958), *Yojimbo* (1961) and *Kagemusha* (*The Shadow Warrior*, 1980), all based on the same mixture of heroic melodrama, moody or athletic acting and laconic directorial wit (e.g. the send-up of *Eisenstein's crowd-scenes in the portrayal of the peasants in *The Seven Samurai*). Unabashed self-consciousness is what makes the style. It works well for Kurosawa too in *Throne of Blood* (1957), a *samurai* reworking of *Macbeth*: stripped of the solemnities of the western scholarly tradition, Shakespeare's play comes across as throat-grabbing *theatre*, in one of the most unboring and plausible versions ever made. (Kurosawa's other literary adaptations, *The Idiot*, 1951, and *The Lower Depths*, 1957, adhering more closely to the western style of the originals, never reinhabit their material in the same enthralling way.)

Kurosawa's most personal films avoid extroversion both in acting and direction. They are slow-moving and thoughtful, rather in the manner of early *Bresson or *Ray. The first of them, *Rashomon* (1950), is his masterpiece. It uses the swaggering talent of Toshiro Mifune (the star of Kurosawa's best *samurai* films) not to impress but to portray hollow barbarity. The story concerns the investigation into a murder and rape; the same events are seen four times, through the accounts of four witnesses to the crime (one of them the murdered man, eerily speaking through a medium). The film's subjects, the nature of reality and the way in which relationships can be used to manipulate truth, are never openly proclaimed, as in the *samurai* stories; they appear often in ironical camera-work (e.g. sudden close-ups, revealing a lie or an exaggeration made for effect) and in the stylization of the script (every effect, every nuance as precisely placed as in *Bergman, say, or *Renoir). The pervasive feeling is of striving through chaos towards order, the spring-cleaning of the turbulent human spirit; its resonances are those of much eastern religious philosophy. This is also the mood of Kurosawa's most intense and moving film, *Living* (1952). In this an elderly council official, suffering from terminal cancer, sets out to discover and assert some meaning in what has so far been a sterile, useless life. The film is about the transfiguration of the soul, the progression from incomprehension through learning towards acceptance; it also has effective points to make about the squalid competence of city bureaucracies. *Derzu Uzala* (1975) also deals with the soul's ennoblement, this time through a close relationship (between a pushy army officer and an enigmatic, possibly saintly old man he meets in the forests of 19th-century Siberia). The film is superbly shot (in colour), and exhibits all Kurosawa's excellence (the action sequences, for example, are as magnificent, and as central, as the depiction of intense personal feeling). It is his *Tempest*: not his greatest work, but a serene recollection of emotion in tranquillity.

Kurosawa's other films include *I Live in Fear* (1955), in mood similar to *Living*, about an old man determined, against all opposition, to move himself and his family to Brazil to avoid death from nuclear fallout. Kurosawa has published *Something like an Autobiography* (1982), particularly interesting on the last ten years. Good studies: D. Richie: *The Films of Akiro Kurosawa* (1965); *'Rashomon': A Film by Akiro Kurosawa* (1969).

LANG, Fritz (1890–1976)
German director

The importance of Lang's influence on later directors is shown by the fact that many of his own films now seem routine, even tame: others have used the grammar he devised to make better psychological thrillers and far more atmospheric horror films. But without him, directors as diverse as *Carné, Clouzot, *Hitchcock, *Huston and Whale (creator of *Frankenstein*) would have begun their careers bereft of a vocabulary.

The greatest influence on Lang's own style was the artistic movement expressionism (see page 538). From this comes his fascination with the workings of the disturbed or neurotic subconscious mind, his use of distortion, selection and violent emphasis to express extreme emotion, and his obsessive political pessimism. His characters are hunted victims, driven distracted by huge forces, both internal and external, which they do not understand and cannot control. Their torment is to continue living, and their only release is hysterical action, often insane or criminal. Lang's style is as ponderously diagrammatic as *Eisenstein's, but he lacks the political optimism and the plain humanity that lighten Eisenstein's best work.

Lang's films are at their best when neurotic fantasy rules everything, when there is no attempt at objective narrative. In three of them, *Dr Mabuse the Gambler* (1922), *The Testament of Dr Mabuse* (1932) and *The Thousand Eyes of Dr Mabuse* (1960), the central figure is a maniac magician, a satanic conjurer bent (in the vortex of his own mind) on world domination. In *Destiny* (1921) Death is the central character; *Metropolis* (1926) is set in a nightmare future world of lowering skyscrapers, robotized worker-slaves, and love flourishing like a weed on a compost heap – a world, like that of Lang's own style, in which 'restraint' is a word unknown.

The Kafkaesque element in Lang's work is most notable in a series of thrillers with a single, bewildered individual at their heart. The archetype is Peter Lorre, the cringing child-murderer of *M* (1931), Lang's masterpiece; but Spencer Tracy in *Fury* (1936), Henry Fonda in *You Only Live Once* (1937), Edward G. Robinson in *The Woman in the Window* (1944) and Glenn Ford in *The Big Heat* (1953) all play characters driven to desperate action by remorseless circumstance.

The problem with Lang's films is not atmosphere or psychological verisimilitude, but plot. (Lack of structure is an endemic failing of all expressionist art.) He often abandons coherence altogether, or ties up loose ends in whatever arbitrary manner will serve to end the film. The love-affair in *Metropolis* and the sickly ending of *The Woman in the Window* are the worst examples, but they illustrate a consistent failing: Lang deals in remorseless pressure, and this is cancelled by the slightest hint of irrelevance or implausibility. Tight plotting, where the conclusion is an inevitable result of what has gone before, is really only achieved in three films, *M, Fury* and *You Only Live Once*. This makes them (together with the Dr Mabuse fantasies, where arbitrariness is the point) the most consistent and satisfying of all Lang's works.

Good studies: P. Bogdanovich: *Fritz Lang in America* (1968); P. M. Jensen: *The Cinema of Fritz Lang* (1969). Good critical essays: S. Jenkins (ed.): *Fritz Lang* (1981).

LOSEY, Joseph (1909–84)
American director

A large part of Losey's output consists of hardboiled thrillers, similar in style to those of *Chabrol, Clouzot and (for political content as well as atmosphere) Costa-Gavras. The best of them (*The Prowler*, 1951, *The Big Night*, 1951, *Blind Date*, 1959, *The Criminal*, 1960, and *The Damned*, 1961) have a Dostoievskian obsession with poverty and oppression as the seedbeds of crime: Losey is strongly on the side of the weak, though he charts their destruction or degradation with detachment, not sympathy. In the 1960s he made a series of enigmatic films about destructive personal relationships. Scripted by Harold Pinter, they blend *Bergman-esque intensity with the arrogant gloss of the French New Wave (*Truffaut is an important influence). *The Servant* (1963) stars Dirk Bogarde as the vessel of apparently motiveless malignity; in *Accident* (1967) he plays a man baffled by the shifts and settlings of a complex emotional relationship. The best of these films is *The Go-Between* (1971), which is both a sumptuously filmed evocation of life among the sunlit Edwardian upper class and a typically laconic presentation of destructive relationships: the uncomprehending boy-victim is beautifully played by Dominic Guard. *Mr Klein* (1976), a story of compromise and lost identity set in Nazi-occupied Paris, has the same mixture of opulence and eeriness, this time to a script (in French) by Franco Solinas. Losey's other films, though always interesting, fall short of this achievement. They include *King and Country* (1964), a court-martial story not unlike *Kubrick's *Paths of Glory*, but concentrating on the relationship between the defending officer (Bogarde) and the accused (Tom Courtenay); two straightforward literary adaptations, *A Doll's House* (1973) and *Galileo* (1974); and a version of Mozart's *Don Giovanni* (1980), well sung but shot in real locations and so stripped of its essential staginess – Mozart intended it to be not life but a charade.

Losey's other films include *Figures in a Landscape* (1970), *The Romantic Englishwoman* (1975) and *The Bout* (1982), a murder story in the best traditions of the French *film noir*. Good studies: T. Milne (ed.): *Losey on Losey* (1967); J. Leahy: *The Cinema of Joseph Losey* (1967).

LUBITSCH, Ernst (1892–1947)
German/American director

In a medium which thrives on romance, Lubitsch was that rare thing, an ironist. His speciality was to turn stories of icing-sugar charm into witty high comedy by means of 'the Lubitsch touch', an element of saturnine self-mockery, a glimpse of skull beneath the skin. If Lubitsch lovers are reflected in a moonlit pool, there is a phallic goldfish darting in the background; when he shows a gondola slipping down the Grand Canal to the strains of 'O Sole Mio', it is a garbage boat. Palaces are revealed as brothels; grandees are crooks, diplomats spies, dry businessmen dewy-eyed fools at heart. No other comedy director but *Wilder has so brilliantly explored the minefield between what is and what we make it seem.

Lubitsch's early German films were costume dramas (*Carmen*, 1918, *Madame Du Barry*, 1919, *Anne Boleyn*, 1920, *Pharaoh's Wife*, 1921). They deal with the private lives behind the façades of history; their heroines are gamines whose lives (it seems) are spent playing charades, peeping out of costumes too stiff and large for them. (The feeling of life as a game is typical of all Lubitsch's heroines: only his men ever concern themselves with reality – and the ones who do are charmless bureaucratic functionaries or fools. The types, first seen in these early films, appear at their most characteristic and effervescent in *Ninotchka*, 1939.)

Lubitsch moved to Hollywood in 1923, to direct Mary Pickford in her first 'grown-up' role, in *Rosita*. He was greatly influenced by *Chaplin's *A Woman of Paris* (1924), a satire on the destructive reality behind the image of Paris as a place of carefree romance; in particular, Adolphe Menjou's role as a dapper seducer served as the archetype for many Lubitsch heroes. (But Lubitsch never became a moralist, as Chaplin was: he thought human life too silly for sermons.) In the next few years, blending the irony learned from Chaplin with the vivacity of his own earlier style, he directed his first truly characteristic films: they include the outstanding *The Marriage Circle* (1924), *Forbidden Paradise* (1924), *Lady Windermere's Fan* (1925) and *So This Is Paris* (1926). In these films parody is generally external (for example *Forbidden Paradise* parodies historical melodrama, *Lady Windermere's Fan* the stiff stage conventions of Wilde's original); the use of self-parody as a crucial ingredient of tart charm, consistent in his later work, is never a feature of his silent films.

Lubitsch's first sound film was *The Love Parade* (1929), starring Maurice Chevalier and Jeanette MacDonald. This musical has uncharacteristic moments of genuine schmaltz – Chevalier had not learned the throwaway charm that underpinned his later performances, his own 'Lubitsch touch' – but, typically, Lubitsch sent it up splendidly in his next film, *Monte Carlo* (1930), in which an operetta star (MacDonald) finds that her life is becoming exactly like operetta, that reality is far less fun than gossamer illusion. This film is as tangy as anything by *Clair, an influence also present in *Trouble in Paradise* (1932), Lubitsch's master-piece. From its opening image (the garbage-gondola), this dazzlingly juggles perception and reality. It is about a suave confidence-trickster (Herbert Marshall) preying on an apparently solid aristocratic society every member of which, as the film proceeds, turns out to be an impostor, fool or crook – only Marshall, who is honest about his own dishonesty, has any morality at all. The dialogue is witty, the direction ice-cool, the performances (especially those of Charles Ruggles and Edward Everett Horton) perfect.

The Lubitsch touch is fragile. If he once lets his characters' amiable amorality drift towards cynicism or sentiment (each of them a form of morality), the soufflé collapses. In *One Hour with You* (1932), *Design for Living* (1933), *The Merry Widow* (1934) and *Angel* (1937), good-humoured heartlessness is judged exactly right. We enjoy the characters' antics (as they do) without the slightest pang for 'meaning' or 'relevance'. When moral commitment does enter a film it wipes out irony. Thus, the wish in *Ninotchka* to give motivation to Ninotchka's wavering loyalties between politics, luxury and love (other than the usual Lubitsch moti-vation 'it might be fun') weakens the story; the anti-Nazi elements in *To Be or Not To Be* (1942), otherwise yet another pirouette through the reality–illusion no-man's land (the film stars Jack Benny as a Shakes-pearean actor), both blunt and date the comedy; the leading character in *Heaven Can Wait* (1943), a rake arguing with Satan for a place in the underworld, seems too emotional, too involved in the outcome of the case he makes. Nevertheless, each of these films is a sophisticated, enjoyable comedy: to criticize them is really only to say that they fall short of Lubitsch's own best work. The truism, for once, is true: like *Capra, like Wilder, he is at his subtlest and funniest when he seems to have least to say.

Good study: H. G. Weinberg: *The Lubitsch Touch* (1968).

LUMET, Sidney (born 1924)
American director

Lumet worked extensively in theatre and television, and many of his films are cinema versions of stage or TV originals – usually competent rather than brilliant. They include *Twelve Angry Men* (1957), a tense drama set in a jury-room, *A View from the Bridge* (1961), *Long Day's Journey into Night* (1962), *The Seagull* (1968), *Equus* (1977) and *The Wiz* (1978), a rock updating of *The Wizard of Oz*. His cinema reputation rests less on these than on a series of polished films in a variety of styles: thrillers (*The Deadly Affair*, 1966; *The Anderson Tapes*, 1971; *Serpico*, 1974; *Dog Day Afternoon*, 1975); 'concerned films' (*Fail Safe*, 1964, a serious reworking of the same theme as *Kubrick's *Dr Strangelove*; *The Group*, 1966, from

Mary McCarthy's novel; *The Hill*, 1965, about military paranoia); comedy (*Bye Bye Braverman*, 1968), and even (latterly) an all-star extravaganza, *Murder on the Orient Express* (1974), based on the novel by Agatha Christie. His three best films explore obsessive neurosis, and he coaxes bravura performances from the stars: Rod Steiger in *The Pawnbroker* (1965), Sean Connery and Ian Bannen in *The Offence* (1973), and Peter Finch in *Network* (1976), a bitter media satire scripted by Paddy Chayevsky.

Lumet's other films include *Prince of the City* (1981), a companion-piece to *Serpico* and *Dog Day Afternoon*, about a 'cop blowing the whistle' on corruption and suffering from it, the splendidly glossy, who-dun-what thriller *Death Trap* (1982), and *Daniel* (1983), a study of the effects on the children of the trial and execution of two alleged Russian spies (based on Doctorow's novel, which is based in turn on the real-life Rosenberg case).

McLAREN, Norman (born 1914)
Scottish / Canadian animator

McLaren stands in the same relationship to the mainstream of animation as John Cage does to 20th-century music. That is, his work is influential on a small experimental group, excellent and enjoyable in its own right, and has a large cult following without ever impinging on the art at large. From the start of his career (with the British GPO Film Unit in the 1930s) he was experimenting with abstract designs drawn directly on to film, and his position from 1941 as head of the animation unit of the National Film Board of Canada allowed him both to create a 'school' and to continue his own experiments. These often show dancing geometric or abstract forms (like animated Klee paintings, or the less figurative ballets of Merce Cunningham); sometimes the music is specially composed, sometimes McLaren uses abstract sound drawn straight on to the sound track. *Fiddle-de-Dee* (1947), *Blinkity-Blank* (1954) and *Mosaic* (1965) are characteristic titles, and characteristic films. Other experiments include the use of animated cutouts (*Alouette*, 1944; the splendid *The Blackbird*, 1958), animated objects (*Chairy Tale*, 1957; *Opening Speech*, 1960) and even three dimensions (*Around is Around*, 1951). McLaren's best known film is *Neighbours* (1952), a more conventional cartoon (that is, involving recognizable human figures) in which a squabble over a boundary fence escalates wittily and inexorably into nuclear war.

MALLE, Louis (born 1932)
French director

Malle's output combines cinematic virtuosity with intellectual fastidiousness; his films are as thoughtful as *Bresson's (a one-time mentor) and as dazzling as *Truffaut's. His favourite subject is innocence, and his favourite location that grey area of morality where 'innocent' behaviour (that is, carefree, pure and undamaged) treads on the corns of inhibited society. Thus, *Lift to the Scaffold* (1957) is about one of the favourite subjects of French *film noir*, the self-tormenting criminal; *The Lovers* (1958) explores sensuality as a true mode of love; *Le Feu Follet* (*A Time to Live and a Time to Die*, 1963) is about a doomed alcoholic; in *Lacombe Lucien* (1974) the central character is an inadequate peasant who creates himself by collaborating with the occupying enemy. These are fine films, the harshness of their subjects lightened by sharpness and restraint in the telling. They are balanced by documentaries (on the Tour de France, Bangkok and Calcutta) and by comedies, sweet or sour: *Viva Maria* (1965) stars Brigitte Bardot and Jeanne Moreau as dance-hostesses involved in a revolution in grand-opera 19th-century South America; *The Thief* (1967) is a relaxed *film noir* parody; *Atlantic City USA* (1980), one of Malle's best films, stars Burt Lancaster as a puffy, ageing hood unexpectedly, bewilderingly given the chance of both the big time and true love.

In Malle's three finest films, the interplay between innocence and corruption is set up by making the central characters children. In *Zazie dans le métro* (1960), a delirious, surrealist farce, the heroine is a hard-talking nine-year-old on a two-day visit to Paris; *Le Souffle au cœur* (1971) centres on an awakening adolescent; in *Pretty Baby* (1978) the heroine is an innocent twelve-year-old in a New Orleans brothel. In each of these films the subject-matter is superficially shocking (Zazie is foul-mouthed; the boy in *Le Souffle au cœur* has his first sexual experience with his mother; the child in *Pretty Baby* watches every aspect of brothel life), and has duly shocked the superficial. But Malle's characters are not anarchic sensationalists: by discovering or coming to terms with Dionysos, they unlock themselves. In *Antonioni, the same discovery leads to despair and death; in Malle it leads to happiness.

Malle's other films include the non-fiction *My Dinnner with André* (1982), a conversation in a Manhattan restaurant between an actor and a theatre director.

MANKIEWICZ, Joseph L. (born 1909)
American film-maker

If, like Mankiewicz, you apply wit and intelligence to second-rate subjects, does that produce excellence? Not always: *Dragonwyck* (1945), *Letter to Three Wives* (1949), *Five Fingers* (1952), *The Honey Pot* (1967) and especially *Sleuth* (1972) have interesting scripts, appealing perform-ances and taut direction – but remain, in the light of day, no more than shiny junk. *The Barefoot Contessa* (1954), *Guys and Dolls* (1955) and *The Quiet American* (1958) are better, because intelligence is applied to the stories as well as to the scripts (two are from notable literary originals); *Julius Caesar* (1953), because it trusts its material, succeeds where more pretentious filmed Shakespeare (e.g. *Olivier's) does not.

Mankiewicz's best film is *All About Eve* (1950). Here he has caustic things to say about the theatrical profession (Bette Davis stars as the clawing, and clawed, Margo Channing) and he says them with bitchery and wit.

Mankiewicz's other films include *Cleopatra* (1962), one of the most notorious of all cinema epics, but one which (if you forget the scandals and ignore the hype) unusually and appealingly shows ancient Romans and Egyptians with a sense of humour as well as of destiny.

MÉLIÈS, Georges (1861–1938)
French illusionist and director

Méliès' films arose out of the techniques of the 19th-century stage illusionist. Initially, he saw the film medium simply as a means of performing transformations and disappearances impossible in three-dimensional reality. Though narrative plots do have their place, his films are really sequences of surreal visual tricks, bound together with the logic of a conjurer's stage act rather than that of story. Like the conjurer, his purpose is not to use the abnormal to shock us, but to show us marvels – illusion creates a comfortable, child's world of endless possibility, and Méliès is not concerned with adult *disillusion*, as later surrealists (e.g. the *Buñuel of *Le Chien andalou* and *L'Âge d'or*) most often are. He made over 1,200 films, some less than a minute long (showing a single illusion or scene), some running for half an hour or more. All are concerned with wonders of one kind or another: typical titles are *The Skipping Cheeses*, *Tunnelling the Channel*, *Balloon Honeymoon*, *In the Ogre's Cave* or *The Ballet Master's Dream*. In many of them he appeared himself, a paunchy, strikingly ugly worker of miracles. Exotic locations (the South Sea Islands, the Wild West, the mysterious East), sensuous women (often suggestively costumed or posed in splendidly vulgar parodies of such famous paintings as *Venus Rising from the Waves* or *The Naked Maja* – another stage tradition), violent action and chases are features of his style. We tend nowadays (when we see his work at all) to see dancing skeletons, space vehicles stuck in the moon's eye, rubber octopuses under a fantastic sea; but of equal interest (and more important for later cinema) are his versions of such enchanted, wondrous or macabre stories as the voyages of Sinbad and the adventures of the Invisible Man, or his depiction of fires, floods, earthquakes, train crashes and horrendous battle scenes. Over 1,100 of his films are lost; of the rest *The Artist's Dream* (1898), *Indiarubber Head* (1901), *Voyage to the Moon* (1902), *The Impossible Voyage* (1904), *20,000 Leagues under the Sea* (1907) and *The Conquest of the Pole* (1912) are representative, and fascinating. Compilation films destroy the power of his images: his work needs to be taken in small doses (as he intended). So taken, it has marvels to show us still.

A fascinating study of the early 'magic' films from which Méliès took off is E. Barnouw: *The Magician and the Cinema* (1981).

MILESTONE, Lewis (1895–1980)
American director

In the 1930s Milestone made a series of tensely dramatic films including the anti-war *All Quiet on the Western Front* (1930), *The Front Page* (1931), *The General Died at Dawn* (1936) and the superb *Of Mice and Men* (1939), his finest achievement. During the Second World War he made worthy action films, the American equivalent of the low-budget, stiff-lipped British school. In *Edge of Darkness* (1943) Errol Flynn all but liberates Norway; in *Purple Heart* (1944) Dana Andrews and Richard Conte are brutally tried after being shot down over Tokyo; in *Walk in the Sun* (1945) the same two stars wipe out a detachment of Germans camped in an Italian farmhouse. After the war Milestone's films (more than a dozen) slumped in quality. *Halls of Montezuma* (1950), for example, is one of the ugliest war-pictures ever made, an obscene and appalling glorification of jingoistic brutality. How could the maker of *All Quiet on the Western Front* descend to this?

MINNELLI, Vincente (born 1910)
American director

Minnelli directed a dozen stylish, inconsequential musicals, including *Meet Me in St Louis* (1944), *An American in Paris* (1951), *The Bandwagon* (1953), *Gigi* (1958) and *On a Clear Day You Can See Forever* (1970). They are softer-edged than the musicals of (say) Sandrich or Donen, replacing wit with charm. The films look delightful: sets, costumes, lighting and colour-processing are sumptuous, and the actors' performances are relaxed and elegant. The same unsophisticated niceness marks Minnelli's comedies too: *Father of the Bride* (1950), *The Reluctant Debutante* (1958), *Goodbye Charlie* (1965). But he has a darker side as well: it lends strength to *Lust for Life* (1956), an above-average bio-graphical picture about Van Gogh, and to two sleekly cynical films about show-business, *The Bad and the Beautiful* (1952, starring Kirk Douglas as a ruthless Hollywood producer) and *Two Weeks in Another Town* (1962, a similar story, this time setting Douglas's venom to work on location in Rome). Like Minnelli's musicals, these films steer clear of subtlety – but (also like the musicals) they are Hollywood entertainment at its sequined best.

MIZOGUCHI, Kenji (1898–1956)
Japanese director

Mizoguchi was a prolific director (he made over eighty films in thirty years), and his work covers the range from satirical comedy to *samurai* and Kabuki subjects. A recurring theme, the self-sacrificing nobility of women, is seen at its most biting in a number of films about prostitutes, whose heroines often have a Cabiria-like vulnerability and simplicity (see Fellini) which transcends their circumstances. *Women in the Night* (1948) and *Street of Shame* (1956) are filmed with unrelenting realism; *Sisters of the Gion* (1936) leavens a painful story with satire. On a different theme (it is his *Les Enfants du paradis*), *The Story of the Last Chrysanthemums* (1939) contrasts performance on the Kabuki stage (symbolizing the rituals of old Japan) with the bustling modernity of the actors' offstage lives.

In the west, Mizoguchi is best known for a group of films in an entirely different style: *The Life of Oharu* (1952), *Ugetsu Monagatari* (*Tales of the Pale Moon after Rain*, 1953), *Sansho Dayu* (*Sansho the Bailiff*, 1955) and *The Princess Yang Kwei Fei* (1955). These are set in remote times (ancient Japan, 8th-century China) and tell mysterious stories about the mingling of natural and supernatural worlds, once again centred on the transfiguring power of women's love. Mizoguchi's characters are dispossessed by war or by cruel overlords; they wander a barren land tenanted by ghosts, brigands and other homeless souls; their only security is the warmth of human love. Some critics have seen the films as allegories of post-nuclear desolation, but they are actually set in the familiar world of Japanese medieval legend, made strikingly modern by the intensity of suffering and resignation shown by the characters. Mizoguchi's cinematic style (in these films) is slow-moving, poetic and mysterious, and his long takes, misty lighting and frequent soft focus give the events a feeling of unreality not unlike that of *Bresson.

MORRISSEY, Paul (born 1939)
American director

Morrissey is the most individual director to emerge from Andy Warhol's experimental 'film-school' in 1960s New York. Earlier products of the group were made by simply pointing the camera at events and letting it run: six hours of a man sleeping (*Sleep*, 1963), eight hours in the life of the Empire State Building (*Empire*, 1964) or crudely lit, badly photographed and gauchely improvised sexual encounters (*Blow Job*, 1964; *Fuck*, 1968). To this interesting but dispiriting underground style (whose chief defect – and perhaps chief point – is pointlessness) Morrissey adds a sharper narrative style and a personal point of view. In some ways, by doing so, he destroys the 'aims' (if there are aims) of the Warhol style; but he also makes it accessible to an outside audience. His films, especially *Flesh* (1968), *Trash* (1970) and *Heat* (1971), are still about grubby, endlessly explicit sex and drug experiences, and the performers are as pimply and charmless as ever – it is punk film-making, no more and no less. But these are not just badly made blue movies. Self-satire gives them life, and we are left wondering not only how the participants manage to keep it up so long (not to say why they bother), but also what they're like in other situations. In short, Morrissey intrigues us with human possibility, turns puppets into people.

A fascinating pendant to the Morrissey/Warhol films is *Edie: The Life and Times of Andy Warhol's Superstar* (1982), by Jean Stein and George Plimpton: in fact a piece of 'oral history' put together from 250 taped interviews. The shattered desolation of 1960s North American life has seldom been so savagely, remorselessly exposed: not even Studs Terkel has ever used other people's words to say so much.

MURNAU, Friedrich Wilhelm (1888–1931)
German director

Nosferatu (1922), a nightmarish, expressionist version of the Dracula story, contains at their most intense every element of Murnau's style. Its latent theme, repressed sexuality, is always implicit in the dark eroticism of the images. Its sets, costumes and make-up are powerfully theatrical and create an atmosphere of melodramatic eeriness in which the actors swim like stifled ghosts. Its camera style (fast, swooping movement which produces a feeling of fluttering alarm, or a long-fixed stare prolonging a scene beyond nerves' endurance) counterpoints rather than underlines the action – we never forget that we are watching conscious contrivance; though illusion is never ruptured, Brechtian alienation is consistently achieved.

Nosferatu is Murnau's masterpiece, because his genius was for atmosphere, and the Nosferatu story is far less important than the way it's told. The success of his other films depends to a greater or lesser degree on how much their stories fight the narrative grandeur of his style. *Faust* (1926) works well because of its supernatural content, and in *Our Daily Bread* (1929), set in the plains of Dakota, and *Tabu* (1931), set in Tahiti, unusual locations provide the essential exotic counterbalance to over-eventful plots. The main interest in *Sunrise* (1927) is the brilliant city set, filmed with no attempt at realism; otherwise, bravura camera-work and acting are at odds with a silly plot. Murnau's best narrative film is *The Last Laugh* (1924), a story of one man's systematic degradation of another as schematic and precise as a Genet play. Here again, as in *Nosferatu*, repressed sexuality is the subtext, and the obvious contrivances of the plot (it follows the unities of time, space and action; cause and effect progress with inexorable, inhuman logic; it is a Greek tragedy whose commenting chorus is the camera) are as satisfying as those in a 'well-made' play. Murnau's work is among the most influential in cinema history; but he never fully achieved his own potential, and his influence is in the end more important than his actual films. *Nosferatu* and *The Last Laugh* should still be seen.

Good study: L. Eisner: *F. W. Murnau* (1972).

NICHOLS, Mike (born 1931)
American director and actor

In the 1950s Nichols formed an outstanding cabaret partnership with Elaine May: in dry, wisecracking dialogue (often improvised) they took a cynical, satirical look at anxious contemporary America. May has since brought the same wryness to film acting and scriptwriting (she appeared in *Luv*, 1967, *Enter Laughing*, 1967, and the Keaton-inspired *A New Leaf*, 1971, which she also wrote and directed); Nichols has had a successful career as a stage director, and has made a handful of distinguished films. In *Who's Afraid of Virginia Woolf?* (1966) he coaxed career-best performances from Elizabeth Taylor and Richard Burton; in *Catch-22* (1970) he admirably caught the sardonic flavour (though not the epic preposterousness) of the original book; in *The Fortune* (1975) he made an enjoyable screwball farce about incompetent crooks and the awful heiress they saddle themselves with. *Silkwood* (1984) is a concerned film (based on a real incident) about the murderous hushing-up of nuclear secrets. His best films are those nearest to the acerbity of his cabaret style. They are *The Graduate* (1967) and *Carnal Knowledge* (1971). Both are about the sexual ambition and social panic of the American male; both rely on performances of wary charm (from, respectively, Dustin Hoffman and Jack Nicholson); both use social satire to temper whimsy into steel.

OLIVIER, Laurence (born 1907)
British actor and director

As actor, Olivier has made more than fifty distinguished films. His screen appeal is due partly to virtuoso technique (his performances are honed to a hair's-breadth; he knows exactly how much acting each part requires, and provides it) and partly to a unique physical mixture of sensuality and menace – in his films of the 1930s and early 1940s in particular (*Wuthering Heights*, 1939; *Rebecca*, 1940; *Lady Hamilton*, 1941) he looks just as a preying mantis must look to its palpitating mate. His two best performances (that is, in other people's films) re-create stage roles both memorable for saurian charm: Dick in *The Devil's Disciple* (1959) and Archie Rice in *The Entertainer* (1960).

Olivier directed himself in five films: *Henry V* (1944), *Hamlet* (1948), *Richard III* (1956), *The Prince and the Showgirl* (1957) and the fine *Three Sisters* (1970). The three Shakespeare adaptations are to cinema exactly what the stage versions of 19th-century actor-managers were to the theatre. Everything that happens is slanted to point up Olivier's own superb starring performance. The text is ruthlessly cut to serve his interpretation of the leading character (the jingoistic Henry V, the 'man who could not make up his mind' in *Hamlet*, the embodiment of hypnotic malice in *Richard III*); the order of events is disturbed to make good climaxes – and the climaxes are all Olivier's; supporting roles, camera-angles, blocking, even set-design and music all point in one direction only; the concept of the star has never been so consummately explored. And yet, as with 19th-century actor-managers, the result is magnificent. Shakespeare may be rolling in his grave – but at least while we're in the cinema, we hardly care.

Good study: J. Cottrell: *Laurence Olivier* (1975). Interesting autobiography: *Confessions of an Actor* (1982).

OLMI, Ermanno (born 1931)
Italian director

Olmi began his film career making documentaries for the Edison-Volta company about its workers' lives and conditions; he has also made television documentaries about the ebb and flow of everyday life (e.g. *During One Summer*, 1971). His feature-films use fictional stories to bind together the same kind of documentary observation: he was inspired to become a film-maker by seeing *Rossellini's *Paisà*, and wherever possible follows Rossellini's method of persuading ordinary people to re-enact the events of their lives (or fictional scenes based on real-life events) before the camera. *The Job* (1961) depicts a first experience of work in factory or dusty office as stifling and repetitious, a denial of humanity; *One Fine Day* (1968) shows how the ordered bourgeois world of a Milanese businessman is shattered after his car hits a pedestrian and he is forced to take cognizance of other people's lives; *The Tree of Wooden Clogs* (1978), Olmi's masterpiece, is a beautifully photographed and unsentimental evocation of peasant lives at the turn of the century. This film is the most powerful statement yet of Olmi's conviction that urban, industrial life is alien to humanity; his view of peasant life, though markedly unsentimental in detail, is of a lost golden age of the human spirit – and his documentary style, seeming to offer observation without the overt political comment of (say) *Bertolucci's *1900* (also about the Italian rural past), is actually sleight-of-hand, dissembling a doctrinaire and controversial (Rousseauian) point of view.

Olmi's other films include *Cammina cammina* (1983), an immensely long, neo-realistic story similar to Kazantzakis's novel *The Greek Passion*, about the effects on a (lovingly observed) peasant community of re-enacting Biblical events (in this case, the story of the Three Wise Men).

PABST, Georg Wilhelm (1885–1967)
Austrian director

Associated for a time with the left-wing politics and eclectic populism of Brecht (whose *Threepenny Opera* he filmed in 1931), Pabst is particularly remembered for a number of grim dramas made in the 1920s and 1930s. They include *Westfront 1918* (1930), a war story, *Comradeship* (1931), about a mining disaster, and several films dealing with the destructive power of eroticism: *Joyless Street* (1925), *The Love of Jeanne Ney* (1927) and *Diary of a Lost Girl* (1929). The finest of these films, his masterpiece, is *Pandora's Box* (1928). This is based on Wedekind's plays *Lulu* and *Earth Spirit*, and stars Louise Brooks as a sultry prostitute, a destroying angel finally murdered by Jack the Ripper. The realism of this film (Pabst is like an expressionist *Rossellini, *Godard's grandfather) is combined with a notably detached technique. Corrupt sensuality may be the theme, but it is recorded with a camera as still and unblinking as an insect's eye. Pabst's later films (nearly two dozen) are far less interesting: the rise of the Nazis and the 1939–45 war made him cautious both in the choice of themes and in technique. There was a brief return to form in *The Trial* (1948), an attack on anti-Semitism, and in the tense thriller *Ten Days to Die* (1955), but the rest is silence.

PASOLINI, Pier Paolo (1922–75)
Italian director and writer

Pasolini was a Marxist, a nihilist and a believer in violence as both the symbol and the cure of late-20th-century decadence. At the beginning of his career he worked with *Fellini (on *Cabiria*) and with *Bertolucci: both were important influences on his style, which is an amalgam of realism and bizarre places and events filmed with unfussy virtuosity. *Accatone* (1961), about a pimp who falls in love, tries to earn an honest living, fails and dies in a road accident, is directly in the social mode of Fellini's *I vitelloni*, and draws its strength from underplayed performances and from lovingly filmed landscapes of urban dereliction (littered streets, crumbling buildings, scrap yards – the deserts of modern city life). Two other films make use of modern settings. *Theorem* (1968) is a Buñuelesque satire on the middle class. A desirable young man (unmotivated, a destroying angel) arrives unannounced at the home of a rich industrialist; he arouses convulsive passion in father, mother, son, daughter and servant; he does not rape them, nor they him – they are raped by themselves, by their own nature and desires, and are driven insane, whereupon he leaves. *Pigsty* (1969) sets a story of medieval cannibalism against a modern story of blackmail (one industrialist coercing another to merge businesses by threatening to reveal his rival's son's sexual obsession with pigs).

These stories are as intriguing as they are uncompromising: unlike *Godard, say, Pasolini never lets pessimistic messages swamp his films' entertainment value, and we are always fascinated to see what happens next. His vision of human beings as destiny's puppets, blind wanderers in the wrecked landscape of their own souls, reached its most perfect expression not in modern stories, but in films set in the distant past. In *The Gospel According to St Matthew* (1964) Christ is seen as an intellectual visionary, a dissident. Pasolini follows Matthew to the letter (he uses for example only the sparse Bible dialogue); he makes no comment, but dispassionately leaves the film to make its own statements of despair or hope – and (unlike filmed lives of Christ by some committed Christians) the result is both moving and restrained. *Oedipus rex* (1967) and *Medea* (1969) are versions of Greek tragedy, strongly blending ritual (inspired by documentary of primitive tribes whose pounding and dancing are meaningful to them but fascinatingly incomprehensible to the spectator) and a passionate, realistic acting style. In *Decameron* (1971), *Canterbury Tales* (1971) and *Salò* (1975) human beings the ritualistic puppets appear again, this time in endless, joyless sexual encounters in glowing medieval settings of sterile richness: the territory not of Brueghel but of Bosch.

Pasolini's films are bleak and stunning. No other director has so ably caught that prevalent late 1960s mood of anarchic intellectual savagery. He belongs with the students on the barricades. Bertolucci and *Fassbinder – and, in a different style, *Scorsese and *Coppola – share his view of the sterility of conventional life in a world in which violence is the only dynamic force. But all four of them are finally softer-centred: they seduce us with story, and the medium outweighs the message. Pasolini's films are just as interesting to watch, but never once lose intellectual control.

Pasolini's *Poems* were published in a bilingual edition in 1982 (translations by MacAfee and Martinengo), and his *Essays* appeared in English (trans. Hood) in the same year. E. Siciliano: *Pasolini: A Biography* (English edn 1982) is particularly good on the interaction between Pasolini's life and his art, and on his sordid and mysterious death (he was found beaten and broken in Ostia in 1975, perhaps the victim of gangland or anti-homosexual violence).

POLANSKI, Roman (born 1933)
Polish director and writer

Polanski made his reputation with three surrealistic short films (*Two Men and a Wardrobe*, 1958; *The Fat Man and the Thin Man*, 1961; *Mammals*, 1962), and consolidated it with the feature *Knife in the Water* (1962), a sexual anecdote (about a married couple and a hitchhiker on a sailing trip) as warm and spare as early *Bergman (*Summer with Monika*; *Smiles of a Summer Night*). Shortly afterwards he left Poland for the west, and completely changed his style. His western films are obsessed with the darker corners of the mind, those in which perversion and occultism walk hand in hand with psychological disorder. Sometimes morbid psychology is uppermost, as in *Repulsion* (1965), about a mental breakdown, *Cul-de-Sac* (1966), a Genet-like story of domination, humiliation and violence between a married couple and an intruder, and *The Tenant* (1976), based on the story of Jack the Ripper. At other times the occult is paramount, as in *Rosemary's Baby* (1968), about witchcraft, and the creepy and nasty *Macbeth* (1971). His best film (after *Knife in the Water*) is *Chinatown* (1974), a private-eye thriller where tongue-in-cheek jokiness (in the manner of Penn's *Bonny and Clyde*) distances horrors depicted with otherwise repulsive glee. It is hard, even so (and despite a sensitive version of Hardy's *Tess of the D'Urbervilles* (1980) – an aberration or, hopefully, a portent?) to see Polanski as anything but a prancing nihilist, happy to turn his outstanding gifts to exploitation instead of art.

Wide-eyed autobiography: *Roman* (1984). Good, unblinking study: B. Leeming: *Polanski* (1982).

PUDOVKIN, Vsevolod (1893–1953)
Russian director

Trained as a scientist, Pudovkin was working in a government laboratory, debating a change to a career in the visual arts or the theatre, when Lenin's 1919 showings of *Intolerance* (see Eisenstein) directed his ambitions, and he joined the State Film School. His first important films were *Mechanics of the Brain* (1926), a documentary about Pavlov, and a terse reworking of Gorki's enormous novel *Mother* (1926). This film – Pudovkin's masterpiece – characteristically takes a story of blunt simplicity (about a peasant woman who, as a result of the suffering and death of her children under Tsarist oppression, comes to see the need for revolution, makes an impassioned speech from the dock, and is finally executed by the Tsar's soldiers, an early martyr for the workers' cause) and tells it in a highly charged and poetic manner. In particular, Pudovkin's fondness for nature metaphors (ripples in pools, blocks of ice jostling down a river, birds and clouds in the sky, all mirroring events or human feelings in the story) is a use of the pathetic fallacy as ruthless as anything in 19th-century romantic verse.

Pudovkin's metaphors, like Eisenstein's, are blatant and dazzling; but his personal message, his propaganda, lacks the fervour of Eisenstein's work. He is far less committed to what he is telling us, and his technical brilliance thus serves not poetry but dilettantism. This is particularly apparent in *The End of St Petersburg* (1927), which recounts the same events in the same locations as Eisenstein's *October*. Eisenstein has a point of view, a controlling theme, which binds his film; Pudovkin is a detached documentarist spectacularly fulfilling a government commission. When Eisenstein's workers (for example) surge to the gates or gape at works of art, they are human beings with emotions we can recognize; when Pudovkin's do the same things, because he never allows them individual character, they look like puppets performing a propaganda script. *Storm over Asia* (1928), about a poor trapper set up as a puppet monarch in British-held Mongolia, is more artful, perhaps because Pudovkin's anger at the forces of oppression (as in *Mother*) involves him more closely with his characters. There is also some excellent anti-imperialist satire: unusually for a Russian film, *Storm over Asia* contains several scenes of unforced farce.

As his career proceeded, Pudovkin's interest in technique began to swamp his work. His films became ever more experimental, more self-involved, more detached from the audience. This led to problems with the authorities, and these, combined with the effects of a car accident in 1935, led to serious eclipse. *The Deserter* (1933) and *General Suvorov* (1941) are interesting, but in general his later work in no way matches the quality of the three great silent features.

Pudovkin's book *Film Technique and Film Acting* (English edn 1958) is a classic account of the aesthetics of film, technical in places but accessible and of remarkable general interest. Good study (of Eisenstein, Dovtzenko and Vertov as well as Pudovkin): H. Marshall: *Masters of the Soviet Cinema* (1983).

RAY, Satyajit (born 1921)
Indian director

There is a huge – and hugely popular – vernacular film industry in India, and its products stand in the same relationship to Ray's work as television soap-opera does to *Three Sisters* or *The Pillars of the Community*. Indian musicals – most popular films are musicals – are quickly made, glossy and frivolous; Ray's work is painstaking and deeply felt. Indian musicals seethe with incident; Ray's films, often almost plotless, depend on atmosphere and character. The actors in Indian musicals swagger and strut; Ray's actors (often amateurs) perform in a quiet, realistic style, with the camera as observer rather than conspirator. The true analogue for both Ray's themes and style is Chekhov. Like Chekhov, Ray shows a society in the process of sluggish change, and the effects of decadence or radicalism on individual lives; like Chekhov's, his style is still and economical, and makes its points by irony, by the accumulation of small details, by gentleness.

Ray came to film-making in his early thirties, after some years in commercial art. The direct inspiration was *Renoir's visit to India in 1950 to film *The River* – and Renoir's films are an important influence on Ray's style. Ray's first film was *Pather Panchali* (*Little Song of the Road*, 1955) which with *Aparajito* (*The Unvanquished*, 1956) and *Apur Sansai* (*The World of Apu*, 1959) form the connected group 'the Apu trilogy', one of his finest works. The story centres on Apu, the child of a close family in rural India, and shows how, as he grows to maturity, his education and longing for a career in the wider world gradually distance him from his family and from his own strong roots. This is both a familiar plot and a parable about India at large; what gives it uniqueness is Ray's attention to the detail of village and family life and to the mosaic of small emotional events which determines human relationships. These are also the qualities of *Jalsaghar* (*The Music Room*, 1958), about a country landowner who evades modern life by inviting musicians to play for him in his crumbling mansion, and of *Charulata* (1964), a study of a disintegrating marriage similar in theme and poetry to Hesse's novel *Rosshalde*.

In several of Ray's films, observation shades agreeably into satire. *Paras Pathar* (1957), about a poor city worker, is full of pungent social comment; *Devi* (*The Goddess*, 1960), the story of a girl whose family believes she is a reincarnation of Kali, the goddess of death, combines black humour (in Ray's treatment of the relatives) with compassion (in his treatment of the bewildered girl). *Mahanagar* (*The Big City*, 1963) deals with a woman trying to balance her career (in a mordantly observed commercial world) with the claims of a traditional marriage. There are a dozen lesser films in a variety of styles, varying from *Kanchenjunga* (1962), a 'village' film in sumptuous colour, to *Company Limited* (1971), a needly satire on big business.

Ray's best films, apart from the Apu trilogy, are *Days and Nights in the Forest* (1970), somewhat like a modern Indian *As You Like It*, *The Chess Players* (1977), a comedy about two gentlemen so obsessed with chess that they miss the greater political game being played outside (the film is set in the British Raj in 1856) and *The Home and the World* (1984), about the effects on friendship of conflicting political loyalties. In each of them, Ray's characteristically delicate social observation is combined with warmth and wit: they are fully achieved works of art, with every component in balance.

Ray's essays and other writings are collected in *Our Films, Their Films* (1976). Good studies: M. Seton: *Portrait of a Director: Satyajit Ray* (1971); C. Dasgupta: *The Cinema of Satyajit Ray* (1981), particularly good on Ray's relationship to his Indian background.

REED, Carol (1906–76)
British director

Reed was a competent craftsman for whom, just once in his career, creative lightning struck. His early films are slight, low-budget British cinema fare: even the best, *The Stars Look Down* (1939), about a mine disaster, *Night Train to Munich* (1940), a *Hitchcocky spy story, and *The Way Ahead* (1944), about a group of civilians welded into an army unit and fighting in North Africa, are quite unmemorable once you leave the cinema. Memorability, the clinching ingredient, came in three 1940s films Reed made to scripts by Graham Greene: *Odd Man Out* (1947), *The Fallen Idol* (1948) and *The Third Man* (1949), his masterpiece. Greene's works are consistently trivialized in screen adaptations, soft balloons to those who know the original stories – but these films stand up well: not so much adaptations as alternatives, they almost make you forget the books. They depend on atmosphere, acting and music: no prose on the page could equal James Mason's hurt doggedness in *Odd Man Out*, the enigmatic (and unexplained) menace of Ralph Richardson's performance in *The Fallen Idol*, or the counterpoint of zither, bombed Vienna and Orson Welles's piggy eyes in *The Third Man*. All are Greeneish qualities, essential to the stories – and all are present only in the films. After this peak, Reed slid back down to the valleys of his earlier style. Of his dozen later films, only *Our Man in Havana* (1959), another Greene adaptation, and the spectacular musical *Oliver!* (1968) stand out.

RENOIR, Jean (1894–1979)
French director, writer and actor

To those who doubt that comedy is a serious dramatic form, a viable language for statements about the human condition, Renoir's films are a convincing answer. He never loses sight of the ridiculous, the artificial, the frivolous in human behaviour. No film of his, however serious, is free of these elements; when he seems most playful, he is at his most profound. But he is not a comedy director, in the way of *Lubitsch, *Wilder or even *Clair. In their work the jokes are all-important, and their purpose is to entertain; in Renoir comedy is blended with other elements (particularly robust romanticism and true-to-life sentimentality) to make a series of comments on human life. His method seems to be to set his camera up to observe, to let his characters (always self-motivated, never merely the puppets of a directorial message) act out their lives as they themselves decide. He uses long takes, so that scenes can develop at the pace of their dramatic meaning and not that of flashy editing. He uses deep focus (a process in which objects in the far and middle distance are as sharply defined as those in the foreground) and sets his human characters against wide, high landscapes or in front of windows, with the result that their momentary concerns seem part of a larger pattern, their truth and illusion aspects of the balance of the universe. When we remember a Renoir film, we remember not only the bustling people, but the surrounding landscapes too, whether leafy and sunlit (*Une Partie de campagne* or *La Règle du jeu*), icy (*La Grande Illusion*) or primitive and predatory (*The River* or *The Golden Coach*). In this, he is a true child of impressionist painting (his father was Auguste Renoir): his landscapes sometimes seem a stage-set for people, his people sometimes a stage-set for landscape – both landscapes and people have vital force. He is a grand illusionist; his people never seem to be manipulated for the sake of art (as happens in Clair or in *Bergman, where form consistently determines theme), and his work is at its most artful when it seems at its most humane, when it appears to replace analysis with narrative.

The first characteristic Renoir film was *Boudu sauvé des eaux* (*Boudu Saved from Drowning*, 1932), in which Michel Simon plays an anarchic tramp given shelter by an absurd bourgeois family whose life is systematically demolished by his Pan-like outrageousness. The empty-headed bourgeoisie, its life a charm-bracelet of fussy rituals, is a recurring Renoir target. The townees picnicking in *Une Partie de campagne* (1936) are funny, the grim provincials of the Pagnolesque *Toni* (1935) and *The Crime of Monsieur Lange* (1936) are serious – but all mistake custom for the sap of life. In *The Diary of a Chambermaid* (1946), *The Golden Coach* (1953) and *French Cancan* (1955), the most successful of his later films, people play games – murderous games in *The Diary of a Chambermaid*, children-of-paradise actors' games in the other two films – and they are real people because playing is their choice, because games reflect feelings instead of replacing them.

Renoir's claim to be one of the greatest cinema masters rests principally on three films: *La Grande Illusion* (1937), *La Bête humaine* (1938) and *La Règle du jeu* (1939). Each is unique, yet all share the same vision: that farce and tragedy have the same pace and moral weight in human affairs, that to be meaningful the human comedy must be human as well as comic, ridiculous as well as deep. *La Grande Illusion* is a film about loyalty. It deals with French prisoners-of-war in the 1914–18 war, their escape attempts and eventual success – but its theme is the conflict of loyalties which makes a person: loyalty to country, to class, to friend, to lover, to race and to creed. The shifts and pulls between these loyalties are beautifully contrived; at one level, the script is as precise as a diagram. But because Renoir lets his characters speak louder than his own authorial voice, the story's humanity is its most pronounced feature, and the film makes its anti-war point by implication and not by rhetoric. (What is the 'great illusion'? Perhaps the metaphor of reality we create for ourselves, the code of life by which we live.) *La Bête humaine*, adapted from Zola, is a schematic tale of murders and claustrophobic guilt. Its greatness lies in the character of the central figure, Lantier, who struggles to control by reason and self-discipline the 'human animal' lurking inside himself. His capitulation to bestial unreason – he kills first his lover's husband, then his lover and finally himself – is a reversal of the genial surrender to Pan preached in *Boudu sauvé des eaux* or *Une Partie de campagne*: the demonic can destroy as well as liberate. Pessimism also dominates *La Règle du jeu*, a galvanic farce peopled by characters from Feydeau and Beaumarchais. These aristocrats, playing out their decadent, immoral lives, are marionettes, straw rulers in a cardboard world. Their society is dead, and their giggly games are the muscle-spasms of a rigidifying corpse. Made at the time of the 'phoney war', this is Renoir's most farcical and bitterest film. In all his other work joking is an assertion of humanity; in this the characters joke because there is no hope left. Like *La Bête humaine*, the film is flawed by its pessimism; *La Grande Illusion* is Renoir's masterpiece because it confronts the world's darkness and shows how human beings, simply because they are human, need not be afraid of it.

Renoir's other films include an early, funny, Feydeau adaptation, *On purge bébé* (1931), *Déjeuner sur l'herbe* (1959, in the mood of *Une Partie de campagne*) and *Le Caporal épinglé* (1962). He published a marvellous evocation of life with his painter father: *Renoir, My Father* (1962) – attacked as fiction, it remains superb. More factual and far less informative (it smacks of the recording-tape): *My Life and My Films* (1974). He also wrote a novel, *The Notebooks of Captain George* (1966). Good study: A. Bazin (ed. F. Truffaut): *Jean Renoir* (English edn 1973). Recommended for enthusiasts: P. Gilliatt: *Jean Renoir: Essays, Conversations, Reviews* (1975).

RESNAIS, Alain (born 1922)
French director

Resnais is much concerned with the nature of reality, and particularly with the contrast between what actually happened in the past and the construct our memory makes of it. Thus, in *Guernica* (1950), he intercuts an exploration of Picasso's painting with newspaper photographs and reports of the horrific event which occasioned it; in *Night and Fog* (1955) a glacial camera tour of the ruins of the Auschwitz death-camp is blended with harrowing old photographs and newsreels of what happened there. These short documentaries (and there are half a dozen others, of less significance) foreshadow the detached style of his later films: the commentary is oblique and uninvolved, leaving the images alone to do powerful work. In *Hiroshima mon amour* (1959), his first feature-film, the camera is again a cool observer, apparently there merely to record what happens, and this alienation-technique is precisely what gives the film its eerie pull. The story, cutting between a modern love-affair in Hiroshima, the atomic devastation of the town in 1945 and the heroine's love-affair with a German soldier at the time of that devastation, blends soap-opera sentimentality (one form of human memory) with the dry-mouthed actuality of nuclear destruction (another: our mental editing of objective fact) in a non-narrative style which makes it both hard to follow and unforgettable. In particular, Resnais makes almost obsessive use of the 'flash-cut', in which a character looks at something in the present and momentarily sees the same something, or a related object, as it was in the past. (Thus the woman, embracing her modern Japanese lover, keeps 'reading' his limbs and features as those either of radiation victims or of her earlier lover.)

In *Hiroshima mon amour*, when the film cuts back, 'reality' is exactly as it was before the cut: we have moved, as it were, from *A* to *B* to *A*. But in *Last Year at Marienbad* (1961) and *Muriel* (1963) we often cut back to a slightly altered reality (*A* to *B* and back to *A1*). This increases the mystery already created in these films by minimal plots, half-audible dialogue and narrative-by-association instead of narrative-by-consequence. We are walking in dream-landscapes, and there is no guide except our own invention. *Last Year at Marienbad* appears to be about a civilized, not to say etiolated, love-affair at a mysterious spa; *Muriel* is an Iris Murdoch-like tangle of love-relationships (involving the past as well as the present) – and that is all we need to know. In these films (and in *Providence*, 1977, about a dying writer, his family, the ghosts of his past and his fiction) the spectator often feels that he or she is being told things of considerable significance, even beauty, but with very few clues to what that significance might actually be. This irritates those who expect explicitness from films. But Resnais' precise imprecision is nearer to music than to cinema – and who would spell out the meaning of a symphony?

Last Year at Marienbad and *Muriel* are the peak of Resnais' work so far. Each of his remaining features centres on single characters and explores their feelings and memories in a much more clear-cut narrative style. *The War is Over* (1966) deals with the self-doubt of a middle-aged political exile, and his search through his past (in the Spanish civil war) for clues about his present crisis of belief. *I Love You, I Love You* (1968) is about a man projected back in time to relive and re-examine a disastrous love-affair. *Stavisky* (1974) is an elegant reconstruction of the life of a famous confidence-trickster in 1930s France, a man who made other people's misapprehensions of reality his chequebook and his toy. *My American Uncle* (1980) blends a melodramatic story (about three decent, ordinary people trying to make sense of the maze of 20th-century life) with *Godardesque footnotes, analyses and even personal appearances by the real-life Skinnerian biologist Henri Laborit. *Life Is a Story* (1983) similarly interweaves a modern fairy story (complete with prince, beautiful girl and dragon), a seminar on the use of the imagination and the account of a drug-induced experiment in reincarnation. Each of these is a mesmeric, absorbing film; but Resnais' masterpieces are none the less his earlier works, in which, appearing to say less, he had far more news to tell.

Good studies: J. Ward: *Alain Resnais or the Theme of Time* (1968); J. Monaco: *Alain Resnais* (1978).

RIEFENSTAHL, Leni (born 1902)
German director

A woman of prodigiously diverse abilities, Riefenstahl trained as a painter, worked as a ballet-dancer, and took part both as actress and production assistant in a number of films about mountaineering and skiing (notably the splendidly named *The White Hell of Pitz Palü*, 1929, and *The Blue Light*, 1932, of which she was also co-director). In 1933 she made a short documentary, *Victory of Faith*, about the Nazi party, and this led to her two major achievements, both to commissions from Hitler: *Triumph of the Will* (1934), a record of the 1934 Nuremberg Rally, and *Olympia* (1938), the official film of the 1936 Olympic Games. Both films are remarkable for geometric, expressionist composition: Riefenstahl's view of people in the mass is of magnificently choreographed automata, marching and chanting in well-drilled lines. She intercuts individual close-ups, rather in the manner of *Eisenstein, and is adept at showing heroic effort – no one has better caught the athlete's achievement of grace through sweat and toil. She saw her work as apolitical, a glorification of human dignity and prowess. But her frequent sequences of Hitler and his entourage (usually shot adoringly from below, dwarfing ordinary people), her vision of human beings fulfilling themselves by submission to order, and her humourless glorification of blond, heroic youth lay too close to Nazi philosophy for post-war comfort. Of her later films *Tiefland*

(1952) is bland, and the self-styled anthropological study *Black Cargo* (1956) now appears offensively racialist. In the two great Nazi films her talent reached a simultaneous zenith (of visual richness) and nadir (of sensitivity and taste). Like *Griffith's *The Birth of a Nation*, these films demonstrate the way in which the cinema awkwardly, embarrassingly refutes Sartre's argument that there can be no good right-wing art – that is, unless Griffith is no good, unless Riefenstahl is no artist.

ROHMER, Eric (born 1920)
French director and critic

As critic for *Cahiers du cinéma* from 1951, and its editor-in-chief from 1958 to 1963, Rohmer established a dogmatic style of film analysis, often incomprehensible to those outside the industry, but a profound influence on many writers and directors, notably those of the French New Wave and the 1970s generation of 'movie brats'. His own films are quiet tales of affection, longing and (sometimes) discreet adultery, the cinema equivalent of the short stories of Guy de Maupassant. The best of them are three comedies (from the series of six 'Moral Tales'), *My Night with Maude* (1968), *Claire's Knee* (1970) and *Love in the Afternoon* (1972), and an atmospheric costume-piece, *Die Marquise von O . . .* (1976), a dream-like story of seduction, regret and acceptance based on the enigmatic novel by Kleist. Like his criticism, Rohmer's (deliberately, rather conceitedly casual) films are too esoteric for mass release. His style is like *Truffaut's, but he lacks Truffaut's clinching populism.

Rohmer's other films include a second six-film series, 'Comedies and Proverbs', whose best parts to date are *A Good Marriage* (1982) and *Pauline at the Beach* (1983).

ROSSELLINI, Roberto (1906–77)
Italian director

Three films from the start of Rossellini's career dwarf his later work. All tell sombre fictional stories and make use of natural locations, some unprofessional actors and a structure as tight and unemotional as a news report. (Documentary drama is, today, a familiar television form, and verisimilitude is commonplace; but in 1940s cinema, to audiences who thought 'realism' was the shiny hardness of Hollywood gangster films or the psychological thumbscrews of *Carné, Rossellini's approach, subsequently dubbed 'neo-realism', must have been as fresh an experience as walking on the moon.) *Rome, Open City* (1945), his masterpiece, is a grim story of Nazi oppression and torture in wartime Rome, and of the doomed bravery of those who opposed it. Marvellous performances by Anna Magnani and Aldo Fabrizzi lacerate the heart. (To describe what they do as 'performances' seems wrong. They live the parts; it is like seeing your neighbour torn to death before your eyes.) The torture-scenes involving Marcello Pagliero are terrible. *Paisà* (1947) is a sequence of six linked stories showing the effects of the war on country people. Its interest today is not so much for the stories as for its remarkable empathy with the life of the countryside – readers of John Berger's book *Pig Earth*, about French peasant farmers, may be struck by a similarity of mood. *Germany, Year Zero* (1947) is another glimpse into Hell: a small boy in occupied Berlin, trying desperately to feed his family, is forced into black-market operation and finally murder. The story is like that of *de Sica's *Shoeshine*, but de Sica's film is lit with the warmth of hope, while Rossellini's is bleak and black.

The war was Rossellini's great inspiration – just as it was Goya's – but he could hardly have gone on sanely producing work of such unremitting harshness and despair. He made many post-war films, on a variety of subjects; but only *Stromboli* (1949), a tough drama of peasant life, a meticulous biography of St Francis (*Francesco, giullare di dio*, 1950) and *General della Rovere* (1959, about a man who agrees to impersonate a famous resistance leader, and is seduced by his role into actually leading the resistance) have anything like the intensity of his earlier work. He turned to the stage and to television, in which he worked exclusively for the last fifteen years of his life. (Of his television work, *The Rise of Louis XIV*, 1966, is outstanding; *Socrates*, 1968, perhaps because its theme is too quiet and too remote, is an impressive flop.)

Good study: J. L. Guarner; *Roberto Rossellini* (English edn 1970).

RUSSELL, Ken (born 1927)
British director

The brilliance and restraint of Russell's television work (a series of dramatized-documentary lives, principally of composers, including *Elgar*, 1962, *The Debussy Film*, 1965, and *A Song of Summer*, 1968, on Delius), and the faithfulness of his feature-film version of *Women in Love*, 1969 (one of the best Lawrence films made), hardly prepared audiences for his extraordinary 1970s metamorphosis into the Naughty Boy Who Loves to Shock, the apostle of the very worst of taste. His films are still brilliant, but restraint has ruptured into hysteria: instead of seducing the senses, these films rape. *The Music Lovers* (1970), ostensibly about Tchaikovsky, and *Mahler* (1974), ostensibly about Mahler, are Freudian catalogues of the nightmares of repression; *Savage Messiah* (1972) is lovingly about artistic madness; *Lisztomania* (1975) ridiculously over-presents the performer as superman. Russell's view of the tortured artist would have more validity if he appeared to have the slightest idea about how creative work is done. Neither Tchaikovsky nor Mahler, for example, wrote their music by shaking their fists at the sky or by surrendering to spermy fantasies of flagellation and anal eroticism. Only when Russell's theme matches his gaudy imagination does a film really work: *The Devils* (1971), a satanic version of Huxley's *The Devils of Loudun*, *Altered States* (1981, to a Chayevsky script), about a drug-hallucinated scientist who regresses to a caveman, and *Tommy* (1975), a dyspeptic rock opera, its images as raucous as its score, are, with *Women in Love*, his most unified and successful cinema works. *The Boy Friend* (1971) turns Sandy Wilson's water-colour musical into an affectionate parody of Busby *Berkeley; *Valentino* (1977) is an uncharacteristically flaccid portrayal of the artist as sensual extrovert.

SCHLESINGER, John (born 1925)
British director

Schlesinger's varied and variable output includes three literary adaptations, *A Kind of Loving* (1962), *Far from the Madding Crowd* (1967) and *Day of the Locust* (1975); a pair of comedies set, somewhat shakily, in the North of England, *Billy Liar* (1963) and *Yanks* (1979); and a chilly thriller, *Marathon Man* (1976). These competent, never very exciting films frame a trio of bitter social comedies, each set with microscopic precision in its period and dealing with individuals trying to make sense of their own baffling and finally overwhelming lives. *Darling* (1965) pins down 1960s London, its modish media men and modern girls swinging like Tarzan from tree to cardboard tree; *Midnight Cowboy* (1970) is a memorable study of two hurt failures, welded by loneliness; *Sunday Bloody Sunday* (1971), again set in swinging London, is a kind of love-triangle (man plus woman plus man – but which character loves which of these?), with acerbic performances and a glacial directorial style not unlike *Losey's in *Accident*. These are streamlined, enjoyable films; but none the less Schlesinger gives the impression that his best is still to come.

SCORSESE, Martin (born 1942)
American director

Of all the young American directors whose work reflects the amoral, atheistic and unglamorous 1970s – those for whom humanity's is a terminal case – Scorsese is the only one who tackles the issues instead of merely depicting their consequences. *Bogdanovich, *Coppola and *Spielberg, his nearest rivals, are glossier and shallower; Scorsese's films are quiet and understated, and he regularly allows his characters a simple humanity which, we are made to feel, may be their means of escape from the despair and imprisonment of urban life. In *Mean Streets* (1973) and *Alice Doesn't Live Here Any More* (1974), his best films so far, the human quality is affection. The puppy gangsters of *Mean Streets*, with their put-on sneers and pimply charades of toughness, never lose the human warmth of their Italian-immigrant background; the flailing, failing adult relationships of *Alice Doesn't Live Here Any More* are cunningly balanced against a sympathetic and beautifully portrayed relationship between the 'heroine' and her twelve-year-old son, the still centre that will rescue both their lives. At first sight, *Taxi Driver* (1976) and its parallel *King of Comedy* (1983) are harsher, with *Godardesque scenes of violence and insanity. But in each of them the hero's motives, despite the bizarre behaviour they induce, are noble and memorable: in *Taxi Driver* we are even made to feel that another person acting from the same motives in other circumstances might succeed in doing good. Redemption never *happens* in a Scorsese film, but it remains a possibility. *New York, New York* (1977), the incredibly and uncharacteristically noisy *The Last Waltz* (1978), the filmed last concert of the rock group The Band, and *Raging Bull* (1980), starring Robert de Niro as a boxer who destroys his career and finds himself, are lesser works, but never blur the fact that, of all his contemporaries, Scorsese is the man to watch.

SENNETT, Mack (1880–1960)
American producer, director and actor

Sennett was not an outstanding film-maker. His acting was ludicrous and his directing method consisted in pointing a camera at the performers and making sure that everyone stayed in shot. His genius was for organization. Particularly at the Keystone Studios after 1912, he created a factory system for film comedy as firmly structured and loosely disciplined as *commedia dell'arte* had been for stage comedy 400 years before. A Keystone comedy is built on a series of rigid conventions. The motivating forces are greed, sex, revenge and incompetent ambition; the characters are a mixture of ordinary people in a surrealist world (Mabel Normand, Fatty Arbuckle) and surrealist zanies manipulating everyday reality (Chester Conklin, the Keystone Cops); the films are structured round battles (as often against buildings, railroads, automobiles and the forces of nature as against people) or as chases (the hero is as often chased as chasing, and much use is made of circus animals – lions, elephants, monkeys – as well as of people and of mechanical objects like bicycles, cars and bombs, which are invested with a malignant anti-human will of their own). Once the theme of a scene was set, Sennett left his comedians free to improvise: the strength of his films is in the freewheeling brilliance of individual performers, and the feeling that each joke, however familiar or part of a recognized tradition (pratfalls, juggling, acrobatic fights and the like), is an inspiration uniquely suited to its moment in the plot. Sennett's affable working method attracted a large group of outstanding artists, and allowed them room to experiment.

Later, as film-making grew more precise – and more expensive – the inspirational Keystone style (best seen today, perhaps, in the feature *Tillie's Punctured Romance*, 1916) was replaced by meticulously planned and scripted comedy, not less funny, but more dependent on the genius of a single controlling individual. For modern audiences, used to more sophisticated styles of film comedy, the most satisfactory Sennett films are not the brilliant, ramshackle Keystone shorts, but a series of longer, fully scripted comedies he masterminded for Paramount in the 1920s, starring Ben Turpin and Billy Bevan. Turpin's incredible face (cross-eyes, large nose, huge moustache and gap teeth) made him an ideal star for romantic parody. His comic athletics parody Fairbanks; his romantic scenes parody Valentino; his martial or sinister roles parody von Stroheim. (Typical titles are *Mud and Sand*, *The Eek of Araby* and *Nudnick of the North*.) Bevan played a chubby, walrus-moustached little man forever at the mercy of animals and machinery. A typical film is *Super-Hooper-Dyne Lizzies* (1924), in which he starts pushing his stalled automobile along the street, only to collect without noticing a huge line of vehicles which he shoves all over town and finally, climactically, over a cliff-edge in the Hollywood Hills.

This fast-paced slapstick, based on incident not character, did not long survive the arrival of sound in 1929. (As soon as comedians speak they acquire character, and a different comic style is needed; early microphones also required static acting, and this was death to slapstick.) *Chaplin resisted sound until 1936; *Keaton's career declined; only Lloyd and Laurel and Hardy (*only!*) adapted and grew. Turpin, Bevan and the other exponents of Sennett's dizzy style were quickly eclipsed – to comedy's great loss. Of all the consequences of the microphone, the decline of slapstick (or its watering down, by such pale reflections of the great Sennett stars as the Dead End Kids, the Three Stooges or Abbott and Costello) is one of the most deplorable. Sennett organized, not to say created, screen comedy: he is a founding father as vital to cinema as *Griffith or *De Mille themselves.

'As-told-to' autobiography: *King of Comedy* (1954). Good study: K. C. Lahue and T. Brewer: *Kops and Custard* (1968).

SJÖSTRÖM, Victor (1879–1960)
Swedish director and actor

After an outstanding career as a stage actor, Sjöström entered the film industry in 1913, and in the next ten years directed over fifty features: he is, for European cinema, a founding figure as crucial as *Griffith in Hollywood or *Eisenstein in the USSR. His best films involve a typical Scandinavian integration of people and their surroundings. In *Terje Vigen* (1917) the harsh coastal setting is as much a mirror of the bleakness of the central character (a fisherman, played by Sjöström himself) as the Suffolk landscape is in Britten's opera *Peter Grimes*; in *Körkalen* (*The Phantom Carriage*, 1921) houses, trees and furniture take on surreal and claustrophobic force. In 1923 Sjöström went to Hollywood, changed his name to Seastrom and made a number of films including the fine *The Wind* (1928), an atmospheric film about a girl (Lillian Gish) on a lonely Texas farmstead who kills an intruder during a dust-storm and then tortures herself with remorse into near-insanity. This film, though hammily acted (the restless, ever-present wind is the most consistent character), is technically Sjöström's best: the scoured landscapes, the dust stirring in the wind and the claustrophobic interior of the farmhouse (mirroring the heroine's mind) are superbly realized. Persistent studio interference led Sjöström finally to leave Hollywood in 1928, and indeed (with two minor exceptions) to give up directing entirely for acting. His most memorable performance was also his last, as the elderly, tormented Professor Borg in *Bergman's *Wild Strawberries*.

SPIELBERG, Steven (born 1946)
American director

Spielberg's first important feature was a savage anti-media comedy, *Sugarland Express* (1973). Its hero and heroine are running from the law, towing a procession of reporters, TV cameramen and autograph-hunters. It's a trivial world (but deadly: they are finally shot to death), and it is sharply and deftly satirized. His next two films, *Jaws* (1975) and *Close Encounters of the Third Kind* (1977, revised and tightened 1980), tackle triviality in a different way – by trying to mend it, to create philosophical systems which might just fill the void in the late-20th-century soul. *Jaws* offers the Hemingway solution of bravery: Man beats Shark by doggedness. In *Close Encounters* we are given the plastic model of a transcendental experience: the alien as a benevolent super-being observes our ant-like human predicament without ever changing it. In both films, Spielberg's entertainer's touch is sure and sharp – he once said 'I love telling stories the way Rudyard Kipling told stories' – but his philosophy is nothing: ersatz humanism, ersatz religion, as much a mirage of thought as von Däniken's chariots of the gods are a mirage of science. There is no message in *1941* (1979) – and not much entertainment either. The piece is a costly, overblown farce about small-town would-be air-aces fighting off a non-existent Japanese attack in the days after Pearl Harbor. Much less pretentious, and more successful, is *Raiders of the Lost Ark* (1981), a rumbustious treasure-hunting story, whose ambience and stiff-upper-lip heroics are a homage to the adventure serials of the 1930s. It and its super-violent sequel *Indiana Jones and the Temple of Doom* (1984) are said to be the first of a series of ripping yarns, and (for those cinema-goers not afraid to watch films cowering behind their seats) bode well. *E.T. – Extra Terrestrial* (1982), the story of a small boy's affection for a hyper-intelligent and lonely Thing from outer space, could be (has often been, in horror versions of the same idea) embarrassing and awful, but is actually both touching and sensitive, a spin-off from one of the best ideas of *Close Encounters* (the delight of the innocent in the appearance and behaviour of extra-terrestrial beings).

Spielberg's other films include *Duel* (1971). Originally made for television, this is about an innocent driver on a California freeway being terrorized by a homicidal maniac in a giant, predatory truck. The theme (Man against Irrational Monster) is quintessential Spielberg, and the treatment is full both of the careful human detail and the brilliant action sequences characteristic of his later work.

STERNBERG, Josef von (1894–1969)

Austrian/American director

The image of the Hollywood director as a refugee from the Prussian nobility, complete with monocle, duelling-scar, jodhpurs, riding-crop and the manners of an irascible auk was one which Sternberg worked assiduously to create: he was always his own most successful star. His films, too, have a spurious aristocratic gloss: their technical accomplishment (they are virtuoso displays of lighting and montage) gives kitsch the momentary appearance of art. Typical early films are *Underworld* (1927), *The Dragnet* (1928) and *The Docks of New York* (1928), precursors of the great Hollywood gangster films of the 1930s. Sternberg's ability to make sleazy low-life seem both dazzling and entertaining led to a German commission, *The Blue Angel* (1930), a version of Heinrich Mann's novel about a schoolmaster who falls in love with a cabaret performer and is humiliated and destroyed by her. In other hands (for example those of Sjöberg, whose *Frenzy* has a similar theme) this plot might have led to realistic tragedy; in Sternberg's it led to a vehicle for the world-weary sexuality of Marlene Dietrich, who became an international star. (Emil Jannings, who played the schoolmaster, received less attention. His part is hammy, pathetic and ludicrous; all human vitality is hers; the destroying angel gets all the best lines.) Dietrich and Sternberg continued to work together in Hollywood, and made a series of films more or less repeating her role as a heavy-lidded, sultry good-time girl (occasionally with a heart of gold): *Morocco* (1930), *Dishonoured* (1931), *Shanghai Express* (1932), *Blonde Venus* (1932) and *The Devil is a Woman* (1935). In *The Scarlet Empress* (1934), the apogee of these extraordinary films (as perverse and brilliant in their way as Mae West's were in theirs), Dietrich plays the German whore-aristocrat who married mad Grand Duke Peter of Russia and eventually succeeded him as the Empress Catherine II.

As well as these Dietrich vehicles, Sternberg directed a version of Dreiser's novel *An American Tragedy* (1931), in part based on a script by *Eisenstein, who had abandoned the project after studio interference. The first half of this film (a harsh seduction) is his finest non-Dietrich achievement. He made a sombre *Crime and Punishment* (1935) with Peter Lorre, and part of what would have been a distinguished *I, Claudius* (1937) with Charles Laughton, if it had not been abandoned after a few days' shooting. At this point his career declined. He made only five more films, and of them only *The Shanghai Gesture* (1941), about blackmail and betrayal in an oriental gambling den, shows anything like the quality of his earlier work. (Dietrich, too, made nothing better than her films with him. Their styles were complementary; each was the other's Frankenstein.)

Lively, self-regarding autobiography: *Fun in a Chinese Laundry* (1965). Good study: J. Baxter: *The Cinema of Josef von Sternberg* (1971).

STILLER, Mauritz (1883–1928)
Swedish director

Stiller's films are of two kinds: witty comedies, in the style of a 20th-century Holberg or Beaumarchais (the best, and best known, is *Erotikon*, 1920), and historical dramas in a serious, landscape-dominated Swedish style, silent equivalents of *Bergman's *The Seventh Seal* (*Song of the Scarlet Flower*, 1919; *Sir Arne's Treasure*, 1919). His finest film is *The Atonement of Gösta Berling* (1924). This, although worth seeing in its own right, is also famous as the film which brought Garbo (and Stiller himself) to the notice of Hollywood. Ironically, Stiller was prevented by studio squabbles from actually directing Garbo in Hollywood. She moved on to work with others, and he, after directing Pola Negri in the workmanlike *Hotel Imperial* (1927) and *The Woman on Trial* (1927) – how wonderful they could have been with Garbo! – retired to Sweden. His early death robbed cinema of an outstanding talent; his finished work was as good as *Sjöström's, and he promised a great deal more.

STURGES, Preston (1898–1959)
American writer and director

After a decade of writing likeable but unmemorable films for others, Sturges went on in the 1940s to direct a dozen stylish comedies, all to his own barbed scripts. (A typical piece of dialogue, from *Sullivan's Travels*, runs: 'The play died in Pittsburgh.' 'What do they know in Pittsburgh?' 'They know what they like.' 'Then why do they live in Pittsburgh?') The films are brittle satire, not unlike the novels of Peter de Vries; Sturges's wit is less fantastical than *Lubitsch's, harder-edged than *Wilder's – and his characters are as poised and heartless as their own wisecracks. *The Great McGinty* (1940) sends up American politics, *Sullivan's Travels* (1941, for many the best of Sturges's films) the pretensions of film-making itself, *The Miracle of Morgan's Creek* (1944) and *Hail the Conquering Hero* (1944) provincial attitudes and aspirations. His most savage films are *The Lady Eve* (1941), about card-sharps on a luxury liner, *The Palm Beach Story* (1942), a sex-comedy as eccentric and hilarious as Wilder's *Some Like It Hot*, and *Unfaithfully Yours* (1948), about an orchestral conductor fantasizing (while conducting) about murdering his wife. *Mad Wednesday* (1946), starring Harold Lloyd in a sour sequel to his own *The Freshman*, shows Sturges's wit beginning to curdle into misanthropy; after it he made only three more films, none a match for the mellow masterpieces of his earlier years.

SUCKSDORFF, Arne (born 1917)
Swedish documentarist

Nowadays television is the true medium for the nature documentary, in fact for most kinds of documentary. The main drive in cinema seems to be for narrative, and large-screen nature films often lack cohesion or point. Sucksdorff's solution to this problem was to give his films a gentle narrative framework, while concentrating on the natural observations made, so to speak, *en route*. Thus, *The West Wind* (1942) is shaped by a journey (the annual migration of the Lapps), *Rhythm of the City* (1946) by the progress of the day and of the seasons, *The Wind and the River* (1951) by the journey of the river itself. In *The Great Adventure* (1953), his masterpiece, beautiful sequences of the animals and birds of the Swedish countryside are linked by a simple story of a boy and his pet otter. In some later films, notably *The Boy in the Tree* (1961) and *My Home is Copacabana* (1965), created elements are more intrusive, but in *The Flute and the Arrow* (1957) and *Forbush and the Penguins* (1971) the blend between the events of nature and the human observer is exactly right. Like the documentaries of Haanstra, Sucksdorff's films are rarely seen outside specialist cinemas or clubs. They deserve wider currency.

TARKOVSKY, Andrei (born 1932)
Russian director

With a few notable exceptions such as Kozintsev's *Hamlet* (1964, starring Innokenti Smoktunovsky), Russian cinema has made little impression in the west since the death of *Eisenstein. The chances are that Tarkovsky is the man to change all that. He has made only a handful of films (*Ivan's Childhood*, 1962; *Andrei Rublov*, 1966; *Solaris*, 1971; *The Mirror*, 1974; *Stalker*, 1980; *Nostalgia*, 1983); but it is clear from them that he combines a view of the world as eerie as Kafka's with a personal style owing debts to *Bergman, *Kurosawa and the European New Wave. His first two films are about individual spiritual development. *Ivan's Childhood* is a *Fellini-like story about a child fighting with a group of partisans; *Andrei Rublov* tells the life of a religious painter at odds with the violence of medieval society – the effect is as if Hermann Hesse had worked with Bergman on *The Seventh Seal*. In *The Mirror* Tarkovsky moved from narrative into the territory of *Resnais, intercutting memories (of childhood under Stalin, of the Second World War) with enigmatic scenes of the present day. It is a hard film to follow, depending for its effect less on narrative than on the 'poetic' juxtaposition of apparently unrelated images – and (for the non-Russian-speaker) the need to read subtitles too makes several viewings essential if it is to make any sense at all. *Solaris* and *Stalker* are just as powerful, and easier to take in. They are science-fiction allegories, set in a future world which is a misted mirror of our own. The detail is realistic, the time often 'real time' without editing – if someone walks across a cornfield, we follow every single step – and the acting superbly naturalistic. But the themes – *Solaris* is about astronauts forced to come to terms with their own past selves, *Stalker* about metaphysics, the search for inner happiness – are complex and opaque, often lateral to the events of the actual stories. *Nostalgia*, about a writer on a nostalgic trip to the Italian countryside (the film is in Italian) is a lengthy, poetic exploration of Proust's notion of the 'landscape of memory': visually ravishing, but enigmatic and extremely slow.

Fellini, Bergman, Resnais, Kafka, Hesse – the list of influences is long and suggests a brilliant cinematographer stunningly filming slow, difficult stories. That's exactly what Tarkovsky is, and does. His work repels as many as it fascinates; those who are fascinated rate him among the greatest 'serious' directors at work in film today.

TATI, Jacques (1908–82)
French actor, director and writer

Tati was the natural heir to the great silent comedians. His art is that of the sight gag: it depends partly on his own extraordinary, graceful body (like a spring-heeled pipe-cleaner) and partly on brilliant exaggeration of the quirks of ordinary human behaviour. Except in his first feature, he rarely speaks. The sound-tracks of his films are a collage of music, multi-lingual mutterings and grunts – he makes superb use of the squawks of radios, tannoys, desk-communicators and telephones – and a *musique concrète* of natural sound-effects (walking feet, clanking machinery, puttering car-engines, tennis-balls – you've only to mention the 'pyoing' of the restaurant door in *M. Hulot's Holiday* to make any Tati-lover smile).

Tati was particularly concerned with the increasing mechanization of our lives, the way in which machines and systems grow like weeds while human beings dehumanize and mechanize themselves. This theme was first seen in his 1930s cabaret acts, in which he deftly and gracefully parodied the players of different sports. Several short films were made of these (e.g. *Oscar the Tennis Player*, 1932; *Tough Guy Wanted*, 1934), and Tati performs one of the most famous of them, playing both horse and rider galloping elegantly round the ring, in his rather uncharacteristic television film, chiefly a compilation of circus acts, *Parade* (1973). The interplay between human machine and machine human is a recurring theme in his major films. In *Jour de fête* (1947) the postman hero François (Tati) sees a film on the streamlining of the American postal service, and determines to streamline himself, with disastrous results. In *M. Hulot's Holiday* (1951), Tati's masterpiece, the guests at a high-summer holiday resort enjoy themselves like animated dolls, fascinated by the anarchic human-ness of Hulot. In *Mon Oncle* (1958) big business is sterile, plastic and efficient; human beings (even when handling a boiled egg) are germ-ridden interruptions of the perfect world. In *Playtime* (1967) big-city conformity oppresses and degrades the humans until they burst out, under Hulot's unwitting influence, in monstrous, orgasmic saturnalia. In *Traffic* (1971) the automobile and its gadgets rule; human beings are reduced to picking their noses in traffic jams in the rain.

Hulot himself (the Tati character) never fully involves himself in the frantic absurdities of the mechanical world. His silence makes him an observer – and his mere existence has a catastrophic effect on any machine, any human system of order, any notion of symmetry. (The station tannoy in *M. Hulot's Holiday* has hysteria, though Hulot is nowhere near; the pipe-extruding machine he operates in *Mon Oncle* begins to churn out coloured balloons, serpents and sausages; the truck he uses in *Traffic* continually grinds to a halt, in the machine equivalent of a nervous breakdown.) In *Playtime* Tati takes Hulot's detachment a stage further. The plot is minimal, and Hulot's own contribution is much smaller and more haphazard than in the earlier films. The main interest is in the antics of the other characters: the influence of Tati's friend, the documentarist Haanstra, with his view of the Human Zoo, is clearly seen. For some, this film is the climax of Tati's quiet style; for others, the lunatic centrality of Hulot in the other films, a 20th-century Pan thrusting open the windows of the soul, leaving delightful chaos and irrationality wherever he goes, makes them his finest work. Either way, he was as committed a social critic as *Chaplin, as rueful a poet of the hostility of the universe as *Keaton; he was also the only solo screen comedian to rival them in performing elegance and in the genius and unrepeatable funniness of his ideas.

Good study: J. Harding: *Jacques Tati* (1984).

TRUFFAUT, François (1932–84)
French director, writer and actor

In the 1950s Truffaut wrote criticism for *Cahiers du cinéma*; his views were a delightful mixture of a breath of fresh air (reassessments of such 'entertainment' directors as *Welles and *Hitchcock, for example) and cerebral philosophizing difficult to relate to anything but itself. After his first feature, *Les Quatre Cent Coups* (*Sowing Wild Oats*, 1959), he made over thirty films, in an eclectic mixture of styles and moods, but all with marked directorial identity and a sure entertainment touch – unlike some directors who progressed from critical theory to artistic practice, he had a real feeling for the popular audience. He made Hitchcockian thrillers (e.g. *Shoot the Pianist*, 1960), nostalgic melodrama (*The Last Metro*, 1980, set in the Occupation), futuristic fantasy (*Fahrenheit 451*, 1966), tender tragi-comedy of relationships (*Jules and Jim*, 1961; *Anne and Muriel*, 1971), black farce (*A Gorgeous Girl Like Me*, 1972), and two intense dramas set in the past and based on real incidents (*The Savage Child*, 1970, about the 'civilizing' of an 18th-century boy found living among animals, and *The Story of Adèle H.*, 1975, based on the obsessive diaries of Victor Hugo's daughter). His most outstanding films are *La Nuit américaine* (*Day for Night*, 1973), an amiable satire on film-making, *The Green Room* (1978), a haunting film about bereavement and the resilience of the human spirit, and the splendid series of films starring Jean-Pierre Léaud as Antoine Doinel (a character in part based on Truffaut himself). The first of these films, *Les Quatre Cent Coups*, shows the fourteen-year-old Antoine at the mercy of society, learning to steal, lie and cheat but still retaining his personal dignity and freedom (a recurring Truffaut theme). The cycle continues with a pair of light comedies showing Antoine coping with young adulthood and especially with the delights of flirtation and seduction (*Antoine and Colette*, part of the international multi-episode film *Love at Twenty*, 1962; *Stolen Kisses*, 1968). Finally come two comedies of maturity, in a bitter-sweet style close to that of *Jules and Jim*: *Bed and Board* (1970), the story of Antoine's stormy marriage, and *Love on the Run* (1979), in which the female-beleaguered hero, now thirty, looks back over his crowded life.

Truffaut's work combines intellectuality, good humour and earthiness. Like Balzac, he produced 'comedies' – in the sense that his work is about *la comédie humaine*, the spice and especially the tears in things. This quality, and the maintenance in balance of head and heart, gives his work distinction: its surface energy is underpinned by intellectual strength and emotional depth.

Truffaut's other films include *La Peau douce* (*Silken Skin*, 1963), *The Bride Wore Black* (1967), *Mississippi Mermaid* (1969) and *The Woman Next Door* (1981). As well as his book on *Hitchcock* (1967), he also published an interesting 'artistic autobiography', *The Films in My Life* (1979). Good interim study: A. Insdorf: *François Truffaut* (1978).

VISCONTI, Luchino (1906–76)
Italian director

Three major strands in Visconti's life were also the vital influences on his films. First, he was born into one of the great Italian noble families and brought up in surroundings of fastidious luxury bordering on decadence. Second, he was attracted to the theatre: his friends included leading theatrical and operatic stars, and he mounted lavish opera productions at La Scala, Milan, and many notable stage plays in Rome. Third, the rise of fascism and the Second World War brought him into sympathy with workers' revolutionary movements, and his feeling for the lives and aspirations of ordinary people was always as powerful as for the artificialities of the stage or of aristocratic life.

Visconti made one film in neo-realist style, using real people to act out situations from their own lives. *La terra trema* (1948) is set among poor fishermen, and was the first of an uncompleted trilogy about Sicilian peasant life. But this use of amateurs was never repeated. His films generally overlay the documentary clarity and sympathy of neo-realism with a patina of bravura acting (he pushed stars, in particular, to give

deeply felt performances without losing their starriness), sumptuous
visual beauty (even his blood and mud ravish the eye), and a self-
conscious refinement of style not at all like the neo-realist films of
*Fellini, *Olmi and *Rossellini. *Ossessione* (*Obsession*, 1942) is a
magnificent version of James M. Cain's *The Postman Always Rings
Twice*, a story of lust, murder and guilt as trashily compulsive as any
of the novels of Zola. *Bellissima* (1951) contrasts – how original! – the
hollowness of the film world (it is about a mother ambitious for her
daughter) with reality. *Senso* (1954) is a powerful drama of betrayal,
both political and sexual (a woman takes an enemy lover during the
Risorgimento, and later denounces him to his own side), given a high-art
sheen by the use of music by Bruckner and Verdi. *Rocco and His
Brothers* (1960), about a poor South Italian family who come to Milan to
find work, is, after *La terra trema*, Visconti's most restrained and most
moving film.

The tendency in *Senso* towards self-conscious elevation of style
blossoms in Visconti's later films into decadence. No one has better
expressed the sensuality of over-ripeness, the bloom on the peach just
before it rots. In *White Nights* (1957, based on Dostoievski), *The Stranger*
(1967, based on Camus) and even the late *Conversation Piece* (1974) and
The Intruder (1976), the beauty of the photography is at odds with the
bluntness of the stories; but in *Vaghe stelle dell'orsa* (*Of a Thousand
Delights/Sandra*, 1965), an updating of the Electra story to German-
occupied Italy, style and theme are in accord: despite its politically
precise location, the film has an elusive, emblematic feeling, as if these
specific characters are acting out for us the movements of a mysterious,
timeless myth. In *The Leopard* (1963) and *The Damned* (1970), both
about the disintegration of great families, the impression of self-absorption in both characters and direction is even more marked: we feel we are
watching slow-moving, impressive charades of vital importance to the
participants but peripheral to the spectator. Of all Visconti's films these
are the grandest and the least successful, because his style bites its own
tail. In *Death in Venice* (1971), based on Mann's story of a dying novelist
(changed in the film to a composer, thus allowing the lavish use of Mahler
on the soundtrack) racked and enraptured by the sight of a beautiful boy,
and in *Ludwig* (1973), about Wagner's crazy patron Ludwig II of Bavaria,
Visconti's baroque style is exactly right, for fastidious corruption is what
animates the characters. He planned to film Proust, even prepared a
screenplay – and it could have been his masterpiece, the sensitivities of
author and director perfectly entwined. He is a grand artist of the cinema,
and his films are impressive and enjoyable. Hollowness was a persistent
problem, but when he solved it (as in his earliest and latest films) his
work was fine.

Good study: G. Servadio: *Luchino Visconti* (1982).

WAJDA, Andrzej (born 1926)
Polish director

Wajda's great theme is war, and particularly the way in which the individual is simultaneously ennobled and degraded by the need for courageous action. His Second-World-War trilogy *A Generation* (1954), *Kanal* (1957) and *Ashes and Diamonds* (1958) combines messages of strident simplicity (about communism, integrity and friendship) with a depiction of horrors as realistic and unbearable as anything in *Rossellini. After the trilogy (and the less successful *Lotna*, 1959) problems of political censorship sometimes led him to choose less controversial themes, replacing political anger with charming, stylish whimsy. (Typical are *Innocent Sorcerers* (1959) and *The Birch Wood* (1970), both on the pains of adolescent love, *Gates to Paradise* (1967), on the Children's Crusade, and *Hunting Flies* (1969), a comedy.) But side by side with these innocuous exercises, as if slipped in under the censor's guard, are several steely political parables. *Landscape after Battle* (1970) is set in a concentration camp after the American liberation: only the Poles remain, awaiting repatriation, racked by the memory of past suffering. *Everything for Sale* (1968) is a pessimistic film about the artist's role in contemporary society – a similar theme to *Fellini's *Eight and a Half*, and treated in a similarly bitter and elusive style. In *Rough Treatment* (1978), Wajda adds even more anguish to the central theme by making his hero a political journalist suddenly stripped of his career and fighting back. These later political films – they also include two *Godardesque pieces, incorporating real events (and newsreel) in the fiction, *Man of Marble* (1977) on the workers' movement of the 1950s, and its sequel *Man of Iron* (1981), centred on the 1980 Gdansk riots – are obsessive, bleak, and in the context of modern Poland, brave, but in the last analysis they lack the epic dimension which makes Wajda's early trilogy still his greatest work.

Wajda's other films include the Chekhovianly autumnal *The Young Ladies of Wilko* (1979), *A German Love Story* (1983, based on Hochhuth's novel) and *The Danton Affair* (1982), which uses Büchner's play *Danton's Death* as a neat parable about stifling 1980s bureaucracies. Good study, as far as it goes: B. Michatek: *The Cinema of Andrzej Wajda* (1973).

WELLES, Orson (born 1915)
American director and actor

Citizen Kane (1941), Welles's first film, is one of the most lauded in the history of cinema: forty years on, it is still widely considered one of the greatest pictures ever made. Its greatness lies partly in its cunning story – with true cinematic magic it makes melodrama (in this case the story of a megalomaniac tycoon politician) seem to resonate with philosophical truth – but chiefly in the magnificence of Welles's direction and Gregg Toland's photography: it is an encyclopaedia of technical skills and tricks, but uses all of them with breathtaking audacity and originality. Above all, the impact of a single creative personality, Welles's own, is felt in every frame: like all masterpieces, *Citizen Kane* puts us directly in touch with its creator's mind and heart.

Welles's subsequent films include three distinguished versions of Shakespeare (*Macbeth*, 1948, *Othello*, 1951, and *Chimes at Midnight*, 1961, a reworking of the Falstaff sequences from *Henry IV*), a romantic thriller (*Lady from Shanghai*, 1948), *The Trial* (1963), based on Kafka's novel, and *F for Fake* (1973), a ruminative, unsettling film about art forgery. His best films are *The Magnificent Ambersons* (1942), about an engulfing, decadent mid-western family, and his nearest equivalent in cinema genius to *Citizen Kane*; *Confidential Report/Mister Arkadin* (1955), whose story (about the posthumous assessment, by his friends and enemies, of a successful and ambitious man) is like an overstated, under-financed *Citizen Kane*; and *Touch of Evil* (1958), the sombre study of a corrupt, bloated police chief, a film whose style is a virtuoso parody of the B feature film (in the way that Beethoven's *Diabelli Variations* could be called a parody on the 19th-century salon waltz).

Welles's career has seemed to some to illustrate the cliché about there being only one direction to travel if you start at the top. His acting has lent baroque bulk to dozens of films, some good, some terrible (though he himself is rarely less than good, and in some films – *The Third Man*, *Compulsion*, *Catch-22* – is magnificent). His own films have been sporadic, penny-pinched and inconsistent; his tireless self-publicizing in the minor media, though amiably done, looks like cynical laziness – why doesn't he buckle to and make another *Citizen Kane*, people querulously ask. His answer, that he has preserved his independence in a fawning, hostile industry, makes him sound like Gulliver in Lilliput – and perhaps he is. In any case, how could his genius be described as wasted? He has directed and starred in a dozen outstanding films, more than many distinguished directors ever make; he may never have bettered *Citizen Kane*, but neither has anyone else; he remains, for the whole industry, a paradigm both of excellence and of the way jealous pigmies dismantle excellence.

A hilarious view of Welles at work on the four-year *Othello* is Michael MacLiammoir's *Put but Money in Thy Purse* (1955). MacLiammoir played Iago. Good studies: R. Gottesman (ed.): *Focus on 'Citizen Kane'* (1971); *Focus on Orson Welles* (1976). Good survey: J. McBride: *Orson Welles* (1972).

WILDER, Billy (born 1906)
Austrian/American director and writer

Wilder is a needle-tongued moralist. He has no pity for his characters and no compassion for their sufferings. They are heartlessly observed, whether what happens to them is funny or sad, whether they bring it on themselves or are the victims of malignant fate. This detachment gives a tone of uncompromising harshness to his 'serious' films, the thrillers *Five Graves to Cairo* (1943) and *Double Indemnity* (1944), the study of alcoholism *The Lost Weekend* (1945) and the attack on gutter journalism *Ace in the Hole* (1951). Nevertheless, there *is* compromise. Wilder systematically subordinates realism to entertainment. We never believe that the insurance office of *Double Indemnity* or the hospital of *The Lost Weekend* are real – they are stage-sets, and in them Wilder's characters perform plays of life. This artificiality is clearly ideal for ironical comedy, Wilder's chief interest; but its rules, and especially its blunting of the edges of comment, are just as important to his non-comic films, and are the actual theme of two of the best of them, *Sunset Boulevard* (1950) and *Fedora* (1978), about the image we create of life and what happens when we try to pin it down. Wilder is fascinated by role-playing (a characteristic feature of both comedy and wit), and never more so than when it is used for serious purposes. In *Witness for the Prosecution* (1958), for example, the gross barrister played by Charles Laughton is as fascinating for his excess as his success; in *The Private Life of Sherlock Holmes* (1970) the mystery of Holmes himself is far more interesting than the mystery he solves.

Wilder began his Hollywood career as a writer, and had a hand in the scripts of most of his own films. He wrote a number of stylish comedies for other men: *Midnight*, the charming *Ball of Fire* (for *Hawks), and two *Lubitsch films, *Bluebeard's Eighth Wife* and *Ninotchka*. His own early films are mainly serious (those 1940s films mentioned above), but include the joky *The Major and the Minor* (1942), in which Ginger Rogers pretends to be a child in order to travel half-fare on a train, and is 'taken care of' by Ray Milland, and the riotous but now dated *A Foreign Affair* (1948), set in occupied Berlin. His great period was the 1950s and 1960s, when he produced a string of fanged farces, often taking specific moral questions (e.g., in *The Apartment*, 1960, the contrast between bought sex and love) or accepted values (e.g. loyalty in *Stalag 17*, 1953, the capitalist ethic in *One, Two, Three*, 1961, and justice in *The Fortune Cookie*, 1966) and turning them on their heads. The starting-point is close to both *Capra and *Lubitsch, but Wilder's cocktail of sentimentality and acid is very much his own.

It is important to the effect of a Wilder comedy that his leading actors possess charm and vulnerability, and also that they crack words like whips. They must always be equivocal: it must never be clear whether

they are all they seem. William Holden in *Sunset Boulevard* projects
hard-boiled innocence – and Wilder makes use of the same duality in
Stalag 17, where Holden plays an apparently cynical villain who turns out
to have been a hero all along. Fred MacMurray, cast apparently against
type as the villain of *Double Indemnity* (while Edward G. Robinson
plays an honest man), reappears as the heartless boss in *The Apartment*
– and our view of his apparent amiability is coloured by what we know of
the teeth behind the grin in his earlier films. *The Seven Year Itch* (1955)
and *Some Like It Hot* (1959) make use of Marilyn Monroe's fluffy
vulnerability; *Some Like It Hot* also depends on Tony Curtis's well-
known ability in roles requiring tongue-in-cheek self-parody. The best
Wilder actor is Jack Lemmon, whose hurt eyes and hurtful tongue exactly
suit this wry, dry style. In *Some Like It Hot, The Apartment, The Fortune
Cookie*, and the marvellously sour *Buddy Buddy* (1981), Wilder's best
comedies, Lemmon moves in an instant from irritability to eagerness,
from smiles to sulks, from despair to hope – and his performances match
every twist and turn of quicksilver, house-of-mirror scripts.

Good biography – well worth persevering with, despite its relentlessly buttonholing,
showbiz-journalism style – is M. Zolotow: *Billy Wilder in Hollywood* (1977).

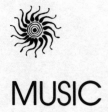

MUSIC

INTRODUCTION

KEY DATES

1909   First recording of a complete symphony (Beethoven's 5th): modern symbiosis of concert music and technology begins here

1913   First performance of Stravinsky's *The Rite of Spring*. Not the most radical work ever composed, or the most scandalous première ever held; its significance is its uncompromising greatness, its demonstration that modernist techniques and musical excellence are not incompatible

1921   Schoenberg's *Suite for Piano*, Op. 25: though several composers had been experimenting with 12-note composition in the 1910s, this was the first work to use the technique systematically, authoritatively and convincingly

1922   Establishment of ISCM (International Society for Contemporary Music), an important forum for new music in Europe and later throughout the world. (Hanson's Rochester Festivals of American music, begun in 1925, and the Copland–Sessions concert series, begun in 1928, opened American ears to 20th-century music in a similar way)

1933   Hitler's assumption of power: in the next decade, advanced composers in Europe either fled (among them Bartók, Hindemith and Schoenberg), went underground or were silenced. Nazi ostracism of culture caused a halt in musical experiment which lasted until the late 1940s, and led to a surge of activity in the 1950s in which the art is still engrossed

1948   First LP records issued in USA (1950 in UK)

1951   First electronic-music studio established (in Cologne, for West German Radio)

1955   Bill Haley's *Rock Around the Clock*: if pop and rock have an official birth-date, this is it

1965   Moog's synthesizer applied the techniques of computer-memory to music, allowing the 'live' performance of electronic sound

1977   Establishment of IRCAM (Institute for the Research and Co-ordination of Acoustics and Music) in Paris, under Boulez

THE IMPORTANCE OF RECORDING

In the first year of its life (1885), Brahms's *Symphony 4* was performed over forty times in twenty different towns – an exceptionally large number, appropriate for a major work by a leading composer. A century later, anyone who wants can hear the same symphony forty times in a single day in his or her own living-room. Works composed to be rare, cherished experiences – it is unlikely that anyone, including the composers, expected to hear Bach's *B Minor Mass* or Mahler's *Symphony 5* more than a dozen times in a lifetime – have become as common as sliced bread. Edison invented the phonograph in 1877; the first million-selling record (Caruso singing 'On with the Motley') appeared a generation later, in 1902; nowadays recordings are as ubiquitous, as profitable and as much a Pandora's box of quality as paperback books.

As with fiction, the main effect on music of mass-production has been to split the art. In Mozart's day composers as happily wrote dance-music as symphonies; Brahms and Johann Strauss were friends, and considered themselves practitioners of the same art; by contrast, there is today a gulf between minority music (say a Shostakovich symphony) and that meant for mass enjoyment (say a Beatles song) which fills musicians of all kinds with complacency rather than alarm. 'Pop' and 'classical' music are different worlds, whose inhabitants seldom meet, and there is even, now, a third group, sitting smugly in the middle and indifferent to both extremes: those who enjoy 'easy listening', and stretch their ears neither to left nor right.

What matters in all this – for what people choose to listen to, or to enrich themselves by providing, is their own affair – is the effect the recording industry has had on composers. The majority have accepted it eagerly: most music nowadays is created primarily for disc or cassette, and live performances are a means of promotion rather than a main activity. In 'serious' music, where live performance is still the norm, costs have soared to the point where only the known is safe: young composers seeking performance are well advised, today, not to write large orchestral works or operas unless they have a commission firmly pocketed. Their dilemma is further increased by the availability and familiarity of a mass of earlier music, much of it of daunting quality. When Brahms wrote his *Symphony 4*, his chief rivals were his own contemporaries and a few great, known predecessors such as Beethoven; composers today write for a market saturated with the past, and their work is often judged not against that of their contemporaries but against a whole tradition, whether relevant or not.

WELCOMING THE PAST

Faced with this problem, composers have reacted in two different but equally energetic ways. Some have regarded past tradition as exhausted, and have set about devising new languages, ways of reinventing their art. Others have treated tradition as a still living, still growing organism, and have chosen to walk further down established paths. For this group, four kinds of activity already established in the 19th century have been particularly useful: the symphonic tradition (largely German or Austrian in origin), the operatic and choral tradition (largely Italian or French, with the overwhelming exception of Wagner), the romantic tradition (ranging from Berlioz's large-scale self-exploration to the more intimate work of people like Chopin), and the nationalist, folk-based tradition (favoured especially in eastern Europe and in Russia).

Anyone writing symphonies in this century has to come to terms with the towering achievements in the form of composers like Beethoven, Brahms and Mahler. Beethoven's first symphony was itself a development from the grand but still emotionally decorous form of Haydn or Mozart; a century later, Mahler could claim that a symphony 'should contain the world'. The combination of length and intellectual complexity had made symphonies, for many 19th-century composers, the pinnacle of creative endeavour, and by 1900 audiences had come to share the view that they were the best the art of music had to offer, eclipsing sonatas and quartets (their stylistic siblings) in scale, concertos in concentration and operas in seriousness of purpose. Mahler's later symphonies were designed to fill most of an evening, to dominate any concert they were played in, and his musical language was suitably elaborate, pushing at what seemed the limits of both harmonic and performing possibility. Since Mahler's death (in 1911), the symphonic tradition has been continued by many fine composers (notably Nielsen, Sibelius and Shostakovich), and what once looked like boundaries have proved a mirage: their musical style may be no more radical than Mahler's, but they have developed the idea of 'symphony' in wholly 20th-century ways (for example, by using techniques of block-juxtaposition instead of development). Other composers, using more radical idioms and avoiding the word symphony, have written works of traditional symphonic stature in other forms: good examples are Debussy's *La Mer*, Berg's *Chamber Concerto*, Bartók's *String Quartets* and Messiaen's *From the Canyons to the Stars*.

At first sight it might seem that the traditions of vocal music offer composers today less scope: the forms of the art-song, of church music and of opera were well established long before the 20th century, and the need to tailor music to the human voice precludes over-zealous innovation. To some extent this is true. 20th-century grand opera (whether Puccini's, Britten's or Henze's), for all the quality of individual works, makes few advances on the art of Verdi or Meyerbeer; much 20th-century church music and art-song is skilled pastiche. But where advances have been made, they are as stunning for their success as their unexpectedness – and as with symphonies, it is the existence of tradition, and their use of it, that validates experiment. Berg's *Wozzeck*, though wholly 20th-century in sound and thought, is formally a step along the path from Verdi's *Otello*; Penderecki's *St Luke Passion*, at first hearing so dissonantly different from Bach's Passions as to seem malicious parody, makes in the end a similar impact on heart and mind, and by the same means (letting the music reveal rather than declare the meaning behind the words). The most radical-seeming vocal medium of the century, music-theatre (the range is from Schoenberg's *Pierrot lunaire* to Maxwell Davies's *Eight Songs for a Mad King* and Henze's *We Come to the River*), is an extension of ideas about the expressive possibilities of his art first formulated and then practised by that apparently quintessential 19th-century composer Wagner.

Another Wagnerian legacy, the feeling that form and harmony need not conform to objective rules but can be adapted to the composer's creative needs, is evident in many of the 20th century's leading traditionalists. At the beginning of the century the prevailing view was that Wagnerian harmony was a tired old medium, fit only to express the most decadent and overheated romantic thought. But although some composers (Franck, Delius) succumbed to the hothouse, the majority took from Wagner only what chords they needed, and based their romanticism less on his fevered example than on the more robust self-exegeses of Berlioz or the pictorialism of Liszt. The works of the grandest 'late romantics' (Strauss, Scriabin, the young Schoenberg) restore to music the objectivity, the feeling of space between creator and listener, which Wagner had replaced with a summons to wallow; no one thought of building shrines to *Also Sprach Zarathustra* or *Verklärte Nacht* (as Bayreuth was built for *The Ring* and *Parsifal*) – and if they had, few worshippers would have made the pilgrimage. Romantic objectivity underlies other, apparently more exotic scores, from Debussy's *Nocturnes* to Stravinsky's *The Rite of Spring* and Bartók's *The Miraculous Mandarin*: however emotionally expressive (not to say expressionist) its content, the music has a voice of its own and says things with it which have nothing to do with the works' 'stories' or their creators' racing pulses. The next stage, for some composers, was neo-classicism, with its deliberate cold-compressing of emotion; for many other 'traditionalists', the balance between romantic passion and expressive dandyism was a main creative resource.

A feature of 20th-century life reflected in music more than in the other arts has been the growth of national identity. In the 19th century, when many nations were still forming, nationalism in music was a tentative and somewhat garish force: however deep the creative impulse behind them, Liszt's *Hungarian Rhapsodies*, Dvořák's Czech folk-dance works, and the explicitly 'Russian' compositions of Mussorgsky, Borodin and Tchaikovsky add no more than a nationalist gloss to music based on other things (symphonic or concerto form; ballet). From the start of the 20th century, by contrast, most composers of stature who used national material dug deeper, making folk ideas the foundation of their art and not its veneer. The best-known example is Bartók, whose personal idiom radically changed – and found its voice – after his 1900s folk-research. But composers as disparate as Ives, Falla and Vaughan Williams turned local inspiration into personal art in the same apparently self-effacing but peremptory way.

Each of these approaches to tradition illustrates a typical 20th-century trend (not confined to music or indeed to the arts): the move towards eclecticism. Tradition had formerly been a guarantor of stability and respectability; now it began to be treated, with ruthlessness, as the trigger of the new.

NEW SOUNDS

The first attempts to dispense with tradition and make new sounds in keeping with a brand-new age were made in the 1910s, as a result of the same new-broom philosophy which gave rise to futurism in Italy and to the Bauhaus in Germany. In his 1913 book *The Art of Sound* Luigi Russolo proposed that traditional instruments should be replaced by 'noise-makers': bangers, buzzers, cracklers, hissers, howlers, gurglers, roarers and rumblers. He invented instruments, wrote music for them (e.g. *Dawn in the City*, 1914), and gave concerts wherever halls could be found to accommodate what looks, in photographs, like a solemn freak-show, ranks of evening-suited, walrus-whiskered gentlemen creaking, wheezing and hooting to order. Russolo's music has not endured, any more than its child *musique concrète* (christened by Pierre Schaeffer in 1948). In this, recordings of natural sounds (bird-song, waves, traffic, wind) are blended by slicing and splicing tape: the result depends for its appeal on ingenuity and surprise rather than musicality, and sounds now less like symphonies than what it is, a collage of sound effects. While serious composers failed with noise, wisecrackers had a field day: the most lasting works to incorporate noise-machines or recorded sound effects are Satie's Dada ballets *Parade* and *Relâche* and the whizz-bang-wallop records of Spike Jones and his City Slickers. A gramophone record of a nightingale (whose number is solemnly given in the score) is played in Respighi's *Pines of Rome* (1924); but until electronic instruments became more sophisticated in the 1950s and 1960s, experiments in the replacing of notes and scales were as frail as lighter-than-air flying-machines look from our space-age vantage-point.

More fruitful experiments were made, also in the 1910s, not to dispense with traditional notes but to forge them into patterns unknown before. On the face of it, this kind of experiment seemed doomed. Not only did it fly in the face of the physics of sound – the harmonic series, which provides every single basic sound, in nature, with an aura of accompanying notes, ethereal and hard to hear but recognizably ordered into a 'major chord' and a 'modal scale' – but the view was strong that the romantics, and later composers like Strauss and Debussy, had taken as many liberties with conventional harmony as were conceivable. For a couple of decades the attempt to abandon harmony led to a chaotic atonal style, chords and sounds jumbling against one another in an anarchic riot which worked well when disciplined by words (e.g. in short songs) but whose logic, in works for larger instrumental forces, escaped the ear. The charitable took this for the musical equivalent of expressionist painting; to the less patient it was uneasily reminiscent of revolutionary crowds storming the Winter Palace or massing in Sarajevo. In the 1920s Schoenberg, the high-priest of atonality, developed 12-note serialism; although this satisfied the analyst, making the organization of notes symmetrical and logical on paper, it produced sounds which seemed (and to many, still seem) indistinguishable from atonality and just as unseductive and disorderly. Further developments in serialization, notably those of Webern, combined with the replacement elsewhere of romantic excess by neo-classical severity, led to a music whose texture is delicate, open and unrhetorical, but whose logic still tends to be cerebral rather than sensual.

By 1933, when the Nazis came to power in Germany and fascists throughout Europe began condemning 'advanced' music as decadent and anti-art, the breach between living composers and their audience was complete. Orchestras, opera-houses, chamber groups and solo performers had plenty of outstanding 'old' music to offer, and the majority of music-lovers feasted on it, pushing their contemporaries to the edge of the plate and experimentalists right off the table. Only in fine art (the aesthetic response to which is, after music, the most subjective and emotional) did the name of modernism so comprehensively – and justifiably, despite occasional masterpieces – stink.

SYNTHESIS

When the artistic depression inaugurated in Europe by fascism ended in the late 1940s (and, in Russia, when the Zhdanov doctrine was revoked in the early 1950s), the fifteen-year gap had badly dated many musical experiments. In particular, 12-note compositions with a Schoenbergian, atonal sound tended to be produced only by elderly composers reaching for former styles after long silence, or by 'avant-garde' composers in countries musically a generation behind the times (e.g. the USA, USSR and UK, all of which discovered serial music in the 1950s). In Europe, experiment continued where it had left off; but this time, instead of aiming for general acceptability – as Schoenberg and Bartók, even at their wildest, had done – avant-garde composers retreated into a defensive and inbred isolationism: there is no more grotesque decade in musical aesthetics than the 1950s, when composers were ready to scream rape the minute they were offered a mass recording contract or a performance beside traditional music in a regular concert-hall. The young Berio, Boulez and Stockhausen, and their less talented cohorts such as Nono, provided music of daunting – not to say self-defeating – complexity for coterie audiences, and collected a small but belligerent army of listeners and critics who declared their experiments the saving of the art, and who still, standing high and dry on their own pretensions, blandly pretend that there is no horizon, that their island is the world.

In the 1960s Boulez and Stockhausen moved on, fast; indeed, musicians everywhere began to relax, to open themselves to their listeners in a way not seen (in experimental circles) for half a century. The rise of pop and rock music to a position of intellectual respectability, and the advent of electronic instruments (whose possibilities rock musicians were the first to take seriously) gave a new lift to sagging creativity, and earlier systems, whether Russolo's, Schoenberg's or Webern's, began to be treated less as sole roads to salvation and more as single resources among many. The variety of stylistic choices open to composers has led, in the last two decades, to music becoming less pretentious, more discriminatory and far more accessible to audiences. Genius has become eclectic rather than exclusive: Messiaen uses 12-note systems, blues harmony, bird-song and rhythms from ancient Greece and India; Maxwell Davies integrates medieval plainchant and Webernian cerebration; Stockhausen uses electronic instruments to solemnize a mystical marriage of eastern and western styles. Above all, musical activity is once more seen as a unified, if multi-faceted, phenomenon. Composers are free to express their own individuality in each new work instead of opting for this or that exclusive style; audiences no longer have to be partisan for tradition or for novelty, and can judge each new piece on what it has to say. The gestation-period has been long and painful, but music, once the sickliest of all 20th-century arts, now thrives: future generations may well look back on this age of Messiaen, Tippett, Boulez, Henze and Stockhausen with the same awe as we regard the 19th century.

▣

Here and there in this section, really bad reviews are quoted. All have been taken or translated from Nicolas Slonimski's hilarious *Lexicon of Musical Invective* (1965), a collection of philistine reviews from Beethoven's time onwards. The splenetic energy of these attacks, parasites hating the hosts they feed on, is one guarantee of music's continuing health – who bothers to kick a corpse?

ANTHEIL, George (1900–1959)
American composer and pianist

Antheil wrote one of the most notorious avant-garde pieces of the 1920s, *Ballet mécanique* (1926). Its score included parts for eight pianos, eight xylophones, doorbells, car-horns, anvils and an aeroplane propeller (engagingly upgraded, in the 1950s revision, to a recorded jet engine). Its first performance provoked a scandal to rival that of *Stravinsky's *Rite of Spring*; critics and audiences loved to hate it; Antheil was hailed as 'the harbinger of tomorrow's music' – and is still solemnly memorialized in textbooks (with Russolo, 1910s inventor of and composer for 'noise machines') as the father of *musique concrète* (music built from a collage of natural sounds) and the grandfather of today's electronic music. In fact he was nothing of the kind, merely the musical equivalent of such painters as Picabia or Duchamp, a talented playboy thoroughly enjoying himself. His autobiography *The Bad Boy of Music* (1945) makes this plain: it begins with a zestful account of his adventures among the 1920s French smart-art set, and goes on to detail his no less uproarious years as a film-composer in Hollywood. His 'serious' music (including six symphonies, four piano sonatas and three operas) is negligible; his ballet and his autobiography are essential works for anyone interested in seeing just what fun could be had by pandering to other people's wide-eyed credulity about what constituted art.

BABBITT, Milton (born 1916)
American composer and teacher

A mathematician as well as a musician – and, from 1938, a Princeton professor – Babbitt was faced early by the gulf between the serial complexities of the music he wrote and the fallibility of the performers who had to play it. At first he solved (or at least lessened) the problem by scaling down his forces: he wrote little for orchestra, and concentrated on solo piano works (e.g. *3 Compositions*, 1947) and on chamber music (e.g. *Composition for 4 Instruments*, 1948; *String Quartets 1 and 2*, 1948, 1954; *Woodwind Quartet*, 1953). These are in a spare, cerebral style similar to *Webern's; the fast music has a delirious and spectral quality, as if written to accompany film of skittering insects. In 1959 Babbitt was given access to the Mark II RCA synthesizer at the Columbia–Princeton Center, a machine which could generate (or imitate) any kind of sound, taking its instructions from the composer in the form of punched-paper tape. (Compositions involving this machine are not random, like some later electronic music; they are as strictly determined, as subject to mathematics, as the most rigorously constructed 'orthodox' scores.) The possibilities electronic sound-generation offered Babbitt for complexity and for accuracy in performance affected all his later work. Some of it is exclusively electronic (e.g. *Composition for Synthesizer*, 1961; *Ensembles* *for Synthesizer*, 1962); but most of it blends electronic and human sounds, producing results which are ethereal and delicately wrought, the musical equivalent of paintings by Klee or the pointillistes. Typical works are *Philomel* (1964) for soprano and tape, *Concerti* (1974) for violin, orchestra and tape, and *Reflections* (1974) for piano and tape. Two further *String Quartets* (No. 3, 1970; No. 4, 1970), for humans alone, are more relaxed and outgoing than Babbitt's pre-electronic music; not his most characteristic scores, they are nevertheless his most accessible.

Babbitt's other works include *Relata I and II* for orchestra (1965; 1968); *Music for the Mass* (1941) and *More Phenomena* (1977) for choir; *Partitions* (1957) and its splendid re-composition *Post-Partitions* (1966) for piano, and *Phenomena* (1974) for soprano and tape.

BARBER, Samuel (1910–81)
American composer

Barber is one of the few contemporary 'serious' composers whose music is familiar to millions: his *Adagio for Strings* (1938, an arrangement made for Toscanini of the slow movement of his 1936 *String Quartet*) is a serene processional which became world-famous when it was played on television throughout the day of President Kennedy's death in 1963. Though it is hardly Barber's best work, its blend of tunefulness and harmonic astringency is typical of his music. Like *Walton in Britain and *Prokofiev in Russia, Barber was stylistically a late-romantic, influenced by few of the harsher experiments of 20th-century music (though he made agreeable use of the harmony and spiky motor-rhythms of jazz). His best music, written in the 1930s and 1940s, includes the score for Martha Graham's ballet *Medea/Cave of the Heart*, two symphonies, relaxed concertos for violin, cello and piano, sonatas for cello and for piano (an excellent piece), and several vocal works including *Dover Beach, Knoxville: Summer of 1915, Andromache's Farewell* and many songs. After the disastrous critical reception of his opera *Antony and Cleopatra* (it was commissioned for the glittering 1966 opening of the Lincoln Center, New York; Zeffirelli's costume designs and production, described by one critic as 'artifice masquerading with a great flourish as art', flattened the music – and the music hardly put up a fight), his career faltered. None the less, he was one of the best second-rank composers of the century, and a handful of works (*Piano Sonata, Violin Concerto, Knoxville*, even *Adagio for Strings*) deserve their popularity.

Barber's other works include the operas *Vanessa* (1958) and *A Hand of Bridge* (1959), the ballet *Souvenirs* (1955), three *Essays* for *Orchestra* (1938; 1942; 1978), the vocal works *Hermit Songs* (1953) and *Prayers of Kierkegaard* (1954), the *Capricorn Concerto* (1944) for small orchestra and *Summer Music* (1956) for wind quintet.

BARTÓK, Béla (1881–1945)
Hungarian composer

In his teens and twenties, Bartók's formidable creativity – he was one of the most productive composers of the century – was hampered by the lack of a truly individual style. Although his early works have personality, they are heavily influenced by Bach and Liszt (of whose piano music he was a virtuoso exponent) and by Richard *Strauss (whose tone-poem *Also Sprach Zarathustra* inspired him in 1903 to write an epic Hungarian equivalent, *Kossuth*). His *Piano Quintet* (1904), *Rhapsody* for piano and orchestra (1904) and two cheerful orchestral *Suites* (1905; 1907) are close kin to Liszt's *Hungarian Rhapsodies* and Brahms's *Hungarian Dances*, with the result that they sound now (to ears used to later Bartók) workmanlike but anodyne.

In 1905, with *Kodály, Bartók began a systematic collection of Magyar folk-music, touring the country districts and recording his discoveries on wax cylinders and in notebooks. (The fruits of this labour were published thirty years later, in the form of an encyclopaedic archive of 2,000 pieces.) His folk-music studies began immediately to affect his own musical style: although many of his works between 1905 and 1917 are exploratory in feeling, and the folk-influences are not fully absorbed, the seeds were sown which led, in works from *String Quartet 2* onwards, to the 'mature' style in which all his later music was composed. In the 19th century, composers who used Hungarian folk-music (they included Schubert and Johann Strauss as well as Brahms and Liszt) 'straightened out' its scales and rhythms to suit prevailing taste: the result was a blood-stirring 'gipsy' style which bore little relation to the originals. Bartók, by contrast, let the un-western scales and irregular rhythms (based on the cadences of Magyar speech) stand unaltered, and devised a style of accompaniment which took its chords from notes of the tune, not from pre-existing notions of 'good harmony': the result is simple, true to the original, and highly exotic to ears used to conventional sounds. He published many folk-song arrangements in this style for voice and piano and for piano solo; more importantly, he began to absorb the harmonies, rhythms and melodic structures of folk-music into his own composing style.

Simultaneously with this folk-research, Bartók was Professor of Piano at the Budapest Conservatory, and a respected recitalist. He wrote extensively for piano: a *Sonata* (1926), three *Concertos* (1926; 1931; 1945), several suites (including *Out of Doors*, 1926), dozens of short pieces (including *Allegro barbaro*, 1911, whose clashing discords and pulsing rhythms once seemed to sum up 'modern music' at its most alarming), and *Mikrokosmos* ('Small World', 1926–39), a set of 153 teaching pieces leading the pupil progressively from five-finger exercises to concert platform and through every available 20th-century piano style. (*44 Duos*, 1931, performs the same pedagogic function for two violins.) The piano is also a partner in two *Sonatas* (1921; 1922) with violin –

among the most 'advanced' and dissonant pieces of their time – and in Bartók's songs, both folk-arrangements and originals.

Bartók's main achievement is in instrumental music: this is the ideal vehicle for his fusion of complex counterpoint, dissonant harmony and rhythmic patterns more intricate than in any previous art-music. His six *String Quartets* (1909; 1917; 1927; 1928; 1934; 1939) are among the peaks of the repertoire: they make as few concessions, either to players or audience, as Beethoven's late quartets, and also share with them a feeling of certainty of aims and methods which is paralleled in Bartók's output only by *Music for Strings, Percussion and Celesta* (1936), one of his most characteristic and thoroughgoing works. His orchestral music, because of its need to accommodate to larger forces and to a less single-minded audience, tempers the austerity of his chamber-music style with colourful scoring and a dash of exuberant romanticism. (His 'night-music' slow movements, full of insect-like rustlings and chirpings, are particularly evocative.) The one-act opera *Bluebeard's Castle* (1911, in effect a fifty-minute symphony with two voices), the ballet *The Miraculous Mandarin* (1919) and *Violin Concerto 2* (1938; No. 1 is an immature early work) are outstandingly lush and approachable; *Concerto for Orchestra* (1943) and *Piano Concerto 3* (1945), written during his anguished wartime exile in America, are in a deliberately straightforward style, and are an excellent (and deservedly popular) introduction to his music.

During his lifetime Bartók's work was regarded as the epitome of all that was nastiest and most alienating in 20th-century music: even more than the sounds themselves, the feeling his compositions give of unswerving conviction, of lack of compromise, tended to frighten off critics and listeners alike. In the forty years since his death, however, his works have entered the repertoire, their difficulties have disappeared and their quality has become apparent. His stature in 20th-century music is akin to Beethoven's in the 19th century: he was utterly original, simultaneously revealing new musical possibilities in every form he used and creating a body of masterworks few of his contemporaries could match.

Bartók's other works include the ballet *The Wooden Prince* (1916), *Dance Suite* (1923), *Cantata Profana* (1930) for chorus and orchestra, *Sonata for Two Pianos and Percussion* (1937), *Divertimento* (1939) for strings and *Sonata* (1944) for solo violin. Good study: H. Stevens: *The Life and Music of Béla Bartók* (rev. edn 1964; includes music examples). B. Suchoff (ed.): *Béla Bartók: Essays* (1976).

BAX, Arnold (1883–1953)
British composer

With Yeats, Bax was one of the chief enthusiasts for the Celtic revival in the arts. His best works are folk-inspired songs (e.g. *Three Irish Songs*, 1922), choral pieces (e.g. *St Patrick's Breastplate*, 1923), and a series of orchestral tone-poems as expressive of their Celtic background as *Sibelius's are of Finnish mythology: typical titles are *In the Faery Hills*

(1909), *The Garden of Fand* (1913), *Tintagel* (1917) and *The Tale the Pine Trees Knew* (1931). The shortness of these works, and their adherence to specific stories or themes (the 'garden of Fand', for example, is the sea), keep Bax's luxuriant invention in check and discipline the music: his style lacks the energetic musical impetus which wings even the smallest Sibelius score, and his longer works (e.g. the seven *Symphonies*, 1921, 1925, 1929, 1931, 1932, 1934, 1939, for devotees – and, in another sense, for detractors – the quintessence of his art) tend to the same kind of elegiac meandering, relieved by occasional passages of greater dynamism, like Powys's novels or De la Mare's nature-poetry. The fault, in each case, is the same: the clothing of elusive subject-matter in rhapsodic forms, instead of the brisk corseting which would control it and give it shape. Perhaps conscious of this improvisatory slackness, Bax in later music tried to incorporate a more sprightly, neo-classical formality. Sometimes, e.g. in his 1938 *Violin Concerto*, this worked well, but in general neo-classical objectivity fought with his lush inspiration to damaging effect. It is for his earlier works (especially the tone-poems and *Symphonies 3 and 7*) that his name will live.

Bax's other works include four piano sonatas, three string quartets, a quantity of other chamber music, a cello concerto, and numerous vocal works including the beautiful neo-Renaissance motet *Mater ora filium* (1921). He also wrote prose and poetry (under the pseudonym Dermot O'Byrne), and published an autobiography, *Farewell, My Youth* (1943). Massive but fine study: L. Foreman: *Bax: A Composer and His Times* (1983).

BERG, Alban (1885–1935)
Austrian composer

Until he was nineteen, Berg had no particular intention of being a composer. He had a small private income and a post in the Viennese civil service; he threw himself with gusto into the avant-garde artistic life of the time, and his friends included the painters Klimt and Kokoschka, the poet Altenberg (an early Dadaist), the architect Gropius and such composers as Mahler and *Schoenberg. In 1904 Berg began composition lessons with Schoenberg, and he, Schoenberg and *Webern became so closely identified as a group (Vienna at the time was a great place for groups and cliques) that they were nicknamed the 'second Viennese school' (the first had included Haydn, Beethoven and Schubert). From this time on, though he worked slowly, producing one major work every two years or so, Berg concentrated on composition.

Berg's early enthusiasm for expressionist and *art-nouveau* styles remained with him throughout his life, and materially affected his composing style. His music resembles *art-nouveau* painting in its combination of strictly disciplined forms and styles – rondos, fugues, passacaglias etc. underlie even his operatic scenes, and he made extensive use, when he needed firm harmonic control, of the 12-note system – with overt and exuberant emotionalism, seen for example in the markings for the movements of his *Lyric Suite* (1926) for string quartet: 'jovially', 'amorously', 'mysteriously', 'with passion' and 'desolately'. His largest works are two operas based on grim expressionist plays, Büchner's *Woyzeck*, about a down-trodden soldier who kills the girl he loves, and Wedekind's *Earth Spirit* and *Pandora's Box*, conflated by Berg into a single story, *Lulu*, about an amoral woman preying on men until she is murdered by Jack the Ripper. (Berg's choice of this subject may have been influenced by Pabst's atmospheric and erotic film, *Pandora's Box*, made in 1928 and starring the hypnotically sensuous Louise Brooks.) Berg's operas (*Wozzeck*, 1925; *Lulu*, 1935, completed 1979 – the third act, left incomplete by Berg, could only be added after his widow's death) treat these doom-laden tales with a strong sense of musical and dramatic impetus, and with a compassion for the characters which elevates what might otherwise be sordidly sensational material.

Apart from opera, Berg's main works are instrumental. Several (*Piano Sonata*, 1908; *String Quartet*, 1910; *Three Pieces for Orchestra*, 1914) are in an intensely emotional style, a musical counterpart to the swirling expressionist paintings of Kokoschka; others (notably *Chamber Concerto*, 1925, for violin, piano and wind orchestra, and *Lyric Suite*) are in a more cerebral and disciplined style (despite the emotive instructions on the score of *Lyric Suite*). His masterpiece, with *Wozzeck*, is a *Violin Concerto* (1935) written in memory of Gropius's eighteen-year-old daughter Manon. Its scheme is highly pictorial (the girl's innocence is depicted by a lilting Carinthian folk-tune, her beauty by an ecstatic theme for solo violin, the approach of death by lurching orchestral chords, and the Christian resignation of her parents and friends by direct quotation, harmony and all, of Bach's setting of the chorale 'It Is Enough'); its musical fabric is woven from a 12-note row organized to conform both with the open strings of the violin and the key of G minor; none of this preliminary cerebration (typical of Berg's painstaking approach to his art) is, however, audible in the music, which sounds as unified, fresh and urgently inspired as if it had been composed at a single sitting.

Berg's other works include several sets of songs (among them *Five Altenberg Songs*, 1912), *Four Pieces* (1913) for clarinet and piano, and a concert aria, *Wine* (1929), for soprano and orchestra, on poems by Baudelaire. He also issued sections of other works in orchestral arrangements: three movements from the *Lyric Suite*, three fragments from *Wozzeck*, a *Lulu-Symphony*. Good study: M. Carner: *Alban Berg: The Man and the Work* (rev. edn 1983; this includes music examples, but is particularly lucid on the ways Berg put the 12-note system to work). Interesting correspondence: H. Berg (ed.): *Alban Berg: Letters to His Wife* (1971).

BERIO, Luciano (born 1925)
Italian composer

In his thirties Berio ran the electronic-music department of Italian Radio; in his fifties, he was head of the 'electro-acoustical section' of IRCAM, the Paris institute for musical research run by *Boulez. Though pure electronic music is only a fragment of his enormous output (half a dozen works out of over 100), Berio adapted the techniques of electronic composition to music produced by ordinary performers. In particular, he is fond of peppering his works with quotations from his own or other people's music, snippets which are distorted and worked upon in performance in much the same way as an electronic composer manipulates and transforms components of pre-recorded or specially generated sound. Berio's *Sinfonia* (1969), for example, involves his eight soloists (the work was composed for the close-harmony group Swingle II) and orchestra in aleatory improvisation on material including elements from Mahler, Beethoven, Wagner, *Ravel, Johann Strauss and Richard *Strauss; in *Circles* (1960), written for his then wife, the singer-actress Cathy Berberian, the soloist screams, whistles, whispers and grunts as well as singing, and her performance is echoed and 'commented upon' by an instrumental group. Fascination with the mechanics of performance led to Berio's most sustained series of compositions, eleven *Sequenzas* (1958–present day) for such avant-garde soloists as Berberian, Globokar (trombone), Holliger (oboe) and Yamashta (percussion). These works are as vivid, and as extraordinary, as some of Paganini's or Liszt's must have sounded to 19th-century audiences – and may prove as musically ephemeral. Berio has reworked several of them, adding 'commentary' by instrumental groups and tape-modulation: the series, called *Chemins*, is typical of his appealingly unserious, let's-see-what-fun-we-can-have approach to music-making, and places him well towards the Dada end of the avant-garde.

Berio's other works include *Opera* (a three-act piece which originated in 1960 and is still growing as new commentaries are added to the original material), *Coro* (1969), Neruda poems reworked for no less than forty voices and instruments, *Concerto for 2 Pianos* (1973), with *Sinfonia* his most substantial work, *A-ronne* (1974), a 'radiophonic documentary' for eight speaking voices and tape-modulator, and *A King Listening* (1984), a luscious, lavish theatre-piece using ideas from Shakespeare's *Tempest*. Interesting self-revelation: *Two Interviews* (trs. Osmond-Smith, 1984).

BERNSTEIN, Leonard (born 1918)
American composer and conductor

Bernstein has always had the knack of introducing music to a wide audience without patronizing simplification or lowering of brows: as a conductor, he popularized Mahler's symphonies; in his 1950s television lectures he zestfully explained matters as abstruse as counterpoint and tempo; his compositions range from Broadway hits to 12-note symphonies. As a composer he is best known for his musicals *On the Town* (1944, the basis of a Gene Kelly/Frank Sinatra film), *Wonderful Town* (1953) and especially *West Side Story* (1957), for the jazz ballet *Fancy Free* (1944) and for the film score for *On the Waterfront* (1954). He also wrote three symphonies, the second of which (1949) is a meditation on Auden's poem *The Age of Anxiety* with a musical range from extreme dissonance to bouncy solo-piano jazz, and the third (1963) is a setting of *Kaddish* for speaker, singers and orchestra. His *Chichester Psalms* (1965), written for the 900th anniversary of Chichester Cathedral, England, his *Mass* (1971), written for the opening of Lincoln Center, New York (and including a part for dancer), and his *Songfest* (1976), composed to celebrate the American Bicentennial, are in an equally eclectic and engaging variety of styles – but the over-riding impression, as always with Bernstein, is of a single mind firmly in control, of attractive unity made from diversity. No one has ever trodden the borderline between 'serious' and 'popular' music with such stylish ease.

Bernstein's other works include the ballet *Facsimile* (1946), *Serenade after Plato's Symposium* (1954) for violin and orchestra, and the musical comedy *Candide* (1956), with a libretto, after Voltaire, by Lillian Hellman, and an overture as popular with modern orchestras and audiences as any by Rossini. His television lectures, published as *The Joy of Music* (1960), are as lively and informative to read as they were to see. His autobiography *Findings* (1983) is showbiz rather than musical, but none the worse for that.

BLACHER, Boris (1903–75)
German composer

Blacher made his gesture to musical serious-mindedness by inventing a technical device, 'variable meters'. (He organized the beats of each bar to fit pre-ordained and regularly repeated patterns, as the semitones of the scale are in 12-note music: a typical sequence might be 3–4–5–4–3 etc.) None the less, the effect of his work is anything but intellectual: helped by cheerful tunes and uncluttered harmony, his music is jazzy, rhythmically unexpected, and full of wit: its nearest analogues are the lighter scores of *Milhaud, or *Copland's *El salón México*. He wrote operas (one of them incorporating electronic sounds, another, *Abstract Opera No. 1*, 1953, a storyless sequence of 'moods' – fear, love, pain, etc. – expressed in nonsense-sounds), chamber music (including five string quartets) and many pieces for orchestra (including seven concertos, for various instruments). The best introductions to his accomplished, fluent music are *Variations on a Theme of Paganini* (1947), *Orchestral Ornaments* (1953, a particularly lively example of variable meter) and *Trumpet Concerto* (1970).

BLISS, Arthur (1891–1975)
British composer

Bliss was one of those dedicated camp-followers who, in every art, use with style and panache the language perfected by greater contemporaries, and make it accessible to audiences unwilling to walk always on the peaks. Thus, his early works (typical are *Rout*, 1919, for soprano and chamber group, all nonsense-syllables, ragtime rhythms and 'wrong-note' harmony, and the aptly named *Mêlée fantasque*, 1921, for orchestra) have a reach-me-down 1920s piquancy derived from *Stravinsky or *Ravel, and his later music affects a late-Edwardian style mid-way between *Elgar and *Walton (typical pieces are *Clarinet Quintet*, 1932, *Piano Concerto*, 1939, and the marches and fanfares he wrote as Master of the Queen's Music from 1953). Unlike most journeymen, however, Bliss several times transcended well-worn language to create works of real distinction: his *Colour Symphony* (1922) is as good as anything by Elgar, his *Music for Strings* (1935) is a masterpiece to rank with *Bartók's *Divertimento*, and his film score for *Things to Come* (1935, later made into a concert suite) rivals Walton's music for *Hamlet* or *Henry V*.

Other worthwhile works by Bliss include the elegiac, pastoral song-cycle *Lie Strewn the White Flocks* (1929), the anti-war choral symphony *Morning Heroes* (1930) and the ballets *Checkmate* (1937) and *Miracle in the Gorbals* (1944).

BLOCH, Ernest (1880–1959)
Swiss/American composer

Bloch's best-known works are an attempt to express in music the grandeur he found in Old Testament legend and history. To a style which was basically late-romantic (derived from Mussorgsky, Rimsky-Korsakov and other late-19th-century Russians) he added the scales and intervals of traditional Jewish sacred music: the result, if at times reminiscent of the music for a De Mille Biblical epic, is at its best compellingly passionate and austere – *Israel Symphony* (1916), *Schelomo* (*Solomon*, 1916) for cello and orchestra, *Baal shem* (1923) for violin and orchestra, and above all his huge choral setting of *Avodath hakodesh* (*Sacred Service*, 1934). Some of the splendour and waywardness of this music (relatable to no western tradition, it sometimes seems like a demandingly assertive party-guest in concerts of 'ordinary' works; Bloch's compositions are best programmed with nothing but each other) spills over into his other works, which are in a harder-edged, more dissonant style reminiscent of *Roussel or early *Bartók. His best pieces in this manner are two *Concerti grossi* (1925; 1953), a fine *Violin Concerto* (1938) and five deeply felt *String Quartets* (1916; 1946; 1951; 1954; 1956), neglected today in favour of Bartók's (whose excellence they rival) and *Shostakovich's (which they eclipse).

Bloch's other major works include the opera *Macbeth* (1910), *Concerto Symphonique* (1948) for piano and orchestra, *Suite* (1919) for viola and orchestra, and *Symphony in E flat* (1955). Interesting writings: *Essays on the Philosophy of Music* (trs. Palmer, 1984).

BOULEZ, Pierre (born 1925)
French composer and conductor

Boulez's first half-dozen works (*Sonatina for Flute and Piano*, 1946; *Piano Sonatas 1 and 2*, 1946, 1948; *Livre pour quatuor*, 1949; *Le Visage nuptial*, 1947) announced him as one of the most radical and talented members of the then avant-garde: they are formidably difficult to perform, and in an advanced serial idiom whose complexities take many hearings (and even devoted study of programme analyses and scores) fully to understand. His interest in mathematical systems led him first to 'total serialism' (in which dynamics, speeds, rhythms and methods of attack were all subject, like the notes, to pre-arranged numerical ordering – typical works are *Polyphonie X*, 1951, for eighteen instruments and *Structures Book I*, 1952, for two pianos, his most uncompromising composition) and then to electronic music (*Études I and II* for tape, 1952). Finally, in 1955, he produced one of the great 'hits' of the avant-garde, *Le Marteau sans maître* ('The Masterless Hammer'), a set of nine atmospheric poetry-settings as coherent and self-confident as *Schoenberg's *Pierrot lunaire*, which it superficially resembles, and *Britten's *Serenade*, which it does not.

At this point, Boulez's career changed direction. Beginning with a period as music-director for the Barrault–Renaud theatre company, he began conducting. He established the Domaine Musicale concerts of contemporary music in Paris in 1953, and spent the next thirteen years travelling and conducting across the world (he was, for example, chief conductor of the BBC Symphony Orchestra from 1971 to 1975, and of the New York Philharmonic from 1971 to 1974; he conducted the centenary production of Wagner's *Ring* at Bayreuth in 1976, a staging whose novelty set Wagner-purists foaming at the mouth). His work as a conductor was crucially important for public acceptance of 20th-century music: he regularly programmed *Schoenberg, *Berg, *Webern and others, persuasively urging them on orchestras and audiences. (He was particularly successful with Webern.) His own compositions became more sporadic, owing partly to shortage of time and partly to an expressed reluctance ever to finish a work, to declare it complete – and his style continually mellowed, so that works which at first were as strenuous and difficult as they were short became, with every revision, larger and more appealing to the ear. (A good example is *Éclats*, a chamber-music piece on which he worked from 1965 to 1971, and which eventually became the scintillating *Éclats/Multiples*, 1976, for large orchestra.)

In 1977 Boulez returned to Paris to head IRCAM (Institute for the

Research and Co-ordination of Acoustics and Music); since then his music has involved a blend of live performers and electronics, and his works have returned to the mastery of his earlier style, without ever surrendering to its audience-alienating complexity. A characteristic late piece, and a masterpiece, is *Répons* (begun 1981, revised 1982 and still evolving). In this, a small orchestra is placed in the centre of the hall, with the audience sitting all round it; six soloists sit at points outside and around the audience; the musical fabric is controlled and electronically modulated by a computer-operator at one side. The methods by which the sounds are made are as complex as ever (they range from total serialization to aleatory improvisation), but the effect is gentle and agreeable, as if several Far-Eastern groups (*gamelans* from Java, *samisen*-players from Japan, Indian sitarists) had strayed into a more orthodox concert of the western avant-garde. But the work is more than tinkly surface: just as the music itself grows at each performance, as composer and performers see new possibilities in the original notes, so it grows in the listener's mind, until what was sensually attractive becomes also intellectually engrossing and satisfying. This interaction between composer, performer and listener precisely fulfils Boulez's often-stated ambitions for the art of music as a whole.

Boulez's other music includes the partly aleatory *Piano Sonata 3* (1956–7), *Structures Book II* for two pianos (1957–62), *Pli selon pli* (1957–65), 'improvisations on Mallarmé' for soprano and orchestra, and *Domaines* for clarinet, instruments and tape (begun 1961, still incomplete). Those of his writings available in English include *Notes of an Apprenticeship* (1968), *Boulez on Music Today* (1971) and the particularly revealing *Conversations with Célestin Deliège* (1977). Brief study (helpful, though sometimes technical): P. Griffiths: *Boulez* (1978).

BRIDGE, Frank (1879–1941)
British composer

For some years after his death, Bridge was chiefly remembered as *Britten's composition teacher and as a composer in a gently pastoral, outmoded 'British-rhapsodic' style, like downmarket *Delius or more than usually vapid *Vaughan Williams. (The worst of these works are his 'Phantasy' quartets and trio of the 1900s; the best are his solo songs, e.g. *Go Not Happy Day* or *Love Went A-Riding*.) In the 1960s and 1970s, as his later music began to be performed, he was shown to be a far tougher, more modern-minded composer, with a visionary style embracing pungent dissonance as well as pastoral: *Ives's music offers a parallel. Most of Bridge's best later music is for small forces (five string quartets, string trio, violin sonata, piano sonata and so on); his masterpiece, however, is a large-scale work for cello and orchestra, *Oration* (1930). It may be that his reputation is as inflated now as it was once depressed: he is a composer (again like Ives) assessment of whose quality depends very much on each listener's subjective taste. None the less, the indications are that much of his post-1920 music is made to last.

Bridge's other works include the orchestral tone-poems *The Sea* (1911), *Summer* (1914) and *Enter Spring* (1927), and a shapely *Sonata* (1917) for cello and piano.

BRITTEN, Benjamin (1913–76)
British composer

With the exception of *Stravinsky, Britten was the most internationally successful 'serious' composer of the century: in his heyday, as a rival once remarked, 'Ben only has to sneeze and it's immediately performed, published and recorded'; his works (many premièred at the Aldeburgh Festival, which he founded in 1948) were written for leading performers (Pears, Brain, Rostropovich, Fischer-Dieskau), and their circulation was usually guaranteed by 'definitive' recordings made by the original artists. His *Variations and Fugue on a Theme of Purcell* (*Young Person's Guide to the Orchestra*, 1946) was once as popular as *Prokofiev's *Peter and the Wolf*, and introduced classical music to countless thousands; his children's pieces (of which the best is the miracle-play opera *Noye's Fludde*, 1958, with parts for performers of every kind from professional soloists to infants wearing animal-masks and their seniors tapping coffee-mugs to simulate raindrops) are regularly performed and enjoyed throughout the world.

The reason for Britten's success is less the 'common touch' which denigrators often attribute to him than inspired technical competence. His 'ear', his ability to find exactly the chord, phrase or instrumental sound for every eventuality, was one of the surest in the business – a good example is his casting of the fairies in *A Midsummer Night's Dream* (1960) as boys, whose unearthly, fluty singing is topped by making their king, Oberon, a counter-tenor. His finest works are vocal, and the range is from opera (*Peter Grimes*, 1945; *Billy Budd*, 1951; *The Turn of the Screw*, 1954; *A Midsummer Night's Dream*; *Three Church Parables*, 1964, 1966, 1968) to song-cycles as intense as Wolf's (*Holy Sonnets of John Donne*, 1945; *Winter Words*, 1953; *The Poet's Echo*, 1965). His vocal masterpieces are the song-cycles for voice and orchestra *Les Illuminations* (1939) and *Serenade* (1943), and the magnificent *War Requiem* (1961), which intersperses a choral-and-orchestral setting of the Requiem Mass as grand as Verdi's with bitter poems on the futility of war by Wilfred Owen, scored for two solo voices and chamber orchestra.

Britten's orchestral and instrumental works, though no less numerous, are slenderer: lacking the prop of words, his musical gestures tend to pall on repetition. His best pieces either consist of short, well-contrasted episodes (*Variations on a Theme of Frank Bridge*, 1937, for strings; *Four Sea Interludes from Peter Grimes*, 1944, for orchestra), are consciously depictive (*Sinfonia da Requiem*, 1940 – elegiac feelings always inspired him), or are fuelled by virtuosity in performance (*String Quartets 2 and 3*, 1945, 1975; *Sonata*, 1961, *Cello Symphony*, 1963 and three solo *Suites*, 1964, 1967, 1971, all written for the dazzling cellist Rostropovich). These are the peaks of an enormous output, of steady quality: for over forty years, Britten produced at least one worthwhile or striking work a year.

Of Britten's other works, the most significant are *Piano Concerto* (1938), *Violin Concerto* (1939), the operas *Albert Herring* (1947) and *Death in Venice* (1973), the vocal *Canticles I–V* (1947; 1952; 1954; 1971; 1974) and *Six Hölderlin Fragments* (1958). Good picture-book: D. Mitchell and J. Evans (eds.): *Benjamin Britten: Pictures from a Life* (1978). Good critical studies: P. Evans: *The Music of Benjamin Britten* (1979) (technical); M. Kennedy: *Britten* (1981) (clear and untechnical).

CAGE, John (born 1912)
American composer

The combination of Dada inspiration and genius, rare in all the arts, is virtually non-existent in music, where the element of performance allows Dada ideas a brief, brilliant flourish followed by long oblivion. The exception to this rule is Cage. His music is not only spectacular in performance, but lasting: it both survives in its own right and has influenced almost every musician who has worked with it. He is devoted, he has said, to 'the principle of originality', and his starting-point is the bankruptcy of the western musical tradition: this claim usefully frees him to make 'music' of any kind and in any way he chooses, since knowing that he has nothing to say, and saying it, 'is poetry'. From this philosophy spring his more lunatic-fringe works, e.g. *4'33"* (which consists of a player sitting in silence at a piano while the audience coughs, shuffles, whispers, sniggers or otherwise copes as best it can), or *Theatre Piece* (1960), a 'happening' in which a man is slung upside-down with a sliced watermelon in a bag, a nude cellist smokes a cigar, a Japanese waves flags and dozens of balloons are released and popped.

Of Cage's more serious contributions to music, to what he claims is a systematic exploration of the natures of sound and silence, the most important were the invention of the 'prepared piano' and the music he wrote for it. To 'prepare' a piano, you stick an assortment of objects (rubber erasers, corks, clothes-pegs, paper-clips, pieces of cloth) against selected strings: this modifies both the sound and the (usually perfectly straightforward) musical patterns you play on the keys. The sound is partly a piano's (somewhat muffled and tinny), and partly like that of an extremely discreet percussion ensemble, a *gamelan* from outer space. Cage's *Sonatas and Interludes* (1948) for prepared piano and his *Concert* (1951) for prepared piano and orchestra are major works: long, hypnotic pieces (their influence on such men as *Ligeti and *Reich is marked) which seduce the willing listener into a species of receptive trance. (Cage is a Zen Buddhist, and the link between music and self-discovery through meditation is central to his art.) In other works Cage introduces aleatory elements, by basing performance-choices on the rolling of dice (the notes they indicate are chosen in advance by reference to the *I Ching* or *Book* *of Changes*), or by encouraging each member of an orchestra to decide independently what part of the score to play next. (*Atlas eclipticalis*, 1962, for orchestra and tape, is a piece of this kind.)

Cage has been as widely mocked as he has been imitated, and his music has not so far found its way into regular concert programmes (as Ligeti's or Reich's works have). It may be that his fate will be merely to have paved the way for others. If that happens, the loss will be ours, for underneath its posed frivolity, his music has elegance and strength.

Cage's 'happenings' (or 'intermedia events', as he poker-facedly calls them) include *Musicircus* (1967), *HPSCHD* (1969, for seven harpsichords and 'at least fifty-one tape machines') and *Renga* (1976, composed for the American Bicentennial). His more serious work includes *Imaginary Landscapes I–V* (1939–62), *Music for Piano* (1952–6) and *String Quartet* (1950). Of his vigorous writings and lectures, typical collections are *Silence* (1961), *A Year from Monday* (1967) and *Empty Words* (1980). Useful essays by others: R. Kostelanetz (ed.): *John Cage* (1970).

CARTER, Elliott (born 1908)
American composer

Before and during the Second World War, Carter's music was astringently neo-classical: his harmony recalled *Ravel's, his rhythm and orchestration *Stravinsky's. (Typical works are *Symphony 1*, 1942, and *Holiday Overture*, 1944, for orchestra, the ballet *Pocahontas*, 1939, and several choral pieces including *To Music*, 1937, and *The Defence of Corinth*, 1941.) The style reappears in some late vocal works (e.g. *A Mirror in Which to Dwell*, 1975; *6 Poems by Elizabeth Bishop*, 1976), and in the Couperin-inspired *Sonata* (1952) for flute, oboe, cello and harpsichord, his most beguiling score.

In the mid-1940s, beginning with *Piano Sonata* (1946), Carter began experimenting with serial and aleatory methods of organization, and finally evolved a style as rigorous as *Bartók's, as forceful as *Tippett's, in which he has since composed a dozen outstanding works. (Like Bartók's and Tippett's music, his is hard to play and initially thorny on the ear, and this has made its acceptance a slow process; it is only as players and listeners have caught him up, learnt his language, that his genius has become apparent.) Rather than with 12-note series, he works with harmonic 'cells' of three or four notes, building intricate counterpoint from them much as Bach did with his short fugue subjects. (Carter builds his cells into chords as well as themes, and so produces a degree of piercing dissonance.) He allows the rhythm of each individual player's music to grow by its own linear impulse, apparently independent of the others: the music often appears to be moving at several speeds at once. These procedures make some of Carter's works sound complex even after repeated hearings: his three *String Quartets* (1951; 1959; 1972), for example, though regarded by many as his finest achievement, never ingratiate. In his larger-scale compositions, however, the technique is somewhat eased to allow clarity of performance, and his earlier neo-classical leanings also lend the music grace: *Variations* (1955) for orchestra, *Double Concerto* (1961) for harpsichord, piano and two orchestras, *Concerto for Orchestra* (1969), *Symphony for Three Orchestras* (1977) and *Triple Duo* (1983).

Carter's other works include *Quintet* (1948) and *Eight Études and a Fantasy* (1950) for woodwind, *Syringa* (1978), for baritone (singing in ancient Greek), contralto (singing about the same themes, simultaneously, in English) and chamber group, *Night Fantasies* (1980) for piano, and *To Sleep, to Thunder* (1982), setting Robert Lowell. His *Collected Writings* (1977) shed light on his composing methods and general musical philosophy; they usefully complement A. Edwards: *Flawed Words and Stubborn Sounds: A Conversation with Elliott Carter* (1971), and D. Schiff: *The Music of Elliott Carter* (1983), highly technical, but useful.

CHÁVEZ, Carlos (1899–1978)
Mexican composer and conductor

There is a tendency for nationalist music (e.g. Borodin's in Russia or Albeniz's in Spain) to sound agreeable but lightweight, picture-postcard local colour taking the place of profundity. Chávez, a vigorous propagandist for and conductor of Mexican music, and the inspirer of a whole 'national' style, belongs to a far rarer tradition. He works local inspiration (in his case pre-Colombian Mexican Indian music) into the fabric of his scores, so that although exotic elements are at the music's heart, the composer's own personality and individuality dominate. (*Falla's Spanishness, *Vaughan Williams's Englishness and *Sibelius's Finnishness are similar.) The bulk of Chávez's work is orchestral: six massive symphonies (No. 2, *Sinfonia India*, 1935, and No. 4, *Sinfonia Romantica*, 1953, are outstanding), *Piano Concerto* (1940), *Violin Concerto* (1950) and a grand opera, *The Visitors* (1957; libretto by Chester Kallman, who worked, with Auden, for *Henze and *Stravinsky). In its romantic energy, its grandeur, and its absorption of ethnic inspiration, Chávez's music is analogous to *Bloch's – and, like Bloch, he is under-represented in today's concert programmes and record catalogues.

Chávez's other works include the ballets *New Fire* (1921) and *Horse Power* (1927). Of his few directly 'Mexican' works, the most colourful are *Xochipilli Macuilxochitl* (1940, using folk-instruments and themes) and the three-movement *Toccata* (1942) for six percussionists, a work as unexpectedly substantial as it is bizarre. Interesting lectures (on music in general and national music in particular): *Musical Thought* (1960).

COPLAND, Aaron (born 1900)
American composer

In his twenties, Copland was the French-educated *enfant terrible* of American music. From Paris he brought back all manner of ideas on scoring and dissonance for which the staid subscription-audiences and Brahms-and-Wagner-oriented critics of the time were hardly ready. He then compounded the felony by stirring jazz into his style. His works of the time included *Symphony for Organ and Orchestra/Symphony 1* (1924), *Music for the Theater* (1925) and the particularly jazzy *Dance Symphony* (1925) and *Piano Concerto* (1926); they attracted phrases like the following (from a *New York Telegram* notice of the *Piano Concerto*): '. . . a tremendous fracas . . . gargantuan dance measures, as of a herd of elephants . . . Rhythm runs away with rhythm and key shatters its sabre against key . . .' Perhaps because of such remarks, and fearing that he might become the darling of a navel-scanning clique, Copland in the 1930s set out to simplify his style, to produce music which 'ordinary Americans' could understand. He wrote film scores (for such straight-down-the-line movies as *Of Mice and Men*, *Our Town* and *The Red Pony*); he arranged American folk-tunes and set Emily Dickinson; he wrote a work (*Lincoln Portrait*, 1942) incorporating extracts from the Gettysburgh Address, and composed an opera (*The Tender Land*, 1954) and an overture (*Outdoor Overture*, 1938) for high schools. Above all, he eliminated pungent unprepared dissonance in favour of a sparer harmonic style which has since been so endlessly imitated in films set in the 'wide open spaces' (especially westerns) that it now seems quintessentially American.

This deliberate reduction of difficulty, without dilution of quality, led to some of Copland's finest scores: by the end of the 1940s he was regarded as America's leading composer, the dean of a respectable national school. Devotees may lament his departure from the mould-breaking audacities of his youth – and he himself occasionally reverted to a stiffer style, even using 12-note processes in such works as *Piano Sonata* (1941), *Violin Sonata* (1943), *Piano Quartet* (1950) and the orchestral *Connotations* (1962) and *Inscape* (1967) – but for most music-lovers, his 'American' works are some of the most accessible 'serious' music composed this century.

Copland was at his happiest writing for orchestra. *El salón México* (1936) is a breezy sound-picture of a crowded Mexican dance-hall, full of popular tunes and syncopated rhythms; *Billy the Kid* (1938) and *Rodeo* (1942) apply the same methods to cowboy themes and cowboy melodies, to jaunty effect; *Appalachian Spring* (1944), his most ecstatic score, is a ballet about a Shaker wedding, and draws on the dignified dances and home-spun hymn-tunes of the people it depicts; *Symphony 3* (1946) is that rare thing, a 'modern symphony' as appealing to the ear as to the intellect; *Clarinet Concerto* (1948), composed for Benny Goodman, blends such classical ideas as fugue and aria with the bounce mandatory in a work commissioned by the 'king of Swing'. If the flight from radicalism always produced works of this quality, more 20th-century composers might usefully be persuaded that Less is More.

Copland's other noteworthy works include *Short Symphony* (1934), *Quiet City* (1941), *Dance Panels* (1959), *Nonet for Strings* (1960) and *Music for a Great City* (1964). His *Fanfare for the Common Man* (1942), his single most popular piece – it was even turned into a 1970s disco hit – was agreeably incorporated into the finale of *Symphony 3*. He published several books on music for the ordinary listener: *What to Listen For in Music* (1939); *Music and Imagination* (1952); *The New Music* (rev. 1968). Good studies: A. Berger: *Aaron Copland* (1953); J. Smith: *Aaron Copland* (1955). Reticent autobiography: A. Copland and V. Perlis: *Copland: 1900 Through 1942* (1984).

COWELL, Henry (1897–1965)
American composer and pianist

Cowell's life was, in Lady Bracknell's phrase, crowded with incident. In the 1920s he toured the United States giving recitals of piano pieces in a spiced-up folk idiom (like Percy Grainger's) and enlivened by what he called 'secondal harmonies', clusters of notes produced by pressing down whole clumps of keys with the palm of the hand, the forearms or suitable lengths of wood. (When this palled, he reached inside to twang the strings, and knocked on the sound-board underneath.) Later, as a result of world tours, he became a combination of wild avant-gardist (well up in *Schoenberg, *Bartók and other 1930s bugbears) and mystic: his aim was to synthesize European, Persian, Japanese, Indian and early American musical traditions into a single, universal style. Many of his 1,000 compositions further this ambition: of his twenty symphonies, for example, No. 3 is entitled *Gaelic*, No. 13 *Madras*, No. 16 *Icelandic*; there are two concertos for Japanese *koto* and western orchestra; in *Concerto grosso* (1963) each of the first four movements is based on the music of a different continent, and the fifth movement blends all previous material. Cowell's most lasting work, influenced by his friend *Ives, is a quieter, more serene exploration of the hymns, folk-songs and square-dances of the 19th-century American pioneers. His *Hymns and Fuguing Tunes* (nearly two dozen, for various instruments) show this style at its most appealing, and this restrained music is also the basis of his fine, Ivesian *Sonata 1* (1945) for violin and piano, *Symphonies 4 and 7* (1946; 1947) and *String Quartet 5* (1956). In addition to composing and playing, Cowell was a one-man polemicist for other people's new music, publishing, lecturing and teaching wherever opportunity arose. To dismiss him as an eccentric is to miss the best of him.

DALLAPICCOLA, Luigi (1904–75)
Italian composer

The musical inspiration of Dallapiccola's small but spectacular output was a love of early Italian vocal composers (such as Gesualdo and Monteverdi) and of *Webern; his subjects came equally from ancient Greece and from his own struggle for political and artistic freedom (he was persecuted by the fascists for marrying a Jewess and for his 'anti-musical' leanings towards serialism). His elegant style is heard at its most refined in several short song-cycles for voice and chamber group: *Greek Lyrics* (comprising *Five Sappho Fragments*, 1942, *Six Songs of Alcaeus*, 1943, and *Two Anacreon Lyrics*, 1945), *Concerto for Christmas Night 1956* (1957) and *Commiato* ('Farewell', 1972). In his major works he combined fastidious technique with racked, expressionist subject-matter, and the resulting tension between content and form produces music of extraordinary emotional intensity: Dallapiccola's are among the very few serial works which regularly reduce audiences to tears. His subjects are always imprisonment and the quest for freedom, sometimes literal (as in the choral-and-orchestral *Songs of Imprisonment*, 1941, and *Songs of Liberation*, 1955, and in the powerful short opera *The Prisoner*, 1948, Kafkaesque or Camusian in effect but actually based on Villers de l'Isle Adam's 1880s play *Tormented by Hope*), and sometimes existential (as in the operas *Night Flight*, 1939, and *Ulysses*, 1968, and in the oratorio *Job*, 1950, in which Saint-Exupéry's lone pilot, Homer's wandering hero and the tormented Old Testament sage are each seen as a symbol of restless human aspiration).

Dallapiccola's other music includes *Six Choruses of Michelangelo* (1933), *Variations for Orchestra* (1954, a reworking of his *Annalibera's Notebook*, a piano work written for his daughter), *A Little Night Music* (1954), for small orchestra, his most Webernian piece, and *Tartiniana* (1954) for violin and orchestra, which ear-ticklingly subjects melodic lines by the 18th-century composer Tartini to every conceivable permutation of 20th-century serial technique. Good study, covering all major works except *Ulysses*: R. Vlad: *Luigi Dallapiccola* (1957).

DAVIES, Peter Maxwell (born 1934)
British composer

Few composers of his generation have been as prolific or as fine as Maxwell Davies: though his style is utterly different, he rivals *Stockhausen for fecundity (a rare quality in post-*Webernian serial composers) and *Tippett for his ability to use the most intractable-seeming ideas and the thorniest of means to make works of exhilarating approachability. His use of contemporary serialism is tempered by composition-techniques imitated from the Middle Ages, in particular the ideas of a *cantus firmus* (a line of long, sustained notes binding together a quickly moving surrounding texture) and of development by constant, minute changes in the basic musical shapes: his works, instead of progressing from theme to theme (as Haydn's or Brahms's do), move with a kaleidoscope ebb and flow, their growth as imperceptible as a plant's.

Medieval techniques were especially prominent in Maxwell Davies's early music; often actual medieval themes formed the basis for his ceaselessly permutative style. Characteristic works are *Ricercar and Doubles* (1959) for chamber group, the carol-sequence *O magnum mysterium* (1960) and the two long orchestral *Fantasias on an In Nomine by John Taverner* (1962; 1964). In the mid-1960s he founded a music-theatre group (Pierrot Players, later rechristened The Fires of London), and wrote for it a series of pieces as remarkable for their instrumental virtuosity as for their theatrical panache. In *Eight Songs for a Mad King* (1969), in which George III vainly tries to coax from mechanical birds the music he hears inside his head, vocal and instrumental pyrotechnics egg each other on to stunning effect; *Vesalii icones* (1969) is a concerto-like piece for cello and chamber group, the solo cello providing the 'voice' for a dancer enacting both the Stations of the Cross and the gory anatomical drawings of Vesalius: *Revelation and Fall* (1968), *Miss Donnithorne's Maggot* (1974) and *The Medium* (1982) explore madness and hysteria, giving the solo soprano spectacular shrieks and gibbering as well as song; *Le Jongleur de Notre Dame* (1978) adds a mime artist and a children's percussion band to the standard vocal soloist and chamber group. As well as these highly dramatic concert works, Maxwell Davies has also composed a meaty (or at any rate sinewy) opera, *Taverner* (1972), based on the life of the 16th-century composer who may or may not also have been an anti-Catholic 'secret agent': its scoring, like that of the music-theatre works, gives prominent parts to virtuoso instrumental soloists.

In 1970 Maxwell Davies settled on the island of Hoy in the Orkneys, and many of his subsequent works (e.g. the short opera *The Martyrdom of St Magnus*, 1977, and its pendants *Hymn to St Magnus*, 1972, and *The Blind Fiddler*, 1976) are on specifically Orcadian themes. In addition, his music in general has acquired a bleak expansiveness which some commentators see as a response to the tossing seas and empty horizon of his home: his *Symphonies 1 and 2* (1976; 1980), for example, without abandoning the musical principle of growth-by-metamorphosis, have a spaciousness and grandeur reminiscent of *Sibelius. Isolation has led to Maxwell Davies's most fruitful period yet, and to some of his noblest works: the symphonies, *Stone Litany* (1973), *A Mirror of Whitening Light* (1977), *Piano Sonata* (1981, modelled on the late Beethoven sonatas as the symphonies are modelled on Sibelius), a massive *Organ Sonata* (1983), and the big chamber works *Ave maris stella* (1975) and *Image, Reflection, Shadow* (1982). The scale of these works, and their combination of intellectual intensity and musical authority, are reminiscent of *Messiaen at his grandest (*Et exspecto resurrectionem mortuorum*; *From the Canyons to the Stars*), and confirm

Maxwell Davies not only as an original and a mystic, but as one of the leading composers of the age.

Maxwell Davies's other major works include *St Thomas' Wake* (1969), *Worlde's Blis* (1969) and *Five Klee Pictures* (1976) for orchestra, the triptych *Into the Labyrinth*, *Sinfonia concertante* and *Sinfonietta accademica* (1983) for chamber orchestra, the supernatural short opera *The Lighthouse* (1980), the supernatural theatre-piece *The No. 11 Bus* (1984), which treats the Apocalypse in the joky, surrealist manner of *Ligeti's *Le Grand Macabre*, and the score for Russell's film of religious hysteria and persecution *The Devils* (1971). Good study: P. Griffiths: *Peter Maxwell Davies* (1982).

DEBUSSY, Claude (1862–1918)
French composer

It was Debussy's ambition to create, or revive, a specifically French voice in music, a modern style to equal those of impressionist painting and poetry (on whose rationale, see page 541). In the late 19th century the majority of French musicians trod in the footsteps either of Wagner (César Franck and his pupils) or of Weber (Saint-Saëns and his pupils). The Prix de Rome (which gave the winner a four-year stay in Rome) had since its inception in 1803 fostered a style of pallid academic orthodoxy, Handelian choral fugues and Gluckish musical depictions of the flames, sunsets and heartbeats mentioned in the texts. It was this tradition that Debussy wanted to sweep away – not by creating a new, equally dogmatic school but simply by ridding his own style of cobwebby conventions.

His preferences were eclectic: the uncluttered lines of French 16th-century vocal music (e.g. the *chansons* of Claude le Jeune), the pictorial, highly decorated harpsichord pieces of such 18th-century composers as Couperin and Rameau, the exotic scales and sounds of Far-Eastern music (which he heard at the Paris Exhibition of 1889). To these he added a wish to create sound-equivalents of the subjective art of the impressionists and symbolists: work whose creator's vision was set directly down regardless of its conformity with the received views of others or even with reality itself. (Thus, a Manet poppy-field, a Verlaine description of moonlight or a Debussy piece entitled *Goldfish* tells us nothing *objective* about its subject, but is concerned with the way it appears to the artist and the associations it has for him. When Debussy is described as an 'impressionist' composer – a term which enrages his partisans – this is what is meant.)

The best vehicle for the new style was piano music. (Since Chopin, indeed since Beethoven, composers had regularly used the piano for harmonic and textural experiments, particularly those seeking to depict moods of reverie or fantasy.) Debussy's fourteen books of piano music span his career and contain some of his finest work. At first (e.g. in *2 arabesques*, 1888, and *Suite bergamasque*, 1890–1905) the music is pretty but prone to lumpish experiment (*Clair de lune*, from *Suite bergamasque*, works beautifully both as an evocation of moonlight and as music; *Passepied*, from the same suite, clod-hops in half a dozen styles). In the suite *Pour le piano* (1901) Debussy first produced the synthesis of clean-fingered virtuosity and elusive, unorthodox harmony that mark his mature style; there followed a series of masterworks to equal the output of Chopin or Schumann themselves: *Estampes* ('Engravings', 1903), *Images I and II* ('Pictures', 1905; 1907), *L'Isle joyeuse* ('The Happy Island', 1904, a musical response to Watteau's painting *L'Embarquement pour Cythère*), *Children's Corner Suite* (1908), *12 Studies* (1915), *En blanc et noir* ('Black and White', 1915, for two pianos) and above all the twenty-four pictorial *Preludes* (Book I 1910, Book II 1913) which contain some of his best-known and most characteristic pieces (*The Submerged Cathedral*; *The Girl with Flaxen Hair*; *Minstrels*; *What the West Wind Saw*).

It was in his vocal music that Debussy most closely approached the literary artists he admired. He favoured a cool, neo-classical lyrical style, an unlikely but workable blend of British Pre-Raphaelite other-worldliness and the exquisite gush of Verlaine or Mallarmé. He set cycles of poems by Verlaine (*Ariettes oubliées*, 1888; *Fêtes galantes*, 1892, 1904) and by Mallarmé (*Trois Poèmes de Mallarmé*, 1913), and also a charming group of neo-Grecian poems by Louÿs (who claimed they were by an hitherto unknown ancient poetess), *Songs of Bilitis* (1897). His opera *Pelléas and Mélisande* (1902) was based on Maeterlinck's dreamlike, hallucinatory play, its style reminiscent both of Poe and of Perrault's fairy-tales; he set Rossetti's *Blessed Damozel* (1888) for choir and orchestra, and paid homage to the 16th century in *Three Songs of Charles d'Orléans* (1908) for choir and *Three Ballads of François Villon* (1910) swaggeringly set for voice and orchestra.

The bulk of Debussy's work is suites or cycles of short pieces organized to express contrasting or complementary moods. In his instrumental music, he came up against the problem of using a gestural style to create large-scale, abstract works without the solid constructional techniques of the Germans or the seamless rhapsody of Wagner. His chamber works (*String Quartet*, 1893; *Sonatas* for cello and piano, 1915, flute, viola and harp, 1915, and violin and piano, 1917) solve the problem by ignoring it: they are suites in all but name, unprofound music given the appearance of sonata-unity by the repetition of ideas from movement to movement. Of his orchestral works, two (*Nocturnes*, 1899, musical impressions of three Whistler paintings, and *Images*, 1910, impressions of England, Spain and rural France) are suites, and a third, *L'Après-midi d'un faune* ('A Faun's Afternoon', 1894 – one American critic breezily asked 'When may we look forward to *A Faun's Quarter-after-Five*?') is a tone-poem after Mallarmé's languorous, not to say decadent, verses of adolescent sexual longing in a sunny ancient Greek forest. In *La Mer* ('The Sea', 1905) and the ballet *Jeux* ('Games', 1912), Debussy used a style of ceaseless metamorphosis, achieving symphonic growth by the repetition of short melodic fragments. The result is a unity and intellectual density missing in his other music – the robust new style, in fact, towards which he had been working throughout his career. These scores crown his work, and though he died before he could further explore the style, it crucially influenced the development of 20th-century music (many of whose composers were, like Debussy, in flight from ponderous 19th-century German certainties), and its effects can be seen in the work of men as diverse as *Stravinsky, *Messiaen, *Boulez, *Stockhausen and Maxwell *Davies.

In the 1900s Debussy wrote a series of trenchant magazine articles on music, later published in book form as *Monsieur Croche the Dilettante-Hater* (English edn *Debussy on Music*, trans. Langham Smith, 1977). Debussy's stylish and revealing *Letters* still await English translation, a preposterous state of affairs, in view of the nonentities (musical and otherwise) whose letters *are* available. Good study: E. Lockspeiser: *Debussy: His Life and Mind* (rev. Langham Smith, 1980).

DELIUS, Frederick (1862–1934)
British composer

Encouraged by fanatical supporters (among them Sir Thomas Beecham, who plucked his music from obscurity and made it famous), Delius regularly tried his hand at large-scale works, and failed. (His operas *Koanga*, 1897, and *Fennimore and Gerda*, 1910, his Nietzsche-cantata *A Mass of Life*, 1905, and his five lumbering concertos, of which only the *Violin Concerto*, 1916, has claims on art, utterly lack coherence: they have pleasant moments, but in general, thanks to poor construction, fall over their own pretensions.) His genius was for miniatures, rhapsodic, autumnal meditations meltingly harmonized (in a personal version of the 'endless modulation' of Wagner's *Tristan and Isolde*) and beautifully scored for orchestra, sound-poems trembling on the edge of decadence. His best works are single-movement idylls (*In a Summer Garden*, 1908; *Summer Night on the River*, 1911; *On Hearing the First Cuckoo in Spring*, 1912), or longer pieces given shape by variation-form (e.g. *Brigg Fair: An English Rhapsody*, 1907) or by the poems he set (e.g. *Appalachia*, 1902; *Sea Drift*, 1904; *Songs of Sunset*, 1908, all for voice and orchestra). His 'problem' was that he perfected a style early in life and could thereafter do little more than repeat himself; his 'glory' was that the style was one of ravishing beauty, and led to a handful of the loveliest pieces in the repertoire.

Delius's other worthwhile works include the opera *A Village Romeo and Juliet* (1901), *North Country Sketches* (1914), the choral *Songs of Farewell* (1930) and *Sonata 2* (1924) for violin and piano. Interesting memoirs: E. Fenby: *Delius As I Knew Him* (1936), by his devoted amanuensis; T. Beecham: *Frederick Delius* (1959). Good, enthusiastic study: A. Jefferson: *Delius* (1972). See also L. Carley (ed.): *Delius: A Life in Letters 1862–1908* (1983; a second volume is to follow).

ELGAR, Edward (1857–1934)
British composer

There is more than a grain of truth in the conventional views of Elgar, that he single-handedly woke British music from a 200-year-long doze, and that he epitomized the Edwardian imperial twilight in sound. He was the first British composer of genius since Purcell – we were excellent at craftsmen, Arnes and Wesleys and Sullivans, but distinctly short on Mozarts or Berliozes – and his minor works (e.g. the five *Pomp and Circumstance* marches, of which No. 1, 1901, is *Land of Hope and Glory*) are as unironically ceremonial as the Trooping of the Colour or the Opening of Parliament. But the true Elgar – maybe this was true of thinking Edwardians generally – has a secret soul, and mysticism and introversion regularly undercut surface strut. His first work of world stature, *Enigma Variations* (1899), contains musical impressions of a dozen friends, identified only by nicknames or initials; his *Violin Concerto* (1910) has the mysterious epigraph (in Spanish) 'Here is enshrined the soul of . . .', and a similar note on his *Symphony 2* (1911) is 'Rarely, rarely comest thou, spirit of delight'; his major choral work, his deepest bow in the direction of the 'British cathedral tradition', is a setting of Newman's *The Dream of Gerontius* (1900), about a dying Catholic's vision of his soul being received in heaven. Even when the duality in Elgar's work is less signposted, it exists – and gives the music depth. *Symphony 1* (1908), despite sections of spectacular swagger, keeps returning to a sombre march theme, the ghost of ceremony; the heart of *Falstaff* (1913, Elgar's orchestral masterpiece) is not joviality or pageantry, but an elegiac episode picturing Falstaff's lost innocence (based on his description, in Shakespeare's *Henry IV*, of his childhood as a page-boy); *Cello Concerto* (1919) is a score of most un-Edwardian introspection, alternating fast, spectral whisperings with slower passages (notably the slow movement itself) of heartrending intensity.

Together with the breezy *Cockaigne* overture (1901) and *Introduction and Allegro* (1905) for strings, these works are the best of Elgar. He wrote shelves more music, most of it for special occasions or amateur use (the range is from choral cantatas like *Caractacus*, 1898, to part-songs and pretty pieces for 'light orchestra' like *Salut d'amour*, 1888): like *Sibelius, he was as happy to turn out miniatures as masterworks. He contradicts the supposed British tradition of the gifted but bumbling amateur: his technique was as surefooted as Brahms's, his orchestration as sumptuous as Richard *Strauss's. There has been critical discussion about whether he was a 'gentleman' (he was certainly the darling of the upper-class establishment) or a 'player' – and the question is as irrelevant as it would be for Haydn or *Debussy. He was a composer of memorable and splendid music, and no more need be said.

Elgar's other works include the oratorios *The Apostles* (1903) and *The Kingdom*

(1906), *Sea Pictures* (1899) for voice and orchestra, two *Wand of Youth Suites* (1907, 1908) and *Piano Quintet* (1919). Interesting letters, some briskly business-like, others intimate and sad: P. M. Young (ed.): *Letters of Edward Elgar and Other Writings* (1956). Good study: M. Kennedy: *Elgar* (1968). Also recommended: C. Redwood (ed.): *An Elgar Companion* (1983).

FALLA, Manuel de (1876–1946)
Spanish composer

The chief inspiration of Falla's music is the Moorish-influenced folk-music of Andalusia, whose characteristics are long-held single notes suddenly breaking off in tumbles of short sounds, melodies based on restricted scales of three or four notes, and hypnotically repeated rhythms like those of *flamenco*. As well as folk-elements (which give his works a hot-blooded sway, best heard in such popular pieces as *2 Spanish Dances* from *La vida breve*, 1905, or *Ritual Fire Dance* from *Love the Magician*, 1915), his style is also notable for a coolness and dandyish poise – its effects exactly calculated, not a chord out of place – which some see as typical of the *hidalgo* tradition in Spanish life and others as a link with such neo-classical contemporaries as *Ravel and *Stravinsky. He spent several years in Paris, and worked with Diaghilev and Picasso; the cosmopolitan edge this gave his music tempers its Spanishness, and raises him above more parochial composers like Albeniz or Granados, his immediate predecessors. Apart from his stage works (*La vida breve, Love the Magician, The Three-Cornered Hat*, 1919, and the tiny opera *Master Peter's Puppet Show*, 1922, based on an episode from *Don Quixote*), his finest works are all small-scale: *7 Popular Spanish Songs* (1914), *Fantasia baetica* ('Spanish Fantasy', 1919) for piano solo, and a bustling *Concerto* (1926) for harpsichord and five instruments, a combination of Scarlattian trills and runs and throbbing melodies accompanied by guitar-like chords.

Falla's other works include *4 Spanish Pieces* (1908), the sensuously atmospheric *Nights in the Gardens of Spain* (1916) for piano and orchestra, and the unfinished choral cantata *Atlantis* (completed after his death by Halffter, and still under-performed). Good study: J. Pahissa: *Manuel de Falla. His Life and Works* (English edn 1954).

FELDMAN, Morton (born 1926)
American composer

Avant-garde music in the 1950s acquired a fearsome (and largely justified) reputation with non-devotees: despite programme-notes detailing every complexity of its making, its actual sound was a mixture of abstruse mathematical formulations perceptible to the ear only as chaos and squeaks, scrapes and bangs often at the extremes of aural tolerance. In this Martian wilderness, Feldman's music offered a welcome friendly face. He admired the drip-paintings of Pollock and the abstract expressionism of de Kooning, and his music stands to their work as *Debussy's does to Seurat's or *Webern's to Klee's. His pieces are usually short, murmurously quiet ('consonant' in an avant-garde way), and scored for small forces, often including oscillators and other electronic equipment. He tends to compose on graph paper, not music-staves, giving the performers hints (e.g. 'low, plucked notes, quiet, 4 seconds') rather than the peremptory instructions of more formal music. Typical pieces are *Projections I–V* for chamber ensemble, *4 Songs to e.e. cummings*, for voice, cello and piano, and *Structures* for orchestra; his rustling, chirruping ballet-score for Merce Cunningham, *Summerspace* (1966), is the quintessence of his understated art.

FOSS, Lukas (born 1922)
American composer and pianist

A pupil of *Hindemith, Foss wrote his quota of sturdily contrapuntal, anonymous music: symphonies (notably *Symphony of Chorales*, 1958, each movement based on a Bach chorale), concertos (for piano, 1944, 1951; for oboe, 1950 – a fine work), cantatas (e.g. *Song of Songs*, 1946) and operas (e.g. *The Jumping Frog of Calaveras County*, 1950, after the Mark Twain story). He seemed set to be one of modern music's most accomplished also-rans – and his career as a solo pianist (his recordings include Hindemith's *Four Temperaments* and the glittering piano part in Bernstein's *The Age of Anxiety*) seemed to confirm that he found composition an occupation for wet afternoons. In 1957, however, he formed a group (Improvisation Chamber Ensemble) to specialize in prompted improvisation, the classical-music equivalent of (say) the Modern Jazz Quartet. (The group's stated objective was to 'restore surprise' in music: not to surprise the audience, which only heard each work once, but to surprise the performers and so trigger their creativity.) Foss's 'compositions' for this group include *Time Cycle* (1960), on texts by Auden, Housman, Nietzsche and Kafka, and *Concerto for Improvising Instruments and Orchestra* (1960), in which the orchestral music, fully notated, provides a frame and stimulus for the soloists. His later music blends improvisation and formality in much the same way, producing agreeable results somewhat in the manner of the saner *Cage: *Elytres* (1964) for instrumental group plus 'distant violins', *Phorion* (1967), in which the first movement of Bach's E major violin partita is dismembered and passed round the orchestra ('as the sea washes pebbles on the beach'), and the quotation-packed *Baroque Variations* (1967), a Cook's tour of the 18th-century repertoire, are typically engaging works. Foss is a minor figure, but his music is fun to play, and no hardship at all to hear.

GERHARD, Roberto (1896–1970)
Spanish/British composer

Until the 1950s Gerhard's style was a happy marriage of serial techniques and the colour and rhythm of Spanish folk-music; the line between his music and *Falla's (especially *Master Peter's Puppet Show* and *Harpsichord Concerto*) was clear. The style served him well, not only in abstract works (*Violin Concerto*, 1945; *Viola Sonata*, 1950) but also in ballet (*Ariel*, 1936; *Soirées de Barcelone*, 1938; *Pandora*, 1944; *Don Quixote*, 1950, a particularly perky score), and in opera (*The Duenna*, 1949, which restores Sheridan's play to its Spanish setting, to delightful effect). In the 1950s he 'strengthened' his style, in particular avoiding the repetition of themes and subjects which had been a staple of musical construction since Handel's day. Though one result is that each bar or section becomes interesting in its own right, another is that it can take several hearings for the musical flow, the architecture, to become apparent to the ear. (For some it never does, and Gerhard is the epitome of incomprehensible genius; those whose perseverance is rewarded find him one of *Schoenberg's most sparkling followers.) In this second style (somewhat like *Carter's in sound) he wrote four symphonies, two string quartets, lively *Concertos* (for harpsichord and strings, 1956; for orchestra, 1965), and a series of chamber works named after signs of the zodiac (the best are *Libra*, 1968, and *Leo*, 1969).

Gerhard's other works include *Nonet* (1956), *Hymnody* (1963), *Epithalamium* (1966) and *The Plague* (1964), which surrounds extracts from Camus's novel (spoken or sung) with a musical argument as expressive as it is dissonant.

GERSHWIN, George (1898–1937)
American composer

Musicologists regularly praise Gershwin for his craftsmanship, for the harmonic and rhythmic subtleties underlying even his most commercial songs (*I Got Rhythm* and *Lady Be Good* are favourite examples): he seldom slips, we are assured, into the reach-me-down strumming of Berlin's accompaniments or the melodic clichés of Rodgers or Kern. Music-lovers, by contrast, love Gershwin because he wrote some of the best tunes in the business. His Broadway shows (which include *Oh, Kay*, 1926, with lyrics by Wodehouse, *Funny Face*, 1927, and the riotous *Girl Crazy*, 1930) and his film musicals (e.g. *Shall We Dance?*, 1937, and *The Goldwyn Follies*, 1938) turn silly plots to gold by the quality of the music: a line of Gershwin notes makes the most banal lyrics (e.g. those of *Swanee*, *Love Walked In* or *Nice Work If You Can Get It*) seem like profound statements couched in unforgettable poetry. In his concert works, Gershwin's melodic and rhythmic gifts triumph in a similar way over episodic construction – who cares that the stitches show, when the garments are so stylish? His best-known works are *Rhapsody in Blue* (1924), *Piano Concerto* (1925, the model for, and sound-twin of, *Ravel's *Piano Concerto in G*), the tone-poem *An American in Paris* (1928, later the core of a Gene Kelly film), and *3 Preludes* (1926) for piano solo. His finest work, *Porgy and Bess* (1935), is a grand opera with show-tunes instead of arias; in other hands (*Carousel* springs to mind) the mixture is cutely pretentious, but Gershwin, thanks (again) to the strength of his material (*Summer Time*; *I Got Plenty of Nothin'*; *Bess, You Is My Woman Now*), triumphantly succeeds.

Gershwin's other 'serious' works include *Cuban Overture* (1932) and *I Got Rhythm Variations* (1934) for piano and orchestra. Good study: D. Ewen: *A Journey to Greatness: The Life and Music of George Gershwin* (1956).

GINASTERA, Alberto (1916–83)
Argentinian composer

The power of *Stravinsky's *The Rite of Spring*, its ferocious musical energy, was so great that (almost alone of his works) it swallowed up imitations and founded no tradition. Ginastera's music is the exception. He was drawn to the pre-Colombian cultures of South America, societies founded on ritual and on violence like those of the Aztecs, Mayans and Incas, and the organized frenzy of *The Rite of Spring* offered a model for expressing primitivism and barbarism in disciplined sound. Ginastera's 'Indian' works (the most memorable are the ballet *Panambi*, 1937–40, *Variaciones concertantes* for orchestra, 1953, and the savage *Cantata for Magic America* for soprano and percussion, 1960) take the notion of picture-postcard nationalism to hitherto unheard extremes: they are like abrupt glimpses into an extraordinary past, an alien world as self-contained and self-absorbed as it is strange. In his operas, *Don Rodrigo* (1964), *Bomarzo* (1967) and *Beatrice Cenci* (1971), although the subjects are far from Indian, the treatment is just as uncompromising: *Bomarzo*, in particular, in which stone statues come to lumpish, guttural and mindless life, and which Ginastera himself described as made up of 'sex, violence and hallucination', is one of the most extreme spectacles ever seen on the opera stage, compulsively magnificent or horrible, according to taste. In the 1950s Ginastera began using serial and electronic methods – and paradoxically, instead of making his music harder on the ear, this sharpened it up and gave it an agility and grace hitherto lacking. His five concertos (especially *Harp Concerto*, 1956, and *Violin Concerto*, 1963), his *Concerto for Strings* (1965) and *Symphonic Studies* (1967), and above all his chamber music (*Piano Quintet*, 1963; *String Quartet 3*, with soprano soloist, 1973), are accessibly, even appealingly, neo-classical. He was that rare thing, an artist working in an advanced idiom who never forgets his audience: whether he set out to shock or intrigue, his music was calculated for maximum effect, and it works.

Ginastera's other music includes two church works, *Psalm 150* (1938) and *Turbae ad passionem Gregorianam* (1974), the guitar pieces and sonatas which seem *de rigueur* for all South American composers, a clangy *Piano Sonata* (1952), and three *Pampeanas* (the Argentinian equivalent of *Villa-Lobos's *Bachianas Brasileiras*), of which No. 3 ('Pastoral Symphony', 1954) is at once the most engaging and the best.

HÁBA, Alois (1893–1973)
Czech composer

Like Magritte in painting or Jarry in drama, Hába was utterly original, convinced of the rightness of what he was doing, and seemed a misguided fool to as many of his audience as thought him a genius. Instead of the twelve semitones into which the octave is normally divided (any twelve notes of the piano, black and white in order, up or down), he invented systems of quarter-tones, one-third-tones, one-seventh-tones and even four-fifths-tones, and when conventional instruments were unable to play his works, had pianos, clarinets and trumpets purpose-built. (There was no need to tailor-make string instruments or human voices to cope with microtones: the problem here was helping players and singers cope.) To the untutored listener, habituated to semitones by some 800 years of music and by the basic physical laws of sound, Hába's music can sound prettily or ear-piercingly out of tune. But for those who warm to his experiments – and both Far-Eastern music and modern electronic music also deal in microtones, without provoking riots in the streets – there are several hundred Hába works to enjoy, ranging from quarter-tone operas (e.g. *The Mother*, 1931), one-sixth-tone string quartets and concertos for microtone-playing soloists (*Violin Concerto*, 1954; *Viola Concerto*, 1956) and conventional, if *Schoenbergian, orchestras. He was a footnote to music – and like many footnotes, if you're in the mood, as fascinating as the text.

HANSON, Howard (born 1896)
American conductor and composer

As conductor of the Eastman-Rochester Symphony Orchestra, Hanson directed more than 1,500 first performances of new music (over thirty-five works a year for forty years); much of the music he introduced has remained in the repertory. His own music is expansive and late-Romantic in style (somewhere between *Nielsen's and *Barber's), and expresses such qualities as austerity, restlessness and heroic grandeur (three of his own favourite terms for it). Its core is six large symphonies, often programmatic: No. 1 (1921) and No. 2 (1930) reflect Scandinavian hero-sagas; No. 4 (1943), like *Britten's then-recent *Sinfonia da requiem*, is a wordless expression of sections from the mass for the dead; No. 5 (1955) is based on St John's account of the first Easter. He also composed an opera (*Merry Mount*, 1933) set in 19th-century New England, and several impressive choral works, ranging from *Lament for Beowulf* (1926) to *Song of Democracy* (1957) and *Song of Human Rights* (1963). He wasted little time on trivia: each of his works tackles big themes in a big way, and is a weighty addition to the repertoire.

Hanson's other works include the choral *Heroic Elegy* (1927), *Piano Concerto* (1948) and *Mosaics* (1958) and *Bold Island Suite* (1961) for orchestra. He published an influential textbook, *Harmonic Materials of Modern Music* (1960).

HARRIS, Roy (1898–1979)
American composer

Like *Vaughan Williams, Harris was generous to a fault about accepting commissions, writing music for anyone who asked, with few heart-searchings about self-repetition or lapses in quality. (He composed, for example, an orchestral fantasy on *When Johnny Comes Marching Home*, 1935, and a choral *Ode to Friendship*, 1944; he anticipated Vaughan Williams's *Harmonica Rhapsody* by writing an *Accordion Concerto* in 1946.) For his wife, the concert pianist Johana Duffy, he wrote two concertos and a *Piano Quintet* (1937) in a tougher idiom involving passacaglias, toccatas and fugues. His best work is in his fifteen symphonies. Some are of largely American interest (No. 4, 1940, for high schools, is based on Old American songs; No. 6, 1944, reflects on the Gettysburgh Address, No. 9, 1963, on the Constitution, and No. 10, 1965, on the life of Lincoln); but the majority are straightforward concert pieces, in an idiom moving from *Sibelius-inspired 'wide-open-spaces' music to jazzy fugues. It is a skilful and likeable output, popular with audiences who prefer their modernism without tears – and once or twice (as in the magnificent *Symphony 3*, 1939) Harris surpassed himself.

HENZE, Hans Werner (born 1926)
German composer

During the reign of the Nazis, German musicians were quarantined against radicalism: 'degenerate' artists (i.e., almost by definition, those interested in experiment) were murdered, silenced or compelled to emigrate, and those who remained kept their styles accessible (like *Orff) or lived in a state of permanent uneasiness with the regime (like *Strauss, who was in any case too old and famous to silence, and whose reputation allowed him to collaborate with Jews unscathed). The end of the Second World War was thus also an end to artistic segregation. German composers of Henze's generation suddenly discovered *Stravinsky, *Schoenberg and other banned degenerates; opportunities for performance, especially of large-scale works, multiplied a hundredfold as the return to normal civic life began. Henze took eager advantage of the situation, creating an eclectic style (incorporating *Stravinskian precision, serial harmony and a melodic directness like that of *Weill's theatre-pieces), and using it in half a dozen striking operas, a dazzling parallel to *Britten's output of the 1940s and 1950s. He wrote an updating of the Manon Lescaut story, *Boulevard Solitude* (1951), three fantasy-operas as rococo as fairy-tales, *King Stag* (1955, rev. 1964), *The Prince of Homburg* (1958) and the satirical *The Young Lord* (1964), and two sombre works to librettos by Auden and Kallman, *Elegy for Young Lovers* (1961), a morality about artistic desperation, and *The Bassarids* (1965), based on Euripides' *Bacchae*.

Despite (or because of) his triumph in the most bourgeois and capitalist of all musical forms, Henze moved ever further left in his political thinking, and after the 1968 student uprisings allied himself firmly with Marxist social revolutionaries. He spent some time in Cuba; he worked to make his musical style accessible to everyone; he abandoned the gorgeous formality of the opera-house for raucous, symbolic music-theatre which could be performed in any kind of hall or square with a minimum of props and no backstage fuss: characteristic works are *The Raft of the Medusa* (1968), *Essay on Pigs* (1969), *El Cimarrón* (1970), a meditation on freedom based on the life-story of a runaway slave, and *We Come to the River* (1975), to a harshly didactic libretto by Edward Bond. The musical rigours of these works – for all their avowed populism, they are noisy, discordant and uncompromisingly avant-garde – were somewhat tempered in the pieces Henze wrote for Montepulciano, a decaying agricultural community near Siena, Italy, where he established a people's music festival and had considerable success providing artistic stimulus for amateurs, children, and the many students and young professionals who flocked to join him. (A typical Montepulciano work is a recomposition of an 18th-century *commedia dell'arte* opera, with parts for everyone from professional orchestral musicians to the town band and unemployed youths plucked from the backstreets.)

Simultaneously with his stage works, Henze poured out instrumental and vocal music of dazzling quality. His output includes six symphonies, half a dozen concertos (the finest are for oboe, harp and strings, 1966, and for double bass, 1966), string quartets, sonatas and shorter works for piano, guitar (several large works based on Shakespeare), solo violin and harpsichord, and above all a series of luscious vocal cantatas, music whose sensual elegance is far removed from the harsh lecturing of the theatre-pieces: *Novae de infinito laudes* (1962); *Being Beauteous* (1963, setting Rimbaud); *Muses of Sicily* (1966, setting Virgil).

Henze's other works include a dozen ballets (among them *Undine*, 1957, and *Orpheus*, 1979), the large orchestral fantasies *Heliogabalus imperator* (1972) and *The Hunt of the Maenads* (1978, in part based on his opera *The Bassarids*), the cantata *Voices* (1973), and two wind quintets (1952; *Autumn*, 1976). His articles and essays, as stimulating and revealing as they are polemical, were published in English as *Music and Politics: Collected Writings 1953–81* (1982).

HINDEMITH, Paul (1895–1963)
German composer

Hindemith is a 20th-century counterpart to the anonymous guild-masters who built the medieval cathedrals: an artisan of genius, speaking the language of his trade with unrivalled fluency, making expertise a wondrous thing. But the medieval artisans were working with an aim which clinched their art and raised common utterance to the level of poetry: every piece of coloured glass, carved stone or painted wood was set in place to the glory of God, to express, as perfectly as human creations could, transcendental feeling and aspiration – and because he lacked any such driving-force (he was a Christian, but this rarely motivated his music), Hindemith produced work after work of magnificent routine. His aim was to write *gebrauchsmusik*, music for use, and disposability was no problem: tomorrow's ideas would be just as serviceable as today's. His ambition was to write in every form of music, to provide at least one piece for every instrument and every vocal combination – and he very nearly succeeded.

In such a welter of music, it was inevitable that several works should rise above the humdrum brilliance of the rest, that some awkwardness of phrase or unlikeliness of harmony would stimulate creativity. (In fact, the less Hindemith concentrated on technical perfection, the better his music was.) In the 1920s, in particular, while evolving the baked-bean blandness of his mature style, he composed several pieces in a shockingly (then) modernist idiom brewed from jazz, *Bartókian discord, jagged scoring and harmony which cheerfully piled up three or four keys at once. This style gives life to his seven *Kammermusiken* ('Chambermusics') of the 1920s, whether they be solo concertos (No. 4, for violin, is especially sprightly) or 20th-century Brandenburg concertos, Bach with a very wicked grin (No. 1; No. 6). At the same period he wrote his first solo sonatas (the six for string instruments in Opus 11 are excellent), string quartets (No. 3, 1921, was influenced by Bartók and *Debussy, to healthy effect), and the Rilke song-cycle *The Life of Mary* (1923), one of his best pieces, revised (i.e. made less spiky) and orchestrated in 1948.

In the 1930s, hounded by the Nazis, Hindemith left Germany and settled in the USA. The cause of his expulsion was ostensibly that he had worked with Jewish artists (he had) and slandered Hitler (he hadn't); more probably it was the subject-matter of his opera *Mathis der Maler* (1934), in which an episode from the life of the medieval painter Mathias Grünewald (the painting of the Isenheim altar-piece) is made the peg for some pointed reflections on artistic freedom. (The theme caught Hindemith's imagination: the opera, and the symphony *Mathis der Maler* quarried from its music in 1934, are among his best works.) Travelling, and the commissions it led to, produced some likeable pieces: *Concert Music for Brass and Strings* (1930), written for the 50th anniversary of the Boston Symphony Orchestra, *Funeral Music* (1936), written in one day in a BBC studio to mark the death of George V, *Symphonic Metamorphoses of Themes by Carl Maria von Weber* (1943), whose lunatic-professor title conceals a jolly orchestral suite sumptuously upholstering Weber's tinkly tunes. Other works can be singled out – the folk-song-based viola concerto *Der Schwanendreher* (1935), the ballet *Nobilissima visione* (1938), on the life of St Francis, the moving choral requiem *When Lilacs Last in the Dooryard Bloom'd* (1946) to words by Whitman, the *Horn Concerto* (1949) – but pointing them out is like soliciting admiration for individual plums on a laden tree.

Apart from music, Hindemith published a lengthy and excellent manual on the techniques of 20th-century music, *The Craft of Musical Composition* (1937–41), and some challenging lectures, *A Composer's World* (1950). Good study (sometimes technical): I. Kemp: *Paul Hindemith* (1970).

HOLST, Gustav (1874–1934)
British composer

The concert-going public has firmly, if harshly, made up its mind about Holst: in *The Planets* (1916) he composed one of the longest-lasting lollipops in the orchestral repertoire – a piece so familiar that most competent players can get through it virtually from memory – and practically nothing else. *The Planets* takes seven of the nine planets – Earth is unrepresented, and Holst refused to add a new movement in 1930 when Pluto's discovery was announced – and explores their astrological associations (bellicosity, jollity, mysticism, etc.) in music whose steely dazzle teeters on the brink of film-score explicitness. The work's success is due to whistleable tunes, uncomplicated harmonies and above all emotional warmth – qualities veiled in or absent from the rest of Holst's cold-hearted output. He was a mystic, and his best work is to texts of somewhat daunting aloofness: *Hymn of Jesus* (1917) sets the apocryphal Acts of St John, *Savitri* (1908) is a one-act opera based on a Hindu myth, *Hymns from the Rig Veda* (1910) uses Indian sacred texts, and *Egdon Heath* (1927) is a chilly musical counterpart to Hardy's description of wasteland in *The Return of the Native*. Holst's devotees make claims for these and slighter works like *St Paul's Suite* (1913) for strings or the ballet from the one-act opera *The Perfect Fool* (1922); he is, none the less, likely to remain the 'one-work composer' most people think he is.

Holst's other works include *Ode to Death* (1919, words by Whitman), two folk-music-inspired *Suites* for military band (1909; 1911), and a one-act comic opera based on a bawdy medieval anecdote, *The Wandering Scholar* (1930). Good, if partisan, study (by his daughter): I. Holst: *The Music of Gustav Holst* (1951).

HONEGGER, Arthur (1892–1955)
Swiss composer

Like the music of his compatriot *Martin, Honegger's work raises questions about the relationship between showmanship and acceptability. How can music so serious and so well-turned remain so grey? Only his short pieces (*Summer Pastoral*, 1920; *Pacific 231*, 1923, a sound-portrait of a steam-engine; *Concerto da camera*, 1948, for flute, cor anglais and strings) linger in the memory; each time one of his five symphonies is played, the listener thinks 'Ah yes', but an hour later the music once again slips the mind. One reason is that for all their craftsmanship and personality, his works are short on good ideas. Certainly his best music is not in abstract forms (he wrote sonatas, quartets and concertos, all agreeable wallpaper), but in flamboyant stage-works where the notes enhance rather than lead the words: *King David* (1921), *Judith* (1925), *Phèdre* (1926), *Antigone* (1927) and above all *Joan of Arc at the Stake* (1935). His *Christmas Cantata* (1953) works characteristic dull magic on that most familiar of material, Christmas carols: equipped with earnest counterpoint and muddy harmony, they become the musical equivalent of Lewis Carroll's Cheshire cat.

IVES, Charles (1874–1954)
American composer

Though he trained as a musician, Ives went into the insurance business (and in due course became a millionaire). His composing was a weekend activity; he allowed few works to be published or performed in his lifetime; he stopped writing altogether in the 1920s. Since the discovery of his music after his death, he has been a cult figure, regarded as the father of American music, a man who perfected many avant-garde techniques (polytonality; serialism; aleatory procedures) decades before anyone else. His true status is nearer that of Douanier Rousseau in painting or Thomas Wolfe in literature. Like Rousseau, he was a genius whose choice of naïve styles made his work, for all its clamorous personality, limited in scope; like Wolfe, he poured out page after page of material, incoherently magnificent, with indifference to its future once the ink was dry.

Ives's music is notorious both for horrendous effects (four or five keys, tunes or blocks of sound all heard at once, a reminiscence of his hearing, as a youth, several bands converging on the same vantage-point), and for his insertion of gems from the popular repertoire (*Columbia, America, From Greenland's Icy Mountains, Taps*) into his pieces whether they fitted or not. These quotations and references are what make his music 'American': such works as *Three Places in New England* (1914), *Holidays Symphony* (1913, including *The Fourth of July*, one of his most characterful pieces) or the *Concord Piano Sonata* (1915, evocations of Thoreau,

Emerson, the Allcotts and Hawthorne) have for non-Americans an exoticism he can hardly have intended, quite different from the patch-work-quilt reassurance they offer those who share his culture. In his finest works the general musical argument is adorned, not choked, by quotations: *Symphony 3* (1911), for example, though based on hymn-tunes, is no more specialized than Bach's works using Lutheran chorales – and no less rewarding to hear.

Despite the richness of Ives's concert music – his ideas are a well from which every subsequent American composer is claimed to have drawn a style – his best pieces tend to be short, impressionistic and suitable for domestic use. His 140 songs, some less than twenty bars long, are as accessible as they are impressive: they range from wide-eyed ballads (e.g. *Two Little Flowers*; *The Children's Hour*), like upmarket Stephen Foster, to pieces of engaging and preposterous difficulty (e.g. *Duty*, whose piano part offers the performer not so much notes to play as an ideal to aim for: chords of eleven notes, spread over a metre of the piano's keyboard, stretch the imagination as well as the fingers). For those new to his music, good samples are *The Unanswered Question* (1906) for orchestra, *The Housatonic at Stockbridge*, a murmurous river-piece from *Three Places in New England*, and *Variations on America* (1891), as rumbustious and vulgar as a circus-act.

Ives's other works include the gigantic *Symphony 4* (posthumous), which needs three conductors and sounds like a collage of all the music ever written, a dozen psalm settings for chorus, and several chamber works including four violin sonatas and two string quartets (No. 1, 1896, is straightforward; No. 2, 1913, gives each player his own harmony and rhythm, and is full of instructions like *andante emasculata* and *con fistiswatto*). Ives's prose (as polemical as his notes) is collected in *Essays Before a Sonata and Other Writings by Charles Ives* (ed. Boatwright, 1961) and *Charles E. Ives: Memos* (ed. Kirkpatrick, 1972). Good studies: H. and S. *Cowell: *Charles Ives and His Music* (1955 – partisan and sometimes technical, but a classic); H. W. Hitchcock: *Ives* (1977).

JANÁČEK, Leoš (1854–1928)
Czech composer

Until his 60s, Janáček was little more than a talented camp-follower of Dvořák, clothing Czech folk-songs and folk-rhythms in chirpy but now old-fashioned-seeming harmonic dress. (*Lachian Dances*, 1890, for orchestra, *Moravian National Dances*, 1891, for piano duet, and *4 Moravian Choruses*, 1904, are typical.) Then, at the end of the First World War, three events changed his life: the formation of the Czech republic, the success of his opera *Jenůfa*, and his love-affair with a girl forty years his junior. In the last ten years of his life he wrote like an impassioned adolescent, flinging on to paper a dozen works as fresh as they are personal: it was as though he had reinvented Czech folk-music and its artistic possibilities overnight. Like *Bartók, he developed a rhythmic style based on ordinary speech-patterns: irregularly grouped handfuls of short notes, repeated and rotated over long-held, throbbing chords. The effect is simultaneously abrupt and beckoning, a no-nonsense romanticism which satisfies the ear and tickles the intellect; it is 'modern' (i.e. clean, neo-classical, without frills) and '19th-century' (i.e. vague, poetic and sensuous) both at once. The style suited opera (and its musical strength is shown by the success of Janáček's operas even in translation): as well as *Jenůfa* and *Katya Kabanová* (1921), whose subjects are passion and jealousy, Janáček's major works include *The Excursions of Mr Brouček* (1917), about a man who goes to the moon, *The Cunning Little Vixen* (1923), a charming allegory set among forest animals, *The Makropoulos Affair* (1925), based on Čapek's fantastic play about a 300-year-old woman, and a version of Dostoievski's *The House of the Dead* (1928) set in a prison-colony. Direct results of Janáček's love-affair are a song-cycle, *Diary of One Who Disappeared* (1919), and two deeply felt string quartets (No. 1, *Kreutzer Sonata*, 1923; No. 2, *Intimate Letters*, 1928). Even the more abstract works of his old age bustle with young man's energy: the wind sextet *Youth* (1924), an engaging blend of his old and new folk-styles, *Sinfonietta* (1926), written for an athletics festival and rich in breezy fanfares and woodwind flourishes, and the *Glagolitic Mass* (1926), which eschews liturgical solemnity in favour of a pagan exuberance looking back to *Stravinsky's *Les Noces* and forward to *Orff's *Carmina Burana*.

Janáček's other works include a full-blooded orchestral fantasy after Gogol's epic poem *Taras Bulba* (1918), several piano pieces including the suite *On Overgrown Paths* (1901), and the terse *Concertino* (1925) and *Capriccio* (1926) for piano and chamber group. Good studies: H. Hollander: *Janáček: His Life and Works* (1963; technical in parts); E. Chisholm: *The Operas of Leoš Janáček* (1971).

KHACHATURIAN, Aram (1903–78)
Russian composer and administrator

At nineteen, knowing little about music, Khachaturian presented himself at a Moscow conservatory and declared that he meant to become a composer; not long afterwards he was winning prizes. The same spectacular determination served him, and Russian music generally, well in 1953. The Central Committee of the Communist Party, in one of its periodic rushes of brains to the buttocks, had condemned many prominent composers as bourgeois formalists, and virtually silenced them; Khachaturian published an article damning this decision and suggesting that composers got on with their own creative business – and the result was not an instant trip to Siberia for him, but a revoking of the Committee decision which rehabilitated, among others, *Prokofiev, *Shostakovich and Khachaturian himself. He also has the distinction of having written a handful of the best-known pieces of 'serious' music of the century: *Sabre Dance*, from his ballet *Gayane* (1942, an otherwise anaemic saga of skullduggery on a collective farm), was a dance-band and orchestral hit throughout the world; the *adagio* from his ballet *Spartacus* (1956, offering the spectacle of gladiators in tights) was used as theme-music for a British TV series (*The Onedin Line*) and from there graduated to every advertisement ever showing Victorian sailing-ships or tumbling seas, and to the lush pastures of the 'popular classical' repertoire; his *Piano Concerto* (1937), though condemned in its day as one of the most vulgar pieces of music ever committed to paper, once rivalled Grieg's or Tchaikovsky's in popularity. All these pieces – indeed, all Khachaturian's works – clothe folk-ideas from his native Armenia in sumptuous, late-19th-century orchestral dress: they are as zestful, and as brashly effective, as anything by Borodin. The bigger his music is, the better: his three symphonies (1934; 1943; 1947) and his violin and cello concertos (1940; 1946) tower above everything else he wrote.

Khachaturian's other main works include a *Violin Sonata* (1932), a vigorous *Piano Sonata* (1961) and a *Trio* for violin, clarinet and piano (1932).

KODÁLY, Zoltán (1882–1967)
Hungarian teacher and composer

Kodály's 'method' of music education is widely used. He believed that singing is the foundation of musical skill, and devised a course, based on vocalizing, which takes students from infancy to mastery; at every point he provided tuneful and effective music, much of it based on the Hungarian folk-songs he collected with *Bartók in the 1900s. He travelled throughout Hungary, conducting and lecturing, and came to be regarded as a national hero of the arts, the Albert Schweitzer of Hungarian music. His compositions, though few, are effective and popular. His best-known work is the orchestral suite from *Háry János* (1927, a play-with-songs about a boastful soldier in the Napoleonic wars, a Švejk-like anti-hero): its use of the jangling *cimbalom* and of dashing *czardas*-rhythms guarantees success. Other folk-inspired works are the grave choral *Psalmus Hungaricus* (1923, composed for a festival celebrating the unification of Budapest) and three colourful orchestral works, *Dances of Marosszék* (1930), *Dances of Galánta* (1933) and *Peacock Variations* (1939). His other instrumental music, though ambitious (it includes two string quartets, *Concerto for Orchestra*, 1940, and *Symphony*, 1961), lacks folk-inspiration and is worthy rather than distinguished, like warmed-up Dohnanyi; the exceptions are two fine sonatas, pinnacles of the repertory, for cello and piano (1909) and for unaccompanied cello (1915).

Kodály's other music includes *Te Deum* (1936), *Missa brevis* (1944) and many other choral works, *Summer Evening* (1906) for orchestra, and numerous songs, some arrangements of folk-tunes. He published an authoritative study of *Hungarian Folk-Music* (1937, English edn 1960), valuable for anyone interested in the roots of his own or Bartók's work. Good study: P. M. Young: *Zoltán Kodály, A Hungarian Musician* (1964).

LIGETI, György (born 1923)
Hungarian composer

International fame of an oblique kind – millions knew his work, dozens his name – came to Ligeti when his *Requiem* (1965) was used as the 'Jupiter' music in Kubrick's film *2001*: its impression of thousands of individual voices murmuring prayers, of a huge sound-edifice built from tiny fragments, seemed emblematic of the human aspiration which Kubrick sought to express. Ligeti calls his technique 'micropolyphony'; it consists of myriads of notes and phrases endlessly repeated, a sound-continuum from which single events (high cries, low thuds) from time to time stand out. (He has been called a musical minimalist, but his work is analogous less to Malevich's paintings of white squares on white than to the pullulating abstracts of Dubuffet or Pollock.) Apart from the *Requiem* and its choral partners *Lux aeterna* (1966) and *Clocks and Clouds* (1973), his most striking endless-belt works are for orchestra (*Atmospheres*, 1961; *Lontano*, 1967; *Melodien*, 1971) and for solo instruments (*Volumina*, 1962, for organ; *Continuum*, 1968, for harpsichord). He has also written joke-pieces (e.g. *Symphonic Poem* for 100 metronomes) and a number of larger-scale works in which micropolyphony contrasts with bolder themes and gestures, somewhat in the manner of *Boulez: the best are two concertos of catherine-wheel dazzle, for cello (1966) and for flute and oboe (1972), and three pieces (*Monument*; *Self-Portrait*; *Movement*, 1976) for two pianos.

Ligeti's other music includes a strident experimental opera, *Le Grand Macabre* (1978), whose title is all too accurate, and several chamber pieces including two string quartets (1954; 1968), *10 Pieces for Wind Quintet* (1968) and a sparkling *Chamber Concerto* (1970) for thirteen instruments. Interesting interviews: *Ligeti in Conversation* (1984). Good study: P. Griffiths: *Ligeti* (1984).

LUTOSŁAVSKI, Witold (born 1913)
Polish composer

Lutosławski's career was hampered by the events and aftermath of the Second World War. Until the mid-1950s he wrote little of substance, chiefly folk-song arrangements (e.g. *Folk-Melodies for Piano*, 1945; *20 Polish Carols*, 1946) or instrumental pieces in an agreeable but insubstantial neo-classical style, sawdust from *Stravinsky's workshop. (*Paganini Variations*, 1941, *Symphony 1*, 1947, and the popular *Concerto for Orchestra*, 1954, are typical.) Then, when stylistic censorship relaxed, he began to explore serial and aleatory techniques – and found his style. The 'new' Lutosławski – a composer of the stature of *Sessions or *Tippett – first became apparent in the 12-note *Funeral Music* (1958), composed in memory of *Bartók, and in the lively *Venetian Games* (1961), *String Quartet* (1964) and *Symphony 2* (1967). In his finest music, Lutosławski combines straightforwardly notated music with passages intended for controlled improvisation, and the result is exuberantly avant-garde without being precious or intimidating: his pieces are particularly enjoyable in live performance. He is inspired by virtuosity, and all his works involve display and contest (the players appearing to challenge and enthuse each other), whether they are vocal (*Three Michaux Poems*, 1963; *Paroles tissées*, 1965; *The Spaces of Sleep*, 1978), abstract-instrumental (*String Quartet*; *Livre for Orchestra*, 1968; *Preludes and Fugue for Strings*, 1972; *Mi-Parti*, 1976; *Chain I*, 1983; *Symphony 3*, 1983) or actual concertos (*Cello Concerto*, 1970; *Concerto for Oboe and Harp*, 1979). For anyone doubting that traditional instrumental techniques (and the disciplines of orchestral playing) have any place in the avant-garde, Lutosławski's works provide an answer as persuasive as it is unequivocal: without reference to the styles of the 19th century, he writes sounds which delight players, satisfy pundits, and charm without pandering to their audience.

Good interim study (partly technical): S. Stucky: *Lutosławski and His Music* (1983).

LUTYENS, Elizabeth (1906–83)
British composer

Early in her thirties, Lutyens began to write 12-note music a generation ahead of most other British composers and several decades before concert promoters and audiences were ready. Her works have attracted a devoted but small following – a pity, since they are immaculately constructed and not at all cacophonous. She wrote chamber music (including six chamber concertos, a trio, a sextet and six string quartets), and several big orchestral pieces (notably concertos for horn and viola, and *Music for Orchestra I, II, and III*). But her best pieces, those most likely to settle in the repertoire, are sensitive cantatas for solo voices and chamber group, reminiscent in spare beauty of those of *Dallapiccola: *Ô saisons, Ô châteaux* (1946), *The Valley of Hatsuse* (1965), *And Suddenly It's Evening* (1967), *Elegy of the Flowers* (1979). If she had been a painter (of the order of de Staël) people would hang her canvases; if she had been a poet (of the order of Amy Lowell) people would buy her books; because she was a serial composer (of the order of *Gerhard) audiences stay away in droves – and the loss is theirs.

Lutyens' other works include *The Country of the Stars* (1963) for chorus, *Plenum I, II and III* for chamber groups, and several sets of delicate, *Weberny songs. Her no-holds-barred autobiography, *A Goldfish Bowl*, a monument to indomitability, and to creative arrogance in the face of public indifference, was published in 1972.

MALIPIERO, Gian Francesco (1882–1973)
Italian scholar and composer

Like the British instrument-maker Arnold Dolmetsch, Malipiero began pushing the frontiers of music back beyond 1700 at a time when most contemporaries thought that God created sound with the romantics (and, in Italy, romantic opera) specifically in mind. He unearthed from libraries and published hundreds of works by baroque composers (Corelli, Galuppi, Tartini, Vivaldi) and by their great Venetian predecessors; he made the first complete edition of Monteverdi, an enormous task; time-travelling still further, he edited Renaissance vocal works and collections of Gregorian chant. Until 1913, composing took second place, and his works were conservative and piffling; then, after going to the first performance of *Stravinsky's *The Rite of Spring*, he decided to radicalize his style, and made a bonfire of his early works. For the next sixty years he poured out music owing as much to the 18th as to the 20th century: analogous to Pre-Raphaelite art in its re-creation of distant styles and techniques, and close in sound to *Debussy's more forthright scores (*String Quartet*; *3 Villon Ballades*), it has been unjustly neglected since his death. From his enormous catalogue (which includes sixteen operas, thirteen symphonies, twelve concertos and eight string quartets) the most ear-catching works are *Impressioni dal vero I, II and III* for orchestra, the choral *Requiem* (1938) and *Virgil's Aeneid* (no less; 1944), the gently pastoral *Symphony 2* (1936) and the busy, Vivaldi-with-teeth *Violin Concerto 2* (1963).

MARTIN, Frank (1890–1974)
Swiss composer

To be Switzerland's greatest composer is an accolade to rival being Miss Virgin Islands or New Zealand's poet laureate – a view Martin's music endorses by being earnestly but unmemorably excellent. He used 12-note rows as the basis of harmony and melody, but devised them to fit recognizable keys and chords: the result is like mellow *Bartók or gritty *Barber. The bulk of his output – it includes two operas (one a setting of Shakespeare's *Tempest*, 1956), half a dozen concertos, chamber works and six large choral works of which the most striking is *Le Vin herbé* ('The Magic Potion', 1941), an oratorio based on the story of Tristan and Isolde – is routine, but a handful of instrumental works stand out, chiefly because Martin scored them for ear-catching orchestral combinations. This aural inventiveness makes his *Concerto for Seven Wind Instruments and Strings* (1949) and *Harpsichord Concerto* (1952) worth repeated hearings, and places his one masterpiece, *Petite Symphonie concertante* (1946) for piano, harp, harpsichord and strings, in the heady class of *Bloch's *Concerti grossi* or *Martinů's *Double Concerto*.

Martin's other works include *Six Monologues from Everyman* (1943) for voice and orchestra, the oratorios *In terra pax* (1944) and *Pilate* (1964), and a set of strikingly scored, closely argued *Studies* (1956) for string orchestra.

MARTINŮ, Bohuslav (1890–1959)
Czech composer

In an art almost entirely given over to isms of one kind or another (many of them incomprehensible or terrifying to non-practitioners), less attention is paid than perhaps should be to work like Martinů's, intended primarily to delight. He followed no schemes save those he needed from bar to bar: his music is a blend of Dvořákian tunefulness, jazz, unexpected rhythms (groups of seven, nine or eleven bubbling against the four or six of the basic beat), and harmonies as likely to be learned from Glenn Miller as from Tchaikovsky. This kind of insouciance is normally reserved, nowadays, for 'light' music; the miracle is that for all his pawnbroker inspiration, Martinů made works of substantial and convincing art. He was prolific (nine operas, sixteen concertos, six symphonies, a dozen chamber works), and his inspiration sometimes slipped (several symphonies, for example, and all his cello works, rate *beta* grades). But at his best (e.g. *Harpsichord Concerto*, 1935, *Three Ricercari*, 1938, *Toccata and Two Canzonas*, 1946, or *Frescoes of Piero della Francesca*, 1955) he outsparkled every serious composer in the business, and in one or two works (*Double Concerto*, 1938; the opera *Julietta*, 1938; *Memorial to Lidice*, 1943) he walked with *Copland or *Britten at their most inspired.

Good study; M. Safranek: *Bohuslav Martinů* (English edn 1962).

MESSIAEN, Olivier (born 1908)
French composer

Few composers in history have worked so many private symbols and obsessions into their music. Messiaen's subject, love, allows him to range – often in the same work – between expressions of transcendental passion (the legend of Tristan and Isolde is a potent influence) and those of the communion between God, the Holy Ghost and the ecstatic Roman Catholic communicant. His rhythms are based on the metres of Greek poetry (choriambics or dochmiacs rather than straightforward dactyls or spondees), on Indian *talas* and on mathematical series of his own. His melody and harmony draw on bird-song, *Schoenbergian note-rows and a system of his own (called 'modes of limited transposition') which produces either churning discords or added-note chords as saccharine as any improvised by a cinema organist. Over-riding everything is a view of the mystical unity of all creation, a world in which canyons and stars join with birds, human beings and angels to hymn the glory of God on high.

If all this was apparent to the listener, hearing Messiaen would be like bathing in syrup. But in general (and particularly if one ignores arch movement-titles like 'Turmoil of Rainbows' or 'Praise to the Eternity of God'), the influences impinge on the music no more than (say) Mozart's Masonic symbols do on *The Magic Flute*. To the uninitiated, Messiaen's music is forceful and clamorous, a succession of sounds (some sweet, some monumentally dissonant) which engross or repel according to the listener's mood. As with Wagner's *Ring*, anyone drawn by the initial attractiveness of the music will find a rich soup of associations to nourish enjoyment: Messiaen's religious works (e.g. *The Ascension*, 1933, *Visions of the Amen*, 1943, *Regards on the Child Jesus*, 1944, *The Transfiguration*, 1969, and especially his orchestral depiction of the last judgement, *Et exspecto resurrectionem mortuorum*, 1964, and his vast opera *St Francis of Assisi*, 1983) offer an experience of dominating and demanding grandeur akin only to that of *Parsifal* or the *B Minor Mass*, and which caused *Poulenc to liken him to the painter Rouault ('prodigious divination of colour ... visionary tone ... mysticism bordering on exacerbated paganism ...'). The same apocalyptic energy fills his works on themes of earthly love and nature-symbolism, *Poems for Mi* (1936), *Harâwi, Song of Love and Death* (1945), and the gigantic *Turangalîla Symphony* (1948) and *From the Canyons to the Stars* (1976).

Anyone intrigued by Messiaen but reluctant to plunge into the larger pieces may find more accessible his bird-song works, notably two piano concertos (*Réveil des oiseaux*, 'Dawn Chorus', 1935, and *Oiseaux exotiques*, 'Exotic Birds', 1956), which are entirely built from bird-calls (the scores even tell us which bird is which), but which sound uncluttered and objective. (Later bird-works, e.g. *Catalogue of Birds* for piano, 1958, and *Chronocromie*, 'Time-Colouring', 1960, for orchestra, use the same procedures to make longer, more demanding scores.)

Messiaen is unique. Though he was a respected teacher (among others, of *Boulez and *Stockhausen), no composers of significance have used his style. Performances of his music attract enthusiastic audiences, and records (especially of *Turangalîla*, a 20th-century orchestral hit) sell well. His future reputation is impossible to assess: our great-grandchildren may regard him as we do Wagner, the brand that lit a thousand fires, or like *Scriabin, a soggy firework. For now, in the 1980s, he is a colossus, a creator whose work appears to match its extraordinary sources of inspiration and to offer receptive listeners the same ecstatic, quasi-mystical experience which led him to write it down.

Messiaen's other works include *Cinq Rechants* (1949) for choir, the splendidly jangly *Cantéjodayâ* (1948) for piano, *The Nativity* (1935) and *Meditation on the Holy Trinity* (1969) for organ, and *Quartet for the End of Time* (1941), a chamber-music vision of the apocalypse composed in a concentration camp. The diversity and complexity of his inspiration have made him a happy hunting-ground for scholars; the least pretentious book on him (technical but readable) is R. Sherlaw Johnson: *Messiaen* (1975), and *Conversations with Olivier Messiaen* (ed. Samuel, 1976), though not without solemnities and preciousness, is helpful to non-devotees and essential reading for every fan.

MILHAUD, Darius (1892–1974)
French composer

The 14th and 15th of Milhaud's eighteen string quartets can be played separately, or together as an octet – and that distinguishes them from all the others. Not since medieval times, when composers wrote music which 'worked' just as well backwards or upside-down, has anyone married such technical expertise to such vapidity, and many of Milhaud's larger works (twelve symphonies, a dozen operas and a score of concertos) lapse into note-spinning. He was at his best when reworking folk-material (e.g. *Carnaval d'Aix*, 1926, a sprightly suite of Provençal tunes arranged for piano and orchestra; *Scaramouche*, 1939, for two pianos, with a bouncy samba-finale), or when unusual words or ideas caught his attention (e.g. *Flower Catalogue*, 1921, extracts set verbatim for voice and orchestra, or the six tiny *Symphonies* of 1917–22, some less than five minutes long exploring the possibilities of polytonality). His most successful works, because the showiness of the medium suits his demonstrative style, are ballets: he wrote twelve altogether, ranging from joky Parisian spoofs (*Le Bœuf sur le toit*, 'The Ox on the Roof', 1919, named after a nightclub, and *Les Mariés de la Tour Eiffel*, 'The Eiffel Tower Newly-Weds', 1920, both with surrealist scenarios by Cocteau) to jazz (*The Creation of the World*, 1923, about a negro Adam and Eve, has a score full of Dixieland harmonies and features a sugary saxophone) and to serious works on lofty themes (e.g. *Jacob's Dreams*, 1949). He is easy to dismiss as a hack of genius; and yet every work you hear comes up fresh and likeable. Pirandello had the same ability: to marry old tricks to brilliant sleight-of-hand, and seem to make magic.

Milhaud's hundreds of other works include *La Cheminée du roi René* (1939), a limpid suite for wind quintet, *The Household Muse* (1945), a set of gentle piano pieces inspired by domestic routine, and – at the other end of the spectrum of endeavour – an enormous and impressive Biblical opera, *David* (1954). His *Notes Without Music, an Autobiography*, a happy book by a happy man, appeared in 1949.

NIELSEN, Carl (1865–1931)
Danish composer

Until his forties, Nielsen composed in a forthright Brahmsian style: there was little to distinguish his string quartets, songs, piano pieces and even his first *Symphony* (1892) from anyone else's. The exception is *Hymnus amoris* ('Hymn of Love', 1896), a choral cantata whose melodious lyricism is worlds away from Germanic severities. In 1906, with his opera *Maskarade* (from a *commedia dell'arte* farce by Holberg, Goldoni's Danish counterpart), he began a series of works which temper Teutonic thoroughness with a cheerfulness and waywardness which some see as typically Danish but are really signs of his own individuality (certainly no one else has imitated them). His symphonies, for example, are built on big tunes as well as counterpoint; his concertos are tailor-made for the temperament of the original artists (the fastidious soloist in *Flute Concerto*, 1926, for example, fights a musical battle against belches and farts from a bass trombone which keeps trying to drag the music into alien keys); many of his smaller works are on Danish themes (e.g. the choral *Springtime on Fyn*, 1921, or the orchestral tone-poem *A Fantasy-Trip to the Faroe Isles*, 1927).

The core of Nielsen's work is six symphonies, three of them peaks of the repertoire. No. 3 (*Sinfonia espansiva*, 1911) is in a line from Dvořák's sunny symphonies, with a surging, romantic first movement, a beautiful pastoral slow movement (complete with two wordless solo voices) and a finale based on a catchy chorale-like melody. No. 4 (splendidly subtitled *Det Uudslukkelige*, 'The Inextinguishable', 1916) takes the form of a confrontation between savage, chaotic music and a serene melody which finally dominates – the piece, composed during the First World War, was deliberately programmatic and optimistic. No. 5 (1922), Nielsen's finest work in any form, is a huge holdall of symphonic form, its two movements bulging with everything from development sections to fugues; its musical energy and air of constructional inevitability are particularly *Sibelius-like, as is Nielsen's way of clinching his argument with singable tunes. Ranking with the symphonies are a Brahmsian *Violin Concerto* (1911), a mellifluous *Wind Quintet* (1922) and a *Clarinet Concerto* (1928) the originality of whose construction rivals that of *Symphony 5*.

Unlike Sibelius, Nielsen never had success outside Scandinavia in his lifetime: it was not until the 1960s that his works entered the repertoire of British and American orchestras, and he is still underplayed in Europe. It is hard to see why, as his music towers above that of other 20th-century traditionalists, and comparisons with Dvořák, Brahms and Sibelius are not over-praise.

Nielsen's other works include *Pan and Syrinx* (1917), a pastoral tone-poem, two violin sonatas (the second, 1912, is fine), *Theme and Variations* (1916) and *Suite* (1919) for piano, and the grittily contrapuntal *Commotio* (1931) for organ. His prose memoir *My Childhood on Fyn* (1927) is a minor autobiographical classic, akin to Renoir's *My Father* or Laurie Lee's *Cider with Rosie*. Good study (with music examples, but with notably untechnical and helpful prose): R. Simpson: *Carl Nielsen, Symphonist* (1952). (Simpson himself is a fine, Nielsenish composer: particularly recommendable are his symphonies and string quartets, many of them influenced by late Beethoven.)

ORFF, Carl (1895–1982)
German composer

Orff's system of music education, *Schoolwork*, has been used throughout the world. Unlike *Kodály's (which is based on singing) it uses percussion and tuned instruments, building up complicated textures by adding layer after layer of simple patterns. Each part is easy – the basis is usually a

nursery-rhyme – but the whole performance can demand as much concentration and creativity as the teacher chooses, and there is scope for the
pupils to make up parts of their own. At its simplest, Orff's *Schoolwork* is
what every kindergarten percussion band aspires to; at its most sophisticated, it is only one step from thoroughgoing adult performance.

In his concert music, Orff also set out to produce sophisticated effects by
the simplest of means. He reduced harmony to a series of chords as plain as
those of a rock 'n' roll band; he wrote tunes as memorable as nursery songs;
he scored his music for enormous forces but simply and directly (pounding
rhythms and supporting chords, always at the service of the voice); he
wrote no counterpoint, no music not for voices, nothing abstract. His chief
output is for the stage, and seeks to reproduce the stark effect of classical
Greek tragedy. He wrote settings of Sophocles and Aeschylus (*Antigone*,
1948; *Oedipus the King*, 1959; *Prometheus*, 1967), operas based on Grimm
folk-tales (*The Moon*, 1938; *The Wise Woman*, 1942), and Biblical dramas
(*The Play of Christ's Resurrection*, 1955; *The Christmas Story*, 1960; *Play of
the End of Time*, 1971). His chief work is a trilogy of stage works called
Trionfi ('Triumphs'). This employs all three theatre arts (drama, ballet,
opera), and is chiefly a celebration of earthly pleasure. *Carmina Burana*
(1936), settings of lusty medieval poems, deals with spring, wine and love –
and contains one of the most explicit musical depictions of the sexual act
ever composed, the moment of penetration appropriately coinciding with
the entire evening's musical climax. *Catulli carmina* (1942), less colourful,
sets Catullus in the original Latin, and *Trionfo di Afrodite* (1951) is an
ebullient depiction of a rustic wedding, a pagan counterpart to *Stravinsky's *Les Noces*. The last two cantatas are neglected in favour of *Carmina
Burana*, a piece deplored by the learned but enthusiastically received by
audiences. It is music as brash and as cunning as Brueghel's peasant
paintings or Rabelais' *Gargantua*; few 20th-century works communicate
so joyously or so disarmingly.

Orff's other compositions include the 'Bavarian stage-piece' *The Wife of Bernauer*
(1945), several choral cantatas including *Nänie and Dithyrambs* (1956), and
arrangements of half a dozen Monteverdi vocal works including *Orfeo* (1940).
Good study: A. Liess: *Carl Orff* (1966).

PENDERECKI, Krzysztof (born 1933)
Polish composer

Penderecki's coming of age coincided with the opening-up of Polish music
to avant-garde procedures, and he exploited them eagerly in such works as
Threnody for the Victims of Hiroshima (1960), in which fifty-two string-
players independently slither, pluck and chirr, using the wood as well as the
hair of their bows and happily playing above as well as below the bridge.
The extraordinary assault this music makes on the ear concentrates the
mind, paradoxically, not on the sounds themselves but on Penderecki's
subject-matter; in other, similar works (e.g. *Anaklasis*, 1960, for forty-two

strings and percussion, or the orchestral *De natura sonoris*, 'On the Nature of Sound', I and I I, 1966 and 1971) lack of an objective correlative unfocuses the experience, leaving the gestures impressive but meaningless. The best of Penderecki's abstract works solve this problem by centring the music on a virtuoso soloist (*Cello Concerto*, 1972, *Violin Concerto*, 1979) or by using pre-existent styles or forms as steadying-points (e.g. *Actions* for jazz group, 1971; *Symphony*, 1973). His best music applies his experimental techniques to (often religious) words, and once again the effects enhance rather than inhibit meaning. In *Stabat mater* (1963), the spectacular *St Luke's Passion* (1966), *Utrenja* (*The Entombment and Resurrection of Christ*, 1971) and *The Song of Songs* (1972), the combination of whistling, whispering, ululating and straightforward, dissonant singing brings out the universal meanings of hackneyed choral texts in much the same way as *Ligeti's endless-belt music seems to open up ordinary semitones and semiquavers: the listener hardly wants to hear all Penderecki's works one after another, but taken singly they offer an engrossing experience – it is hard to hear them impassively. His two operas, *The Devils of Loudun* (1969) and *Paradise Lost* (1978), perhaps because the context for the music is more overtly dramatic, are less coherent; his work needs the objective framework of concert performance to achieve its musical equivalent of Brecht's alienation effect.

Penderecki's many other works include *Sonata* (1964) for cello and orchestra, *The Dream of Jacob* (1974) for orchestra, *Dies irae* (1967) and *Cosmogony* (1970) for choir and orchestra, and two string quartets (1960; 1968) which are breathtaking compendia of his extraordinary effects.

PISTON, Walter (1894–1976)
American composer and teacher

Except that his inspiration was instrumental rather than vocal, Piston was an American counterpart to *Britten. His music is fluent and characterful, and uses the techniques of modernism without ever becoming unapproachable: when people say 'he makes us hear C major as if he'd just invented it', this is the sort of music they have in mind. The best introduction to his work is his jazzy ballet-suite *The Incredible Flutist* (1938), whose chirpy tunes and 'wrong-note' harmony are reminiscent of such fastidiously frivolous French composers as Ibert or Françaix. He wrote half a dozen concertos in a more serious version of the same approachable style: those for viola (1957) and clarinet (1967) are particularly enjoyable. His most lasting work is in large abstract forms: five string quartets (No. 4, 1951, is outstanding) and eight heavyweight symphonies; these are nowadays neglected in favour of similar works by *Harris (in the USA) and *Prokofiev (virtually everywhere), which they outclass.

Piston's other works include the orchestral *3 New England Sketches* (1959), more like *Martinů's orchestral suites than the *Ives pieces their title suggests, a *Piano*

Quintet (1949) and a graceful *Flute Quintet* (1952) and *String Sextet* (1964). As the author of three lucid university textbooks, *Harmony* (1941), *Counterpoint* (1947) and *Orchestration* (1955), he taught several generations of American composers most of what they know.

POULENC, Francis (1899–1963)
French composer

There are two faces to Poulenc's music. He composed a large number of instrumental pieces in an undemanding, uncomplicated style, parroting *Stravinsky when he felt serious and Cole Porter when he didn't. The quality of relaxed bravado about his piano suites (e.g. *3 Mouvements perpétuels*, 1918; *10 Promenades*, 1924; *Suite française*, 1935) and his ballets (*Les Biches*, 1923; *Les Animaux modèles*, 1941) intrigues without engagement and pleases without satisfaction, and several of his larger works, e.g. the posturing *Stabat mater* (1950) and *Gloria* (1959), country cousins of *Stravinsky's *Oedipus rex*, bustle with the same agreeable but second-rate inspiration. At other times, he was fired to write music of real substance. His thirty-two song-cycles, in particular – the range is from surrealist squibs to utterances of profound emotion, often in the same cycle: good examples are *Tel jour, telle nuit* (1937), setting Éluard, and *Banalités* (1940), setting Apollinaire – rival Fauré or Duparc, their inspiration. This seriousness also appears in his convent-opera *Dialogues des Carmélites* (1956), from Bernanos's novel, and in his Saint-Saëns-like *Organ Concerto* (1938) and *Flute Sonata* (1947). He was a miniaturist, and seems to have cared little about the originality of what he wrote; but at its level, a slight thing expertly thrown off, his music seldom fails to please.

Poulenc's many other works include concertos for harpsichord (1928), two pianos (1932) and one piano (1949), various chamber pieces including *Sextet* (1940) for piano and wind quintet, and a delightful children's work, *The Story of Babar the Little Elephant* (1945), for speaker and piano. Good biography: H. Hell: *Francis Poulenc* (1959).

PROKOFIEV, Sergei (1891–1953)
Russian composer

In the world of 20th-century music, Prokofiev is a multi-lingual interpreter mistaken for a poet. 150 years ago, the most popular 'serious' composer was not Beethoven but Spohr, and Prokofiev has inherited Spohr's pasteboard crown. The reason is that in an art devoted primarily to the evocation and expression of emotion, both men rigorously excluded feeling from their scores, thus leaving their dexterous technique and unfailing invention high and dry. In the heartless 1920s, when Prokofiev made his name (and, indeed, in the 1820s when Spohr made his), absence of emotion hardly mattered, and the music made its way by being glitteringly accessible both to audiences and performers. One after another, Prokofiev took the prevailing languages of modern music – *Rite* *of Spring* dissonance, neo-classical elegance, 'wrong-note' cheekiness, neo-romantic heroics – and homogenized them for popular consumption: his music lay well under the fingers (it was much easier to play than *Stravinsky's, for example) and flattered audiences into thinking themselves at ease with the avant-garde. Galsworthy and Cather once worked similar tricks in fiction; Fowles and Didion do so now.

Prokofiev's third-rate excellence is heard at its most naked in his ballets, particularly *Romeo and Juliet* (1935) and *Cinderella* (1944), which pick up the stylistic gauntlet (actually a mauve kid glove) thrown down by Tchaikovsky's *The Nutcracker*: strings of personable short 'numbers' are each equipped with a simple tune, a distinctive and danceable rhythm and ear-tickling orchestration or harmony, with nothing ever to trouble the artistic sense. When he applied the same style to grander pieces, notably opera, Prokofiev flopped because lack of memorability or emotional profundity crippled the music. *The Fiery Angel* (rev. 1927) and *War and Peace* (1942, continually revised) are pretentious failures, screen-music masquerading as art; *Love of Three Oranges* (1921) and *The Duenna* (1941) are better because their stories are thistledown comedy, and even they are best known because of light-weight orchestral suites quarried from the scores. Prokofiev's other works in larger forms include seven symphonies (which demonstrate the greatness of *Shostakovich), half a dozen concertos (Nos. 1 and 2 for violin, 1913 and 1935, are the best) and several big chamber pieces in which the poverty of his thinking, stripped of orchestral glitter, is remorselessly revealed.

The catalogue would be even fuller of inadequacy – Prokofiev wrote a lot of music – were it not for his consciously lighter works, and his music for his own instrument, the piano. In the suite (originally for a film) *Lieutenant Kije* (1934) and the story for speaker and orchestra *Peter and the Wolf* (1936) he tapped the genius which elsewhere eluded him. Not a note is out of place; the music unobtrusively does what it sets out to do; passages like Kije's sleigh-ride and the slinky-cat theme from *Peter and the Wolf* haunt the mind. The piano music is stiffened by virtuosity, the display element concentrating Prokofiev's imagination. He wrote five concertos (No. 3, 1921, is the sugariest and most popular; Nos. 1 and 2, 1911 and 1913, are the shortest, most self-conscious, and best), and ten sonatas, whose steely pyrotechnics and epigrammatic brevity place them in a line from Liszt's more extrovert pieces, and which add biting harmonies and earnestness of purpose (not a tune in earshot) to bracing effect.

In the end, the best approach to Prokofiev's music is to give up critical agonizing and lie back to enjoy it. Seduction is his forte, and in such works as *Symphony 1* ('Classical Symphony', 1917), *Lieutenant Kije*, *Peter and the Wolf*, the suites from *Romeo and Juliet* and *Piano Concerto 1*, it is accomplished with ease and charm.

Prokofiev's other music includes several large choral cantatas to Soviet texts (e.g. *Cantata on the 20th Anniversary of the October Revolution*, 1937), half a dozen sets of songs (notably *Five Akhmatova Songs*, 1916), and film music (e.g. for

Eisenstein's *Alexander Nevsky*, a score which he reworked as a cantata in 1939). His autobiographical and other writings are collected in *Materials, Articles, Interviews* (1978) and *Prokofiev by Prokofiev* (1979), and good accounts of his sad life – he blamed his creative dilemmas, with at least some justice, on persecution by the authorities – are given in I. Nestyev: *Sergei Prokofiev: His Musical Times* (1960) and C. Samuel: *Prokofiev* (English edn 1971).

RAKHMANINOV, Sergei (1873–1943)
Russian composer and pianist

At the beginning of his career Rakhmaninov was a successful conductor, particularly of opera (he was principal conductor at the Bolshoi in the 1900s, and his own three operas were well received there). He was also active as a solo pianist, and after the revolution settled down to pursue this career in Europe and the USA. These other activities curtailed his composing: he wrote less than fifty works altogether, many of them sets of songs or of short piano pieces (e.g. the popular *Preludes* and *Études-tableaux*) designed for his own use. His composing credo, as he said in an interview with the American critic David Ewen, was 'to make my music speak simply and directly what is in my heart at the time I am composing. If there is love, bitterness, sadness or religion, these moods become part of the music . . .' This forthright romanticism, coupled with gifts for melody, bitter-sweet Tchaikovskian harmony and coruscating virtuosity, has made his music for piano and orchestra dominate the repertoire. His four concertos (1891; 1901; 1909; 1926), especially Nos. 2 and 3 – No. 2 became a world 'pop' when it was used as the theme music of the film *Brief Encounter* – and his *Paganini Rhapsody* (1934), whose 18th variation was detached and made into a sentimental ballad, are so familiar that it is easy to miss how good the music is. These warhorses are sturdy as well as mettlesome; the construction of the 2nd and 3rd concertos is as effective as anything by Brahms, and the play of moods in the *Paganini Rhapsody* is as intellectually extrovert as its pianism is sensual. Less showy but no less well-wrought are the 2nd and 3rd of Rakhmaninov's three symphonies (1907; 1936 – No. 2 is especially fine, a sibling of Tchaikovsky's *Pathétique*), his choral symphony *The Bells* (1913) and his *Cello Sonata* (1901), a work as unexpected (from a virtuoso pianist) and as satisfying as Chopin's.

Rakhmaninov's other music includes several large works for use in the Russian Orthodox liturgy (notably *Easter Vigil*, 1915), two piano sonatas (1907; 1913), two ebullient *Suites* for two pianos (No. 2, 1901, is a prancing stable-mate to *Piano Concerto 2*), and an atmospheric orchestral sea-picture after Böcklin's painting *The Isle of the Dead* (1909). Good biography: S. Bertensson and J. Leyda: *Sergei Rakhmaninov: A Lifetime in Music* (1965); good study (partly technical): P. Piggott: *Rakhmaninov* (1978).

RAVEL, Maurice (1875-1937)
French composer

*Stravinsky, who had a phrase for everyone (usually uncomplimentary), called Ravel a 'clockmaker of genius', and it is easy to agree. Ravel's music is meticulously put together – his 'ear' for harmonic refinement, for the exact 'voicing' of chords (laying them out for instruments so that every note makes a specific effect instead of contributing to a blur of sound), and for piquancy of scoring, was unequalled this century, save perhaps by Stravinsky's own – but once the surface enchantment of his work dissolves, there is often an unsatisfying lack of heart. In this, he is like many baroque composers (Scarlatti and Telemann, for example), and like them, he is at his best when effectiveness rather than affectiveness is called for. His virtuoso piano music, from the delicate *Sonatine* (1905) to the barnstorming *Gaspard de la nuit* (1908, which he deliberately composed to be the hardest piece of music ever written for the instrument), shows his ability at peak, but when the element of individual endeavour is removed by (brilliant) orchestral transcription, as in *Valses nobles et sentimentales* (1911) or the suite *Le Tombeau de Couperin* (1917), the music's essential *salon* quality is revealed. In his larger works, notably the ballet *Daphnis and Chloe* (1912) and the opera *L'Enfant et les sortilèges* (1925) he looked for feeling and found sentimentality: *Debussy (in *Jeux*) showed how ballet-music could be emotionally profound without sacrificing intimacy or dandyism, and *Janáček (in *The Cunning Little Vixen*) demonstrated how to write an opera about animals without tweeness or patronizing. Ravel's best music is either heartless (the two piano concertos, both 1931; the orgiastic orchestral *tours de force La Valse*, 1920, and *Bolero*, 1928, and the ice-cool *Introduction and Allegro*, 1906, for harp and chamber group, commissioned by a harp-manufacturer to show off his latest line) or else is unselfconsciously simple and – a crucial quality – short, like the *Mother Goose Suite* (1908) composed as a children's piano duet and later arranged as a pellucid ballet score. Debussy devised for French music a forward-looking, adaptable and new language; Ravel, for all the beauty of his scores – few composers have consistently produced sounds so ravishing – led it right back up the *cul-de-sac* it had been exploring for years before Debussy came.

Ravel's other works include a joky one-act opera, *L'Heure espagnole* (1907), an agreeable *String Quartet* (1903) and *Piano Trio* (1914), and several sets of songs, the most striking of which is *Histoires naturelles* (1906). His *Pavane for a Dead Infanta* (1899), originally the result of an afternoon's dalliance with a piano, was orchestrated in 1910 and for a time ousted all his other music from popular attention. His orchestration of Mussorgsky's *Pictures at an Exhibition* has been a showpiece for sixty years, eclipsing Mussorgsky's piano original. Of the many books about Ravel – the exquisiteness of so many individual works has encouraged people to think him a more interesting composer than he is – the simplest and best (despite occasional technicality) is R. Nichols: *Ravel* (1977).

REICH, Steve (born 1936)
American composer

In *Satie's piano piece *Vexations* the performer is told to play the same twelve bars 840 times without variation, and Reich's music develops this principle. A single musical idea – chord, group of notes, rhythm – is repeated quietly, inexorably and unemotionally until the piece ends. It could be done using a tape-loop, except that from time to time, as the flow proceeds, minute small changes are introduced: one note of the chord is altered or prolonged, the rhythm skips a beat, the 'melody' rises where once it fell. The effect (if you survive the first five minutes) is hypnotic and restful, a musical counterpart to Hartung's reeds-rippled-by-breeze paintings. Reich's admirers talk of African drumming or Zen Buddhism, but the analogy is more that wallpaper whose pattern may or may not be regular, and which gently occupies the mind as you tease it out. A characteristic work, an excellent sample of his executive-toy wares, is *Phase Patterns for Four Organs* (1970), which he himself described as 'one chord growing in time'. *Piano Store* (1969) applies the same principles to a 'storeful of pianos', and *Drumming* (1971) uses glockenspiels, marimbas and voices as well as drums. Other composers to use the style well are Brian Chapple (e.g. in *Concert Piece*, 1969, for eight pianos) and La Monte Young, who, in addition to comparatively 'straight' works like *The Tortoise, His Dreams and Journeys* (1964), has written pieces like *Composition 5* (1960), in which the performer, like some disarming Nabokovian charlatan, seduces his audience by freeing a cloud of butterflies.

ROUSSEL, Albert (1869–1937)
French composer

Until he was twenty-five Roussel worked in the merchant navy, travelling round the Indo-Chinese ports frequented by Conrad and promoted to glory in the tales of Maugham and Josef von Sternberg's Marlene Dietrich films. In 1909 he became professor of counterpoint at the Schola Cantorum in Paris. His music also tacks between the poles of exoticism and academicism. Many of his works take themes and colour from the East, either drawing directly on oriental traditions (*Padmavati*, 1918, for example, is an opera-ballet treating an Indian legend in much the same way as Borodin's *Prince Igor*) or finding in ancient Greek ideas a pagan sensuality very far from the stiff-upper-lip scholarly classicism of the time. (Good examples are his mythological suite *Flute Players*, 1917, and his *Ravellian ballet *Bacchus and Ariadne*, 1930.) His academic interests led to a large body of abstract works in a no-nonsense 'conservatoire' style, in which muscular construction tends to outweigh inspiration: his four symphonies (the best is No. 3, 1930) recall *Prokofiev, his chamber music (notably *String Trio*, 1937) Ravel or *Holst, his *Piano Concerto*

(1927) Busoni. In a few works, usually short, he made an appealing and personal synthesis of styles: *Suite in F* (1926) for orchestra, his songs (especially *2 Songs from the Chinese*, 1908) and above all his ballet *The Spider's Banquet* (1912), inspired by Fabre's anthropomorphic book on insect behaviour, are jewels in a somewhat over-carpentered wooden crown.

Roussel's other works include two violin sonatas, a string quartet, an agreeably light-weight *Trio* (1929) for flute, viola and cello, and *Sinfonietta* (1934) for strings. Good study: B. Dean: *Albert Roussel* (1961).

RUBBRA, Edmund (born 1901)
English composer and teacher

As lecturer in music at Oxford from 1947 to 1968, and at the London Guildhall School of Music, Rubbra taught many leading post-war British composers: his importance in the UK was analogous to *Piston's in the USA. He was a prolific composer, in a personal style which blended complex counterpoint (derived from Palestrina or the English madrigalists) with scoring as ponderous and romantic as that of Brahms. The effect is to make his larger instrumental works (which include eleven symphonies, half a dozen concertos and four string quartets) intriguing but muddy, so that it takes several hearings to learn their subtleties; exceptions are the fleet-footed *Symphony 5* (1949) and the meditative, graceful *Piano Concerto* (1959). Rubbra's finest works are settings of Catholic words (three masses, and motets such as *Stabat mater* or *Lauda Sion*); their clean texture (uncluttered by orchestral doubling, where several instruments earnestly try to put across the same melodic line) and their 'endless melody' recall both his admired Renaissance predecessors and the robust ecstasies of such British cathedral composers as Stanford and Howells.

Rubbra's other works include several chamber pieces (his *Piano Trio 1*, 1948, and *Oboe Sonata*, 1958, are excellent) and numerous groups of songs of which the best are the Brahmsian *3 Psalms* (1947).

SATIE, Erik (1866–1925)
French composer

Satie is revered in histories of 20th-century music as an influential precursor of *Debussy (he 'invented' unprepared discords as a colouristic device), of neo-classicism (he proclaimed the inability of music to depict or evoke emotion) and of *musique concrète*, aleatory music and other avant-garde techniques (he included parts for typewriters, rattles and whistles in the score of his surrealist ballet *Parade*, 1917; he dispensed with bar-lines in several piano works; he peppered his scores with *Cagy instructions like 'any way you like' and 'play from the head'). To most people he is also known as an eccentric, who at the first performance (during a 1920 art-exhibition) of his *Furniture Music* scurried round beseeching the audience to talk, and who gave his pieces titles like *In Horse Costume* (1911) or *Things Seen to Left and Right (Without Glasses)* (1914). He was a Rosicrucian and a Montmartre cabaret pianist, a friend of Cocteau and Picasso whose favourite art was that of the Middle Ages, a recluse who delighted in company, a character from Balzac strayed into the gayer age of Gide. His music consists chiefly of short piano pieces, whose gentle melodies and plain harmonies belie both their extravagant titles and absurd running commentaries (e.g., in *Dried-Up Embryos*, 1913, the instruction 'like a nightingale with toothache', or in *Bureaucratic Sonatina*, 1917, such remarks as 'he dreams of promotion'). His most famous works are *3 Gymnopédies* (1888, the first nowadays as well established in the popular repertoire as Bach's *Air on the G String* or Fauré's *Pavane*), *3 Pear-Shaped Pieces* (1903, actually seven pieces), and the splendid *Sports and Diversions* (1914), thumbnail sketches of twenty different pastimes (boating, tennis, skipping), a musical precursor of Tati's 1930s cabaret act. His most serious composition is also his longest and best: *Socrates* (1919), a setting of passages from Plato which manages to be as undemonstrative and at the same time as moving as the original placid prose.

Good study: R. Myers: *Erik Satie* (1948).

SCHOENBERG, Arnold (1874–1951)
Austrian composer and teacher

In 1913, after a Berlin concert, the critic of the newspaper *Signale* wrote: 'Fifteen intrepid musicians gave us Schoenberg's Chamber Symphony. "Chamber-of-horrors symphony" would be a better title . . . A hundred listeners sat impassively as this storm of dissonance roared past. But people of courage still exist. At the beginning of the concert it was threatened that the Chamber Symphony would be played twice, and none the less most of the audience stayed put. Or perhaps it was not so much courage, as simple fear that such cunningly created chaos might one day become the art of the future.' In 1981, still puzzling it out, the musicologist Malcolm Macdonald wrote: 'He may yet be seen, not as modern music's *monstre sacré*, the composer audiences most like to hate, but as the last great custodian of the ethical (as opposed to aesthetic) values of musical Romanticism, and their chief deliverer into the modern world.'

These appraisals stand at the beginning and end of the long process of understanding Schoenberg's artistic intentions, the battle to unfetter musical expression which he himself once likened to swimming through a boiling sea and which some less tolerant listeners still think a dogged but pointless exercise. His goal was 'pure expression', a musical statement of its creator's psychic state as unequivocal and revealing as the case-histories of his contemporary Freud. (It was less apparent in the 1900s than today just how devious the monologues of Freud's patients, and his interpretations, actually were.) Schoenberg's aims were close to those of the expressionists in art – he himself was a talented painter, in a style close to Munch or Kokoschka – and his early compositions concerned themselves, in expressionist style, with the depiction of neurotic states of mind. A good example is *Verklärte Nacht* ('Transfigured Night', 1899). A man and woman walk through a forest in moonlight; she tearfully confesses unfaithfulness; he forgives her; they walk on, their love transfiguring the gloom. This story inspired in Schoenberg a score turbulent with contrast, the harmony and musical texture changing with every new flicker of emotion, the chords (none more alarming than those of Wagner's *Tristan and Isolde*) used somewhat schematically – unusual or discordant harmony expressing dismay or anxiety, straightforward harmony expressing love's security – but with a sensuality and melodiousness he never again achieved. If the 'ethical values of Romanticism' are at the heart of this music, so is one of its chief aesthetic purposes, to rouse and satisfy emotion in its audience.

As Schoenberg's music moved further along the expressionist path (in such pieces as *Erwartung*, 'Expectation', 1909, *Gurrelieder*, 1911, and *Die glückliche Hand*, 'The Lucky Hand', 1913), late-19th-century harmonic procedures, which had already in *Verklärte Nacht* been pushed to expressive extremes, began to collapse under the intensity of emotion they were expected to encompass. The chords became so bizarre, and their changes so frequent and so unrelatable to any previous musical experience – even in Mahler's or *Strauss's most 'advanced' harmony, the ghost of Beethoven still lurks – that the effect is anarchic rather than precise, delirious and incoherent rather than explicit. The music makes demands not only on its hearers' aural tolerance but also on their emotions; there is none of the objective distance between artist and audience which characterizes (say) a Mozart score; these works demand emotional complicity in the consumer in the same way as Kandinsky's paintings or Strindberg's plays. This invitation to share in what often seems neurotic or self-indulgent breast-beating is the most 'difficult' thing about Schoenberg's music – and for those drawn to it, it can be one of its greatest pleasures.

The collapse of traditional harmony in Schoenberg's music was complete by 1909, the year of his first atonal masterpiece *5 Orchestral Pieces* (each of which is a sequence of sounds devised to be individually striking and ordered according to a logic which is internal, is the music's own, and conforms to no external 'rules'). For a decade thereafter he worked at a variety of projects, seeking to find new ways of disciplining what must have seemed a riot of musical possibility; most pieces were either abandoned or else finished years later, and the chief successes of the time are *Pierrot lunaire* (1912), which solves the problem of organization by using twenty-one very short, atmospheric poems as the basis for the music, and a number of aphoristic songs and piano pieces.

In the late 1910s he began experimenting with 12-note serial organization, in which the notes of the chromatic scale would be 'related only to one another' (that is, given independence from keys, traditional chords or modes), and in 1921 he published his first entirely 12-note work, a *Suite* for piano whose movements share forms with Bach's harpsichord suites (gavotte, jig, minuet), but whose harmony is like Schoenberg's earlier atonal music with all its expressionist emotionalism pared away.

In the next thirty years Schoenberg produced a couple of dozen works each of which was as stylistically unpredictable as the last: he never settled down to repeat himself, never formulated a definitive 'Schoenberg style'. Some of his pieces (e.g. *Accompaniment to a Film Scene*, 1930, or the huge opera *Moses and Aaron*, 1932, which supplies a Biblical story with Freudian and Nietzschean layers of meaning in the manner of Mann's novel *Joseph and His Brothers*) are still expressionist in intention and technique, while others (notably *String Quartet 3*, 1927, *Variations for Orchestra*, 1928, and the fine, late *String Trio*, 1946) use objective classical forms, as in the piano *Suite*, to the music's gain. In the 1930s he escaped from the Nazis to California, and American old age led (as it did with *Bartók) to a relaxation of technique: *String Quartet 4* (1936), *Piano Concerto* (1942) and the dramatic ghetto-narrative *A Survivor from Warsaw* (1947), although no one but a fanatic would call them beautiful, are his most approachable and audience-conscious scores for half a century.

On paper, Schoenberg's music is intriguing and engrossing. The note-patterns are created and manipulated with driving intellectuality and logic; the flow from idea to idea is as seductive as it is unexpected. For this reason, his work has been exhaustively analysed and has influenced both the composition and academic study of music throughout the world. (As a teacher, he himself combined formidable intellectual integrity with personal charm: his pupils seem, if they were wise, to have anticipated his criticisms before they went to him, and gone chiefly for the pleasure of sharing his enthusiasm for examining the nuts and bolts that made the art.) The fact that he has rarely beguiled audiences, that for all its cerebral distinction his music still sounds to many as chaotic and ugly as it did to the *Signale* critic in 1913, is a sad but serious flaw: *pace* Macdonald, it is little use being the custodian of ethical (or any other) values if you fail in the artist's other primary duty to his or her audience, to entertain.

Schoenberg's other works include a large symphonic poem after Maeterlinck, *Pelléas and Mélisande* (1903), *Serenade* (1923) and *Suite* (1926) for chamber group, *Violin Concerto* (1936) and an impassioned setting of Byron's anti-tyrannical *Ode to Napoleon* (1942) for speaker and instruments. His books include *Selected Letters* (ed. Stein, 1964) and *Style and Idea* (1975). In the nature of things, books about him tend to be technical; the briefest and least formidable are C. Rosen: *Schoenberg* (1975) and M. Macdonald: *Schoenberg* (1976).

SCHULLER, Gunther (born 1925)
American composer

A horn-player, Schuller has specialized in instrumental works: as with Malcolm Arnold's music in Britain, part of the pleasure his pieces give is a sense of exhilarating virtuosity, of cheeky challenges urbanely met. His interests range from jazz to *Webern, and in the 1950s he invented 'third-stream' music, in which jazz and classical players work together. (*Symphonic Tribute to Duke Ellington*, 1955, *Concertino*, 1959, for jazz quartet and orchestra, and *American Triptych*, 1965, after paintings by Calder, Pollock and Davis, are his most lively pieces in this style, which was also used, in the same decade, by Rolf Lieberman in Switzerland and Matyas Seiber in Britain.) Schuller's most thorough-going third-stream work is an opera, *The Visitation* (1966), which sets the story of Kafka's *The Trial* in an American university (where its hero is a bullied negro), and uses jazz sequences to propel the plot without incongruity. The opera's style is reminiscent both of *Gershwin's *Porgy and Bess* and of *Henze's *Boulevard Solitude*; despite its mixture of inspirations and influences, it works. The breadth of Schuller's interests is also shown in his orchestral *7 Studies on Themes of Paul Klee* (1959), a sound-tour of seven Klee pictures (including *Arabian Town* and *The Twittering Machine*) which offers a virtuoso, and delightful, 20th-century counterpart to Mussorgsky's *Pictures at an Exhibition*. Schuller's later works apply the same sunny extroversion to more abstract forms, notably a *Symphony* (1965) and half a dozen concertos (of which the finest are *Double Bass Concerto*, 1968, and *Violin Concerto*, 1976).

Schuller's other works include the *Stravinskyish ballet *Variants* (1961), *Museum Piece* (1970), a concerto for Renaissance instruments and modern orchestra, and many chamber pieces including two string quartets and an exuberant *Wind Quintet* (1958).

SCHUMAN, William (born 1910)
American composer and administrator

When a composer's music is famous in his own country and largely unknown outside it, the reason is usually parochialism, a local viewpoint not for export. (Finzi's rhapsodic Englishness and Schmidt's post-Mahlerian Austrianness are good examples. Neither folk-song modalities nor endless *ländler* tickle the international palate as much as *aficionados* think the music deserves.) In Schuman's case, apart from one piece incomprehensible to most non-Americans (the baseball opera *The Mighty Casey*, 1953), it is hard to see why the music fails to travel. Its inspiration is often American enough – he set Whitman, and wrote works in honour both of the New England countryside and the social-realist painter Ben Shahn – but the language is straightforwardly and appealingly international-modern, like *Walton's, full of busy rhythms, catchy tunes and harmony which is pungent but rarely cacophonous. The best of his works are seven symphonies (he wrote nine, but withdrew the first two; No. 5, 1943, for strings, and No. 8, 1962, are especially Waltonian), concertos for cello and for violin, and a series of powerful ballets to exploit the taloned talent of Martha Graham (*Night Journey*, 1948; *Judith*, 1948; *The Witch of Endor*, 1965). In addition to composing, Schuman had an influential career as an administrator: among other things, he ran the Juilliard School of Music, the music-publishing firm Schirmer (a good friend to 20th-century American composers) and the Lincoln Center for the Performing Arts.

Good interim study: V. Persichetti and F. Schreiber: *William Schuman* (1954).

SCRIABIN, Alexander (1872–1915)
Russian composer and mystic

Scriabin's early career was as a starry composer-pianist, Chopin's heir. In the 1890s and early 1900s he toured Russia and Europe, performing his own music, and wrote pieces for the purpose (studies, preludes, mazurkas, even a showy *Concerto*, 1898) which followed the tradition, in Chopin's music, of blending virtuoso technical demands with refined, experimental harmony. (He even emulated Chopin by composing two orchestral works, *Symphonies 1 and 2*, which appeared to show that his talents were best accommodated at the keyboard.) During the 1900s his career dramatically changed. He studied theosophy and the philosophy of Nietzsche, and convinced himself that there was a mystical road to human enlightenment, and that the spirit-guide would be an artist-superman such as himself. Schumann's and Wolf's neurotic sensibility had led them to despair and tragedy; the same kind of romantic over-sensitivity produced in Scriabin an equally insane but more joyous ebullience: he went on another – highly successful – European tour proclaiming himself nothing less than the Messiah. He wrote works to support this view, some (e.g. the last half-dozen of his ten piano sonatas, music of demonic ferocity quite unlike the scented showing-off of his earlier works) at once intimate and driven, the rest a series of attempts at the grand artistic synthesis which would unblinker and rescue humanity. Although the rationale of these pieces (*Divine Poem*, 1904; *Poem of Ecstasy*, 1908; *Prometheus*, 1910, all dazzlingly conceived and scored for orchestra) now seems absurdly dated and pretentious, and their techniques (ranging from mystic chords to colour-organs projecting lights to match each sound) eerily foreshadow the psychedelic psycho-drivel of the 1960s, the music itself is often excellent: Scriabin's preposterous ambitions released in him a creative originality and energy which clinched his already formidable skill.

A wide-eyed, period account of Scriabin is A. E. Hull: *A Great Russian Tone Poet: Scriabin* (1916); less optimistic and more up-to-date (alas?) is F. Bower: *The New Scriabin: Enigma and Answers* (1973), based on an earlier biography and making exemplary use of Scriabin's own letters.

SESSIONS, Roger (born 1896)
American composer

In a distinguished academic career (he worked in the universities of Boston, Princeton, Yale and Berkeley, California, and at the Juilliard School) Sessions taught many of the most eclectic American composers of the century (among them *Babbitt and the fine symphonist David Diamond). With *Copland in the 1920s, he began a series of contemporary music concerts in New York; he was a director of the League of Composers, and US president of the International Society for Contemporary Music. Few men, in short, have worked harder on behalf of their artistic contemporaries. His compositions are few (a couple of dozen), but – like *Hanson's in all but sound – of immense power and seriousness. His style is dissonant and demanding, somewhere between *Bartók's uncompromising 1920s scores and the later music of *Tippett; he makes free use of serial technique; his music would be dauntingly ugly if it were not for the feeling of a vigorous intellect at work in every piece – Bach's *B Minor Mass* or *St Matthew Passion* give a similar impression of order hard-won (but triumphantly won) from musical complexity. Sessions' works range from operas (*The Trial of Lucullus*, 1947, based on Brecht's anti-Nazi play; *Montezuma*, 1963, whose harsh view of pre-Colombian South America anticipates Herzog's 1970s films) and choral works (e.g. Whitman's *When Lilacs Last in the Dooryard Bloom'd*, 1970, also set by *Hindemith) to eight symphonies (Nos. 2, 1946, and 8, 1968, are especially grand), concertos for piano, violin and violin and cello, a compact *Concerto for Orchestra* (1981), and chamber works including two *Ivesy string quartets.

SHOSTAKOVICH, Dmitri (1906–75)
Russian composer

If Schubert's movements were (as Schumann said) like country walks, then listening to Shostakovich is like driving down an autobahn. The notes and harmonies flow past, pleasantly and undemandingly; occasionally there is a change of gear or scenery, to remind us that we're travelling; it's only at the end of a movement or work that we realize that ground has been covered and progress made. Apart from a few uncharacteristic early works, none of his compositions are tougher on the ear than César Franck's; apart from frequent passages which seem in their context like sardonic grimness (if music can be either sardonic or grim), his works are as even-textured as a child's storybook.

Part of the reason is his unending aesthetic battle with the authorities. Every time he produced 'difficult' harmony or music with depth of meaning, he was denounced. His opera *Lady Macbeth of Mtsensk* (1932) offended Stalin because it contained a (highly explicit) bedroom scene, and dropped out of the repertoire until Stalin's death, when it was revised and restaged as *Katarina Ismailova* (1956); his *Symphony 9* (1945), with other works, was dismissed by the cultural commissar Zhdanov in 1948 as decadent and formalist, because instead of reflecting the Soviet triumph in the Second World War it was cheerful and frivolous; his setting, in *Symphony 13* (1962), of Yevtushenko's poem *Babi Yar* on Soviet extermination of the Jews, was hissed from the concert-hall. Shostakovich's public response to such criticisms was to grovel. He wrote breast-beating apologies in magazines ('I know that the Party is right . . . I accept . . . stern but paternal solicitude . . .'); he subtitled his *Symphony 5* (1937) 'A Soviet artist's practical creative reply to just criticism'; he wrote cantatas to jingoistic texts (e.g. *The Song of the Forests*, 1949, on a reafforestation scheme, or *The Sun Shines Over our Motherland*, 1952, on the happy relationship between Russian weather and endeavour). Three years after his death, a book was published (*Testimony: The Memoirs of Shostakovich*, ed. Volkov, 1979) depicting him as an embittered hypocrite whose acceptance of Lenin Medals and Stalin Prizes was intended as savage irony, and whose misery led to an obsession with death which haunts his scores. Even if this book is genuine – its worth has been disputed – the vast amount of 'people's music' Shostakovich wrote offers testimony of a different kind, pointing either to a remarkably cynical attitude to his own day-to-day work or to a case of equally remarkable artistic schizophrenia.

Despite the contradictions and unpredictable quality of his music, Shostakovich wrote some of the century's most satisfying works. On his day, and particularly in instrumental music, he outstripped competition. *Symphony 10* (1953), for example, is a deeply felt, affecting piece whose success results, in true symphonic style, from the development and transformation of its themes: it is a masterpiece, and would not have worked so well in any other form. *Symphony 5*, for all its flag-waving finale, is stirring and characterful; *Symphony 14* (1969), a song-cycle on the theme of death inspired by the orchestral song-cycles of Shostakovich's friend *Britten, shares their quality. His concertos (especially *Violin Concerto 1*, 1948, *Piano Concerto 2*, 1957, and *Cello Concerto 1*, 1959) are effective and memorable; his ballet suites (notably *The Age of Gold*, 1930) and film scores (notably *The Gadfly*, 1955) are as witty as anything composed in 1920s France. It is likely, once the controversies over his personality and career fade and the bulk of his music is forgotten, that he will be remembered as a symphonist in a line from Mahler and Tchaikovsky, for quality as well as style.

Shostakovich's other works include fifteen string quartets (Nos. 8–15 outrank the others), an excellent *Piano Quintet* (1940), and several piano pieces including *24 Preludes* (1933) and *24 Preludes and Fugues* (1951). Apart from *Testimony* (mentioned above, and essential reading), the best books on him are D. Rabinovich: *Dmitri Shostakovich* (1959) and the collection of critical essays *Shostakovich: The Man and His Music* (ed. Norris, 1982).

SIBELIUS, Jean (1865-1957)
Finnish composer

In the 1930s it was fashionable for European critics (especially British) to hail Sibelius as the greatest composer since Beethoven, and to proclaim his symphonies and symphonic poems the only hope for an art otherwise overrun with *Stravinskys, *Bartóks and *Schoenbergs. Whether this claim was true or not, making it involved ignoring a pile of Sibelius's own compositions, perfectly estimable but of an irresponsible cheerfulness incompatible with the role chosen for him of Man of Destiny. Over 120 of his 150 opus numbers are collections of songs or short pieces, written very often as incidental music for plays and as cheerily tuneful as his 'serious' works are solemn and profound. *Valse triste* (1904), which he foolishly sold outright to his publishers, thus handing them a fortune in exchange for a month's rent, the suites *Karelia* (1893), *King Christian II* (1898) and *Pelléas and Mélisande* (1905), and such songs as *Autumn Evening* (1904) and *Flower Song* (1917) are among the best light music of their age: of 'serious' composers, only Schubert and Fauré had the same deft touch. Tunefulness also bubbles through several of Sibelius's larger scores, notably the tone-poems *The Swan of Tuonela* (No. 3 of *Four Lemminkainen Legends*, 1895), *Finlandia* (1899), whose central tune was used for the English-language hymn *Be Still, My Soul*, and above all the Tchaikovskian *Violin Concerto* (1903).

Side by side with this impressive but low-profile creativity (which he kept up throughout his life), Sibelius produced a group of orchestral masterpieces on the most sonorous and epic scale. He took from Liszt the idea of the symphonic poem (the depiction in sound of a mood or story derived from literature, fine art or legend), and used it to present the landscape and epic history of Finland. Several of the works are straightforward, general evocations of grandeur (e.g. *En Saga*, 'A Saga', rev. 1901) or landscape (e.g. *Tapiola*, 1926, a vision of Finland as the home of the forest-god Tapio); others – among them the finest – are based on stories from the legend-cycle *Kalevala*: *Pohjola's Daughter* (1906), *Luonnotar* (1913), *The Bard* (1914). The culmination of this bleakly majestical style is his seven symphonies, which replace the narrative structure of symphonic poems with a developmental form entirely Sibelius's own: whereas most symphonic composers begin their works by stating themes or ideas which are then developed, Sibelius tends to begin with hints and fragments, gradually increasing tension until it is released by a final, complete statement of the themes to which a whole movement or work has been aspiring. His first two symphonies (1899; 1902), still the most played, are least characteristic, looking back towards Tchaikovsky rather than forward to Sibelius's own maturity. Thereafter, each symphony is formally and harmonically unlike all the others (No. 4, 1911, for example, is based on the normally shunned, tense interval the tritone, known in medieval times as 'the devil in music'; No. 7, 1924, is in a single packed movement); unity in the cycle is achieved by such recurring devices as intermezzo-like slow movements in an apotheosis of Sibelius's light-music style (e.g. those in No. 3, 1907, and No. 6, 1923), repetition of blocks of material from movement to movement (notably in Nos. 4 and 6), and above all the building up, in the last movements, of an all-engulfing 'big tune' (those in Nos. 2, 3 and 5, 1915, are particularly striking). This intellectual power, combined with the individuality and immediate recognizability of his harmony, has meant that Sibelius has (contrary to 1930s predictions) had few imitators and started no school. For all the 19th-century approachability of his music, it is both revolutionary and unique.

Good studies: R. Layton: *Sibelius* (1965; partly technical); *Sibelius and His World* (1970; untechnical, and well illustrated).

SKALKOTTAS, Nikos (1904–49)
Greek composer and violinist

Skalkottas was a tantalizing musical might-have-been. In the 1920s he was among *Schoenberg's most brilliant pupils, as fine a composer as *Berg or *Gerhard; then, in 1933, he returned to Greece, worked for the rest of his life in the back desks of the Athens Symphony Orchestra, and hid his compositions in a drawer. After his death they were taken out, and found to be excellent. (There are over 150: symphonies, suites, concertos, piano pieces, songs and chamber works.) Whenever they are played – and few are repertory pieces – they please audiences, rouse critics and make scholars fall over themselves to assert Skalkottas's greatness. Unfortunately, his day was the 1930s and his hard-working Schoenbergian idiom may now sound dated. Until his music is better known, its quality can only be taken on trust; for the present, pieces like *Greek Dances* (1936) or *Concertino* (1939) for oboe and piano – two of the Skalkottas works which *are* performed – seem to bear out the extravagant claims made for him. Bruckner was once as little-known.

STOCKHAUSEN, Karlheinz (born 1928)
German composer

Stockhausen's starting-points are the same as *Cage's: the exhaustion of all previous composing systems and musical methods, and the need utterly to rethink and reinvent the art of communication in sound. His work is analogous to New Fiction in its use of a rationale as abstruse as it is dogmatic; it is analogous to 1960s Beat poetry in its quasi-mystical, quasi-Far-Eastern methods – one piece instructs the players, without offering them notes or chords, to empty their minds, and when they are thinking of nothing, to begin to play – and in its attraction of a large, vociferous and 'far-out' audience. As with all artists who gather disciples rather than spectators, the uncommitted may feel doubts about the general relevance or importance of Stockhausen's work; but for the converted, and especially while he is alive to guide performances himself – he usually modulates the sounds by means of an electronic console – its claims are large and irresistible.

The key components of Stockhausen's 'compositions' are blocks of material (often extracts from earlier pieces), detailed verbal instructions (often supplemented by a series of signs: plus, minus, exclamation, etc.), and a carefully controlled use of chance. The players improvise round the given material according to their instructions and their psychic identification with the mood of the performance, and the sound is processed through loudspeakers by one or more technicians. In some early works, e.g. *Groups*, 1957, and *Square*, 1960, loudspeakers were replaced by groups of performers placed along the walls of the auditorium surrounding the spectators. For music of this kind, live performance is essential; recordings can only be souvenirs of real experience. (The same is not true of some of Stockhausen's earlier pieces for tape, in which the finished recording, mastered by the composer, *is* the performance: characteristic are *Song of the Young Man*, 1956, and *Hymnen*, 'National Anthems', 1967.)

Stockhausen's early works (e.g. *Kontrapunkte*, 'Counterpoints', 1953, *Moments*, 1964, or *Piano Pieces I–XI*) are less representative of his output or philosophy than his evening-long 1970s works with electronics, such as *Sternklang* ('Music of the Stars', 1971), *Inori* ('Adorations', 1974), *Sirius* (1975) or *Light* (1977–present). The musical ancestors of these pieces are *Scriabin's tone-poems and the huge, ecstatic scores of *Messiaen (once Stockhausen's teacher); but the impact of Stockhausen's work is more mystical than musical, and he himself considers the sounds less an end than a means. His set of 'operas', one for each day of the week (*Thursday*, 1982, and *Saturday*, 1984, so far exist) will, when completed, be as all-embracing a statement of his philosophy-for-humanity, and very probably as demanding in its musical and theatrical needs, as Wagner's *Ring* was for our great-great-grandparents.

Books on Stockhausen tend either to unhelpful musical technicality or to philosophical ramble. J. Cott: *Stockhausen: Conversations with the Composer* (1974) is useful, though its argument can be headache-making to follow; the most lucid musical account for the general reader is J. Harvey: *The Music of Stockhausen: An Introduction* (1975).

STRAUSS, Richard (1864–1949)
German composer and conductor

In the 1910s there would have been no question about Strauss's place: at the head of the avant-garde. His symphonic poems (notably *Don Juan*, 1889, *Death and Transfiguration*, 1890, *Till Eulenspiegel*, 1895, *Also Sprach Zarathustra*, 1896, and *Ein Heldenleben*, 1899) were regarded as some of the most extreme and forward-looking scores ever written for romantic orchestra, and his operas *Salome* (1905, a setting of Wilde's barbaric and erotic play) and *Elektra* (1909) scandalized capacity audiences throughout the world. In his fifties, however, he relaxed his 'advanced' style, abandoned dissonance and turned instead to a mellow, harmonious idiom derived equally from Wagner and from Viennese operetta. Lehár is the main inspiration of his stage masterpiece, the comic opera *Der Rosenkavalier* (1911); its ecstatic tunes (for example in the scene of the presentation of the rose) are as sumptuous as those in *The Merry Widow* or *The Land of Smiles*, and its waltz-sequences out-swirl every other Strauss in sight. Strauss however adds to this confectioner's sugar symphonic breadth and power: for all their sweetness, his operas are as controlled and organized as Mozart's. He produced a string of urbane and lyrical works in this vein, including *Ariadne auf Naxos* (1912), *Die Frau ohne Schatten* (1919) and *Arabella* (1933), all to librettos by Hofmannsthal (who also wrote *Rosenkavalier*), and *Capriccio* (1942), to a libretto by Clemens Krauss. In his extreme old age he used the same warm style for non-operatic music: *Metamorphoses* (1945) and *Oboe Concerto* (1946), although they could have been composed at any time in the previous 100 years, are outstanding works, and *Four Last Songs* (1948), for soprano (always his favourite voice) and orchestra, crown his output. He was a splendid anachronism, ignoring every development in the art since Wagner; he thought of himself as a craftsman rather than a genius; his music's place in the repertoire is secure.

Strauss's other works include *Don Quixote* (1898) for cello and orchestra, two horn concertos (1883; 1942), eight other operas including *Intermezzo* (1924) and *Daphne* (1938), and over 200 songs. Good biographies: W. Schuh: *Richard Strauss: A Chronicle of the Early Years, 1864–1898* (1982); A. Jefferson: *Richard Strauss* (1973). *The Strauss–Hofmannstahl Correspondence* (English edn 1961) offers fascinating glimpses into a collaboration conducted largely by letter. Good technical account: N. Del Mar: *Richard Strauss, a Critical Commentary on His Life and Works* (3 vols., 1962–72).

STRAVINSKY, Igor (1882–1971)
Russian composer

It is rare for a composer of Stravinsky's stature to found his career not on operas, symphonies or chamber music but on ballet. Ballet music tends to be pretty but insubstantial, the handmaid of the dance; Stravinsky's ballet scores eclipse the stage, and work as well if not better in the concert-hall. He made his reputation writing for Diaghilev's Ballets Russes; many of his finest neo-classical works were written for ballets choreographed by Balanchine; more than sixty of his compositions altogether, whether composed for the stage or not, have been used for ballet scores. The reason is rhythmic alertness. Though his music is by no means easy to dance to, it derives and communicates energy by a combination of rhythmic variety and directness which many composers have imitated but none excelled; rhythmic dynamism is at the heart of every Stravinsky score, whether meant for theatre or concert-hall.

In the 1910s, at the time of his successes with the Ballets Russes, Stravinsky's work – like that of many White Russians contemplating artistic or political exile in the west – was full of nostalgia for the Motherland. *The Firebird* (1910) is based on a Russian fairy-tale; *Petrushka* (1911) is set during the St Petersburg Easter Fair and uses several Russian nursery songs; *The Rite of Spring* (1913) depicts a pagan ritual in stone-age Russia; *Les Noces* (1914–23) is a dynamic presentation of a peasant wedding. The style, derived originally from Borodin's or Rimsky-Korsakov's colourful exoticism, leans more and more towards shattering polytonal dissonance (the piling-up of chords from two or more keys at once); the première of *The Rite of Spring* was one of the most notorious theatre scandals of its day, and the work's ritualized rhythms and hammered discords led one Paris wit to rechristen it, instead of *Le Sacre*, *Le Massacre du printemps*. As Stravinsky settled, reluctantly, to the idea of exile, his style retreated from orgiastic complexity – only *The Nightingale* (1914) inhabits anything like the same world – to a more 'stripped-down' idiom (his phrase) influenced by *Debussy and *Satie and looking further back, for musical methods to the 18th century and for stories very often to ancient Greece. The jazz-inspired theatre-piece *The Soldier's Tale* (1918) announced the new Stravinsky; *Symphonies of Wind Instruments* (1920, a processional composed in Debussy's memory) and the leanly neo-classical *Octet* (1923) for wind instruments confirmed the wide potential of the new style. (Stravinsky's flight from barbarity, and his rediscovery of the past, were paralleled by several other artists, notably *Strauss, Picasso and Gide. It was as if the First World War, the most barbarous event in human history up to that time, had taken their experimental breath away. Others, however, ignored it: for *Bartók, *Schoenberg, Kokoschka and Joyce, for example, the 1920s and 1930s were decades of even more extreme experiment.)

Stravinsky's neo-classical period lasted for thirty years and produced most of his finest scores. They range from operas and ballets on classical themes (*Oedipus rex*, 1927; *Apollo*, 1928; *Orpheus*, 1947) to such abstract works as the 20th-century *concerto grosso Dumbarton Oaks* (1938), *Symphony in C* (1940), the *Symphony in 3 Movements* (1945, his most radical and rhythmically dynamic work since *The Rite of Spring*) and a series of jaunty concertos (notably for piano, 1924, for violin, 1931, and for two pianos without orchestra, 1935). At the same period, Stravinsky also revealed his impulse towards church music, which came to rival dance as the dominant feature of his work. His *Symphony of Psalms* (1930), as objective as a Byzantine triptych, and his *Mass* (1948), with its unlikely blend of Monteverdian vocal writing and declamatory speech-rhythms, are major scores.

In his sixties, Stravinsky's neo-classical style became somewhat tired. (His opera *The Rake's Progress*, 1951, for example, depends more for success on its brilliant libretto, by Auden and Kallman, than on truly original or memorable music.) He began stiffening it with elements of serialism (which he had hitherto wittily and mercilessly mocked): the first hybrids (*Cantata*, 1952; *Septet*, 1953; *Canticum sacrum*, 1955) were more intriguing than satisfactory, but gradually, and particularly after he made a study of *Webern's music, he regained his panache, and the music of his seventies and eighties includes some of his most extrovert and unequivocal scores (the ballet *Agon*, 1957; *Orchestral Variations*, 1964; above all *Requiem Canticles*, 1966, his most notable religious work since *Symphony of Psalms*).

Stravinsky produced a vast amount of music, much of it so clamorous with personality that it out-manoeuvres criticism. He created his own standard – and not without effort: there are dozens of short works, chips from his workshop, and the path to greatness is littered with such pretentious failures as *Persephone* (1934), an uneasy melodrama, and the late religious works *Threni* (1958) and *Abraham and Isaac* (1963), which communicate neither awe nor ecstasy behind their uningratiating sounds. His influence was enormous: in the freeing of orchestration and rhythm from 19th-century ponderousness (the result of a search for symphonic weight), almost every subsequent composer, from *Ravel to *Stockhausen, is in his debt. He is one of the half-dozen most dominant creative figures of the century: like Picasso, Joyce or Chaplin (and like no previous composer since Beethoven), he seemed to redefine and reinvigorate his art each time he practised it.

Stravinsky's many other works include the ballets *Pulcinella* (1920) and *Danses concertantes* (1942), a witty *Capriccio* (1929) for piano and orchestra, *Duo concertant* (1932) for violin and piano, and several piano works ranging from a spikily neo-classical *Sonata* (1924) to a tongue-in-cheek, gloriously galumphing *Tango* (1940). His writings include *Autobiography/Chronicles of My Life* (English edn 1936), the Harvard lectures *Poetics of Music* (1947), and a series of 'conversations' with his amanuensis Robert Craft which veer from dogmatic malice to common sense and are wittily bitchy about almost everyone he knew: *Conversations with Igor Stravinsky* (1959), *Memories and Commentaries* (1960), *Expositions and Developments* (1962), *Dialogues and a Diary* (1963), *Themes and Episodes* (1966), *Retrospectives and Conclusions* (1969). Of the vast range of books by others – the Stravinsky industry is second only to that surrounding Proust – many are meretricious and ephemeral; the most interesting include R. Craft: *Stravinsky in Pictures and Documents* (1978, the best of Craft's otherwise somewhat self-serving memorials), and E. W. White: *Stravinsky* (rev. edn 1979), a huge compendium of documents, analysis and commentary on every single work Stravinsky wrote, and a model of how studies of creative artists should be made.

SZYMANOWSKI, Karol (1882–1937)
Polish composer

Like the painter Derain, Szymanowski began his career by showing just what he could do with other men's styles. His first two symphonies (1907; 1908) use the language of *Strauss's steamier symphonic poems (*Death* *and Transfiguration*; *Also Sprach Zarathustra*); his *Preludes* (1900), *Studies* (1902) and *Sonata 1* (1905) for piano agreeably pillage *Scriabin; his *Metopes* (1915) for piano, *Myths* (1915) for violin and piano and the choral symphony *Song of the Night* (1916), on ancient Persian poems, wear the perfumed slippers of *Ravel's most exotic scores. At the end of the First World War he soaked himself in Polish folk-music, and added its angular simplicities to his heady style: his historical opera *King Roger* (1924) and ballet *Harnasie* (1926) echo *Bartók and foreshadow *Kodály. Despite its second-hand clothes, this music is rarely second-rate; even so, its whirl of influences makes it hard to take in at first, and Szymanowski remains something of a special taste. In a few later pieces, notably *Stabat mater* (1926), the *Mazurkas* (1926; 1934) for piano and *Violin Concerto 2* (1933) he synthesized everything he'd learned, and the effect was as if a ventriloquist's dummy began speaking Shakespeare.

Szymanowski's other works include *Symphonie concertante* (1932) for piano and orchestra, two string quartets (1917; 1927) and 100 songs, of which the best are *4 Tagore Songs* (1918) and the two sets of *Love Songs of Hafiz* (1910; 1914), to more of the Middle-Eastern poetry he admired. Good study (partly technical): C. Palmer: *Szymanowski* (1981).

THOMSON, Virgil (born 1896)
American critic and composer

As a musical commentator, Thomson worked hard for modernism: his newspaper reviews (collected in *The Musical Scene*, 1945, *The Art of Judging Music*, 1948, and *Music Right and Left*, 1951) are forthright, clear-headed and enthusiastic about the kind of music his fellow-critics (e.g. Olin Downes) wittily and unhelpfully rubbished. His own music avoids isms, affecting instead a melodic and harmonic simplicity learned from *Satie and a back-to-our-roots Americanness like the plainer scores of *Ives. His opera *Four Saints in Three Acts* (1928) became notorious for its nonsense-libretto by Gertrude Stein – a typical 'aria' runs 'Let Lucy Lily Lily Lucy Lucy let Lucy Lucy Lily Lily Lily Lily' – and for being composed, against fashionable trends, with nursery-rhyme tunes and hymn-tune harmonies; his *Louisiana Story* (1948), based on music for Flaherty's film, uses Cayun folk-tunes to depict such bizarre but homely activities as playing tag with a pet raccoon or stealing alligators' eggs. Thomson's most enduring works are his three symphonies (No. 1, 'Symphony on a Hymn Tune', 1928, is magnificent), his *Cello Concerto* (1950), pleasingly devised as the self-portrait of a 'healthy, happy man', and his *Missa pro defunctis/Mass for the Dead* (1960), a collage of every kind of music from hymns to waltzes, a vision of the Day of Judgement as an uninhibited but never sacrilegious romp.

Thomson's other works include the ballet *Filling Station* (1937), composed at a time when downbeat ballet locations were all the rage, two other operas – *The*

Mother of Us All, 1948, has an almost comprehensible libretto by Stein – and chamber works including four piano sonatas and three string quartets (No. 2, 1932, is identical, in all but scoring, with *Symphony 3*). Splendidly penny-plain autobiography, like that by a character from a Cheever novel: *Virgil Thomson* (1966).

TIPPETT, Michael (born 1905)
British composer

There are two sides to Tippett's creative personality. When he writes music, it is lyrical, full of energy – he creates finger-snapping fast movements, one of the rarest compositional gifts – and convincingly single-minded. When he writes, or speaks, words, his thought becomes woolly, convoluted, interminable and as arch as that of an archdeacon essaying the latest slang. This Jekyll-and-Hyde personality would hardly matter – no one needs to watch Tippett interviews or read essays as contorted as those in his books *Moving into Aquarius* (2nd edn 1974) and *Music of the Angels* (1980) – except that Tippett's main work marries words and music, and his four operas dominate and direct his career. *The Midsummer Marriage* (1952) and *King Priam* (1961) are musically the best, their expressive modes (respectively lyricism and athleticism) being at once attractive and comprehensible, however much one might wish the words translated into Icelandic or Afghan. In *The Knot Garden* (1970) the gibberish of the libretto (ostensibly influenced by Eliot's plays) disables the music, making the piece a garbled and baffling charade; *The Ice Break* (1976) makes even less apparent sense and has the unendearing characteristic of seeming more opaque the more you hear it. In all four cases, the music derived from or inspired by the operas is better than the operas themselves. *The Midsummer Marriage* gave rise to some of Tippett's most ecstatic scores, hedonism expressed in sound: *Ritual Dances* (1953), *Fantasia Concertante on a Theme of Corelli* (1953), and above all *Piano Concerto* (1955, a worthy stable-mate to Beethoven's *Concerto 4* which inspired it) and the *Stravinskian *Symphony 2* (1957). From *King Priam* derives the bouncy *Concerto for Orchestra* (1963), whose fast movements have a lean energy Tippett never surpassed; *The Knot Garden* gave rise to *Symphony 3* (1972), whose first three movements are among Tippett's finest orchestral music and whose finale (four 'blues' for soprano and orchestra) is reminiscent of Bessie Smith (or of Gertrude Stein reworking *Indian Love Lyrics*) and crowns the piece (or cuts its throat); after *The Ice Break* came *Symphony 4* (1977), *String Quartet 4* (1979) and *Triple Concerto* (1979), works coupling the vitality of Tippett's earliest music with a block-construction – progress by juxtaposition of material rather than by development – with which all his 1960s and 1970s music had been experimenting. This process reached a climax in *The Mask of Time* (1984), an enormous ninety-minute choral work, part song-cycle part oratorio, on Tippett's great preoccupation, the violence inherent in humankind and our power to rise above it. It is as capacious an anthology of Tippett's creative techniques and obsessions as *Messiaen's *St Francis* is of his – and non-devotees may find it similarly dissonant and indigestible.

Tippett's finest music of all was either written to other people's words (e.g. the song-cycle *The Heart's Assurance*, 1951, and the complex choral work *Vision of St Augustine*, 1965), or is purely instrumental (*Concerto for Double String Orchestra*, 1939; *String Quartet 3*, 1946). The exception is his oratorio *A Child of Our Time* (1941), an outcry against inhumanity whose specific theme (a Nazi atrocity) is generalized both by the use of negro spirituals, magisterially and movingly punctuating the action, and by a pithy libretto drawing out the resonances of the action without Tippett's usual ethical and verbal overkill. Like *Messiaen, if you are sympathetic to his obsessions, he is a composer of overwhelming impact (he was once the subject of a campus cult, the lapel-badges inviting the world to 'turn on to Tippett'); if you turn off the words and simply hear the notes, he is a flawed genius, but still demanding and magnificent in a way few less-risk-taking contemporaries ever are.

Tippett's other works include four piano sonatas (No. 1, 1937, and No. 3, 1973, are outstanding), and several light suites of which the most agreeable is *Suite for the Birthday of Prince Charles* (1948) and the most substantial is *Divertimento on Sellinger's Round* (1954). Good study (partly technical, and more sympathetic to Tippett's cerebration than this article): M. Bowen: *Michael Tippett* (1982).

VARÈSE, Edgard (1883–1965)
French/American composer

One of a kind, Varèse set out in each of his dozen compositions to explore, thoroughly and rigorously, one particular way of organizing sound. His technical means were complex – multiple rhythm, total serialization – but they matter less than the results, which sound like a cross between *Ives's noisier works and the 1950s music of *Boulez. Varèse is still regularly praised as 'ahead of his time' – indeed, he is a posthumous *guru* of the avant-garde, earning such poker-faced praise as *Stockhausen's comment 'Varèse is alone in his generation in . . . having heralded . . . a modern formulation of compositional relationships whose true significance can only today be recognized . . .'; equally, he was a critics' joy, offering plenty of opportunities for pumping hot air into flaccid copy. This 1933 review of *Ionisation*, from the Havana *Evening Telegram*, is typical – and incidentally gives, for all its hyperbole, a clear layman's impression of the score: '*Ionization* by Varèse, a symphony of noises which represents the wondrous actions of ions within the atom, recalls schooldays in the chemical laboratory where hydrogen sulphide was produced to the merriment of students and the horror of teachers. Anvils clanged, maracas jittered, drums thumped, sirens wailed, and there was hell to pay. Director Slonimsky performed the . . . feat of keeping one section of the orchestra in one rhythm with his left hand and another section in a different time with the right, and if you think that's easy, try patting your head with your left hand and rubbing your stomach with your right . . .' Varèse's music is often at the extremes of discord, and never sets out to please; but for all that, its earnestness and single-mindedness give it, in these days of turgid and philosophically indeterminate modern scores, considerable audience appeal, like a case of samples satisfying even those who never rush to buy. Until the mid-1930s Varèse composed for live performers: *Amériques* (1922), *Hyperprism* (1923), *Octandre* (1923), *Intégrales* (1925), *Arcana* (1927) and the egregious *Ionisation* (1931); then, having decided that the future of music lay in (so far undeveloped) electronics, he gave up composing – with the exception of one *jeu d'esprit*, *Density 21.5* (1936), exploiting the sound-possibilities of a platinum flute – until electronics caught up with his inspiration in the 1950s. His last works, however (e.g. *Déserts*, 1954, *Poème électronique*, 1958, *Nocturnal*, 1961), have a wished-for experimentalism his earlier, more committed pieces lack.

Fascinating account (by Varèse's wife) of his early artistic struggles: L. Varèse: *Varèse: A Looking-Glass Diary* (1972). Good, solemn study: F. Ouellette: *Edgard Varèse* (English edn 1968).

VAUGHAN WILLIAMS, Ralph (1872–1958)
British composer

For two generations the British have been proclaiming Vaughan Williams one of their greatest composers, somewhat to the bafflement of outsiders who fail to respond to his seemingly endless rhapsodic meditations, the musical equivalent of Constable's golden cornfields and thatched cottages, and just as enervating in more than a single dose. A good deal of Vaughan Williams's music *is* cut from traditional tweed: for all their beauty, works like *On Wenlock Edge* (1909), *The Lark Ascending* (1920), *Serenade to Music* (1938), even the *Pastoral Symphony* (No. 3, 1921), are unlikely ever to have more than insular appeal. Others of his (nearly 500) works are ecstatic lumber from the English choral tradition, and the outside world would surely sleep untroubled by the lack of the *G Minor Mass* (1921), *Sancta civitas* (1925), *5 Tudor Portraits* (1935) and the popular but dreadful carol-oratorio *Hodie* (1954). His lighter pieces – even when they are finely made as *Linden Lea* (1901), the *Wasps* overture (1909, Aristophanes in a Mummerset smock) or *English Folksong Suite* (1923) – remain trivia.

Vaughan Williams's claim on world attention rests on a handful of works which handle the same mystical, pastoral inspiration in a more disciplined way, so that the associations of the music are not external but its own. Each of his *Symphonies 4, 5 and 6* (1935; 1943; 1947), for example, the crown of his work, is a self-contained and self-explanatory statement, Nos. 4 and 6 abrasive, No. 5 a placidly eloquent counterpart to the Bunyan opera *The Pilgrim's Progress* (1925–41) whose themes it shares but whose sprawl it avoids. Another pendant to this opera is the fine ballet *Job*, 1930, inspired by Blake's Bible-illustrations and, like *Stravinsky's *The Rite of Spring*, so urgent in its musical affirmations that it bursts from theatre-pit to concert-hall, demanding an audience's full attention. Less 'objective' (that is, more easily relatable to the English tradition) is *Fantasia on a Theme by Thomas Tallis* (1910), Vaughan Williams's noblest work in any form. This meditation on a Renaissance hymn-tune, for solo string quartet and double string orchestra, was composed for a cathedral festival and intended to fill a resonant medieval building with layers of overlapping sound; even in the more pristine acoustic of concert-hall or recording-studio it achieves the same serene effect, wrapping the listener in harmony and inducing that sense of surrender to the experience (akin to theatre's suspension of disbelief) which is regularly claimed as an effect of art but is actually rare – and which Vaughan Williams's music, for his devotees, more reliably brings about than that of many of his contemporaries.

The best of Vaughan Williams's other works include *5 Mystical Songs* (1911), *A London Symphony* (No. 2, 1914), *Violin Concerto/Concerto accademico* (1925), the short opera *Riders to the Sea* (1932), based on Synge's play, and two beautiful short anthems, *O Taste and See* (1952) and *Silence and Music* (1953). He made many folk-song arrangements (e.g. *5 English Folksongs*, 1913, for unaccompanied choir), and edited the innovative *English Hymnal* (1906), which restored many fine tunes to church use. His writings on music are *National Music* (1934) and *Heirs and Rebels* (1959). Good study of his life (by his second wife): U. Vaughan Williams: *R. V. W.: A Biography of Ralph Vaughan Williams* (1964); good study of his work (not overly technical, and covering most of the ground without breathlessness): M. Kennedy: *The Works of Ralph Vaughan Williams* (1964).

VILLA-LOBOS, Heitor (1887–1959)
Brazilian composer

It takes about twenty minutes to write down a single page of orchestral score, and even a five-minute work may run to a dozen pages. To compose over 2,000 pieces, therefore (as Villa-Lobos did), is a daunting activity in terms of time alone: one piece a fortnight for seventy years, with time off for holidays and good behaviour. In such a welter of notes, quality is a matter of luck rather than calculation, and many of Villa-Lobos's works (which include twelve symphonies, ten concertos and seventeen string quartets – at least) are of more value to manufacturers of printer's ink than to audiences. His best pieces are based on Brazilian Indian themes or rhythms, treating them in the same dissonant, neo-barbaric way as *Chávez' Mexican scores. (*Stravinsky's *The Rite of Spring* is a distant ancestor.) There are two main series: fourteen pieces called *Chôros* and nine called *Bachianas Brasileiras*. The *Chôros* tend to be longer and more ethnic than the *Bachianas Brasileiras*, which are conscious efforts to marry Brazilian inspiration with Bachian or other European musical techniques. *Bachianas Brasileiras 2* (1931, whose final toccata, 'The little train of the Caipira', pictures a one-track jungle steam-train) and *Bachianas Brasileiras 5* (1938, a lovely, partly wordless song for soprano and eight cellos) are justly popular. Of Villa-Lobos's other music, the guitar pieces (studies, preludes, a concerto) are well-known but anodyne, the best of the large works are *Cello Concerto 2* (1953) and *Symphony 12* (1957) – commissioned by North American orchestras, they sacrifice local colour to careful musical construction – and the finest work of all is in such specifically Brazilian pieces as *Rudepoema* (1926, best in its piano-and-orchestral version) and the four suites *Discovery of Brazil* (1936–42).

WALTON, William (1902–83)
British composer

Walton's dazzling public career began when he was 'taken up' by the Sitwell family in the 1920s – his and their entertainment *Façade* (1921) was one of the most deliciously naughty pieces of its age – continued in the 1930s and 1940s when he wrote scores for some admired British films (notably Olivier's Shakespeare films), and moved into a serene final phase in the 1960s, when he began precociously to be regarded as the Grand Old Man of British music. Though his reputation was founded on slight pieces (and fostered by such orchestral bobbydazzlers as *Portsmouth Point*, 1925, *Johannesburg Festival Overture*, 1956, and *Capriccio burlesco*, 1968), his name will live less for these than for a handful of masterpieces written in his thirties. He composed them slowly and carefully, producing just one outstanding work in each of three major forms. His *Viola Concerto* (1929), oratorio *Belshazzar's Feast* (1931) and above all his *Symphony 1* (1935) – one of the finest British compositions of the century, at least as good as *Sibelius's *Symphony 5* which inspired it – are achievements as substantial as Brahms's; his *Violin Concerto* (1939), though less fine than its viola counterpart, is that rare thing, a thoughtful showpiece, rivalling Tchaikovsky's concerto for energy and Lalo's *Symphonie espagnole* for zest. After the critical savaging of his opera *Troilus and Cressida* (1954) his career collapsed: his subsequent large works (including a second symphony and a cello concerto) are clouded mirrors of the music of his great decade. Like *Barber, he outlived his time, but in that time, few composers wrote better works.

Walton's other music includes the Elgarian coronation marches *Crown Imperial* (1937) and *Orb and Sceptre* (1953), a colourful *Gloria* (1960) for choir and orchestra, a swaggering orchestral *Partita* (1957), and chamber music including a *Violin Sonata* (1949) and a *String Quartet* (1947) which doubles as *Sonata for String Orchestra* (1972). Good studies: F. Howes: *The Music of William Walton* (1965); N. Tierney: *Sir William Walton: His Life and Music* (1985).

WEBERN, Anton (1883–1945)
Austrian composer

Of all this century's revolutionaries, Webern was the most unlikely. He it was who first allied 12-note composition to the rigorous musical disciplines of the Middle Ages (canon, inversion, mirror-forms), and applied serial principles to orchestration and melody: innovations which led others to the total serialization – the well-spring of most avant-garde and electronic music since the 1950s. And yet, compared say to Wagner, whose impact on 19th-century composers was similar, he was the least flamboyant of mould-breakers. His pieces are very short (6 *Bagatelles*, 1913, uses only fifty-six bars of half a dozen notes each; there is more ink in a single *Strauss symphonic poem than in Webern's entire output); they are very quiet (the few loud climaxes are as brief and startling as a sneeze in church); in many of them only one instrument plays at a time, and chords or overlapping sounds are rare; a favourite ploy is to pass the notes of a 12-note row (or tune) from instrument to instrument, each player taking one note as if in a relay race, while the rest of the ensemble busies itself with – equally etiolated – versions of the same group, upside-down, backwards or beginning on different notes. It is music unfleshed, without concessions or self-indulgence, the equivalent of a Cummings *haiku* or one of Beckett's less teeming plays.

For a time, performers were as baffled by the music as audiences. Even when Robert Craft recorded Webern's entire works (on four LPs) in the 1950s, the musicians played the notes tolerably well, but none of the expression: it was scaffolding rather than buildings. In particular, the passing of the notes of a theme from instrument to instrument eluded orchestral players, with the result that the notes came out as meaningless single sounds. Gradually, however, as singers and string quartets in particular became familiar with the music, they performed it with the same warmth and expressive intensity as any other work, and Webern's compositions were revealed to have sensual as well as intellectual appeal. (The same transformation was worked on the orchestral scores by *Boulez in the 1970s: his complete recorded edition appeared in 1979, and is a bouquet of delights.)

This process of rediscovery changed critical assessment not only of Webern's output as a whole, but of individual works within it. Formerly, it was those of his instrumental pieces which could be readily analysed on the page which had been most highly regarded: the intellectually compact *Symphony* (1928) and *Concerto* (1934), in particular, were favourite works with the avant-garde, and their aridity and austerity were hardly noticed in face of the awesome dexterity of their construction. With more sensual performance, attention shifted to the more loosely constructed and (by comparison) more vulgarly emotional vocal works, notably sets of songs to words by Webern's friend Hildegard Jone (*3 Songs*, 1934; *3 Songs*, 1935 – Webern's titles are as laconic as his pieces), and to three works for soloists, chorus and orchestra, *Das Augenlicht* ('Eyesight', 1935), *Cantata 1* (1939) and *Cantata 2* (1943). In these, although the compositional procedures are as complicated and the music is as skeletal as ever, the use of voices and the human concerns of the texts (love, religious awe, joy in nature) reveal in Webern an eloquence, even a hot-bloodedness, which some critics have seen as typically Viennese, linking him with such unlikely compatriots as Schubert or Lehár. This is over-enthusiastic: to the layperson, the music still takes several hearings to reveal its warmth – and Webern's most accessible pieces remain the earliest, the *Bagatelles, 5 Pieces for Strings* (1909, later sumptuously arranged for string orchestra) and the epigrammatic *6 Pieces for Orchestra* (1910).

Webern's other works include an often-played but uncharacteristic *Passacaglia* (1908) for orchestra, various highly wrought chamber pieces including *String Trio* (1927), *Quartet* (1930) for violin, clarinet, saxophone and piano, and *String Quartet* (1938), and the unusually lavish *Variations* (1940) for large orchestra. Among his arrangements – he earned his living as a conductor and by arranging music for his publishers – is a fascinating version of the six-part ricercare from Bach's *Musical Offering*, applying to cerebral music from the past Webern's own principle of passing the theme from instrument to instrument, and revealing unsuspected avant-garde tendencies inside Bach's notes. Background information helpful to the enjoyment of his music is gleanable from his book *The Path to the New Music* (English edn 1963) and from his *Letters to Hildegard Jone and Josef Humplik* (English edn 1967). Studies of his music are without exception technical and complex; the most thorough is H. Moldenhauer: *Anton Webern: A Chronicle of His Life and Works* (1978).

WEILL, Kurt (1900–1950)
German/American composer

The modern passion for completeness has led to investigation of Weill's early concert music (two symphonies, a violin concerto, a string quartet) which he would surely have deplored. He came to favour a 'people's music of today', an up-to-the-minute, comprehensible and attractive music which would be as disposable as paperback fiction, and his earnestly *Hindemithian works of the 1920s hardly fit this bill. His 'new' style was announced in *The Threepenny Opera* (1927), to a libretto by Hauptmann and Brecht updating Gay's *Beggar's Opera* to the age of flappers and gangsters; its hit song *Mack the Knife* epitomizes the harsh sweetness of his favoured style. In view of his opinions about the disposability of music, it is ironical that so much of his work survives – and the reason is less its quality (no higher or lower than that of any other 'concerned' Broadway composer) than its edginess: it seems to capture exactly the cynical sentimentality of the 1930s, the mood of such plays and films as *Scarface, The Blue Angel, Main Street* and even *Waiting for Lefty*. Weill's Broadway successes included *Johnny Johnson* (1936), *Knickerbocker Holiday* (1938, the first of several collaborations with Maxwell Anderson) and *One Touch of Venus* (1943); his more 'serious' works (i.e., those with no less commitment but less good tunes) include *Rise and Fall of the City of Mahagonny* (1929, with Brecht) and a pretentious ballet-with-songs, *Seven Deadly Sins* (1933). He sold his talent not for popularity but for populism; except for Brecht he was the equal of the playwrights he worked with (Kaiser, Anderson, Rice); he was less a magnificent failure than a dull success.

Good study (especially of the musicals): D. Jarman: *Kurt Weill* (1983).

XENAKIS, Yannis (born 1922)
Greek/French composer and architect

In the 1950s Xenakis worked as an architect (with Le Corbusier), but since the 1960s he has devoted himself to teaching and writing music, in Paris and the USA. He invented what he calls 'stochastic' music, after the mathematical idea that the probable pattern of future actions can be predicted in advance. (This is a central element in modern computer maths; gamblers have worked on the principle for millennia.) Xenakis begins a piece by plotting, often with a computer, the possible paths his notes might take (i.e. their speed, duration and location, high or low), and the results which might follow each decision; when the computations are finished he begins his score. Some of his pieces are electronic (e.g. the egregious *Hibiki-hana-ma*, 1970, which requires 800 loudspeakers for ideal performance), but most use human performers, thus restoring the personal involvement with sounds which his creative process tends to lack. His works normally have titles in Greek (e.g. *Eonta*, 'Beings', 1964; *Antikthon*, 'Counter-earth', 1971), but understanding their point is seldom essential to enjoy the music (if 'enjoy' is the word when sounds are so piercing and seem so random). His most accessible compositions, for ordinary listeners, are either based on well-known Greek tragedies, and thus have a graspable programme (*The Suppliants*, 1964; *Oresteia*, 1966; *Medea*, 1967), or use performing virtuosity to seduce the listeners (e.g. *Terretektor*, 1966, and *Nomos gamma*, 1968, the players of which are scattered – alarmingly or agreeably, depending on your threshold of embarrassment – among the audience).

Xenakis's other works include *Pithoprakta* (1956), *Duel* (1959), for two orchestras, *Persephassa* ('Persephone', 1969) for six percussion-players, and the breathtaking *Nomos alpha* (1966) for solo cello.

PAINTING AND SCULPTURE

INTRODUCTION

KEY DATES

1905 Fauvist exhibition in Paris: paintings (by, e.g., Matisse, Rouault, Vlaminck) whose blaring colours and direct emotion challenged every sensibility of late-19th-century art

1907 Cézanne commemorative exhibition in Paris: influential because of (a) his view that paintings represent a personal viewpoint (supremacy of the artist) but are also and equally about coloured marks on canvas (importance of abstract order in art); (b) the challenging greatness of his own work

1907 Picasso's *Les Demoiselles d'Avignon*

1911 Kandinsky painted first influential abstracts, and published *Concerning the Spiritual in Art* (widely read theoretical work on the abstract 'composition' of pictures, as if they were pieces of music)

1916 Cabaret Voltaire (home of early Dada) opened in Berlin: beginnings of surrealism

1937 Nazi exhibitions of 'degenerate art': devastating for many individual artists, but by hindsight a validation by oppression of almost everything 20th-century artists were trying to do

1948 Pollock exhibited first 'drip painting' in New York: beginning of great period of American abstract art

ARTIST AND SOCIETY

To many observers the progress of 20th-century art has seemed a journey from optimism to despair, from energy to nullity. How full of hope the travellers set out, each with a bright new compass and a neat map of his or her own devising – and how trackless and full of dragons the wilderness turned out to be! Whether the collapse in communication has been caused by the obtuseness of artists or the blindness of their audience, the fact remains that at the beginning of the century most artists felt that the news they had to bring was relevant to society (however reluctantly society might agree); nowadays most art claims relevance only to itself.

The first major cause is the collapse, in both artists and society, of moral self-confidence. The progressive awfulness of 20th-century wars and the lurch towards the apocalypse on the one hand, and on the other the rise throughout the world of guilt-ridden liberals as a species of social class, have removed from society that universal smugness which always used to lead to the commissioning of art. What are the great periods and areas of artistic excellence? Ancient Greece, Renaissance Italy, 19th-century Europe – each also a boom time for aristocratic arrogance, opulent business enterprise and military and imperial conceit. In times of totalitarian rule or of doubt (Rome, the dark ages, the reformation, our own century), art as a universal moral force goes underground.

Political nervousness in this century (manifested as much in arrogant absolutism as in self-questioning) has been matched by a phenomenon even more significant for fine art: the collapse of religion as a social binding force. Each of the greatest societies of the past was based on a firm sense of moral order stemming from a 'proper' hierarchy of human beings and gods; even those people (Plato, Luther, Marx) who challenged existing certainties – in the name of new ones – validated their radicalism by making it a mirror image of something already, unchallengeably, *there*. In such an atmosphere both artist and patron could draw themes and inspiration from a common moral stock, which gave a sound platform for comment, acceptance or revolt. But the moral absolutisms of the Olympian system, Buddhism or Christianity (to name three religions which inspired some of the world's greatest art) are no longer available. For a contemporary artist to introduce Christian iconography into his or her work is as much a symptom of nostalgia or eccentricity as would be references to bho trees or the metamorphoses of lusty Zeus.

At the beginning of the century it seemed to many artists that religious moral certainty could be replaced with social or political polemic, that art had a programmatic role to play in the improvement of society. Most of the 'isms' of the 1900s and 1910s produced high-flown manifestos proclaiming art as a redemptive and restructuring force. The futurists, for example (founded 1909), sought to replace 'the burden of the past' with a new order dedicated to speed, efficiency and cleansing change. The expressionists (a term first used in 1911) sought, good Freudians all, to replace Nature with the Id as a source of reference and inspiration: by unlocking and revealing emotion they hoped to purge the soul. The surrealists, particularly in the early 1920s, claimed their system as a way of life rather than an artistic method: their aim was to replace stifling bourgeois 'reality' with the meta-reality of the unfettered imagination. In the 19th century, preoccupation with self had been a decadent but creative component of romanticism; in the 20th, it became a respectable but increasingly sterile norm.

The problem with these programmes (and there were many others of less artistic significance) was that so far from being misunderstood or rejected they were quickly absorbed into the standard 20th-century cast of thought: yesterday's radicalism became today's orthodoxy. This placed the artists themselves in the awkwardly comfortable position of successful revolutionaries: their sails hung slack and they had nowhere left to go. Futurism became the preferred artistic style of oppressive totalitarianism (not at all what its founders had in mind) until the grand-opera rhetoric and mindless barbarism of the dictators destroyed both its credentials and its credibility. Surrealism became fashionable and was transmuted into shop-window chic. Expressionism remained a powerful voice for protest until the atrocities against which it protested became so huge as to strike all protest dumb – what picture on a wall could ever make an adequate comment on the holocaust or the bombing of Hiroshima?

There was a further snag for artists who tried to promote programmes for a better life. Their masters, the dictators and politicians who set about realizing such programmes (or their crude parodies), had no time for them at all. The artist is by nature a dissident; for the dictator or the apparatchik, art is a sickness which the state must purge. For many European artists in the 1930s another form of officially diagnosed 'sickness' made life sicker still: that of Jewishness or sympathy with 'Jewish culture'. The toll of artists who were condemned as decadent, committed suicide, were murdered or abandoned creativity is unparalleled since the days of the Inquisition. The only beneficiary, if anyone can be described as the 'beneficiary' of such anguish, was America. As with every form of art, painting and sculpture in the USA were boosted by brilliant religious or political refugees (Grosz, Mondrian, Chagall and Léger, to name only four) at just the right moment to lend wings to their own already vigorous adolescence. America – the one truly self-confident modern state, at least until Nixon and Vietnam – has been the most consistent high-growth, high-energy area in the fine arts of this century.

ARTIST AND AUDIENCE

The second major cause of the declining role for art was the amputation of the audience. The growth of mass consumption in the arts, and of mass-produced art to satisfy it, has led not to the hostility towards the avant-garde characteristic of more bourgeois-élitist times, but to indifference. There is a hunger for art, but it is satisfied on the one hand by the junk food of pictorial calendars, jigsaw puzzles, magazine illustrations and fashionable kitsch (Oh those autumn scenes, Tolkien posters and clothes-peg wishing wells!), and on the other by cheap, excellent reproductions of what is by consensus (i.e. by a combination of what learned authorities declare is good and marketing managers declare will sell) 'great art', the top ten exhibits from the *Musée imaginaire*. There was a time when great art-works of the past were a challenge and a stimulus to new creativity; now, their ubiquity and cult-status stifle. If you can't rival *Hunters in the Snow* or *Sunflowers*, why paint at all?

The circle of incomprehension is completed by a galvanic, grimacing avant-garde, screaming to be noticed, reviled or ignored by the public (and – to their shame – by many of the critics and teachers who inform public taste, usually a generation out of phase), and finally proving to general applause that 'modern art', though never a threat, is both incomprehensible and ridiculous. Publicity and the thing publicized,

advertisement and the article advertised, become one. The avant-garde
artists of the late 20th century – they might be creating 'mandarin art',
'fetish art', 'illusionist art', or be exponents of 'high-tech' or 'performance'
art – produce chiefly for their peers, working in a mutually admiring and
exclusive clique; they are endlessly self-justifying and seem, to the
outsider, as bewilderingly contemptuous of 'accepted standards' as those
who accept those standards are of them.

What is wrong in this is not the split between experiment and mass
audience – it has always been a function of artists to educate and stretch
their audience – but the extraordinary width of the 20th-century gulf.
Can it be a symptom of the low moral standing of art today that very few
people, on either side of the gulf, seem to care that it exists or try to make
bridges? (In the 1910s the avant-garde, just as esoteric, cared very much
about educating the public; in the 1980s the avant-garde, punk-rocker-
like, draws strength from its alienation from the crass lump.) There is (in
art as in music) a serious danger that the avant-garde will one day vanish
into the navel it has been so long and so smugly contemplating – and that
can hardly be good for art.

Another symptom is the ikon status of works of art themselves.
Museums are the cathedrals of our secular age, paintings and sculptures
its relics, books of prints its holy books. Just as 16th–18th-century artists
gradually promoted landscape from the background to some crucial
human or divine activity into a main pictorial theme, so in the 20th
century we have promoted the artist's signature. It is hardly enough –
hardly possible – to say 'That's a fine picture' unless you back it up with
the artist's name and what it cost. (You can bank on the greatness of
Matisse.) This phenomenon – it must end, but when? – produces in many
creative artists the not unnatural desire to hop aboard the gravy-train, to
become themselves a realizable asset for someone else – and the net
result of that is to fill wall after wall with assets. In earlier centuries
patrons demonstrated social eminence by the art they hung; now we
demonstrate our credit-rating. The general public, which has no credit-
rating, has about as much stake in this as the beggar in a Renaissance
street.

ARTIST AND MATERIALS

The wary pluralism brought about in art by separation from moral
engagement and alienation from the audience has been aggravated, for
many creators, by a third phenomenon: the unexpected and paradoxical
undermining of self-confidence produced by an unprecedented freedom
of choice in materials, styles and media. 20th-century artists are in the
position of Bluebeard's wife in the fairy tale: having learned the secret of
every room in the house, they find that they have lost the secret of
themselves. To the materials and methods traditional to art for centuries
we have added the infinite possibilities of *laissez-faire*. There are no

'right' styles or materials; the only rule is that there are no rules. Even the creative monopoly of hand and eye can be challenged: mechanically produced art is commonplace and electronic art is on the way.

The most influential new techniques have been those of mass-production art. Metal-press, photographic etching and the myriad possibilities of plastic have created forms of fine art hitherto unknown, from Gabo sculptures to the cranked-up commercial art of Op and Pop. Film cameras and electron microscropes have revealed undreamed-of forms and symmetries in nature (and led to art as far apart as Duchamp's Muybridge-inspired *Nude Descending a Staircase* and the amoeba-creatures of Miró and Klee). The exploration and manipulation of light, from infra-red photography to the laser beam, have changed our whole perception of shade and colour. Most important of all, the clamour of advertising and admonitory art in modern urban society – we can go for miles without seeing anything not artificial – has made us more susceptible to, and wary of, images than the people of any previous age.

COMING TO TERMS

Faced with the ubiquity of art and artefact, which cuts down their status from the main providers of images to one among many, not by any means necessarily the most effective or significant, modern artists have pursued integrity in one of three ways. Some have accepted the law of the ants' nest, achieving 'meaningful' identity by adhering to movements and accommodating themselves to this programme or to that. Artists have always done this to some extent, from Athenian red-figure potters to the Pre-Raphaelites. But the movements of the past, unprocessed by modern communications, were usually small-scale and local. 20th-century movements spread world-wide, fast, and joining artistic movements has nowadays become a socio-aesthetic obligation – 'tell me who you eat with and I'll tell you who you are'. Sheltering under the commodious cubist umbrella allowed individuality of expression to such diverse stylists as Braque, Gris, Lipchitz and Léger; surrealism made bedfellows of Ernst, Magritte and Klee; pop art embraced talents as disparate as Hockney, Rauschenberg and Johns. The simple division of art into abstract and figurative enabled many emerging artists to find their own true voices: Mondrian and Brancusi, for example, discovered themselves only when they made the decisive step of embracing abstraction; Léger's best work began when he combined figures with abstract shapes.

The second self-validating path is to go into the commercial world and bend its will to yours. In the 20th century there have been just as many fine artists who have worked to commission as at any other time – and like artists of other times they have walked the borderline between surrendering individuality to a general official style and producing work so radical as to frighten off their patrons. Portraits by Kokoschka and Picasso, for example, are as recognizably portraits as those by Holbein or

Gainsborough – and they are no less recognizably personal works of art. Modern art continues to be commissioned for public buildings: the sculptures and paintings that adorn Coventry Cathedral, the Pompidou Centre, the United Nations Building or Lincoln Center (to name four 20th-century Parthenons at random) are as representative of the best art of our times as St Peter's (say) is of its. Apart from this large-scale public art, many artists have taken 'popular' 20th-century styles, images and techniques (in particular those of billboard and magazine advertising) and made them personal. The light and space of Hockney's swimming-pool paintings, for example, are clearly learned from billboard art, and their smoothness also owes much to a modern medium, acrylic paint. Vasarély's work also draws on our familiarity with huge billboards, images whose size and vulgarity would have overwhelmed our great-grandparents; his blurring, hallucinatory geometric shapes also owe much to electronic images, from those of the radar screen to computer holographs. Oldenburg takes ordinary objects from daily life and makes them wonderful.

The third and thorniest path is the one which leads to the ivory tower. The artist comes to terms with society by stepping aside, going his or her own way, letting the world follow as best it can. The danger here is that the world will simply make an excuse and leave: the art of people as diverse as Munch, Kandinsky and Soutine, for example, is so personal that it repels as many as it fascinates. But if your ivory tower is properly accessible to the public, if it has stairs, direction-signs and floor-plans, even the most outlandish-seeming and esoteric images will make their point. Picasso and Braque, for example, even when their early cubism was at its most bizarre and abstract, were careful to provide clues (in the picture-title, in small references within the picture to recognizable shapes, in the incorporation of newspapers, tickets and pieces of chair-cane) which could lead spectators into the experience or at least give them a peg on which to hang hostility. (The process is analogous to Stravinsky's distortion of conventional harmony at the same time.) Klee and Pollock gave their least representational works simple representational titles like 'Red Balloon' or 'Lavender Mist' – and by the time you've scanned the picture to see how it could possibly have earned its name, you've been drawn into its meaning and it communicates. The statues of Moore make their starting-point the reinterpretation of familiar sculptural themes (mother and child, grandee, reclining nude) and move from this familiar base to fascinating, uncharted territory.

The greatest modern artists never forget that art is a performance, that it requires an audience. They are conscious not only of their own role as creators, as performers, but also of the role of their audience. (Art as genuine anti-communication is a feature only of the most inbred and piffling avant-garde – and it can only be fake art. *All* aesthetics postulate response.) The work need not be easy – no one takes in Kandinsky or Mondrian in five minutes – but it needs a point of access, an initial pull which intrigues and whets the appetite. In former times this point of access was often the shared religious or social experience of artist and spectator; nowadays the references are more often to other art: parodic in the widest sense, they ask a certain knowledge and sophistication in the spectator. 20th-century artists have had first to invent a vocabulary, then to teach it to the rest of us. Now that their speech is known, we can explore what they have to say – and what else is such a dialogue but a civilizing, moral force?

◙

Illustrations being unfortunately out of the question in a book of this kind, I have replaced them with brief descriptions of essential or characteristic works. (Sources are given for the benefit of energetic world-travellers; all the works are also reproduced in standard histories of modern art or in books on particular artists.) As knowing the size of an art-work is vital to envisaging it, I have given dimensions, in centimetres unless otherwise declared. The abbreviations are: Coll. = collection; M = museum; A = art; MMA, NY = Museum of Modern Art, New York; MAM = Musée de l'Art Moderne.

ARP, Jean (or Hans) (1887–1966)
French (or German) artist

A founder of Dada, Arp never lost the naughty-boy impishness characteristic of the movement. Throughout his life he teased his public and
deflected attention from the seriousness of his work by supplying it with
irrelevant, often preposterous titles. *Head with Three Annoying Objects*
(1930; 36×26×19; artist's estate) and *To Be Lost in the Woods* (1932;
Coll. Benjamin Dunkelman, Toronto), for example, are actually just
lumps and bumps of bronze, looking like large sea-smoothed pebbles
stuck together; *To Be Lost in the Woods* places them on an angular
cubist pedestal. The titles tell us everything and nothing about the art in
the same way as his 1916 *Portrait of Tristan Tzara* (51×47×20, Art
Museum, Geneva), which consists of five jigsaw-like flat wooden shapes
painted green and pink and stuck together, tells us nothing about Tzara
or itself.

Unlike some of his fellow-Dadaists, however (see Duchamp), Arp has
more than jauntiness to offer. At first sight his works are pert or shocking
in the approved Dada way; that they survive a second or third sight is due
to satisfying shape and texture, to the evidence of genuine visual
imagination. Even the notorious paper collages (rectangles of torn paper
fluttered at random on to a backing sheet and glued where they fall)
make pleasing patterns, because there are only a few torn scraps and
their placing – for all Arp's claims – is regular. Two of the best are
Squares Arranged According to the Laws of Chance (1917; 48×35; MMA,
NY) and *Composition* (1937; 30×22; Philadelphia MA), three scraps of
glued paper with an elegant abstract pattern drawn on top. After 1930 he
worked principally as a sculptor, producing smooth, rounded pieces not
unlike those of *Moore. Good examples are *Human Concretion on Oval
Bowl* (1935; 65×73×53; artist's estate) and the larger (113 cm high)
Human Lunar Spectral (1957; Smithsonian, Washington). These, and his
paper collages, are likely to be lasting work.

Arp also wrote poetry, collected in *Moonsand* (1960), *Pensive Flames* (1961) and
The Dream Captain's Log-Book (1965). A good selection of his writing in general
is *On My Way: Poetry and Essays 1912–1947* (1948). Good critical works: C.
Giedion-Welcker: *Jean Arp* (1957); H. Read: *Arp* (1968); E. Trier: *Jean Arp;
Sculpture* (1968).

BACON, Francis (born 1909)
Irish painter

Bacon's work reached maturity in the early 1950s (and he subsequently
destroyed much of his previous painting). His style is a nightmarish blend
of expressionism (tortured Kafka figures in poses of enigmatic agony)

and cubism (*Picasso's *Guernica* is a major influence). He sometimes reworks in his own style paintings by other artists. For example, his *Head Surrounded by Sides of Beef* (1954; 126×120; Art Inst., Chicago), a characteristic work, is modelled on Velasquez – but Bacon's grandee sits on a chair in the cold store of an abattoir, his face blurred as if by a stocking mask, his mouth open in a soundless scream. Often Bacon sets his tormented characters in doorless rooms or cubes of distorting glass; as they writhe and scream, we are made to feel like the spectators of some efficient and clinical ritual of torture. *Study for a Crouching Nude* (1952; 195×135; Detroit Inst. of Arts) and the splendid 'Pope' series (e.g. *Pope II*, 1951; 198×152; Kunsthalle, Mannheim) are typical: gaunt, twisted figures blurred almost to transparency by the surrounding glass. This enigmatic holocaust-art (the horrific 1945 newsreels of Dachau survivors seem never far from Bacon's imagination) is his finest achievement; when he makes more specific references (e.g. in *Three Studies for a Crucifixion*, 1962; each 195×143; Guggenheim, NY), particularity tends to dissipate the effect.

Good introductions: D. Sylvester: *Interviews with Francis Bacon* (1975); J. Russell: *Francis Bacon* (1979).

BECKMANN, Max (1884–1950)
German painter

There is no human comfort in Beckmann's work. He crowds his canvases with figures as tortured as those of Brueghel or Bosch, but painted with the lanky shapes and flat colours of 20th-century expressionism. The allegorical effect of paintings like *Family Picture* (1920; 100×62; MMA, NY) is as strong as that of anything by (say) Botticelli – but Botticelli's paintings are also sensuous and beautiful, whereas if you fail to 'read' the meaning of Beckmann's, you're left with a baffling jumble of coloured shapes. His finest work, the triptych *Departure* (1933; 212×100, 212×113, 212×100; MMA, NY), one of a series painted shortly before he fled from the Nazis to America, makes a powerful statement because the events it depicts are universally familiar. In the end, one of the main reasons for the greatness of the Christian art of the Middle Ages and Renaissance was that it was radiant with the shared hope of artist and spectator; to be (as Beckmann was) an iconographer not of religion but of bleak political oppression is to paint visions of sterility inimical (unless you are Goya or Bosch) to 'art'. Or perhaps the failing, in the end, was Beckmann's own: unlike Goya or Bosch, he never managed to transcend his own despair.

Good introductions: F. Fischer: *Max Beckmann* (1973); C. Kessler: *Max Beckmann's Triptychs* (1970).

BONNARD, Pierre (1867–1947)
French painter

In the 1890s Bonnard was a member of the group known as Nabis (see page 543). Their aim was to produce art in an uncluttered, sumptuous style; their chief influences were Gauguin and Japanese prints. Bonnard's work from this period was produced chiefly for the theatre: posters (similar both in appearance and in refined raucousness to those of Toulouse-Lautrec), programme illustrations and stage designs. At the end of this period he first began painting his life-long model and companion Marthe (after twenty years, dear reader, he married her), and developed the mature style characteristic of his best-known work. His subjects are landscapes (chiefly of the South of France) and interiors; Marthe figures in many of the paintings, usually nude and often in enigmatic poses (bent over, prone in the bath, gazing over her shoulder, back view looking out of a window).

Because of its domestic content, Bonnard's style was christened Intimism; because of the kaleidoscopic dazzle of his handling of colour and light (in a prismatic style not unlike that of Monet or Sisley) he was often called – indeed he ruefully called himself – 'the last of the impressionists'. But the impressionists painted refractions of what they *saw*; increasingly as he grew older Bonnard painted what he *remembered*. In particular with Marthe he looked beyond ageing reality and painted radiant youth; pictures such as *Nude in a Bathroom* (1932; 119×15; Coll. Mrs Wolfgang Schoenborn, NY) blend the ideal and the actual with an equivocal, hesitant feeling quite unlike the impressionists' bright certainties. This elusiveness, coupled with the intimacy of his subject-matter, makes Bonnard an especially personal artist. Not only small canvases (such as *Interior*, 1898; 51×34; North Carolina MA, Raleigh) but even his larger works (for example *The Abduction of Europa*, 1925; 150×115; Toledo MA, Ohio; or *Signac and His Friends, Sailing*, 1928; 132×122; Kunsthaus, Zurich) have the self-communing quality of a diary, a piece of chamber-music or a water-colour sketch.

Good critical biography: D. Sutton: *Bonnard and His Environment* (1957).

BRANCUSI, Constantin (1876–1957)
Romanian sculptor

Some of Brancusi's early work was influenced by Rodin, for example *Sleep* (1908; 26 cm high; National Gallery, Bucharest), in which the face of a sleeping girl half-emerges from the rough marble block from which it is carved. By 1910 the same face has become abstracted into its geometrical lineaments (in *Sleeping Muse*; 28 cm high; Smithsonian, Washington) – and this reduction of objects to still recognizable but abstract shapes remained the main feature of Brancusi's style throughout his life. Some of his works are reminiscent of the primitive art of the New World – Mayan (*The Kiss*, 1912; 57 cm high; Philadelphia MA), American Indian (*King of Kings*, a 1920s wooden totem figure 295 cm tall; Guggenheim, NY) or Eskimo sealstone carving (*The Miracle*, 1936; 107 cm high; Guggenheim, NY) – but in general he favoured extreme simplicity, smooth ovals, highly polished and with the minimum amount of contours to suggest features (e.g. *Mlle Pogany*, 1931; 43 cm high; Philadelphia MA), or quill-shaped uprights (e.g. the beautiful series of *Birds in Space* carved in the 1920s). He said of his etiolated sculptures: 'Don't look for obscure formulas or mysteries. It's pure joy I'm giving you' – and the soaring grace of his art certainly contrasts with the lumpish solidity of what he called the 'beefsteak sculpture' of the 19th century. His masterpiece is four huge metal columns made for the Tirgu Jiu National Park in Romania; *Endless Column* (1937), the finest of them, is an obelisk made from seventeen slender octahedrons and standing over 28 metres high. It is at once like Romanian geometric peasant art and chains of chemical elements from a scientific textbook, but it adds to these reminiscences the feeling of lightness and aspiration, of frozen movement, which characterizes all Brancusi's work.

Good introductions: D. Lewis: *Brancusi* (1957); S. Geist: *Brancusi* (1968).

BRAQUE, Georges (1882–1963)
French painter

Braque's style is one of deceptive simplicity. The elements of painting – particularly composition and colour – are presented with a refined clarity which conceals sophistication: it is a wide-eyed, child's view of how a modern artist, or a wide-eyed child, might see the world. In his earliest work (e.g. *Seated Nude*, 1906; 60×49; Milwaukee Art Center) he favours bright colours and simple shapes like those of Cézanne – but already present are the distortion and geometric organization which led, very soon, to his first cubist pictures (e.g. *Houses at L'Estaque*, 1908; 73×60; Kunstmuseum, Bern). To begin with, his cubist pictures were exactly that: an arrangement of cubes coloured to give an impression of landscape or form, superior versions of the 'blocking-out' of a picture recommended in textbooks of drawing. He developed the style in close association with *Picasso; in fact there was a period when their styles were so alike as to seem interchangeable (Braque's cubist portraits, e.g. *The Portuguese*, 1911; 115×75; Öffentliche Kunstsammlung, Basel, and Picasso's *Man Smoking a Pipe*, 1911; Braque's collages, e.g. *The Clarinet*, 1913; 120×93; private coll., NY, and Picasso's 1913 *Bottle, Glass and Violin*). As the techniques of cubism became more refined, the two men's styles diverged. Braque still regularly painted cubist pictures with the best of them (e.g. the splendid *Still Life: Le Jour*, 1929; 145×115; National Gallery, Washington), but in general he softened and blurred the jaggedness of cubism, in particular by shading the colours at the lines of geometric intersection instead of letting them snarl, imperatively territorial, across a black dividing-line. The union of angularity and sensuality, by Cézanne out of *Gris, produced some of his finest work: characteristic pictures are *Nude Woman with Basket of Fruit* (1926; 167×73; National Gallery, Washington), *Woman with a Mandolin* (1937; 128×98; MMA, NY) and the dazzling set of *Studio* pictures (e.g. *Studio II*, 1949; 160×132; Kunstsammlung Nordrhein-Westphalen, Düsseldorf). Braque lacks the challenge of the very greatest artists: his paintings reassure rather than reassess the observer. But is there any reason to dismiss art simply designed to delight the eye?

Good autobiographical essays: *Le Jour et la nuit* (1952). Good biographical studies: J. Russell: *Georges Braque* (1959); E. Mullins: *Braque* (1968).

CALDER, Alexander (1898–1976)
American sculptor

As well as sculpture, Calder produced abstract paintings and book illustrations in an airy, fantastical style derived from *Klee and especially *Miró. But his principal work is his sculpture. He invented the *mobile*, or sculpture that moves – elegant, often massive structures of wire and flat, leaf-like shapes which move gently in the breeze. Some hang from the ceiling (e.g. *Lobster Trap and Fish Tail*, 1939; *c.* 255 cm high and 285 in diameter; MMA, NY); others stand on the floor (e.g. *Red Petals*, 1942; 275 cm high; Arts Club, Chicago). The apotheosis of the mobile is his *Four Elements* (1962). This consists of four huge motorized shapes of coloured metal (the tallest nine metres high), which twist and writhe to form random abstract patterns. It stands in the car park of the Stockholm Museum of Modern Art, and either exhilarates observers or reminds them of modern street-furniture (kiosks, lamps, traffic signals) gone haywire. When Calder used the same style in sculptures which didn't move, they were called (by his friend *Arp) *stabiles*. In fact these are his most impressive creations. They often take the form of huge monumental structures in public places; a fine example is the 28-metre-high *Man*, an arching, upward-reaching construction in stainless steel made for Expo 67 in Montreal.

Good introductions: H. H. Arnason: *Calder* (1966); J. Lipman: *Calder's Universe* (1976).

CHAGALL, Marc (born 1887)
Russian/French painter

Chagall's gorgeously coloured, velvet-textured dream-visions (like those of a Jewish Douanier Rousseau) are the nearest equivalent in painting to the surrealist films of Cocteau. Disembodied limbs and heads float in space; cats have human faces, people seven fingers and green heads; trains run upside-down and wallpaper blossoms with country scenes. His symbolism is private, but never obscure: whatever the pictures actually mean, they are gaudy and joyful, visions as artless and as sophisticated as those of a knowing child. Characteristic works are *Paris Through the Window* (1913; 135×130; Guggenheim, NY), an extraordinary, teasing evocation of the never-never Paris of the mind, and *Me and the Village* (1911; 193×152; MMA, NY), a sensuous collage of faces and scenes from the Russian Jewish life of Chagall's childhood, images as specific and as universal as those in the stories of Isaac Singer. In later life he turned from memory to mysticism, and produced a large body of public religious art: stained-glass windows (of the twelve tribes of Israel) for a Jerusalem synagogue (1961), mosaics and tapestries for the Israeli Knesset (1966), stained glass for Chichester Cathedral, England (1978).

Good interim introduction: F. Meyer: *Marc Chagall* (1964).

CHIRICO, Giorgio de (1888–1978)
Italian painter

Chirico's early work combines a notably clean-lined, simple technique (geometric buildings, plain as scenery-flats, throwing immense dark shadows; elegant figures in classical draperies; bright yellow sunlight and sea-green clouds) with surrealist conjunctions of such unrelated objects as cannons and artichokes, easels and tombstones. The combination of obscure symbolism and clear expression is as menacing and bewildering as in, say, the bleaker films of Bergman – what are Chirico's people *doing* in those empty marble squares and palaces? In *The Soothsayer's Recompense* (1913; 177×133; Philadelphia MA) the classical statue of a girl reclines outside what appears to be a Moroccan desert fort, until you see the clock and the train passing behind a high brick wall. In *The Disquieting Muses* (1916; 95×65; Gianni Mattioli Foundation, Milan), three statues wait, surrounded by a bizarre luggage of boxes and ovals, like people queueing for a bus. But they wait at one end of an enormous Palladian piazza; one has a mannequin's blank-faced wooden head, another no head at all; in the background are a medieval castle and a modern factory. Pictures like these (typical of Chirico's enigmatic art) are absorbing to look at – does it really matter what they mean? After several decades of painting in this style (and of making naughtily exact copies of his works for anyone who asked), in the 1930s Chirico abandoned surrealism for a much more formal, logical style, close to that of the architectural painters of the Renaissance. Here he had little new to say; it is for his earlier, more elusive art that he will be remembered.

Chirico's *Memoirs of My Life* were published in English in 1971. Good introduction: J. T. Soby: *Giorgio de Chirico* (1955).

DALI, Salvador (born 1904)
Spanish painter

In Dali, the mixture of respect and cynicism with which creative artists often view their patrons has been carried to its logical conclusion: a crafty showman, he has invented himself as the paying public's idea of a crazy genius, a wild man driven by his own ungovernable talent and governable moustache. He produces just the kitsch-art such a 'genius' might: his dream-symbols (whether blazing giraffes, locust-jewellery or the use of Millet's *The Angelus* – of all things – as a sexual fetish) symbolize nothing except the Woolworth's view of what dream-in-art might be – not surrealist images, but images of surrealism advertising themselves for mass appeal. Technical wizardry is an essential part of this approach – the public must be able to recognize what is cosily to baffle it (now you see it and now you see it again – or do you?). Dali consistently uses a superb Renaissance *trompe-l'œil* technique – his bread is crusty as well as crumby – concealing lack of imagination by brilliant cleverness. *Trompe l'imagination*, in fact. Do the oozing easel- (or violin-) shapes and bony figures of *The Birth of Liquid Desire* (1932; 110×95; Guggenheim, NY) mean anything at all? What is the point of those soft watches in *The Persistence of Memory* (1931; 32×23; MMA, NY)? Why is Christ floating on his cross above that dazzling sunset sky in *The Crucifixion* (1951; 202×114; Glasgow Art Gallery)? While you ponder these questions, trying to reach into the artist's subconscious mind, or into your own, the paintings flash brightly at you, pretty as parrots – and *that*'s their point. (Dali's work seems designed for reproduction on the tea-towels of yesterday's smart art set.) In his sixties Dali began making sumptuous surrealist jewellery, and it is the quintessence of his art: designed to surprise but not to shock, to impress but not to move, to communicate by dazzle and not by depth. The centrepiece was a ruby heart that actually beat – an expensive transplant not for the breast but for the purse.

The most revealing account of Dali's life and thought is his own self-serving writings *Diary of a Genius* (1966) and *Dali by Dali* (1970). A more balanced assessment is in D. Ades: *Dali* (1983).

DELAUNAY, Robert (1885–1941)
French painter

Delaunay believed that colour was the chief determinant of form and emotional meaning. His early pictures, though figurative, distort the shapes of reality to enhance colour-harmonies: his many paintings of Parisian scenes incorporating the Eiffel Tower, for example, are similar to the early cubist pictures of *Picasso or *Braque, except that in their work shapes dominate, whereas in Delaunay's the forms are determined by colour not geometry. (A characteristic work from this series is *Eiffel Tower in Trees*, 1909; 125×91; Guggenheim, NY.) Other pictures, though they have figurative titles, are really abstract designs. Some are like gaudily coloured marquetry (e.g. *Homage to Blériot*, 1914; 245×245; Kunstmuseum, Basel), others like mosaics (e.g. the dazzling *Window on the City No. 4 (La Ville)*, 1911; 128×112; Guggenheim, NY). He developed the idea of the 'colour disc', a circular painting of curved abstract shapes whose placing and emotional relationship are based on the demands of the colour wheel: *Discs: Sun and Moon* (1913; diameter 135 cm; State Museum, Amsterdam) is typical. The culmination of this kind of abstraction, decorative rather than intellectual, came in a series of vast murals painted for the 1937 Paris Universal Exhibition.

DERAIN, André (1880–1954)
French painter

Derain's early art was dazzling. He could turn his hand to any style and produce brilliant work. *London Bridge* (1906; 97×65; MMA, NY), for example, is a *Dufy-like splurge of fauvist pinks and blues, *Morning Light* (1905; 75×65; private coll., Rome) a sumptuous pointillist forest-scene, *The Bagpiper* (1911; 185×150; Minneapolis Institute of Arts) a velvety landscape borrowed from Douanier Rousseau. After the 1914–18 war, the momentum of his painting faltered. There are occasional masterpieces (e.g. *The Table*, 1921; 128×95; Metropolitan MA, NY – a solemn cubist still-life in greens and browns – and some African-inspired 'primitive' wood-carvings of the 1950s), but on the whole self-confidence seems to have been replaced by diffidence. Perhaps, from the start, eclectic brilliance disguised the fact that he had nothing very personal to say.

Interesting: *Letters to Vlaminck* (1955). Good study: D. Sutton: *André Derain* (1959).

DIX, Otto (1891–1969)
German painter

Like *Grosz, Dix painted bitter studies of the 20th-century psychic wilderness. But where Grosz's work is alert and sly with wit, Dix's is aseptic and hopeless. He first became known for nightmarish war paintings, scenes of torn bodies, jagged tree-stumps and churned mud in a style as coldly romantic as that of Böcklin or Doré. In the 1920s he painted portraits in a naïve style (like shattered Rockwell) whose predominant themes are apathy and hopelessness: typical are *The Artist's Parents* (1921; 115×99; Kunstmuseum, Basel) and *Dr Mayer-Hermann* (1926; 147×97; MMA, NY). Harassed and finally banned by the Nazis, he turned after the war to religious subjects – though even these suggest alienation and neurosis rather than certainty or warmth. If the unsmiling characters in the novels of Lenz or the films of Bergman have pictures on their walls, those pictures are by Dix.

Good collection (with German text): O. Dix: *Gemälde und Graphik von 1912–1957* (1957). Good study: E. Löffler: *Otto Dix: Life and Work* (English edn 1983).

DUBUFFET, Jean (born 1901)
French artist

After a comparatively late professional start (aged forty-one; he was formerly in the wine trade) Dubuffet produced a huge and varied body of work. He was particularly well-known for what he called 'brute art': harsh images of naked human figures, like graffiti or the work of the insane (which he studied and collected in the 1930s). The figures' square bodies, tiny heads and feet and crude sexual organs are like those in South American Indian art; Dubuffet's medium (oil paint made lustreless with sand, mud, cement and gravel) emphasizes texture and weight in a way reminiscent of abstract artists such as *Pollock or *de Staël. Excellent examples are *Pièce de boucherie: Corps de dame* (1951; 117×89; Sidney Janis Gallery, NY) and *The Gypsy* (1954; 90×72; Alex Hillman Coll.). In his sixties, Dubuffet carried his idea of figurative abstraction still further, in a style to which he gave the (meaningless) name *l'hourloupe* (he was an inventive theorizer and self-publicist). Here, human figures are reduced to geometric jigsaw-puzzle pieces or fat squiggles; the canvas seethes with them, like a tray of maggots. (A good example is *Nunc stans*, 1965; 160×67; Guggenheim, NY.) In a third style – one to which he returned throughout his career – Dubuffet blends the joyful colours and pin-figure people of children's art with swirling, abstract backgrounds to produce on canvas a sophisticated version of street art. *Site avec 2 personnages* (1975; 90×72; Pace Gallery, NY) is typical.

Dubuffet's writings (so far available only in French) include *Prospectus et tous écrits suivants* (1967) and *Asphyxiante culture* (1968). Good interim study: P. Selz: *The Work of Jean Dubuffet* (1962).

DUCHAMP, Marcel (1887–1968)
French artist

Duchamp retired from painting in the mid-1920s, to become a dealer (and a fanatical chess player). But he was never really a committed artist at all: his commitment was to the destruction of artistic snobbery. And in this, he failed. We still solemnly visit in galleries or worry over reproductions of his moustachioed Mona Lisa or 'ready-mades' such as the urinal signed 'R. Mutt' and entitled 'Fountain'. Duchamp's real painting is in a confident but second-hand early cubist style. *Portrait of Chess-Players* (1911; 100×100; Philadelphia MA) is typical, and *Nude*

Descending a Staircase II (1912; 145×88; Philadelphia MA), a tumbling cadenza of brown cubist shapes, like the multi-image photographs of movement popular at the time, is at once the most accomplished, best known and emptiest. (It used to be cited by philistines as typical of the preposterousness of 'modern art'. It is not preposterous – merely unserious and second-rate.) Duchamp's other notorious 'masterpiece' is *The Bride Stripped Bare by Her Bachelors, Even (Large Glass)* (1915–23; 272×172; Philadelphia MA). This consists of two panels of plate glass (cracked in transit and carefully repaired by Duchamp – the cracks adding the final random touch), each with a delicate surrealist machine painted on it in soft blues, browns and greys. It is pretty to look at – and its 'meaning' is expounded at length in its other essential component, an accompanying booklet. Are we foolish to take this seriously, or to assume any serious intention on Duchamp's part? It's the final irony that Dada art now plumps up many a solemn thesis.

Duchamp's literary work is anthologized in *The Essential Writings of Marcel Duchamp* (1973). Good introduction: A. Schwarz: *Complete Works of Marcel Duchamp* (1970). Duchamp debunked: O. Paz: *Marcel Duchamp: Appearance Stripped Bare* (English trans. 1980).

DUCHAMP-VILLON, Raymond (1876–1918)
French sculptor

Brother of *Duchamp and *Villon, Duchamp-Villon was a promising sculptor who died young after being gassed in the First World War. His best-known work is a series of cubist horses (e.g. *Horse*, 1914; 40 cm high; Coll. Ed Kaufmann Jr, NY), but there are also portrait-heads and satisfying human figures (e.g. *Seated Woman*, 1914; 62 cm high; Yale University Art Gallery).

Good study (of all three brothers): J. J. Sweeney: *Jacques Villon, Raymond Duchamp-Villon, Marcel Duchamp* (1957).

DUFY, Raoul (1877–1953)
French artist

Initially an impressionist, Dufy was inspired by *Matisse's *Luxe, calme et volupté* to investigate the simple shapes and bright colours of the fauvists. His gay, uncomplicated holiday scenes of regattas, race-meetings, circuses and sunny landscapes have been the envy and aspiration of amateur painters ever since. *Street Decked with Flags, Le Havre* (1906; 80×65; MAM, Paris) is typical: unpretentious and 'spontaneous', but braced and strengthened with touches of modernity (cubist house-shapes in the background; a man and a straw hat enigmatically painted on the foreground flag; the people all with their backs to us). A later painting, the Matisse-like *Indian Model in the Studio at Impasse Guelma* (1928; 77×61; Coll. A. D. Mouradian,

Paris), shows several characteristic canvases, and also the kind of textile designs for which Dufy later became known, a perfect vehicle for his unassuming inspiration and fastidious technique.

Good study: R. Cogniat: *Raoul Dufy* (1962).

EPSTEIN, Jacob (1880–1959)
American/British sculptor

Epstein's free-standing sculpture is in a beetling, lumpish style derived from Rodin (especially from such rough-hewn works as *The Burghers of Calais* or *Balzac*). *The Visitation* (1926–55; 165 cm high; Smithsonian, Washington) or *Smuts* (1957; Houses of Parliament, London), for example, have a heroic weight which has more to do with Epstein's handling of his material (bronze) than with his subject-matter. His monumental art is at its most typical in public places or on buildings: good examples are the brooding *Tomb of Oscar Wilde* (1911; Père Lachaise cemetery, Paris), the expressionist marble frieze on the London Transport Building, Westminster (1929), and the huge bronze *Archangel Michael* – suggesting heaven's bulky majesty rather than spirituality or grace – which juts from one wall of Coventry Cathedral (1962). Even by the Victorian standards of British civic sculpture, Epstein's work looks graceless and clumsy – and perhaps this challenge to accepted ideas constituted his main 'idea'. He depicted the New Testament in terms of the Old; he was an ancient modern, sculpture's Cecil B. De Mille. This may help to explain his remarkable fame in his own lifetime – but whatever will our great-grandchildren think of his work, or of the worthies who commissioned it?

Excellent study: R. Buckle: *Jacob Epstein Sculptor* (1963).

ERNST, Max (1891–1976)
German artist

Many of Ernst's best early works are surrealist collages. In the tiny *Here Everything is Floating*, for example (1920; 12×10; MMA, NY), an anatomical drawing of a beetle is turned upside-down, equipped with a smoking funnel and becomes a steam-boat in a sea which also includes a skeletal fish; in *People in a Railway Carriage*, from the 'pictorial novel' *Une Semaine de bonté ou les sept éléments capitaux* (1934; 27×21), a 19th-century bourgeois straight from Doré apprehensively shares a train compartment with a man tied with ropes, a half-naked girl bound to a torturer's rack and a Russian-looking *mujik* with a sheep's head. This is narrative art for the inhabitants of Babel. His paintings range from *Dix-like visions of horror (e.g. *The Horde*, 1927; 143×112; State Museum, Amsterdam – twisted heraldic creatures with a corrugated texture generated by *frottage*, rubbing the paper over a rough material – or the grim green tree-stumps of *La Grande Forêt*, 1927; 146×114; Kunst-museum, Basel), to bland surrealist canvases as elegantly enigmatic as those of *Chirico (e.g. *Two Children Are Threatened by a Nightingale*, 1924; 45×32; MMA, NY, in which a menacing wooden picture-frame and two enormous matches grab attention, or *Oedipus rex*, 1922; 116×89; private coll., Paris, a nightmare assemblage of fingers, arrows, an eyeball, the heads of a bull and a huge bird and a meticulously drawn brick wall). He also made impressive, bony sculptures (e.g. the chess-fantasy *The King Playing with the Queen*, 1954; 98 cm high; MMA, NY). These, and his Dix-like paintings, are his finest work.

Ernst's own writings (useful for information on all surrealist intentions) include *Les Malheurs des immortels* (1922), *La Femme 100 têtes* (1929) and the comparatively mature *Vus à travers un tempérament* (1953). Good introduction: V. Schneede: *The Essential Max Ernst* (1973).

GABO, Naum (1890–1977)
Russian sculptor

Gabo's work is not so much sculpture as the skeleton of sculpture: bare ribs, exposed armatures, transparent angles and planes and curves. In particular, he dispenses with mass (the overwhelming feature of earlier sculpture) in favour of the constructivist ideal of depicting 'movement in space'. His constructions, to the uninitiated, often look like machines of the future – or at least those of science-fiction films – poised to begin working as soon as the spectator looks away. He worked with artificial materials (glass, plastic, nylon) or with rods and rectangular slivers of polished wood. A typical piece, *Column* (1923; 105 cm high; Guggenheim, NY), consists of several ruler-shaped plastic pillars of different heights set on end on a pedestal of three metal discs and bound with rings of transparent plastic, one of which is set diagonally: the filter-unit for a cubist aquarium. Another, *Spiral Theme* (1941; 24×24×13; Tate, London), is a hollow oval of clear plastic with inset frets and braces – a Martian mandolin. This is not public art – it is for private enjoyment in uncluttered, airy rooms – and Gabo made only one major piece of public sculpture, a huge (25·5 metres high) aeolian-harp-shaped construction of wire and concrete for the Bijenkorf department store, Rotterdam (1957). Its use of wire extends the idea of his 'thread-sculpture' of the 1940s: frames of transparent plastic supporting loom-like traceries of nylon thread. In his youth, Gabo's constructivist vision was of this kind of art serving and decorating a wholly modern world, washed clean and pure. (The Korda film of Wells's *Things to Come* had constructivist designs.) The vision was never realized, perhaps because humanity itself, the one unstreamlinable material, polluted it; its most substantial remnants are Gabo's abstracts, vibrant with idealism, the ghosts of what might have been.

Good introduction: T. Newman: *Naum Gabo: The Constructive Process* (1976).

GIACOMETTI, Alberto (1901–66)
Swiss sculptor

Giacometti's early work was surrealist or cubist in inspiration. *Spoon Woman*, for example (1926; 142 cm high; Guggenheim, NY), is exactly what the title says; *Cube* (1935; 92 cm high; Kunsthaus, Zurich) could have fallen straight out of a *Braque landscape; *The Palace at 4 a.m.* (1933; 72×62×39; MMA, NY) is a scaffolding house filled with surrealist objects (a pterodactyl, a *Chirico mannequin, a seahorse-tail in a scaffolding cage). In the 1940s his style changed. He began making elongated, spindly figures, like ash-people from Pompeii or rust-eaten toys from bronze-age graves. They are elegant and bleak, art for the survivors of the apocalypse. A typical example, *Forest* (1950; 65×60×57; Maeght Foundation, Saint-Paul, France), consists of eight burnt-match-stick people on a butcher's-block-shaped plinth, looking out at the spectator with an air of sad, hieratic menace. The same blend of etiolated grace and hopelessness is present in Giacometti's painted portraits (e.g. *The Artist's Mother*, 1950; 86×59; MMA, NY).

Interesting appraisal: J. Genet: *Alberto Giacometti* (1962). Good study: R. Hohl: *Alberto Giacometti* (1972).

GONZÁLEZ, Julio (1876–1942)
Spanish sculptor

González worked for a time as a painter, but in 1908 abandoned art for the family business (gold- and silver-work). In the mid-1920s his friend *Picasso asked him for technical advice on the making of metal sculpture, and this reawakened his interest. The form of his sculptures owes less to the bronzes of the past (generally made in moulds) than to the shaping and welding of 'cold' metal characteristic of commercial wrought-iron work. Most of his pieces are in a simple cubist style (e.g. *Cactus Man II*, 1931; 78 cm high; MAM, Paris), and he never achieved the quality either of Picasso or of contemporaries such as *Lipchitz. One work (*Montserrat*, 1937; 163 cm high; State Museum, Amsterdam) does stand out. In this, González's anti-fascist feelings are realized in the solid, defiant form of a stylized mother and her child (the child shield-shaped, her guarantee against extinction): a rare example of political art transcending its circumstances to make a large human point.

Good study (incorporating González' own comments): A. C. Ritchie: *Julio González* (1956).

GRIS, Juan (1887–1927)
Spanish painter

In paintings such as *The Man in the Café* (1912; 125×89; Philadelphia MA) or *Chessboard* (1915; 92×73; Art Inst., Chicago), Gris agreeably combined a particularly clear, doctrinaire form of cubism with colours as dazzling as those of *Léger. His pictures have the simplicity and directness of posters; in fact he had considerable success as a magazine- and book-illustrator. From the beginning he was particularly interested in the formal aspect of cubism, in the intrinsic possibilities of geometry rather than its presence in and relationship with the natural objects being depicted. This led him, towards the end of his life, to paint in an austere, almost abstract style, filling each canvas not with the hundreds of shapes of earlier cubism but with a dozen large, single-coloured shapes in symmetrical relationship. *Guitar with Sheet of Music* (1926; 80×65; Saidenberg Coll., NY), for example, shows a yellow guitar and white music on a brown table with a red cloth, framed against blue sky seen through a window. But these 'meanings' are less important than the harmony of lines and angles: pure abstraction, if he had lived, was beckoning.

Good studies: R. Rosenblum: *Juan Gris: His Life and Work* (English trans. 1969); M. Rosenthal: *Juan Gris* (1984).

GROSZ, George (1893–1959)
German painter

Grosz is the Hogarth of the 20th century, a fine painter corrupted (or elevated) by political disgust into a bilious satirist. When his satire is overt (as in the etchings of bald capitalists and their sleazy tarts in the collection *The Face of the Ruling Class*, 1921, or in paintings of arrogantly lacerated Prussians like those in *Pillars of Society*, 1926; 195×108; National Gallery, Berlin), he is as savage as Juvenal, as monumental and grotesque as Gillray. But when his satire is covert, when corruption seems endemic to the human condition rather than to specific individuals (as in the comfortless *Portrait of Max Hermann-Neisse*, 1924; 100×93; Stadtliche Kunsthalle, Mannheim), he terrifies. Grosz fled from (hardly surprising) official persecution to America in the 1930s – and painted warm, sensual nudes and city-scapes until the Second World War filled him once more with despair and bile. (See for example the Bosch-like *A Piece of My World II*, 1939; 140×100; Grosz estate, Princeton.) He is a stunning artist, and an enigma – was he promoted to excellence or diverted from it by his appalling theme?

Good, if disingenuous autobiography: *A Small Yes and a Big No* (English version 1982). Good study: H. Bittner (ed.): *George Grosz* (1965).

HARTUNG, Hans (born 1904)
German/French painter

Hartung is a leading exponent of that kind of abstract painting sometimes called 'tachisme', that is, concerned not with shapes (as is that of, say, *Mondrian or *Nicholson) but with the actual marks the brush makes on the canvas. It is the extended equivalent of pointillism: instead of dots, lines and patches of colour merge and mesh to make large areas of indefinite shape. The mesh-effect (something like light seen through waving grass) is the most striking feature of his work; his paintings shimmer in the same way as *Riley's or *Vasarély's, though he has none of their geometric precision. Much of his work is untitled, though some paintings are identified by dates and numbers like opus numbers in music. There are good examples of his painting in the Tate (London), Guggenheim (NY), MAM (Paris) and the Philadelphia MA.

HEPWORTH, Barbara (1903–75)
British sculptor

Hepworth's work was influenced by *Arp and by *Brancusi. *Two Segments and a Sphere*, for example (1936; 30 cm high; Florsheim Foundation, Chicago), is just what its title says, two slices from a sphere (like wedges of cheese) with a smaller, complete sphere balanced on the upper edge; *Wave* (1944; 47 cm high; Havinden Coll., UK) is a curved mollusc shape in polished and blue-painted wood, its interior laced with wire; *Figure: Churinga* (1952; 122 cm high; Walker Art Center, Minneapolis) is a gourd-shaped, hollowed and beautifully textured block of mahogany. Texture and finish are of the utmost importance in all her works, whether monumental, like *Single Form* (1963; a 460cm-high bronze palette shape erected outside the Dag Hammerskjöld Memorial Library at the United Nations, NY), or miniature and domestic, like the groups of white marble figures she made in the 1950s (e.g. *Group III (Evocation)*, 1952; 22 cm high; Margaret Gardner Coll., UK). Like *Moore, she made a number of huge sculptures for open-air sites in the Cornish hills, and for new towns such as Harlow and Hatfield. These and her miniatures are her most impressive works.

Useful: B. Hepworth: *A Pictorial Autobiography* (1970). Good introductory study: J. P. Hodin: *Barbara Hepworth* (1961). Splendidly hot-blooded, if brief, memoir, gorgeously gossipy on Hepworth in her Hampstead thirties: M. Gardiner: *Barbara Hepworth: A Memoir* (1982).

HOCKNEY, David (born 1937)
British artist

Hockney's early paintings are full of squat, matchstick-limbed figures, *Dubuffet shapes drawn with meticulous thin lines and decorated with private jokes and verbal references in a style akin to *Klee: We Two Boys Together Clinging (1961; 153×122; Arts Council of Great Britain) is typical. In the mid-1960s he worked in California, and produced a series of shower- and pool-scenes notable for their simple geometric shapes, bright pinks, greens and blues, and dazzling effects of movement in still water. The best-known is A Bigger Splash (1967; 244×244; Marchioness of Dufferin and Ava Coll., London); the best is Portrait of an Artist (Pool with Two Figures) (1971; 275×214; private coll., UK). He has made many drawings and etchings (e.g. the witty *Picasso-homage Artist and Model, 1974; 81×61), and a large number of impressive portraits, of both single subjects and pairs of people sharing a room but not communicating (e.g. Gregory Masurovsky and Shirley Goldfarb, 1974; 214×122; Kasmin Ltd, London).

In the early 1980s Hockney abandoned painting in favour of 'joiners', collages of photographs showing a brief 'story' (e.g. a girl walking down steps with a cup of tea) in a kind of time-lapse, frozen-narrative form. The effect is as if comic strips or film story-boards had been cut up and grouped in a surrealistic tumble like *Duchamp's Nude Descending a Staircase, except that Hockney's pictures are subtler than comic strips and far more explicit and eye-ravishing than Duchamp's painting. Hockney says that they will outlive his own painting and drawing – but don't hold your breath. They are, in fact, like all his other work, decorative rather than profound, other-worldly rather than 'contemporary'. His art has no commitment to anything but the process of making art itself, and makes no demands on spectators but that they should enjoy it – which in the present world has a paradoxical effect of happy defiance, colourful insolence.

Splendid (and beautifully, comprehensively, illustrated) autobiography: David Hockney (1976). Hockney 'starred' (somewhat archly and unwillingly) in the biographical film A Bigger Splash (1974).

HOFMANN, Hans (1880–1966)
German/American painter

Hofmann was an influential teacher, first in Munich and then (after 1932) in the USA. His early work followed *Delaunay's ideas on the dominance of colour; most of these paintings, however, were destroyed in a studio fire in the late 1930s, and he is chiefly known for the virtuoso abstracts of his later years. These range from dribbles, whorls and squiggles – he influenced both *Pollock and de *Kooning – to thickly painted, cheerful groups of rectangles in brash, bright colours (e.g. *The Gate*, 1960; 187×124; Guggenheim, NY). He is, like *Dufy, not a great painter but a delightful one; his uncomplicated canvases give the illusion of ease, provoke creative empathy – if you or I painted abstracts for pleasure, might they not look just like these?

Interesting writings: *Search for the Real* (1967). Good study: W. C. Seitz: *Hans Hofmann* (1963).

HOPPER, Edward (1882–1967)
American painter

A (reluctant) commercial artist for several years, Hopper reflected in his magazine illustrations and advertisements the environment and aspirations of middle-brow, middle-income middle Americans, the Mr and Mrs Average of the mail-order catalogue. It was a world where every man was natty, every woman smart, every emotion passionate and clear – and it accorded very ill with the underlying secretiveness and pessimism of Hopper's own nature. His 'real' art – widely represented in US galleries, though rare in Europe, and with titles like *Early Sunday Morning*, *Western Motel*, *Room in New York* or *Woman in the Sun* – shows, with devastating harshness and irony, exactly the same scenes as his commercial work: shaded windows in sunny walls, apartments and soda-fountains, brilliantined men and bee-sting-lipped women in offices and cafés or standing on sidewalks gazing at their reflections in the windows of empty stores. His world – for all the claims that he is a 'realistic' painter – has no reality: his people are mannequins, his city-scapes *Chirico stage-sets notable for savage top-lighting and threatening shadows. Light is Hopper's chief weapon – the America he shows us is immensely familiar, but it is the never-never America of Warner Brothers movies, and is lit and angled to the same merciless effect. Apart from Chirico, his nearest equivalents are Degas (for bleached, cruel colour) and *Munch (for eeriness). His individuality and visual richness do, in the end, transcend his lonely viewpoint; but he remains attractive rather than first-rate, a painterly equivalent of Carson McCullers but never of Kafka.

Good study: G. Levin: *Edward Hopper: The Art and the Artist* (1982).

JOHNS, Jasper (born 1930)
American artist

If one of the purposes of art is to make us see the familiar with fresh eyes, then Johns' earnest pop art fulfils it perfectly. His heavily painted targets and American flags, or his beer-cans bronzed for immortality like babies' shoes, place ordinary objects in a startling new context, and – if trendier critics are to be believed – 'de-identify them' in the process. (Duchamp, thou art translated!) But Johns is a deeper and more serious artist than this might suggest. His 1970s paintings (though they still use numbers, figures and made-over objects from real life, often glued on to the canvas and painted over – a collage of tins, nails, chains and brushes) have the same feeling of personality and choice as *Picasso's cubist collages, often of the same kind of 'ready-mades', in the 1920s. Some of them (e.g. the triptych *Voices Two*, 1971; 180×125 each panel; Kunstmuseum, Basel), for all their cheeky technique, are images of considerable dignity and power. Those are also the qualities of what is perhaps his best work of all: designs and costumes for the Merce Cunningham Dance Company, to which he has been artistic adviser since 1966.

Good study: M. Crichton: *Jasper Johns* (1978).

JONES, Allen (born 1937)
British artist

Not so much pop art as fetish art, Jones's work draws its glossy style from fashion-plates (Erté, rather unexpectedly, is an influence) and its inspiration from the world of 1950s erotic magazines. His women have long legs, pointed breasts, bland unchallenging faces and pouting lips; they wear high heels, stockings and suspender belts; they are dehumanized and anti-feminine, the art world's bunny girls. In a characteristic canvas, *Holding Power* (1974; 240×120; Waddington Galleries, London), a stripper receives the plaudits (and Freudian hats) of an unseen audience. But her lower half is dressed (shoes, stockings, leotard), her upper half a spotlit silhouette, a shape as simple and eloquent as a paper cutout by *Matisse. As well as paintings, Jones has made a large number of 'sculptures', in which his fantasy-women alarmingly become full-size, three-dimensional and lifelike – except that they are bent double backwards supporting tables, or fitted with coat-hangers and outstretched trays for drinks. Illusionist sculpture of this kind is increasingly common (de Andrea and Hanson in the USA, and Monro and Davies in Britain, for example, have filled galleries with people who look as real as the spectators who come to view them); but Jones's figures lead the field, not least because of his powerful, puritan vision of the plastic sensuality of our Madison-Avenue world. Clockwork orange juice, anyone?

KANDINSKY, Vassili (1866–1944)
Russian painter

Kandinsky was a genius with little talent. He wrote an important (and still interesting) book on the aesthetics of 'modern' art, *Concerning the Spiritual in Art* (1910); he taught at the Bauhaus; his theories and teaching were vital influences on 20th-century abstract painting; his importance generally is analogous to Schoenberg's in music. But his pictures rarely haunt the memory: he lacks the clinching individuality of many of his less great followers.

One of the problems is a jostle of theory. Like the composers Wagner and Scriabin, Kandinsky believed in the possibility of a single, ultimate art-work, a gathering together of every facet of human aesthetic creativity. Wagner conceived stage settings, action and lighting himself, as integral parts of his music-dramas (for which he also wrote the words as well as the music); Scriabin experimented with 'light-organs' and evolved complex theories about the 'colour-values' of musical notes and chords; Kandinsky spoke of the 'resonance' of painting, of its 'developing the same energies as music'. The trouble is that music is, precisely, energetic, that it moves and grows, whereas paintings are still. The realization of Kandinsky's theories is paint not on canvas but on animated film – and indeed the films of Norman McLaren (images drawn directly on to the film stock, often with a drawn music track as well) seem excellently to represent what he was trying to do. His own canvases are like the whole of one such film crammed into a single frame; without sequence, their images seem illogical and cluttered. *Chagall's textures and colours come to mind (Kandinsky often has a similar mystery and sensuality); but Chagall's pictures assemble recognizable objects and thus have an objective correlative, whereas Kandinsky's merely teem with shapes. The series of *Compositions* is typical: tumbling lines, shapes and blurs, like abstract dreams of landscape (*Composition II*, 1910; 129×97; Guggenheim, NY) or shipwreck (*Composition VII*, 1913; 300×200; Tretyakov Gallery, Moscow).

In the 1920s, under the influence of *Klee, Kandinsky's work did at times replace this kaleidoscopic jazziness with a sort of order (e.g. *White Line, No. 232*, 1920; 99×80; Mme Kandinsky Coll., Neuilly-sur-Seine, France), and some of his later paintings (e.g. *Blue Sky*, 1940; 100×73; MAM, Paris, a group of *Miró creatures dancing and tumbling in a cloudless blue sky) do please as well as intrigue the eye. But they are essentially derivative (see especially the expressionist searchlights of *Shrill-Peaceful Pink*, 1924; 62×47; Wallrauf-Richatz Museum, Cologne), and lack the chaotic intensity of his earlier canvases. His best legacy is the work he inspired in others.

Kandinsky's other theoretical writings include *From Print and Line to Plane* (English edn 1947). (His *Complete Writings on Art*, ed. K. C. Lindsay and P. Vergo, were published in English in 1982.) Good introduction: W. Grohmann: *Wassily Kandinsky – Life and Work* (1959). Particularly well illustrated: P. Weiss: *Kandinsky in Munich: The Formative Jugendstil Years* (1979).

KIRCHNER, Ernst (1880–1938)
German painter

A founder-member of the Brücke group (see page 536), in 1906 Kirchner published its manifesto in the form of a squat-lettered, mock-medieval black woodcut: youth, freedom from establishment techniques, unfettered self-expression. His paintings are a jumble of influences, especially those of primitive art and of 'free spirits' like Gauguin and *Matisse. *Self-Portrait with Model*, for example (1910; 147×100; Kunsthalle, Hamburg), blends the plain shapes and flat colours of Matisse with a heavy-lidded eroticism like that of Schiele. *Marketplace with Red Tower* (1915; 119×89; Folkwang Museum, Essen) is like a *Delaunay streetscene reworked by Gauguin. His most successful works – and he is a pleasant enough painter, if derivative – are his many scenes of prostitutes walking in busy city streets. The subject-matter is impressionist, the style fauvist, the social comment blunt. After war service Kirchner suffered a breakdown in both mental and physical health. He spent his last twenty years in Switzerland, sometimes in sanatoria; in 1937 his paintings were condemned by the Nazis; in 1938 he killed himself.

Good study: W. Grohmann: *E. L. Kirchner* (1961).

KITAJ, Ron (born 1932)
American painter

Kitaj worked in Britain in the 1950s and 1960s, and was a friend and associate of *Hockney. His paintings are an extraordinary amalgam of diverse influences. They are as cluttered as those of the surrealists, and are organized in a take-it-or-leave-it early cubist way, though colour and shapes follow fauvism. Perspective is often avoided. Though the pictures tell stories, their dominant shapes are those of the ceramics of *Matisse. All of which suggests that Kitaj's work has personality, but no maturity. Characteristic canvases are *London by Night, Part I* (1964; 182×133; Marlborough Fine Art Ltd, London) and the politically clamorous *The Murder of Rosa Luxemburg* (1960; 150×150; private coll.). He returned to the USA in the late 1960s (and has several pictures in such places as the MMA, NY), but has had little effect on contemporary American art. In the late 1970s, he began a long series of nudes, like Degas in inspiration and execution. He is an individual, lonely figure, akin to the British painter Peter Blake: a talented enigma.

Well-illustrated account: J. Ashbery, J. Shannon, J. Livingston, J. Hyman: *Kitaj: Paintings, Drawings, Pastels* (1983).

KLEE, Paul (1879–1940)
Swiss painter

Klee taught art (at the Bauhaus, 1921–31; at Düsseldorf Academy, 1931–3) and published numerous articles, diaries and notebooks on the subject of style and creativity. His pictures combine clarity and simplicity of shapes with an alert, bright fantasy not unlike that of *Miró. He famously described his artistic method as 'taking a line for a walk': that is, the picture begins with one of the basic abstract elements (a line, a dot, a blob of colour) and grows and develops in an organic way, controlled partly by technical caprice ('what can this shape or line do next?') and partly by Klee's own fantasy. His images are surreal, a map of his own subconscious mind; but most are gentle, pastel dreams, with neither the imaginative clamorousness nor the covert sexuality of much surrealist art (*Chirico, *Dali, *Magritte). His interest in art as decoration, and his fascination with such technical matters as *Delaunay's colour-wheels, give his pictures not only a unique feeling of *process* (they are anatomies of art, stepwise demonstrations of creation), but also a detailed and engrossing personal iconography (they are full of arrows, pointers, clusters of small shapes and objects which seem to have obsessive private significance; their 'poetic' titles are an essential part of their meaning).

All through his career, Klee produced both abstract and figurative art. Sometimes (as in *Hammamet with the Mosque*, 1914; 21×18; Coll. Berggruen, Paris) the picture begins figuratively but develops into a set of abstract shapes. Sometimes (as in *The Red Balloon*, 1922; 31×28; Guggenheim, NY) the starting-point is abstract, and it is not until the very end (in this case, the title) that figurative meaning appears. In some of his most attractive works, thousands of tiny shapes are pulled into overall meaning by a single controlling line or colour-band. In *A Garden for Orpheus* (1926; 46×32; Kunstmuseum, Berne), diamonds, stars, crosses and pyramids are built up on a pale yellow background with black pen-strokes – it is like a manual of hatching and shading – until the title reveals that each shape is a different kind of plant or foliage. *Ad Parnassum* (1932; 124×99; Kunstmuseum, Berne) is an abstract mosaic of tiny coloured rectangles (whose minute lack of symmetry – typical of Klee – is part of their charm: they are organic, not mechanical); it is however dominated by the inverted V of a roof, an arched door-shape and a perfect circle set like a sun in the mosaic sky. Even in purely abstract works (e.g. *In the Current Six Thresholds*, 1929; 42×42; Guggenheim, NY) the impression is of warmth and joy, patterns chosen for their beauty and arranged to seduce both mind and eye.

This feeling of selection – each element in the picture chosen for its own individual grace – is one of the two vital features of Klee's work. The other is colour. No other 20th-century painter but *Rothko has made rectangles of colour shimmer and glow with such warmth – and Rothko put only two or three huge rectangles on each canvas, whereas Klee crowded his colour in dozens, sometimes hundreds, of tiny areas. In *Battle Scene from the Comic Opera 'The Seafarer'* (1923; 51×37; Coll. Frau T. Dürst-Haass, Switzerland) a pink-and-yellow helmeted warrior in a pink boat delicately spears one of three pink-and-purple fish. The rest of the picture consists of blue sea and brown land, criss-crossed by thin lines which divide them into wobbling squares, like ceramic tiles pushed over sideways, or tilled fields seen from a high-flying aircraft. The single dominating line of the painting, the coastline, is a flattened S-shape placed horizontally across the centre, and echoed in the S-shapes of the serpent-fish. No two tiny squares are identically coloured: blues and browns wash over the whole canvas in constant variation. It is a quiet picture, its radiance not muted but intimate, its appeal a sensuality of the intellect. *Flagged Town* (1927; 30×21; private coll., Berne) has the same intimate charm. It is as if a Rothko (blue) had been overpainted with a network of fine white lines, a drawing of castles and palaces made by a tipsy architect. Then six flags (red, yellow and blue-grey), a crescent moon and a brown circle (without 'meaning' – but it gathers the picture and draws the eye) are superimposed.

Like Webern's music, Klee's paintings once seemed unemotional and aloof to the point of coldness – even he once said they lacked 'passionate warmth'. Certainly his emotional restraint makes most other artists seem shouting extroverts. But the limpidity and elegance of his work, its quiet dazzle, has its own appeal.

Of Klee's writings, the most useful are *On Modern Art* (1948), a discussion of the aesthetic dilemma (or self-imposed isolation) of the 20th-century artist, and the jottings about his own and other people's art collected in *The Thinking Eye* (2nd edn 1964) and *The Nature of Nature* (English edn 1973). Good introductions: W. Haftmann: *The Mind and Work of Paul Klee* (English trans. 1954); J. S. Pierce: *Paul Klee and Primitive Art* (1975). An intriguing, albeit scholarly, read is A. Kagan, *Paul Klee: Art and Music* (1983), whose starting-point is the analogy frequently drawn between Klee's art and the processes of music, and which investigates Klee's debt to musical procedures. (Musical knowledge useful.)

KLIMT, Gustav (1862–1918)
Austrian artist

Apart from its intrinsic merit, Klimt's work is an important bridge between late-19th-century *art nouveau* (his erotic drawings are in a direct line from those of Beardsley) and the violent expressionism of such men as *Kokoschka and Schiele. In particular, he blends ostentatiously meticulous draughtsmanship with headlong subject-matter, and his demonstration that nightmare emotion need not lead to indiscipline was an important factor in the development of German art. (*Grosz, for example, owes him debts.) A canvas which illustrates these qualities is *Death and Life* (1908/1911; 195×176; Coll. Preleuthover, Vienna). On the left, a grinning skeleton, in a gaudy *Klee-cloak of crosses, flags and circles, contemplates a bedful of people on the right: mother, father, granny, child and friends, wrapped in what looks like a number of particularly colourful patchwork quilts. The theme and decorative style in part suggest Morris (or even Millais's *Ophelia*); but the abstraction and exuberance of the patterns are wholly 20th-century in style, quite unlike the heavy, carpet-like patterns in *art nouveau*. Klimt's drawings and paintings (e.g. the much-reproduced *Woman with a Black Feather Hat*, 1910; 79×62; Coll. Fogaraszy, Graz) are also full of calculated eroticism – and this appears also in his murals and mosaics for public buildings. (His sensual ceilings and wicked walls for Vienna University made scandal in 1903.)

Good study: F. Novotny and J. Dobai: *Gustav Klimt* (1968).

KLINE, Franz (1910–62)
American painter

Kline's early work is figurative, in a heavily drawn, boldly coloured style derived from such painters as *Nolde and *Rouault. In the early 1950s he changed his style, and became a leading exponent of abstract expressionism. (This uses paint with all the jagged force of the expressionists, but concentrates on abstract shapes instead of figures.) Kline's canvases are large, and often painted in three tones only: black, white and grey. The darker shades are sloshed and splashed across the background in broad, haphazard lines. The result reminds some people of oriental calligraphy, others of the strokes with which an intemperate distemperer attacks a wall. As with so many other stylistic pioneers, Kline's influence is greater than his work. Those who made a language out of his broken syllables include Tworkov, Gorky and especially de *Kooning. Characteristic Kline pictures are *Accent grave* (1955; 188×128; Cleveland MA) and *Mahoning* (1956; 250×250; Whitney MMA, NY).

KOKOSCHKA, Oskar (1886–1980)
Austrian painter

The individuality and strength of Kokoschka's work come from a tempering of expressionist style (the depiction of emotion by means of heightened colour and distortion) with the elegant disciplines of *art nouveau*. His many portraits, for example, seem not merely to depict the sitters but to analyse them, to make them emblems of emotional states or moods – he himself remarked that he painted them 'in their anxiety and pain'. Anxiety and pain there may be, but Kokoschka depicts them with a calm introversion (the emotions are similar in picture after picture: they are his and not his subjects') very far from the hysterical anguish of other expressionist painters, e.g. *Beckmann or *Nolde. We are drawn into the quietness of such paintings as *Hans Tietze and Erica Tietze-Conrat* (1909; 135×76; MMA, NY) or *Portrait of Marcel von Nemes*, 1929; 133×94; Neue Galerie, Linz); it is only as we 'read' them that underlying tension becomes apparent (in the hands, the eyes, the clashing background colours) – and it is this gentle *growth* in their meaning that gives them power. Outside portraiture, Kokoschka's pictures are more overt. The magnificent *The Bride of the Wind*, for example (1914; 217×178; Kunstmuseum, Basel), shows a woman asleep beside her pensive lover (a self-portrait of Kokoschka) in a whirling blue landscape suggesting a beach beside a stormy sea at night.

In later life Kokoschka travelled widely, and painted many landscapes. His pictures of London are characteristic: they are a mixture of depiction (simple lines) and emotional suggestion (eerie jumbles of clashing colours), at once uncomfortable and satisfying. *View of the Thames*, for example (1926; 128×89; Albright-Knox Art Gallery, NY), clearly shows the Embankment, Cleopatra's Needle and the smoky docks – but this is no actual Thames, it is a churning, storm-lurid river of the mind set in the same dour, bustling city as Turner painted and Doré drew.

Kokoschka's autobiography *My Life* was published in English in 1974. Good introduction: J. P. Hodin: *Kokoschka* (1966).

KOLLWITZ, Käthe (1867–1945)
German artist

Kollwitz lived in Berlin for fifty of its most traumatic years (1891–1943), and her grim art reflects the agony of the century: it is as if the girl in *Munch's *The Scream* (1893) had had to respond to every subsequent horror from the Western Front to Auschwitz. Kollwitz's expressionist images of frozen pain are close to Munch; she has tenderness and humanity, but they are emotions icy with despair. Much of her work is in black and white: drawings, lithographs and chilly bronze sculptures. Her etchings of rioting workers or peasants (e.g. *Weavers' Rising*, 1893–7) are reminiscent of newspaper scenes from the Paris Commune of 1871; but her work is best when it replaces specific political references with general comment on the bleakness of human life (e.g. the lithograph *Bread*, 1924, which shows a weeping woman with her back to us and two terrified children clinging to her skirts – an emblematic group from an Eisenstein film). Her greatest theme is that of mother and child. The sculpture *Mother and Child (Pietà)*, for example (1917/1954; 72 cm high; Smithsonian, Washington), is a characteristically comfortless reinterpretation of a standard Renaissance motive. Art of this quality, on themes like this, raises disturbing questions about purpose – both the artist's and the spectator's. Is the artist's function a moral one, to warn, shock or improve? And does not our 'pleasure' in the artwork – all Kollwitz's pieces have sombre aesthetic appeal – involve an uneasy mixture of intellectual appreciation and emotional voyeurism? These scenes should arouse pity and horror – does the beauty in their depiction not fight with that?

H. Bittner (ed.): *Käthe Kollwitz: Drawings* (1959).

KOONING, Willem de (born 1904)
Dutch/American painter

Although he lived and worked in the USA from 1923, de Kooning did not become well known until the late 1940s; since then his achievement has been substantial and influential. His figurative paintings (e.g. the series *Women* of the 1950s) take their starting-point from *Picasso and their style from a blend of *Pollock and *Rouault. *Woman I*, for example (1952; 189×145; MMA, NY), is a next-door neighbour of Picasso's *Les Demoiselles d'Avignon*. She is sitting facing us, a comfortable, large-bosomed lady in skirt and sensible shoes. But her face is a grinning primitive mask and her torso (chiefly white) is overpainted with broad strokes and gashes of paint, as if *Kline had been invited to finish off the canvas. The background (except that it is not background, because the painting is without perspective) is an abstract turmoil of pinks, blues, yellows, whites and blacks. Despite the apparent chaos of the brush-strokes, the picture's effect is hieratic and reposeful; its blend of horror and stillness is again reminiscent of *Les Demoiselles d'Avignon*. (In other paintings in the *Women* series, e.g. *Woman VI*, 1953; 172×146; MA, Carnegie Institute, Pittsburgh, the hurrying abstract background swallows the human figure.) De Kooning's fully abstract works have the same vigorous swagger. It is as if he has streaked paint-tubes at random across the canvas – and then ordered the randomness and made it speak. (The method is analogous to *Klee's, except that de Kooning's walk is taken not with a line but with a broad ribbon of thick, unmixed colour.) *Composition* (1955; 198×173; Guggenheim, NY) is warm with pillar-box reds, yellows and browns – a dominating canvas, not strident but much too grand for the living room. In their sensuality and brashness, such large de Koonings are a 20th-century equivalent of those vast Victorian allegorical and hunting scenes made for the hallways and committee-rooms of public buildings. He is the Alma-Tadema of 20th-century Corporate Humanity.

The best introduction to de Kooning is *De Kooning* (1974) by Harold Rosenberg, whose book on modern art in general, *The Anxious Object* (1964), is comforting and stimulating to general readers baffled by what may (or may not) be going on.

KUPKA, Frantisek (1871–1957)
Czech painter

Kupka was interested in psychic phenomena (he was a spiritualist, at one time a professional medium), and his paintings are inspired by theories of the mystical meanings of shape and colour. They are abstracts, each a strong, simple statement of a single theme. *Disks of Newton (Study for Fugue in Two Colours)* (1912; 98×72; Philadelphia MA) – the title, with its suggested union between art, music and science, is typical – is a pretty pattern of coloured wheels and circles, reminiscent of *Delaunay's colour-wheel paintings or his *Homage to Blériot. Amorpha, Fugue for Two Colours* (1912; 220×211; National Gallery, Prague) and its smaller sister *Amorpha, Fugue for Two Colours II* (1912; 110 × 67; Cleveland MA) consist of cubist whorls and crescents, with the colour applied in iridescent dabs and dashes, like feathers or fish-scales. More individual and more forward-looking – they bring to mind *Nicholson or such 1970s figures as Marden or Stella – are his canvases of rectangles: *Vertical Planes* (1913; 198×116; artist's estate), a group of five ruler-shapes in black, white, grey and (just one) violet, is typical. He was a perfectionist, often destroying or repainting earlier works. His output is small, perhaps no more than a grace-note to the main theme of 20th-century art.

Good study: L. Vachtova: *Kupka* (1968).

LAURENS, Henri (1885–1954)
French sculptor

Laurens was a Parisian, a friend of *Picasso and *Braque during the evolution of cubism in the 1910s. He worked as a stage designer (notably for Diaghilev in the 1920s) and as a book illustrator. His chief works are sculptures, in a rigorous and consistent cubist style like that of *Lipchitz, though he lacks Lipchitz's liberating fantasy. In his best sculptures, those of the 1920s, he often painted the finished stone. *Guitar and Clarinet*, for example (1920; 36×32×8; Smithsonian, Washington), is a relief-carving painted in browns and yellows, like a *Gris still-life in three dimensions. Apart from satisfying images, his work offers the spectator the pleasure of seeing two distinct media not surrendering their individuality yet married to good effect.

Good study: C. Goldscheider: *Laurens* (English edn 1959).

LÉGER, Fernand (1881–1955)
French artist

At first sight, there is a hint of the nursery about Léger's work. The shapes are simple and unequivocal: a bicycle is a bicycle, a cup a cup, a rose a rose. (Gertrude Stein's idea of 'pure meaning' is not irrelevant.) The colours are matt and pure; each shape has a single colour, without gradation. (Thus, a Léger tree is a straight-sided, rectangular brown column topped by a green circle with scalloped edges, the whole thing surrounded by a heavy black outline.) His pictures look like designs for children's wallpaper, or for those plywood jigsaw puzzles where each piece is a complete object or shape. The designer's modern nursery world is heavily cubist; so is Léger's. A typical picture in this style is *The Outing/Homage to Louis David* (1949; 182×152; MAM, Paris). Two women and a man in cycling clothes pose in a stiff group with two men in heavy suits. One of the men holds a pipe; the other has a straw hat on his head and a child in his arms. There are bicycles, a tree, sand, and a group of love-birds in a bright blue sky. It is a child's dream of a Sunday outing: the symbols of domestic endeavour leading to happiness are perfectly clear.

But Léger is not a nursery artist, and these are not nursery scenes. Why, in *The Outing*, are all the faces those of bland, unemotional dummies? Why is the grouping of the figures as stylized and stiff as in an early Victorian photograph? Why do the cycling-outfits look more like circus acrobats' leotards? Why does the green foliage seem so venomous? An elusive point of view, sardonic and satirical, has been painted into the picture – and its presence is indicated in the piece of paper held by one of the girls, with the painting's title clearly written on it.

This wide-eyed symbolism, like the geometric forms and plain bright colours, gives Léger's work a strongly surrealist edge – or rather, he shows the surrealist aspect of ordinary life. Another picture in this style, *The Great Constructors* (1950; 295×197; Musée F. Léger, Biot, France), shows a scene of men at work on the steel-girder skeleton of a modern skyscraper. But they are *not* at work: they stand in an emblematic group (emblematic of what?) like a chorus-line frozen in mid-dance; they are eclipsed and dominated by the soaring geometry of the building, as the people in *The Outing* are by plants. Is Léger (an earnest socialist) portraying humanity out of harmony with its environment? (A further complexity of symbolism, in this picture, is a series of references to Renaissance paintings of Christ being taken from the cross. Is modern skyscraper society destroying religion, or restoring it?) The same kind of ambiguity is present in one of the largest and finest of Léger's late works, *The Great Parade* (1954; 392×270; Guggenheim, NY). This is the culmination of a series of circus paintings, and shows a dozen figures in symbolic poses. But the figures are dominated by a huge superimposed figure 10 in red, and a horizontal purple stripe across the middle of the picture. (If it were an advertisement, these would be bands for copy.) And what are those square, round-windowed boxes everywhere – cameras, cigarette-packets, *washing-machines*?

If Léger's figurative paintings, however equivocal and baffling their ultimate meaning, are a celebration of 20th-century life, his many abstracts and near-abstracts celebrate machine-shapes in the same uncluttered, child's-puzzle way. *Mechanical Element*, for example (1924; 128×96; Kunsthaus, Zurich), is a pattern of straight-edged shapes – abstract marquetry, or a masonic dream of art – with a single curved shape (phallus? boxing-glove?) ballooning out at one side, the only thing painted with perspective. It is a cheerful picture, more cluttered than, say, *Mondrian and far more teasing. In other pictures Léger emulates *Klee and indicates possible 'meaning' for an abstract composition in his title. *The City* (1919; 293×231; Philadelphia MA) is a kaleidoscope of futuristic shapes, bound together by four cubist mannequins which appear from behind pillars or rectangles, like pedestrians turning into modern streets clamorous with architecture.

Léger's vision of mechanical people is not unique, and the surface features of his style have become commonplace in posters, street-maps and the ubiquitous advertising 'logo' of the modern world. (Some of his own most striking work is on public buildings, for example the gigantic murals he made for the UN building, NY.) What is unique is the irony he adds, the over-riding feeling in all his work that machines, like people, are essentially absurd. His view of human beings themselves, as ritualizing automata, is close to that of the playwright Ionesco – and like Ionesco, he presents his essentially nihilistic philosophy with disarming warmth and heart.

Good study: P. de Francie: *Fernand Léger* (1983).

LEWIS, Percy Wyndham: see page 131.

LIBERMAN, Alexander (born 1912)
American artist

When you crush an automobile in a hydraulic press, you end up with a neat cube of compacted metal – or the beginnings of a Liberman junk-metal sculpture. For those who find ruins attractive (and which of us would honestly choose to have the Parthenon as pristine as in Pericles' day?) his ruined pipes, tanks and cylinders have nostalgic power, the rusty wracks of the industrial age. In the 1970s he began making 'new' metal sculptures. These often look like cardboard models – tubes, pyramids, curved rectangles – except, that is, for their enormous size. *Argo*, for example (1974; 4·5 m×9·5 m×10·8 m; Coll. Bradley Family Foundation, Inc.), looks like the stage-set for some gigantic futurist opera.

Liberman's paintings are examples of 'minimal art': the presentation of a single form (circle, line, rectangle) or texture (matt or gloss paint; bare canvas) whose point, according to one contemporary critic (T. B. Hess), is 'to invite concentrated meditation . . . it is you'. If this kind of art is coloured (as it is by such painters as Budd, Kelly or Resnick) it has a shimmering intensity that can seduce the eye. But what of the black-and-white circles (two each, large and small) of Liberman's *Diptych – One Way* (1950; 186×150; Emmerich Gallery, NY)? Is this Californian-Buddhist art, as Hess claims, *you*? Or is it another metamorphosis of Liberman's good old friend, junk?

LICHTENSTEIN, Roy (born 1923)
American artist

The pop art of which Lichtenstein is a leading exponent is based on parody. In the world outside the arts the word 'parody' has a limited meaning, with overtones of satire and distortion. But to an artist it means basing his or her work on an earlier work of art, dismantling and re-creating it for his or her own purposes (which need not include lampoon), using it as a foundation both of meaning and of style. Renaissance composers wrote parody Masses in this way (taking over the music of popular songs, church motets or other such works); playwrights, among them Shakespeare, regularly reworked earlier source-material; in fine art, the use of pre-existent material as a kind of objective correlative is commonplace. What distinguished Lichtenstein's work, at first, was the ephemeral nature of the 'works' he parodied, many of them outside the usual (snobbish) view of what constituted 'art'. He used the images of advertising, the movies and comic strips, taking small details (a hand holding a cigarette, a foot pressing the pedal of a garbage pail) and magnifying them on giant canvases painted in flat, hard colours and imitating the dots and lines of the pulp-newspaper printing-process of the original material. Typical works on this style are *Whaam* (1963; 400×170; Tate, London) and *As I Opened Fire* (1964; 520×170; Stedelijk Museum, Amsterdam), both based on war-action comic strips, or *Art* (1962; 170×90; Locksley Shea Gallery, Minneapolis), which consists simply of the word ART, like an information sign writ large. In his later work, Lichtenstein has parodied more upmarket material, notably paintings by *Picasso and *Matisse. His *Artist's Studio: The Dance*, for example (1974; 320×240; private coll., NY), shows – still in the same flat newsprint style – a table with brushes in a pot, a straw-covered wine-bottle, a plate of lemons and a vase of flowers (the usual cubist bric-à-braque), and behind it on the studio wall, a black-and-white version of Matisse's *The Dance*. He is telling us, as always, things about our attitude to 'art' – and as often with pop artists, we are left entirely in the dark about *his* attitude to art. The question that arises is how long orthodox art can go on honouring the cheques that such parodists cash on its account. Will the time not come when their drafts are returned to drawer, and the giggling has to stop – or be taken seriously?

Good introduction: D. Waldman: *Roy Lichtenstein* (1971). Good (if poker-faced) study of the whole pop art phenomenon: L. Alloway: *American Pop Art* (1974).

LIPCHITZ, Jacques (1891–1973)
Lithuanian/French sculptor

Lipchitz's early work is as rigorously cubist as that of *Laurens or *Duchamp-Villon. *Head*, for example (1915; 60 cm high; Smithsonian, Washington), reduces a helmeted warrior's head to a dozen planes and curves; *Sailor with a Guitar* (1914; 75 cm high; artist's estate) steps straight out of a canvas by *Braque or *Gris. In the 1920s he developed a more individual style, openwork groups in which the figures appear to be constructed from a single, twisted girder – a sculptural equivalent of *Picasso's single-line drawings of the same period. Good examples are *Joie de vivre* (1927/1960; 330 cm high; Whitney MMA, NY), which shows two entwined dancers on a plinth, and the famous *Figure* (1930; 217 cm high; Guggenheim, NY), like a *Miró fantasy-creature in three-dimensional bronze. In yet a third style, he produced roly-poly, dumpling figures, often in savage embrace. *Prometheus Strangling the Vulture* (1944; 242 cm high; Walker Art Center, Minneapolis), one of many groups illustrating Greek legends, is typical – and remarkable because despite their heaviness the figures seem to be flying in the air, in a modern version of the ancient world's sculptures of *Winged Victory*. In his later years Lipchitz was often commissioned to make religious and political works, ranging from the small bronze altar-piece *Notre Dame de Liesse* (1948; 83 cm high; artist's estate) to the huge *Government of the People* (1968) made for the city of Philadelphia. Some of his works, for all their power, are remarkably ugly (e.g. the *Sailor* and *Prometheus* mentioned above), and others can suggest to unmoved spectators those ultra-modern sculptures sent up in countless campus satires on contemporary art. But at his best (e.g. *Joie de vivre* or the *Madonna* described above) he combines grace and energy in a way matched by no other sculptor of such uncompromising futurist modernity, and equalled only by such giants as Picasso and *Moore.

Good studies: R. J. Goldwater: *Lipchitz* (English edn 1959); A. M. Hammacher: *Jacques Lipchitz: His Sculpture* (1960).

MAGRITTE, René (1898–1967)
Belgian painter

There is a widespread belief, in our advanced society, that any kind of silly behaviour (swallowing goldfish, running three-legged races backwards, dressing as clowns and intimidating passers-by) is validated and elevated if it is done for charity. Saturnalia is not legitimate in itself: it must be justified by moral earnestness. Exactly the same solemnity informs opinions of Magritte's surrealist art (not least his own opinions). If you paint a silly picture (showing for example a table set for a meal, with a plate of juicy ham – in the centre of which is an unwinking eye) the joke is not enough in itself: the picture must be dignified by a solemn title (*Portrait*) before it can be hung (in the MMA, NY; its dimensions, if they matter, are 72×49).

Magritte is less a surrealist than a punster, a music-hall artiste. A true surrealist – *Chagall or *Chirico come to mind, as well as the great masters of surrealism in art, *Picasso, *Miró or *Klee – tries to define the indefinable, to make clear-cut images of the meta-reality of dreams, to paint hauntings. Magritte tells us jokes, and (unless you like old jokes) once they're told, they're dead. There is nothing to *ponder* in a painting of a pipe called *Ceci n'est pas une pipe* ('This isn't a pipe', 1929; 76×62; Los Angeles County MA), or in a picture of an easel in front of a window through which can be seen exactly the landscape on the easel, even if it's coyly captioned *The Human Condition I* (1933; 99×79; private coll.). Magritte is one of the few artists whose pictures can be clearly described in words – and that raises doubts not only about the inherent 'mystery' claimed for them but also about their validity as works of *visual* art. Even *Dali's soft watches have mystery – a quality which Magritte's room-filling apple, for example (*The Listening Chamber*, 1953; 99×78; private coll.), conspicuously lacks.

It is only fair to say that not everyone shares this view of Magritte's work. Some find menace or claustrophobia in many of his works (e.g. in *The False Mirror*, 1928; 80×53; MMA, NY, a close-up of a single staring eye whose cornea is replaced by a cloudy sky), and eroticism in others (e.g. *Perspective: Madame Récamier of David*; 81×61; private coll., which replaces David's lady reclining on an elegant chaise-longue with a reclining coffin). One authority (George Melly) has said: 'He is a secret agent; his object is to bring into disrepute the whole apparatus of bourgeois reality. Like all saboteurs, he avoids detection by dressing and behaving exactly like everybody else.'

Ceci n'est pas une pipe.

Good introductions: D. Sylvester: *Magritte* (1969); H. Torcyner: *Magritte: Ideas and Images* (1977). Magritte's own writings are anthologized in French in *Manifestes et autres écrits* (1972).

MAILLOL, Aristide (1861–1944)
French sculptor

Maillol began his career as an *art-nouveau* painter and illustrator, and first took up sculpture in his forties. His works are almost indistinguishable from the sculptures of Hellenistic Greece: sensuous nudes, stone or bronze worked into a smooth facsimile of flesh. There is no idealization, no distortion: this is how human beings are. (Even the flat, ordinary faces of his models are faithfully reproduced.) Many of the figures are in classical poses: *The Mediterranean* (1901; 103 cm high; MMA, NY) shows a girl sitting on the ground, one knee raised to support her crooked arm, on which her pensive head rests – the conventional Greek pose for showing the 'spirit' of a river or a sea; the enigmatically entitled *Young Cyclist* (1908; 97 cm high; MAM, Paris) is a naked youth gazing at the ground in the pose of a *Hermes* or *Young Apollo* from antiquity. In other sculptures, the pose is more modern: *Night*, for example (1902; 104 cm high; Coll. Diana Vierny, Paris), shows a young girl sitting on the ground, her head resting on folded arms on upbent knees – a pose which combines sensuality with an evocation of sadness and meditation. Maillol is a throwback to the past, a 20th-century artist in nothing but dates. His best work (e.g. the ecstatic, tumbling nude called *The River*, 1943; 225×134; MMA, NY) is as good as anything by Myron, his master and his inspiration from ancient Greece.

Good study: W. George: *Aristide Maillol* (1965).

MALEVICH, Kasimir (1878–1935)
Russian painter

In his early work (basically similar in appearance to that of *Léger), Malevich used elements of every available radical style, from impressionism to futurism, to produce what he called 'nonsense realism', a representation of physical sensations by collages of shapes and images. *Woman Beside an Advertising Pillar* (1914; 71×64; Stedelijk Museum, Amsterdam), a typical early work, shows neither a woman nor an advertising pillar. It is a painted collage of fragments from advertisements: lettering, people's limbs and half-clear objects – is that a lemon, this a bicycle wheel? – overlaid with large coloured rectangles. In 1913 he produced the first piece of suprematist art, one of the ikons of the century, an emblem for both admirers and detractors of modern art. This is *Basic Suprematist Element* (1913; State Museum, Leningrad). It consists of a grey square drawn in pencil on a square white sheet of paper. The suprematist aim, in Malevich's own words, 'to free art from the burden of the object', was followed in many other such 'pictures', e.g. *White on White* (1918; 81×81; MMA, NY), a white square tilted on a white background, as if just about to fall out of the painting. Some of his works, thanks to the use of colour, are less minimal. The vertical arm of *Large Cross on White*, for example (1922; 83×68; Stedelijk Museum, Amsterdam), is a glowing red, and in *Suprematist Painting* (1916; 86×74; Stedelijk Museum, Amsterdam) a score of rectangles, widely varied in shape and colour, slant diagonally across the canvas like a shower of *Mondrian rain. The seriousness of Malevich's artistic intentions is certified by the fact that in 1922, having decided that he had nothing more to paint, he stopped.

Malevich's prolific writing includes *The Non-Objective World* (1927) and *Essays in Art* (1968). Good study: L. Zdanova: *Malevich: Suprematism and Revolution in Russian Art* (1983).

418 · Painting and Sculpture

MANZÙ, Giacomo (born 1908)
Italian sculptor

Predominantly a religious artist, Manzù is internationally known for his magnificent bronze doors for Salzburg Cathedral (1958) and for St Peter's, Rome (1964). These have panels in low relief, on the theme of death; their mixture of savagery and devotion follows directly from the work of such earlier church artists as Grünewald and Donatello. Manzù's non-church works are in a more modern idiom, owing debts to Rodin and Degas, and to the paintings of *Modigliani. His series of *Cardinals* (e.g. *Large Standing Cardinal*, 1954; 166 cm high; Smithsonian, Washington) gives the figures an equivocal, aloof menace (they are like cardinals in a Buñuel film); their withdrawn gaze is a feature of all his work. He has also made a number of attractive nudes, sometimes seating them (again, like Degas) on meticulously realistic modern chairs. One of the finest is the ecstatic – sunbathing? – *Young Girl on a Chair* (1955; 110 cm high; Smithsonian, Washington), a pigtailed, Nabokovian bronze nymphet.

Good study: J. Rewald: *Manzù* (1967).

MATISSE, Henri (1869–1954)
French artist

In *Notes of a Painter* (1908) Matisse revealingly and disingenuously claimed for his art no more than the status of pretty furniture, '. . . a soothing, calming influence on the mind, something like a good armchair which provides relaxation from physical fatigue'. This was an old-fashioned, *art-nouveau* attitude, out of line with the bustling programmes of moral improvement attached to many early 20th-century artistic isms; but Matisse's unpretentious aesthetic hedonism worked and has survived, while the aims of many of his more strident colleagues (futurists, constructivists, surrealists) have drained away leaving their actual works sometimes embarrassingly high and dry. Instead of challenging the spectator, Matisse's paintings massage him or her; they demand enjoyment not action; they involve (and perhaps 'improve') through harmonious expression. These are the effects of much oriental art, especially calligraphy, and Matisse's work has the same aloofness. It is an art, as he himself wrote, 'of balance, of purity and serenity, devoid of troubling or depressing subject-matter'; it is art for meditation and not for a hasty glance.

The way of achieving this serenity was harmony, particularly of colour. Matisse increasingly restricted his subject-matter to human figures (often nude, usually at ease in sumptuous, sunny rooms), to landscape seen through a window, to studio and parlour scenes. Its banality is banished by his idea of a 'room of earthly delights': his interiors are full of extravagant geometrical ornament (another oriental trait), and are painted in a sensuous kaleidoscope of colours, silky and simple. *The Hindu Pose*, for example (1923; 72×59; Coll. Mr and Mrs D. Stralem, NY), shows a nude girl sitting cross-legged on a sofa with her arms folded behind her head. Beside her, on a carpet, is a tall blue vase of flowers. In the background are panelled cupboard doors and a window with the shutters open. What dominates the picture are the sofa-covering (a check-pattern of blue, white and black dots), the luscious pink of the girl's body (Matisse could paint flesh with a sensuality to match Renoir himself) and the balancing purple of the flowers, the gaudy reds and yellows of the carpet picked up in a red-and-yellow curtain behind her head, and everything unified and held in balance by a broad black band of shadow and by the necklace round the girl's neck. In a later picture, *Pink Nude* (1935; 92×66; Baltimore MA), colour-pattern and geometry rule all. A nude girl reclines on a blue-and-white checked sofa; her body is reduced to a black outline coloured pink without highlights. The balances between pink, blue and the red of the wall behind, and between the check pattern of the sofa, the square window panes and the curves and ovals of the girl are the painting's point.

The formal simplicity of *Pink Nude* became the hallmark of Matisse's style. In his youth he was a fauvist, a colleague of *Derain and *Vlaminck, and his colours never abandoned the brightness and gaiety of fauvism. (A good example is *Open Window, Collioure*, 1905; 55×46; Coll. Mr and Mrs J. H. Whitney, NY, a tumble of greens, pinks and reds.) As his work developed he reduced and simplified the shapes which contained the colour: the three nude figures of *Bathers with a Turtle*, for example (1908; 220×179; City Art Museum of St Louis, Missouri), for all their sensual curves, are emblems rather than representations of humanity. They clearly foreshadow both the near-abstract geometric people (red, on blue and green) of *Dance* and *Music* (1910; each 290×256; Hermitage, Leningrad – there is another version of *Dance* in the MMA, NY) and the simply outlined, smiling women of *Music* (1939; 114×114; Albright-Knox Gallery, Buffalo). At the end of his life, twisted with arthritis, he carried figure-simplification to its logical conclusion, cutting flowing, elegant shapes from coloured paper and assembling them on painted backgrounds. Some (e.g. *The Snail*, 1953; 261×261; Tate, London) are abstract patterns whose point is their colour; others (e.g. the gigantic *The Negress*, 1952; 847×448; Galerie Beyeler, Basel) combine geometric patterns with human figures composed of a handful of elegantly cut paper shapes. His interest in shape led him, especially at the start of his career, to sculpture (e.g. *Decorative Figure*, 1908; 71 cm high; Smithsonian, Washington), and at the end of his life to design one of his most serene and reposeful works, aesthetic beauty at the service of meditation, the Chapel of the Rosary at Vence in France (consecrated 1951).

Of all artists, Matisse's work defies verbal description. If, as has been said, art aspires to the condition of music, then his achieves it. It is at once demanding and deferential; its expressive power is immense, but depends for completion on the spectator's mood – you can be 'not in the mood' for Matisse, just as you can for Bach. His eminence in 20th-century art (as high as *Picasso's) is due less to his influence than to the fact that he painted so many eloquent and unforgettable pictures, quite simply more masterpieces than almost anyone else.

Good introductions: A. Barr: *Matisse, His Art and His Public* (1951); N. Watkins: *Matisse* (1984). Gorgeously illustrated: J. Guichard-Meli: *Matisse Cutouts* (1984).

MIRÓ, Joan (1893–1983)
Spanish artist

In conception and execution, surrealism was primarily a bourgeois art-form. Its intention was to prise open the closed mind and shuttered perception of 'everyman' (identified, for this purpose, as a furled-umbrella Belgian clerk) and to show ordinary people the wonders lurking in their own Ids. Those wonders were, more often than not, utilitarian objects (pipes, fob-watches, ladders, tailor's dummies) set in the deserts, parks and marble piazzas of the imagination: a travel-brochure dream of freedom. The paradox is that because this art constantly refers to the objects which are (in the surrealists' minds at least) the prison-bars of the everyday, it is less a parable of freedom than a reminder of imprisonment: surrealist paintings are more often disorienting than comforting, gloomy rather than zestful, sterile rather than creative.

Some of Miró's work, it is true, is cut to this uncomfortable pattern. *Still Life with Old Shoe*, for example (1937; 115×80; MMA, NY), depicts ordinary objects (a bottle, a fork stuck in a fruit, a loaf whose cut end reveals a skull, an old shoe) with all the wished-for plasticity and ooze of *Dali. It tells us nothing at all (though it was claimed in the 1930s to be an anti-fascist tract); its effect is clever and depressing. But in general, and although he claimed to be 'a tragic pessimist at heart', his paintings forsake mundane ugliness for a gay, fastidious fantasy nearer to *Kandinsky and *Klee than to doctrinaire surrealism. The painting which announced this style, a masterpiece, was *The Harlequin's Carnival* (1925; 93×66; Albright-Knox Gallery, Buffalo). This shows a large well-lit room with no furniture but a table and a ladder (equipped, as most Miró ladders are, with an enormous ear). The room is filled with bizarre creatures and objects in the middle of a party. Each of them seems to metamorphose as we look at it: hour-glasses smile and dance, butterflies turn into dragons and starfish glow like stars. The only person not having fun is a Chirico-like mannequin, with a cigar in one hand and a clay pipe in his mouth; he is standing next to a jack-in-the-box which is actually a dragon-fly. The colours are the bright blues, yellows and warm browns of a child's paint-box.

Miró painted scores of pictures of this kind. Whatever the creatures are – insect-life from a Douanier Rousseau jungle, algae and hydrae from a botanist's microscope or twittering visitors from outer space – they are both delightful and comforting, a painted equivalent to the 'insect-music' of Bartók or Martinů. Like Klee, Miró is more concerned with pattern and colour than with 'meaning'; he lets his fantasy lead each picture where it will, and then gives the finished result a teasing title. *Dutch Interior II*, for example (1928; 91×72; Coll. Peggy Guggenheim, Venice), ostensibly a transformation of Jan Steen's painting *The Cat's Dancing-Lesson*, in fact is neither Dutch nor set in an interior – though it does include a guitar and a dancing cat. The three extraordinary creatures (bull? beetle? fish?) of *Nursery Decoration* (1938; 315×79; Weil Coll., St Louis, Missouri) are really ballooning abstract shapes in black and orange on a blue background, given creatureness by the addition of hypnotic Miró eyes and open mouths – and most of Miró's paintings can be 'read' this way. Some of his later works are 'pure' abstracts, and for all their extreme simplicity, they shed none of the riot of his figurative art. *Yellow-Orange (Mural Painting I)*, for example (1962; 350×266; Galerie Maeght, Paris), is no more than a huge orange rectangle with (on the right) three black plant-like tendrils and (on the left) two small black circles – and yet you feel that something innocent and wide-eyed is hidden in the picture watching you.

If surrealism's purpose is to refashion, rather than merely to subvert, bourgeois reality, then Miró is a true surrealist. His fantasy includes delight and charm as well as menace; his absorbed or watchful figures more often dance than fight; his living balloons and spirals, liveried in primary colours, intrigue the mind and entrance the eye. It is not child's art – too sophisticated and sensuous – but it is childlike for openness and charm. Miró is that rare 20th-century being, someone who has listened to Freud and smiled.

Good introductions: J. Dupin: *Joan Miró: Life and Work* (1962); R. Penrose: *Miró* (1970).

MODIGLIANI, Amedeo (1884–1920)
Italian artist

Known in his adopted Paris as *le peintre maudit* (a pun on his corrupt life-style and his nickname Modi), Modigliani lived the truly accursed life of one touched by the angel of death or the presentiment of a Hollywood biopic. He suffered from tuberculosis, and added to its ravages the self-inflicted wounds of heroin addiction and alcoholism. He was contemptuous of formal art training; his apologists (and like many a charming, doomed genius, he had plenty of those) explained this on the grounds that he had a 'perfect intuitive understanding' of every aspect of technique, whether that of Botticelli (an important influence), African sculpture or cubism. He originally intended to be a sculptor, and his long-necked, flat-nosed, 'cycladic' stone heads are among his most elegant works. (Fine examples are *Head*, 1911; 64 cm high; Guggenheim,

NY, and *Head*, 1911; 58 cm high; Musées Nationaux, Paris.) His paintings are almost all portraits, usually full face, the subject sitting with clasped hands or shown from the waist up. Apart from a few children and male friends (e.g. *The Sculptor Lipchitz and His Wife*, 1916; 81×54; Art Inst., Chicago), most of his subjects are women. Typically they are given slim hands, swan necks and thin oval faces with long flat noses. The eyes are tiny almonds, either pupil-less and opaque or with dark button-pupils. The more easy-going of these portraits (e.g. *Portrait of a Girl (Victoria)*, 1917; 81×60; Tate, London) have been much reproduced, and indeed have inspired much of the kitsch 'modern art' sold in chain stores. They are typical of Modigliani, but not of his best work. This is more enigmatic, and the figure-distortion is less mannered and more integral to the design of the picture or the delineation of the sitter's character. He favours thick, van Gogh paint textures, especially in backgrounds, and solemn cubist faces (e.g. *Chaim Soutine Seated at a Table*, 1917; 92×60; National Gallery of Art, Washington). There are also many nudes, notable for shimmering flesh (Goya's *La maja desnuda* comes to mind) and expressions of ironical, come-hither soulfulness or post-coital sleepiness. *Reclining Nude* (1917; 92×60; Staatsgalerie, Stuttgart) shows, characteristically, how Modigliani's obsessive energy and outstanding skill, even with such limited subject-matter, work together to produce a masterpiece. He is like the composer Rackmaninov: endless imitation of his manner in popular media has made it over-familiar, so that the true quality of the original is hard to appreciate. (Like Rackmaninov, too, he was not above being seduced by his own fluency.) But a handful of his works, including those mentioned here, are excellent.

Good accounts: J. Modigliani: *Modigliani: Man and Myth* (1959); F. Russoli: *Modigliani* (English trans. 1958).

MOHOLY-NAGY, László (1895–1946)
Hungarian artist and designer

In the 1920s Moholy-Nagy was a professor at the Bauhaus, particularly concerned with industrial design. In 1937 he founded the New Bauhaus in Chicago (now part of the Illinois Institute of Technology). His teaching at these two institutions, his books (e.g. *Vision in Motion*, 1947; *The New Vision and Abstract of an Artist*, 1949) and his own multifarious artistic activities (e.g. the invention of *photograms*, abstract photographs created by placing objects on photographic papers and admitting light – no camera or film) were seminal influences on dozens of artists and industrial designers in the 1920s–40s. His effect on others is his enduring legacy: his own art-works (e.g. the extraordinary sculpture, really a bizarre machine with moving parts, *Light-Space Modulator*, 1930; 149 cm high; Harvard University) have, now, more curiosity value than aesthetic punch.

Good study: S. Moholy-Nagy: *Moholy-Nagy: Experiment in Totality* (1950); K. Passuth: *Moholy-Nagy* (1984).

MONDRIAN, Piet (1872–1944)
Dutch painter

Mondrian spent the first forty years of his life seeking for an individual style, stripping down his art even as he refined his name (originally Pieter Cornelis Mondriaan). His early paintings are competent landscapes and flower-pictures in a realist style which looks at its best (e.g. in *Farm at Duivendrecht*, 1908; 108×85; Gemeentemuseum, The Hague) as if Vermeer and van Gogh had lent him one brush each. In the late 1900s he began experimenting with expressionist colour, particularly in paintings of mills, churches and trees (e.g. *The Red Tree*, 1908; 99×70; Gemeentemuseum, The Hague). In the *Tree* series his style gradually moved from realism to a semi-abstract form of cubism close to that of early *Braque (e.g. *Composition in Blue, Grey and Pink*, 1913; 115×88; Kröller-Müller Museum, Otterlo – a masterpiece). Next he spent some years experimenting with pictures built up from scores of overlapping black crosses, the haphazard rectangles so formed being coloured pink, blue and brown (e.g. *Composition*, 1916; 120×75; Guggenheim, NY). From this time onwards he painted no more figurative pictures.

So far, the sense of onward movement in Mondrian's style is stronger than any feeling of style itself. The crystallizing influence was his meeting, in the late 1910s, with the theosophist author Schoenmaekers. As a result of pondering Schoenmaekers' theories of art and life, Mondrian evolved his own revolutionary picture-style and gave it the dry name Neo-plasticism. Its dogma is as austere as its name: no curved lines, no angles except the right-angle, no colours but red, blue and yellow balanced against shades of grey. With few exceptions, all his subsequent paintings conform to this: it is the 'Mondrian look', and its philosophical rationale was tirelessly explored in the art magazine *De Stijl*, which he helped to found in 1917. The first picture to use the style with rigour was *Composition. Colour Planes with Grey Contours* (1918; 60×49; Max Brill, Zurich and Ulm). This consists of rectangles of various shapes and sizes, separated by thick black lines – the effect is of an abstract stained-glass window, panes of opaque colour lit from behind.

For the remaining quarter-century of his life, Mondrian explored this style with vigour and variety. His paintings are always rectangular, often square; some are set on the diagonal, as diamonds. (The black lines which separate or compose the rectangles are, however, always horizontal or vertical.) Some paintings consist of a handful of complete rectangles, others of partial rectangles sliced off by the picture-edges. The colours are always grey, red, blue and yellow – and Mondrian found more shades of each than any other artist. Some paintings suggest repose or meditation (e.g. *Composition with Red, Yellow and Blue*, 1922; 50×42; State Museum, Amsterdam – in which the coloured rectangles are crowded to the edges of the canvas by a large square pool of shimmering grey); others bustle with energy (e.g. the extraordinary *Composition with Yellow Square*, 1936; 73×66; Philadelphia MA, one yellow square set bottom right on a grey canvas crisscrossed by six broad black lines).

To many people, seeing Mondrian's pictures only reproduced in books, they look like nothing more or less than designs for floor-tiles – and indeed some have been used for just that (e.g. *Composition with Yellow Lines – yellow* lines, an innovation – 1933; diagonal 133 cm; Gemeente-museum, The Hague). But reproduced, whether in books or on the floor, they lose all their mystery and most of their point. Their size (much too large for tiles) and their vertical position on a wall are vital; their surfaces are rough-textured and show brush-strokes on canvas in a way few reproductions catch. They control and dominate a room. (Mondrian himself hung several in the same room, so that the wall itself becomes a composite art-work, a super-Mondrian.) He spent his last years in America, where his work influenced a generation of abstract artists, and where he painted some delightfully bustling and uncharacteristic pictures (the rectangles grey, the lines yellow, blue and red; no black). A good example, and a masterpiece, is *Broadway Boogie-Woogie* (1943; 127×127; MMA, NY). Both these gay pictures and more severe earlier works such as *Composition with Red and Black* (1936; 104×102; MMA, NY) demonstrate the fertility of his genius. Unlike many of his imitators (he is easy to imitate, hard to equal), he had a genuine rationale, a 'vision'; as he said himself, 'To deal exclusively with relationships, creating them and seeking to balance them in art and in life: this is the beautiful task of today; to do this is to prepare for the future.'

Of Mondrian's writings, *Plastic Art and Pure Plastic Art and Other Essays* (1947) are the most informative, offering both an aesthetic autobiography and useful side-glimpses of many aspects of the development of 20th-century art. Good introduction: H. L. C. Jaffé: *Mondrian* (1970).

MOORE, Henry (born 1898)
British sculptor

In a 19th-century poet's recipe for the creation of sculpture, Gautier wrote: '*Sculpte, limne, ciselle,/Que ton rêve flottant/Se scelle/dans le bloc résistant*' ('Sculpt, limn, chisel, so that your floating dream seals itself in the resisting block'). For Moore, the dream is the block's dream, already there, and his work is to release it and give it form. For many 20th-century sculptors modern plastics, and plastic processes such as moulding and welding, have been a main inspiration, affecting the appearance of their work whatever its actual medium – *Gabo's wooden sculptures, for example, imitate his plastic sculptures in mass, form and finish. Moore's natural medium is worked stone: his pieces often retain the chisel-marks, or have the *objet-trouvé* look of stone on a hillside or of weathered statues from the distant past. (In fact ancient statues were a formative influence.

Pieces like *Reclining Figure*, 1929; 84 cm long; City Art Gallery, Leeds, derive both their chunkiness and their enigmatic, serene facial expressions from pre-Colombian South American art. Both qualities became characteristic of Moore's work.) His bronzes, his wood sculptures, even his drawings, all have the same solid grace as his stone carvings; he is concerned less with movement than with density and mass.

Part of his output consists of abstract shapes, rather in the manner of *Arp. However, Arp's shapes, for all their figurative titles, are purely abstract, whereas Moore's shapes, even with abstract titles, always suggest human or animal form. Good examples are *Composition* (1932; 32 cm high; Atlanta Art Museum, Georgia), a smooth wooden oval with contours and sockets like those of a worn bone, and *Double Oval* (1966; 60 cm high; Marlborough Fine Art, London), two pierced ovals like the heads of Eskimo bone needles, whose delicacy in this size is deceptive, as his later reworking (in plaster, 420 cm high) shows. His most characteristic work takes abstract figures and the contours of eggs and bones and reveals in them implicit human shapes. Many of his finest sculptures are of reclining people; they range from the early, cubist-headed *Reclining Woman* (1930; 90 cm long; National Gallery of Canada, Ottawa) to the monumental *Lincoln Center Reclining Figure* (1965; 480 cm high; Lincoln Center, N Y), two huge, rough shapes, like dolmens or storm-worked rocks remade in bronze. He is also known for 'statues with holes in them', the stocky people of his early work hollowed out and given lightness and grace. The feeling that you can see through these sculptures, that their settings are inside them as well as around them, gives them particularity and dramatic emphasis. (A fine example is the bronze *Reclining Mother and Child*, 1961; 84×215×135; Walker Art Center, Minneapolis.) The feeling for setting is important to Moore. Many of his works were designed for specific sites, some even carved *in situ*. For others, he worried and experimented until he found the ideal site. *King and Queen*, for example (1953; 163 cm high), which shows a serene seated bronze couple, with flattened torsos and spindly limbs and wearing masks and crowns, was made in an edition of four. It looks fine in an exhibition (e.g. in the Hirshhorn Museum and Sculpture Garden, Smithsonian, Washington), but its full regality and grandeur are only seen in the site Moore finally found, on a stone plinth high in the barren moorland of Glenkiln, Scotland.

As well as sculpture, Moore has made thousands of drawings, ranging from sketches and notes for future work to finished drawings complete in themselves. Particularly fine are his *Sheep Sketchbook* (1980) – which, Leonardo-like, shows us sheep both as familiar and as emblematic objects: the mother with her lamb, a large shape balancing a smaller one, is a new version of a persistent Moore theme – and the powerful wartime drawings of people sheltering from air-raids in the London Underground and of coal-miners in his native Yorkshire.

Sculpture, by its nature, offers the artist less scope for formal and thematic variety than painting or drawing; certainly Moore's work revolves round half a dozen obsessively repeated themes. But in every other respect – and particularly in the feeling his work gives of joy in the act of creating, craftsman's zest in getting to grips with his medium – his only 20th-century rival for protean energy, and perhaps for greatness, is *Picasso.

A good selection of Moore's own (occasional) writings is R. James (ed.): *Henry Moore on Sculpture* (1966). Exhaustive, 4-volume study: D. Sylvester and A. Bowness (eds.): *Henry Moore: Sculpture and Drawings* (1957–77). Well-illustrated study, particularly good on the evolution of works from first sketches to finished sculptures: W. S. Liebermann: *Henry Moore: 60 Years of His Art* (1983).

MOTHERWELL, Robert (born 1915)
American painter

As editor of the *Documents of Modern Art* series (1944–57), Motherwell wrote well and influentially about the problems of art in the contemporary world, and particularly about the balance between art as decoration and as an ethical force. As a painter, he is chiefly known for his enormous series (more than 150 canvases) of *Spanish Elegies*. These range in size from small (e.g. *At Five in the Afternoon*, 1949; 50×37; artist's coll.) to huge (e.g. *Elegy to the Spanish Republic No. 100*, 1975; 600×210; artist's coll.); many are black and white, or black and white plus one other colour; all consist of three or four large, jagged shapes splattered on the white background, like hulks silhouetted against harsh light. He also made many large paper-and-cardboard collages, and a variety of cheerful prints. But his vast, glowering *Elegies* are his major work: art stripped to raucous gestures, gallery-dominating, with little decorative appeal but clamorous, rhetorical, unforgettable.

MUNCH, Edvard (1863–1944)
Norwegian painter

The Scream (1893; 91×73; National Gallery, Oslo) is, in art, where the tortured 20th century of Kafka and of Freud begins. Under a swirling, blood-red sky a lonely figure hurtles at us across a bridge, followed by two indistinct and watchful companions (passers-by? keepers? assassins?). The figure's hands are clamped round its face, and its mouth is open in a ghastly expressionist scream which concentrates all the neurotic tension and hysteria of the whole picture. Munch was a friend of Strindberg, and this painting inhabits the same straitjacketed world as the characters in Strindberg's plays. It is typical of a major strand in Munch's large output (over 1,000 canvases): if human beings truly are, in Ryle's phrase, 'the ghosts in the machine', then alcoholic, mentally unstable Munch is their eeriest spirit medium. The pedestrians in *Evening on Karl Johan Street* (1892; 121×84; Rasmus Meyers Samlinger, Bergen), out for a stroll in top hats and elegant evening clothes, walk towards us in the pink half-light with the flat faces and empty eyes of the Living Dead; the terrified, naked girl of *Puberty* (1894; 151×110; National Gallery, Oslo) is numb with the awareness of human misery, not joy.

This is Munch's most characteristic style, and his recurring, depressing theme. But he was also, in other moods, a colourist as joyous as van Gogh: thick streaks of paint, jutting from the canvas, as in the superb picture of two horses ploughing (*Horse-Team*, 1919; 145×110; National Gallery, Oslo) or the peaceful blue snowscape of *Starry Night* (1924; 120×100; National Gallery, Oslo). Some of his finest work, the murals painted in the 1910s for the University of Oslo, glow with a burnished radiance belying his reputation as a gloom-ridden neurotic: *The Sun* (1916; 780×455; Oslo University), the central painting of the Assembly Hall, is a Schiele-like dazzle of light and energy. Munch is a painter of enormous power, whose scope far exceeds what is generally known of him outside Scandinavia. In this, as in so much else, the comparison with Strindberg prevails.

Good introductions: J. P. Hodin: *Edvard Munch: Norway's Genius* (1945); J. B. Smith: *Munch* (1977).

NEWMAN, Barnett (1905–70)
American painter

Like *Rothko, Newman aimed at producing a quasi-religious abstract art, 'an art that would suggest the mysterious sublime rather than the beautiful', 'a poetic outcry'. His means were very large canvases, usually painted in a single glowing colour, sometimes cut by one or more thin vertical lines in another colour. A good example is *Covenant* (1949; 150×120; Smithsonian, Washington): it consists of a red rectangle with one brown vertical line and one yellow, and shimmers like the after-image you get from staring at the sun. In *The Word* (1954; 225×175; Coll. S.I. Newhouse, Jr) there are three vertical panels, black, blue-grey and blue; a single red line slices across the centre panel. The mystical effect in Rothko is produced in part by the blurry, seeping edges of his colours; in Newman, where the divisions are precise and hard, the effect is much less romantic, more Zen than Christian (despite such Christian titles as *Stations of the Cross*). It is hard to describe in words the emotional power of Newman's work. To declare that a canvas contains 'three rectangles and two verticals' is to say nothing of the feeling of opaqueness and depth, of a mysterious pool of calm. His work, in the end, may prove fugitive, dependent on a fashionable mood, but for the moment it seems to speak exactly to our condition.

NICHOLSON, Ben (1894–1982)
British artist

Nicholson's many painted reliefs are an abstract equivalent of such delicate, refined classical works as the *Mourning Athene* in the Acropolis Museum, Athens. A good example is *White Relief* (1934; 95×71×3; Tate, London). Two rectangular panels are superimposed, the upper one incised with a circle and a square, and with smaller rectangles snipped off at the upper and lower left-hand corners. The whole is carved from wood and painted white, so that the shadows form additional contours (in the Tate it is lit from above, which makes the shapes' lower edges seem dark and hard). Other reliefs are painted in pale colours, and the paint surface is then scuffed with sandpaper; a particularly beautiful example is *Painted Relief (Plover's Egg Blue)* (1940; 46×46; Coll. Helen Sutherland, Cumberland), a series of *Mondrian shapes in blues, greens, white and black. Nicholson's paintings have the same extreme refinement, whether cubist abstracts (e.g. *Feb. 1952 (Carafe)*, 1952; 85×45; Walker Art Center, Minneapolis) or landscapes (e.g. *November 11 1947 (Mousehole)*, 1947; 58×46; British Council, London – a *Klee-delicate drawing of his favourite Cornish landscape, incorporating in the foreground a cubist still-life of bottle and palettes). In his later work, landscapes and abstract reliefs merge. *Saronikos*, for example (1966; 129×73; Marlborough Gallery, NY), consists of three rectangles (two orange-grey, one orange) on a blue background – at once a set of simple, satisfying shapes and a classical evocation of whitewashed houses against a marvellously blue Aegean sky.

Good, illustrated introduction: H. Read: *Ben Nicholson: Drawings, Paintings and Reliefs 1911–68* (1969).

NOLAND, Kenneth (born 1924)
American painter

Together with such equally serious and talented contemporaries as Kelly, Louis, Olitsky and Stella, Noland was subjected in the 1960s to a preposterous and stifling campaign of adulation. The critics endlessly described and analysed each new work, substituting explication for experience until catalogue swallowed exhibition, verbiage gobbled art. (It was also a phenomenon of avant-garde music criticism of the 1960s and 1970s, the people who explained each work regarding themselves as at least the equal of its creator.) This barrage of garbage (gabbage?) effectively concealed the fact that Noland (and those other painters named above) produces pretty work, but nothing of world-shattering importance – he is no *Matisse, and has no aspiration to such eminence. His work is a development of the Abstract Expressionism of such men as *Newman and *Rothko, though he is concerned less with mystical emotion than with the aesthetic quality of flat paint on flat (often unsized) canvas. His paintings, to the layperson, often look like the bright patterns of mass-produced fabrics, writ huge. *A Warm Sound in a Grey Field*, for example (1961; 206×202; private coll., NY), consists of concentric rings of black, green and red on a throbbing grey-green ground: a poncho-pattern to hang on the wall. *Graded Exposure* (1967; 572×222; Coll. Mrs S. G. Rautbord, Chicago) contrasts vertical stripes (greens, yellows, reds) with a blue ground – the pattern for a giant's deckchair. Many of Noland's paintings vary the shape of the canvas, preferring diamonds to rectangles or angling one edge of a square towards the diagonal. The uncharacteristically tiny *Mach II*, for example (1964; 42×22; Coll. Mr and Mrs J. Powers, Colorado), is a squat diamond shape painted with regular chevrons (one each) of yellow, blue, brown, green and red. Despite critical attention and surface prettiness, it is doubtful if this jolly art will mark or indeed survive the century.

Good introduction: K. Moffat: *Kenneth Noland* (1977).

NOLDE, Emil (1867–1956)
German artist

Fired by the zeal to produce a 'great German art', a 'second period' equal to that of Dürer, Holbein and Grünewald, Nolde spent much of his time in the 1900s and 1910s painting expressionist versions of religious subjects (e.g. *The Last Supper*, 1909; 106×84; State Art Museum, Copenhagen), culminating in the polyptych *Life of Christ* (1912; 8 panels 99×84, centre panel 216×187; Nolde Foundation, Seebüll). The content of the pictures is rather at odds with their style, which is as hysterical and shattered as that of *Beckmann: their emotional power, instead of drawing the spectators into the experience, tends to send them reeling. In this respect, at least, Nolde's aspirations outran his talent. Only his woodcuts (e.g. *Prophet*, 1912; Kunstmuseum der Stadt, Düsseldorf – a bearded, sorrowing face like a *Rouault drawing) approach anywhere near the strength-through-style of his revered 'first period' artists. He joined the Nazis in the 1920s, but was subsequently one of the artists most vilified by them as degenerate.

Good study: P. Selz: *Emil Nolde* (1963).

OLDENBURG, Claes (born 1929)
American artist

Oldenburg's delightful work belongs in the cuddly-toy cupboard of modern art: stuffed vinyl typewriters, car-engines, toilets and drum-kits, ice-cream cones and hamburgers big enough to sit on. He further mocked those earnest museum curators and city elders who, calling such soft art 'significant' (indeed, 'a disturbing commentary on the values of contemporary life'), place it in galleries and on public show, by proposing a series of outrageous and hilarious public monuments: a peeled banana for Times Square, a giant lipstick for Piccadilly Circus, a 4-metre-high clothes-peg, a King-Kong sized teddy bear for Central Park, a 4-metre-high baseball catcher's mitt complete with ball. The clothes-peg and catcher's mitt have actually been erected; not so the others, or his most splendid and 'serious' proposal yet, an enormous concrete war memorial to be set up at some busy city intersection, halting all traffic. Clearly his sense of irony still outruns that of his patrons.

Oldenburg's writings include *Injun and Other Histories* (1966); *Notes* (1968); *Notes in Hand* (1971); *Raw Notes* (1973) and the important *Photo Log* (1976). Good study: B. Rose: *Claes Oldenburg* (1971).

OROZCO, José (1883–1949)
Mexican artist

The combination of revolutionary politics, fervent Catholicism and a gaudy stylistic mixture of expressionism with Mexican primitive art makes Orozco a figure of major impact if not significance. His main work is vast murals, often to revolutionary government commissions. They combine propaganda with the clamorous symbolism of Catholic art: the blacksmith at his anvil, for example, forging a new democracy, may well have stigmata and wear a crown of thorns. Size of theme never daunted him: a typical work, the 1930s series of murals for the Baker Library, Dartmouth College, New Hampshire, tells the story of the Americas all the way from Quetzalcoatl to the Second Coming. Its naïve, brash authority makes it clamorous to live with (or to read by) – can this really be a modern equivalent of, say, Raphael's frescoes in the Vatican?

Good study: A. M. Reed: *Orozco* (1956).

PASMORE, Victor (born 1908)
British artist

In the 1930s and 1940s Pasmore painted in an admired realistic style like a 20th-century blend of Whistler and Turner. In the late 1940s he turned to abstract painting: his whorls and lines (e.g. in *The Snowstorm*, 1951; 150×117; Arts Council, London) interestingly foreshadow the later 'jigsaw' style of *Dubuffet. In the 1960s he began making constructions of metal and perspex similar to those of *Gabo. He was an influential figure in the 1960s; but as this clutch of comparisons suggests, he is more of a competent craftsman than an original talent. His work satisfies more because of its confident intentions and fastidious style than because it stands (as *Nicholson's, say, or *Hepworth's does) in the front rank of British art.

PECHSTEIN, Max (1881–1953)
German artist

A member of the Brücke group led by *Kirchner in the 1900s, Pechstein developed an easy, colourful style blending expressionist colour (and heavy outline) with an exoticism learned from Gauguin (he visited the South Seas himself in the 1910s). His paintings are hardly original – he was dismissed by Kirchner as a 'Matissist', and the influence of *Rouault is also marked – but they are cheerful and competent, and particularly striking for sumptuous reds and blues. His career was interrupted by the Nazis; after the Second World War he became a respected teacher in Berlin. In every art there are well-liked practitioners who follow the creative pack with skill but no originality, whose work we are nevertheless glad to see. As Huston is to movies, Weidman to the 20th-century American novel, so Pechstein is to expressionist painting: convenience food, but expertly prepared.

PICABIA, Francis (1879–1953)
French artist

Picabia was a wealthy, engaging and energetic camp-follower of the naughtier fashionable trends. In the 1910s he was a competent cubist: *Dances at the Spring*, for example (1912; 119×118; Philadelphia MA), is a joyful tumble of activity, a second cousin of *Duchamp's *Nude Descending a Staircase*. He then espoused Dada, and indeed brought the movement to America: *Tableau Dada* (published in the magazine *Canibale*, April 1920) shows a grotesque masturbating monkey surrounded by picture-titles like 'Portrait of Rembrandt' and 'Still Life'. His most original work – and he is a witty dilettante rather than a serious artist – is a number of obscurely titled canvases showing unlikely machines (e.g. *Amorous Procession*, 1917; 96×73; Coll. Morton G. Neumann, Chicago – which depicts, if anything, a vacuum pump or a piece of primitive anaesthetic equipment, certainly nothing either amorous or processional). In the 1930s, like *Dali, he affected a style of photographic realism – except that his paintings were not of floppy watches or blazing giraffes but of meticulously lifelike nudes. Towards the end of his career, a butterfly returning to his favourite flower, he returned to the cubism of his earliest manner. Not an outstanding artist, but a colourist who had outstanding fun with art.

Picabia himself published *Poèmes et dessins de la fille née sans mère* (1918), a typically fanciful and inconsequential book. Good study (French text): M. Sanouillet: *Picabia* (1964).

PICASSO, Pablo (1881–1973)
Spanish artist

Like his contemporary Stravinsky, Picasso was regularly attacked for being a stylistic chameleon, for changing idioms like shirts. What marks his vast output, however – like Stravinsky's – is not diversity but unity. His unique personality is present in every work; he disconcerted his critics not by changing styles but because he seemed regularly and prescriptively to reinvent the nature of art itself. For protean energy, technical mastery, originality, characterfulness and wit his work is rivalled only by that of Leonardo (and he is wittier than Leonardo); his legacy is not merely hundreds of masterpieces but a wholly new and all-pervasive climate for modern art. If all other 20th-century art disappeared overnight, Picasso's work would still single-handedly make clear what modern art had tried to do, and the quality and scope of its achievement.

Any one of five hundred large pictures would serve to illustrate Picasso's genius. But he lavished himself on tiny objects too, and one of them, the small sculpture *Woman Reading* (1953; 36×15; private coll.) shows every component of his mastery. A girl lies on a wooden bench, head propped on hands, absorbed in a book. Her dress is green; her hair and the bench are brown. The first impression the piece gives is of inevitability: that's exactly how girls reading *are*; every real girl subsequently seen reading will be reminiscent of this sculpture; life and art do not imitate, they merge. The very distortions – she has a swan-neck, praying-mantis head and sausage fingers – instead of distracting, give the piece style and satisfy the senses. The cockiness of its construction – her body is a sliver of firewood, her legs are bolts and one of her arms is a discarded wood-screw – is balanced and completed by the composure and concentration of her pose, achieved seemingly by no more than three painted lines (delineating her eyes) and the placing of those sausage-fingers in relation to her ears. The witty exactness of Picasso's technique, coupled with the simplicity of what the sculpture 'says' (a common mood, precisely caught), produce exhilaration. This is not armchair art for a tired business executive; it makes you fizz with eagerness to create for yourself.

Picasso's earliest work – he painted his first masterpieces in his early teens – begins in a rich 'old master' style (Rembrandt and Hals are influences) and progresses to a restrained fauvism derived partly from Cézanne, the paintings of the 'blue' and 'pink' periods (so called because of their predominant colours). These show waif-like figures, usually in family groups and often acrobats, jugglers or other circus artistes. Life, for these people, is immeasurably sad – but they are performers, not 'real' people, and their choice of this particular life gives their sadness a distancing irony typical of all Picasso's art. (Stravinsky's 1911 ballet *Petrushka*, about a puppet who falls agonizingly in love, draws on the same duality between performance and experience.) The greatest picture in this style, *La Vie* (1903; 197×127; Cleveland MA), shows a naked couple on the left (possibly artist and model; she embraces him, he turns away), on the right an older woman ('Experience'?) holding a child, and in the background two paintings, one of an embracing couple, the other of a desolate single figure. The picture's meaning (apart from over-riding melancholy) is enigmatic and private; its force comes from intensity of emotion and from elegance of form – it is as carefully organized as a Mantegna.

The enigmatic figure-groups of the blue and pink periods reach apotheosis in *Les Demoiselles d'Avignon* (1907; 244×234; MMA, NY). This is the most influential and one of the ugliest things Picasso made. Like *Matisse's *Luxe, calme et volupté* it galvanized other artists into effervescent creativity; no masterpiece, it is nevertheless a work as seminal for the 20th century as *Ulysses* or *The Rite of Spring*. It shows five nude figures, aspiring to the condition of cubism, with African-mask faces; they stand in the listlessly provocative postures of bored whores, not in a brothel but in a cubist cave complete with a foreground still-life of pears, apples and grapes. The figures are coloured mannequin orange and pink, and the rocks (or draperies?) behind them are brown and blue. The painting redirected Picasso's own creative energy (though he refused to exhibit it for another twenty years, on the grounds that it was unfinished): it is the beginning of his first radical shift of style, to cubism. For the next half-dozen years, together with *Braque, he enthusiastically explored every possibility of cubism, from geometrical pattern-making (e.g. *Vollard*, 1910; 92×65; Pushkin Museum, Moscow) to collages of journals, pieces of rope and cane (e.g. *Still Life with Chaircaning*, 1912; 35×27; artist's estate).

The effect of the First World War produced in him (as, again, in Stravinsky) an introversion of emotion expressed in an exploration of the art of the classical past. In Picasso's case this led to a large number of drawings in elegant, fine lines (e.g. *Portrait of Igor Stravinsky*, 1920; 47×61; private coll., USA), or drawings of centaurs and other mythical creatures (e.g. *Nessus and Deianeira*, 1920; 26×21; MMA, NY), and to paintings of beefy sculptural women at rest or energetically enjoying themselves (e.g. the clumping, *Chirico ecstatics of *The Race*, 1922; 42×32; artist's estate). Classical styles and themes thereafter coexisted in his work with cubism (he never again worked exclusively in any single mode); classical elegance of line even lends poise to such bright cubist masterpieces as *Three Musicians* (1921; 219×197; MMA, NY) or *Still Life with Saucepan* (1945; 104×83; artist's estate). However, neither a return to antiquity nor cubist pirouettes could exorcise emotion; hysterical grief and anger are present in several paintings of the 1930s (e.g. *Crucifixion*, 1930; 65×51; artist's estate), and reach climax in dozens of gory bullfight drawings and in the huge, tormented *Guernica* (1937; 763×343; MMA, NY). This vast ikon, writhing horses' heads, howling human faces, plunging limbs, all in a grey room lit by a single harsh bulb, is in its way as ugly as *Les Demoiselles d'Avignon* – and stifles the spectator in much the same way. (Most of Picasso's art invites you in, suggests a smiling dialogue; both these paintings, by contrast, shout messages so shrill as to pre-empt response.)

For the rest of his life Picasso continued to work in each of these styles, seemingly as his fancy took him. He produced sculpture (among his most elegant work), ceramics, drawings, engravings and paintings of every kind, portraits and still-lifes, landscapes and allegorical and mythical scenes. (A particularly delightful work is his *La Joie de vivre*, 1946; 245×118; Musée Grimaldi, Antibes – a group of *Miró creatures dancing by the seaside, intended as an act of homage to Matisse.) He became to some extent the prisoner of his own reputation: the most famous painter of the age was happy to sign a dozen quick daubs a week, if that was his mood, and there was a risk that the world would be saturated with trifles. The best work of this period is not his paintings (save for an admired series of meditations on paintings by others, e.g. forty-four variations of Velazquez' *Las Meninas*, 1957): it is his serene ceramics, old man's art as cheerful and relaxed as Matisse's paper-cuts. By now, a decade after his death, the ephemera are already being forgotten – and we are left with a mind-boggling array of masterworks, prolific and protean excellence that creates its own standard and beggars it.

Good studies: W. Boeck and J. Sabartes: *Picasso* (1965); T. Hilton: *Picasso* (1975). Outstanding critical study: J. Berger: *The Success and Failure of Picasso* (1965). Useful anthology: M. McCully (ed.): *A Picasso Anthology: Documents, Criticism, Reminiscences* (1981).

POLLOCK, Jackson (1912–56)
American painter

In the 1950s Pollock's method, known as action painting, provided clear proof to philistines that the lunatics had finally taken over the asylum of modern art. Instead of using brushes like a 'regular' painter, he dribbled and splashed paint direct from the cans over sheets of canvas tacked to the floor. The theory that this might one day produce a great painting was held to be analogous to the view that a monkey pounding a typewriter might in a millennium produce one line of *Hamlet*. But the main function of philistines is to be routed, and Pollock's canvases can now be seen as a triumphant justification of his method: they are unique (he has never had a successful imitator) and they are certainly fine art. One of the finest is also one of the first: *Number One* (1948; 220×170; MMA, NY), a series of delicate brown and white scribbles on a grey-brown ground, conjuring up images (if images help) of barbed wire, autumn leaves and sand. There are intriguing – and compositionally crucial – dots of yellow and red scattered sparsely over the canvas. It may have no meaning, in the sense that *The Laughing Cavalier*, say, can be said to have meaning; but it is both stimulating and satisfying to the senses – and is *The Laughing Cavalier*, say, really anything more than that? Later, further to confound the philistines, Pollock began to combine his action technique with broad, fast brushwork as clear as *Klee's, though replacing Klee's pin-thin lines with distemper-brush swathes. *Ocean Greyness* (1953; 226×144; Guggenheim, NY) is a snarl of fish-jaw shapes in orange, yellow and black against a busy action-painted blue-black ground. It is like a view into a nightmare aquarium; it is a masterpiece.

Good study: B. H. Friedman: *Jackson Pollock: Energy Made Visible* (1973).

RAUSCHENBERG, Robert (born 1925)
American artist

The Dada roots of American pop art are clearly exposed in Rauschenberg's 'combine' paintings of the 1950s. They combine paint with ready-made objects such as newspapers, pieces of fabric, even bedspreads and – in *Monogram* (1959; 180×180×120; Leo Castelli Gallery, NY), the most notorious – a stuffed ram rammed into an automobile tyre. What is Dada about these art-works is their combination of silliness (or pointless point?), ugliness and earnest tongue-in-cheek explanation for anyone foolish enough to listen. Rauschenberg, an inventive artist, soon moved on from this pricy posturing and began making delicately coloured silk-screen collages, still using magazine pictures and fabric to create the images: *Blue Urchin* (1974; 190×122; Sonnabend Gallery, NY) is typical. The works of this phase are prettier than his 1950s combines, but even so Rauschenberg, like many of his colleagues, has not solved the problem – perhaps doesn't care to solve the problem – of how to make art about the banality of life anything but banal.

Good interim study: A. Forge: *Robert Rauschenberg* (1969).

RAY, Man (1890–1977)
American artist and photographer

A surrealist, *Magritte without the talent, Ray produced minor works in every conceivable style, from harsh *Chirico staginess (e.g. *La Rue Férou*, 1952; 77×58; Coll. Samuel Siegler, New Jersey) to straightforward cubism (e.g. *Knight's Move*, 1946; 36×36; private coll., London). He made a large number of silly 'sculptures' (e.g. a mobile of coat-hangers; the joky *Cadeau*, 1921, a flat-iron studded with tacks; a classical torso, roped; *Ballet français*, 1956, a floor-brush – *balai*, geddit? – set upright in a plastic plinth). His best work is his photographs, whether straightforward Hollywood starpics, Voguish fashion-plates or 'Rayographs' – treated photographs, where extra light is introduced to the plate or the film, producing (often beautifully) distorted or enhanced images. His album of 'solarized' photographs *The Age of Light* (1934) is his most serious and lasting work.

Ray's other books include *Facile* (1935, with poems by Éluard); *Man Ray* (1944); *Revolving Doors* (1972). Visual puns of all kinds: *Objects of My Affection* (1983). Good studies: L. Aragon, J. Arp, etc.: *Man Ray: Sixty Years of Liberties* (1971), and the more solemn Arturo Schwartz: *Man Ray* (1977). Gorgeous portrait-anthology: *Man Ray Photographs* (1982).

RILEY, Bridget (born 1931)
British artist

Op art (the art of optical illusion), developed by *Vasarély, was a 1960s phenomenon which led to quality work from only two artists, Vasarély himself and Riley. Riley's paintings, often black and white, consist of regular lines or shapes (somewhat like computer holograms) cunningly organized so that they seem to writhe and blur as you look at them. The effect for some spectators is calming, for others disorienting and disturbing. A characteristic picture (in its largeness, its simplicity, and the fact that you can't look at it for long without going cross-eyed – op art is an optometrist's dream as well as a psychiatrist's) is *Late Morning* (1967; 354×222; Tate, London). It consists of hundreds of straight parallel verticals: blue, red, white, red, blue, white, blue, red, white, red, blue . . .

RIVERA, Diego (1886–1957)
Mexican painter

Originally a Paris-trained cubist, Rivera returned to Mexico in the 1920s, espoused revolutionary politics and abandoned modernism for a 'people's style' which turned out to be a blend of 19th-century realism with brash colours and simplified shapes learned from Gauguin. He used this style to paint huge murals on public buildings, as busy as those of *Orozco, but less raucous and more relaxed. His *Workers of the Revolution*, for example (1929; Palacio Nacional, Mexico City), shows dozens of earnest middle-class intellectuals (the *peons* are represented by backs and *sombreros*) looking sternly out towards an idealistic future. In sporting clubs everywhere this mural's ancestors proliferate: team-photographs, group portraits of the committees of yesteryear. Its narrative style (as opposed to the didacticism of Orozco or *Siqueiros) is typical of Rivera's striking but essentially gentle art – if political murals an acre large can ever be described as 'gentle art'.

Rivera's books (texts by Bertram D. Wolfe) are *Portrait of America* (1934) and *Portrait of Mexico* (1937). Wolfe also wrote Rivera's biography: *The Fabulous Life of Diego Rivera* (1963), a starry-eyed, if not exactly fabulous, read.

ROTHKO, Mark (1903–70)
American painter

Rothko's smaller paintings often combine whorls, dancing lines and dozens of tiny shapes reminiscent of stick beings and animals or the insect people of *Miró or *Klee, all executed in clean, bright colours and confident, uncluttered strokes. A good example is *Baptismal Scene* (1945; 49×35, Whitney Museum of American Art, NY). He is best known, however, for paintings in a different style altogether. They are often very large, designed to fill or dominate one wall of a public room; each consists of two or three single-coloured rectangles, whose irregular edges blur and bleed into one another as tie-dyeing stains cloth. Within each rectangle, too, the colour is not hard or constant, but iridescent and shifting: like *Riley's lines, Rothko's colours seem to shimmer and move before your eyes. This movement, combined with dominating size, evokes in many spectators the feeling that these paintings have a transcendental quality, that abstract Rothko is the ideal religious painter for a non-religious age. (Indeed, eight of his most powerful canvases were painted in the 1960s for the interior walls of an octagonal 'secular chapel' at St Thomas University, Houston, Texas.) At his best, for example in the dazzling *No. 8* (1952; 201×170; Coll. Mr and Mrs Burton Tremaine, Connecticut) or the huge, brooding *Two Openings in Black over Wine* (1958; 381×226; Tate, London), he proves that religious or not, abstract art can through shape and colour alone be imbued with grandeur, mystery and compelling emotional intensity.

Excellent study: D. Waldman: *Mark Rothko* (1978).

ROUAULT, Georges (1871–1958)
French painter

Rouault's early training was as a maker of stained-glass windows, and his art always favoured the bold shapes, leaded outlines and gaudy colours of this medium. His themes are two, the satanic shambles of everyday life and the redeeming power of Catholic religion, and his symbols are loud and clear: for decadence and despair sour prostitutes, capering lawyers and shattered clowns, for Christianity the standard Biblical crew. His paintings of disgust rival *Nolde's for blazing colour and *Grosz's for viciousness. A typical canvas, *The Old Clown* (1917; 101×75; Coll. Niarchos, Paris), shows an empty-eyed clown staring out in despair from a violent fauvist landscape, the hoarse emotion of the picture deriving from harsh black outlines and colour so slapdash it seems to have been flung on to the canvas in a frenzy. Another work, *Before a Mirror* (1906; 69×52; MAM, Paris), shows a baggy nude woman fixing her hair, her distorted reflection glowering back at her from a mirror; again, the lines and colours seem to have been plastered on in a paroxysm of disgust and rage. Rouault's later religious works, though still as clamorously emotional, are more hieratic, processionals from a technicolor expressionist epic film. *The Old King*, for example (1916/1937; 76×53; Carnegie Inst,. Pittsburgh), shows a heavy-bearded Old Testament monarch (Nebuchadnezzar?) posed as in ancient Persian art – but the picture is less the depiction of any specific individual than a majestic conglomeration of colour panels (sunburst reds, yellows and greens) separated by wide black bands. Rouault's limited themes and oppressive, repetitive style make him, perhaps, an artist to look at once in a while rather than every day; but his paintings (and engravings, e.g. the illustrations to *Père Ubu* and *Les Fleurs du mal*) are some of the most dramatic and turbulent of the century.

Good study: P. Courthion: *Rouault* (1962).

SCHWITTERS, Kurt (1887–1948)
German painter

A forerunner of such 1960s American artists as *Johns and *Rauschenberg, Schwitters made extensive use of garbage in his pictures, which are collages of paper, string, wood, bottle-tops and labels, all controlled and organized by the surrounding paint. A good example is *Star Picture (Merz Picture 25A)* (1920; 104×79; Kunstsammlung Nordrhein-Westphalen, Düsseldorf), in which a wooden batten, a piece of netting, some string, tickets and labels invade and are swallowed by a bustling cubist canvas. He was for years regarded as a Dadaist, but his work is too elegant and lasting for that. (He christened it 'Merz art', after a fragment of a label *Kommerz und Privatbank* in one of his pictures.) One of his obsessive activities was the creation of *Merzbauen* ('Merz houses'), abstract sculpture-artwork-garbage-tips which took over the whole interiors of houses as fungus takes over logs. He made three such nests, in successive homes in Hanover, Norway and the Lake District. Each took years to assemble; the first two were destroyed by the Germans, and the third is now preserved by Newcastle University. Schwitters was a witty, consistent painter, the only Dadaist to produce art of any objective stature. Perhaps that's why the Dadaists disowned him as heartily as he did them.

Good studies: S. Themerson: *Kurt Schwitters in England* (1958); W. Schmalenbach: *Kurt Schwitters* (1967).

SHAHN, Ben (1898–1969)
American painter

A 1930s 'social realist', Shahn used the styles of advertisement-hoardings and naïve painting to produce sharp propaganda art, influential in its day but now as dated as the subjects on which it speaks. He worked with *Rivera on murals for Radio City, and also provided New Deal murals for the Bronx Post Office, NY, and the Social Security Building, Washington. His most celebrated work is a series of anti-establishment drawings and paintings inspired by the Sacco–Vanzetti case in the late 1920s.

Good study: J. T. Soby: *Ben Shahn: His Graphic Art* (1957).

SICKERT, Walter (1860–1942)
British painter

If Sickert had been born a decade earlier and a thousand kilometres further south, he would probably have become one of the leading impressionists. As it is, his work (an amiable and talented pendant to that of Degas) lacks direction: it is skilful and decorative, but seems to stand aside from its time, to have nothing much to say. His best pictures are seaside scenes (greyer than the impressionists', because Brighton is no sunny Mediterranean resort), pictures of music-hall performers and their audiences, and scenes of London backstreets in the manner of a dour Utrillo. In his later years, marked decline set in, and he began squaring up photographs, picture postcards and other ephemeral objects, and painting large copies in a garish, slapdash style: unlike *Picasso's or *Matisse's late works, these are the rags of talent – and perhaps indications that Sickert was never the great master he once seemed to some to be. His eccentric memoirs, *A Free House* (1947), a combination of flamboyant wit and anti-everything bile, are an invigoratingly disorderly and scabrous read.

Good study: L. Browse: *Sickert* (1960).

SIGNAC, Paul (1863–1935)
French painter

Signac was a talented, enthusiastic follower of Seurat, an encouraging patron and friend to many younger or less prosperous artists (e.g. *Bonnard and the young *Matisse), and a noted apologist of neo-impressionism (a minor movement combining Seurat's dot-technique with an over-careful, hieratic style, the pictures as self-consciously 'posed' as those of *art nouveau*). Signac's main works are landscapes and seascapes, second-rate but pretty (typical is the blue-and-red-dotted *Port of Marseilles*, 1911; 135×125; Musée du Luxembourg); he was a good team-member with neither the ambition nor the ability for leadership.

SIQUEIROS, David (1896–1974)
Mexican painter

The most violent and political of all South American artists, Siqueiros spent a good part of his life in gaol. When he was free, and in favour, he painted huge murals with the best of them (i.e. *Orozco and *Rivera): a good example is *Liberation of Chile* (1942; 259 square metres; Escuela México, Chillán). He also produced a large body of easel paintings, in a style reminiscent of *Rouault for colour and heaviness of outline, and of *Dix for rhetorical despair. The irony is that despite his aim of 'socializing artistic expression, destroying bourgeois individualism', he is one of the most individual, most bought and most admired (by bourgeois art connoisseurs) of all Mexican painters.

SMITH, David (1906-65)
American sculptor

Smith's style is rooted in the welded metal sculpture of *González, but with a lightness and grace (learned from *Gabo) which González, a lesser talent, never achieved. His work is occasionally figurative (e.g. *The Royal Bird*, 1948; 148×54×22; Walker Art Center, Minneapolis – harsh and skeletal, like squawking, predatory Meccano). But his best work is the series of large, abstract *Cubi* he made in the 1960s. Each of these stands 2–3 metres high, and consists of a number of stainless steel cubes welded together in patterns like the ideograms of some calligraphic Far-Eastern script or like children's bricks precariously piled to challenge gravity. There is a score of them, dispersed in galleries and museums as far apart as Dallas, Boston, New York and London. Smith's work is somewhat limited (he has nothing like the scope of *Lipchitz, for example); but within its range it has an authority and grandeur much abstract sculpture lacks. He was to steel, perhaps, what *Newman was to paint.

Good books: E. Fry and M. McClintick: *David Smith, Painter, Sculptor, Draughtsman* (1983); S. E. Marcus: *David Smith: The Sculptor and His Work* (1984).

SMITH, Matthew (1879-1959)
British painter

A disciple of *Matisse, Smith spent much of his creative life in France, and produced a body of colourful work like a lighthearted, lightweight van Gogh. His best paintings are nudes (e.g. *Fitzroy Street Nude No. 2*, 1916; 100×75; British Council, London, a boldly coloured Matissian odalisque sitting in a cane chair with one arm bent behind her head), but there are also attractive landscapes. Though finally derivative, Smith is an enjoyable painter, on a level with *Modigliani or Augustus John.

Good study: P. Hendy: *Matthew Smith* (1944).

SOULAGES, Pierre (born 1919)
French painter

The recipe for a Soulages abstract is simple. You cover your canvas with a single colour, thickly applied. Then you take a house-decorator's brush (if the canvas is large) or a broad palette-knife (if the canvas is small) and make a dozen or so vertical and horizontal strokes across it in one other colour, preferably black. Then you date the picture – the date serves also as a title – and sit back to await a buyer. Mechanically followed, this recipe reliably produces abstracts as kitsch as the charging elephants or flamenco dancers of the realist school. But when the recipe is followed with flair, when the cook puts imagination into the dish, the result has something of the intensity of *Motherwell. There are 'good' Soulages in the Tate, London, the MAM, Paris, and the Guggenheim, NY; there are 'poor' Soulages almost everywhere else. The distinction, unfortunately, like the painting recipe itself, seems purely arbitrary. One person's meat . . .

Good (partial) study: J. J. Sweeney: *Soulages: Paintings Since 1963* (1968).

SOUTINE, Chaim (1894–1943)
Russian/French painter

Like his friend *Modigliani, Soutine was nicknamed a '*peintre maudit*', one whose lifestyle (a dissipated, self-destructive fugue) marked him for early death. In Modigliani's work obsession and neurosis are governed by classically cool technique; in Soutine's, they dominate. His canvases shriek with undifferentiated disgust and rage, as if he found the physical act of painting simultaneously comforting and infuriating. The nearest analogues for the fervour of his colour (harsh, without gradations, as thick as mud) are *Rouault and van Gogh at his most tormented; his virulent content is close to *Nolde or to *Bacon. His most notorious paintings are of slaughtered animals (e.g. *Side of Beef*, 1925; 138×105; Albright-Knox Gallery, Buffalo, NY, where the disembowelled carcase seems to howl its agony down a nightmare tunnel of black and blue). But he also painted portraits (e.g. the sour, red-suited manikin *The Page-Boy* 1927; 98×80; MAM, Paris) – no painter since Rembrandt, no less, has so consistently managed to imply the blood and raw flesh that lurk beneath skin – and 'landscapes' in which trees, sky and land are churned into the whirling, hysterical jungle which haunts bad dreams. *Landscape at Ceret* (1921; 85×60; Tate, London) is typical of these decompositions: if you flung a pot of stew over the canvas and painted it in strident colours, you'd get results like these. There is no questioning the quality of Soutine's talent – the comparisons with van Gogh and Rembrandt, in this respect, at least, are fair – but lack of control is an inhibiting factor in all his work. With van Gogh (even at his maddest), with Rembrandt, we can always see the artist's disciplining mind and hand at work; with Soutine, for all his brilliance, we eavesdrop on insanity.

Good study: M. Wheeler: *Soutine* (1950).

SPENCER, Stanley (1891–1959)
British painter

The combination in Spencer of a forceful naïve style – though academically trained, he painted in a manner reminiscent of *Orozco, Lowry or even Grandma Moses – with complex personal symbolism, religious and erotic, produces art which is clamorous, difficult and often hideous. (The spectator needs to 'read' each painting as he or she might an essay – and Spencer's images carry meanings as tough as any of the words in Orwell, say, or Eliot.) His most abiding vision is of the crucifixion or the day of judgement taking place in the backstreets of 1930s British provincial towns: while the soldiers hammer or the sheeted dead arise, washing flaps on lines hung over trim vegetable gardens or Sunday lawns. In *Christ Carrying the Cross*, for example (1920; 151×141; Tate, London), the procession walks down not the Via Dolorosa but a British street past a red-brick house, from every window of which gossipy neighbours lean and peer – and the window-curtains, fluttering in the breeze, are disposed like angels' wings. The symbolism of such Christian pictures, though arcane and disturbing, at least has a recognizable external correlative. In Spencer's 'erotic' pictures – domestic scenes crammed with sensual messages (e.g. the silk stockings, plump legs and bouncy bottoms which dominate *The Nursery*, 1936; 91×76; MMA, NY) – the effect is at once secretive and shocking: whatever these paintings 'mean', they give a whole new meaning to the phrase 'rude art'. In his time Spencer has been both neglected and wildly over-praised. His paintings are dating fast; his art is interesting for what it says rather than for what it is, and may not endure. He has been compared with Blake; Rossetti, alas, may be nearer the mark.

Good study of the man: *Stanley Spencer: The Man: Correspondence and Reminiscences* (1979), edited by John Rothenstein, whose *Modern English Painters 1952–1974* (1976) is lucid, dispassionate and a standard work.

STAËL, Nicolas de (1914–55)
Russian/Belgian artist

A pupil of *Braque, unhappy de Staël (he died by suicide) painted some of the happiest and most charming abstracts of the century. He favoured a patchwork-quilt effect, the painting built up of pillars and piles of coloured cubes. His line is as graceful as *Klee's, but his paint is thicker and his pictures are more loosely organized. Like Braque, he offers the spectator no messages, merely images to delight eye and brain. Good examples are *Untitled* (1951; 157×72; Coll. Mr and Mrs Lee A. Ault, NY), a column of red, green, grey and dark-blue rectangles on a background of broad swathes of brown, green and red, and *Roofs* (1952; 200×150; MAM, Paris), in which the coloured squares (predominantly dark blue) cluster in the bottom third of the canvas like a *Dufy town, while the top two-thirds depict a sun-bleached blue-and-silver sky. In the over-solemn world of abstract art, de Staël offers the treat of a sunny smile.

SUTHERLAND, Graham (1903–80)
British painter

Sutherland often worked to establishment commissions, notably for portraits and large-scale religious art. His uncompromising style, close to that of 1910s cubist *Picasso, equally often shocked or infuriated his patrons – his portrait of Churchill, for example (showing a broody, senile old bulldog of a man) was first hidden in a cellar by the Churchill family and then destroyed. His most lasting works are his many desolate landscapes (influenced by his experience as a war artist in the 1940s – gaunt trees, mud, thistles and fungus under grey-green skies), and his religious works, of which the best known and finest is the bee-shaped tapestry *Christ in Majesty* made for Coventry Cathedral in 1962. Though his work is good, it is too streamlined, too blandly 'modern', to offer genuine individuality. He is like the composer Hindemith: he makes all the right noises, with distinction and efficiency – and that's all he does.

Good biography: R. Berthoud: *Graham Sutherland: A Biography* (1982).

TOBEY, Mark (1890–1976)
American painter

Drawn to the Far East, Tobey studied Zen Buddhism, the Bahai faith and the techniques of Chinese painting. He evolved a powerful abstract style which he called 'white writing': it consists of scribbles and scratches of white covering the whole surface of a canvas prepared in one other basic colour. Sometimes the lines are bold and scattered, as in *Above the Earth* (1953; 98×74; Art Inst., Chicago), which divides into large jagged panels like panes of broken glass; often they are multitudinous and squiggly, like the drip paintings of *Pollock – a good example is *Shadow Spirits of the Forest* (1961; 62×47; Kunstsammlung Nordrhein-Westphalen, Düsseldorf), a jazzy scribble of white on brown. Apart from its own distinction, Tobey's art was a beneficial influence not only on the Pollock generation but also on the 'pattern painters' and 'systematic abstractionists' of the 1970s. Whenever meticulousness and precision govern the placing of hundreds of tiny repeated shapes on a canvas, his style has made its mark.

Good interim study: C. Roberts: *Mark Tobey* (1959).

VASARÉLY, Victor (born 1908)
Hungarian/French artist

In his book *Yellow Manifesto* (1955) Vasarély set out his aims, and they can stand for those of a whole generation of artists who have tried to come to terms both with the techniques of the mass media and with the apathy to fine art engendered in a public made somnolent rather than receptive by those media. His intention was to replace the old notion that a work of art is a unique entity (i.e. one unrepeatable canvas or sculpture) produced by a unique individual, with 'social art' in which the artist's idea (his or her chief creative contribution) would be mass-produced by every available modern technique and made universally available for mass consumption. The logical extension of this process might seem to be a world-wide Coca-Cola sign (or a *Warhol multi-Coca-Cola-bottle 'work'); but Vasarély's process differs from those because he begins from an original creative idea, not from a banal *donnée* plucked from the rubbish-tip of the consumer society. The idea of destroying the élitism of art is a worthy one; even so, it could be argued that uniqueness (a form of élitism) is one of art's crucial ingredients, and that Vasarély's own excellence, as opposed to the emptiness of a thousand imitators, arises from his own unique talent. Apart from *Riley, he is the only producer of op art so far to have consistently made works of (a) beauty and (b) lasting quality. They consist of symmetrical geometric shapes painted in flat colours and organized so that they appear to move and alter as you look at them. Some of his smaller works (e.g. *Hat Tupa*, 1972; 91×77; Gallery Denise René, NY – a cube emerging from a deep black background as if floating towards us through space, and with a surface decorated with squares of colour distorted in such a way that it seems to bulge outwards as if it contains a sphere inside) are as restful as they are pretty – Vasarély seldom challenges his spectators, seldom give them eye-ache, as op art by others so often does. His larger works (e.g. the 3–4-metre-high, free-standing creations in the Vasarély Foundation, Aix-en-Provence) are both more dominating and less personal: this *is* hoarding-art, but its use of optical effects makes it hallucinatory and menacing instead of reassuring and ignorable like a regular advertisement.

This kind of art is analogous to electronic music. It is the first attempt for half a century to do something genuinely new, to produce truly 'modern' work using none of the techniques, media or themes of the past. We are too close to assess it; but it certainly deserves attention (and is aesthetically as well as theoretically interesting); its existence shows that the carcase of fine art, despite many enthusiastic embalmers, is by no means yet dead.

Good study: M. Joray (ed): *Vasarély* (1965).

VILLON, Jacques (1875–1963)
French artist

Quieter than his less-talented brother *Duchamp, less talented than his quiet brother *Duchamp-Villon, Villon painted a large number of gentle cubist canvases (e.g. *Soldiers Marching*, 1913; 91×64; Coll. Louis Carré, Paris – soft planes of grey, brown and purple, with no harsh lines to break the dream-like effect). In the 1930s he moved on to equally

restrained abstracts (e.g. *Abstraction*, 1932; 66×54; Philadelphia MA –
a cubic plinth painted in perspective, with a single line whiplashed across
the middle). He also painted landscapes (e.g. *Between Toulouse and
Albi*; 1949; 78×54; MAM, Paris – a study in delicate shades of green),
and made prints. All of it is minor but agreeable work, murmuring rather
than shouting, as discreet as a monastery waiting room.

Good study (in French): D. Vallier: *Jacques Villon: œuvres de 1897 à 1956* (1957).
(See also Duchamp-Villon.)

VLAMINCK, Maurice (1876–1958)
French artist

A racing cyclist, a violinist, Vlaminck was a self-taught artist proud to
claim that he'd never once set foot in the Louvre. He was passionate in
his allegiances – to his friend *Derain, to van Gogh, to Cézanne – and his
paintings are a mish-mash of all his favourite styles. The best are
landscapes, bright and uncomplicated (e.g. *The Circus*, 1906; 72×59;
Galerie Beyeler, Basel, which shows a jazzy *Dufy street with a circus-
tent in a field to one side), or wintry and plain (e.g. the tiny *Hamlet in the
Snow*, 1943; 17×13; owner unknown, whose placidity and order are
reminiscent of no less an artist than Hobbema). Taken overall, Vlaminck's
work is easy to dismiss as derivative and routine. But whenever you look
at an individual canvas, busy, energetic and colourful, this judgement
seems unfair. It's not really that *he* was no good, more that the painters
he admired and imitated were better. He was, in fact, the talented
amateur he always claimed to be.

Good study: J. Selz: *Vlaminck* (1963).

VUILLARD, Édouard (1868–1940)
French painter

Vuillard was a friend and colleague of *Bonnard, and his paintings are
similar to Bonnard's both in their intimate themes and the quiet
lusciousness of their style. *Interior at l'Étang-la-Ville*, for example (1893;
36×34; Smith College MA, Northampton, Mass.), shows women dress-
making in a cosy room complete with gorgeous dotted Bonnard wallpaper;
Portrait of Claude Bernheim de Villiers (1906; 96×68; MAM, Paris)
shows a sailor-suited child in one corner of a huge, brightly tapestried
sofa; *Place Vintimille* (1908; two panels each 190×63; Thannhauser Coll.,
NY) is a sunny city scene designed – in true Nabis style – to be mounted
on a screen for the sitting-room. None the less, Vuillard was *not*
Bonnard – and the reason was that he lacked a Marthe. Marthe gave
Bonnard an obsessive, private focus for intimism, allowed emotion to
underpin decoration. Without such an emotional focus Vuillard's art,

though no less relaxed, has an objective coolness, a decorative aloofness like that of *art nouveau*.

Good study: C. Roger-Marx: *Vuillard. His Life and Work* (1946).

WARHOL, Andy (born 1930)
American artist

It was a symptom of the fashionable sterility and sterile fashionableness of 'art' in the early 1960s that Warhol made such a profound impact not only on critics and the hungry public but also on workers in the arts themselves. He is the last, limp flourish of a long tradition of negativism in 20th-century art, a Dadaist dedicated to anti-art, to personality without individuality, creation without creativity. (He called it 'eliminating the artist's personal signature'.) To this end, he tossed out brushes and paint in favour of the mechanical reproductive techniques of commercial art, especially silk-screen printing and photo-etching. He took familiar objects (soup-cans, bottles, photographs of famous people) and multiplied them endlessly and without variation till they became frozen ikons of their own banality. The public, unaccountably, flocked to see and to buy, declaring that a 'picture' consisting of seven identical rows of Coca-Cola bottles, or a room entirely filled with images of Mao Tse-tung, was art. (That makes the government health warning on a cigarette-packet poetry.) The world soon moved on – Warhol himself moved on, to dismantle films (see Morrissey, page 265) – and multi-images of Marilyn Monroe are now as dated as hulahoops. Where does that leave Warhol's art? On the wall, is the unfortunate answer – at the kind of prices investors pay or have paid, even ephemera must be classed as art.

Good studies: J. Coplam: *Andy Warhol* (1971); S. Koch: *Andy Warhol: Stargazer* (1973). A splendidly acerbic counter to the euphoria of the 1960s is S. Gablik: *Has Modernism Failed?* (1984).

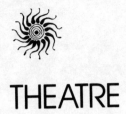

THEATRE

INTRODUCTION

KEY DATES

1888 Strindberg's *Miss Julie*, whose foreword, setting out the aims of the theatre of naturalism, was far more influential than his actual plays. Championship by Archer and Shaw of Ibsen in London led to wide European currency of 'theatre of ideas'

1896 Scandalous first performance of Jarry's *Ubu roi*: irresponsible, Dadaist modernism, the theatre of rude shocks, launched on its long career

1909 First Paris season of Diaghilev's Ballets Russes, presenting the latest ideas (in art, music, dance and theatrical style) to an enthusiastic public

1921 Pirandello's *Six Characters in Search of an Author*. Its questioning of the meaning of theatrical realism was particularly influential in the USA

1924 O'Neill's *Desire under the Elms*: the first great 'intellectual' play of the USA, a forceful counterblast to the Broadway musical revue or to the melodramas of Belasco. Hughes's fifteen-minute *Danger* (set in a coal-mine; the first specially written radio play) broadcast in London

1926 Stanislavski's *An Actor Prepares* (to become the Bible of the 'method' school of acting) published

1930 Pirandello's *The Man with a Flower in his Mouth* was the first play ever shown (experimentally) on television

1947 Clurman and Strasberg's Actors' Studio set up in New York: 'method' acting established in the USA

1949 First Berlin Ensemble production (Brecht's *Mother Courage*). Its techniques, including group improvisation, have been influential on experimental theatre-groups ever since

1950 Ionesco's *The Bald Soprano*, with Beckett's (very different) *Waiting for Godot* (1952) one of the earliest and most programmatic masterworks of the Theatre of the Absurd

1956 Osborne's *Look Back in Anger* not only buries the conception of the 'well-made' play (theatre tailored for the affluent, middle-aged middle class), but dances on its grave

1962 Albee's *Who's Afraid of Virginia Woolf?*, the first US masterpiece using 'Absurd' techniques

THE NINETEENTH-CENTURY LEGACY

Of all the arts, theatre reached this century in the most parlous state, least helpfully dowered by the generations immediately preceding it. Most other arts – music, painting, architecture, literature – reached high peaks of excellence in the 19th century, and were regarded both by their exponents and their consumers as fit vehicles for the maturest and most creative minds; even the occasional 'wildness' of some artists was treated as a symptom of raffish genius rather than of degeneracy. The stage, by contrast, was a trade for mountebanks. In the Victorian social hierarchy, actors ranked with thieves and prostitutes; even the greatest (Kean, Macready, Deburau) were honoured more by the rest of the artistic community than by 'people of quality'. The theatre was the home of sententious or lurid melodrama (well into this century, Irving earned most of his living not from *King Lear* but from *The Bells*), of pantomime, rustic comedy and freak shows (e.g. Sarah Bernhardt, wooden leg and all, travestying *Hamlet*).

In such a situation, writers of distinction were even rarer than great performers. The last German plays to treat noble themes in a noble manner were those of Schiller (died 1805) and Goethe (died 1832); in Britain the greatest 19th-century playwright was not Byron (whose plays, like Goethe's, were magnificently unstageable) but Boucicault; in France Dumas, Hugo and Zola all wrote plays in the prevailing modes, and proved that their greatness lay in other fields; only in Russia (notably with Pushkin, Ostrovsky and Turgenev) was the torch of dramatic art held high – and even there, compared with the dazzle of Elizabethan England or 17th-century France, its light was a fitful flicker.

In France and Britain at least, one of the chief reasons for this degeneracy was a strong feeling, on the part of the authorities, that the theatre was no place for new ideas. Its purpose was the entertainment of a heterogeneous and illiterate mob, and the presentation of radical or revolutionary material was rigorously forbidden. In France, the grip of traditionalism was so strong that Hugo's *Hernani* (1830) provoked a riot as much for its anti-royalism (only a generation after Louis Capet lost his head) as for its loose verse (so unlike the strict metre of Racine); in Britain, the Lord Chamberlain's office refused to license plays in which God, the Bible, the state, successful criminals (including, at one stage, Robin Hood) or royalty were mentioned, and decreed (to one hapless pantomime impresario) that 'the scene in which Lord Palmerston turns into a Cabinet Pudding is to be omitted'. (The stage is no longer important enough – that is, no longer a large enough mass medium – to attract such censorship; but a brief reflection on the themes warily or trivially treated, or not treated at all, by today's mass medium television – the range is from urban deprivation to the home life of Presidents and the nuclear apocalypse – will show how little establishment apprehensions, or the times, have changed.)

THE THEATRE OF IDEAS

Improvement was long overdue. When it came, the impetus was not from pantomime-ridden Britain, France (where Scribe and Sardou ruled) or Germany (whose characteristic drama was sentimental comedy or sententious historical epic like Raupach's sixteen-play-long *History and Destiny of the Hohenstaufen Family*), but from Calvinist Scandinavia. In the 1870s Bjørnson began writing plays embodying philosophical or moral ideas (*The Bankrupt*, for example, is about irresponsibility in business); in 1877 Ibsen wrote *The Pillars of the Community* (an attack on bourgeois complacency, and the first of his great series of social dramas); in 1888 Strindberg, in the preface to *Miss Julie*, set out the aims of the new thinking-person's theatre with commendable, if polemical, clarity. He began

> I have long thought of the theatre – in common with most other art – as a *Biblia pauperum*, a Bible in pictures for the illiterate. I see the playwright as a preacher peddling the ideas of his time in popular form (popular enough for the middle classes, mainstay of theatre audiences, to grasp without taxing their brains too much . . .)

and continued, milling away right and left,

> My tragedy *The Father* was recently criticized for being too gloomy – as if anyone wanted cheerful tragedies. Everybody clamours for what is known as 'the joy of life', and theatre managers insist on farces, as if the joy of life consisted in being ridiculous and portraying all humanity as suffering from St Vitus' dance.

The fact that Strindberg's argument was placed in a preface, and not in the play itself, is significant. Many of Strindberg's and Ibsen's followers regarded the publication of their plays in book form as just as important an activity as performance, allowing the dissemination of their ideas to a far wider circle than the audience sitting in a theatre. (A good example of this practice, undercutting the theatre as a valid vehicle for ideas even as it proclaims it, is Shaw, who equipped his published plays with lengthy prologues and page-long explanatory stage-directions intended for the reader's eye and very far removed from the curt 'two paces up left' of the actors' script.) For a time, the ideas in plays were more important than the plays themselves, and needed longer pondering than the two-hour span of the average night's performance. We remember the principal British 'playwrights of ideas' for other things than their dramatic or philosophical excellence: Henry Arthur Jones is no more than Shaw's shadow (Wilde said, 'The first rule for a young playwright is not to write like Jones. The second and third rules are the same'); Granville Barker is known less for his plays than for his Shakespeare commentaries, Pinero less for serious drama than for farce. Ibsen and Shaw apart, it was a generation before the theatre of ideas settled down (e.g. in O'Casey's 1920s plays for the Dublin Abbey Theatre), and began to combine instruction with entertainment.

DIALECTICAL THEATRE

The notion that plays are not incompatible with intellect was by no means a discovery only of the Ibsenists. Theorists such as Nietzsche had long been advocating a return to the glorious harmony of Apollonian intellectuality and Dionysian exuberance in Greek classical tragedy or in Shakespeare; advanced thinkers like Freud used theatrical methods (in his case, encouraging his patients to improvise prompted monologues) to achieve non-theatrical ends, and stressed – as theatre did – the expression of emotion as a therapeutic force. When the 1871 Paris Exhibition brought Far-Eastern theatre-troupes to Europe for the first time, and showed that (contrary to the practice of Ibsen or Chekhov) the illusion of reality was not essential for stage effect, the floodgates were open for theatrical experiments of every kind, from actors imitating puppets (in Jarry's *Ubu roi*) to the rambling dream-logic of Maeterlinck or the two-dimensional symbolism of Kaiser and Wedekind.

Ever since those early experimental days, dialectic has continued to hold the stage. At first (since all theatre tends to mirror rather than to redraw its audience, and the first audiences of the theatre of ideas were comfortably middle-class) ideas were presented in a neat, naturalistic and well-made style. The industrial-relations problems of pre-1914 Britain, for example, were cosily packaged in Galsworthy's *Strife*, where no one 'idea' wins (the protagonists of both sides are destroyed by that quintessential middle-class – not to say Aristotelian – flaw, 'going too far'); the financial problems of 1920s America were sent up (and trivialized) by Rice's *The Adding Machine*; in 1930s and 1940s Britain, Priestley saw to problems of identity and Rattigan to those of conscience; 1940s American decency was given an identity by Wilder, and its fear of fascism was sugar-coated by Odets and Hellman. The audience for such plays was seduced by ideas, not educated, and left the theatre warmly applauding its own open-mindedness. Robert Sherwood, one of the most successful 1930s writers of 'problem plays', spoke for all his decent colleagues when he ruefully remarked: 'The trouble is that I start off with a big message and end with nothing but good entertainment.'

But even as well-made drama (and the well-made films created in its image) went imperturbably on presenting argument in terms of instances (e.g. in Sherwood's *The Petrified Forest*, dramatizing the moral problem of confronting fascism as the conflict between a cowardly aesthete and a sadistic escaped convict), and thus letting us look at pictures rather than reflect on issues, revolution was again afoot in Europe. In *The Theatre and Its Double* (1933, only two years before *The Petrified Forest*), Artaud wrote

movies ... murdering us with second-hand reproductions which, filtered through machines, cannot *unite us* with our sensibility, have maintained us for ... years in an ineffectual torpor, in which all our faculties appear to be foundering.

In the anguished, catastrophic period we live in, we feel an urgent need for a theatre which events do not exceed, whose resonance is deep within us, dominating the instability of the times.

At the same period, Brecht said that the theatre should shock, not cosset its audience, and to ram his messages down the throats of a complacent public devised a raucous, flamboyant and continuously unexpected show, drawing strength from Far-Eastern production-techniques and employing every trick of preacher's or politician's rhetoric. The drama of previous ages was no longer the armature for discreet explorations of 'difficult' modern themes (as it was for such giants as O'Neill or Eliot as well as for minor masters like Anouilh or Giraudoux): Brecht and his followers cannibalized what they wanted from the Greek tragedians, Shakespeare or Jonson, and junked the rest. Their methods were designed to send the audience from the theatre in a state of shock; once the shock wore off, their hope was that ideas would germinate in the spectators' minds.

Theatre audiences have, however, proved remarkably resistant to this kind of polemic: it is, after all, the act of a masochist to pay good money to be shocked out of your complacency or insulted where you sit. Not only that, but much of the anti-realistic repertoire of dialectical drama was borrowed from more down-market entertainment (e.g. music-hall, fairground or circus) and offended as many of the bourgeoisie as it enticed. Since the demise of the well-made play – or rather its translation to television after the 1950s theatrical revolution led by Osborne, Ionesco and Beckett – dialectical theatre has become the art of a minority. To sit in a large audience, in a subsidized theatre, watching an established dialectical masterpiece (say, Brecht's *The Caucasian Chalk Circle*) is to be among people doing their duty by greatness rather than enjoying themselves; most polemical drama takes place on pocket-handkerchief stages above pubs or very far off Broadway, and tends to outrage the majority more by its existence than by its messages. (The fury roused in Britain in 1980 by Brenton's *The Romans in Britain* was largely at the fact that a National Theatre, financed by the tax-payer, should put on what one popular newspaper called 'pinko dross'; Mary Whitehouse, the anti-permissiveness campaigner and guardian of born-again middle-class morality, was able to sue the play's director without bothering to see the play.) We remember the furore over Hochhuth's *Soldiers* more easily than the point of the play itself (the accusation that Churchill connived at the murder of Sikorski); the dialectical bombs dropped by even such fine writers as Bond, Bullins or Fugard make large noises in small spaces, and hurt no one. That work of such excellence should fail to make its point, while cosy moral dramas like Odets' *The Country Girl* or Rattigan's *The Winslow Boy* are remembered *precisely* for their messages, is a comment not on dialectical theatre, but on the nature of theatre, and its audience, at large.

ENTERTAINMENT AND METAPHOR

The vital factor remains entertainment. However much some may wish it otherwise, the theatre is less a matter of sermons than of good evenings out; unless there is a show, there is no show. Throughout this century, commercial managements have taken to their bosoms only those 'serious' plays which are also 'engrossing human dramas' (Tennessee Williams's output springs to mind), or mould-breaking plays (like Beckett's *Waiting for Godot*, Osborne's *Look Back in Anger* or Frisch's *The Fire-Raisers*) which have served their time on the avant-garde fringe until their quality becomes undeniably obvious (that is, it can be argued, until their teeth are drawn). Despite Strindberg's claims, we like to see *ourselves* in plays, not the lay-figures of moral tracts or symbols of any other kind (like clowns): for most theatregoers, empathy with the characters' dilemmas involves and depends on empathy with the characters themselves.

Many commercial managements, and many writers of quality, have turned away from messages altogether. This century's drama is rich in plays written purely for entertainment. The farces, for example, of Feydeau, Travers, Kaufman and Hart, Barry and Orton are among the best of any age, and exploit the possibilities of theatre with unrivalled dispatch and verve. The 'light tragedy' favoured by boulevard audiences has had superb light-comedy equivalents, plays of manners ranging from Shaw's *You Never Can Tell* or *The Devil's Disciple* (which, as he pointed out himself, were a hundred times more popular than his 'thoughtful plays' such as *The Apple Cart* or *Back to Methuselah*) to the work of such craftsmen as Anouilh, Fry, Albee or Stoppard.

The tension between plays-of-message and plays-of-entertainment was caused, for the first half of the century at least, by the lack of a convincing and unifying metaphor of life. For theatre *is* a metaphor for reality, not its simulacrum, and many of this century's dramatic experiments are failed attempts to find changing metaphors for a changing situation. (Expressionism, for example, tried to depict the urgency and irrationality of emotional states; the many 1930s plays based on classical models tried to use past civilizations as templates for our own.) Some outstanding playwrights (Shaw, O'Casey, Wilder, Miller) succeeded in saying what they wanted despite cumbersome and intractable forms; others (notably O'Neill and Brecht, whose work is for many as unwatchable as it is great) found that their messages exploded form. Despite individual master-pieces, pre-1950s theatre was in a chaotic state, living through that kind of adolescent frenzy which most other arts outgrew a century ago.

Maturity – or the discovery of exactly the right metaphor to fit the age – came in the 1950s with the rise of the Theatre of the Absurd. This linked a fertile theme (humanity's feeling of existential loneliness) with a fertile style (galvanic nonsense, combining jerky silent-film movement with the 'psycho-babble' of mid-20th-century communications). The blend was unlikely, and in the hands of some of its early users (Adamov,

Simpson, Gelber) produced nothing more than modish silliness. But once the style settled down, it proved as successful a metaphor for contemporary society as mythological tragedy was for ancient Athens or historical morality for Elizabethan England, and led to as many masterpieces. While the great plays of the first half of the century (*Mourning Becomes Electra*; *Six Characters in Search of an Author*; *Murder in the Cathedral*; *The Skin of Our Teeth*) often seem excellent in spite of themselves, today's masterpieces (Ionesco's *The Chairs* or *The Killer*, Beckett's *Waiting for Godot*, Frisch's *Andorra*, Dürrenmatt's *The Physicists*, Bond's *Bingo*) seem relaxed and easy, a harmonious marriage of content and style. As Dürrenmatt himself wrote, in the preface to *Four Plays* (1965),

> The task of art – in so far as art can have a task at all – and hence also the task of drama today, is to create something concrete, something that has form. This can be accomplished best by comedy . . . which presupposes an unformed world, a world turned upside-down, a world about to fold like ours . . . The comical exists to form what is formless, to create order out of chaos.

◙

As in other sections, I have concentrated in this one on creative figures whose work is still available, that is (with the sole exception of Diaghilev) on writers and choreographers rather than on directors or performers. This is manifestly unfair – Stanislavski and Brook, for example (to say nothing of outstanding artists like Barrault or Olivier), were as influential on 20th-century drama as Shaw or Ionesco – but their work is more easily accessible to those within the profession than to the outsider looking for an overview. The guide offered here is to makers of blueprints; the study of interpretation is matter for a different book.

ADAMOV, Arthur (1908–70)
French playwright

In his earliest plays (not written until his forties) Adamov was influenced by *Ionesco, and by the ideas of 'ritual theatre' and 'theatre of cruelty' put forward by Artaud (in *The Theatre and Its Double*, 1933, a seminal book for the 1950s avant-garde). His plays combine absurd incidents (a man locks himself for a fortnight in a cupboard; a man loses his limbs one by one on stage) with the images and events of nightmare (collapse of identity; guilt; violence; the police state) – for Adamov's characters, the sun never shines and all fruit comes from the Dead Sea. His most successful plays in this vein are *Professor Taranne* (1953), about a man whose character disintegrates under the weight of neurotic guilt, *Ping-Pong* (1955), in which life is reduced – literally – to games of zany, zen ping-pong with neither bats nor ball, and *Paolo Paoli* (1957), which examines the socio-economic causes of the First World War in so far as they affect a merchant of ingenious toys made from butterflies' wings. In the 1960s Adamov broadened his scope to produce a kind of absurdist historical epic (e.g. *The Sorcerers*, 1962, a pageant about racism; *Spring 71*, 1961, about the Paris Commune; *Saint Europe*, 1966, in which Charlemagne is reincarnated as Charles de Gaulle). Compared with Ionesco or *Brecht he is a slight figure; but his work has been influential, and *Professor Taranne* and *Ping-Pong*, at least, deserve to last.

Adamov's other plays include *Off Limits* (1969) and *If Summer Came Back* (1969). He also wrote two volumes of involuted autobiography, *The Confession* (1946) and *Man and Boy* (1969).

AILEY, Alvin (born 1931)
American choreographer

A varied performing career (as classical ballet dancer, actor and dancer in film musicals) equipped Ailey on the one hand with an eclectic musical taste (embracing both Samuel Barber and Pink Floyd), and on the other with a precise idea of what is theatrically and artistically effective (by no means as standard a qualification for avant-garde choreographers as it ought to be). His ballets – most written for his own company, the Alvin Ailey City Center Dance Theater, New York – are, in their way, stage journalism, striking and entertaining rather than memorable; his importance lies less in any single work than in his influence on the visual style of contemporary ballet. His dancers are often costumed in yards of flowing cloth, supported on frames, pastel-coloured and subtly lit: when they move it is as if the set itself is shifting and regrouping itself somewhere else. This style can be traced back to Japanese classical theatre, but Ailey – perhaps influenced by Busby Berkeley's surrealist towers of frames, cloth and human limbs – has brought it so far into the modern age that his tableaux and *pas d'action* also look like animated sculptures by Brancusi, Giacometti or David Smith. The dance-style is suitably statuesque, alternately posing the dancers for visual rather than for narrative effect (Ailey pays little heed to story) and giving them wild outbursts of movement derived from whirling dervishes or African tribal dance. These effects can be seen at their simplest in *Labyrinth/Ariadne* (1963, music by Jolivet) or *Cry* (1971, music by Alice Coltrane); his most satisfying work dates from the 1970s, and ranges from *Mass* (1971, music by Bernstein) and *The Lark Ascending* (1972, music by Vaughan Williams) to a series of abstract ballets to music by Duke Ellington.

ALBEE, Edward (born 1928)
American playwright

Albee has from the start been a restless, experimental writer. His early plays (especially *The Zoo Story*, 1958, *The Sandbox*, 1959, and *The American Dream*, 1960) were influenced by *Ionesco – and one of his best later works, *A Delicate Balance* (1966), depends on the absurdist *coup* of one couple moving in, unheralded, to live in another's house. His more recent plays owe debts to *Beckett, especially the radio play *Listening* (1977), and the splendid *Box-Mao-Box* (1968), in which a stream-of-consciousness monologue from a middle-aged woman is juxtaposed with quotations from the thoughts of Chairman Mao and the cracker-barrel poet Will Carleton. In *Counting the Ways* (1976), two characters in twenty-one scenes live out an entire marriage.

The chief qualities of this output, striking theatrical ideas and dialogue carefully structured to follow the external pattern of the play rather than the needs of the characters, are repeated in Albee's major works, *Who's Afraid of Virginia Woolf?* (1962), *Tiny Alice* (1964) and *A Delicate Balance*. *Who's Afraid of Virginia Woolf?* is one of the best American post-war plays, of a stature analogous to that of Heller's *Catch-22* in fiction, and with a markedly similar use of savagery and absurdist wit to flesh despair. George and Martha lacerate each other with words, replacing concern with rhetoric: their relationship is a hollow edifice built on the life of the son they never had (another Ionescan – not to say Ibsenish – device). Only in the last act, when George 'kills' the son, are they able to face each other and the future. Are George and Martha symbols (as their names suggest) for the USA? Or a homosexual couple, Martha *en travestie*? No matter: the play succeeds by stinging rhetoric and not by messages. Albee declares himself a technician and never a tragedian – *Miller, for example, would have made the play's flatly sentimental ending work, whereas in Albee it comes as simply the last in a series of theatrical surprises.

Tiny Alice borrows style from Strindberg. The raucous central female role is as close to Laura in *The Father* as to Martha in *Who's Afraid of Virginia Woolf?*, and the religious symbolism (the play even contains the death of a priest in crucifix-position) is florid and neurotic in the manner of Strindberg's *Dream Play*. *A Delicate Balance*, superficially on the same theme as *Who's Afraid of Virginia Woolf?* (our depredations of those we love), and just as barnstorming in performance, offers a more varied situation (four interrelated characters tearing each other, not two), and is less violently rhetorical – though Tobias's huge Act Three monologue, the turning-point of the action, exhibits the usual Albee combination of theatrical brilliance and heartlessness. (It is a *show*, a coruscating 'turn', by no means inevitable from what we know of the character or what has gone before.) Albee produced nothing to equal it until *The Man Who Had Three Arms* (1983). This is a huge, furious monologue by a once-famous, now not-famous dramatist (called 'Himself', no less): two lacerating hours about what fame does to the artist. (This is a theme of recent novels by both Roth and Updike; Albee is less funny, but far more raucously brilliant, than either of them.)

Albee's other plays include *The Death of Bessie Smith* (1960), *All Over* (1971), *Seascape* (1975), *The Lady from DuBuque* (1980), adaptations of McCullers' *The Ballad of the Sad Café* (1963) and Nabokov's *Lolita* (1980), and a musical version of Capote's *Breakfast at Tiffany's* (1966). Good brief survey: R. Hayman: *Albee* (1971).

ANDERSON, Maxwell (1888–1959)
American playwright

Anderson's best plays – his output was large and variable – are verse tragedies drawing structure from Aristotle (*peripeteia*, *anagnorisis* and the unities are all painstakingly observed) and style from Shakespeare (particularly the Histories). They include *Joan of Lorraine* (1946, reworked as a screenplay for *Joan of Arc*, 1948), and three talky Tudor dramas, *Elizabeth the Queen* (1930), *Mary of Scotland* (1933) and *Anne of the Thousand Days* (1948, later filmed). He also wrote for the musical stage (notably *Knickerbocker Holiday*, 1938, and *Lost in the Stars*, 1949, both with music by Weill, and the latter based on Paton's novel *Cry, the Beloved Country*), and for films (most effectively in his contribution to the script of *All Quiet on the Western Front*, 1930). His finest work of all (perhaps because it has American roots and so involves his emotions at first, not second, hand) is a pair of tragedies on modern themes. *Winterset* (1935), set in the New York slums, is about a man obsessed with avenging his murdered father (overtones of *Hamlet*) who falls tragically in love (overtones of *Romeo and Juliet*) and is murdered in his turn. It is a successful mixture of sensational content with classy structure: poetry apart (and Anderson is no poet), Shakespeare is by no means traduced by the comparison. *Key Largo* (1939, later filmed) is about a man haunted by an act of cowardice, who redeems himself before our eyes by sacrificing himself for his companions.

Anderson is a minor master, a middlebrow intellectual with few pretensions (despite his exalted models). His plays raise interesting issues and discuss them interestingly; he is the rococo *Rattigan of the USA.

In addition to plays, Anderson published two books of meaty essays, *The Essence of Tragedy* (1939) and *The Bases of Artistic Creation* (1942), and a lighter volume, *Off Broadway: Essays about Theatre* (1947). Good introduction: A. S. Shivers: *Anderson* (1976).

ANOUILH, Jean (born 1910)
French playwright

Enormously prolific, Anouilh famously divided his output into categories such as *pièces noires* (dark plays) and *pièces roses* (rosy plays). His serious work centres on four plays exploring mythological or historical themes: *Eurydice/Legend of Lovers* (1941), *Antigone* (1944), *The Lark* (1953, about Joan of Arc) and *Becket* (1959). In each of them events follow their traditional course, but the characters are given modern sensibilities and rationale, and contemporary resonances are exploited to the full: *Antigone*, for example, about freedom of conscience, gained great power from the circumstances in which it was written, the German occupation of France. A constant theme in all these plays (also present in the comedies) is the nature of innocence and of those who would corrupt it: Anouilh's favourite heroes are naïve young girls or honourable middle-aged men, and in each case the play's action involves them in facing and coping with compromise.

Anouilh's most characteristic plays are his *pièces roses*: bitter-sweet comedies leaning sometimes towards the elegant slapstick of René Clair, sometimes towards the warm-heartedness and whimsy of Ealing comedy. Almost without exception they involve masquerade: *Thieves' Carnival* (1938) is about a trio of romantic confidence tricksters; *Léocadia/Time Remembered* (1940) concerns a young girl dressed up by an outrageous aristocratic lady (a superb part) to distract grieving Prince Charming, her nephew; *Traveller Without Luggage* (1937) and *Colombe* (1951) are about the stage; *L'Invitation au château/Ring Round the Moon* (1947) – the quintessential Anouilh *pièce rose* – is a merrygoround of mistaken identities engineered by a pair of handsome twins, played by the same actor, who only just fails to come on to the stage when he is already there. The gaiety of these plays is enhanced by songs, costume-balls, carnivals and (often) the setting and costumes of an Edwardian country house-party. The characters are gorgeous, self-conscious peacocks – Anouilh has a marvellous line in eccentric actresses and elderly aristocrats. In two plays, *Waltz of the Toreadors* (1952) and *Poor Bitos* (1956), without sacrificing froth, he deepens the drama by showing us leading characters at odds with themselves. The ageing General in *Waltz of the Toreadors* is a fool to all around him, and the play shows his gradual realization of his own hollowness; *Poor Bitos* shows the search for identity of a man whose character everyone else moulds to suit themselves, a counterpart to *Ionesco's Bérenger.

Hugely popular in the 1940s and 1950s, Anouilh was eclipsed in the 1960s, when black comedy and social realism swamped the theatre. He is still out of fashion; but he is a master of stagecraft and of enigmatic dialogue; his plays are exotic and entertaining, and will return.

Anouilh's recent plays include the rebarbatively reactionary *Chers Zoiseaux* (1976) and *La Culotte* (1978), and a nostalgic study of a rich, underrated and unfashionable writer, *The Navel* (1981). Good introduction: H. G. McIntyre: *The Theatre of Jean Anouilh* (1961).

ARDEN, John (born 1930)
British playwright

The most accomplished Brechtian dramatist since *Brecht, Arden combines polemic and theatricality to an extent unequalled by any of his younger contemporaries (e.g. *Brenton or *Keefe). His plays deal with topical, political themes, but use a fable-structure which both distances and elevates them, so avoiding the obsolescence endemic to agit-prop theatre. His most powerful plays deal with the welfare state (*Live Like Pigs*, 1958), pacifism (*Serjeant Musgrave's Dance*, 1959 – his masterpiece, as pungent as a medieval morality), the need for political order and civic corruption (*The Workhouse Donkey*, 1963, his most Brechtian work, even down to the songs). In the 1960s he began collaborating with Margaretta d'Arcy, and together they adopted a stance towards production as uncompromising as the contents of their plays, which has tended to inhibit performances. When the work *is* performed or published, its quality shines. *The Island of the Mighty* (1972), for example, a rambling trilogy on the relationship of the artist and society centred on the time-straddling figures of King Arthur and Merlin, is like *Peer Gynt* or *Back to Methuselah*: unstageably magnificent, clamorous with potential, an essential work which (alas) elbows itself aside from general accessibility (thanks to a huge cast, dozens of scenes and above all its exacting demand that the audience follows and agrees with every twist of argument – there is no quarter for heterodoxy here). When they choose, or accept, technical discipline (as in their children's play *The Royal Pardon*, 1966, or their impressive radio play *Pearl*, 1978, on the history of Ireland and its 'problem'), Arden and d'Arcy are unbeatable; in general, however, because of their reluctance to agree that formal discipline can be a liberating force, they choke ideas with words. Arden's solo radio play, *The Old Man Sleeps Alone* (1982), together with his novel *Silence Among the Weapons* (see below), marks a superb return to form. Perhaps the shenanigans of the 1970s were nothing more, and he is about to enter a late, great phase.

The causes of Arden's and d'Arcy's disaffection with the professional theatre (which came to a head in 1972, when they picketed the theatre and interrupted performances during the RSC run of *The Island of the Mighty* in London) are set out in a piece of witty polemic, *To Present the Pretence* (1978). Arden's first novel, *Silence Among the Weapons* (1982), is an excellent (and unpolemical) historical tale set in Ancient Rome. Good brief introduction: F. Gray: *John Arden* (1982).

ARRABAL, Fernando (born 1932)
Spanish/French playwright

Theatrical Dadaism is alive and well, and its wetnurse is Arrabal. He has invented what he calls 'panic theatre', a presentation of horrific and horrible happenings (coprophagy, castration, cannibalism) in a stiff-legged, surrealistic style derived from circus clowning or Keystone comedy. It is unique, and it has the authority of its uniqueness – who is to say, for example, if Arrabal's plays are as ephemeral as pop art (they are certainly as brash) or will last, and grow, as the paintings of the great surrealists have grown? Characteristic titles – culled from an enormous output – are *The Two Executioners* (1958), *The Solemn Communion* (1958), *Ceremony for a Murdered Black* (1965), *The Architect and the Emperor of Assyria* (1967), *Erotic Bestiality* (1969) and *A Turtle Called Dostoievski* (1969).

BALANCHINE, George (1904–83)
Russian/American choreographer

From the start (seven years at the Imperial Ballet Academy) Balanchine was drawn to choreography, and away from the older, 'narrative' fashion in Russian ballet (typified by Petipa's great Tchaikovsky ballets) towards a severer style, in which uncluttered choreography was set to clear-lined music against plain scenery, and story took second place to movement. His first great success was *Apollon Musagète*, choreographed for *Diaghilev's Ballets Russes in 1928, to a pellucid neo-classical score by Stravinsky. The neo-classical idiom, much in vogue in the 1930s (it enticed, among others, such influential artists as *Cocteau, Gide, Picasso and Hindemith), became the basis of all Balanchine's subsequent work. His preference for abstraction (highlighting dance for its own sake, regardless of plot), for geometric patterns (using arms and legs in a stylized way unknown in dance before him) and for the balletic use of movements from popular dance (e.g. Bluebell Girls high-kicks and Astaire arm-movements) and from ice-dancing and gymnastics, were vital influences on almost all later choreographers, particularly in the USA, where he founded the American Ballet (later the New York City Ballet) in 1935. Balanchine choreographed several hundred ballets, to scores by every composer of worth from Monteverdi to Webern; but his greatest work was always in collaboration with Stravinsky, with whom he created a dozen original ballets and to whose concert works he choreographed several dozen more. (The quintessential Balanchine–Stravinsky ballets are *Apollo* and *Orpheus*, 1948, on Greek subjects, *Pulcinella*, 1972, in *commedia dell'arte* style, and *Danses concertantes*, 1944, *Agon*, 1957, *Movements*, 1963, and *Symphony in Three Movements*, 1972, all abstract or pure-dance ballets.) Balanchine also worked in television (pioneering the creation of ballets specifically for the cameras), and in 1930s Hollywood: his influence on dance musicals can be seen in other people's films as diverse as *The Goldwyn Follies* (1938) and *West Side Story* (1957).

BARRIE, James Matthew (1860–1937)
British playwright and journalist

Running through English letters of the last 150 years there is a distinct faery or elven streak, a genteel folk-memory of much tougher medieval elves and sprites (those whose apotheoses are Shakespeare's Puck and Ariel). For some reason – perhaps because children too are seen as 'little people' – it surfaces most frequently in writing about or for the young: *The Water Babies* and the poems of Walter de la Mare are characteristic examples. Barrie's early books (mainly collections of newspaper articles, and with tell-all titles like *Auld Licht Idylls*, 1888), and his charming, appalling plays, carry the trend to its unearthly apogee. *Peter Pan* (1904), who never grows up, *Dear Brutus* (1917), a drawing-room-comedy *Midsummer Night's Dream* where life's previous mistakes can be wiped out if you agree to enter 'the wood of the second chance', and *Mary Rose* (1920), with its vision of the island 'that likes to be visited' (the asylum into which the heroine herself eventually escapes) – all three carry whimsy to the point where the audience must writhe in ecstasy, or retch. Barrie demands total surrender: lose hold on his gossamer reality, and you blow away. Do his fey conceits really evoke a pre-pubescent golden age? All who believe in fairies, shout yes, together, now.

Barrie's many other plays include the sentimental *Quality Street* (1902), and two rather more robust comedies of manners, *The Admirable Crichton* (1902) and *What Every Woman Knows* (1908). He also published novels (*The Little Minister*, 1891, and *Sentimental Tommy*, 1896, are typical titles), and a discreet autobiography, *The Greenwood Hat* (1930). Splendid biography, good both on Barrie's robustness and his sentimentality: A. Birkin: *J. M. Barrie and the Lost Boys* (1979).

BARRY, Philip (1896–1949)
American playwright

At first sight, Barry seems to belong to that group of skilful, graceful comic craftsmen which includes Neil Simon, Alan Ayckbourn and Sacha Guitry: surefire winners on their day, whose slight but splendid works are guaranteed to put a bottom on every seat. Certainly comedy comes no higher than in Barry's *Holiday* (1928), *The Animal Kingdom* (1932) and especially *The Philadelphia Story* (1939), his funniest play (filmed in 1940, and musically remade as *High Society* in 1955). But he produced serious work as well (in a style not unlike that of *Wilder), and although it currently suffers from the general unfashionableness of all 1930s serious drama, it merits attention. He wrote on politics (*Liberty Jones*, 1941), theology (*John*, 1927, about John the Baptist) and self-discovery (*Hotel Universe*, 1930). His best play of this kind is *Here Come the Clowns* (1938), whose theme and general style – it is about a malign magician who induces seedy actors in a cafe to shed their surface selves and reveal their true natures – is reminiscent both of *O'Neill's *The Iceman Cometh* and Carné's *Les Enfants du paradis*.

A useful anthology of Barry's work is *States of Grace: Eight Plays* (ed. Gill, 1975). Apart from plays, he published one other work, the novel *Liar in Heaven* (1938).

BECKETT, Samuel (born 1906)
Irish/French playwright, poet and novelist
Ever since the appearance of *Waiting for Godot* (1952), Beckett's work has been the cult that came to stay, the centre of an immense critical industry whose explanations, if heeded, can totally obscure what is actually simple, pure and clear. His novels (especially *Murphy*, 1938; *Molloy*, 1951; *Watt*, 1953; *Malone Dies*, 1955, and *The Unnameable*, 1958) and his plays (notably *Waiting for Godot*; *Endgame*, 1957; *Krapp's Last Tape*, 1958; *Happy Days*, 1961; *Not I*, 1968) depict humanity stripped of the present but richly dowered by memories: though present actions are meaningless or ritual, recollection warms the mind with hope. Beckett's heroes are beggars in a post-apocalyptic wilderness or cripples deprived of movement, limbs or senses; the characters in *Play* (1963) are dead, in urns, the protagonist of *Not I* is reduced to a spotlit, jabbering mouth.
The strength of Beckett's drama lies less in his 'philosophy' than in his skill with words. The *fons et origo* of his work is Molly Bloom's soliloquy at the close of Joyce's *Ulysses*: Beckett's whole output is an exploration of the possibilities for language and for character-revelation suggested by that one speech. He is also fascinated by the grave slapstick comedians of silent films, particularly in old age when their skill has become an aura, a memory. The shifting, double-act, busy-doing-nothing relationship of Vladimir and Estragon in *Waiting for Godot* is based on that of Laurel and Hardy; Hamm in *Endgame* is a crippled Chaplin; *Film* (1964) was made by septuagenarian Buster Keaton, the 'great stone face' seamed and lined as if by ineffable experience. The timing of silent comedy also affects the dramatic pointing of the plays: Beckett, when he directs them himself, is obsessive about the placing and duration of even the smallest pause. (Many elderly vaudevillians, men like Bert Lahr or Max Wall, have had successes in his work, using their old music-hall timing and drawing on the audience's memory of their own real-life past acts.)

Although the dialogue-plays (*Waiting for Godot*, *Endgame* and *Happy Days*) are Beckett's best, the monologue remains his most characteristic form. His novels are rambling, first-person narratives, often with no other characters except those in the narrator's mind; and from *Krapp's Last Tape* onwards, the plays have tended increasingly towards verbal anorexia: even *Happy Days*, where there are secondary characters, is chiefly a bravura solo for the actress playing Winnie. Beckett's works in the 1970s also became ever shorter, more aphoristic and elliptical. (His admirers call this distillation; his detractors don't.)

Whatever the ultimate status of Beckett's work, there is no doubt that he is the greatest single influence on post-war theatre since *Brecht, and that his plays (like Brecht's) will survive less for their subtexts and overtones (if any) than because they work uncannily well on stage. His novels are peripheral, but the delights of the plays, enlivened by the performing dimension, are self-renewing and manifold.

Beckett's many other plays include the enigmatic *Play* (1963) and *Eh Joe* (1967, originally for television), and the 30-second-long *Breath* (1969). He has also published poetry (*Collected Poems in English and French*, 1977), short stories (*More Bricks than Kicks*, 1934), and a study of Proust (*Proust*, 1931), which reveals as much of his own creative purpose as it does of Proust's. Good introduction: R. Coe: *Samuel Beckett* (1966). Good, packed anthology: J. Calder (ed.): *A Samuel Beckett Reader* (1984). J. Fletcher (ed.): *A Student's Guide to the Plays of Samuel Beckett* (1978).

BETTI, Ugo (1892–1953)
Italian playwright

A lawyer by profession (and, from 1930, a high-court judge), Betti wrote a novel, many short stories, and a couple of dozen plays. Although his method and manner were close to *Pirandello – his style, a combination of realistic action and neurotic characters, stops, like Pirandello's, only just this side of melodrama – the underlying theme of his work is quite different. Pirandello is concerned with illusion and delusion, Betti with the tragic results of the breakdown of order (religious, moral, ethical) in a personality or a society. There is thus a Catholic firmness to his plays which tempers the (often) steamy action. The plays best known in English are *Summertime* (1942), a comedy about two lovers whose relationship deepens the more everyone else attempts to end it, *The Queen and the Rebels* (1949), a Pirandellian piece about a prostitute mistaken for a queen who becomes the part she plays, and *The Burnt Flowerbed* (1952), a rather tract-like morality about political duty and self-sacrifice. The first two of these – and especially *The Queen and the Rebels*, his masterpiece – reveal Betti as a minor master whose work is serious and durable.

Among the best of Betti's other plays are the surrealist *Inspection* (1942), the Pirandellian *Corruption in the Palace of Justice* (1947), and *Goat Island* (1948), the story of a man brutalizing, and brutalized by, three peasant women, told in a style reminiscent of Rossellini's neo-realist films.

BOND, Edward (born 1935)
British playwright

Bond began his public theatrical career (with the immature *The Pope's Wedding*, 1962) at the same time as the British Lord Chamberlain was ending his, and for a time it seemed as if Bond plays were specifically designed to provoke censorious apoplexy. The baby-stoning scene in *Saved* (1965), and the plot of *Early Morning* (1968) – Prince Albert and Disraeli engineer a *coup* to dethrone Queen Victoria, who is engaged in a lesbian affair with Florence Nightingale – were seen by many as gratuitous excess, distracted drama for far-from-distracted times. But the times got worse, and in *Narrow Road to the Deep North* (1968 – a watershed date for radical politics) Bond found in Japanese legend and *Brechtian theatrical techniques a way to discipline his rage, to direct his audience's anger at the matter of each play and not its manner.

None the less, his work is still obsessive about violence and decay. He himself said, in his introduction to *Lear* (1971, a reworking of Shakespeare's themes in terms of the contemporary wasteland), 'I write about violence as naturally as Jane Austen wrote about manners. Violence shapes and obsesses our society, and if we do not stop being violent we have no future. People who do not want writers to write about violence want to stop them writing about us and our time. It would be immoral not to write about violence.' The Jacobean disgust this suggests is the well-spring of his art (just as it is for *Keefe's plays, and for the films of such men as Coppola, Fassbinder and Scorsese). But as that quotation implies, Bond (unlike those other play- and film-makers, and unlike most of the Jacobeans) has also room in his work for hope: he is one of the few agit-prop playwrights not afraid of compassion. *Bingo* (1974), about the artistic and moral exhaustion of Shakespeare, leading to his suicide, and *The Fool* (1976), about the mad poet John Clare – and the artist as society's fool – make substantial statements about redeeming vision: the visionary suffers and dies, but his idea lives on as a healing force.

The idea of the cathartic power of violence is both Puritan and inquisitional: there is more than a hint of flagellation, of torturing into paradise, in all Bond's work. In *The Sea* (1973), the Trojan war adaptation *The Woman* (1978), and the grim *Summer* (1982) we are shown people driven past the extremes of suffering – and 'cured' by it: *Summer*, in particular, shows how acceptance of suffering, and of the evil which causes it, is a creative force in human character. Only in *The Worlds* (1979), about a political kidnapping and its corrosive effects on the personalities of the terrorists, does Bond blunt his edge: this is an untypically relaxed play, serene despite its theme, middle-aged as if Bond has become a *guru* of radical theatre. It was published, too, with ninety pages of 'activist papers', poems and short essays on such subjects as The

Worlds, Weapons, The New Fascism, Types of Drama and Aesthetics. This is (as it was with Brecht) a sombre artistic trend: pamphleteers are ten a penny, but playwrights of Bond's distinction are few.

Bond's other works include the script for Antonioni's film *Blow-Up* (1967), the libretto for Henze's music-theatre piece *We Come to the River* (1975), translations of Chekhov's *Three Sisters* and Wedekind's *Spring Awakening*, and what must be the only Brechtian musical comedy set among exploiting 18th-century aristocrats and their vengeful tenants, *Restoration* (1981). Good critical study: M. Hay and P. Roberts: *Bond: A Study of His Plays* (1980).

BRECHT, Bertolt (1898–1956)
German playwright

Lamentably, the average English-speaking theatregoer still knows Brecht less as a great playwright than as a legend (the man who spoke out at the 1947 Unamerican Activities hearings), the author of two likeable but minor musical plays (*The Rise and Fall of the State of Mahogonny*, 1927, and *The Threepenny Opera*, 1928, a nimble updating of *The Beggar's Opera*), and above all as the theoretician who created 'epic theatre' and the 'alienation effect'. Brecht's influence is still more common in our theatres than Brecht's own work.

'Epic theatre' demands that drama should be dialectical as well as rhetorical, that is that it should enter into a dialogue with its spectators, involve them in critical thinking instead of gulled acceptance of what they are shown. The 'alienation effect' prevents the spectators from suspending disbelief by constantly reminding them that what they are watching is artificial, a self-conscious 'show' with a distinct argument apart from entertainment. (Songs, commentaries, critical monologues by characters not part of the main action or by characters who step aside from their roles in the main action – these are the chief means of producing the effect.) The methods and results of epic theatre are antithetical to those of 'realistic theatre' (e.g. the plays of Ibsen), where a careful illusion of reality is preserved, and although 'issues' are discussed and arguments put forward just as much as in Brechtian drama, they are absorbed into the general flow of characterization and illusion, and the characters never break that flow. Thus Brecht's work, though it cut across the theatre practice of its time (it was, for example, alien to Stanislavski's method of production), was in a direct line from the 'theatres of convention' of ancient Greece, Japan or the Elizabethans.

This demanding stage-style, coupled with radical politics (there seems to be no successful agit-prop theatre of the Right – except possibly for rightist politics themselves), kept Brecht from mass public favour in his own lifetime. Certainly there are dialectical *longueurs* in his plays (though never as many as in those of his myriad disciples), and the ramshackle structure – he intended them to be revised for each production, and much of his time with the Berlin Ensemble in the 1950s was spent in reworking them with a close-knit company of actors – can alienate even a patient audience right out of the theatre. But a handful of them are masterworks, whose theatrical power renews itself with each performance in ways which have nothing to do with messages. (This is, of course, not at all what Brecht intended. But the same is true of Aeschylus or Shakespeare: long after the political and philosophical topicality of their work has disappeared, the plays remain.)

Brecht's finest plays are all concerned with the nature of individual heroism, and of compromise. Galileo, in *Galileo* (1943), though deserted by his disciples after his capitulation to the threats of the Inquisition, redeems his physical cowardice by moral bravery, continuing to work on his book in secret and smuggling it out for publication. The prostitute heroine of *The Good Woman of Setzuan* (1943, a satiric and ironic masterpiece) has to invent a wicked *alter ego* to outwit business parasites who prey on her after the gods reward her with gold for virtue; as she is gradually corrupted (the instinct for survival over-riding her moral uprightness), so the gods, too, become subject to human anxiety and despair. *Mother Courage* (1941), an indomitable survivor who triumphs over every kind of adversity including the loss of all her children, is unaware of the devastating irony (shown to the audience: the play is dialectical theatre at its best) that her troubles all stem from an original moral flaw, that she makes her living by selling goods to soldiers of both sides, and so lives by compromise as well as by others' deaths. (The play is an obverse image of Gorki's novel *Mother*, which Brecht adapted for the stage in 1931: there, suffering and deprivation lead to the heroine's moral ennoblement, and she becomes a revolutionary martyr.) *The Caucasian Chalk Circle* (written 1945; first performed, in English, 1948) is a huge (and lumbering) allegory about warfare, justice, personal integrity, roguery – all human life is here. (The play has seventy speaking parts and a dozen locations. Of all Brecht's works it relies most on the ingenuity and collective endeavour of the acting-company. In this, as in everything else, it is his quintessential work.)

If these four plays are Brecht's masterworks, his lesser plays offer similar pleasures and challenges on a smaller scale. The best are *Puntila and Matti* (1948, an updating of the theme of *Don Quixote*), *The Resistible Rise of Arturo Ui* (1941, an allegory about Hitler which draws strength from *Jarry's *Ubu roi*), *The Trial of Joan of Arc at Rouen, 1431* (1952), and *Schweik in the Second World War* (1957, a reworking and extension of Hašek's novel). Of his early plays, thorny with doctrinaire Marxism, the most accessible are *A Man's a Man* (1926) and *St Joan of the Stockyards* (1931): these, more than anything else he wrote, conform to what he called his 'anti-Aristotelian' theory that drama, so far from purging the spectators, should rouse them to political action, make them run from the theatre to change the world. There are also several important adaptations (most written in the 1950s for the Berlin Ensemble): *Antigone, Coriolanus, Edward II, Don Juan, The Recruiting Officer*. He also produced novels and poetry, of less significance: it is his theoretical and practical theatre work, and above all the four great plays, which place him among the dozen or so greatest (as well as most influential) figures in all 20th-century arts.

Brecht's other writings include one film-script (*Hangmen Also Die*, 1942), a large quantity of theoretical writing on drama (a good selection is *Brecht on Theatre*, ed. Willett, 1964), and some poetry, which alone of his work resists translation. Good introduction, making ample use of Brecht's own writings: R. Hayman: *Bertolt Brecht* (1983). Good critical essays: G. Bartram and A. Wayne: *Brecht in Perspective* (1982).

BRENTON, Howard (born 1942)
British playwright

A left-wing playwright of great talent, Brenton has not yet written the play which will clinch his artistic reputation: the *agent provocateur* still outweighs the dramatist. His view of our decadent, raped society is shared by many playwrights of his generation (e.g. *Arden, *Bond, Handke, *Keefe, Poliakoff): they take the generalized peevishness of *Osborne's angry young men and exalt it to a cosmic force. Brenton has focused several plays by projecting his rage and dismay on to historical cult-figures (*Christie in Love*, 1969; *Scott of the Antarctic*, 1971; *Hitler Dances*, 1972; *Bloody Poetry*, 1984, about Shelley and Byron); he also used pre-existing plays as platforms, in *Measure for Measure* (1972) and in *The Churchill Play* (1974), about a performance before visiting dignitaries to a 1984 British concentration camp of the 'Churchill play', a fascinating political variant on *Weiss's *The Marat/Sade*. Brenton's most notorious plays are *Brassneck* (1973, written with David Hare) and *The Romans in Britain* (1980), a sprawling epic whose scope embraces both oppressed Druids and the Irish Problem. It occasioned a summons for the director on the charge of pimping for buggery (when it should, perhaps, have been for boring the public). Brenton's best plays (in the sense that polemic and entertainment work for and not against each other) are *The Churchill Play*, *Epsom Downs* (1977), a Jonsonesque spectacular (shades of *Bartholomew Fair*) seeing the Derby-day crowds as a microcosm of shattered, shabby Britain, *Weapons of Happiness* (1976), a study of workers' revolution in a London factory, seen (unflatteringly) in terms of the 1968 Czech uprising against the Russians, and *The Genius* (1983), a fine, quiet piece about a US mathematician escaping to teach at a British university and getting involved in nuclear protest.

Brenton's other plays include *Wesley* (1970), *Magnificence* (with David Hare, 1973), and a particularly glum depiction of left-wing committee politics, *Thirteenth Night* (1981). He also published a version of *Brecht's *Galileo* which occasioned a lively debate on the ethics of adapting someone else's well-known, well-regarded work.

BRIDIE, James (1888–1951)
British playwright

If *Shaw had never existed, Bridie's star would stand higher than it does. His plays offer the Shavian mixture of sharp characterization, lively incident and garrulous talk, and add to it a dash of that pawky, self-satisfied Scottish directness familiar from the characters in John Buchan's novels. His output was large (over thirty plays) and variable, but his best work is certainly a match for Shaw's. It includes *Tobias and the Angel* (1930), an agreeably ironical reworking of the Book of Tobit in the Apocrypha; *The Anatomist* (1930), subtitled 'a lamentable comedy of Knox, Burke, Hare and the West Port murders' and lively with discussion of medical ethics; *Mr Bolfry* (1943), about two young men who recite a spell one stormy night and raise an urbanely, Shavianly discursive Devil; and two ebullient comedies, *Forrigan Reel* (1944) and *Daphne Laureola* (1949). He is often chided for his Scottishness, and it is true that some of his plays need subtitles for Sassenachs; but his best work is perfectly comprehensible and surefootedly holds the stage.

Bridie's other plays include *A Sleeping Clergyman* (1933) and the biographical study *John Knox* (1949), which uses *Brecht's alienation technique by adding commentary on the action from two 20th-century characters who regard Knox and his contemporaries, in the main action, as ghosts.

BULLINS, Ed (born 1935)
American playwright

Bullins was from 1968 to 1973 a leading figure in the New Lafayette Theater in Harlem, New York, and since then has been producer-director for The Surviving Theater, New York City: professional, experimental, black theatre groups for which most of his forty plays (to date) were originally written. They explore the life of American blacks, particularly in the working-class ghettos of the big cities, and are usually experimental in form and sharp in dialogue, drawing on the rhythms and *argot* of the streets. (It is a tribute to Bullins' writing skill that this does not make them incomprehensible, even to non-American non-blacks: they have been produced with marked success outside the United States.) Typical of these fast, brash plays – more theatrical journalism than literature – are *The Electronic Nigger* (1968), *Goin' a Buffalo* (1969), *The Pig Pen* (1970, one of a group of four polemically anti-white *Dynamite Plays*), and *You Gonna Let Me Take You Out Tonight, Baby* (1972). Apart from these short works (usually one-act), Bullins has written several musical plays (e.g. *Home Party*, 1973; *Home Boy*, 1976) and more ambitious longer works including *The Duplex: A Black Love Fable in Four Movements* (1970). He is working on a cycle of twenty plays depicting the whole experience of American blacks in the 20th century; when completed (half a dozen plays are so far written) this will clearly be a major work. He has been rather grandly compared with Chekhov (for precise nostalgia) and with *O'Neill (for theatrical ambition). He reminds one more of Jonson: for the brilliant use of street-*argot*, for theatrical energy, and for making universal drama out of subject-matter which is hermetic, exclusive and parochial.

In addition to his theatre work, Bullins has produced fiction (*The Hungered One*, short stories, 1971; *The Reluctant Rapist*, a novel, 1973), and edited volumes of plays by himself and others (e.g. *New Plays from the Black Theatre*, 1969; *The New Lafayette Theater Presents*, 1974).

ČAPEK, Karel (1890–1938)
Czech playwright and novelist

As well as a quantity of light, agreeable work (books satirizing national characteristics, e.g. *Letters from England*, 1925; utopian science-fiction, e.g. *The Absolute at Large*, 1922), Čapek wrote several anguished and anxious political novels, reflecting the turbulent history of Czechoslovakian democracy between the two world wars: the best of them is the trilogy *Hordubal* (1933), *Meteor* (1934) and *An Ordinary Life* (1935). He is, however, better known outside Czechoslovakia for three fantastical, absurdist plays written in collaboration with his brother Josef. *R.U.R.* (1921) is about robots, rashly given souls by their maker, who proceed to exterminate humanity. *The Insect Play* (1921) is a comedy projecting the loves, hopes and rivalries of humanity on to insects: its nearest analogue (for quality as well as general atmosphere) is Aristophanes' *Birds*. In *Adam the Creator* (1927) Adam, dissatisfied with God's world, destroys all created beings, whereupon God gives him a lump of clay and invites him to do better. (He fails, and agrees to leave God's world in God's good hands.) Described thus baldly, Čapek's plays sound like simplistic tracts; what gives them life is not their message, but irony, riotous caricature and proliferating incident: like the operas of Janáček (whose *The Makropoulos Affair* is based on a Čapek play), or like Hašek's *The Good Soldier Švejk*, they teem.

Čapek's other works include short stories (*Wayside Crosses*, 1917; *Tales from Two Pockets*, 1929), the novels *Krakatit/An Atomic Fantasy* (1924) and *The War with the Newts* (1937), and the plays *The Outlaw* (1911/1920), a comedy, and *The Mother* (1938), a surrealist tragedy.

CHAYEFSKY, Paddy (born 1923)
American playwright

The transient nature of television drama (in the 1950s, when Chayefsky began, plays were broadcast live, and therefore vanished as soon as they were seen), coupled with its documentary-realist manner (surrealism and

Brechtian techniques rarely work on the small screen; even such compressed works as Strindberg's *Dream Play* and *Beckett's *Eh Joe*, the latter conceived for television, seem overlong and overblown) make writing for television a perilous exercise for the playwright who wants his or her work to last. Chayefsky has surmounted the problem by reworking his best TV scripts for other media and for publication: he thus seems (and perhaps is) a more substantial writer than some of his peers. (The same is true of *Mercer in the UK.) His most lauded play is *Marty* (1953), about an unprepossessing man in search of love; its crisp, 'tape-recorder-ear' (i.e. highly stylized) dialogue style, characteristic of Chayefsky and ideal for the medium, recurs in *Middle of the Night* (1954) and *The Bachelor Party* (1957), and is the main appeal of Chayefsky's stage-play *The Tenth Man* (1959). His other stage-plays aim higher and fall flatter. *The Passion of Josef D* (1964) provides Stalin with a spiritual odyssey; *The Latent Heterosexual* (1968) is about the individual battling the conglomerate state (a favourite Chayefsky theme). In his movie screenplays (his best work), he abandoned television decencies for wisecracking satire. *The Hospital* (1971) is a farce about medical bureaucracy; *Network* (1976), about an insane newscaster promoted by his TV bosses as a species of martyr-saint, definitively bites the hand that once fed Chayefsky. Why is it, even so, that compared to the work of even a mediocre stage dramatist (*Odets, say, who wrote in much the same 'honest' vein as Chayefsky's TV work), all this talented, diverse output seems like yak yak yak?

Chayefsky's other screenplays include *The Goddess* (1958, later adapted for the stage), *Middle of the Night* (1959), *The Americanization of Emily* (1964) and the Ken Russell drug-hallucination film *Altered States* (1978), based on his own novel.

CLAUDEL, Paul: see page 75.

COCTEAU, Jean (1889–1963)
French writer, director and artist

One of the great artistic chameleons of the century, Cocteau started from *Diaghilev's 1909 challenge '*Étonne-moi!*', and later (in *Orpheus*, 1926) announced that the artist's task is 'to throw a bomb'. Perhaps because of this, Anglo-Saxon critics (never fond of explosions) have rarely taken him seriously or to their hearts. Their grumbles were stoked, not quenched, by the fact that in every field Cocteau chose he produced work of outstanding quality. He wrote novels (notably the Gidean *Les Enfants terribles*, 1929, a partly autobiographical, partly fantastical book about adolescents); he wrote librettos for opera (Stravinsky's *Oedipus rex*) and ballet (Satie's *Parade*; Milhaud's *Le Bœuf sur le toit*); he worked in the visual arts (his Picassian drawings and ceramics are particularly good); above all, he wrote and directed several films, three at least of which (*The Blood of a Poet*, 1930; *Beauty and the Beast*, 1945; *Orpheus*, 1950) had wide influence (on New Wave directors in particular) and depict dream-states with a striking mixture of economy, poetry and sensuality.

Cocteau's plays begin with updatings of Greek myth and tragedy. Some (e.g. *Antigone*, 1922) are straightforward adaptations, but others are more personal: *Orpheus* turns the legend of Orpheus and Eurydice into surrealist farce, anticipating *Ionesco's style by thirty years; *The Infernal Machine* (1934) blends the supernatural ingredients of Sophocles' *King Oedipus* with the bustle of contemporary political intrigue, and also makes Oedipus and Jocasta a civilized upper-middle-class couple, exchanging aphorisms while the jaws of the gods' trap close. In the same style are his free version of Shakespeare's *Romeo and Juliet* (1918), from which he claimed to have stripped the exotic flesh (the poetry) in order to reveal the tough skeleton (the story), and *The Knights of the Round Table* (1937), a jolly mixture of Shavian talk and pantomime, complete with magic effects from Merlin. His other plays include *The Human Voice* (1930, the half-hour monologue of a heart-broken woman pleading with her lover on the telephone), *Les Parents terribles* (1938, a boulevard tragedy about incestuous family relationships), a Racinian verse-tragedy called *Renaud and Armide* (1943), and two plays close in style to *Shaw, the 'Ruritanian drama' *The Eagle Has Two Heads* (1946) and the 'play of ideas' *Bacchus* (1951).

It is an inchoate and glittering output, amply satisfying Diaghilev's demand for astonishment. Some of it (the poetry; the ballets; *Romeo and Juliet, The Knights of the Round Table* and *Renaud and Armide*) is merely smart; but a large body of it (the novel *Les Enfants terribles*; the films *Beauty and the Beast* and *Orpheus*; the plays *The Human Voice, The Infernal Machine* and *Les Parents terribles*) produces not only bomb-explosions to startle the complacent, but also that 'rehabilitation of the commonplace' (his phrase) which is an essential element of art.

Good biography: F. Steegmuller: *Cocteau, a Biography* (1970).

COWARD, Noël (1899–1973)
British playwright, actor, composer and director

There was a time when Coward's clipped performances eclipsed his plays. His aphoristic arrogance – St John Ervine called him 'Savonarola in evening dress' – and his apparent view of human beings as the butts of Divine irony, seemed the quintessence of both the dandyish twenties and the cynical thirties; like Wilde, he had 'nothing to declare but his genius' – and who could ask for more? As time passes, however, and the memory of his personality fades, his plays grow stronger. They cover a wide range, from country-house melodrama (*The Vortex*, 1924, a steamy tale of adultery, bitchiness, self-delusion and drug-taking – possibly sending up the glum theories of Pound, Wyndham Lewis and the other Vorticists) and graceful musical comedy (*Bitter Sweet*, 1929) to patriotic dramas such as *Cavalcade* (1931) and *This Happy Breed* (1942), which miraculously stop short of mawkishness – we look for dramatic sleight-of-hand, and find genuine sentiment. Two of his last plays, and most serious, are among his best: *Waiting in the Wings* (1960), set in a rest-home for elderly actresses, and *A Song at Twilight* (1966), about an ageing writer tormented by his homosexual past.

Coward's finest plays are high-society comedies with intricate plots and bejewelled dialogue – his epigrams are as preening as Wilde's, but his characters are better drawn; the wit seems part of what the people are, their own showing-off not the author's. The narcissistic, ignorant Bliss family of *Hay Fever* (1925), the quarrelling lovers of *Private Lives* (1930) and *Design for Living* (1933), the 'court' fawning on the vain playwright-hero of *Present Laughter* (1943) and the dotty spirit-medium and bitchy wives – one living, one dead – of *Blithe Spirit* (1941) are comic characters as robust as any in Goldsmith, say, or Sheridan. Character and dialogue are always in perfect balance; Coward worked in a great tradition, and served it as well as it served him.

Bearing in mind, no doubt, Bertrand Russell's remark that the truth is 'what the police require us to tell', Coward produced two entertaining volumes of autobiography, *Present Indicative* (1937) and *Future Indefinite* (1954). The picture should be rounded out by his *Diaries* (ed. Payn and Morley, 1982), and by Sheridan Morley's less witty but shrewder assessment, *A Talent to Amuse* (1969). Gorgeous picture-book: C. Lesley, G. Payn and S. Morley: *Noël Coward and His Friends* (1979). Superb critical study of the plays: J. Lahr: *Coward the Playwright* (1982).

DIAGHILEV, Sergei (1872–1929)
Russian impresario

Though he himself created nothing, Diaghilev was the greatest single influence on the arts of the 20th century. His genius was for enthusiasm: he had a greedy eagerness for new work of all kinds, and also the knack of enthusing a large, cosmopolitan and fashionable audience. What Diaghilev liked today became inevitably part of tomorrow's European high culture: the avant-garde, if not respectable, was at least *de rigueur*; esoteric artistic scandal became the order of each day. At twenty-seven Diaghilev (with Bakst and Benois) founded a fine-arts magazine, *The World of Art*, which championed the modernism of the time (that is, everything from European *art nouveau*, which it introduced to fashionable St Petersburg, to the first stirrings of impressionism, expressionism and even futurism). Despite his iconoclastic views (or perhaps because of them – St Petersburg society, like many groups of self-conscious art-connoisseurs, loved being outraged), he was appointed director of the Maryinsky Theatre, and spent several years importing interesting European productions and exporting Russian ones (for example Chaliapin's 1908 *Boris Godunov*). In 1909 his ballet company had a triumphant season in Paris, and its success led to the foundation of the Ballets Russes, which was Diaghilev's artistic vehicle, and the cultural hub of Europe, for the next twenty years.

The success of the Ballets Russes, and their lasting effect on the arts, was due in part to the galvanic social effects of the Russian revolution, which scattered an interest in Russian culture (to say nothing of wealthy expatriates to finance it) to every important European town. Wherever the Ballets Russes (or the many talented individuals who struck out from them on their own) went, there were appreciative, knowledgeable and demanding audiences; if the hunger for what Diaghilev provided arose partly from Tsarist nostalgia, the fact that he fed it not with Tsarist art but with novelty guaranteed the spread and success of that novelty everywhere. Acceptability was the result not only of the Russianness of what the Ballets Russes and their attendant art-exhibitions offered, but also of Diaghilev's unique ability to spot creative talent and give it unpredictable but irresistible impetus. (Ballet, with opera one of the most synthetic and multi-faceted of theatre arts, was an ideal vehicle; of all 20th-century artists, only writers owe Diaghilev nothing.)

Diaghilev's instructions to artists ranged from general encouragement (for example his invitation to *Cocteau, '*Étonne-moi!*') to strict prescription (for example his exact direction of Stravinsky's early career). His method was usually to form an 'interesting' creative team, give it a project and await results. A good example of what this process might achieve is *L'Après-midi d'un faune* (1912), whose theme was languorous decadence (the day-dreams of an adolescent faun on a summer afternoon), and which had music by Debussy, décor by Bakst and choreography by *Nijinsky. Other typical collaborative works – all different; one of Diaghilev's most cunning inspirations was never to repeat a theme – were *Petrushka* (1911), the quintessential White Russian ballet, nostalgically evoking the old St Petersburg Easter fair, with music by Stravinsky, décor by Benois and choreography by *Fokine; *Parade* (1917), with a surrealist story by Cocteau, music by Satie, cubist décor by Picasso and choreography by *Massine; and the futurist *Pas d'acier* (1927), set in a factory, with music by Prokofiev, décor by Yakulov and choreography by Massine (whom Diaghilev originally intended to work with the young Meyerhold).

Diaghilev's enormous influence can be seen in a simple list of the great artists who found their feet, or did some of their most striking work, for the Ballets Russes: the painters Derain, Picasso, Chirico and Rouault, the composers Falla, Prokofiev and above all Stravinsky, the dancers/choreographers Fokine, Nijinsky, Massine and *Balanchine. Not only that, but the sixty-eight ballets created for the Ballets Russes include a quantity of masterworks unrivalled by any other company: Diaghilev's artistic legacy – works which would not exist except for him – includes *The Rite of Spring, Jeux, The Three-Cornered Hat, Les Sylphides, Parade, La Boutique fantasque* and *Apollon musagète*. Only the moguls of the great Hollywood film studios have ever rivalled

Diaghilev's sponsorship of talent; only Maecenas (the arts minister of the Roman emperor Augustus) ever equalled him for the quality of work he consistently drew from others.

Good biography: R. Buckle: *Diaghilev* (1981).

DUNCAN, Isadora (1878–1927)
American dancer

At first sight, Duncan looks more like a fashionable fad than a creative artist. Everything about her, from her free-flowing garments and her passionate approval of Bolshevism to her sensational death (strangled by her own scarf during a joy-ride on the Côte d'Azur), reads like the wilder inventions of P. G. Wodehouse or Evelyn Waugh; she was the self-servingly unconventional twenties personified. Her performances too – in a random, inspirational style supposedly re-creating ancient Greek dance: they involved throwing her body about in a sinuous frenzy, ecstatic or brooding as the mood took her – ally her more closely to such other early 20th-century eccentrics as Ellis or Gurdjieff than to such a disciplined, meticulous art-form as ballet.

Nevertheless, and although her own performances now seem ridiculous rather than inspired, she played a vital role in freeing ballet from the rigid formalism, the tyranny of the *maître de danse*, which had by the end of the 19th century begun to dominate or even to transcend its aesthetic qualities. She reasserted the importance of the performer, the creative role of each dancer's individual inspiration. This new libertarianism (artistic democracy replacing the old company hierarchy), allied in particular to the 'loose' company style of the (equally fashionable) Ballets Russes (each dancer in, say, *Polovtsian Dances* or *Petrushka* given a solo identity and a solo role, however brief), became the foundation of all later, 'modern' choreography, from that of *Balanchine to the present avant-garde. Just as the old system ideally suited (and still suits) long-established companies in permanent homes, so the new freedom, with its accent on individual responsibility, was perfect for the many smaller, touring or experimental companies characteristic of this century.

It is unlikely that Duncan herself would have recognized this development as hers. She would probably have regarded as a much more characteristic legacy the eurhythmics or 'music-and-movement' classes in many 1930s–60s schools, or massive celebrations of movement and the beauty of the human body such as those of the 1936 Berlin Olympics or the Spartakiade and other eastern European or Chinese communist displays still given today. To have inspired both these and the work of choreographers like *Graham, Cunningham and Béjart is an extraordinary, bizarre achievement – especially, perhaps, for someone whose only aim was to express her own soul in dance.

Good, sensational biography: A. R. Macdougall: *Isadora – a Revolutionary in Art and Love* (1960); good assessment: V. Seroff: *The Real Isadora* (1971).

DURAS, Marguerite (born 1914)
French dramatist and novelist

Duras's plays are often reworkings of her novels, and vice versa. This means that the novels tend to be largely in dialogue, and to have small casts; the plays tend more towards static conversation or monologue than towards incident. Her style is mannered (reminiscent both of *Beckett and of Ivy Compton-Burnett), and her subject-matter is usually restricted to the relationship of a single couple (e.g. in the film *Une aussi longue absence*, 1961) or to the teasing-out of a single character's state of mind (e.g. that of the old lady in *The Square*, 1965). She is also interested in the elusiveness of language, and in the dramatic presentation of states of mind. All these traits – characteristic preoccupations of the 1950s French New Wave, whether in fiction or the cinema – can be seen at their best in her novel *The Sailor from Gibraltar* (1952) and her script for Resnais's film *Hiroshima mon amour* (1959) – and an objection to both these works, that despite intellectually sophisticated methods, they tell stories of novelettish soft-centredness, can be levelled at much of her output: novels like *The Little Horses of Tarquinia* (1953), or *Moderato cantabile* (1958), for example, are Françoise Sagan made over for the O-Level intellectual set. Her best work is for film and theatre, and its quality comes from the addition to emotional sentimentality and absurd linguistic style of a strengthening exoticism of plot: the atomic-holocaust overtones of *Hiroshima mon amour*, incest (*Days in the Trees*, 1965), gruesome murder (*L'Amante anglaise*, 1968), paranoia (*Susanna Andler*, 1970) or political oppression (*A Man Came to See Me*, 1968, conversations between a Russian dissident and his judge, after the trial). Together with *The Square*~(a convincing piece about loneliness), these are her most persuasive work.

Duras's other novels (or *'textes'* as she prefers to call them) include *The Rapture of Lol V. Stein* (1964), *The Vice-Consul* (1966), *Destroy . . .* (*Détruire, dit-elle*, 1969), *Love* (1971) and *India Song* (1973).

DÜRRENMATT, Friedrich (born 1921)
Swiss playwright and novelist

As well as for plays, Dürrenmatt is known as a painter and as a writer of crime fiction (e.g. *The Quarry*, 1953; *Traps*, 1956; *The Pledge*, 1958). His current project, *Materials*, is a six-volume panorama (part essay, part novel) of the modern world, which he sees as a combination of desolation (where the only enemy of humankind is itself) and labyrinth (where the raging Minotaur waits). This view of sick and sorry society also prevails in his theatre work, though it is generally expressed there in terms of

Absurd comedy. In *Romulus the Great* (1949) the collapse of the Roman empire is a grotesque domestic farce presided over by an unflappable chicken farmer (the emperor Romulus) and a businesslike German invader, a trouser-manufacturer who wants everyone to abandon civilized standards by wearing his products. In *The Marriage of Mr Mississippi* (1952), a couple attempts to live, and to expiate guilt, by rigorous, Old Testament honesty – and fails. *An Angel Comes to Babylon* (1953) begins with God sending a beautiful girl to marry the lowliest man on earth, and ends with the building of the tower of Babel.

Dürrenmatt's best-known plays are *The Visit* (1956), *The Physicists* (1962) and *The Anabaptists* (1968). *The Visit* is about a millionairess who offers her native village a fortune in exchange for a man's life. The villagers, after debating the issue very thoroughly, hunt down and kill the man – and so destroy themselves by greed and guilt. The hero of *The Physicists* retreats to a lunatic asylum rather than divulge scientific knowledge which could destroy the world. Two other 'physicists' (spies, disguised as Newton and Einstein) follow him to change his mind – and the asylum director locks all three of them away as a first step towards world domination. *The Anabaptists* (a reworking of Dürrenmatt's first stage play *Thus It Is Written*, 1947) is about a deluded actor caught up in an even more deluded world of conflicting religious ideologies (the 1533 siege of Catholic Munster by the Anabaptists). The play is a Chinese-box puzzle – who is play-acting and who is real? – and its ultimate point, as often with Dürrenmatt, is that there is no point.

Dürrenmatt's nihilistic content and all-or-nothing farcical style make him an uncomfortable writer. He says, loudly and consistently, that there is nothing to be said, that the world is corrupt beyond hope and that all existential leaps are doomed. Many writers have shared this vision, including such playwrights as Büchner, Wedekind, Strindberg, *Jarry and *Genet. They also share – those five, at least – an unsmiling, take-it-or-leave-it zeal which in Dürrenmatt can alienate audience sympathy. Despite its witty absurdity, his style is as glum as mud: his farces hector when they should beckon and feint when they should stab. His work is like a contest of styles between Aristophanes and *Brecht – and Brechtian earnestness, alas, wins every bout.

Dürrenmatt's other original stage-works include *Frank V* ('a farce with songs'), *Hercules and the Augean Stables* (1963, a mythological burlesque), *The Meteor* (1966), *Portrait of a Planet* (1971), *The Conformer* (1973) and *The Deadline* (1977). He has also written radio plays (including the fine *Incident at Twilight*, 1956), and reworked plays by Shakespeare (*King John* – improved; *Titus Andronicus* – not improved), Strindberg (*The Dance of Death*, appealingly reworked as the comedy *Play Strindberg*, 1969) and Goethe (*Urfaust*). He is a voluminous essayist (see especially *Connections*, 1976, on a journey he made to Israel), and a short-story writer whose best work (e.g. *Die Stadt: Prosa I–IV*, 1952) has yet to be translated.

ELIOT, Thomas Stearns: see page 85.

FO, Dario (born 1926)
Italian playwright, director and actor

The more intellectual and literary our theatre becomes – and, never mind 'high' tragedy and comedy, even such avowedly populist manifestations as agit-prop drama draw on an arsenal of highbrow effects from and allusions to Jacobean drama, miracle plays, Japanese theatre and Aristotle, to say nothing of the writings of Marx, Freud and other polemicists – the more we should be reminded that theatre need not be like that, that except in the last 400 years it was never like that at all. Fo's scripts are not finished works: they are literary skeletons, the armature for performance. On to them he and his company graft topical allusions, improvised insult and repartee, comic tricks and skilled routines (juggling, pratfalling, mime) taken from the circus and the fairground. The performances contain songs, slapstick, dancing and conjuring as well as dramatic action and formal dialogue. What makes them plays instead of variety bills is Fo's original idea, the triggering and binding theme. His ancestors are Aristophanes, court jesters and the pantaloons and columbines of *commedia dell'arte* – and like them, he provides a spectacle which is as satirical as it is extravagant.

Until the political uprisings of 1968 gave his work a committed social and ethical drive, Fo's plays were genial, general satire: titles like *Corpses Disappear and Women Strip* (1958) and *Anyone Who Robs a Foot Is Lucky in Love* (1961) are typical of their cheerful anarchy, and only occasionally – as in *The Lady's To Be Removed* (1967), in which clowns go to heaven and find it a Disneyland stuffed with toys – are the satirical shafts specifically aimed. After 1968, however, political involvement gave Fo's rambling satire wings. *Grand Pantomime with Banners and Small and Medium Puppets* (1969), for example, is a George-and-the-Dragon confrontation between communism, fascism and capitalism, and, because this is a Fo play, capitalism, in the shape of a pretty girl, wins easily. In *The Accidental Death of an Anarchist* (1970), based on a real incident (a death in police custody), such serious themes as police accountability and the clash between left- and right-wing politics are made the targets of a lunatic Punch-and-Judy show. *Mistero buffo* ('Mystery Farce', 1978) is a superb one-man re-creation of medieval mystery plays, culminating in a burlesque (and biliously hilarious) presentation of a luxury-loving, barbaric pope (human decadence personified) coming face to face with Christ in the *Via Dolorosa* procession.

It is absurd to try to describe a Fo spectacular in words. Everything depends on the show itself, on the theatrical impact of costumes, songs, dialogue and performing tricks. He is a lord of misrule, a magician; to see him in action is to understand why Dionysos, god of ecstasy and intoxication, is also the patron of drama. In solemn words, Fo's frivolous farces make points about human nature and human life, and make them just as forcefully as highbrow art. His work is the essence of what theatre is, and does.

In its genial way, Fo's theatre is the living embodiment of the theories of the Russian director Meyerhold (1874–1940), who devised an integrated style of production drawing on circus, cabaret, gymnastics and dance as well as 'standard' actors' skills. Meyerhold's theories are lucidly explained in Braun (ed.), *Meyerhold on Theatre* (1969) – reading which is as stimulating, though hardly as funny, as visiting a performance staged by Fo.

FOKINE, Mikhail (1880–1942)
Russian choreographer

It is a measure of how far 'traditional' ballet has travelled since Fokine's day that his stylistic innovations now seem commonplace. He took the ossified formal style of traditional ballet (based as much on beautiful groupings and tableaux as on actual dance, the soloists like animated, romantic statuary) and without materially altering its basic movements, used it to tell dramatic stories in a wholly dramatic way. His basic principle was that every part of a dancer's body, every movement, should be part of the narrative flow, just like the rhythms of the music; décor, score and choreography were harmoniously linked, none dominant and all serving the same dramatic end. A typical Fokine ballet, showing these principles admirably applied, is *The Dying Swan* (1907), created for Pavlova. As we watch, we are invited to do that rare thing in ballet, suspend disbelief; the dancer's movements do not *symbolize* real actions (as, say, the wing-beatings and pirouettes in Ivanov's *Swan Lake* do), they *represent* them; still photographs of Pavlova as the swan are unsatisfactory, incomplete, random moments snatched from a continuous performance – something rarely the case in 19th-century ballet photos (*Giselle*, for example, photographs like a series of village wedding snaps).

This plasticity is seen at its greatest in Fokine's dazzling series of ballets for *Diaghilev, including *Les Sylphides* (1909), *Sheherazade* (1910), *The Firebird* (1910), *The Spectre of the Rose* (1911), *Petrushka* (1911), *Daphnis and Chloe* (1912) and *The Golden Cockerel* (1914). In each of them forward impetus never flags: the momentum of the music is exactly matched in dance. We are drawn into the story of *Petrushka*, or the single emotional mood of *The Spectre of the Rose*, in a way which makes 'excerpts' (based on the display of dance-steps) impossible or absurd. Ballet, in short, as Fokine claimed it should be, is made primarily a theatrical, dramatic show.

After the First World War, and his break with Diaghilev, Fokine's career declined: he spent the rest of his life as a touring, 'guest' choreographer, and none of his later work matches the brilliance of his seven greatest years. His legacy is, first, the large number of narrative ballets in traditional style, all following his dramatic precepts and showing his influence, which are staple repertoire for most great companies today (the Ashton and Mac-Millan ballets for the British Royal Ballet are good examples), and second, the string of masterpieces he choreographed for Diaghilev, at once the foundation and the ornament of 20th-century ballet style.

FRISCH, Max (born 1911)
Swiss playwright and novelist

In the 1930s Frisch worked as a journalist, in the 1950s as an architect; it was not until the mid-1950s that he began to write full-time. The liberating influence seems to have been not so much his friend *Brecht (on whom see his two fascinating books of *Diaries*, 1950 and 1972) as the arrival of *Ionesco's first play *The Bald Soprano* in the early 1950s. Until then, Frisch's anti-realistic methods (involving his characters, for example, in passing on the stage from 'reality' to 'dream' and back) had been somewhat awkwardly derived from films (especially those of Carné and *Cocteau) and from plays like *Wilder's *Our Town* and *The Skin of Our Teeth*. The awkwardness arose because the styles of these models had been devised for stories of fantasy and humanist optimism, and hardly suited Frisch's harsher visions. In *Santa Cruz* (1946) and *When the War Was Over* (1949) people try to substitute dream-existences for reality, and fail; in the anti-war *Now They're Singing Again* (1945) twenty-one surrealist scenes display the effects of the murders of twenty-one hostages on their families, their killers and their killers' wartime enemies. *The Chinese Wall* (1946) is a complicated anti-war farce in which historical figures (Caesar, Columbus, Don Juan) give evidence in support of a philosopher who wants to prevent the building of the Great Wall of China on the grounds that it will lead inevitably to nuclear war.

The defect of these plays is their lumbering, anecdotal style, which slows them down and hampers allegory with the trappings of realistic characterization and dialogue. Ionesco's influence taught Frisch brevity, the power of the absurd to bypass explanation. In *Count Öderland* (1951), a public prosecutor preparing a case day-dreams that he is a revolutionary hero, a terrorist – and then finds that his dream has actually taken place. (This ending is the Ionescan touch, violently establishing that there is no boundary between fantasy and actuality, truth and dream.) In *Don Juan, or the Love of Geometry* (1953) the hero fakes death at the statue's hands in order to escape from the career the world has forced on him (libertine) to the one he himself prefers (geometrician). Ionesco's influence here allows Frisch to breathe new life into a creaking old story (by making Juan the prey of heartless society, instead of the other way about) and also, in the study of geometry, to find a ludicrous but apt metaphor for the search for order in human life.

These two plays announce the theme of Frisch's major work: the individual's struggle to find his or her own reality, by conforming to or rebelling against the conventions of society. In his first truly great play, *The Fire-Raisers* (1958), the hero Biedermann is a bourgeois industrialist who has lived his life self-righteously according to 'the rules', taking his chances but harming nobody – if an unfortunate employee committed suicide, that was *his* choice; Biedermann's hands are clean. He accepts into his house two thugs who make no secret of their intention to burn it down: his upbringing, his character and the conventions of his society make it impossible for him to believe that anyone can gratuitously do harm to him who has done no harm.

The idea of conformity as a destructive force is also at the heart of Frisch's stage masterpiece, *Andorra* (1961). This tells of a small independent republic threatened by a totalitarian enemy. Gradually the people begin to reveal the same anti-Semitic thought-patterns as their enemy. They turn on the 'hero' (an anti-social outcast named Andri – who in the end turns out not to have been a Jew at all, if that ever mattered), desert or betray him one by one and collaborate in his humiliation and eventual death. The play's dramatic scenes are interspersed with speeches made by each of the main characters directly to the audience, deliberately reminiscent of the defence-speeches at the Nuremberg trials. Once again the Absurd style (Andorra is a 'model' of society, a state consisting of a single town square, at once unique and typical) allows Frisch a bluntness of parable impossible by other means.

Though Frisch wrote several other plays, *The Fire-Raisers* and *Andorra* are his finest theatre work. He reached the same heights twice in novels – as with his plays, perfect marriage of theme and style came late, after several immature works. *I'm Not Stiller* (1954) is about a man falsely imprisoned, accused of being someone else – or is that someone else his real self? (The Pirandellian aspects of this theme were further explored in a less detached, less absurdist – and less good – book, *Let My Name be Gantenbein/A Wilderness of Mirrors*, 1964; absence of irony makes it an anguished, uncomfortable read.) The hero of *Homo faber* (1957), a conforming, neutral man, falls in love with a young girl, and the self-discovery this unlocks destroys him. (The book has a bitter secondary theme based on the myth of Oedipus.) *Montauk* (1976) treats with rueful irony a similar theme: the love of an elderly writer for the young publisher's assistant he meets on a visit to New York.

Frisch was regarded in the 1950s as an interesting but unimportant writer, a pilot fish swimming alongside the absurdist giants. As time has passed, however, and history has begun uneasily to reflect his picture of it, his work has constantly increased its stature: of all post-war European dramatists, he is the one most likely (so far) to be still performed a century from now.

Frisch's other plays include *Biography, a Game* (1967), about a man given the chance to relive his life, and *Triptych* (1978), a sombre vision of the after-life as a series of endless repetitions, like a post-nuclear version of *Sartre's *Huis-clos*. The best of his later novels (as often, on the subject of identity) is *Bluebeard* (1982).

FRY, Christopher (born 1907)
British playwright

In the 1940s and early 1950s (until *Osborne) there was a vogue in the British theatre for verse-drama. It was fuelled by Olivier's Shakespeare films and by post-war performances of medieval mystery plays; its leading authors were Eliot and Fry. Eliot's work, apart from *Murder in the Cathedral*, was always the delight of a highbrow minority; Fry's was widely enjoyed and performed by everyone from prestigious professional companies to groups of village amateurs. The reason is that his themes were comfortable – he was a verse *Rattigan – and his lines were witty and easy on the ear: in fact, apart from occasional luxuriance among the adjectives, you might almost think you were hearing prose. It was perhaps just this middlebrow urbanity that led, as soon as the angry young men arrived, to Fry's almost total eclipse. (He began writing gargantuan screenplays: *Ben Hur*, 1959; *Barabbas*, 1960; *The Bible*, 1964.)

Many of Fry's plays have religious themes. *The Boy with a Cart* (1937) is about St Cuthman; *The Firstborn* (1948) is a study of Moses; *Thor, With Angels* (1948) is a jolly account of the conversion to Christianity of a 6th-century farming family; *A Sleep of Prisoners* (1951) shows four wartime soldiers imprisoned in a church: loss of temper leads to attempted murder, and provokes in them dreams of Cain and Abel, David and Absalom, Abraham and Isaac, and Shadrak, Meshak and Abednego. Interspersed with this religious output (actually more humanist than anglican, as for all its surface Christianity it concerns the reconciliation of individual human beings) are Fry's comedies. These begin with *A Phoenix Too Frequent* (1946), a dramatization of the story of the widow of Ephesus from Petronius's *Satyricon*, and continue with four 'comedies of mood', one for each season of the year: *The Lady's Not for Burning* (1948), about alchemy, witchcraft, belief and love, *Venus Observed* (1950), an *Anouilh-like piece about old age and love, *The Dark is Light Enough* (1954), a 'wintry comedy' about compromise, set in the 1848 Hungarian revolution, and *A Yard of Sun* (1970), about the resolution of the tensions caused in an Italian family by different allegiances in the Second World War. Serious themes treated in a light-hearted way – and with such charming characters! – these are Fry's hallmarks. Not for nothing was he the (brilliant) translator of Anouilh's *Ring Round the Moon* and *Giraudoux's *The Lark* and *Tiger at the Gates*. He never over-reached himself (except perhaps in *Curtmantle*, 1962, a dull political drama about Henry II). If his early stature was exaggerated, his 1950s decline was undeserved: he is too likeable and competent a dramatist to be crushed by fashion's whim.

FUGARD, Athol (born 1932)
South African playwright

Fugard is a talented artist whose work has unhappily been engulfed by politics. His early plays (e.g. *No-Good Friday*, 1959; *The Blood Knot*, 1961; *People Are Living There*, 1969), although not bare of politics, are chiefly studies of well-drawn people at emotional crisis-points (the pressure coming from within, not from outside). *The Blood Knot*, about the tormented relationship of two brothers, is a tragedy worthy of *Miller; in *People Are Living There*, a Pintery tragi-comedy, the landlady of a Johannesburg boarding house, abandoned by her lover, holds a defiant party with her other lodgers to exorcise her pain. With the success of *Boesman and Lena* (1969), however, political anger began to dominate Fugard's work. He became an international spokesman (not least after his passport was withdrawn) against the brutalities of *apartheid*, and his plays, though no less theatrically effective, began to describe the effects of systems on people rather than people themselves. Thus, *Sizwe Bansi Is Dead* (1972), *Statements after an Arrest under the Immorality Act* (1974) and *Dimetos* (1975) are powerful demonstrations of specific suffering and specific injustice – but their chief purpose is political, not theatrical, and they are unlikely to outlive the *apartheid* state they seek to undermine. Fugard's one masterpiece – and his only play satisfactorily to marry politics and dramatics – is *The Island* (1973). In it, two political prisoners rehearse and discuss the Creon/Antigone arguments from Sophocles' *Antigone*, as they prepare to present them before their gaolers – an idea which allows Fugard both an ordered discussion of the prisoner-of-conscience theme and a striking final *coup de théâtre*, one of the most chilling moments in contemporary drama since *Weiss's *The Investigation*.

Fugard's other plays include *Hello and Goodbye* (1965), *Botticelli* (1976), *A Lesson from Aloes* (1980), and the acerbically funny *Master Harold and the Boys* (1982). Fascinating journals, on both politics and drama: M. Benson (ed.): *Athol Fugard: Notebooks 1960–1977* (1984).

GENET, Jean (born 1910)
French playwright and novelist

The events of Genet's early life (he was a tramp, thief, homosexual pimp and prostitute and a convict only paroled from life imprisonment after a 1948 petition by *Sartre, Gide, *Cocteau and others) provided his work with sensational themes which tend to pre-empt discussion of its actual quality. (Discussion is also hampered by the existence of Sartre's extraordinary endorsement *Saint Genet*, 1952. A joke?) His novels (the best are *Our Lady of the Flowers*, 1943; *Querelle de Brest*, 1947, and the fantasy-autobiography *The Thief's Journal*, 1949) discuss obscene and obsessional subject-matter (sexual, scatological and sadistic, often all at once) in exquisite prose – he is an upmarket Henry Miller, the only pornographer who could qualify for the Académie Française. His books leave the reader stunned with admiration, but never moved. His plays belong firmly to Artaud's Theatre of Cruelty: they are sadomasochistic pantomimes of sexual fantasy and degradation. In *The Maids* (1947), 'mistress' and 'maid' take turns to assault and humiliate one another; in *The Balcony* (1957), the clients in a brothel dress as bishops, queens and policemen and play out fantasy-scenes of insult and self-abasement; in *The Blacks* (1958), black actors play out before a white court the sex-murder of a white woman, whose coffined body lies centre-stage; the court joins in the enactment, and its members are bloodily murdered, after which they jump up, tear off their masks and reveal that they are blacks too. *The Screens* (1961) is a violent parable about the Algerian revolt, whose images of buggery and brutality have prevented frequent staging. Despite the claims of Sartre and others, it is hard to believe that all this work has any point at all – unless the brilliant sensuality and bestiality of its assault on the audience and its stylish linguistic prancing offer some kind of catharsis. Is flagellation really fun?

Good introduction, cooler than Sartre's: P. Thody: *Jean Genet, A Critical Appraisal* (1968).

GHELDERODE, Michel de (1898–1962)
Belgian playwright

Ghelderode's work is the nearest modern equivalent to the bustling mystery plays performed on carts in medieval processions – the holiday entertainment painted by Foucquet or Vinckebooms and described by Chaucer and Villon. He takes Biblical, folkloric or chivalric themes and treats them in a fast-moving, open-air style: busy plots, bright characters, colourful costumes and uproarious dialogue. A good example of his religious moralities is *Barabbas* (1928): this focuses the events of Holy Week on the figure of a coarse criminal, a buffoon whose last meeting with Christ is in a fairground overshadowed by Calvary. A good example of Ghelderode's secular work is his 'farce to make you sad' *Pantagleize* (1929): a simple, honest man sets out to say 'Lovely day!' to everyone he meets, unaware that this is the watch-word for a group of anarchists who promptly elect him leader of their revolution. The play is an extravagant charade, full of vaudeville routines, cartoon characters and circus acts, an animated updating of Brueghel's *Flemish Fair*. Superficially, Ghelderode seems like *Fo, but he lacks Fo's satiric impulse, replacing it with folksy geniality or Roman Catholic rigour. There are more than fifty plays, many written for the Flemish Popular Theatre Group; he also wrote picaresque, Rabelaisian novels, short stories, and books on Flemish history and culture.

GIRAUDOUX, Jean (1882–1944)
French playwright

A professional diplomat, Giraudoux had a tremendous stage vogue in France in the 1930s and in the English-speaking world in the 1940s and 1950s, thanks in part to the popularity of his one-time protégé *Anouilh. He wrote fifteen plays, most of them ironical comedies based on well-known stories from the Bible or ancient myth. He reshaped traditional material to suit his own whimsical and sentimental view of human affairs, in which whole empires can be thrown away for the sake of a pretty girl or a witty exit-line. His greatest creations are his heroines, who combine the dewy charm of Anouilh's young girls with the ability of *Shaw's to talk and talk. It is a theatre of bitter-sweet frivolity, well-turned and charming. Among his best plays are three superbly translated by Christopher *Fry (the only translator to match Giraudoux's limpid cadences phrase by elegant phrase): *Judith* (1931, based on the Biblical story of Judith and Holofernes), *Tiger at the Gates/The Trojan War Will Not Take Place* (1935, which does for Troy what Shaw's *Caesar and Cleopatra* did for Egypt) and *Duel of Angels/For Lucrece* (1953, a 19th-century French provincial version of the Rape of Lucretia). Other noteworthy plays are *Amphitryon 38* (1929), about Zeus's courtship of Alcmena, the future mother of Hercules – and one of Giraudoux's most sophisticated and formidable ladies, *Electra* (1937), *Ondine* (1939) and *The Madwoman of Chaillot* (1945), about a miracle-working woman in a romanticized, Tatiesque Paris who uses her magic to stop the city being pulled down to make way for oil-wells. (This play depends on the same view, that the whimsical will inherit the earth, as *Kaufman and Hart's robuster *You Can't Take It with You*.) Giraudoux belongs with Anouilh, Fry and Shaw – and that means that his work is now markedly out of favour. But for all their whimsy, his plays are sturdily made, and may return.

Among Giraudoux's other plays are two set in the 20th century, *Siegfried* (1928), about the effects on a hero of the First World War, and *Intermezzo* (1933), set in a Clochemerlian provincial town afflicted by a ghost (it is a stylistic equivalent to the films of Renoir or even of René Clair). Good introduction: L. LeSage: *Jean Giraudoux: His Life and Works* (1959).

GRAHAM, Martha (born 1894)
American dancer and choreographer

Graham began as a dancer, in the 1920s, founded her own company in 1929, and from then until the mid-1970s was a dominant figure in 20th-century ballet, training or influencing almost every subsequent practitioner of 'modern dance'. One of the foundations of her style was ancient Greek dancing: she started from the same point (freely expressive movement) as *Duncan, but stiffened the performance by a rigorous use of formal steps and by rejecting abstract emotion in favour of the telling in dance of particularly dramatic myths: her most lasting works of this kind are *Cave of the Heart* (1946), on the story of Medea, *Clytemnestra* (1958), *Phaedra* (1962) and *Circe* (1963). Her second main source of inspiration was folk-dance, particularly American. She is, in this, somewhat like a ballet version of the dramatist Paul Eliot *Green: there are few aspects of American life unrepresented in her output, from the grave Shaker wedding-ceremonial of *Appalachian Spring* (1944) to the determined athletics of *Secular Games* (1962).

As Graham grew older, she evolved for her company a distinctive style, blending avant-garde gymnastics with ritual or folk-dance movements (see especially *Acrobats of God*, 1960; *The Archaic Hours*, 1969; *Holy Jungle*, 1974), and for herself and her soloists a freely expressive form of music-theatre, an eclectic mixture of Japanese mime, Duncanish self-expression, traditional ballet positions and Theatre of the Absurd surrealism: her best ballets in this style (highly influential on younger choreographers in the 1970s) are *Deaths and Entrances* (1943), *The Witch of Endor* (1965) and the particularly striking *Lucifer* (1975).

In 1957 Graham made a film about her methods and style, *A Dancer's World*; her later development is charted in *The Notebooks of Martha Graham* (1973).

GRASS, Günter: see page 101.

GREEN, Paul Eliot (1894–1981)
American playwright

Green invented 'symphonic drama': that is, the creation for a specific area of a spectacular pageant about some incident from local history (e.g. the Louisiana Purchase or the ride of Paul Revere), and using, as well as professional and amateur actors, local people, bands, dance-groups, firemen, policemen and anyone else who cared to come along. It is colourful, patchwork-quilt theatre, and the movement has blanketed the United States; Green himself provided scripts for over sixty different areas. The rest of his enormous output includes several musicals (an American version of *Carmen*, 1954; *Johnny Johnson*, 'the biography of a common man', with music by Weill, 1936; *The Stephen Foster Story*, 1959), and a number of sensitive dramas on social issues, of which the best are *In Abraham's Bosom* (1926), about an ambitious, persecuted black teacher in the Deep South, and *The House of Connelly* (1931), about a rich Southern boy who falls in love with the daughter of a poor white tenant farmer: it is a combination of *Romeo and Juliet* and *The Magnificent Ambersons*, and it works. The lasting power of his plays is due partly to the honesty of his themes (he actually is what is claimed for so many, 'close to the people') and partly to the vigour of his writing. His talent is not unlike Mark Twain's: he said things relevant to his audience (though not always comfortable for them), and said them well.

In the late 1970s, the idea of 'symphonic drama' was introduced to the UK by the playwright Ann Jellicoe, best-known for *The Knack* (1961). The British communities chosen were generally in the south of England, and the playwrights involved included Howard Barker, Charles *Wood and Jellicoe herself.

GREENE, Graham: see page 104.

HECHT, Ben (1894–1964) and **MacARTHUR, Charles** (1895–1956)
American playwrights

Both men worked independently (Hecht was a prolific writer of short stories and a polemical Zionist), and with other collaborators; but their best work was done together. They formed a film production company in 1934, and together or separately contributed to the scripts of more than eighty films, ranging from rubbish (*Hallelujah, I'm a Bum*, 1933; *Rasputin and the Empress*, 1933; *Gunga Din*, 1939) to such quality kitsch as *Crime Without Passion* (1934), *Wuthering Heights* (1939) and *Notorious* (1946). Their chief stage legacy, rising well above kitsch, is a pair of sharp farces, notable for satiric bite and fast, wisecracking wit – a foretaste of the films of Preston Sturges or Billy Wilder. *The Front Page* (staged 1928, first filmed 1931) is about the newspaper business, the lengths to which reporters will go to get a scoop including jilting their loved ones and hiding murderers in roll-top desks. *Twentieth Century* (staged 1932, filmed 1934) sends up the theatre business; the part of the maniacal producer, bullying his actress on a train-journey (the play's title is the name of a famous cross-continental train) gave John Barrymore one of his best screen roles.

Good autobiography: B. Hecht: *Gaily, Gaily* (1963). Good biography: B. Hecht: *Charlie: The Improbable Life and Times of Charles MacArthur* (1957).

HELLMAN, Lillian (1905–84)
American playwright and memoirist

A Jewish intellectual from the Deep South, friend of Dorothy Parker and companion of Dashiell Hammett, Hellman was at the centre of left-wing liberalism in the 1930s and 1940s; her courageous stand during the McCarthy hearings was the high point in a distinguished and varied life. Her plays, modelled on the social dramas of Ibsen, depict close-knit societies torn apart by outsize characters or bizarre events: the cat is let out of every bag, each cupboard contains its skeleton and no confrontation fails to end in tears. In *The Children's Hour* (1934), a spiteful child's charge of lesbianism destroys the careers and lives of two innocent schoolmistresses – a prescient plot, foreshadowing McCarthy by a decade. In *The Little Foxes* (1939), the larger-than-life members of a Southern household bicker and snarl over business and family supremacy: Regina, the wife (played in the 1941 film by Bette Davis – and just her part), out-flounces the family and steals the show. (This play influenced almost every subsequent drama about sulky Southerners, from Welles's film *The Magnificent Ambersons* to the hugely successful 1970s television soap opera *Dallas*.) The tendency to melodrama in these plays was sent up by Hellman herself in an uproarious sequel to *The Little Foxes*, *Another Part of the Forest* (1946), about an earlier episode in the life of the same family, a business enterprise in which everyone pretends to be Red Riding Hood and is really a big, bad wolf. Hellman also wrote two well-regarded wartime plays (now dated) about creeping fascism, *Watch on the Rhine* (1941) and *The Searching Wind* (1944), and the book for Bernstein's smash-flop musical *Candide* (1956). Her later plays, *The Autumn Garden* (1951, like *Shaw's *Heartbreak House* set in the Deep South) and *Toys in the Attic* (1960, about the disintegration of a family oppressed by incest-guilt and blackmail), add to the style and themes of her pre-war work a reflectiveness of mood nearer to Chekhov than to Ibsen. Her plays have been over-rated, and (*The Little Foxes* apart) their reputation has not been helped by starry, mediocre film versions. (It is also true that she put more intellectual vigour into life than art.) Her work is understated, effective and personal – a theatrical equivalent, perhaps, of the novels of Carson McCullers or François Mauriac.

As well as plays, Hellman wrote a novella, *Maybe* (1980), and a trilogy of memoirs: *An Unfinished Woman* (1969), *Pentimento* (1973) and *Scoundrel Time* (1976), published together as *Three* (1979). These were generally regarded as both stylish and honest – except by Mary McCarthy, who famously described their author as a phoney whose every word, including 'and' and 'but', was a lie. Good, impartial study: B. F. Dick: *Hellman in Hollywood* (1983).

HOCHHUTH, Rolf (born 1931)
German playwright

With Hochhuth's *The Representative/The Deputy* (1963) the political blockbuster reached the stage. The play lasts for six hours, is in (limp) blank verse, and is an exhaustively documented attack on Pope Pius XXII for conniving at the Nazi persecution of the Jews. What prevents it from being no more than a laborious washing of yesterday's dirty surplices is the blazing passion of the argument: Hochhuth rants, rages, pleads and parodies with the fervour of a latter-day Victor Hugo working for the Red Brigades. It may not be art (unless Wouk's *Exodus* or Haley's *Roots* are art), but for political rhetoric it rivals such screen epics as Griffith's *The Birth of a Nation* or Eisenstein's *October*. Hochhuth has since repeated the trick twice more, in *Soldiers* (1967), about Churchill's decision to bomb Dresden in 1945, and in *Guerillas* (1970), about a 1968 plot for a socialist revolution in the United States. (The latter was followed in 1984 by *Judith*, an exhaustive presentation of the moral arguments for assassinating a US president who authorizes the making, and use, of nerve-gas.) It seems unlikely that his work is anything but Wagnerian cardboard – and drama (especially in such a rhetorical and heroic form) seems a self-defeating vehicle for such fully documented argument. But it still provided a succession of remarkable theatrical shocks – and both *The Birth of a Nation* and *October* were also dismissed in their day as sensational ephemera.

Hochhuth's other plays include *The Midwife* (1972), *Lysistrata and NATO* (1975), and the comparatively restrained *Death of a Hunter* (1977), a monologue supposedly spoken by Hemingway before he shot himself. He has also published a 'documentary novel' modelled on Capote's *In Cold Blood*, *A German Love-Story* (1980).

INGE, William (1913–73)
American playwright

Inge appeared from nowhere in the early 1950s, wrote four plays whose popular success was matched by critical approval, then lapsed into a string of increasingly unconvincing works, chiefly experimental one-acters, in the 1960s. His four good plays show him a stable-companion to *Miller: with compassion, humour and honesty he portrays the lives of inarticulate people caught up and driven by events or feelings they cannot control. *Come Back, Little Sheba* (1950) is about a garrulous, emotionally retarded housewife married to a failed doctor, a drunk; *Picnic* (1953) tells of a destructive angel, Hal, who in a single day wrecks the lives of two young sisters; *Bus Stop* (1955) shows the doomed passion of a cowhand for a seductive showgirl; *The Dark at the Top of the Stairs* (1957) is about one of those self-rending families (bellowing husband, desperate wife, blowsy sister-in-law) beloved by realistic playwrights from Ibsen onwards. All four of these plays were made into excellent films (*Bus Stop* with Marilyn Monroe); but the realism and sunny locations of film dissipate their claustrophobia, which needs a stage 'box set'. Inge lacks the feeling of cosmic inevitability which makes Miller a great tragedian: all his characters' burdens, one feels, would disappear if they were simply rehoused or given a seaside holiday. That they never are is, none the less, a kind of tragedy, and it is certainly true to life: they belong to the drab, trapped America of Hopper's paintings and Updike's *Rabbit* books.

IONESCO, Eugène (born 1912)
Romanian/French playwright

Although he is not himself consistently a great playwright – his vast output includes more than its share of dross – Ionesco was the consistent instigator of greatness in others. His use of the Absurd as a stylistic method ranks, for its liberating effect on other creative artists, with the invention of cubism in painting, modular structure in architecture or the 12-note system in music. Until Ionesco, surrealism was a haphazard, disjointed and static style, pirouetting round its own pointlessness. In fine art (its most widespread manifestation) it led to elaborate jokiness or to a jejune 'philosophy' of bafflement; in music and drama it seldom rose above the level of a revue-sketch or an undergraduate prank. Only in fiction (e.g. in the work of Kafka and Joyce) was it put to serious constructive use, the articulation of a coherent vision – and this, not the 1920s theatrical prancing of *Cocteau and the Dadaists, was Ionesco's starting point. He is above all a philosopher, and his plays are attempts to analyse and describe what he calls 'the void at the centre of things', the precipice over whose brink human beings are always nerving themselves to look. (His views on life and the theatre are set out in *Notes and Counternotes*, 1962, and further explored in Claude Bonnefoy's *Conversations with Eugène Ionesco*, 1966.)

It is the fact that what happens in his plays is an illustration of something else, and not (as with the Dadaists) simply there for its own bright sake, that gives his best work depth. He normally starts from a single illogical idea (e.g. that people are turning into rhinoceroses or can walk on air) and then explores and exploits it with remorseless, hairsplitting French logic: apart from its ludicrous premise, a page of Ionescan dialogue reads like the example from a dissertation on casuistry. In this, he is in the great farce tradition of Labiche or Feydeau, both of whose plays depend as much on logic as on the ludicrous. But he adds a philosophical (sometimes even tragic) dimension by setting his hero at odds with the surrounding world in things which matter: life and death, for example, instead of (as with the farceurs) mistaken identity or loss of dignity. ('Absurd' in this context means 'out of step' or 'alien' as much as 'daft'. The phrase 'theatre of the absurd' comes from Martin Esslin's book *The Theatre of the Absurd*, 1961, essential for understanding the whole genre.) The people in *The Bald Soprano* (1950, Ionesco's first play) struggle to maintain the façade of polite manners (symbolized by their language, a farrago of formal sentences from a language phrasebook) while the world disintegrates around them; in *Rhinoceros* (1960, seen by some as a parable about engulfing totalitarianism) the hero is the outsider, the only person unable to turn into a rhinoceros; in *A Stroll in the Air* (1963) the hero, alone of humankind, can walk on air, but his stroll leads to a nightmare nuclear-devastated landscape which none of his earthbound compatriots can see.

Many contemporary playwrights, especially in the 1950s, eagerly parroted the surrealist elements in Ionesco's plays: the giant, ever-growing corpse in *Amédée* (1954), the lecture given by a dumb orator to an audience of empty chairs in *The Chairs* (1952, a superb play), the masks, gibberish and mechanical strutting of the characters in *Jacques* (1955). This led to disproportionate praise of Ionesco's slighter works, in which the surrealist *donnée* is everything: funny but unprofound one-acters like *The Lesson* (1951), *Maid to Marry* (1953), *Foursome* (1959) and *Madness for Two or More* (1962). Some of his full-length plays (e.g. *Amédée* or *The King Must Die*, 1962) show the same galvanic dazzle: they are sketches extended to fill whole evenings, and nothing else. But in his most elaborate work (*Rhinoceros*; *A Stroll in the Air*; *Hunger and Thirst*, 1966; *The Man with the Luggage*, 1975) he has deeper things to say (chiefly about the alienation of men and women from themselves, the 'absurdity' of the whole human condition). If he is a less great dramatist than some of those he has influenced (e.g. *Beckett or *Frisch), the reason is that even in these more philosophically pretentious plays he is still easily tempted into shallowness, still ready to sacrifice meaning to effect.

Ionesco's finest play, *Tueur sans gages/The Killer* (1959), avoids the trap of facility. Its hero (his frequent hero, the bullied, ineffectual, passionately normal Bérenger) lives in a beautiful city, a le Corbusian *ville radieuse*, whose inhabitants are nevertheless terrified to go outdoors for fear of a mysterious, arbitrary killer. Bérenger refuses to submit to this mass hysteria, finds evidence of the killer's identity – which the police disdain because they are too busy directing traffic to deal with crime – and finally meets the killer (an idiot dwarf), attempts to reason him out of his homicidal mania, fails and agrees to be killed himself. Like many of Ionesco's final acts, the confrontation between Bérenger and the Killer is deep, long – Bérenger's plea is made in a single thirty-minute speech – and somewhat tedious: he tends to construct his plays on a downward progression from eventful first-act bustle to a talky finale, and though this may serve his theme it can under-stimulate his audience. The play (reminiscent of Camus, another influence) is an existentialist parable, futile or profound, depending on your view of Ionesco's nihilistic philosophy, a combination of pointful farce and anguished argument. Above all, it uses to stunning effect the theatre's power to express, instantaneously, by means of single emblematic actions or tableaux, ideas which would require pages of exposition in other forms. Like Beckett's *Waiting for Godot* and Frisch's *Andorra*, it shows the power of the theatre of the absurd to transcend apparently limiting means and produce universal and satisfying plays.

Ionesco's non-dramatic writings include a novel, *The Hermit* (1973), and two autobiographical volumes, *Journal in Crumbs* (1967) and *Present Past, Past Present* (1968). Good, brief introduction: R. Coe: *Ionesco* (1961).

JARRY, Alfred (1873–1907)
French playwright and novelist

The first performance in 1896 of *Ubu roi* was a theatrical scandal on the scale of those caused by Hugo's *Hernani* in 1830 and Stravinsky's *Rite of Spring* in 1913; the play has continued to have scandalous (and not entirely deserved) success ever since. It began life as a schoolboy skit against a despised teacher, and retains a fifteen-year-old's relish for smutty hyperbole. Ubu is a monstrous bourgeois vulgarian, a figure of gargantuan stupidity and scatological excess, the beast in humankind made flesh. He rises to eminence (the throne of Poland) because his vulgarity beggars opposition; in the end his grossness defeats even itself, and he is deposed and overthrown. The play is a disconnected charade – it was conceived for puppets, and first performed by actors aping puppets – and its dislocated style, surrealist language and obsessive naughtiness made it a prime influence on Dadaists, surrealists, and eventually the theatre of the absurd. It has been dwarfed by its own progeny; it is now no more than a historical curiosity, a great-grandparent whose former vigour is difficult to imagine from the husk that remains. Jarry wrote several other scenes from Ubu's life (*Ubu Chained*, 1899; *Cuckold Ubu*, published 1944), and a number of novels exploring in a rambling, Rabelaisian style the surrealist, zen-like philosophy of Pataphysics (his invention, and another game for fifteen-year-olds), which consists largely in providing lunatic-logic answers to unanswerable questions. What *is* the metaphysical potential of a fart . . . ?

Good critical work: R. Shattuck: *The Banquet Years* (1958).

KAISER, Georg (1878–1945)
German playwright

One of the leading expressionist playwrights, Kaiser derived a style from Strindberg and a mood from Munch. The expressionist aim is to strip away the inessentials in human character, unlocking and revealing the true potential of the soul. (That the process more often ends in despair than hope is, perhaps, a statement about the condition of the expressionists rather than about that of humankind. The Hungarian poet Balász wrote the quintessential expressionist drama in his libretto for Bartók's opera *Bluebeard's Castle* (1911). One by one, the doors to Bluebeard's soul are unlocked, and at the end absolute knowledge leaves no other consummation possible but death.) Kaiser's multitudinous plays (over seventy), and especially the trilogy *Coral* (1917), *Gas I* (1918) and *Gas II* (1920), about ambitious and altruistic businessmen whose quest for human happiness leads only to universal war, are both characteristic of their time and prescient allegories. His best-known plays, though still favouring the disjointed structure of expressionist art (dream-logic, not rationality), flesh the characters of nightmare with human personality: his people may be emblems whose philosophical meaning extends far beyond the plot, but they also have a personality and local interest which engages and holds our sympathy. The clerk in *From Morning Till Midnight* (1916), who embezzles money and spends it in a whirligig spree in search of happiness, is fully drawn and engagingly pathetic, a blend of Chaplin's tramp and Kafka's K. *The Burghers of Calais* (1914) deploys its action in set-piece scenes and formal speeches, but the (often anonymous) figures nevertheless have vivacity and vitality: they are as intriguing as (say) the individual cartoon-figures on the Bayeux tapestry. The children lost at sea in *The Raft of the Medusa* (1943), although their plight – there are thirteen on the raft, and one must be killed for survival's sake – is somewhat heavily symbolic of the human predicament, are warmly drawn, particularly the leader Allan, who refuses to consent to murder, is defeated (by sexual awakening) and finally chooses to die at sea rather than be rescued and 'return to accursed life'. (This story was later turned into an expressionist music-drama by Henze.) Kaiser's plays are gloom-and-doom-ridden, in the best expressionist tradition; but for spectators resilient enough to stay the course, they unerringly catch and express 'the ache in things'.

Good introduction: B. J. Kenworthy: *Georg Kaiser* (1957).

KAUFMAN, George (1889–1961) and HART, Moss (1904–61)
American playwrights

Individually or together, Kaufman and Hart were responsible for more than fifty hit Broadway shows in the 1930s, chiefly musicals and musical revues, and including (in Kaufman's case) the Marx Brothers' *The Cocoanuts* (1925) and *Animal Crackers* (1928). (He also wrote their film *A Night at the Opera*, 1935.) Their most enduring work is three classic comedies: *Once in a Lifetime* (1930), *You Can't Take It with You* (1936), and *The Man Who Came to Dinner* (1939). *Once in a Lifetime* shows the Marx-like turning upside-down of a film studio: the more inane the hero's proposals ('use no lights'; 'demolish the building') the more famous and successful he becomes. *You Can't Take It with You* and *The Man Who Came to Dinner* show dotty, self-absorbed and wisecracking families (the farce equivalent of the Glass family in Salinger's stories): the Vanderhofs in *You Can't Take It with You* are devoted to the premise 'all that matters in life is happiness', the polite hosts in *The Man Who Came to Dinner* are terrorized by an egomaniac guest who breaks a leg and refuses to leave for weeks. The specific targets of some of their satire are now forgotten (even Alexander Woollcott, source of the monstrous Sheridan Whiteside in *The Man Who Came to Dinner*, is now more famous in this reincarnation than as himself); but the play's hilarity is undiminished, thanks to careful construction – nothing needs more writing control than cumulative chaos – and above all to the wholeheart-edness of the fun and games. Few laughter-machines have ever run so smoothly on such funny lines.

Autobiography: M. Hart: *Act One* (1959). Good biography: M. Goldstein: *George S. Kaufman, His Life, His Theatre* (1979).

KAZANTZAKIS, Nikos: see page 124.

KEEFE, Barrie (born 1945)
British playwright

Keefe is the most brilliant playwright the 'alternative' British theatre has yet produced. Theatre clubs, pub theatres and theatres upstairs are packed with polemicists; Keefe towers above them all. This is not because his messages are better or louder, but because he has superb stage sense. (He is a punk Ben Jonson.) He attacks the police, national and local government, social workers, the clergy, industrialists, lawyers, school-teachers, the royal family: the scope of his fury is nation-wide. He rants at his 'heroes', too, the dispossessed: they are as venal and as vicious as everybody else. It sounds bilious and negative (and in some plays, e.g. the trilogy *Barbarians*, 1977, is). But his best plays have a dexterity and wit which raise them above spleen: there is, for example, a criticism-defying gusto about *Up the Truncheon* (1977), and *Sus* (1979), which dignifies their theme, the confrontation of angry young people and the police. *Gotcha* (1977), about an unemployed school-leaver savaging those who have failed him, is as nihilistic and ranting a play as *Osborne's Look Back in Anger* – and just as emblematic of its time. *A Mad World, My Masters* (1977), a venomous and hilarious farce depicting everyone in royal-jubilee Britain (from social security scrounger and bought policeman to Harley Street abortionist) as a seedy crook, is a black masterpiece just as good as the Jacobean farce whose name it shares. Are Keefe's searing satires meant to change the world he mocks? If so, like every satirical dramatist since Aristophanes, he fails. Are they meant to entertain? If so, he triumphantly succeeds.

Keefe's other plays include *Bastard Angel* (1980), a satire on the rock-music business which draws strength from raw musical numbers, whose pounding energy elevates otherwise limp material. Rock was also the subject of his seven-hour raucous TV series *No Excuses* (1983), simultaneously excoriating and luxuriating in its subject.

KOPIT, Arthur (born 1938)
American playwright

Kopit takes the healthy buttermilk of the American dream and curdles it. His plays are a stage equivalent of Altman's films, a blend of naturalism and Absurdist farce; but where Altman finally succumbs to the dream (his cowboys, army doctors or middle-class wedding-guests are always in the end on the good folks' side), Kopit usually shows how adherence to stereotype leads to despair and death. (His plays begin as farce, then turn inwards and end up no joke at all.) *The Questioning of Nick* (1957, one of nine plays produced while he was still an undergraduate) is about the corrupting effects of adulation in sport; *The Day the Whores Came Out to Play Tennis* (1965, one of three one-act plays together entitled

Chamber Music) is funny about segregation (whores seek to penetrate a suburban tennis club); *Oh Dad, Poor Dad, Mamma's Hung You in the Closet and I'm Feelin' So Sad* (1960) depicts the American mother as a murderous, all-engulfing monster; *Indians* (1968) is about honest motives leading to genocide (it uses the extermination of the American Indians as a parable for Vietnam); *Wings* (1979) painfully depicts mental illness; *End of the World* (1984) is a backstage black farce about a blocked author researching a play on why the human race is hell-bent on nuclear suicide. In all his plays (more than two dozen) Kopit cares more for ideas than for dramatic technique. His plots (again like Altman's films) tend to sprawl and to trail loose ends; he has none of the formal discipline of, say, *Albee. But this take-it-or-leave-it quality is also, in its way, engaging (and it helps to defuse the stories' hysterical element); in this, as in the panache of his Absurd ideas (though his themes are utterly different), Kopit is *Ionesco's nearest American equivalent.

LAGERKVIST, Pär: see page 127

LAURENTS, Arthur (born 1918)
American playwright

Like the films of Stanley Kramer and the novels of Nevil Shute, Laurents' stage works pose questions about depth and artistic seriousness. He tackles big themes (ghettos, deprivation, psychic misery) in a brisk, *Time*-magazine way which raises the issues and then leaves them pat – as if putting on a serious face were enough to make you serious. His book for *West Side Story* (1957) shows his style at peak: it is an entertaining and 'thoughtful' musical – and who would want a musical to tackle serious themes (such as gang warfare or the conflict of loyalties) in depth? Form is elevated by content and content glamorized by form; there is thesis but no argument. In the same way, *Time of the Cuckoo* (1952, later filmed as *Summertime*) appealingly shows us a spinster warming into love – but its psychological acuteness is undercut by a picture-postcard Venetian setting. (Henry James had no such trouble in *Wings of the Dove*.) *Home of the Brave* (1946), about racial intolerance among soldiers on active service, *The Bird Cage* (1950), an allegory about capitalism and exploitation, and *A Clearing in the Woods* (1957), about mental illness, are similarly decent and respectable plays; *Gypsy* (1959) is a splendid musical; *The Way We Were* (1973), after his own novel, is a stylish and touching film. Laurents' work, in sum, is superbly second-rate – does it matter if, judged by the stern intellectual criteria of the highest art, it delivers less than it promises?

LORCA, Federico García: see page 134

MASSINE, Leonid (1895–1979)
Russian choreographer and teacher

An outstanding dancer, Massine took *Nijinsky's place in the Ballets Russes in 1914, but left the company in 1921 to begin a distinguished freelance life as choreographer and ballet-master. He worked for many leading companies (the Ballets Russes de Monte Carlo; Martha *Graham's company in New York; the Sadler's Wells Ballet in London; Ballet International), for the 1920s Cochran revues in London, and for the British cinema (on the choreography of, among other films, *The Red Shoes*, 1946, and *Tales of Hoffmann*, 1951); he studied American Indian dance, and produced a theoretical guide to ballet choreography. While several of his many ballets were important (*Pulcinella*, 1920; *Nobilissima visione*, 1938; *Labyrinth*, 1941), none is outstanding: his main contributions to the art were to spread the influence (and standards) of the new Russian Ballet throughout the world, and to invent a new ballet form, subsequently imitated everywhere. This was 'symphonic ballet', the interpretation in abstract or loosely plotted dance of existing musical works. Previously, ballet scores had been specially composed, or concert works had been used to accompany stories as if they were ballet scores; Massine's innovation was to reverse this procedure, and make dance serve music. His successes in the genre include *Les Présages* (1933, to Tchaikovsky's fifth symphony), *Choreartium* (1933, to Brahms's fourth symphony), *Seventh Symphony* (1938, to Beethoven) and *Red and Black* (1939, to Shostakovich's first symphony). At first sight, symphonic ballet seems merely the extension to a whole dance company of *Duncan's inspirational movement-to-music; but simply because Massine's works used the whole company, they had to be fully disciplined and choreographed. An element of theme (jealousy; rivalry; joy in nature) was often used to bind together otherwise unrelated dances.

Massine's autobiography, *My Life in Ballet* (1960), because of the nature of his life, gives a wide-ranging and catholic view of the whole field of 20th-century dance; it is also delightfully bitchy.

MAUGHAM, William Somerset: see page 148

MAYAKOVSKY, Vladimir (1893–1930)
Russian playwright, commercial artist and poet

There is a tradition of bitter, satirical farce in Russian literature, best known in the west in Gogol's play *The Inspector General*, the 1934 film *Lieutenant Kije* (for which Prokofiev wrote the music) and the 1970s novels of Zinoviev (especially *The Yawning Heights*). It is at once deprecatory and savage, treating the system not as an object of satire in itself, but as a lunatic symbol of the general lunacy of humankind. (This fact is not always noticed by contemporary western critics of the Soviet system, who fall on it with glee, misreading furious affection for denunciation.) Mayakovsky (whose output also includes hundreds of futuristic posters, hectoring pamphlets and reams of pro-bolshevik propaganda verse: he was a tireless, one-man communist manifesto) wrote a number of plays in this saturnine tradition, of which two, *The Bedbug* (1928) and *The Bathhouse* (1930), have classic status. *The Bathhouse* is hard for non-Russians fully to understand (as the humour of *Diary of a Nobody* escapes non-Britons, Benchley non-Americans). But *The Bedbug* has the power of a universal fable. A man and a bedbug are accidentally frozen in a block of ice in 1928, and thawed out fifty years later (in a soullessly perfect futuristic state, a workers' paradise which is also an anti-human hell). They are placed on exhibition, as examples of two parasites found in the old days, *bedbugus normalis* and *bourgeoisius vulgaris*. Lively, funny dialogue and breadth of attack make this play a worthy stable-mate to *Čapek's *The Insect Play* or René Clair's *À nous la liberté* – and like theirs its intention is geniality rather than to change the world.

Mayakovsky's poetry (generally more serious-minded than his plays) includes *A Cloud in Trousers* (1915), *Man* (1918) and *About That* (1923). The best introduction to his work is the anthology *The Bedbug and Selected Poetry* (1961); a good appraisal of his stature is E. J. Brown: *Mayakovsky, a Poet in the Revolution* (1973).

MERCER, David (1928–80)
British playwright

One of the most talented British television playwrights of the 1960s and 1970s, Mercer had international success with the feature-film version of *Morgan/A Suitable Case for Treatment* (1966). In fact this piece, a black comedy about a crazy painter courting his estranged wife by irrepressible and outrageous behaviour, is rather more flamboyant than the rest of his work. He favoured a quieter exploration of personal tension, sometimes in a relationship (e.g. *Let's Murder Vivaldi*, 1967; *You and Me and Him*, 1973), sometimes in a single hunted or paranoid individual (e.g. *The Bankrupt*, 1972; *Find Me*, 1974). The culmination of this style, and his finest screen work, was his script (about a hallucinating, dying author) for Resnais' film *Providence* (1977). His stage plays (apart from *Ride a Cock Horse*, 1965, a garrulous echo of *Look Back in Anger*) all treat the disintegration of personality or society in the same understated way – which makes for superb shock in *Duck Song* (1974), when the scenery starts to disappear, dead characters come to life again, and collapse and renewal take place, *Ionesco-like, before our eyes. Mercer's best stage plays, combining wry humour and psychological acuteness, are *Flint* (1970), about the November–February relationship between a convention-flouting vicar and a young waif just released from prison, and *After Haggerty* (1970), a triangular relationship between the hero (a despairing drama critic), his boorish salt-of-the-earth father and the ex-girlfriend of the previous owner of the hero's flat (Haggerty), left behind like abandoned luggage.

MILLER, Arthur (born 1915)
American playwright

Miller is regularly described as a latter-day Ibsen, and the implication is that he is a 'social' dramatist, a liberal-realist whose characters are emblems or specific instances of social themes. To an extent this is true: his plays deal with wide issues such as the capitalistic ethic (*All My Sons*, 1947), the banality of evil (*The Crucible*, 1953), or the collapse of radical ideals (*After the Fall*, 1964), and one at least (*Incident at Vichy*, 1964, about political altruism) is as schematic a debate as (say) Ibsen's *The Pillars of the Community* or *An Enemy of the People* (of which Miller made an English version in 1950). But his work is also close (far closer) to Ibsen's plays of personal disintegration (*Hedda Gabler*, *The Wild Duck*, *The Woman from the Sea*): he likes to show individuals striving to come to terms with themselves or with outside pressures, and failing because of flaws in their own nature. In *All My Sons*, for example, a father and his son are locked in ideological combat: the father's business ambition has led him to sell defective aircraft parts, and when his son convinces him that this is an immoral and unjustified act, the edifice of his being collapses and he kills himself. (The play has thematic parallels with Ibsen's *The Master-Builder.*) In *A View from the Bridge* (1955), the pressure on the hero, Eddie, from outside – conflict between the old Sicilian family moral hierarchy and the more hedonistic ethic of the America to which the characters have emigrated – is matched by pressure from within (incestuous longing for his niece), until he is destroyed. For all his inarticulacy and 'low' status (he is an illiterate longshoreman), Eddie is an Aristotelian tragic hero, and his inexorable progress towards self-discovery and fall is moving and 'truthful' (that is, relatable to real emotion and experience) in the approved Aristotelian way.

Another lesson learned from Ibsen is powerful theatricality. 'Social' plays and 'problem' plays can be talky; Miller avoids this by the use of heightened naturalistic language (its rhythms as powerfully and purposefully organized as verse), and by the use of stage metaphors as striking as they are precise (Eddie desperately demanding his 'name'; the possession-sequences in *The Crucible*; the proffered handshake and its spurning in *Death of a Salesman*, 1949). The plays' rhetoric gives domestic characters and incidents wider symbolic meaning; but Miller also has an awareness of the drabness and ordinariness of tragedy. We are racked in *Death of a Salesman* by Willy's recognition of his own failure and by his ambition for his son's happiness – but also by the simple mess of non-communication between father, mother and son; *The Crucible* deals with witchcraft, bigotry and superstition (it is famously a parable about

McCarthyism) – but it is also about the disintegration of that skein of small compromises which binds everyday relationships; *The Price* (1968) deals with public duty – and its heroes are appropriately a policeman and a doctor – but its vital theme is the enabling banalities of their relationship with each other and with their father (one of Miller's most robust and comic parts).

Miller's output is small – the half-dozen plays discussed here are the bulk of it – but the single-mindedness and distinction of his work place him among the major dramatists. His quality is due to brevity (every line or move has exact purpose), to linguistic power (only *Osborne, of recent dramatists, can match his rhetoric), and to his over-riding theme, which is (as he himself wrote) 'to discover our own relationship to evil, its reflection of ourselves': a demonstration of how, even in mundane circumstances, original sin persists.

Miller's other plays include the *Riceian, *Greenian 'tapestry-play' *The American Clock* (1980), a sociological saga of a young man growing up in Brooklyn during the Depression. (Like *The Price*, it is partly autobiographical.) His non-dramatic works include a novel about anti-Semitism (*Focus*, 1945), short stories (*I Don't Need You Any More*, 1968), the script for the film *Misfits* (1961), which starred his then wife Marilyn Monroe (also the subject of his play *After the Fall*), and two books of travel journalism illustrated with photographs by his second wife Inge Morath and consciously modelled on Agee's and Walker's 1941 volume *Let Us Now Praise Famous Men* (*In Russia*, 1969; *In the Country*, 1977). Good surveys: D. Welland: *Miller: A Study of His Plays* (1979); N. Carson: *Arthur Miller* (1982).

MONTHERLANT, Henri de (1896–1972)
French playwright and novelist

Although he wrote plays from adolescence onwards, Montherlant's first successes were as a novelist: it was not until 1942, with the first professional production of *The Dead Queen*, that he turned conclusively to drama. There is thus something of a dichotomy in his work. His novels (whose tone is reminiscent of those of Gide) are about the balance in the human character between idealistic hardness (a function of mind) and tenderness (a function of emotion). Like Hemingway, Montherlant was convinced that physical self-testing was the way to express, and to reach, people's essence; like Hemingway, he used sport as a metaphor for the human quest. (His novel *The Bullfighters*, 1927, is as fine on this subject as Hemingway's *Death in the Afternoon*.) But he was more aware than Hemingway that the ideal is as often missed as reached, and his best novels are studies of people who have, because of such character-weaknesses as tenderness or compromise, failed to maintain that zen-like level of self-denial which leads to austere content. *The Bachelors* (1934) is about two old men looking wistfully back at their lives; *The Young Girls* (a tetralogy, 1936–9) is about fiction (its hero is a racked novelist) and love; *Chaos and Night* (1963), about an exiled Spanish revolutionary in old age, deals with political idealism and its withering.

There are several other novels, all concerning Montherlant's themes that human beings are failed angels, and that our failure, because it is caused by positive forces such as love and loyalty, is an ennobling flaw. In his thirteen plays the theme is the same but the tone more tragic. He is a Sophoclean dramatist: his plays show characters whose passionate idealism leads them to irreversible crisis and suffering; their eventual 'recognition' of the 'tragic flaw' in their own natures (usually inflexibility) is the subject-matter of each plot. (The terms suggest a schematic, Aristotelian structure; but, again like Sophocles, Montherlant uses a mechanical framework not for its own sake but as the basis for a much more compassionate examination of the quality of humanity, the frailty which is also strength.) Many of the plays are based on historical characters and events (but shaped and reordered to suit Montherlant's underlying themes, as happens in the work of Racine and Shakespeare – or in the librettos of Verdi's operas, a strikingly similar if simpler counterpart to his work). In *The Dead Queen* (1942), a renaissance king of Portugal, finding that his son has married in secret and is thus unavailable to serve the state's dynastic needs, imprisons him 'for mediocrity'; in *The Master of Santiago* (1947), a daughter sacrifices her own happiness (a long-desired marriage) out of duty to her father, and her father, Abraham-like, accepts her renunciation of happiness as a mirror of his own obedience to God; *Port Royal* (1954), a full-length play in one packed act, shows the noble suffering of a group of nuns who defy both religious and political authority – it is a heroic reversal of the situation in Huxley's *The Devils of Loudun*, and a stunning aural and visual experience in the theatre.

Montherlant's most famous play (not however his best, which is *Port Royal*) is *The City Whose Prince Is a Child* (1951). This is set in a Roman Catholic boarding-school, and is about the conflict of love and duty. A priest, concerned at the relationship between his fourteen-year-old protégé and an older boy, persuades the older boy to replace carnal affection for the younger with a stern educational relationship (based on those between youths and boys in ancient Sparta). The boys meet to settle their new relationship, are discovered and are expelled – to the total spiritual collapse of the priest, who realizes that his own action was motivated by sexual jealousy as well as by pastoral concern. The play's demonstration of the conflict between morality and hedonism is characteristic of Montherlant's work, and it is a conflict also apparent in his style.

Montherlant's other plays include *Nobody's Child* (1943), *Malatesta* (1943), *The Girls We Embrace* (1950), *The Spanish Cardinal* (1960), and *The Civil War* (1965), set in ancient Rome. Good critical introduction: J. Cruickshank: *Montherlant* (1964).

NICHOLS, Peter (born 1927)
British playwright

The nature and style of Nichols's work are aptly summed up in his subtitle to *Forget-Me-Not Lane* (1971): 'Humorous, serious and dramatic selections'. This suggests the kind of variety bill mounted in 1930s and 1940s music-halls: slapstick, garish, jingoistic and smutty, a discontinuous flash-bang-wallop of a show. Use this style with irony, bind with black-comedy plots and add scenes of domestic seriousness, and you have the quintessential Nichols play. Thus, his first success, *A Day in the Death of Joe Egg* (1967), presents the birth and death of a brain-damaged child, 'a human parsnip', as a charade full of songs, tap-dance routines and humorous sketches interspersed with touching dialogue. The result is a deft balance between the hilarious and the pathetic, winsomely out-rageous – and this is also the hallmark of *The National Health* (1969), a parable about individuality and the institution set in a hospital ward (it is *Carry On Doctor* reworked by Kafka), and of *Born in the Gardens* (1980), about the attempts by a go-ahead progressive couple to prise their stick-in-the-mud brother and mother out of the genteel emptiness of their life. (It is a fable about decaying Britain.) In other plays, style outweighs message: the parody makes the play. *Forget-Me-Not Lane* juxtaposes the absurdities of day-to-day family life in the Second World War with the sour effects of that upbringing on the characters a generation later; but the play lives more by its evocation of local beauty contests, radio shows, rationing and the *Daily Mirror* than by depth of theme. *Privates on Parade* (1977) is a bitchy backstage comedy set in an army concert party in Singapore in 1948. *Chez nous* (1974) and *Passion Play* (1981), Nichols's best plays, are black parodies of the 'well-made' West End comedy of the 1950s, respectively about a 'delightful' family and their house-guests in a tax-exile Dordogne farmhouse and the evasions and deceits of a homely, middle-class marriage. Like all Nichols's plays, they salt their laughter sufficiently to make serious points denied to their stylistic models (and *Passion Play* physically embodies the couple's wish-fulfilment selves onstage, to caustic effect); but they also depend on those models for vitality.

Nichols's other works include the book for a Victorian musical about drug-smuggling, *Poppy* (1982), a less successful mixture of romp and seriousness (because of its preachy tone) than some of his plays. Sweet-and-sour autobiography (he does *hate* success): *Feeling You're Behind* (1984).

NIJINSKY, Vaslav (1890–1950)
Russian dancer

Nijinsky's career was as short-lived as it was dazzling. He spent five seasons (1907–11) as leading male dancer at the Maryinsky Ballet, and three seasons with *Diaghilev's Ballets Russes. He quarrelled with Diaghilev in 1914, was interned in Hungary at the outbreak of the First World War, and in 1916 began to show signs of the mental illness which was to keep him dismally in asylums for the rest of his life. He choreographed three new ballets (*L'Après-midi d'un faune*, 1912; *Jeux*, 1913; *The Rite of Spring*, 1913), and danced in a dozen more (notably *Sheherazade*, 1910, *The Spectre of the Rose*, 1911, and *Petrushka*, 1911, all created for him). But his greatest and most lasting influence was on traditional ballet, and in particular on the status of the leading male. In earlier choreography, from Bournonville (early 19th century) onwards, the chief emphasis had been on the prima ballerina; the male dancer's function was to support her and to stand meaningfully still, tasks for which he was rewarded by occasional frenzied solos involving leaps and *entrechats* (scissoring the legs quickly while jumping in the air) whose connection with the plot or the character he played was, to say the least, tenuous. (Male roles of typical pallidity can still be seen in 'original-choreography' versions of *Giselle*, *Coppélia* or *The Nutcracker*.) Nijinsky's dancing was so electrifying and acrobatic (he could do eight *entrechats*, for example, sometimes even ten, to other dancers' six; his legendary final leap in *The Spectre of the Rose* appeared to carry him halfway across the stage) that traditional ballets had, one after another, to be re-choreographed to contain him. The change of emphasis this gave to both dance-style and plot (and its effect on the relative status of male and female ballet stars offstage) has made its mark on all 'traditional' ballet companies since. Star ballerinas have tended to be demure and graceful (Karsavina; Fonteyn) or bonily assertive (*Graham), and male stars have ruled the roost: good contemporary examples are Nureyev and Baryshnikov, a large part of whose choreographic careers has been spent reworking standard roles to suit their own neo-Nijinskian styles.

Nijinsky's influence was not confined to dance. His enormous popular success, and the aggressive masculinity of his performances (helped on occasion – for example in the 1911 Maryinsky *Giselle* or the 1912 Paris *L'Après-midi d'un faune* – by scandalously revealing costumes) routed the prevailing view that male dancers were effeminate or degenerate, and made overt male eroticism in the performing arts possible if not respectable.

Good biography, R. Buckle: *Nijinsky* (1971). Nijinsky's wife Romola published a biography in two volumes, *Nijinsky* (1933), excellent on the Ballets Russes, reticent on Diaghilev's relationship with her husband, and gushing about Romola herself, and the painful *The Last Years of Nijinsky* (1952). Nijinsky's own *Journals* (1952) are a fascinating revelation of his mind: he felt himself (as Colin Wilson pointed out in *The Outsider*) utterly alienated from his world, his century and even his own creative art.

O'CASEY, Sean (1880–1964)
Irish playwright

The roots of O'Casey's art are his 'Dickensian' slum childhood and his decades of left-wing political activism among and on behalf of the Dublin poor. Even in his weakest plays – two-thirds of his output is repetitious blarney – his documentarist's eye for detail and his compassion for the downtrodden elevate tawdry material. (Even a weak one-acter like *Hall of Healing*, 1951, a slice of suffering in a seedy doctor's waiting-room, invests poverty with a pain and dignity which are moving and never sentimental.) He adds to this a poetry of language which seems effortless (in the same way as Dylan Thomas's Welsh cadences), but is actually the result of cunning rhythmic organization: for all their rich imagery, O'Casey's lines are economical, swift and calculated for exact effect.

Compassion, craftsmanship and greatness of theme coincided in the three masterworks O'Casey wrote for the Abbey Theatre, Dublin: *The Shadow of a Gunman* (1923), *Juno and the Paycock* (1924) and *The Plough and the Stars* (1926). In these, precise evocation of impoverished daily life, and lively characterization (not to mention character-inter-action: Juno, for example, is defined as a person as much by her husband's feckless optimism as he is by her heroic determination) are given the dimension of tragedy by dark political themes. Each of the plays contains innocent or weak-willed people swept to their deaths by politics they do not understand: Minnie in *The Shadow of a Gunman* protects the man she loves; Johnny in *Juno and the Paycock* is trapped into informing against his comrades; Bessie in *The Plough and the Stars* dies trying to protect the innocent wife of a political opponent. The pull is always between family loyalty (or loyalty to the larger family of the tenement) and loyalty to cause. Peasant fatalism – husbands, sons and lovers may die, but life goes on – is presented as a heroic force, the substance of life.

It may be, even so, that O'Casey found the Irish troubles a limiting theme. (Or perhaps, in the three Abbey Theatre plays, he said all there was to say.) Certainly in his subsequent work he tried to broaden his subject-matter, and the result was a loss of focus, a lapse into brilliance without distinction. *The Silver Tassie* (1929), rejected by the Abbey Theatre, thus occasioning O'Casey's self-imposed exile in England, is a denunciation of the waste of life in the First World War, and its crippled hero and surrealist second act tend to alienate as many audiences as they enthrall. (We have also had nastier wars, and tougher plays about war's nastiness, since 1929.) *Purple Dust* (written 1940; first performed 1956) is a broguish farce about two vain Englishmen trying to renovate an Irish castle, and being gulled and rooked by jolly Irish workmen – Barry Fitzgerald at his most leprechaunish would have been its ideal star. *Cock-a-Doodle-Dandy* (1949), another farcical comedy, is about faith in demons and spirits as a cultural necessity – and once again a serious point gets lost in Ealing Comedy Oirishness.

In his later years O'Casey attacked the gloom and nihilism of modern theatre (especially that of *Beckett and *Osborne); but the empty Dionysian celebrations in his own late plays are hardly a cogent alternative. Far better, as he did in his three great plays, to face the world's darkness with human warmth, and so make light of it.

In addition to plays O'Casey published a book of stories and essays (*Blasts and Benedictions*, 1967), and an autobiography, rich in theatrical and political polemic, which originally appeared in six volumes, but was republished as one fat book, *Mirror in My House*, in 1964. Good critical study: D. Krause: *O'Casey: The Man and His Work* (1962). B. Atkinson (ed.): *Sean O'Casey: From Times Past* (1983) contains delightful essays and memoirs, particularly revealing of O'Casey's late years. Acerbic, brief life: J. Simmons: *Sean O'Casey* (1984).

ODETS, Clifford (1906–63)
American playwright

Such was the power, once, of Odets' writing that he could make even a Broadway audience believe in the Marxist apocalypse: at the end of *Waiting for Lefty* (1935, a play about a union meeting), we are told, they jumped to their feet and joined the characters in shouting 'Strike!' New Deal optimism, the notion that however awful the human predicament we still had the guts and idealism to pull ourselves through, was the guiding-force of *Awake and Sing* (1935), about a young man in a poor family roused by his grandfather to make his life's struggle revolutionary not materialist, *Golden Boy* (1937) – is the hero to find happiness as violinist or boxer? – and *The Country Girl/Winter Journey* (1950), about an alcoholic actor clawing his way back to dry success. These are the best of Odets' stage plays. He also wrote a number of successful films (*The General Died at Dawn*, 1936; *None But the Lonely Heart*, 1944; *Sweet Smell of Success*, 1957) – and the cinema seems by hindsight the right vehicle for his combination of social-realism and somewhat wooden parable. Out of his experience of Hollywood, and with the stormclouds of McCarthyism gathering round him (he was an ex-communist), he wrote his masterpiece, the one play apart from *The Country Girl* that is likely to survive. This is *The Big Knife* (1949, filmed 1955): the study of an honest man (a film star) at odds with the system (a corrupt film studio), it is at once a pointful allegory about bourgeois society and a backstage drama to rival Wilder's *Sunset Boulevard* or Mankiewicz's *All About Eve*.

Good introduction: H. Cantor: *Odets, Playwright-Poet* (1978).

O'NEILL, Eugene (1888–1953)
American playwright

The son of an actor-manager, O'Neill spent his childhood watching his father ranting and roaring round the country in the melodrama *The*

Count of Monte Cristo; later, as a seaman and in a tuberculosis sanatorium, he read Nietzsche, Strindberg and the Greek tragedians. So his work was formed: powerful stage hokum on the one hand and symbolic solemnity on the other. His first plays were those of a stage Joseph Conrad, depicting humanity as an ill-assorted group of people on a long sea-voyage; the best of them are the tetralogy of one-acters *S.S. Glencairn* (1918), and the sea is also a crucial image in *Anna Christie* (1921, later memorably but over-glamorously filmed with Garbo), an Ibsenish piece about a prostitute 'conquered and purified' by the sea.

In the 1920s O'Neill's work became even more heavily symbolic, and often experimental and tortuous into the bargain. *The Emperor Jones* (1920), about the journey to self-knowledge and death of an escaped convict who has made himself emperor of a superstition-ridden West Indian island, contains six dream-scenes showing visions of the hero's past. In *The Hairy Ape* (1922) a sensitive giant of a man, cast out from a society which finds his appearance bestial, steps into a gorilla-cage and is crushed to death. *The Great God Brown* (1926) is about identity, and involves the use of masks and impersonation. (Is Dion really dead if Brown impersonates him?) *Marco Millions* (1928) depicts Marco Polo as a cross between shrewd businessman and mountebank. And in the finest of these plays, O'Neill combined the style and structure of Greek tragedy with contemporary themes, and produced work as schematic and as powerful as his models. *Desire Under the Elms* (1924) transposes the story of Phaedra and Hippolytus (tyrant husband, second wife and the son she tragically falls in love with) to an 1850s New England puritan setting; the trilogy *Mourning Becomes Electra* (1931) is Aeschylus's *Oresteia* (about the net of guilt and revenge which traps a family, corrupting generation after generation) set in the American Deep South. In the same way, *Strange Interlude* (1928), also about the past haunting the present, is in part an extension of themes from Ibsen's *A Doll's House* (itself influenced by Greek tragedy).

After these great plays – and several lesser ones, including the charming, if uncharacteristic, comedy *Ah! Wilderness!* (1933) – O'Neill's ill-health caused several years of silence. In the late 1930s, however, he resumed work, and three at least of his late plays are among his masterworks. *The Iceman Cometh* (written 1939; first performed 1946) is a rambling, gloomy and compelling reflection on the vanity of hope. In a seedy flophouse, derelicts and failures talk of their hopes and illusions as they wait for – what? Death? The iceman? The play is pretentious, bombastic and brilliant, the climax of O'Neill's lifelong obsession with life as an elusive charade. (However, perhaps as a warning against over-solemnity, he once explained the title as a combining of the Biblical 'Death cometh' and the old husband-wife routine 'Has the iceman come yet, dear?' 'No dear, but he's panting hard.') *Long Day's Journey into Night* (written 1941; first performed 1956), again about the past corrupting the present, draws on O'Neill's own relationship with his father. It observes the unities, showing one day in the life of one family in a single set. It also deals schematically with relationships, one at a time, in the manner of Sophoclean tragedy. Its story is lurid – but for all that, strictly autobiographical (ageing actor-star father neglects family; wife is a drug addict, elder son a wastrel, younger son tubercular; all the hope they have is each other, and they have no hope) – but the intensity of the characterization and O'Neill's over-riding metaphor of the journey through life (no longer a sea-voyage, but just getting through one day at home) make it a draining though exhilarating theatrical experience. *A Touch of the Poet* (1957), the first part of an unfinished eleven-play cycle (on how money corrupts successive generations of a New England family), centres on the marriage between the daughter of an Irish immigrant and the dreamy son of an old landed family. Dreams and delusions are once again the enabling factor in the characters' lives – the boy's mother even has a fantasy-life as mistress of the king of France – and the action is therefore simultaneously about awakening and compromise.

O'Neill is a gigantic playwright, and his dramas are huge in every sense: big themes, outsize characters, inflated language and enormous length. He is in the league of heavyweight novelists like Proust or Mann, and like them he yields nothing to the sipper – the only way to approach him is to risk indigestion and gulp him whole.

Good biography: A. and B. Gelb: *O'Neill* (1962, rev. 1973). Good critical survey: J. J. Raleigh: *The Plays of O'Neill* (1965). Good brief introduction: N. Berlin: *Eugene O'Neill* (1982).

ORTON, Joe (1933–67)
British playwright

Orton's sordid murder (he was bludgeoned to death by his boy-friend) cut short the career of the finest writer of English high farce since *Travers. Travers's shocking themes (lust, greed, deceit) were supplied in Orton with 1960s black-comedy equivalents (transvestism, corpse-snatching, voyeur-ism and murder), but his insouciant approach and the dance of his language are in the truest Travers style. (A Travers character, thrown out of the house, says with Wodehousian detachment and gusto: 'I annoyed him; so just after I'd gone to bed he came up and took me in his arms and ran me out. Ph't'; an Orton detective, listening to the alibis of two young men, says: 'What a coincidence. Don't you agree? Two young men who know each other very well, spend their nights in separate beds. Asleep. It sounds highly unlikely to me.' In each case, the self-absorption of the speaker and the heightened banality of the language work for artificiality and hilarity.) Apart from minor work (television plays and the double bill *Crimes of Passion*, 1967), Orton wrote three major plays. *Entertaining Mr Sloane* (1964) is about a middle-aged couple vying for the affections of their young lodger, who may or may not also be a murderer. *Loot* (1966), about vast amounts of stolen money hidden in the coffin of the hero's mother, is a dazzling exits-and-entrances farce complete with vanishing corpse, sadistic detective and a real British-farce pair of leading men (though Orton's are cheerfully vicious instead of the standard scheming silly asses). *What the Butler Saw* (1969) starts with a psychoanalyst inviting a prospective secretary to strip naked, progresses to the arrival of his wife and her handsome blackmailer, and leads inexorably to a Gordian knot of intrigue and accusation only cut by the *deux-ex-machina* arrival – he climbs down a rope-ladder – of Police Sergeant Match.

As well as plays, Orton published a surreal, deadpan novel, *Head to Toe* (1971), a counterpart to West's *The Dream Life of Balso Snell*: a man is trapped in and on a 100-foot-high human body. Good biography: J. Lahr: *Prick Up Your Ears* (1978).

OSBORNE, John (born 1929)
British playwright

With the first performance of *Look Back in Anger* (1956), the British theatre was officially declared either dead or to have come of age. What was dead was gentility (tea-cups rattling among the plush at matinées of well-made plays); but the age the theatre had come of was adolescence, not maturity. Jimmy Porter, the play's ranting hero (and its only substantial character: the others are paper dolls), hates everything – friends, parents, upbringing, himself – and says so with a vigour and at a length which make Holden Caulfield (in Salinger's novel *Catcher in the Rye*) seem reticent. The tirades we were used to in the theatre at the time were either Shavian urbanity or grand-guignol hysteria; Osborne borrowed a stance (and a rhetorical style) from a much grander model, Shakespeare's Edmund, and gave it the accents of the discontented youth of post-Festival-of-Britain coffee-bars.

His problem ever since – and to some extent the theatre's problem too, as snappish nihilism moved from vogue to cliché to prescribed stance – has been dwindling energy. To depict frustrated people railing against society is one thing; to infuse them with theatrical vigour without fighting the play's theme is quite another. In *The Entertainer* (1957), Osborne gave his hero (a music-hall comedian) the galvanic life of old vaudeville routines – the variety bill has always been a fertile source for British dramatists – and produced both a lively style and a convincing metaphor for sour society. (He was also greatly helped by Olivier's performance in the leading role, as he was by Finney's in *Luther*, 1961, which drew its rhetorical style from Luther's own writings and its metaphor-of-life from the emptiness of Luther's chamber-pot.) But generally in the 1960s his work, though lively, was directionless and slight: adaptations of Lope de Vega's *A Bond Honoured*, Ibsen's *Hedda Gabler* and Shakespeare's *Coriolanus*; the screenplay for *Tom Jones*; sensationalist – then! – dramas about knicker-fetishism (*Under Plain Cover*, 1962) and homosexuality (*A Patriot for Me*, 1965).

The exception to this running on the spot was *Inadmissible Evidence*

(1964), widely regarded then and since as Osborne's best play. Like *Look Back in Anger* and *The Entertainer* it is basically a punctuated monologue, a cosmic grumble. Its central character, a solicitor whose alienation from the world (or the world's from him) has brought him to the edge of breakdown, talks as compulsively to the audience (or to himself) as a patient to a psychiatrist – but where a psychiatrist might respond with help, we offer only applause, and he is left at the end alone and suffering still. The binding agents in the play, serving the same stylistic function as music-hall in *The Entertainer*, are legal ritual and language – and its power, as with all Osborne's work, lies in the extraordinary rhetorical hold the chief character has over the audience, partly feline (playing with it) and partly sexual (wooing it).

Since *Inadmissible Evidence*, Osborne has tended brilliantly to repeat himself. *Time Present* (1968), unusually, has for its central role a female bitch (a sharp-tongued, unhappy actress), but its disgust is otherwise an updating of that in *Look Back in Anger*. *A Hotel in Amsterdam* (1968) is an elegiac, old-fashioned play about the effect of an absent, bullying friend on a group of six characters gathered in a hotel. It was taken at the time to be a parable for the middle class waiting for God (at news of his death, at the end, the characters fall apart) but by hindsight seems closer to *Priestley or *Sherwood than to contemporary reality. *West of Suez* (1971) and *A Sense of Detachment* (1972) cripplingly replace rhetoric with a curious flat irony. (The latter is also repetitive and offensive – it included, for example, the elderly actress Lady Redgrave reading pornography aloud – and was widely claimed in the press to be Osborne's farewell to the theatre. Since then, as if to prove the point, he has written only two other theatre plays.)

Osborne is a major writer, and has had a vital (if baleful) influence not only on British drama but also (such was the loosening impact of Jimmy Porter's rage) on British society itself. It has become fashionable to decry him, as 'no more than' a failed romantic or a heartless technician. But in Jimmy Porter, Archie Rice and Bill Maitland he created three characters to stand with the greatest in our drama, whether as archetypes, emblems, fascinating people, or simply outstanding acting-parts.

Osborne's other stage plays include *Epitaph for George Dillon* (with Anthony Creighton, 1958), *The End of Me Old Cigar* (1975), and *Watch It Come Down* (1976). He is also the author of numerous television plays (notably *A Subject of Scandal and Concern*, 1960, and *Jill and Jack*, 1974), and of a bitter-tongued, absorbing and, so far, incomplete autobiography (*A Better Class of Person*, 1981). Good brief introduction: A. P. Hinchcliffe: *John Osborne* (1983).

PINTER, Harold (born 1930)
British playwright, actor and director

Pinter's plays (a dozen one-acters, including *The Collection*, 1962, *Tea Party*, 1968, *Landscape*, 1969, and the triple bill *Other Places*, 1982, and six full-length plays: *The Birthday Party*, 1957, *The Caretaker*, 1960, *The Homecoming*, 1965, *Old Times*, 1971, *No Man's Land*, 1975, and *Betrayal*, 1978) show groups of people in ordinary domestic surroundings, under threat. Sometimes the threat is extravagant and surrealist, like the two mysterious strangers who menace and eventually lead away the hero – to execution? – in *The Birthday Party*. Sometimes the characters are threatened from inside their imaginations: Aston in *The Caretaker*, for example, fears even more than madness the electro-convulsive therapy designed to cure it, and Davies in the same play is in dread of physical violence. In Pinter's finest plays the threat comes with the arrival of characters from the past, and is the threat of awakened memory: Ann's revisiting of her old lover Kate and Kate's husband Deeley begins *Old Times*; the bringing home to London of someone who may or may not be an American wife is the starting-point of *The Homecoming*. In each case, the play deals not with incident but with the shift in character and relationships caused by threat. Davies in *The Caretaker* turns from sycophant to fascist bully; each of the three characters in *Old Times* discovers new attitudes to love and to himself; the relationships in *The Homecoming* and *No Man's Land* revolve and shift between character and character. In *Betrayal* the whole play is on the Proustian theme of the collapse of present reality into memory (and while the relationships develop, the action of the play moves backwards in time – a surprising, effective theatrical coup, paralleled in the excellent 1983 film by ingenious cross-time cutting).

The prismatic quality in Pinter's plots is matched by the poise of his language. Seen on the page, it has the inconsequentiality and banality of remarks overheard on a bus or in the street; but on the actors' lips, directed with due attention to pace and above all to pauses (the 'Pinter pause', replacing with silence a dozen lines of expository dialogue, is famous, and – by others – notoriously abused), it has the pull of music. (His work can be compared – and a serious point underlies the hyperbole – with the fugues of Bach.) His sense of pace, and above all of the right moment to 'cut' each line or scene, has made him one of the most admired screenwriters of his generation: his scripts for Joseph Losey (in particular *Accident*, *The Servant* and *The Go-Between*) and his so far unfilmed *The Proust Screenplay* (published 1978) are both outstanding in their genre and among his own best works.

Like *Beckett, Pinter has been over-explained and over-praised. His work is unlike anyone else's – superficially it resembles Beckett's in style, but his plots avoid Beckett's absurdism and nihilism, his characters (particularly his women) are far more warmly drawn, and he replaces Beckett's Joycean jokiness with laconic wit. His art is narrow, precise and as specific in its demands and its appeal as poetry.

Pinter's other works include poetry (a good selection is in *Poems and Prose*, 1978) and the admired screenplay of John Fowles's novel *The French Lieutenant's Woman* (filmed 1981). Good introductions: M. Esslin: *Pinter: A Study of His Plays* (3rd edn 1977); B. F. Dukore: *Harold Pinter* (1982).

PIRANDELLO, Luigi (1867–1936)
Italian playwright and story-writer

A professor of Italian at Rome University until 1922, Pirandello was spurred into taking up drama full-time by the international success of *Six Characters in Search of an Author* (1921). He founded an acting company; based at first in Rome, it later toured Europe and the United States giving performances of his plays – and made him the most internationally famous Italian dramatist of his generation. He published six forgettable novels, 250 short stories (rivalling Chekhov's for excellence) and fifty plays, many of them dramatizations of his stories.

A good deal of this large output harks back in style to the *verismo* movement of the late 19th century. This takes down-to-earth, modern stories (often culled from newspaper reports) and teases out every possible emotional and psychological overtone. It was a grand style for opera (particularly for Puccini), where music can intensify emotional meaning; in spoken drama it tends to produce melodrama, ordinary housewives and clerks shouting their inner torment like tragic queens. Pirandello's *Naked* (1922) is absolutely characteristic. The leading character tries to commit suicide, and while she waits for death builds a woman's-magazine scenario about being jilted after a passionate love-affair. She recovers, but the story gets out and she is persecuted by the townspeople as a liar and an immoral fantasist. Stripped of even the illusion of being loved, she commits suicide.

The clash in *Naked* between fantasy and real identity is a main subject in Pirandello's plays (though not in his short stories, which are more anecdotal and naturalistic). In *Right You Are If You Think You Are* (1917), the action hinges on a young girl's identity: if she is the hero's first wife, then she is Signora Frola's daughter; if she is his second wife, then the Signora's daughter is dead and the Signora deluded. In *As You Desire Me* (1930), a woman comes into town claiming to be – and looking exactly like – Bruno Pieri's long-lost wife. Her identity is however not proved: she is willing to remember, say or indeed be whatever Pieri asks, and he is baffled by this lack of character and refuses to make her the one thing she really claims to be, his wife.

In Pirandello's three greatest plays, rhetoric and melodramatically heightened emotion are still present, but distanced by non-realistic stage methods (an anticipation of the alienation-techniques of *Brecht). There is a play within a play, and this allows the characters to examine the claims and falsifications of their role-playing even as they play the roles. In *Each in His Own Way* (1924), actors sit watching a play about the reasons for a girl's suicide – and each (still in his or her role in the play being staged) argues and discusses the slant the play is putting on 'real' motives or on 'real' events. In *Six Characters in Search of an Author* six people interrupt a rehearsal and demand that the actors put on 'their story'; then, as the actors tentatively improvise scenes around the events they hear, the characters quarrel with the interpretation step by step, thus revealing their true motivation – as each himself or herself sees it. The play has been widely taken to be about such abstractions as the true meaning of existence or our perception of it; if so, this resonance hardly lies in the mind, and the main impression left is of a superb stage show about the stage itself. (The trilogy of plays about theatre was completed in 1929 by the less effective *Tonight We Improvise*.) Pirandello's best box-of-mirrors play is *Henry IV* (1922). This is about a rich man who has for years lived under the delusion that he is an 11th-century monarch: he keeps courtiers, treats his visitors as ambassadors and dignitaries, and leads a full royal life. But is he really deluded, or is this a role he has chosen to play? And what will happen when his well-meaning friends try to shock him out of his madness and back to reality?

Pirandello's plays are themselves sleight-of-hand. The illusion is that they are intellectually complex, discussing philosophical abstractions in a deep and thorough way. In fact he is not in the least concerned with intellectual thought. What intrigues him is theatricality itself, the nature of performance – and his teasing illusion–reality theme is never developed, merely used as the enabling factor for the all-important element, the show. He is a provider, in short, of outstandingly convincing three-dollar bills.

Other notable Pirandello plays include *The Pleasure of Respectability* (1917), the harsh – it is like the least sunny novels of Mauriac, the grimmest films of Chabrol – *Man, Beast and Virtue* (1918), and the striking one-acter *The Man With a Flower in His Mouth* (1923 – the first play ever televised, by the BBC in the early 1930s). His essay *Humour* (1908) gives useful insight into his creative intentions. Good critical studies: G. Giudice: *Pirandello* (1963); R. W. Oliver: *Dreams of Passion: The Theatre of Luigi Pirandello* (1979).

PRIESTLEY, John Boynton (1894–1984)
British playwright and novelist

Priestley wrote one of the great middlebrow novels of the century, *The Good Companions* (1929), about the journey round the music-halls and small-town theatres of 1920s Britain of a warmly drawn 'family' of actors, whose quest is equally for artistic success and human happiness. In its quieter way (substituting charm for satire, disappointment for heartbreak, seaside boarding-houses for the London slums) it is Dickensian in variety and breadth. *Angel Pavement* (1930), a similarly crowded tapestry of the lives of those involved in a small firm of London dealers, is almost equally successful, despite surrendering the glamour of backstage life. As well as dozens of other, slighter novels, Priestley also wrote trenchant essays, notably in *English Journey* (1934), an unsentimental study of ordinary people's lives in the Depression.

Priestley's second reputation was as a playwright. His forte here was for taking the conventions of the 'well-made' 1930s play and playing tricks with them. *Dangerous Corner* (1932), for example, is an after-dinner discussion (in a country-house drawing-room) about truth-telling and its effect on our lives. After a melodramatic climax (one of the characters, distressed by the truths that have been told, commits suicide), the whole action begins again, and proceeds to the 'dangerous corner' where the truth-telling began, at which point it takes a different course and ends in a happy dance. (This kind of conjuring-trick with time was repeated in *Time and the Conways*, 1937, *I Have Been Here Before*, 1937, and several other plays.) Priestley's two best plays, however, are less contrived. *An Inspector Calls* (1946) also deals with truth-telling – who is the inspector, and why do the characters tell him so much about themselves? – and sustains suspense through dialogue alone. *When We Are Married* (1938) is a delightful period farce, one of the least affected and most effective of all his works.

The best of Priestley's many other novels include the huge satire on the communications business *The Image Men* (1968, also in two volumes as *Out of Town* and *London End*). He also published three volumes of discursive, chatty autobiography, *Midnight on the Desert* (1936), *Rain upon Godshill* (1937) and the particularly unbuttoned *Instead of the Trees* (1977). Good, plain study: J. Braine: *J. B. Priestley* (1978).

RATTIGAN, Terence (1911–77)
British playwright

There was a time when critics queued up to disparage Rattigan: his plays were written off as slick, superficial, full of glib decency and easy craftsmanship, confected exactly to please his own creation, Aunt Edna (the middle-aged, middle-class maiden aunt who likes a play about nice people and with a recognizable beginning, middle and end). Some of his work certainly supports these criticisms, notably the anyone-for-tennis farce *French Without Tears* (1936), *Ross* (1960, an attempt to present Lawrence of Arabia in the style of *Coward's *Cavalcade*, and coming disastrously a cropper over the issue of homosexuality), and such glamorous and snobbish film-scripts as *The VIPs* (1963) and *The Yellow Rolls Royce* (1964). In his best plays, however, Rattigan used irony and a sense of real pain to get under the skin of Aunt-Edna characters. *The Winslow Boy* (1946), for example, about a decent middle-class family rocked when their son is expelled from school for stealing, has a sturdy dramatic skeleton (the search for truth – can such a boy really be guilty of such a crime?), but its muscle comes from an examination of middle-class character and attitudes, and of family loyalty, which is never overt (as it is in, say, *Osborne's *Look Back in Anger*) but which nevertheless gives the characters depth and propels the play. *The Deep Blue Sea* (1952), which is about a suicidally depressed woman being talked into 'facing life', reaches the prescriptive happy ending (she blinks back her tears and looks to the future) but deepens it, first by showing it not as a comfortable trick but as the inevitable consequence of her character, and second by an undercutting wryness – 'to live without hope is to live without despair' may comfort the heroine, but it offers no comfort to the audience. *Cause célèbre* (1977) is at one level a suspenseful courtroom drama (based on the 1935 Rattenbury murder trial); but its depth comes from a compassionate study of the love-affair between the two defendants, a middle-aged woman and a younger man. These plays, together with the one-acters *The Browning Version* (1948, Rattigan's masterpiece, about a dried-up, despairing school-master) and *Separate Tables* (1954), and the urbanely scandalous *In Praise of Love* (1973), have a memorability and honesty which confound disparagement.

Among Rattigan's other work is the interesting television play *Heart to Heart* (1962), based on his own unhappy experience in a confessional-interview series called *Face to Face*: in Rattigan's play, the interviewee turns the tables and reveals the flaws in his interrogator's life and character. Wish-fulfilment, and marvellous irony: one of his best-conceived and tightest works. Good study: M. Darlow and G. Hodson: *Terence Rattigan: The Man and His Work* (1979).

RICE, Elmer (1892–1967)
American playwright

In the 1930s and 1940s Rice was something of a jobbing dramatist, producing capable plays with a variety of themes and in styles ranging from light comedy (e.g. *The Left Bank*, 1931) to Theatre of Ideas (e.g. *Between Two Worlds*, 1934, in which passengers symbolically travelling on an ocean liner argue the merits of capitalism and communism and end by proposing a marriage of the best elements of both). He also wrote short stories and novels, including *A Voyage to Purilia* (1930), an amiable satire on Hollywood as Utopia. His most lasting plays are *The Adding Machine* (1923), a *Čapek-like fantasy, dated but still interesting, about humankind as an adding-machine – the leading character is called Mr Zero; *Street Scene* (1929), a 'panorama' of tenement life in New York, with a cast of over eighty – it is the grandfather of *Bullins' *Dynamite Plays*; and *Counsellor-at-Law* (1931), about the disintegration of a successful lawyer threatened with exposure for past unethical behaviour. Both *Street Scene* and *Counsellor-at-Law* are reminiscent (in themes, style, characterization and quality) of the novels of Jerome Weidman: that is to say, their thoughtfulness and sharpness of observation lift them above an easy-going, generic style.

SARTRE, Jean-Paul (1905–80)
French philosopher, playwright and novelist

One of the great guru-figures of the intellectual Left (not least in the journal *Modern Times*, which he edited with Beauvoir from 1945), Sartre took the existentialist theories of Kierkegaard and Heidegger out of the realms of philosophical abstraction into the arena of ethics and politics. The starting-point is Nothingness (*le Néant*), which is the natural state of humanity: we simply exist, and have no moral status, understanding or outside determinants of any kind (e.g. God). As each individual comes to terms with this Nothingness, he or she may choose to make a moral decision, a self-defining leap which will establish his or her Being (*l'Être*). For Kierkegaard the leap was the leap of faith, the acceptance of the existence and mystery of God. For non-Christian existentialists like Heidegger and Sartre it was a serious moral choice of any kind (including the choice to make no choice at all). But in each case the decision to make the leap is the crucial act, and opens the way to an ordered ethical existence. By 'defining' themselves, people simultaneously narrow their range of moral choices and free themselves from stifling Nothingness. (The feeling of moral dynamism, of ethical thrust, is crucial to Sartrean philosophy. Once we have chosen we must work, move forward, become involved. The nihilism – or acceptance of Nothingness – of many of his followers, though a valid existentialist choice for them, is quite unlike his own passionate involvement in contemporary affairs.) The philosophy and its implications are clearly, if lengthily, set out in his treatise *Being and Nothingness* (1943).

For writers, Sartrean existentialism could hardly have come at a better time. The feeling that (as Sartre put it) 'Man is a useless passion' was by no means new, but the pain of being had earlier tended to be discussed in terms either of despairing relationships with an aloof, cruel God (see Joyce, Mauriac or Gide) or of such circling explorations of the great Nothingness as are found in Kafka or in Hemingway (who called it *Nada*). For many 20th-century writers human beings were hopeless cases, done-to not doers, disliking both what they saw and what they were. Sartre's novels tackle this problem head-on. *Nausea/The Diary of Antoine Roquentin* (1938) is an (autobiographical) account of a man's agonized search for meaning in his own existence; *The Roads to Freedom* (in three volumes, *The Age of Reason*, 1945; *The Reprieve*, 1945; *Iron in the Soul/Troubled Sleep*, 1949) is an unfinished account of the gathering stormclouds of the Second World War as they overshadow the personal lives of Parisian intellectuals tormented by the simple pressure to take a position which they can justify to each other and to themselves. (In each of these books, Sartre offers no dogmatic solution to the problem of identity; but his critical and ironical stance towards his characters continually suggests that if 20th-century humankind once accepted *responsibility*, it might grow from adolescence to maturity.)

The scope and discursiveness of Sartre's novels make them, for all their gruff honesty, long to read. The best initial approach to his work is through his plays, which demonstrate rather than expound and which are always lively and fast-moving. In *The Flies* (1943), an existentialist reworking of Aeschylus's *Oresteia*, every citizen of Argos, because he or she chooses to do nothing, 'collaborates' in the guilt of Agamemnon's murder – like *Anouilh's *Antigone*, the play had political overtones in German-occupied France. Only Orestes chooses to make the self-defining leap to moral freedom, by killing the killers. (He escapes from Nothingness, but even so the flies of madness pursue him: freedom is not an easy choice.) In *The Devil and the Good Lord* (1951), the hero, an anticlerical leader in 16th-century Germany, tries every means in his power to show that good is possible on earth, even though God is dead. (His altruistic acts, like sharing his land with the poor, all fail because of the pigheadedness or evil of those he is trying to help; his quest for existential good leads him, ironically, not only to commit every kind of crime but also to the fasting, self-flagellation and acceptance of stigmata of the churchmen he despises. In the end he can only rouse the peasants to revolt against injustice by threatening them: he is engulfed by the very evil he is trying to end.) *The Victors/Men Without Shadows* (1946) and *The Condemned of Altona/Loser Wins* (1959) are both about torture: physical torture in *The Victors*, to try to make people (Resistance fighters) renounce their self-defining choices, and in *The Condemned of Altona* the mental pain of a man reliving the events which led him to become a wartime torturer, 'the butcher of Smolensk'. Other plays deal with simpler choices: venality or integrity (*The Respectful Prostitute*, 1946), truth or lies (*Nekrassov*, 1955), illusion or reality (*Kean*, 1953, a reworking of Dumas' play about acting).

Sartre's best plays are *Huis-clos/No Exit/In Camera* (1944) and *Les Mains sales/Crime passionel* (1948). *Huis-clos* takes place in the existentialist hell: not only are the characters dead (no longer existing as physical entities), but they have lost free-will as well, and are condemned forever to the paralysis of each other's company. (Even so, Garcin's line which ends the play, 'All right. Let's start again', suggests a glimmer of hope – for acceptance is itself a defining act.) *Les Mains sales* is about a political idealist ordered, for the Party, to murder a man he admires. (He nerves himself to do it only when he suspects the man of seducing his wife: free choice is pre-empted by passion.) *Les Mains sales* and *Huis-clos* score over Sartre's other plays because, without sacrificing intellectual intensity, they allow in sunshafts of wit and lightness of character; the style embodies the philosophy, and the philosophy binds and validates the action.

There have been better 20th-century novelists than Sartre, and finer playwrights. But few other writers can match his combination of rigour and attractiveness. His works are nobly cerebral from start to finish, but they never desert the market-place for the ivory tower: they have the pulse of real life in them, and their mundane energy leaves no room for pretension or tedium. Unlike some younger dramatists, the violence of whose rage squeezes out hope, he is a romantic telling us a hard but reassuring message: that there *is* choice, and the choice is ours.

Sartre's other philosophical writings include *Imagination* (1936), *The Transcend-*

ence of the Ego (1936), *Psychology of the Imagination* (1940), and *Critique of Dialectical Reason* (1960); see also F. Jeanson: *Sartre par lui-même* (1954). Other writings include studies of Baudelaire (*Baudelaire*, 1947), *Genet (*Saint Genet*, 1952) and – at enormous length, though unfinished – Flaubert (*The Fool of the Family*, 1972) and a volume of short stories (*The Wall/Intimacy*, 1939). For a vivid memoir of Sartre's paranoid, incontinent and miserable last years, see S. de Beauvoir: *Adieux: A Farewell to Sartre* (1984). Whether such intimate and unflinching detail enhances our picture of a great artist and what he or she achieved, or is mere voyeurism, is a matter of debate, but the book exists and is (alas) of undeniable authority.

SHAFFER, Peter (born 1926)
British playwright

Shaffer's minor work follows the traditions of the well-made West End or Broadway play, offering solid psychological drama with recognizable characters in a non-experimental style. *Five Finger Exercise* (1958), about the stresses in a middle-class family, has meaty roles for mother, son and German lodger, and the tension between them makes the play; *Black Comedy* (1965) is a superb one-act farce, full of mistaken identities and the blurting-out of unfortunate truths when the lights go out (and brilliantly, when the lights fuse in this play, the stage lights go up, not down); *The Battle of Shrivings* (1970, reworked, and tautened, as *Shrivings*, 1973) presents a dialectical conflict between two powerful personalities. To this excellent but low-key work Shaffer added theatrical dynamite in *The Royal Hunt of the Sun* (1964). The heart of this play (about the conquest of Peru) is a 'well-made' dramatization of the relationship between the conqueror Pizarro and the conquered god-king Atahuallpa. But their dialogues are surrounded and punctuated by every device of the theatre of spectacle: masks, bird-costumes, dancing, chirruping and crowing on the sound-track, an all-engulfing presentation of the exoticism of Inca civilization. In the same way, *Equus* (1973), essentially showing the relationship between a psychiatrist and a confused boy who has blinded some horses, is tricked out, by dancers and acrobats playing horses, with a poetic, orgiastic presentation of the joy the boy feels in taming, riding and being at one with horses. *Amadeus* (1979) is on the same subject as Pushkin's *Mozart and Salieri*, that is the nature of genius (feckless, dirty-little-boy Mozart) and the consuming jealousy of the merely talented (strait-laced Salieri, his rival). This play, though powerfully conceived, cuts its own throat by presuming to use stretches of Mozart's music under Shaffer's dialogue – an argument Mozart wins without a word. The vulgarity of that idea is, perhaps, typical of a lack of fastidiousness in all Shaffer's work. But tasteful or not, his plays use the medium of theatre with dazzling panache: flat to read and limp when filmed, on stage they never fail to provide a stunning and convincing show.

SHAW, George Bernard (1856–1950)
Irish playwright and polemicist

There was a time when Shaw was regarded as the greatest English-language playwright since Shakespeare. (He did nothing to hinder this opinion. In the preface to *Three Plays for Puritans*, 1901, for example, he lodged his tongue firmly in its favourite place, his cheek, and explained why his *Caesar and Cleopatra*, 1898, was preferable to Shakespeare's *Antony and Cleopatra*. Many readers were scandalized; more believed.) Though his reputation has dwindled since, there is (as so often with Shavian outrageousness) more than a grain of truth behind the blarney. In particular, Shaw rescued English theatre from the trivial, purely-for-entertainment status it had had since Puritan times – his support for Ibsen (notably in his book *The Quintessence of Ibsenism*, 1892) and his polemical theatre-criticism (collected in *Our Theatres in the Nineties*, 1931) stemmed from a firm belief that 'ideas' and their discussion were not incompatible with stage entertainment, and his own plays amply justified that view: whether or not he was as good as Shakespeare, he was certainly better than any of his own contemporaries, even than such estimable 'thinking' dramatists as Pinero or Henry Arthur Jones.

Ibsen's influence is strongest on the structure of Shaw's plays. He worked in a sturdily realist style: we are encouraged to believe that we are watching not an acted drama but real people in real situations, and in several of the plays (*The Devil's Disciple*, 1897; *Captain Brassbound's Conversion*, 1899; *Major Barbara*, 1905) this reality extends to time as well, with elapsed stage time being exactly equivalent to the elapsed time in the story. (Much stage drama, by contrast, makes use of compressed or emblematic time, telescoping or stretching real time to make dramatic points.) Shaw's most Ibsenish play of all (and one of his best) is *Candida* (1895). It is about a strong-minded woman choosing between two weak men, and its settings and characters are more than a little reminiscent of Ibsen's *Hedda Gabler*. But there the resemblance ends, for Shaw has no time at all in his plays for the unsmiling intensity of Ibsen: he replaces it with charm and roguish talk. If *The Devil's Disciple* is about the deceptiveness of appearances and true nobility of character (it owes debts to Dickens's *A Tale of Two Cities*), it is also and predominantly the study of a lovable rogue; *Captain Brassbound's Conversion* is dominated by Lady Cicely, the first of those briskly rational and competent women so common in Shaw, a devastating blend of Fabian Society clear-headedness and upper-middle-class unconventionality which may be a dramatist's trick – she is larger than life, or rather larger than the life of the surrounding play – but which propels the plot; *Major Barbara*, essentially a silly story about wills and mistaken identities, is given solidity by its apparent (but never actual: consider what *O'Casey might have made of it) discussion of 'good works' and its contrast of farcical aristocrats and clean-cut heroine; *Mrs Warren's Profession* (1898) is on the Ibsen theme

of 'the ghost we carry in the cargo' – the heroine's education has been
paid for out of the profits from a chain of brothels – but this revelation is
merely a *frisson* (it might as well have been cleaning windows or
pawnbroking), and the play is really about a tough young woman
choosing her own way in life.

For all the discussions which fill his plays, there is a lack of intellectual
rigour in Shaw. He goes into every corner of each issue, but true analysis
is always undercut by point-making. Shaw the journalist, the twinkly-
eyed guest scandalizing the dinner-table, is present in every character.
He has no idea at all about the Lower Orders: from Brassbound to Bill
Walker, from Doolittle to the common soldiers in *St Joan* (1923), they
are all taken from the working-class stereotypes of the Victorian stage.
He consistently deflates the 'debate' aspect of his plays by happy endings:
The Devil's Disciple ends with a last-minute gallows reprieve, *Man and
Superman* (1905) with the heroine fainting in the arms of the man she
really loves, *Candida* with the *coup-de-théâtre* of a return to the status
quo. (Only *Pygmalion*, 1913, has a wry ending consistent with the development of the plot: given everything but love by Higgins, Eliza walks
out on him, threatening to set up as a rival teacher in phonetics. Whatever
the other metamorphoses in the play, neither her character nor his
undergoes a change of heart.) Because of this pulling-back, Shaw's light
comedies (notably *Arms and the Man*, 1894, *You Never Can Tell*, 1899,
The Doctor's Dilemma, 1906, and *Androcles and the Lion*, 1913) tend
to 'work' better than his more serious drama (e.g. *Misalliance*, 1910;
Heartbreak House, 1921) or than those endlessly urbane late plays such
as *Back to Methuselah* (1923) or *The Apple Cart* (1929) which are full of
good talk, but whose subjects (e.g. the wrong-headedness of Darwinism
or the need for monarchy) hardly make for drama or merit such
ferociously relaxed treatment.

Shaw's best plays harness his preoccupations, talents and influences to
precise characterization and intriguing plots. *Caesar and Cleopatra*,
Pygmalion and *St Joan* all deal with the (again Ibsenish) theme of the
confrontation between innocence and worldliness; all avoid garrulity –
the talk arises from and defines the characters, instead of elbowing them
aside; all keep a balance, in their action, between inevitability and
surprise. They work as *plays*; they would not work so well in other forms.
Together with *The Devil's Disciple*, *Candida*, *You Never Can Tell* and
Major Barbara, though never comparable with Shakespeare, they are
major work.

Shaw's non-dramatic writings are voluminous: tracts, pamphlets, reviews and
journalistic pieces of every kind. The best of them, the political tracts collected in
Essays in Fabian Socialism (1932) and his superb 1890s music criticism (collected
in *Shaw's Music*, 1981) exhibit a characteristic blend of discursive outrageousness
and trenchant common sense. (They are also superbly written, as craftsmanlike
examples of English prose as Bach's fugues are of counterpoint: no one who takes
pleasure in well-turned phrases grouped in elegant, forceful and beautifully
articulated sentences could fail to warm to them.) There are also lively letters,

including *Ellen Terry and Bernard Shaw – a Correspondence* (1931) and *Bernard Shaw and Mrs Patrick Campbell: Their Correspondence* (1952). A useful critical anthology is *The Genius of Shaw* (ed. Holroyd, 1979). The 'standard' biography (a masterpiece of the genre, and full of Shavian talk) is H. Pearson: *Bernard Shaw* (first complete edn 1961). A very funny book, resonant with the sound of egos clashing, is M. Peters: *Bernard Shaw and the Actresses* (1981).

SHEPARD Sam (born 1943)
American playwright and actor

In the 1920s Rachel Crothers' plays summed up what everyone thought 'advanced' drama ought to be (i.e. formally adventurous, psychological, faintly feminist) without themselves ever being advanced. In just the same way Shepard's plays – more than forty since *Cowboys* in 1964 – conform to the 'advanced' stereotypes of the 1960s and 1970s. They are reach-me-down *Beckett, Sears-Roebuck *Ionesco, or (if it is that year's model) anodyne *Albee. His ideas are simple (picnics going wrong; a man waiting for death in the electric chair; a race track; a revivalist service) and his language is often derived from actors' exercises (e.g. one character shouting while another whispers; non-sequitur argument; emotional scenes using words from the phone directory or letters of the alphabet). It is off-the-peg avant-garde theatre, effective, accessible – and durable? Characteristic titles are *Shaved Splits* (1969), *Mad Dog Blues* (1971), *Geography of a Horse Dreamer* (1974), *Suicide in B-Flat* (1976) and *Curse of the Starving Class* (1977). His best-known work, internationally, is his contribution to the screenplay of Antonioni's film *Zabriskie Point* (1970): at the time this, too, seemed no more than fallen petals from the flower people, but it throve and thrives.

Shepard's most successful recent plays are *True West* (1981), at once the study of two warring brothers, one successful and one a failure, and a back-of-screen showbiz farce to rival *Wood's *Has 'Washington' Legs?*, and *Fool for Love* (1984), about two people desperately trying to sort out truth from self-deception in their lives and their marriage, a kind of metaphysical thriller. He also wrote the script for a fine Wim Wenders film, *Paris, Texas* (1984), about a broken family.

SHERWOOD, Robert Emmet (1896–1955)
American playwright

Sherwood's chief claim to be remembered now is as the author of *The Petrified Forest* (1935), the social melodrama which made Humphrey Bogart a stage star and gave him his first important film role (as Duke Mantee, a sadistic thug). His winning formula for plays – which later became clichéd in 'disaster movies' – was to maroon a heterogeneous group of people in an isolated situation under threat (for example shut up in a hotel by the threat of imminent war) and let them act out not only their own fears and tensions but also some crucial moral issue: he was a fervent supporter of Roosevelt, an activist for liberal ideas and against oppression. (His memoir of the war years, *Roosevelt and Hopkins: An Intimate History*, 1948, is a moving account of friendship with noble friends.) His avowed intention was to provide 'moral theatre', with a thought-content above that on offer in what he characteristically called – he never could call a spade a spade – 'the neighbouring cinema places'. He succeeded in *The Petrified Forest* and in *Idiot's Delight* (1936), a presentation of all the arguments for and against the approaching war which ends with two of the characters singing 'Onward Christian Soldiers' as the first bombs are heard outside. His work, otherwise, ranges from historical tableau (*Abe Lincoln in Illinois*, 1938, later filmed) to jingoistic tract (*There Shall Be No Night*, 1940) – and for all its worthy aims, its second-rateness and oyster-smoothness make the spectator feel he or she is being gummed to death. He was also prolific in the cinema (a better medium for him, for all his disparagement of it): his screenplays include *The Ghost Goes West* (1935), *Rebecca* (1940), *The Best Years of Our Lives* (1946, a fine film about soldiers adjusting to post-war lives) and *Man on a Tightrope* (1953, a presentable circus film).

Good critical works: J. S. Brown: *The Worlds of Sherwood* (1965); *The Ordeal of a Playwright* (1970).

SOYINKA, Wole (born 1934)
Nigerian playwright

Soyinka uses Yoruba tribal legends, culture and ritual in the same way as the Greek tragedians used folk-material. That is, he gives his plays exotic strength – very like that of Euripides, whose *The Bacchae* he adapted in 1973 – by filling them with snippets of songs, chants, incantations and dance, and uses the framework of ethnic themes to tell stories of modern human beings caught in the clash of two cultures. (The two cultures are not, as some critics have claimed, black and white; they are those of ancient Africa and the 20th century.) His plays are about the transition from a 'numinous' culture to a more pragmatic and realist one; he sets out (as he wrote of Euripides) to 'evoke awareness of a particular moment in a people's history, yet imbue that moment with a hovering, eternal presence'. It must be said that for non-Yoruba audiences Yoruba culture does often seem thinner and less relevant than the great Greek myths, and this makes some of Soyinka's earlier plays (e.g. *The Lion and the Jewel*, 1957, the *Jero Plays*, 1963, and *The Road*, 1965) seem no more than a talky equivalent of those bare-breasted African dance-groups who perform for tourists. But in his later plays (written after a period of imprisonment during the Nigerian civil war) the 'Greek' quality begins to appear: *Madmen and Specialists* (1971) and *Death and the King's Horseman* (1975), which explores and makes meaningful the ritual suicide of a 20th-century Yoruba chief, are universal and impressive works.

Soyinka's non-dramatic work – generally more political, and angrier, than his plays – includes two Sartrean novels, *The Interpreters* (1965) and *Season of Anomy* (1973), a scholarly treatise, *Myth Literature and the African World* (1976), poetry (notably *Idanre*, 1966, *A Shuttle in the Crypt*, 1973, and *Ogun Abibiman*, 1976, the latter a political allegory patterned on a traditional 'praise poem'), and two books of autobiography, the well-received *Ake, the Years of Childhood* (1982) on his first twelve years, and the polemical and much-reviled *The Man Died* (1972), on his political imprisonment. Helpful study: J. Gibbs (ed.): *Critical Perspectives on Wole Soyinka* (1980).

STOPPARD, Tom (born 1937)
British playwright

What do Rosencrantz and Guildenstern do in the wings of history, while *Hamlet* takes place onstage? *Rosencrantz and Guildenstern Are Dead* (1966) dazzlingly tells us: they play word-games; they speculate about the meaning of *Hamlet*, life, themselves; like Estragon and Vladimir but without even Godot to look forward to, they wait. The play is lively, shallow fun, plucking at the edges of the intellect, turning philosophy (existentialism, in this case) into a party-game. In *Jumpers* (1972) a moral philosopher preparing a learned paper on the Existence of the Absolute is interrupted by a police investigation into the death of one of a team of acrobats his wife has been entertaining in the family home. In *Travesties* (1974) rehearsals for a down-at-heel embassy production of *The Import-ance of Being Earnest* in 1917 Zurich become fantastically interwoven with the debates and schemes of Lenin, the Dadaist poet Tzara and the young James Joyce. These three plays, and one-acters such as *The Real Inspector Hound* (1968), *Dirty Linen* and *New Found Land* (1976), declared Stoppard an intellectual farceur of genius – and he character-istically proceeded to trump his own reputation by adding depth. *Every Good Boy Deserves Favour* (1977) is about a dissident intellectual locked up with a madman who thinks he has an orchestra at hand. (He has: a real orchestra in the theatre. Who is sane and who is mad?) *Professional Foul* (1977), a television play, shows a philosopher lecturing in an eastern-bloc country, and invited to smuggle dissident papers out, to perform in real life the *acte gratuit* about which he talks. *Night and Day* (1978), set in an African country on the brink of revolution, is about the ethics of journalism: whether we help to make the violence we report. *The Real Thing* (1982) is a lesser play, a mellow love-story, in which two couples exchange partners and aphorisms: it is as if Pinter had provided dialogue for an Iris Murdoch plot. Stoppard has the rare gift (in contemporary drama, only *Albee can match him) of making intellectual cleverness great fun; the darkening of themes in his later plays, the move towards substance, may yet make him one of the most important, as well as most attractive, dramatists of his generation.

Stoppard's other work includes a likeable novel (*Lord Malquist and Mr Moon*, 1966), several shorter stage or radio plays (e.g. *Albert's Bridge*, 1967; *Dogg's Hamlet and Cahoot's Macbeth*, 1979), and a hugely funny full-length farce, *On the*

Razzle (1981), an updating of the Nestroy comedy which also served as the basis for *Wilder's *The Matchmaker*: Stoppard's plot is neater than Nestroy's and his lines are wittier than Wilder's. Useful study: J. Hunter: *Tom Stoppard's Plays* (1982).

STOREY, David (born 1933)
British playwright and novelist

Storey leapt to prominence with his novel *This Sporting Life* (1960), in particular after it was filmed (by Lindsay Anderson) in 1963. The combination of gritty realism and symbolism (the book's rugby matches were variously taken as allegories of the class struggle, of the conflict of Marxism and capitalism, and of humanity's urge to survive by force – Konrad Lorenz's book *On Aggression* appeared in 1963, and his ideas were much in vogue) made Storey seem a successor to D. H. Lawrence. His subsequent novels (the best are *Radcliffe*, 1963, *A Temporary Life*, 1973, and the avowedly Lawrentian *Saville*, 1976) have the same meticulous documentation of everyday life, but turn their attention inwards, on the psychological and emotional tensions in the characters rather than on their progress through society. This is also the pattern for two of Storey's early plays, *The Restoration of Arnold Middleton* (1967), the study of a provincial schoolmaster's nervous collapse, and *In Celebration* (1969), about the tensions caused in working-class parents by their children's middle-class success. Three other plays use a framework of carefully observed (and to the ordinary playgoer, slightly recherché) everyday activities to discuss the human conditions: *The Contractor* (1970) shows us ourselves as contractor's men putting up and taking down a wedding marquee, *The Changing Room* (1971) as rugby players before, during and after a match, *Life Class* (1974) as art students sketching a model. (The settings may seem bizarre for such symbolic messages, but they are no more unlikely than a group of people contemplating the cutting-down of an orchard or amateur dramatics on a Russian country estate – and they work just as well.) *Home* (1970) is the outsider in Storey's work: a Pintery dialogue between two old men in a mental home, it was saved in its first production by touching performances from John Gielgud and Ralph Richardson. (Richardson also starred in *Early Days*, 1980, a similar but slighter play about an old man's ebbing grasp on memory.) But austerity is deceptive: *Home* has surface dignity but no substance, and lacks both the energy and the resonance of Storey's major work. As the combination of Lawrence and Chekhov suggests, Storey is an uncompromising (and somewhat sunless) writer, whose work nevertheless has power to move the heart.

Storey's first novel since *Saville* was *A Prodigal Child* (1982). *Present Times* (1984), his most recent, is about the anguish of a forty-seven-year-old ex-rugby player, facing the compromises and problems of coping with a permissive age he doesn't understand. The dialogue (unexpectedly from a playwright) is wooden,

but the plot is solid and 'old-fashioned', in the manner of Maugham or even
*Priestley: a 'good read'.

SYNGE, John Millington (1871–1909)
Irish playwright

In a writing life of less than a decade (his first play did not appear until
1903) Synge laid the foundations for Irish drama, and for much other
20th-century Irish literature: his laconic, poetic style, for example, was
a major influence on early Joyce. He lived in the Aran Islands, and drew
themes and language both from folklore and from the fishermen's
everyday lives. He wrote precisely that kind of 'magical Irishry' which
has since been debased in a thousand lesser hands; in his work it was
new, rich and strong. He wrote four one-act plays (*In the Shadow of the
Glen*, 1903; *Riders to the Sea*, 1904; *The Well of the Saints*, 1905; and *The
Tinker's Wedding*, 1908); the most powerful, *Riders to the Sea*, a mother's
'keening' for five drowned sons, replaces incident with the musical ebb
and flow of words (and was later beautifully set to music by Vaughan
Williams). His one full-length play, *The Playboy of the Western World*
(1907), is a comedy whose feckless, roguish hero Christy (the man who
stumbles into town and into the girls' hearts, claiming to have killed his
father who wanted him to marry an elderly widow – and who is not a whit
disconcerted when his father arrives to fetch him away) is in a great line
from Goldsmith's Tony Lumpkin and Boucicault's Dazzle to Háry
János or the trickster-hero of Gogol's *The Government Inspector*. Only
*O'Casey's *Juno and the Paycock* is a finer 20th-century Irish play.
(Some claim this status for Synge's unfinished *Deirdre of the Sorrows*,
1910, based on an Irish legend; but this is self-conscious and over-ripe,
the kind of folksy navel-contemplation better done by Synge's mentor
Yeats.)

Good, brief introduction: E. Benson: *J. M. Synge* (1982). Good on the folk origins
of Synge's art: T. O. Johnson: *Synge: The Medieval and the Grotesque* (1983).
Synge's letters are currently appearing, in an edition by A. Saddlemeyer: volume
one was published in 1983.

TETLEY, Glen (born 1926)
American choreographer

Originally a dancer (he worked, among others, for *Graham and for
Robbins), Tetley first became prominent as a choreographer for the
Nederlands Dans Teater in the 1960s. In his work, ballet moved from the
classroom – at one point, it had seemed, *Balanchine and his disciples
had elevated class and bar-exercises into a public art-form – back to the
theatre, and to a primarily narrative style. (Romantic ballet had been
based on the genteelly stylized mime and *corps-de-danse* spectacle of
Victorian theatre; in the early 20th century *Duncan, *Nijinsky and

others had asserted the primacy of pure movement; Tetley introduced the harsh new mime-styles of the Theatres of Cruelty and of the Absurd.) The techniques involved were derived partly from Japanese and other Far-Eastern theatre, partly from the neo-medieval mime-style of Marcel Marceau and his pupils, and partly from the jerky, symbolic movement of silent films. This electic idiom, a feature also of much 1960s and 1970s 'music theatre' (e.g. the works of Henze or Maxwell Davies), and of avant-garde theatre directors like Planchon or Brook, was used by Tetley with stunning impact in *Pierrot lunaire* (1962), in which gymnastics on a high scaffolding tower played a prominent part, in *The Anatomy Lesson* (1964), in which the corpse of Rembrandt's painting was given eerie, Frankenstein's-monster life, and in *Sargasso* (1964), a swirling, writhing sea of bodies. Since these pioneering ballets, Tetley has created a number of prestigious avant-garde works (e.g. *Circles*, 1968, and *Labyrinth*, 1972, to music by Berio; *Ziggurat*, 1967, *Field Figures*, 1970, and *Mutations*, 1970, to music by Stockhausen; *Chronocromie*, 1971, to Messiaen's huge score). But he has also turned his talent to several great ballet scores of the early 20th century (e.g. *Daphnis and Chloe* or *The Rite of Spring*), and has shown – a rare achievement in our peremptorily experimental age – that 'mainstream' and 'avant-garde' techniques, so far from being mutually exclusive, can be combined to produce work as serious and unified as it is exhilarating.

TRAVERS, Ben (1886–1980)
British playwright

As Wodehouse was to the novel, so Travers was to the theatre: he did a slight thing with surpassing excellence and made it art. He worked, like Feydeau (his only rival in the field of farce), on the principle of remorseless logic. Each play begins with an absurd deed or decision ('absurd' here meaning nothing metaphysical, but simply 'daft'), and then knits the chain of circumstance until a huge Act Three tangle has to be resolved by another arbitrary move (usually discovery of the concealed or misrepresented truth, or the arrival of a so-far-unseen character). But whereas Feydeau's chief strength is the meticulous dovetailing of absurdity, Travers offers other delights as well. His themes are more varied: suspected adultery, certainly, in *The Cuckoo in the Nest* (1925) and *Rookery Nook* (1926), but also social pretension (*Thark*, 1927), crime (*Plunder*, 1928) and – perhaps uniquely in farce – sexual enslavement (*The Bed Before Yesterday*, 1975). His language is as unique as Runyon's: basically a heightened 1920s slang, it veers off into surrealism at the slightest chance (e.g., from *Rookery Nook*: 'I'll try to put the lid on Gertrude.' 'And Harold.' 'If I get the lid on, he can sit on it.' Or, from *The Bed Before Yesterday*: 'I got the bells. Did you get the bells?' 'What bells?' 'When it happens, you seem to hear bells.' 'Do you?' 'Don't *you*?'). Above all, his characters (written, in the 1920s plays, for the magnificent trio of actors Tom Walls and Ralph Lynn, silly asses, and

Robertson Hare, put-upon grotesque) are tweed-suited zanies in the great tradition, as lively and as memorable as any of Wodehouse's. Perhaps because it needs little explication, critics tend to ignore or undervalue comedy; but if we were looking for the most enjoyable playwrights of the century, Travers's name could head the list.

Travers's nine 'Aldwych' farces, all written with Walls, Lynn and Hare in mind, are *A Cuckoo in the Nest, Rookery Nook, Thark, Plunder, A Cup of Kindness* (1929), *A Night Like This* (1930), *Turkey Time* (1931), *Dirty Work* (1932) and *A Bit of a Test* (1933). (The first three also appeared as Wodehousian novels.) Travers's other farces include *Banana Ridge* (1939) and *She Follows Me About* (1945). He also wrote amiable, forgettable screen comedies (chiefly in the 1930s), light fiction, and two separate autobiographies, *Vale of Laughter* (1957) and *A-Sitting on a Gate* (1978).

WEISS, Peter (1916–82)
German playwright

Weiss's career as a full-time dramatist did not begin until after his conversion to Marxism in the early 1960s. (He had previously been a painter, novelist and film director.) The majority of his early plays are grotesque farces on political themes (reminiscent of those of *Kopit). *The Insurance* (1952), for example, shows in twenty-one scenes the progressive collapse of bourgeois society (symbolized by a Mack-Sennett-like police chief) in favour of an even more imbecile workers' revolution. *How the Pain Was Driven Out of Herr Mockingpott* (1968) is about a clownish fool who sheds his foolishness and becomes a Man only when he rejects the trappings of capitalist society. In Weiss's most famous play – 'Did you see it?' someone asked George Axelrod. 'No, but I read the title' – *The Persecution and Assassination of Jean-Paul Marat as Performed by the Inmates of the Asylum of Charenton under the Direction of the Marquis de Sade*, also known as *The Marat/Sade* (1964), the historical events of the play-within-the-play make one attack on bourgeois society, and its setting makes another: the asylum symbolizes both a concentration-camp and the oppressive capitalist regimes of contemporary Europe. After this onslaught, and influenced perhaps by *Hochhuth, Weiss began to concentrate on historical polemic, often in verse, very long and unremittingly serious. *The Song of the Lusitanian Bogey* (1967), for example, is a panorama of Portuguese colonial rule in Angola, with side-swipes at fascism and racism almost everywhere else; *Discourse on the historical background and the course of the continuous struggle for liberation in Vietnam as an example of the necessity for armed warfare by the oppressed against their oppressors and furthermore on the attempts of the United States of America to annihilate the basic principles of the revolution* (1968) is precisely what it says; *Trotsky in Exile* (1970), as comparatively laconic as its title, is a defence of Trotskyist Marxism (as against Stalinism) interspersed with scenes showing Trotsky's life. The best of these plays is also the angriest: *The Investigation* (1965). This combines scenes from the Auschwitz trials with a denunciation of Weiss's German contemporaries for pretending that the Final Solution was a myth. It is a theme as uncomfortable as it is powerful, and Weiss spares his audience nothing (as the play develops, the accusers round on the spectators, in the very opposite of the alienation-technique). He has awkward things to say, and effective ways of saying them; the flaw is his very breadth of attack – Aristophanes and *Brecht, his great models, both knew how to narrow focus and so direct their aim.

Weiss's artistic and political journey through the blast-zones of 20th-century German history is the basis for three autobiographical novels, *The Shadow of the Coachman's Body* (1961), *Leavetaking* (1961) and *Vanishing Point* (1963). In addition to his original plays, he wrote a fine stage adaptation of Kafka's *The Trial*, one of the most convincing contenders in a crowded field. He also published, in three volumes, *The Aesthetics of the Resistance* (1981), about the German Communist Party and the embodiment of political philosophy in works of art: a fascinating, stimulating, and very long read (German edition only).

WESKER, Arnold (born 1932)
British playwright

When 'the Wesker trilogy' (*Chicken Soup with Barley*, *Roots* and *I'm Talking About Jerusalem*) was first staged complete in 1960, critics leapt to claim it as the most ambitious and impressive achievement of new-wave theatrical realism. The plays show working-class families trying (and failing) to organize, rationalize and put into practice socialist ideals; they are set in mean kitchens and living-rooms, and their characters and dialogue are vigorously true to life. In their conscious dismissal of artifice, their deliberate lowness of key, they set a trend (John Braine, Shelagh Delaney, Waterhouse and Hall were followers) – and, sadly, as the trend dwindled their importance also waned. The problem is that this kind of mundane melodrama works much better, and has been much more done, on television: it is carbolic-soap-opera, and no amount of writing up can make it art. (*The Kitchen*, 1961, ostensibly about believable people, is really a stage equivalent of that curious television hybrid documentary drama: it tells a great deal about the characters' working lives, but nothing of interest about themselves. The people's frustration, however movingly portrayed, is thus a function of environment not self, and fails to convince. Why, we wonder, if the kitchen is so awful, don't they take other jobs? No one asks such questions about King Oedipus.)

Wesker wrote one more play in this style (*Chips with Everything*, 1962, an unromantic account of the training of RAF conscripts), trying to leave flat naturalism with an emblematic, *Brechtian style. It is certainly his liveliest play. Since then he has produced a large amount of work in many different styles, including the plays *Their Very Own and Golden City*, 1964, *The Friends*, 1970, and *The Old Ones*, 1972; all of it is worthy (and inspired by unimpeachable zeal to show ordinary people going about their decent lives), but none of it fires critical or public imagination. The most interesting of his later works is *The Journalists*. This began (1972) as a documentary play about the making of a newspaper, occasioned lawsuits and injunctions from the *Sunday Times* journalists whom Wesker had observed at work, and was finally published (in 1979) as the original play, a diary of the play's conception and its eventual rejection by the Royal Shakespeare Company, and 'the book of the play', a journalistic account of Wesker's time at the *Sunday Times*. (This last section was the best.) *The Journalists* is fascinating not only for what it reveals about journalists, but also for what it tells about its honest and embattled author, a playwright who has consistently been very nearly very good, the Trigorin of the British stage.

Wesker's other plays include *The Four Seasons* (1965), *The Merchant* (1976, a reworking of *The Merchant of Venice*), *Love Letters on Blue Paper* (1977), and – interesting departure, a play about a medieval anchoress – *Caritas* (1981). *Annie Wobbler* (1983) is a series of three linked monologues, a marvellous *tour de force* for the actress, along the lines of the solo scenes in *Caritas*, but somewhat enervating for the audience.

WHITING, John (1917–63)
British playwright

The contradiction in Whiting's work between theme and style makes him a thorny, and for some impossible, dramatist. (He is a 20th-century John Ford.) He wrote in a limpid style close to that of *Anouilh, a prose parallel to the dramatic verse of Eliot or *Fry. But underlying this urbanity is a bleakly misanthropic view of human endeavour and the future of the species – and the effect is as disconcerting as if a kindly dinner-guest gave you a hundred lucid, unemotional and unarguable reasons for committing suicide. *Saint's Day* (1951), an edgy parable about the violence innate in human character and human relationships, which ends with real, hideous violence, outraged the critics – and has since been taken as a masterly precursor of *Pinter's theatre of menace. Even more Pintery is the first of his five plays, *Conditions of Agreement* (written 1948, first staged 1965), a play in which five characters seek to dominate each other: its effect is as if Pinter's screenplay for Losey's film *The Servant* had been provided with additional dialogue by J. B. *Priestley. Whiting's two finest plays are both anti-war. *A Penny for a Song* (1951) is ostensibly a comedy (it has a pair of doddering aristocratic eccentrics straight out of Anouilh, proposing to repulse Napoleon with fire-engines and phrase-book French), but ends with an autumnal wind, a foreglimpse of the death and not the rebirth of humanity. *Marching Song* (1954), about a general imprisoned for seven years after his country's defeat, who is released only to be offered the scapegoat's choice of suicide or a show trial, is bitter about humanity's refusal to recognize that the true cause of war is our inherent violence. Apart from these plays, and a somewhat flat comedy (*The Gates of Summer*, 1956, about archaeologists in 1913 Greece digging so industriously into the past that they fail to see their own immediate future – it is a similar story to Ray's film *The Chess Players*, but lacks Ray's finesse), Whiting's only other major work was *The Devils* (1961), a Brechtian stage adaptation of Huxley's novel *The Devils of Loudun*. (It later formed the basis of the script for Ken Russell's film.)

Whiting straddles a period of transition in the British theatre, from romanticism to nihilism. Because he had a foot in each camp, he pleased neither; but as the fads recede the strength of his own artistic personality becomes more apparent – and it is the Whiting in his plays which gives them, for all their contradictions, lasting quality.

WILDER, Thornton (1897–1975)
American playwright and novelist

Wilder was fascinated by the idea of simultaneity: that time is not progressive and sequential but circular, and that we arrive at understanding of a given moment only by making ourselves aware of the many human viewpoints or experiences which converge on it. In some of his works he starts from a central incident and explores the surrounding circumstances: his novel *The Bridge of San Luis Rey* (1927), for example, starts and ends with the collapse of a bridge, and in between describes the lives and thoughts of the five people killed in the disaster (which is thus seen as the culmination of five separate but contingent realities). In other works he depicts human life as a continuum, enlivened by specific incidents but essentially unchanged despite the passing of the generations: his one-act play *The Long Christmas Dinner* (1931, later set as a turgid opera by Hindemith), for example, shows progressive generations of a family sitting at the same eternal Christmas dinner-table.

The result of this approach to time is that Wilder is able, without labouring the point, to propose a metaphysical component for human life – and this leads to his second major theme, that the world is not a pre-existing, hostile force (as it is for *Beckett, say, or Kafka), but that we have the power to make and remake it, moment by moment, for ourselves. (The idea that happiness is as much in us as misery, and that we find it when we are truest to ourselves, underlies Wilder's novels *Heaven's My Destination*, 1934, and *Theophilus North*, 1973: in each of them the hero searches for and eventually finds – these are optimistic books – his existential leap.) An interest in the classical world (whose metaphysical inquiry seemed to Wilder analogous to that of our own pagan era) led to three other novels: *The Cabala* (1926), in which the pagan gods take up residence, incognito, in the modern USA, *The Woman of Andros* (1930), a reworking of Terence's comedy, and *The Ides of March* (1948), an epistolary novel about the converging events leading to the assassination of Julius Caesar.

Wilder wrote over two dozen one-act plays (the best are in *Plays for Bleecker Street*, 1961), and adapted plays by authors as diverse as Obey, Ibsen and *Sartre (*The Victors*, 1949). But he is chiefly known for three of the classic plays of the 20th century. *The Matchmaker* (1954), a reworking of his *The Merchant of Yonkers* (1938), which is itself based on plays by two other men, is a charming costume comedy, an American *Hobson's Choice* involving a pair of frisky young men, their girls, an irascible elderly gentleman and the merry widow who tames him, the matchmaker herself. (The play was the basis for the vulgar, effervescent musical *Hello, Dolly*.) *Our Town* (1938, excellently filmed in 1940) applies the theory of simultaneity to a small New England town, showing how, as the generations succeed one another (one generation is born, grows up and dies before our eyes) the unchanging qualities of decency and honest aspiration give strength to human life. It could be a mawkish and embarrassing parade of 'niceness'; what saves it is salt in the characterization (particularly that of the women) and utter simplicity – it is as unaffected and moving as Copland's Shaker ballet *Appalachian Spring*. *The Skin of our Teeth* (1942) shows the simultaneity of human affairs over the last 5,000 years, as the Antrobus family move from the stone age to the present day, inventing the wheel and surviving the great flood on the way. It is not, however, so much a play about the resilience of human beings as about what Joyce called 'epiphanies': the moments of happiness or discovery which irradiate our lives. In Joyce they come unawares, by chance; in Wilder, if you work and wait, they come.

Wilder's optimism discomforted the nuclear-age cynics. Critics claimed that his vision of the essential dignity and warmth of humanity was arch sentimentality, and he published little for twenty years (though occasional plays, notably *A Life in the Sun*, 1955, based on Euripides' *Alcestis*, continued to be produced). The novel which broke his silence, *The Eighth Day* (1967), is, after *Our Town*, his finest work. It is about a man who loses his faith in humanity after being falsely accused of murder, and who recovers it by, in effect, beginning creation all over again, showing people the value of the great discoveries of human history, from needles and thread to marriage. Wilder's sacramental humanism (there is no God to interfere; we ourselves weave the 'tapestry of history' of which we are part), and his epiphanic view of human life, are set out with a witty directness which confounds criticism. If the human race is not like this (we are made to feel) then so much the worse for the human race.

Wilder wrote the script of Hitchcock's 1943 film *Shadow of a Doubt* – an unlikely but highly successful venture. Good surveys: M. Goldstein: *The Art of Wilder* (1965); D. Haberman: *The Plays of Wilder* (1967).

WILLIAMS, Tennessee (1911–83)
American playwright

In so far as technique is concerned, Williams was the heir to *O'Neill, and through him to the great actor-managers of the 19th century: the rhetoric and fustian of theatre have seldom been deployed with such hypnotic skill. He invented the most outrageous characters, the steamiest situations and the most extraordinary events – and made us believe in them. It is drama of hysterical excess: there is (as a puritan preacher once reprimanded Byron) 'no hope for them as laughs'. If Williams had also had O'Neill's depth of vision and breadth of theme, he would have been as great a dramatist. But his subjects are limited (sexual repression, neurotic menace and cleansing violence), and his character-invention yields everything in subtlety to Harold Robbins or Grace Metalious.

Williams's plays usually centre on tense females, ravaged by Freudian anxiety and threatened by aggressive and inadequate males. In *The Glass Menagerie* (1945), whose subject is the craving for love, the family contains an emotionally predatory mother, an introverted daughter and a sensitive, artistic son (the play is partly autobiographical). In *A Streetcar Named Desire* (1947, superbly filmed, with Vivien Leigh and Marlon Brando, in 1951), the family contains a wife in sexual enslavement to her brutish husband, and her sister, a demented ex-prostitute clinging to sanity by inventing for herself a genteel past as a schoolteacher. (Rape and madness are the end of it; the only survivor is the ape-husband.) *Summer and Smoke* (1948) stirs religion into the brew: a parson's spinster daughter falls in love with a rakehell, fallen-angel medical student and is corrupted and destroyed by the passions he unlocks in her. In *Cat on a Hot Tin Roof* (1955, also superbly filmed, with Elizabeth Taylor, Paul Newman and Burl Ives, in 1955), domineering 'Big Daddeh' (the play is set in Williams's favourite location, the Deep South) drives his sensitive son to drink and impotence, and the son's wife Maggie saves the situation with a life-giving lie (that she is pregnant) which will eventually wither her marriage even more. (The central image of the play is 'the life-force' which Big Daddy possesses, at least until he develops cancer, and which all the other characters want. Another view of the same force is given in the earthy, erotic tragi-comedy *The Rose Tattoo*, 1951, a play helped towards both tautness and optimism by the fact that the central part was written for Anna Magnani, than whom few actresses exulted or suffered more compellingly.) In the film *Baby Doll* (1956), adolescent sexuality is depicted with a pouty panache which makes Lolita seem chaste. Two other plays, *The Night of the Iguana* (1961), about a phoney preacher, and *In the Bar of a Tokyo Hotel* (1969), about a failing artist, replace racked women in the central roles with tormented men – and allow Williams to hint at an additional neurosis, the guilt of repressed homosexuality.

There are a dozen other, lesser plays (chiefly one-acters, but including at least one full-length piece, the uncharacteristically cheerful 'family comedy' *Period of Adjustment*, 1960). But Williams said nothing new after his big 1940s and 1950s plays: *The Milk Train Doesn't Stop Here Any More* (1962) and *Vieux carré* (1977), the best of his later works, were thin reworkings of previous themes. (He was also a tireless reviser and rewriter of material: each script exists in a multitude of different forms.) His quality is hard to assess. He once seemed a colossus, *Miller's only rival among post-war dramatists. His plays, when revived, still have stunning power. His work is obsessed, exotic, unique: like hell-fire preaching rather than drama, it depends for its effect on the amens of a willing, believing (and some would say gullible) audience.

In addition to plays, Williams published novels (the best, later filmed, was *The Roman Spring of Mrs Stone*, 1950); poems (*In the Winter of Cities*, 1956); *Memoirs* (1970); and four collections of Faulknerish short stories (*Twentyseven Wagons Full of Cotton*, 1946; *One Arm*, 1948; *Hard Candy*, 1956 – the best; *Eight Mortal Ladies Possessed*, 1975). Good introduction to the major work: B. Nelson: *Williams: The Man and His Work*.

WOOD, Charles (born 1932)
British playwright

Peter Ustinov once asked how anyone could take seriously a man who said (as generals do) 'We can take that ridge with minimal loss: only 20,000' – and how anyone could *not* take such a person seriously. This matter, the surrealist deadliness of the military mind, is Wood's great theme. He treated it with deadpan irony in his script for the film *The Charge of the Light Brigade* (1968), at once a satisfying military epic and a cutting attack on the epic convention; it is also the basis for his savage stage-play *Dingo* (1967), in which the Second World War is presented as the inane, smutty antics of a concert-party in the North African desert – exactly true to the tone of actual soldiers on the spot at the time. (Because it made music-hall jokes of Churchill and Montgomery, it was banned in Britain during the Lord Chamberlain's last dismal days; no one seemed to mind that it treated Hitler and Rommel in exactly the same way.)

Wood's second preoccupation (not, perhaps, unrelated) is the manufacture of drama. He is interested in the boredom and frustration involved in writing, acting and filming – and also in the enabling egotism which helps 'creative artists' cope. In *Fill the Stage with Happy Hours* (1966), set in a shabby small-town theatre, the need to perform is all that stands between a family of failed actors and disintegration; *Has 'Washington' Legs?* (1978) presents the making of an epic film about the War of Independence as a hilarious backstage farce, stuffed with every Hollywood cliché ever known. Two other works, the television series *Don't Forget to Write* (1979), about an anguished and absurd writer, and the stage-play *Veterans* (1972), about two elderly actors bitching on the sidelines as they wait to play cameo roles in a film about desert warfare, are deeper, the farce coloured with a sad view of people struggling with emotional stress which is no less painful for being both self-inflicted and ludicrous. With *Dingo*, these are Wood's finest achievements.

Wood's other stage-plays include *Red Star* (1984), about an impressionable Stalin lookalike who gets to play him in a ludicrous epic film and identifies closely with him. In addition to stage and television drama, Wood has also written the scripts for several successful films, including *Help!* (1965, written for the Beatles), *How I Won the War* (1967), *Cuba* (1979), the bilious Stalin–Beria comedy *Red Monarch* (1983), and Tony Palmer's spectacular eight-hour epic *Wagner* (1983).

YEATS, William Butler: see page 202.

ZUCKMAYER, Carl (1896–1977)
German playwright

Zuckmayer's plays are numerous and variable, and range from folk-comedy (e.g. the engaging *The Jolly Vineyard*, 1926, a *Bartered-Bride*-like piece about an elderly landowner, his daughter and the suitors they each prefer for her) to surrealism and documentary drama. (Good examples of this last form are *The Cold Light*, 1956, based on the Fuchs case and dealing with the social responsibility of science, and *The Devil's General*, 1946, which centres on the investigation of sabotage in factories supplying planes for the Luftwaffe in 1941, and is an effective study – comparable in style and mood to *Rattigan's *The Winslow Boy* – of idealist resistance to the totalitarian state. It was well filmed, with Curt Jürgens, in 1956.)

Zuckmayer's best play, *The Captain from Köpenick* (1931), combines social criticism with satirical wit and an amiable folk style. It is based on a true incident, and tells of a Švejk-like soldier who steals an officer's uniform and is able because of it to trick and dominate the citizens of an entire small town. Its strength is partly in the central roles (Clochemerlian townsfolk and a cheerfully amoral hero from the mainstream of central European farce), and partly in its satire on German willingness to follow anyone in uniform (a pointed theme in 1931). Zuckmayer is, overall, a minor figure, but in this play and *The Devil's General* he produced quality work.

As well as plays, Zuckmayer wrote novels, poetry (none of great distinction), and an excellent autobiography, *A Part of Myself* (1966). Overall, he gives the impression of an excellent journeyman who once or twice made works of real art: he was his country's *Priestley.

GLOSSARY
OF TECHNICAL TERMS

ABSTRACT ART

All visual art – including sculpture and photography – is in one sense abstract, as it concerns itself as much with the placing of geometrical shapes in space as with depicting or suggesting reality. In its narrower meaning, however, 'abstract art' means art in which shapes, patterns or forms exist primarily for their own sakes, and the object depicted (if any) is of secondary importance. (Thus, a Moore sculpture of, say, a mother and child, is *not* abstract: though it uses forms characteristic of abstract art, its references are to the real, outside world; a wrought-steel cube by Smith, by contrast, is abstract and concerned exclusively with shapes in space.) The best-known types of abstract art in painting include the squares and lines of Mondrian, the *action paintings of Pollock and the large coloured rectangles of Rothko or Newman.

Excellent, and beautifully illustrated, anthology: A. Pohribny: *Abstract Painting* (English edn, 1979).

ACTION PAINTING

In action painting (a term first used in 1952), the artist's creative *action* is regarded as the crucial factor: each mark he or she makes has individual significance, in contrast to more conventional painting, where the artist's actions are regarded more as means towards an end (the finished work). The best-known exponents of action painting were Pollock (who dribbled, splashed and threw paint on to canvases tacked on the ground) and de Kooning and Motherwell, whose pictures look as if they used their brushes (often house-painter's brushes) to attack rather than (as Botticelli, say, or Seurat did) to woo the canvas. Whereas more conventional art tends to be subjective in both intention and effect, action painting, for all its subjectivity of means, tends to seem objective and depersonalized, as though paint and canvas have married independently of the painter who brought them together.

ALEATORY (or ALEATORIC)

Derived from the Latin word *alea* ('dice'), this adjective is applied to any art-form in which chance is allowed to play a part. Though this can include 'finished' art – Arp's paper collages, for example, depended on random flutterings; Schwitters' *Merzbauen* depended on what objects came to the collecting hand – the main application of aleatory techniques is in the performing arts, and particularly in music. In aleatory music the players are encouraged to choose the sequence of movements, sections or individual chords and notes, or to improvise on a pattern or idea suggested by the composer (e.g. in Ligeti's *Aventures*, on letters of the alphabet; in Lutosłavski's *Preludes and Fugue*, on a series of lines, squares and triangles). Thus, the result differs from player to player and from performance to performance. (Aleatory music is, in conception, close both to Far-Eastern art-music and to jazz, in each of which improvisation on a previously agreed basis is a feature of the performance.) Aleatory procedures have been used in the theatre, and in the recitation of poetry; but there are few signs here that they have progressed beyond the experimental stage. In music, however, composers as established as Boulez, Stockhausen, Ligeti and Lutosbavski use aleatory techniques as an integral, and entirely accepted, component of their work.

ALIENATION EFFECT

This is Brecht's term for the feeling of objectivity, of distance between audience and performers, which was a crucial ingredient of Greek, Japanese, Shakespearean and other 'theatres of convention' (as opposed to the 'theatre of illusion' of 19th-century writers like Ibsen or Chekhov), and which would allow spectators of his drama to understand its polemical messages even as they enjoyed the show. In essence, the effect is achieved by the performers constantly emphasizing that what they are performing *is* a show, and never pretending that it is reality. (The most common way of doing this is to make out-of-character 'asides' to the audience, commenting on the action.) Paradoxically, both in Brecht's own plays and in those of his myriad disciples, the effect achieved is often one of conspiracy-about-performance between actor and audience, and is as engrossing and involving for the spectators as any of the simulations of reality in the theatre of illusion. Is it that a major part of our enjoyment of live theatre is *precisely* the feeling that we are participating in a performance – or is that feeling a measure, today, of how successful and far-reaching Brechtian techniques have been?

Good English-language selection of Brecht's theoretical writings: J. Willett (ed.): *Brecht on Theatre* (1964).

ATONALITY

Tonal music is that in which the listener can constantly relate the harmonies he or she hears to a tonal centre (in the case of many 18th- and 19th-century works, to a specific key, so that a piece can be said to be 'in C' or 'in E flat'); in atonal music, this feeling of harmonic nucleus is replaced by that of a continuum of sound, in which each individual harmony is equal with all the others. Thus, although the word 'atonal' was once (wrongly) applied exclusively to *twelve-note music, it can describe any music in which a feeling of harmonic vagueness, of ebb and flow, predominates: not only works by Messiaen, Varèse or Tippett, but earlier pieces ranging from Bach fugues to Wagner's *Tristan and Isolde* or Debussy's piano preludes. (By the same token, much 20th-century music once regarded as 'atonal', for example Bartók's, can now clearly be heard to have a strong tonal drive, based on the departure from and return to the harmonies of a single all-embracing 'key'.)

BAUHAUS

The aims of the Bauhaus ('Build-house', founded in 1919, broken up by the Nazis in 1933) were to apply the best forms and styles of modern art to ordinary living, and in particular to marry mass-production techniques to the latest ideas in fine design. In practice, Bauhaus creations (exemplified by tubular-metal furniture, variably positionable desk-lamps and cuboid buildings) were stiff to look at and expensive to buy; the Bauhaus idea, however, has influenced the design of consumer goods ever since, as anyone can testify who has sat in a moulded-plastic chair in a high-rise flat, or drunk from an extruded-polystyrene cup. The artists, architects and designers associated with the Bauhaus (and who went on to greater and less anonymous creation) include Breuer, Gropius (its director for the first nine years), Kandinsky, Klee, Mies van der Rohe and Moholy-Nagy.

Good study: H. W. Wingler: *The Bauhaus* (1969). Also recommended: T. Wolfe: *From Bauhaus to Our House* (1982), a marvellously sour polemic against the concept of 'art-for-living' by a writer who never lets even-handedness get in the way of wit.

BILDUNGSROMAN

The *bildungsroman* ('formation-novel') is an 18th- and 19th-century fictional form taken over by many 20th-century writers. It tells, in a quasi-biographical manner, the story of one person's growth from innocence to maturity (and often, on to decline), and shows how its hero is formed by or reacts against outside events and influences. Many of Dickens's novels (e.g. *Nicholas Nickleby, David Copperfield*) show the form at its 19th-century peak; in the 20th century, some writers (most notably Proust, Hesse and Nabokov) have used it in a largely unchanged way, while others have made it lead in other directions. (Mann turned it back to front, moving from confidence to decadence, in *The Magic Mountain*; Pasternak overlaid it in *Doctor Zhivago* with elements of political epic; several writers, from Sartre to McCarthy, used it to show the evolution not of individuals but of groups.)

BLOOMSBURY GROUP

The only things the 'members' of the Bloomsbury Group had in common were that they all at one time or another lived in Bloomsbury, London, that they were friends, and that they have been exhaustively written about by those who took them as some kind of trend-setting intellectual pressure-group. (Their own memoirs, letters and diaries are not the least vociferous advocates of this point of view.) The friends (often nicknamed 'Bloomsberries') included Clive Bell, Roger Fry, Duncan Grant, John Maynard Keynes, Lytton Strachey and Virginia Woolf; others associated with them included E. M. Forster and Katherine Mansfield.

A starry-eyed account is given (by one of the surviving children) in Q. Bell: *Bloomsbury* (1969); more flinty is the view in J. K. Johnstone: *The Bloomsbury Group* (1948).

BRÜCKE, DIE

This phrase ('the bridge') was the name chosen for themselves by a group of young German artists who formed a loose association from 1905 to 1913. The members included Kirchner, Nolde and Pechstein, and the 'bridge' they were seeking to build was between past and future art. They were influenced by primitive and pre-Renaissance art, and particularly by stained glass and the chunky woodblock illustrations of early printed books; their use of bold, flat colour was similar to that of the *fauves, and they also favoured an overt emotionalism which links them with the *expressionists.

BRUTALISM

Dedicated to utility above beauty and to the undecorated use of materials, this architectural movement had a great vogue in the 1950s and 1960s, when every prize-winning new building seemed a monument to bare cement, breeze-blocks and unconcealed ducts and pipes. The chief architects of Brutalism included Rudolph and the Smithsons; among its characteristic relics are several post-war British universities and the graceless new towns in which they are placed; in each case the feeling that buildings come first and human needs nowhere (for all the architects' nobler intentions) is sure and strong.

CONSTRUCTIVISM

Born in Russia just after the revolution, Constructivism was a movement intended to harness new artistic forms (especially *cubism) to the needs of humanity at large. Its main application was in architecture – and its chief monument is the model for a tower, intended to rival the Eiffel

Tower and to be constructed of spiralling steel girders, designed by Tatlin for the Third International but never built – and its influence spread, through the *Bauhaus, to the design of buildings, furniture and household artefacts throughout the world.

CUBISM

One of the quintessential styles of 20th-century painting, cubism was prefigured in the late, increasingly geometric works of Cézanne, and was energetically developed in the 1900s and 1910s by Braque and Picasso (whose *Demoiselles d'Avignon*, 1907, is generally cited as the first 'official' cubist picture). Its starting-point, the division of the objects the artist wishes to depict (houses, trees, fruit, musical instruments, faces) into planes of light and colour, is identical to that of any earlier art; but in cubism the planes are stressed, separated one from another and even outlined until geometric shapes dominate the finished picture. (As well as the cubes which give the style its name, cylinders, pyramids and spheres are common.) At its most extreme (e.g. in Picasso's *Man Smoking a Pipe* or Duchamp's *Nude Descending a Staircase*), a cubist picture can seem to the unconvinced observer little more than a tumble of shapes hard to relate to the picture-title, at its most representational (e.g. in the check tablecloths, plates and fruit of a Gris still-life) little more than a pleasant emphasis of form over content; but at its finest (say in Picasso's 1930s and 1940s portraits of Jacqueline) it becomes just as much the means towards an end as, say, perspective was in the hands of the great artists of the late Middle Ages. With Braque, Gris and Picasso, the chief painters to use the style were Delaunay and Léger; as part of the technical vocabulary of 20th-century painting, however, it has influenced artists of every kind, from Mondrian to Nicholson. (There is little cubist sculpture, and what there is – e.g. the work of Lipchitz – suggests that paint on canvas remains the ideal vehicle for this apparently three-dimensional style.)

Good studies: R. Rosenblum: *Cubism and 20th-Century Art* (1961); D. Cooper: *The Cubist Epoch* (1971).

DADA

Appropriately for a movement founded on nonsense, Dada was born in two quite separate places: in New York in 1913 (where its progenitors were Duchamp, Picabia and Man Ray) and in Zürich in 1916 (where its parents, including the poet Tzara and the artist Arp, found a name for it by sticking a knife into a French dictionary: instead of *Dada*, 'hobby-horse', it might have been christened *Dorémi*, *Réticule*, or anything at all). Its object was to demolish bourgeois art by mocking it: anti-poetry might consist of nonsense-words, anti-music of rude noises, anti-painting of a bucket of whitewash hurled at the spectators or the wall. For a time

– particularly in Dada magazines and Dada cabarets – the idea was voguish, but by the mid-1920s it had been absorbed into such more directed artistic movements as *cubism, *neo-classicism and *surrealism. None the less, the feelings of nihilism and alienation which produced Dada have remained central forces in the arts of the 20th century – vital influences, for example, on Kafka, Picasso, Stravinsky, Ionesco and Beckett. The nonsense-element also lingers (and does avant-garde art no good at all in bourgeois eyes): to compose a piece of 'music' for twelve randomly tuned radios (as Cage did), to wrap the Californian coastline in polythene or walk round East Anglia balancing a plank on your head, call it art, and get grants to do it (all of which happened in the late 1970s) – are these not activities to make Dada's founders dance with joy? The joke is really on those critics who solemnly expound what the Dadaists did, and why.

A good example of such solemnity (for all its clear analysis) is H. Richter: *Dada: Art and Anti-Art* (1965); for those who read French, a less stuffy account is G. Hugnet: *L'Aventure Dada, 1916–1922* (1957).

ELECTRONIC MUSIC

As its name implies, electronic music is generated not by human performers, but by electrical impulses; at first it was recorded on disc or tape, but modern machines such as the synthesizer produce it to order, on the spot, and so allow an element of 'live' performance. Electronic methods are standard in modern rock and pop, but apart from the *ondes martenot* (whose sound is a pure, clear squeal like that of a musical saw) few electronic instruments have found their way into the 'serious' orchestra. On the other hand, several composers of note have consistently produced electronic works, either 'composing' them on tape in the studio (as Cage, Eimert, Babbitt and other pioneers used to do), or using synthesizers and sound-mixers to blend with 'orthodox' performers in live concerts (as Boulez and Stockhausen do). Although many composers have used electronic techniques (apart from those mentioned, the key names include Berio, Ligeti, Penderecki, Pousseur and Xenakis), the whole field – largely because the electronics industry moves ahead so far so fast – remains more suited to constant experiment than to the production of established masterworks, and raises the issue of whether musical machinery, however sophisticated, can ever rival the emotional power generated by human performers making natural sounds.

Good study: P. Griffiths: *A Guide to Electronic Music* (1979).

EXPRESSIONISM

In contrast to pre-19th-century arts (which were principally concerned to depict reality, and used emotion – the artist's or the subject's – as one component of expression and not its guarantor), expressionist art deals directly with the transmission of emotion: it is subjective and incoherent rather than objective and precise. The urge towards the overt expression of feeling began with the romantic movement at the end of the 18th century, but true expressionism was only liberated a century later, when Freud's work made complexes, neuroses and private obsessions acceptable subjects for polite study, and for the arts. In music, although earlier compositions like Berlioz's *Fantastic Symphony* or Wagner's *Tristan and Isolde* are clearly concerned above all with emotion, the term expressionist is generally reserved for the work of such men as Scriabin (e.g. *Poem of Ecstasy*), Strauss (e.g. *Salome*) or the young Schoenberg (whose *Verklärte Nacht* and *Erwartung* are explicit sound-pictures of shifting emotional states). In literature, though the chief expressionists are turn-of-the-century writers like Mallarmé, Huysmans and Maeterlinck, expressionist aims and techniques also influenced later writers like Gide, Proust, Kafka and – in his blunter way – Hemingway. In drama expressionism was the style of men like Strindberg, Wedekind and Kaiser, and hardly survived the 1920s (except in the cinema, where the range is from Murnau and Lang to more modern exponents of Gothic or horrific mystery: both Hitchcock's *Psycho* and Bergman's *The Seventh Seal*, for example, make play with expressionist techniques).

The most lasting expressionist work has been in fine art, and ranges from the harsh canvases of Munch and Kokoschka (which show recognizable people in states of nightmare psychological alarm) or the paintings of Kandinsky (whose aim was to paint abstract emotion, and whose results often seem experimental and chaotic rather than exact) to the much later 'abstract expressionism' of painters like de Kooning, Dubuffet or Motherwell. Many other artists (e.g. Bacon, Chagall, Rouault), though not full-hearted expressionists, have used the emotional fervency and gaudy colour characteristic of the style.

Good studies: J. Willett: *Expressionism* (1971); M. and D. Gerhardus: *Expressionism* (well-illustrated English edn 1979).

FAUVISM

Fauves ('wild animals') was the disparaging name given by the critic Vauxcelles to a group of artists – including Derain, Matisse, Rouault and Vlaminck – exhibiting at the Paris autumn salon of 1905. What disconcerted him – he was comparing their work with Donatello's sculpture – was the dazzle of colour which filled their canvases: large areas of flat, unmodulated colour, often thickly applied and with little resemblance to the natural colours of the objects depicted. (In this respect, fauvism had been anticipated centuries before, by such artists as Mantegna, Rembrandt and El Greco.) Apart from this colouristic brilliance – which had great influence on such *expressionists as Munch and Kokoschka – they had little else in common. Their immediate predecessors included van

Gogh and Gauguin; later painters influenced by their style range from
Dufy and Kandinsky to Soutine, Bacon and Rauschenberg.

Good study: J. E. Muller: *Fauvism* (English edn 1967).

FUTURISM

This artistic movement was founded by Marinetti in 1909, and flourished
for twenty-five years, especially in Italy, until it was engulfed by the neo-
classicizing vulgarities of fascist art. Its object – akin to that of
*constructivism in Russia – was to create an art-form specifically of and
for the modern world, with no references to any previous traditions.
Thus, speed, machine movement and geometrical angularity were features
of the futurist style: its analogues range from the gawkier *cubist canvases
to the unbending modularities of the *Bauhaus. As a style for fine art, it
has proved limited (though several fine artists, e.g. Léger, owe debts to
it); but in every other respect it is all around us still, as the dominant,
whirlwind mode of this century's most striking billboard art, fashion and
theatre and cinema designs.

Good study: M. W. Martin: *Futurist Art and Theory* (1968).

IMAGISM

This poetic movement was founded by Pound and others in 1912. Its
purpose was to dispense with waffle, to present clear images in simple
words and comprehensible syntax, and generally to sweep the emotional
grandiosities of 19th-century poetry into the garbage-can. The work of
many of the imagists themselves (as well as Pound, they included Hilda
Doolittle, Joyce, Amy Lowell and William Carlos Williams, who developed it in the 1930s into an even more rarefied style of his own,
objectivism, in which the poet tries to keep personality rigorously out of
what he or she describes) was often no more than tersely coy, and 20th-
century poetry has never really recovered from the aura of pretentious
preciousness with which the imagists invested it. But at its best (e.g.
much of Pound's own early poetry) it transcends affectation and genuinely
achieves the stripped-down clarity of expression and emotional exactness.
to which it aspires. (It is, for example, streets better – because thought-
out, polished and linguistically precise – than the apparently similar, Far-
Eastern-style Beat poetry of the 1960s and 1970s.) Not only that, but the
stylistic experiments of the imagists had an incalculable effect on most of
the great English-language poets of the century, from Auden and Eliot
to Berryman, Graves and Robert Lowell.

Good, if somewhat technical, study: J. B. Harmer: *Victory in Limbo: Imagism
1907–1917* (1975).

IMPRESSIONISM

The best-known form of impressionism is the French fine-arts movement begun in the 1870s and embracing such major painters as Cézanne, Degas, Monet and Renoir. As the title of Monet's 1874 painting *Impression: Sunrise* (which is thought to have given the style its name) implies, the object is to depict not photographic reality but an impression of reality, the prismatic view of the artist's own eye. Above all, the impressionist painters were concerned with representing light, often dappled by leaves, reflected in water, or scattered into a myriad dots like a newspaper photograph. These formal innovations are the corner-stone of all 'modern' art: though there is no single 'impressionist style' (Turner, Gauguin, Manet and Seurat, for example, were all in their quite different ways impressionists), impressionist techniques and ideas underlie *cubism, *expressionism, *minimalism, and in fact every ism save those following such harsher (more politically or philosophically oriented) paths as *constructivism, *futurism and the like.

Impressionism is also apparent in the arts of literature and music. In both, it implies an evocative, subjective and somewhat misty conjuration of atmosphere, of which Mallarmé's poem of adolescent eroticism *L'Après-midi d'un faune*, and Debussy's tone-poem based on it, are archetypes. Debussy was none the less not really a musical impressionist – his works are too formal and objective – and yields that particular palm to such composers as Delius and Respighi. In literature, impressionism was largely absorbed into other movements, from the dewy-eyed mysticism of the British Pre-Raphaelite poets to the more exotic (and erotic) fancies of such minor writers as Corvo and Firbank (and one major writer, Gide); as in art it very soon evolved, and became the basis for writing of many other kinds, from the precise imprecision of the *imagists (and through them, of much later verse) to the – very different – novels of Hesse, Joyce and Woolf, the plays of Beckett and the film-scripts directed by Carné, Cocteau, Kurosawa and Mizoguchi.

There is no satisfactory overall study of impressionism: the term is too vast and vague. But for fine art, at least, P. Pool: *Impressionism* (1967) is a reasonable starting-point, and – fittingly for a movement whose origins always seem traceable to France – J. Lethève's *Impressionistes et symbolistes devant la presse* (1959) amiably charts the reactions of succeeding generations to this most evocative and evanescent form of art.

INTERNATIONAL STYLE

This style (first described in Hitchcock and Johnson's book *The International Style*, 1932, and named accordingly) has been predominant in world architecture for the last fifty years. Its combination of simple construction-methods (a steel framework filled in with bricks or reinforced concrete, or hung with pre-fabricated wall-and-window panels) and its elegantly severe appearance (most buildings are cuboid; the finish is often bare grey cement) has appealed to architects of every country, and buildings in the style have proliferated even in such culturally inappropriate environments as Japanese or Cambridgeshire villages. Although when used by lesser talents (among them the *Brutalists), the International Style has produced buildings as nasty to look at as they are to live in, all the great 20th-century architects influenced by it (e.g. Aalto, Johnson, Le Corbusier) have adapted it and added to it to suit their own or their clients' fancy; the greatest architects of all (e.g. Mies van der Rohe) have treated it as a basic vocabulary, and created wonders.

A brief, clear survey is given in K. Frampton: *Modern Architecture: A Critical History* (1980).

METHOD ACTING

'The Method' was a style of acting supposedly (though not actually) initiated by Stanislavski at the Moscow Art Theatre (and enshrined in his books *The Actor Prepares*, 1936, *Building a Character*, 1949, and *Creating a Role*, 1961), and which achieved wide currency when it was taken up by the New York Actors' Studio in 1947. In essence, Method acting involves 'living' each role, feeling and experiencing life exactly as the character (instead of applying a veneer of performing-technique willy-nilly to every part, as earlier actors such as Irving were thought to have done): in short, the system seeks to reduce to a teachable method what every talented actor does anyway, whether consciously or not. Combined with the experimental group-techniques of such producers as Brecht, Barrault and Brook, the Method has led to some of the century's most intense theatrical experiences (Brook's production of Weiss's *The Marat/Sade* is a notable example); furthermore, thanks to the Actors' Studio, it directly influenced American film acting (for the better) in the 1950s and 1960s, helped to form the careers of fine film actors like Brando, MacLaine, Newman and Nicholson, and (thanks to their example) led to a raising of acting standards throughout the world. (It signally – and mercifully – failed, however, to change Marilyn Monroe, who briefly 'studied' at the Actors' Studio: star quality is still what makes a star.)

Apart from the Stanislavski books mentioned (engrossing texts for anyone interested in acting technique), the best glimpse of the Method in action is in R. H. Hethman (ed.): *Strasberg at the Actors' Studio* (1965).

MINIMALISM

This term began to be used in the 1960s to describe art which had been reduced to its minimal elements: single lines, squares, circles, colours. Its progenitors included Malevich (who in 1913 launched a movement of his own, Suprematism, with almost identical aims, painted single white squares on white backgrounds, and sold the results); the key 1960s minimalists included Newman, Rothko and Kelly, and the style also influenced much 'pop' art of the time (e.g. the targets and other plain geometrical shapes painted by such people as Noland, and sculpted by Smith and others). There is a strong hint of *Dada about minimalism (which allows artists to 'sign' heaps of bricks, strips of cloth, mounted tiles – objects as commonplace as Duchamp's 'ready-mades'); but reduction in itself is no inhibitor of quality, as the (minimalist-influenced) paintings of Klee and the solarized photos of Man Ray attest.

Good introductions: G. Battcock: *Minimalist Art* (1969); E. Lucie-Smith: *Art in the Seventies* (1980).

NABIS

The Nabis ('prophets') were a group of artists gathered in Paris in 1892, who advocated a calm, reassuring style, painting domestic scenes in bright, clear colours, rather in the manner of the Japanese domestic prints in vogue at the time. The chief 'prophets' – the reason for the name has never been satisfactorily explained, except that they were preaching a technical gospel supposedly learned from Gauguin's South Sea Island canvases – included the sculptor Maillol and the painters Bonnard and Vuillard. Though the movement was never in the main current of modernism, and remained a seductive, tranquil backwater, its gentle influence can be seen in the work of several later artists, notably Dufy and Matisse.

Good introduction: C. Chassé: *The Nabis and Their Period* (English translation 1969).

NEO-CLASSICISM

The formal strength, emotional objectivity and sensual grace of Greek and Roman classical art, literature and architecture have held a consistent appeal for later artists, from the painters of the Renaissance to the dramatists of the 17th and 18th centuries and the civic architects of the 19th century. The attraction is partly in the classical models themselves, and partly in the thought that if you anchor your style on what has proved of lasting greatness from the past, some of its authority and quality may rub off on yours. In the 20th century, a number of writers and artists made use of the past in this way. Gide, Giraudoux, Cocteau and other French writers, for example, used literary models from ancient Greece (and Hesse, in a similar way, is full of reminiscences of medieval literary techniques); Chirico, Maillol and Picasso produced art derived from Greek, Roman or Renaissance originals, and concepts of classical restraint and purity influenced artists as disparate as Brancusi, Gabo, Klee and Nicholson.

The chief 20th-century application of neo-classicism has been in music. As a direct reaction against 19th-century turgidities, many composers in the 1920s began turning back to the small ensembles, unfussy counterpoint and clear harmonies – not of ancient Greece or Rome (whose music is largely unknown), but of Bach, Vivaldi and their early 18th-century contemporaries. The first neo-classical work of genius, Stravinsky's *Pulcinella* (1920), reworks actual pieces by Pergolesi, adding spicy harmony, sharpening the rhythm and dressing up the original in dazzling 20th-century orchestral clothes. (The absence of overt emotion in this *commedia dell'arte* ballet was also a crucial influence on later composers: as well as being technically stripped down and reassembled, neo-classical music is characteristically open and unaffected, in some composers to the extent of take-it-or-leave-it busyness.) Apart from Stravinsky (whose neo-classical period lasted for thirty years, and produced many of his finest works, including *Apollo*, *Symphony in C* and *The Rake's Progress*), leading composers using the neo-classical idiom included Hindemith, Prokofiev, Martinů and, in his individual way, Webern. Looking back on his neo-classical period, Stravinsky said, 'I was a kind of bird, and the 18th century was a nest in which I felt comfortable for laying my eggs' – and when we consider the myriad later composers who learned grace and discipline either from the past or from his reinterpretation of it (they range from Copland and Honegger to Boulez, Ligeti and the young Stockhausen and Henze), we see what a commodious nest it was.

There is no adequate or comprehensive book on neo-classicism. For those who read Italian, M. Praz: *Gusto neoclassico* (2nd edn, 1959) adequately covers fine art; H. Honour: *Neo-Classicism* (1969) deals with architecture (but is weak on the 20th century); for music, the best general introduction is the appropriate section in P. Griffiths: *20th-Century Music* (1980), and the most stimulating and witty account of the neo-classical aesthetic is in Stravinsky's lectures *Poetics of Music* (1940).

NEW FICTION

This was a kind of novel-writing which emerged in France in the late 1950s, at much the same time as *New Wave cinema. Its chief writers were Butor, Robbe-Grillet and Sarraute, and their aim was to abandon the methods of older fiction (e.g. consecutive narrative, orderly characterization and above all authorial and 'philosophical' comment), and to produce a new fiction suitable for a new age. For the general reader, the avant-garde techniques in their work (e.g. dislocated narrative, obsessive attention to apparently trivial or inconsequential details, a feeling of life as ritual or charade) ally it both to the *Theatre of the Absurd (Beckett's and Genet's works – including their novels – are major influences) and to the films of such men as Godard and Resnais. Apart from those mentioned, the finest French new novelist is Duras; outside France – and despite the growth of 'new criticism' in universities everywhere – there are few thoroughgoing exponents, though writers as far apart as Borges, Durrell and Grass use some of the new novelists' techniques.

Good introductions: A. Robbe-Grillet: *Towards a New Fiction* (1963); J. L. Sturrock, *The French New Novel* (1969).

NEW WAVE

This was the name given to a large group of film directors who began working in French cinema in the late 1950s, sweeping aside such established names as Carné, Clément and even Renoir. For all the bitterness felt in the profession at the time, the change was salutary: Chabrol, Godard, Malle, Resnais, Rohmer, Truffaut and Vadim created a vigorous new tradition, capable of infinite variety, from the loose, quasi-documentary style of Godard to the imponderabilities of Resnais and Chabrol's Hitchcockian panache. The 'New Wave style', however, is best exemplified by the films of Truffaut and Malle, and as such has influenced foreign directors from Antonioni to Forman and Kubrick. There have been two subsequent 'New Waves', one in America (led by Coppola, Scorsese and Spielberg) and one in Germany (led by Fassbinder and Herzog).

Good critical anthology: P. Graham (ed.): *The New Wave* (1968); also recommended: J. F. Monaco: *The New Wave: Truffaut, Chabrol, Rohmer, Rivette* (1976); M. Pye and L. Myles: *The Movie Brats: How the Film Generation Took Over Hollywood* (1979).

OP ART

This was a 1960s movement; its name is an attempt to harmonize 'pop' and 'optical' art, and its intention was to dazzle or trick the spectators' eyes (and, in the 1960s, to 'blow their minds') with hallucinatory optical effects. The technique involves abstract patterns of line and colour, so organized that they seem to shimmer and shift as you look at them. Though the style was quickly taken over, and debased, by the advertising profession (and has now been superseded by computer art), it produced, in Riley and Vasarély, two painters of distinction, and influenced others, notably Hockney.

POLYTONALITY

As its name implies, this is a musical style involving the use of several keys at once. Stravinsky's *Petrushka*, for example, makes simultaneous use of F sharp major (the 'black-key scale' on the piano) and C major (the 'white-key scale'); Milhaud wrote several works in the 1910s and

1920s, including a setting of the *Oresteia*, in parts of which each instrument plays in a different key. The effect, in simpler polytonal music (e.g. Holst's *Terzetto* in three keys, or Ives's chorales in four), is often as if conventional harmony has gone inexplicably awry, in the way that some cubist paintings look like conventional pictures seen in a distorting mirror. But in the hands of the greatest composers (notably Bartók, Messiaen, Sibelius and Stravinsky), who use it as one component of style and not as a style in itself, polytonality produces balanced and expressive results – even Milhaud, once he stopped experimenting, turned it to good and serious account (e.g. in *Symphony 6*).

SERIAL MUSIC

Composers of serial music seek to remove randomness from their art by subjecting some or all of its elements – pitch, duration, volume – to external mathematical discipline. In twelve-note music, for example, the twelve notes of the octave (C, C sharp, D, D sharp, etc.) are arranged in a series (e.g. 2, 5, 8, 9, etc., where C is 1, C sharp is 2, and so on); no note may be repeated until the whole series has been played. (This style, developed by Schoenberg in the late 1910s, and formalized by him in 1923, is the single most radical innovation in 20th-century music, as fundamental to it as the development of *cubism was to art.) The series can be used vertically to produce chords and harmonies, or horizontally to produce 'melodies'; it can appear backwards and upside-down, and can begin on any of the twelve chromatic notes – forty-eight permutations are thus available. In addition to pitch, many composers have experimented with rhythmic series: Messiaen used Greek poetic metres and the *talas* of Indian music, Blacher used irregular, rigorously repeated patterns of crotchets and quavers, Stockhausen and Boulez serialized duration according to imposed mathematical rules. The difficulty of performing music in which every note is a different length and pitch from all the others, and needs a different kind of attack – in some Boulez piano works, each finger is playing in a different way – led, in the 1950s and onwards, to the development of electronic and computer-played music, which eliminates the fallible humanity of the player. This art, though enthusiastically enjoyed by its devotees, has remained that of an avant-garde minority; only twelve-note serialism has proved a serious influence on music at large.

The clearest guide to the various styles (though technical), is in A. Whittall: *Music Since the First World War* (1977).

SUPREMATISM: see MINIMALISM

SURREALISM

A child of *Dada, surrealism was christened by Apollinaire in 1917. Its purpose was to break through the barriers imposed on the arts by the need to conform, to a greater or lesser extent, to the 'realism' of life, and so to reach the 'superior realism' of the subconscious, unhindered by such objective correlatives as the trappings of everyday existence. This Freudian activity, it was thought, would liberate the subconscious not only of the artist, but also of his or her spectators: the various subconsciouses would then unite in the face of everyday reality, and so purge it of show or sham. For a time in the 1910s and 1920s surrealism held sway in every art (save architecture, which needs firmer ground to build on than the subconscious); but it soon proved a sterile form in music – even Cage, the greatest surrealist composer, wrote his best works when he disciplined his random plinks and plunks – and became associated chiefly with literature, fine art and drama.

Literary surrealism is a combination of cuteness and hallucination. Sentences, words, even single syllables and letters disengage themselves from syntax and float free, producing in readers either the feeling that they, too, have been liberated into new spheres of meaning, or bafflement. Surrealist poetry (whether by Éluard, Gascoigne, Arp or the *imagists, objectivists and Beat poets they influenced) and surrealist prose (where the range is from Stein to Burroughs, and those influenced include giants like Joyce and Woolf) is pretty more often than beautiful, entertaining more often than meaningful: in short, surface is all and style gobbles form. In fine art, the same problem arises: surrealist images, whether Chirico's piazzas and mannequins, Magritte's room-filling apples, Dali's soft watches or Oldenburg's floppy toilets, tend to absorb the attention for a moment only, and to provide clues to the artist's sense of humour and (often dazzling) technique rather than to the 'superior reality' they seek to reveal. It is like talking with spirits in a séance: good fun while it lasts (if you believe in it), but no substitute for genuine person-to-person dialogue.

In the theatre, where the element of performance essential to surrealism is allowed full scope, the style has had its greatest success and led to work of true substance. Early surrealist drama (its ancestor was Jarry's *Ubu roi*, and its chief 1920s creator was Cocteau, who continued to use it for forty years, notably in his films) was inconsequential, shocking and delightfully ridiculous: Apollinaire's play *The Breasts of Tiresias* or Cocteau's and Satie's ballets *Parade* and *Relâche* ('Theatre closed') are typical, soap-bubbles which only the most earnest ever took for art. But the seeds were sown which thirty years later blossomed into the *Theatre of the Absurd, a genre which transformed drama – and incidentally transformed surrealism, by letting the spectators into the secret (philosophical, moral or otherwise) for which the artwork itself is just a metaphor.

548 · Glossary of Technical Terms

Good introduction: M. Nadeau: *The History of Surrealism* (English edn 1968). Outstanding study of Chirico, Ernst, Magritte and Miró: C. Lauchner and L. Rosenstock: *Four Modern Masters* (1983).

THEATRE OF THE ABSURD

Prefigured by the surrealists, and by such 1930s movements as Artaud's Theatre of Cruelty, the Theatre of the Absurd was born in Paris in the 1950s with the first performances of Ionesco's *The Bald Soprano*. Its premise is philosophical, not hilarious: human beings are creatures without hope or destiny, coping as best they can with an irrational and often hostile universe. Sometimes (as in Ionesco's *Rhinoceros*, where the hero is the only person in the world unable to change into a rhinoceros) the struggle is for conformity, and is as funny as it is painful (failed attempts at betterment being a staple theme of comedy); sometimes (as in Beckett's plays) the heroes have long ago opted out of effort and decided to let the world pass by, and the spectacle of their resignation is tragic (if you find the plays uplifting) or pathetic (if you don't). From the beginning, however, the best Absurd drama hovered between the extremes of farce and tragedy, providing both a striking theatrical show and an underlying moral meaning, however bleak. Apart from Ionesco and Beckett, the chief Absurdist playwrights are Albee, Dürrenmatt, Frisch and Pinter; Absurd techniques have also been used by post-war dramatists of every kind, from Camus, Sartre and Genet to such apparently unlikely figures as Miller and Brecht, and have permeated the work of experimental theatre-groups everywhere. The Absurd style (which consists, chiefly, of pushing an initially ludicrous notion to preposterous but rigorously logical conclusions) has spread to other arts as well, notably to fiction (e.g. the novels of Heller, Márquez and Grass) and to film (where the range is from Bergman and Buñuel to simpler entertainers like Allen or Altman). It is clear, in short, that what seemed in the heyday of the well-made play to be a jolly but flimsy avant-garde preoccupation was in fact one of the three or four seminal artistic movements of the century.

Good study (the book which gave the movement its name): M. Esslin: *The Theatre of the Absurd* (2nd edn 1968).

TWELVE-NOTE MUSIC: see SERIAL MUSIC

INDEX

Page numbers in italics indicate major entries.

General della Rovere (Rossellini), 279
General Line, The (Eisenstein), 238
General Suvorov (Pudovkin), 272
Generation, A (Wajda), 291
Genet, Jean, 239, 477, *483–4*, 544
Genitrix (Mauriac), 149
Genius, The (Brenton), 468
Genius and the Goddess, The (Huxley, A.), 117
genre writing, 44–6, 52
Gentlemen and Ladies (Hill), 113
Geography of a Horse Dreamer (Shepard), 519
Gerhard, Roberto, *329*
German Embassy, St Petersburg (Behrens), 20
German Love-Story, A (Hochhuth), 291, 489; (Wajda), 291
Germany, Year Zero (Rossellini), 279
Gershwin, George, 199, *329–30*, 358
Gertrud (Dreyer), 235; (Hesse), 111
Gertrude's Child (Hughes, R.), 115
Getting Even (Allen), 213
Getting Gertie's Garter (Dwan), 236
Getting of Wisdom, The, 196
Ghelderode, Michel de, *484*
Ghost Goes West, The (Clair), 229; (Sherwood), 520
Ghost in the Machine, The (Koestler), 126
Ghosts (Wharton), 196
Ghost Writer, The (Roth), 172
Giacometti, Alberto, *398*
'Giant Mole, The' (Kafka), 123
Giant's Strength, A (Sinclair), 176
Gide, André, 52, 60, 72, *95–7*, 150, 151, 189, 366, 461, 539, 541, 543
Gift, The (Nabokov), 153–4
Gigi (Minnelli), 264
'Gimpel the Fool' (Singer), 178
Ginastera, Alberto, *330–31*
Ginsberg, Allen, *97–8*
Giovanni's Room (Baldwin), 59
Gipsy Ballads (Lorca), 135
Giraudoux, Jean, 452, 485, 543
Girl Crazy (Gershwin), 329
Girlfriends, The (Antonioni), 215
Girls at Play (Theroux), 185
Girls of Slender Means, The (Spark), 181
Girls We Embrace, The (Montherlant), 500
Girl, 20 (Amis, K.), 56
Girl with the Flaxen Hair, The (Debussy), 324
Giselle (Adam), 502
Gladiators, The (Koestler), 126
Glagolytic Mass (Janáček), 338
Glasgow School of Art (Mackintosh), 31
Glass Bead Game, The (Hesse), 112
'Glass Falling' (MacNeice), 140
Glass House, New Canaan (Johnson), 26

Glass Menagerie, The (William, T.), 530
Glastonbury Romance, A (Powys), 165
Glittering Prizes, The (Raphael), 168–9
Gloria (Cassavetes), 227; (Poulenc), 349; (Walton), 373
Glückliche Hand, Die (Schoenberg), 356
Gnomobile, The (Sinclair), 176–7
Goat Island (Betti), 464
Go-Between, The (Hartley), 105–6; (Losey), 258; (Pinter), 509
God and His Gifts, A (Compton-Burnett), 77
Godard, Jean-Luc, 209, 239, *243–4*, 250, 269, 544–5
Goddess, The (Chayefsky), 471; (Ray, S.), 272
Godfather, The (Coppola), 231
Godfather Part Two, The (Coppola), 231
God Knows (Heller), 108
God's Grace (Malamud), 142
'God's Grandeur' (Hopkins), 114
Gogol, Nikolai Vasilievich, 122, 496
Goin' a Buffalo (Bullins), 469
Going Home (Lessing), 130
'Going My Way' (Day Lewis), 81
Going to Meet the Man (Baldwin), 60
Gold Coast Customs (Sitwell, E.), 179
Gold Diggers of 1933 (Berkeley), 220
Gold Diggers of 1935 (Berkeley), 220
Golden Age, The (Buñuel), 224
Golden Apples, The (Welty), 194
Golden Ass, The (Apuleius, tr. Graves), 102
Golden Boy (Odets), 504
Golden Coach, The (Renoir), 274
Golden Cockerel, The (Fokine), 479
Golden Fleece, The (Graves), 102
Golden Fruits, The (Sarraute), 172
Golden Notebook, The (Lessing), 131
Golding, William, *98–9*, 196
Gold of the Tigers, The (Borges), 68
Gold Rush, The (Chaplin), 210, 229
Goldsworthy Lowes Dickinson (Forster), 91
Goldwyn Follies, The (Gershwin), 329, 462
Goncharov, Ivan Aleksandrovich, 122
Gone with the Wind, 87, 139, 246
Go Not Happy Day (Bridge), 314
González, Julio, 398, 440
Good as Gold (Heller), 108
Goodbye Charlie (Minnelli), 264
Goodbye, Columbus (Roth), 172
Goodbye to All That (Graves), 102
Goodbye to Berlin (Isherwood), 118
Good Companions, The (Priestley), 511
Good Man Is Hard to Find, A (O'Connor), 157
Good Marriage, A (Rohmer), 278
Good Soldier, The (Ford, F. M.), 90